A HISTORY OF THE HABSBURG EMPIRE 1526-1918

A HISTORY OF THE HABSBURG EMPIRE 1526-1918

Robert A. Kann

UNIVERSITY OF CALIFORNIA PRESS
Berkeley / Los Angeles / London

University of California Press
Berkeley and Los Angeles, California
University of California Press, Ltd.
London, England

Library of Congress Catalog Number: 72-97733
Printed in the United States of America

Second printing, with corrections, 1977
First Paperback Printing 1980
ISBN 0-520-04206-9

08 07 06 05 04 03 02 01
15 14 13 12 11 10

The paper used in this publication is both acid-free and totally chlorine-free (TCF). It meets the minimum requirements of ANSI/NISO Z39.48-1992 (R 1997) (*Permanence of Paper*). ∞

To Mady

Contents

Preface

The history of the Habsburg empire began with the union of the Alpine hereditary lands and the crowns of Bohemia, Hungary, and Croatia in 1526–1527. The first background chapter discusses the late medieval history of the hereditary lands more broadly than that of the eastern (Hungarian, Croatian, and Bohemian) crowns, because they were for two and a half centuries the heartlands of Habsburg rule and the nucleus of the evolving empire. From then on the various political units and national groups of the Habsburg lands are covered on a completely equal footing.

A Habsburg empire existed in fact but not in name throughout modern history, long before the proclamation of the Austrian empire of 1804. This declaratory imperial act as a consequence of the French political and military advance into Central Europe was indeed the mere external confirmation of a social and political evolution that had gone on throughout modern history. The succession treaties which came into effect in the sixteenth century could merely institute the premises for this step-by-step evolution of an empire. Not before the end of the first quarter of the seventeenth century was Habsburg rule in the Bohemian lands firmly established and not before the last decade of that century in the Hungarian-Croatian orbit. Consequently this study has to meet several demands. It has to show the rise of the Habsburg power, in Oswald Redlich's words, "Das Werden einer Grossmacht," its subsequent status and action as a great power, and finally its dissolution. It belongs to the paradoxes of which the history of the Habsburg empire is so rich that its official birthday in 1804 does not mark the beginning of an era of leadership in Central Europe. On the contrary, this date is close to the beginning of the disintegration of Habsburg power.

This volume attempts to give equal attention to political, cultural, and socioeconomic history. This has been attempted before, and only the one who sets about this task again, knows the difficulties which the historian has to face when he struggles with the problems of the multinational, multicultural empire. Yet in some respects the approach of this study differs from previous ones. Generally students of Austrian history have tried to give their undertaking as far as possible unified structure by pressing the many-faced problems into the frame of a centralized empire. Such method follows the philosophy of a German-directed centralism, which after 1867 had to yield to a German-Magyar diarchy. In some studies written from this viewpoint a German national and later also Magyar national bias is expressed. Yet in most cases criticism of this kind would be unfair. Frequently authors adopted this centralistic method not as a result of national preference but of methodical convenience. Some works which follow such patterns are outstanding. Their authors have perceived the empire from the center, not because they were biased but because it seemed to them the best way to give structure and coherence to their story. Just the same, such a presentation leads, however unwittingly, to a distorted structure.

The problems of the Habsburg empire can be fully understood only if equal attention is given to the various political entities and ethnic groups which formed it. There is no one stage of action but several stages, which have to be presented in a synchronistic view. This does not mean that all arenas are necessarily of equal importance, and certainly not at the same time. The part of the stage where the action takes place is illuminated, and then it falls back into darkness when history shifts to some other place. It is necessary, however, to keep in mind that specific aspects of history have to be viewed in the first place from the angle of particular groups. This method applies to national and cultural problems but also to political and socioeconomic events. Due attention will be paid to the task of the central administration, and not only in regard to foreign policy, defense, and legal institutions. These are important aspects of the history of the Habsburg empire but not the essence of this history. It rests in the synthesis between supranational and national problems. In correlating them as seen from different angles this study has tried to break new ground.

The most formidable difficulty in a work of limited size and wide scope is the presentation of the cultural evolution of the various national groups. Partly this difficulty results from the fact that the whole book is based primarily on works available in western languages. On the other hand, in the past two decades studies in eastern and central European history and literature, and translations from eastern languages, have increased in quantity and quality, thus diminishing language limitations.

More difficult to solve is the problem of selecting significant authors and artists representative for a national culture. Here one has to navigate between the Scylla of a superabundant number of outstanding works and the Charybdis of heaping name upon name in the manner of a telephone directory without proper evaluation. A perfect solution to this problem, particularly in works of limited size, has to my knowledge not yet been found. An author is bound either to discuss too few significant personalities or to list too many names without necessary analysis. In this dilemma of choice between evils the former seems to me the lesser one and I have acted accordingly.

Several technical problems require brief comment. One is the use of geographical names which in line with the principles traced above cannot be necessarily or uniformly German. I tried to adopt a middle ground between the ethnic-linguistic name of a place and the historical name used throughout an important period of development. In many instances, therefore, more than one name had to be used. The one primarily in use at the time under discussion is stated first, the other, or in some instances others, in parenthesis. The main consideration is that the names used are or become familiar to the reader. Automatic consistency has to yield to this consideration. This flexible approach pertains also to the use of anglicized or vernacular names of individuals. The same principle is applied to the terminology used in referring to the political body with which we are concerned, the Habsburg empire. In another work, *The Multinational Empire,* Vol. I, I discussed the legal and political question to what extent the term "Habsburg empire"—at some times a controversial one—may be used. Furthermore, whether "Austria" refers to the western parts of the Habsburg lands or to the whole, whether "Austria-Hungary" after 1867 stands for two unequal halves of one great power or for one single power, and other debatable questions of this kind were discussed there.

The deductions drawn in the quoted work apply to this volume as well. From the point of view of semantics, as distinguished from politics and law, the problem shrinks indeed to manageable size. The empire is generally understood as the whole area and the total of peoples with which we are concerned. What the term Austria means in specific places can generally be understood within the context. Where doubt exists, the meaning is clarified.

Dates are used sparingly throughout the book but I hope frequently enough to serve as scaffold for the understanding of political history. In the chapters on cultural history, biographical dates have been used where they are helpful to place the efforts of a person with precision within the intellectual currents of his time. They have purposely been omitted where this does not seem necessary. Here the line has to be drawn between a textbook, which this volume is not, and a historical introduction to the problems of the Habsburg empire which it hopes to be.

At this point it is a pleasant duty to express my sincere thanks for continued support of this study to the Research Council of Rutgers University, The American Council of Learned Societies, and the American Philosophical Society. I am obliged to Columbia University Press for permission to have five maps from my study *The Multinational Empire: Nationalism and National Reform in the Habsburg Monarchy 1848–1918* (2 vols., 3rd ed., 1970) reproduced in this book. I am greatly indebted to Mrs. Sophia Kurzweg for her never-failing help in the preparation of a difficult manuscript. Dr. Zdeněk David, Slavic bibliographer of Princeton University, advised me on questions of spelling of Slavic names, bibliographical problems, and selection of Slavic literature. I am indebted to Dr. Denes Koppanyi, Princeton, for advice concerning spelling in Hungarian. Finally and above all my thanks are due to Max Knight, editor of the University of California Press. I have benefited as much from his wise counsel as I have enjoyed our many battles in which he has deployed an impressive array of weapons of critical acumen and wit to make this a better book.

R.A.K.

CHAPTER I

Toward the Union of the Habsburg Lands

The permanent affiliation of the Habsburg dynasty, the ruling house in the German Alpine hereditary lands, with the lands of the Bohemian and Hungarian-Croatian crowns in 1526–1527 initiates the beginning of the history of these realms as an over-all political entity. The designation given to the study of this process indicates the position of the historian. We could speak either of the history of the Habsburg monarchy or of the Habsburg empire.

To speak of the Habsburg "monarchy" implies that the bond between the eastern crowns and the hereditary lands (the *Erblande,* that is, the Alpine domains from the spurs of the Alps in the north to the shores of the Adriatic in the south, from the Bavarian frontier in the west to the Hungarian plains in the east) is the monarchical principle. Seen from the point of view that in 1526–1527 three political systems begin to merge under the rule of the same dynasty, the basic element in the joint history of the Habsburg realms is the common allegiance to the Habsburg scepter.

To speak of the Habsburg "empire," however, as this writer does, implies a closer affiliation. What is an empire? It covers many political, cultural, and social factors of great significance without concentrating unduly on the dynastic element, important as it is as one factor among others. Webster calls such empire "an extended territory usually comprising a group of nations, states, or peoples under the control or domination of a single sovereign power." Such an empire "has a great extent of territory and a great variety of peoples under one rule and often has a ruler with the title of emperor." According to Webster, empire in its original

Latin meaning of *imperium* stands also for "supreme or absolute power, especially of an emperor," and finally the concept empire represents "an extended territory . . . dominated or successfully controlled by a single person, family, or group of interested persons." [1]

If we thus accept the term empire which in our case means Habsburg empire, we can avoid terminological pitfalls of perceiving the history of our subject as that of Austria or of the Austrian lands. In doing so we would neglect the fact that at the time when this history commences only a large part of the Alpine hereditary Habsburg lands was associated with the name of Austria. Subsequently it was extended, by custom rather than by law, to the major, primarily western portions of the lands under the German Habsburg line. Finally the concept of Austria was used also as frequently as incorrectly for all the lands under the rule of the German Habsburgs, ("the house of Austria").[2] By using the term Habsburg empire we can thus steer clear of these contradictions which in a sense are in themselves a characteristic element in the story presented here.

The Habsburgs, beginning with the union of 1526–1527, ruled over wide territories and a great variety of peoples, including Germans, Magyars, Carpatho-Ruthenians, Czechs, Croats, Slovaks, Slovenes, Italians, and Roumanians. The question has been raised whether these peoples, to whom within three centuries Poles, Serbs, and more Italians and Ruthenians were added, lived actually under the control of a single sovereign power, that is, whether they lived in an empire under a sovereign generally referred to as emperor. The title "emperor" of the Habsburgs referred until August 14, 1804 not to the rule over their own lands but to the crown of the Holy Roman Empire. Only afterward can we speak of an Austrian empire under an Austrian emperor. Yet this empire, created by a mere declaratory

[1] Webster's *Third New International Dictionary of the English Language* (Springfield, 1965).

[2] Robert A. Kann, *The Multinational Empire, Nationalism and National Reform in the Habsburg Monarchy*, 1848–1918, 2 vols. (New York, 1950, 2nd reprint 1970), I, 4–28 "Empire and Nationalities." For the literature on the subject see ibid., pp. 346–349.

For a revised and enlarged version, brought up to date to the bibliographical state of 1964, see Robert A. Kann, *Das Nationalitätenproblem der Habsburgermonarchie: Geschichte und Ideengehalt der nationalen Bestrebungen vom Vormärz bis zur Auflösung des Reiches im Jahre 1918* (Graz-Cologne, 1964, 2nd ed.), I, 17–39, 344–350 "Das Reich und die Völker." See also Alphons Lhotsky, "Was heisst Haus Österreich?" *Anzeiger der Philosophisch-Historischen Klasse der österreichischen Akademie der Wissenschaften* (Vienna, 1956), XI, 155–173.

The concept of Austria for the western part of the Habsburg empire was officially introduced only in 1917, one year prior to the empire's dissolution.

act in the face of the pending dissolution of the Holy Roman empire under the duress of the Napoleonic wars, had to yield within two generations to the dualistic union of the two states of the Austro-Hungarian monarchy in 1867. These legal-political qualifications do not invalidate the social and ideological concept of empire. Neither is it nullified by the fact that the imperial crown never fully absorbed the royal honors and privileges of the various Habsburg domains, of which one, the lands of the Holy Hungarian crown of St. Steven, remained for a major part of the history until 1918, fully coordinated and not subordinated to the Habsburg imperial power.[3]

The salient issue of this imperial power is the uniformity of the raison d'être of Habsburg rule in all domains and the common institutions and values in these lands. This kind of unity—if it exists—gives meaning to the idea of a centuries-old empire. Differences of the constitutional status of the ruler in his various lands and their diverse historical traditions recede thereupon into the background as secondary issues.

The Habsburgs ruled from the time when imperial history unfolds in the early sixteenth century to the end of 1918 in their German lands, for all practical purposes, by the law of hereditary succession. The same holds true for most future acquisitions outside of the Hungarian borders and those of the Bohemian lands. But in the lands of the Bohemian crown until 1620, and those of the Holy Hungarian crown of St. Steven until 1687, the Habsburgs ruled by election through the estates. Actually, hereditary succession in the Bohemian and Hungarian lands remained by law and in the Hungarian lands in fact as well conditioned by estates rights.[4] Technically no common, but only individual, allegiances of various political

[3] Ernst R. Huber, *Deutsche Verfassungsgeschichte seit 1789* (Stuttgart, 1957), I, 61–74. Kann, *The Multinational Empire,* I, 18–28, 349–355 and of the same author *Das Nationalitätenproblem,* I, 30–39, 349–356.

[4] Richard Plaschka, "Das böhmische Staatsrecht in tschechischer Sicht," in Ernst Birke and Kurt Oberndorffer, eds., *Das böhmische Staatsrecht in den deutsch-tschechischen Auseinandersetzungen des 19. und 20. Jahrhunderts* (Marburg/Lahn, 1960), pp. 5–14; Ernst C. Hellbling, *Österreichische Verfassungs- und Verwaltungsgeschichte* (Vienna, 1956), pp. 248–58; S. Harrison Thomson, *Czechoslovakia in European History* (Princeton, 1953), pp. 111 ff; Dominic C. Kosáry, *A History of Hungary* (Cleveland, 1941), pp. 33 ff., 94 ff., 132 ff.; Henry Marczali, *Hungary in the Eighteenth Century* (Cambridge, 1910), pp. xvii–lxiv; see also Josef Polišenský, Robert A. Kann, Fran Zwitter, *Der österreichisch-ungarische Ausgleich 1867* in Lúdovít Holotík and Anton Vantuch, eds. (Bratislava, 1971), pp. 14–23, 24–44, 45–75; Stanco Guldescu, *The Croatian-Slavonian Kingdom 1526–1792* (The Hague, 1970), pp. 9–18; L. von Südland, *Die Südslawische Frage und der Weltkrieg* (Vienna, 1918), pp. 30–70.

domains to the Habsburg sovereignty existed. This distinction is reflected before 1526–1527 in the diversity of customs and laws of the peoples under the Habsburgs and in the paucity of common institutions thereafter.

Yet the fact that this joint structure operated throughout four centuries, in spite of pressure from foreign powers and domestic conflicts, indicates the existence of substantial cohesive factors. What they were, how they evolved, worked, weakened, and failed is the concern of this study.

A. The political evolution of the Alpine hereditary lands before 1526

The Erblande, the hereditary lands of the Habsburgs, have to be perceived as the heartland of the future empire. Beginning with the reign of Rudolf of Habsburg in the late 13th century, these lands formed the historic and political nucleus of the dynasty's power. Due to the initially intermittent and later practically permanent connection of Habsburg rule with the crown of the Holy Roman Empire, the dynasty possessed in the eastern Alps and the valley of the Upper Danube a core area and base for her great-power aspirations. Although western central Hungary rather than the eastern parts of the hereditary lands stood for the geographical center of the empire in the last two centuries of its existence, Vienna, the capital of the Austrian Habsburgs, and the immediately surrounding area represented the political, administrative, and economic hub of Habsburg power. The combination of these three factors—the historic-traditional weight of the hereditary lands, their interrelationship with the crown of the Holy Roman Empire, and the administrative-economic power center in Vienna—established a fourth one: the German-speaking Austrians, henceforth referred to as Austro-Germans, who are settled in this area. In terms of political and economic power they became the leading national group of the empire. This primacy was contested only in political matters by the Magyars in the last half century of the empire's existence.

The Austro-Germans claimed this leadership by right basing it primarily on their unquestionable cultural advantages as part of the large German nation over the other peoples under Habsburg rule. This bold assertion, generally upheld in German historiography to varying degrees, but pervasive also in western languages beyond the German orbit, is not acknowledged in this study, unlike the other factual reasons for German supremacy previously referred to. We reject the notion of ideological, cultural, or racial superiority of any people, Germanic, Slavic, or Romance.

In 976, at the time when the Holy Roman emperor Otto II invested a member of the house of Babenberg with the Carolingian Eastern March established by Charlemagne in the later years of his reign, it included only the larger part of what is today Lower Austria. By the middle of the twelfth century the march included a part of the future crownland of Upper Austria as well. Perhaps more important, the so-called *privilegium minus* of 1156 granted by Frederick Barbarossa to Henry II (Jasomirgott) of Babenberg raised the march to a largely autonomous duchy, and limited its obligations to participating in imperial wars and to attending imperial diets. The weakening of the bonds between the empire and its advanced domain to the southeast started with this act of state.[5] The trend accelerated with the enlargement of the Babenberg possessions, in Styria by the end of the twelfth century, in—what is called today—Lower and Upper Austria, Friuli, and Carniola in the first half of the thirteenth century. This evolutionary development stretching over almost three centuries was interrupted when the house of Babenberg expired with the death of the belligerent duke Frederick II in the battle against an invading Magyar force in 1246.

Because of its close connection with other developments in Central Europe, this event turned out to be of far-reaching significance. The vacancy of the Babenberg fiefs in the east coincided practically with the great interregnum in the empire brought about by the death of Frederick II, the last Ghibeline (Hohenstaufen) emperor, in 1250. Hungarian attempts to advance toward the west and expansionist policies by the new king of Bohemia, Přemysl Ottokar II, who moved into the vacated Babenberg fiefs, created a dynamic new situation. It was cleared up only when in 1273 the princes of the empire elected a king Rudolf of Habsburg, a lord endowed with considerable possessions in southwestern Germany.[6] The great showdown between the imperialist ruler of Bohemia and the first Habsburg led to the former's defeat in 1278 and to the joint accession of Rudolf's sons in the Austrian lands and in Styria in 1282. This rule by

[5] See particularly Heinrich Fichtenau, *Von der Mark zum Herzogtum* (Munich, 1958), pp. 36–54; see also Heinrich Mitteis, *Der Staat des hohen Mittelalters: Grundlinien einer vergleichenden Verfassungsgeschichte des Lehnszeitalters* (Weimar, 1968), pp. 254–257.

[6] The rulers of the Holy Roman empire who were not crowned in Rome are properly referred to as king, rex Romanorum, of the Holy Roman empire. Those who were crowned in Rome by the Pope are designated as emperors. This distinction becomes, however, meaningless after the last coronation of an emperor in Rome, that of Frederick III in 1453. All rulers of the Holy empire afterwards, although none of them was crowned in Rome, are generally referred to as emperors.

the Habsburg dynasty lasted until the disintegration of the Habsburg empire in 1918. Yet the decisive importance of the events between 1273 and 1282 goes beyond its dynastic aspects. Rudolf's rule as German king from 1273 to 1291 helped to restore law and order in the empire. But the strengthening of imperial judicial and general administrative institutions, in particular military defense, the collection of custom duties, and the protection of urban development, was not brought about directly by imperial power but by the newly established hereditary dynastic powers of the Habsburgs in the southeast and those of other princes in the west and north. Imperial power was strengthened only when it did not collide with princely power; in a conflict of interests it had to yield. Thus while the Habsburg accession intermittently strengthened imperial power, it did so only in a supplementary way. In the long run, Habsburg power absorbed imperial power and not the other way round. This means a further weakening of ties to the empire.

Was this true also in the national sphere? Using the term *national* in the late Middle Ages with caution, the question is still legitimate, whether the entrenchment of a new German dynasty in the hereditary lands for more than six centuries meant a strengthening of the German impact in eastern Central Europe. Was such impact not even further strengthened by the fact that the Habsburgs bore the imperial crown for more than five of these six centuries? Ottokar II with German help might have advanced Czech economic and cultural development faster and perhaps further had he not been stopped by Rudolf. German national-oriented historiography, on the other hand, has held that the breakdown of Ottokar's great design to establish the rule of his Czech dynasty in the Austrian and imperial lands actually put a stop to a complete Germanization of the core lands of the Bohemian crown—Bohemia, Moravia, and Silesia—since this brilliant ruler had made the widest possible use of the skill of German professional men and craftsmen in his domains.[7] Such far-reaching conclusions, which underrate the solid foundations of Czech national culture and overrate the importance of a superstructure of a highly selective immigration, are hardly warranted. There is indeed little evidence in Ottokar's policy or that of his heirs, who ruled for another generation in the

[7] Typical for this line of thought are the interpretations of Adolf Bachmann, *Geschichte Böhmens,* 2 vols. (Gotha, 1899–1905), I, 556–658, see particularly 593–608; Berthold Bretholz, *Geschichte Böhmens und Mährens,* 4 vols. (Reichenberg, 1924), I, 76–160. Fully objective is the presentation by Karl Richter, "Die böhmischen Länder im Früh- und Hochmittelalter" in *Handbuch der Geschichte der böhmischen Länder,* Karl Bosl, ed. (Stuttgart, 1967), I, 272–305.

Bohemian lands, that a radical wholesale Germanization policy was ever contemplated.

The supremacy and extension of Habsburg rule between the Danube, the Adriatic, and the Little Carpathians in the following century strengthened Germanic influence. Yet this influence in turn was not only shaped by the evolving autonomous power of the Habsburg hereditary lands, but also the social and cultural influence of Czech, Magyar, Slovene, and Italian peoples. The German character of the Habsburg lands in the southeast of the Holy Roman Empire had thus become a complex composite concept, different from that of the southwest, whence the Habsburgs and their entourage had come. These southwestern lands were German, the southeastern were predominantly German, but the ethnic features of many people were superimposed on the German structure.

In the fourteenth century, Habsburg rule was extended to Carinthia, Tirol, Breisgau, Istria and Trieste. The remainder of the Litoral was gained by 1500. The *privilegium maius* of Duke Rudolf the Founder of 1359 strengthened the Habsburgs versus the empire in regard to heredity of fiefs, exemption from taxation, military obligation, and recognition of supreme judicial power.[8] The fact that the *privilegium maius* was in essence a forgery, emphasizes its significance; the *privilegium* is a triumph over legal objections. Within another century the Habsburgs had the rights claimed by the *privilegium* recognized by an emperor from their own house. This proves that Rudolf, shortly after 1359 recognized as archduke, a title which assimilated his status in some respects with that of the seven electors of the empire, had foreseen—and, indeed, influenced—the course of future events.

There were setbacks. By the end of the century the Habsburgs had lost their domains in Switzerland. More important, internal dissension within the dynasty lead to several partition treaties of the Habsburg lands between 1379 and 1396; they delayed the rise of the Habsburg power in Germany. However, from 1438, beginning with the election of Albrecht V of Austria as German king to the extinction of the male line in 1740, only Habsburgs were Holy Roman emperors. The brief reign of the gifted Albrecht, as king the second of his name, is also insofar significant, as his marriage to the daughter of the last Luxemburg emperor established

[8] See particularly "Epilegomena zu den österreichischen Freiheitsbriefen," in Alphons Lhotsky, *Vorträge und Aufsätze,* edited by Hans Wagner and Heinrich Koller (Vienna, 1970), I, 265–282. Ernst K. Winter, *Rudolf IV. von Österreich,* 2 vols. (Vienna, 1934–1936), I, 309–395.

for the first time long-range Habsburg claims to the crowns of Bohemia and Hungary. Similar demands were made before, but now the Habsburg power was sufficiently strong to raise them seriously, though not yet strong enough to have them met in full. The long reign of the undistinguished but tenacious Frederick III (1440–1493), the last emperor crowned in Rome, is filled by a continuous struggle to come into the Bohemian and Hungarian heritage. These claims were blocked at first by the mere existence of Albrecht's late-born son, Ladislas [Posthumus] (1440–1457). Frederick could prevent the son's accession, but he could not secure his own. Foiled later by the powerful Hussite regent and eventually king, George of Poděbrady in Bohemia (1452–1471), the Hungarian regent John Hunyady (as such 1446–1452), and, above all, by his great son, King Matthias Corvinus (1458–1490), Habsburg rule even in Austria was put on the defensive. The victorious Matthias resided in Vienna after 1484. The new feuds about the succession between the various Habsburg lines were resolved in favor of the emperor only in 1490, after the Hungarian king's death. Yet even if Matthias Corvinus had left a legitimate heir and had not been threatened by the advancing Ottoman-Turkish power, an empire approximating the Habsburg power of the coming generations could hardly have been established under Hungarian leadership.

The Hungarian power potential, squeezed between Germans and Turks, as later between Germans and Russians, was too narrow. At the same time, the imperial connections of the Habsburgs in the west were strengthened by the political marriage of Emperor Frederick's son Maximilian with the heiress of Burgundy and the Netherlands in 1577. Accordingly, the new Polish Jagiello dynasty in Bohemia and Hungary had little chance to conduct an active policy against the rising Habsburg power.

Besides, Frederick III's son Maximilian I (1493–1519) was a ruler of greater capabilities than his indecisive, unreliable, but stubborn father. Maximilian's over-all policy was more German-oriented than that of the old emperor but it was characteristic of Habsburg power that foreign policy objectives might have been neglected for a time but hardly ever abandoned. This applies to Maximilian's eastern objectives. In the south the only tangible achievement of the new reign was the succession in Gorizia and Gradisca after the ruling house there had become extinct. The so-called Holy League, in which Maximilian joined the pope and the Republic of Venice against the expansive policy of Charles VIII of France and his successor Louis XII, marked the beginnings of a quarter of a millennium of wars between the Habsburgs and the French. The Holy League failed as completely as a few years later the League of Cambrai, directed now against Venice and cosponsored by the emperor. Only some small Italian domains, until then under Venetian rule, could be joined to Tirol. On the whole, the conflict with France could be sidetracked temporarily as long as merely northern Italy was the issue.

Taking a long-range view, developments in the east were more serious. Turkish forays had threatened southern and western Hungary, and even Styria, during the later years of Frederick III's reign. These hit-and-run attacks could not be stopped under Maximilian, either. Only ten years after his death, the Turks swept through Hungary and laid siege to Vienna in 1529. And yet the Turkish danger is as closely related to the rise of the Habsburgs as the ultimate victory in the east.

In this respect one thinks first of Maximilian's marriage policy, which made the Habsburgs heirs to the crown of Hungary, vacated in the struggle against the Turks. Thereby they became also the chief carriers of the fight against the Turkish advance. When Maximilian concluded the pact of Wiener Neustadt with the Jagiello king Ladislas II of Hungary (Vladislav V of Bohemia) in 1506, according to which Ladislas' daughter should marry the emperor's grandson, Ferdinand, and Ladislas'—not yet born—son Louis was supposed to marry the emperor's granddaughter Maria, he hoped to establish Habsburg claims to the crowns of Bohemia and Hungary.[9] The unexpected death of Louis II of Hungary in the swamps of Mohács in battle against the Turks in 1526 changed the situation radically. Hungary ceased to be a functioning political body and the Habsburg succession moved from the sphere of speculation into that of reality. Considering the steamroller power and speed of the Turkish advance, the unrest in an anti-foreign, and this meant largely anti-Habsburg Hungary, and the religious division in Bohemia, the Habsburgs did not seem to be exactly in luck when Ferdinand succeeded to the crowns of Hungary, Croatia, and Bohemia. Yet the formidable power of the Habsburgs, with its claims to the three crowns, was the only political force in its time and

[9] The actual conclusion of the double marriages in 1515 and 1516 carried him one step further. Yet these rights to succession were mutual and a scion of the house of Jagiello might have succeeded with equal probability in the hereditary lands as the Habsburgs did in Hungary. In fact, the law passed by the Hungarian diet of 1505, according to which a born Hungarian would have to succeed Wladislaw on the throne, seemed to be a major stumbling block for Habsburg ambitions, since its provisions might easily be extended into the future. As to the important peasant riots in Tyrol see Josef Macek, *Der Tiroler Bauernkrieg und Michael Gaismair* (Berlin, 1965), (transl. from the Czech).

place which could have resisted the Turkish advance with or without rights established by marriage. These rights in themselves would have meant nothing without the right constellation of geography, cultural affinity between Christian nations, and corresponding military and political power. To trace the rise of the Habsburg empire to the marriage policy of the dynasty is a patent oversimplification of history.

Where the component geopolitical factor did not exist, as in the two western political marriages—that of Maximilian to the heiress of Burgundy in 1477 and that of his son Philip to Juana, heiress to Castile and Aragon, in 1496—the interrelationship between political marriage and evolution toward empire failed to work. This point has frequently been obscured. Many historians have traced the world position of the house of Habsburg to the Burgundian and Iberian unions of 1477 and 1496 rather than to the ties with the Jagiellons in the east. This is true only to a point. The Burgundian marriage brought the Netherlands under the Habsburg scepter. The Iberian marriage made Charles, the grandson of Ferdinand the Catholic of Aragon and Isabella of Castile, and also of Emperor Maximilian, sovereign of three of the most powerful political entities of his time: the Holy Roman empire, Spain (formed out of the union of Castile and Aragon), and only lastly the crowns of Bohemia, Hungary, and Croatia. They were first linked merely by geographic contiguity to the ancient Habsburg hereditary lands, which had become a political unit beside, rather than of, the empire.

These marriages established the world power of the Habsburgs, unquestionably the greatest, but also the most complex of its time. Within a few years, by the family compact of Brussels of 1522, the Austrian hereditary lands, though still part of the Holy Roman Empire, were transferred from the emperor's to his brother Ferdinand's administration and princely sovereignty. In 1526–1527, the three eastern crowns were added to this new power structure. Within another generation, in 1556, the abdication of Charles V (as king of Spain Charles I) led to the permanent separation of the crown of the Holy Roman Empire from that of Spain. The Netherlands remained a noncontiguous and isolated appendage of the Habsburg crowns, changing from Maximilian's eastern realm to that of Charles V and his heirs in the west. After the richer northern part of the Netherlands was lost less than two generations after Charles' accession, the major portion of the southern half was returned after the War of the Spanish Succession, by the peace of Rastatt of 1714, to eastern control. Parts of the Italian appendages of the Spanish empire came at the same time under the rule of the eastern Habsburg line, usually referred to as the German line. The power which the German Habsburgs derived from the temporary union with the Spanish crown and its immense colonial empire was impressive, and influenced European power politics. Yet the inheritance which the Habsburgs secured through the western political marriages did not lead to the evolution of a specific Habsburg empire. The crowns of Charles V in east and west remained disparate in an administrative, economic, and cultural sense, even when they were united under one head. After his death, until the extinction of the Spanish line in 1700, the bonds between the two branches of the house were reduced to diplomatic and military alliances. The appendages in the Netherlands and Italy, which after the War of the Spanish Succession accrued to the German-Austrian Habsburgs, were never fully integrated into their empire. The last remainders of this heritage were lost in the process of Italian unification in the mid-nineteenth century.

The Jagiello marriages, on the other hand, had supplemented and cemented the contingencies of geographic, economic, and military affinities and also of cultural needs. The western marriages could not supplement bonds that did not exist before; the marriages attempted to create those bonds. Lacking the geographic, social, and cultural prerequisites, they failed to create integration, although they succeeded in increasing political power.

The eastern empire began to emerge under the rule of Maximilian's grandson Ferdinand I. It is necessary to survey here its component parts, first the hereditary lands, that is, predominatly German-speaking possessions of the Habsburgs. Their political evolution in the Middle Ages has already been traced. They included roughly the territories of the present Republic of Austria and most of the German part of former South Tirol and Italian domains as far as Lake Garda. In the south, Carniola, Gorizia and Gradisca, and Trieste were part of the hereditary power and, in line with the provisions of the *privilegia minus* and *maius* of 1156 and 1359, loosely affiliated with the Holy Roman Empire. Inasmuch as the Habsburgs, in addition to their rule in the hereditary lands and the west German possessions (Vorlande),[10] bore the crown of the Holy Roman Empire

[10] The Vorlande, generally referred to also as Vorderösterreich, included Upper Alsatia, the Breisgau, until the 14th century domains in Switzerland, and after the middle of the 18th century also Suebian possessions. The Alsatian territories were lost in the Westphalian peace treaty of 1648, the remainder in the peace of Pressburg of 1805. Actually the terms Vorlande and Vorderösterreich are not fully identical but overlapping. The latter is the wider one. See also Otto Stolz, *Grundriß der österreichischen Verfassungs- und Verwaltungsgeschichte* (Innsbruck, 1951), pp. 71 ff.

from the accession of Albrecht II to the death of Charles VI in 1740 for three centuries without interruption, the extent of this affiliation created no constitutional problem. An emperor from another dynasty would hardly have confirmed the *privilegium maius* as the Habsburg ruler Frederick III did in 1453. A problem, however, was the question of the division of rule in the hereditary lands between the various lines of the Habsburg dynasty themselves; but in 1490 all possessions of the house were reunited under Frederick III, and the Austrian hereditary lands remained united until the death of Ferdinand I in 1564. When the problem of partition reappeared at that time, it affected the struggle between Reformation and Counter Reformation in the hereditary lands.

B. Social and cultural conditions in the hereditary lands before 1526

The hereditary lands represented, in historical terms, the cradle of the future Habsburg empire. For this reason their social and cultural institutions in the transition period from late medieval to early modern history are discussed in this section, whereas similar developments in regard to the eastern crowns, apart from predominantly political issues, will be taken up later.

Institutions and conditions in the hereditary lands in the last century before the union with Hungary were subject to frequent change. The estates, particularly in the Alpine lands, played an increasingly active part in government. They consisted of the high clergy as the first curia, the lords and knights as the second, and the princely towns and markets as the third. Only in Tirol could the free peasants join this third curia. The right of convocation of the diets, in the Alpine lands occasionally also that of general diets of several lands, belonged to the sovereign. The estates were convoked to approve extraordinary taxes, particularly in wartime, rarely regular taxes; the estates had some say in the allocation and collection of taxes. Otherwise, the regalia (mining, minting, hunting, fishing privileges, industrial and commercial semimonopolies, special taxes on Jews etc.) and the income from the princely domains, represented the main financial sources of the administration.

Courts, (*Landrechte*), nominated by the estates and appointed by the sovereign, had jurisdiction over nobles and in general over those who owned lordly estates. Another court, the Chamber Court, (*Hof- or Kammergericht*), composed of counselors selected by the prince, officiated at his residence. It adjudicated issues of direct importance to him. Lower courts (*Landgerichte*) in towns and markets increased in the fourteenth and fifteenth centuries in number and importance. They were still to be distinguished from the mere patrimonial jurisdiction of the lords. The right to judge capital crimes (high crimes) had to be conferred on every single court by the sovereign. Town courts, established by princely privileges, corresponded to the Landgerichte in the countryside. The reintroduction, the so-called Reception of Roman law, enters the Austrian lands relatively late, in substance not before the middle of the fifteenth century.

Secular and ecclesiastic lords held considerable power in a country where more than four-fifths of the population lived outside of towns. Yet apart from the autonomy granted to ecclesiastics and from the estates rights, this power in the late medieval period was more socioeconomic than political. The peasantry, the largest class, lived in various subject relationships to the lords: Feudal contracts between lords and tenants were increasingly restricted to one year and renewed only with one-sided concessions to the lord. Lifelong covenants were more favorable to the peasants and could be transmitted to the heirs or sold. A still more rigid form of lord-subject relationship called for personal services, either by personal labor or by payment of rent in kind, frequently both. Only a small group of free lieges were exempted from such obligations and restricted to payment of rents. Money payments took their place gradually besides those in kind—a change within a very incomplete money economy—to the disadvantage of the peasantry. The peasant riots and revolts in the late fifteenth and sixteenth century in the Austrian lands, resulted to a large extent from the advance of the money economy, for which the commercial towns were better prepared than the lords and peasants.[11]

From the fourteenth to the end of the fifteenth century, a large number of towns were founded in the Alpine lands. Few increased to substantial size, although the flight from the land on the part of the impoverished peasantry favored their growth. Attacks by knights in the thirteenth century, later the threat of Hungarian, Bohemian, Hussite, and Turkish incursions, widespread and deadly plagues, frequently checked their further expansion for a long time. Political power in the towns was shared by the

[11] See Alphons Huber and Alphons Dopsch, *Österreichische Reichsgeschichte* (Vienna, 1901), pp. 61–90; Arnold Luschin v. Ebengreuth, *Österreichische Reichsgeschichte* (Bamberg, 1901), pp. 189–287; Otto Brunner, *Land und Herrschaft: Grundfragen der territorialen Verfassungsgeschichte Österreichs im Mittelalter* (Vienna, 1959, 4th revised ed.), pp. 240–356 and Alphons Lhotsky, *Geschichte Österreichs seit der Mitte des 13. Jahr-hunderts (1281–1358)*, (Vienna, 1967), passim.

wealthy burghers with hereditary citizenship rights. They, above all, were represented in the town councils, although the guilds and brotherhoods of craftsmen also exercised substantial influence. In the late fifteenth century the influence of hereditary patricians was in decline. The two violent conflicts between sovereign and burghers in Vienna at the beginning and after the middle of the fifteenth century, which led to the execution of two mayors, Konrad Vorlauf and Wolfgang Holzer, involved different strata of the burghers: the first, patricians; the second, primarily wealthy immigrant merchants.[12] In both cases Emperor Frederick III violated the rights of the burghers, as he did those of the noble estates in Styria.

Industry and commerce were on the rise. The iron foundries in Styria and glass industry in Tyrol are worth mentioning. Salt, silver, and gold mining in the Alpine lands were significant. A main commerce route between Germany, Bohemia, and Hungary was the Danube. Cloth and salt were being transported downstream, wine and cattle up the river. The hereditary lands profited more from transit traffic—including that from Germany to Italy—than from exports of their own limited industrial goods. In fact, exports of domestic lumber and silver[13] were restricted to protect domestic needs.

Except for the fine arts, medieval culture was on the decline in the hereditary lands in the fifteenth century. Only in the last years did the new humanism, in particular Renaissance culture, show promise at the court of Maximilian I. The great days of knightly chivalry and minnesingers had ended in the fourteenth century. Ecclesiastic chronicles in Latin were frequently historically significant, but the verse novels and rhyme chronicles in German were of greater social than literary interest, except for the poetry of Oswald von Wolkenstein (about 1377–1445). More important were the scholarly chronicles of the historian and one-time rector of the University of Vienna, Thomas Ebendorfer (1387–1464). In his Austrian chronicles, the Kaiser and papal chronicles, he transcended in method and scope considerably the work of other contemporary chroniclers. Still, he belonged to the late medieval world, like the famous astronomers of the University of Vienna in the early fifteenth century, Georg von Peuerbach, Johannes Müller (Regiomontanus), and Johann

[12] See Franz von Krones, *Handbuch der Geschichte Österreichs,* 4 vols. and index vol. (Berlin, 1880–1881), see particularly II, 224 f., 375–391; Hans Tietze, *Wien: Kultur, Kunst, Geschichte* (Vienna, 1931), pp. 100–107.

[13] Ferdinand Tremel, *Der Frühkapitalismus in Innerösterreich* (Graz, 1953), pp. 96–147 and by the same author *Wirtschafts- und Sozialgeschichte Österreichs: Von den Anfängen bis 1955* (Vienna, 1955), pp. 142–229.

von Gmunden. Only the mystical genius of the Copernicus' precursor, Nicolas of Cusa (1401–64), later bishop of Brixen and cardinal, pointed to modern times.

The University of Vienna, founded by Rudolf IV in 1365, developed until the mid-fifteenth century in a fairly satisfactory way, although the crisis of Frederick III's wars and domestic disorders paralyzed the intellectual climate for the next generations. As yet it had been little affected by new ideas evolving farther west.

The coming era of Austrian Renaissance and Humanism is closely related to the personality of the long-time private secretary and diplomatic adviser of Frederick III, Eneas Silvius Piccolomini of Siena (1405–1464), as pope from 1458 to 1464 known as Pius II. Eneas Silvius' literary writings, whether amatory literature, didactic tracts, or travelogues on Bohemia, the Rhineland, Austria, and particularly Vienna, reveal elegance, charm, and keen observation. The Sienese pope may well be called a friend of Austrian culture. Conrad Celtes (1459–1508), the South German poeta laureatus at the courts of Frederick III and Maximilian I, was an Austrian by choice. Neither his Latin poetry and epigrams nor his historical study on Nuremberg are of the first order, but his break with the scholastic method and the direct turn to Humanism were significant. Celtes' colleague and successor, Johannes Cuspinian (1473–1529), who came from the same homegrounds, was an important historian though his work did not have the same breadth as that of Celtes. The Renaissance in Austria was centered in the court; its spread to the burghers and urban culture was more limited than in Germany. Yet it was significant enough to perceive Emperor Maximilian I as the first great Renaissance patron in in the hereditary lands rather than as the cliché of the last knight.

Architecture, sculpture, and painting at the turn from the fifteenth to the sixteenth century, as in the Gothic period earlier, were sponsored by the dynasty, the aristocracy, and, particularly at the height of Gothic art, by the Church. This holds fully true for the great Austrian Gothic art. Even the artistic achievements of urban culture were not primarily determined by the activities of the burghers, despite the dedicated cooperative efforts of the craft guilds.

Because of this only slowly changing social structure, bourgeois Renaissance architecture, sculpture, and painting which in western countries were furthered by a powerful urban upper middle class, played only a minor, though attractive part in Austrian culture. The fine arts, even later, throughout the Baroque age, prospered because of the sponsorship of a counter-reformatory ecclesia triumphans and the rising secular power of the house of Austria and its aristocracy. The social forces which favored this art were still little affected by the demands and values of bourgeois culture.[14]

Feudal and ecclesiastic influence remained dominant in the cultural field. The Church in Austria retained its eminence of status, although it could not be unaffected by the crises of the Babylonian captivity of the popes, papal schism, Waldensian and Hussite heresies in south, west, and north. The foundation of Church-state relations in Austria was the Concordat of Vienna of 1448, the preliminaries of which were negotiated by two of the truly great and greatly different representatives of the Church, Nicholas of Cusa for the Pope Nicholas V, and Eneas Silvius for Emperor Frederick III. The Concordat, which in its principal features remained valid until the dissolution of the Holy Roman Empire, provided for free election of bishops by the cathedral chapters, but subject to confirmation by the pope. The papacy on its part agreed in the next generation to the establishment of the bishoprics of Vienna and Wiener Neustadt, which strengthened the imperial power against the mighty bishop of Passau and the archbishop of Salzburg.[15] This diocesan church organization was the first pillar of ecclesiastic power in the cultural as well as in the political sphere. The second was monasticism.

Yet the great times of monastic culture in Austria were the High Middle Ages and the Baroque period. The fifteenth and sixteenth centuries belong to the intermediate period of crisis in monastic life and of frequent violations of the three vows in orders and secular clergy. Rapid changes may have been partly due to the diminished prestige of the Church, which had suffered from schism and heresies. The liberalizing influence of Italian Renaissance life played a part too. Extremes in the opposite direction, religious craze and zealotry, were manifested in flagellantism and later witchcraft trials. Between these two currents stood the great reformers and crusaders Nicholas of Cusa and Johannes of Capistran, who fought simony and heresy. The powers of the Church in secular affairs were in slow retreat. Church jurisdiction in matters effecting clergy and laymen was frequently contested, even in marital affairs. Of even greater importance were the restrictions imposed on the Church for eco-

[14] Alphons Lhotsky, *Thomas Ebendorfer: Ein österreichischer Geschichtsschreiber* (Stuttgart, 1957); Hans Ankwicz-Kleehofen, *Der Wiener Humanist Johannes Cuspinian* (Graz-Cologne, 1959); Otto Rommel, ed., *Wiener Renaissance* (Vienna, 1947).

[15] Josef Wodka, *Kirche in Österreich* (Vienna, 1959), pp. 170–179; Alois Knöpfler, *Lehrbuch der Kirchengeschichte* (Freiburg i. B., 1920, 6th ed.), pp. 503 f.

nomic reasons, above all in regard to acquisition of landed estates. Furthermore clerical tax exemptions were frequently challenged on the local level. The prohibition of the promulgation of papal bulls and decrees of excommunication ex cathedra without consent by the secular authority as part of the centuries-old conflict between state and Church power existed in the Habsburg lands as in all Catholic countries. But unlike conditions in many of them, it implied here no decline of religious feelings.

Two basic facts should be added to this sketch of social and cultural conditions in the hereditary lands. The first is the scope and objectives of Maximilian I's sweeping administrative reforms. They represented a step in the transition from the feudal state of lord-liege relations to the bureaucratic state of appointed office holders. This transition reached only the higher levels of administration and even here economic matters remained still primarily part of the feudal system. Yet the over-all reorganization of the hereditary lands was based on the new principles of administrative expediency as from now on modified but not voided by historic tradition. Two major administrative units were established, Lower and Upper Austria. The former included the Lower and Upper Austria of today, only approximately within their present boundaries, as well as Styria, Carinthia, and Carniola. Upper Austria then comprised Tirol, Vorarlberg, the Windisch Mark (roughly, the Slovene territories between Styria and Carniola), Gorizia, Istria, Trieste, and the noncontiguous southwestern German domains, the Vorlande or Vorderösterreich. The government of the Lower Austrian unit was in Vienna, that of the Upper Austrian in Innsbruck. The individual lands of which the main units were composed were subdivided into major administrative and smaller judicial districts. The sovereign appointed the chiefs of government of the individual lands, who were to be supported by likewise appointed counselors. Symbol of the preservation of some unity of the administratively divided hereditary lands was the general diet of 1518, convoked by Maximilian the year before his death.

The second fact was the over-all political and national orientation of the regime. Of the two main units, the Lower Austrian lands were clearly German in character; Upper Austrian had a predominantly Slovene and Italian population in the south and southeast. Since the Slovenes lacked a nationally conscious nobility and urban middle class and the Italian domains were fragmentized, these ethnic factors were as yet politically insignificant. Maximilian's political philosophy was clearly

German-oriented. Here, as so often in this imaginative emperor's planning, his designs outran the adminstrative potentialities of the day. The establishment of the Aulic Council (*Hofrat*) as common supreme court for the hereditary lands and the empire, and the Court Chamber (*Hofkammer*) as joint supreme financial body, met opposition from the imperial estates and proved to be unworkable. The same was true for the division of the Holy Roman Empire into ten imperial districts, of which the combined hereditary lands should form just one. The plan was rejected by the electors but also by lesser princes of the empire and by the estates in the hereditary lands. It was no longer compatible with their autonomous development that had begun with the *privilegium minus*.[16]

C. The evolution of the eastern crowns and their status at the time of the union of 1526–1527

The German-ruled and German-oriented lands represented and remained the nucleus of the Habsburg power, to which in 1526–1527 the Bohemian, Hungarian, and Croatian crowns were joined. The lands of the Bohemian crown and those of the Hungarian crown (including its unequal union with the Croatian crown), were more distinct political entities than the hereditary lands. The latter were separated from each other by family compacts that divided sovereignty between the branches of the dynasty for the major part of the high and late medieval period. All hereditary lands were held together, however, by a loose association with the Holy Roman Empire. This flexible concept of the hereditary lands favored political and administrative adjustments when the Habsburg domains became the basis of an evolving new empire. The greater rigidity of the state concepts of the Bohemian and Hungarian-Croatian crowns made such adjustment more difficult, as the history of the following centuries shows.

The hereditary lands had a particularly close connection with the Habsburg-empire concept and its envisaged social structure, in contrast with the greater constitutional and cultural distinctiveness of the eastern crowns. The lands of the Bohemian crown had been under Habsburg rule twice before 1526–1527, in 1306–1307 and in 1437–1439.[17] The first union, under Rudolf III (grandson of Rudolf I, first Habsburg king of

[16] Heinrich Ullmann, *Kaiser Maximilian I,* 2 vols. (reprint), (Vienna, 1967), see I, 292–403, II, 561–657. Huber and Dopsch, *Österreichische Reichsgeschichte,* pp. 87–90.

[17] In theory the Habsburgs' claims in this respect continued until the death of Ladislas Posthumus in 1457.

the Holy Roman Empire), would not be important except that the connection between the young king's accession and the extinction of the house of the Přemyslids which had ruled in the Bohemian lands for four centuries gave his brief reign significance. The Přemyslids, raised to royalty by the German counter king Philip of Swabia at the end of the twelfth century, pursued a policy of close affiliation with the empire and of the influx of German culture into the Bohemian lands. This policy was confirmed by Ottokar II's aspirations to the crown of the Holy Roman Empire, which ended on the battlefield of Dürnkrut in 1278. The house of Luxemburg, which succeeded the Přemyslids in 1310 after a short interlude, made an equally strong contribution to Czech history as the Přemyslids and one not less influenced by German cultural contacts. In fact, the synthesis between Czech and German institutions and achievements from inside and outside the Bohemian lands was elevated under Emperor Charles IV (1347–1378) to the highest levels of national culture in Czech history. Under Charles and his sons until the extinction of the German-Bohemian branch of the house in 1437, the lands of the Bohemian crown, Bohemia, Moravia, Silesia, and Lusatia, unlike the situation under the Přemyslids, were not mere appendages of the Holy Roman Empire. For a brief period they had become its center of power and in many ways also of culture, even under an unworthy king like Václav IV, the older son of Charles IV. Under the last Luxemburg rulers the curious combination of a Bohemian geographic fringe position and a central power position in relation to the empire accentuated the incipient conflict between Czechs and Germans, which was interwoven with the religious aspects of the Hussite movements.[18]

The election of Duke Albrecht V of Austria as king of Bohemia in 1437, his investiture with Moravia, and in the following year his coronation as king of Hungary and election as Roman king in Frankfurt, preceded this development. Albrecht died soon, in 1439. The fact that for the first time the imperial crown and those of the Bohemian and Hungarian lands could be claimed by the same ruler was thus of the very short duration. Moreover, Albrecht's rule was merely based on a relationship through marriage. It was heavily contested by all Hussite factions. And yet we face in this second affiliation of the Bohemian lands with Habsburg rule a chain of events of great historical significance.

[18] Particularly important were in this context the social conflicts between the relatively moderate Calixtines or Utraquists, the social revolutionary Taborites and, later, the Bohemian Brethren, in whose doctrines the religious and social tenets of both trends merged in some measure.

In the first place, Albrecht's possession of the three crowns: of the empire, Bohemia and Hungary, in addition to the rule in the hereditary lands, was not a mere transitory event like Rudolf III's brief kingship one and a half centuries before. Albrecht's claim lived on in his son Ladislas Posthumus (1440–1457), born after the king's death. Had it not been for the personal aspirations of his guardian Frederick of Styria, the later emperor Frederick III, the union of 1526–1527 could have been conceivably established already under a boy king in mid-fifteenth century.

More important were two other themes during Albrecht's brief reign. First, the Turkish threat in the east. Albrecht, who died while preparing for a campaign against the Turks in Hungary, represented one of the major reasons for the later union of the crowns: the necessity to ward off the threatening holocaust of the advancing Turks. Second, Albrecht's contested rule in Bohemia represented the idea of a kind of Counter Reformation there, which throughout the centuries was related to Habsburg rule. For another two decades this particular brand of Counter Reformation was checked by the rule of the truly national Czech king and moderate Hussite leader, George of Poděbrady. After his death, the election in 1471 of Ladislas II, son of the king of Poland from the house of Jagiello, revived the counterreformatory idea. The elevation of Ladislas to the throne of Hungary after the death of Matthias Corvinus accentuated again the common defense interests of Bohemia, Hungary, and now also Poland, against the advancing Turks. Ladislas II and his young son Louis II, the last Jagiello king of Hungary and Bohemia, who died on the battlefield of Mohács in 1526, were too weak to see either policy—defense against the Turks and counterreformatory objectives—through to a successful end. Jointly with the national issue of the struggle between Czechs and Germans, unresolved through the centuries, we face here the ever more accentuated main problems of Czech development within the new union.[19]

The Hungarian crown, under the last Luxemburg ruler Sigismund, after 1386 and throughout the reign of Albrecht II until 1439, was worn also by the king of Bohemia. Here, too, the succession was the result of a marriage. Like the election of Albrecht V of Austria as king of Bohemia, the coronation of Vladislav III, the king of Poland from the house

[19] Karl Richter, "Die böhmischen Länder im Früh- und Hochmittelalter," pp. 257–347 and Ferdinand Seibt, "Die Zeit der Luxemburger und der hussitischen Revolution," pp. 351–568, both in Karl Bosl, ed., *Handbuch,* Vol. I; Count Franz von Lützow, *Bohemia,* revised by H. A. Pichler (London, 1939), pp. 38–202; Robert W. Seton-Watson, *A History of the Czechs and Slovaks* (Hamden, 1965), pp. 23–88; Ernest Denis, *Fin de l'Indépendance Bohême* (Paris, 1890), II, 3–29.

of Jagiello, as king of Hungary in 1440[20] indicated the evolution of a defensive alliance system of the eastern nations against the Turks. The three-cornered struggle for the crown of Hungary among Emperor Frederick III, his ward Ladislas Posthumus, and John Hunyady (and Hunyady's son Matthias Corvinus), presented the further development of this alliance. Although Matthias remained victorious, Frederick after the death of Ladislas Posthumus appropriated the deceased king's claims to the Hungarian crown. Yet Frederick's election as Hungarian king—or rather counter king—against Matthias in 1459 never led to the assumption of power. Just the same, the ambitions of the slow, indecisive, but stubborn and ruthless Frederick paved the way for the double marriages between Jagiellos and Habsburgs, on which the further political destiny of Hungary and Bohemia was to be based.

The significance of the struggle between Frederick and Matthias Corvinus went further. In the first place, the rule of the Hungarian king relied on his support of lesser nobility and towns, but also of the upper strata of the peasant population. They all had much to gain from further centralization of the kingdom. Matthias' opponents were the powerful landed aristocrats who succeeded in securing the election of the weak Jagiello king of Bohemia, who ruled in Hungary henceforward as Ladislas II. Under his son, Louis II, the last Hungarian king before the Habsburg accession, early Protestant thought was studied and cultivated at the court, an incipient development to which Louis's successor Ferdinand I, the first Habsburg ruler in Hungary, put a stop. Yet the late Jagiello rulers of Hungary had made their peace with the Habsburgs, who soon would be heirs to the crowns of Hungary and Bohemia. Like their Jagiello predecessors after the death of Matthias in 1490, the Habsburgs became identified at the beginning of their rule with the interests of the Magyar magnates, who had been opposed to the major reforms associated with the reign of Matthias. Yet neither Jagiellos nor Habsburgs could rely on the gratitude of the national aristocracy. On the contrary, either dynasty had to face increasingly stiffened opposition by the magnates. The weakness of the Jagiello regime had shaken the defense capabilities of Hungary against the Turks. This weakness went back to the reign of Matthias. Had this truly national king not felt that the defeat of the emperor was necessary to establish a workable alliance between Hungary, Bohemia, and Poland, he might not, as often charged, have conducted an offensive western policy at the cost of the neglect of adequate defense against the east.

[20] As king of Hungary Ladislas I.

All this does not mean that Matthias' policy was free of imperialist designs and in that respect very different from that of Frederick III, but he had the ability to appeal successfully to broader strata of the eastern European peoples than Frederick. However, the crushing of the Hungarian peasant revolt of 1514, undid much of Matthias' reform legislation. The great law code of the new Hungary, the Tripartitum of the brilliant but narrow-minded lawyer Stephan Verböczi, identified the political nation for centuries to come with the nobility. Although this concept of nobility included the gentry, it was still narrower than the political and social stratification of Hungary evolved between the Hungarian Magna Charta—the Bulla Aurea of 1222—and Matthias' death. At the eve of the Turkish onslaught, which was to engulf Hungary for one and a half centuries after 1526, the Habsburgs, a foreign dynasty preceded by another foreign one, became heirs to a divided and weakened political nation. They were faced by the threefold evil of foreign occupation, and in a sense deriving from it religious and ethnic division and conflict.

This last conclusion pertained in more than one way also to Croatia-Slavonia-Dalmatia, the triune vassal kingdom of Hungary.[21] The Habsburgs succeeded here in 1527 after due election by the Croatian estates as heirs to the Hungarian rule established in the early twelfth century. They had to face a Turkish occupation with social consequences even more far-reaching than in Hungary proper, and a gradually evolving Southern Slav ethnic problem which was to engulf Hungary and eventually the rising Habsburg power altogether. The union had started under inauspicious beginnings.[22]

The question may be raised at this point whether one can speak of political and institutional bonds between the political entities of the hereditary lands and the lands of the Bohemian and Hungarian-Croatian crowns in 1526–1527. Did any social-political premises exist, furthering the coming process of integration? Undoubtedly the rising Turkish danger from the east accentuated the problem of common defense needs of Christian Europe, as they had existed at the time of the Magyar invasions of Central Europe in the tenth century and of the Mongolian forays into eastern Central Europe in the thirteenth. Both dangers resulted in a measure of political integration. The Turkish advance in the early sixteenth cen-

[21] The rule over Croatia was contested by claims of the Venetian republic.

[22] Bálint Homan, *Geschichte des ungarischen Mittelalters* (Berlin, 1943), Vol. II; Kosáry, *A History of Hungary,* pp. 44–91. Lásló Makkai, in Ervin Pamlényi, ed., *Die Geschichte Ungarns,* (Budapest, 1971), Chapter II, pp. 23–127. Stanko Guldescu, *History of Medieval Croatia* (The Hague, 1964), pp. 215 f. and by the same author *The Croatian-Slavonian Kingdom 1526–1792* (The Hague, 1970), pp. 9–28.

tury represented a more lasting and better organized offensive than previous invasions, yet it might have been fought equally well by mere defensive alliances between the threatened countries.

Cultural ties between the Hungarian and the hereditary lands did exist to some extent under the reign of Matthias Corvinus. His death in 1490 and the hit-and-run attacks of the Turks were not conducive to further cultural progress and to the strengthening of cultural bonds with the west.

As for Bohemia, fairly close ties between the Bohemian and hereditary lands had existed as long as the cultural center of Prague was furthered by the German-Luxemburg rulers, who valued both, the imperial crown and the Czech national tradition. Yet the Hussite wars and the concomitant social upheavals in Bohemia strained cultural relations with Habsburg Austria (and Jagiello Hungary) even more than the political instability brought upon Hungary by the Turkish offensive. The fact that the Jagiello kings ruled in Hungary and the Bohemian lands at the same time changed little in this respect. Basic experiences, the Turkish danger, and the struggle between Matthias Corvinus and Frederick III in western Hungary and eastern Austria, and the social and religious impact of the revolution in Bohemia, were not shared.

In the socioeconomic field Hungary after the death of Matthias was too exposed to the eastern danger to be considered a reliable trading partner with west and north. As for the peasant situation, the reform movement of Matthias was stopped and the peasant revolt of 1514 headed by George Dózsa in the rural towns, although put down with savage ferocity by the authorities, revealed the continuing instability of existing conditions. Undoubtedly this social crisis weakened resistance against the Turkish conquerors.[23]

The union of 1526–1527 occurred at a time when cultural relations between the hereditary lands and the Bohemian crown were weaker than in the late fourteenth century. Strong ties between the hereditary lands and Hungary developed under Matthias Corvinus but they ended with his death. Bohemian, Hungarian, and Austro-German social conditions in the fourteenth and fifteenth centuries showed many similarities. The superiority of the Bohemian urban social structure in the fourteenth century, however, was less marked in the time of troubles of the fifteenth

[23] Peasant revolts followed also in the Habsburg domains of lower Styria, Carinthia, and Carniola, but they did not coincide there with an immediate threat of foreign aggression. Accordingly the impact of these revolts on international relations was limited.

century. Social progress in Hungary, which advanced considerably under Matthias had no chance to develop further. This becomes apparent in the socially backward law code of the Tripartitum Verböczi. Croatia was now almost fully absorbed by the Turkish invasion and had for a long time no major role to play in the social-cultural relationship between the historico-political entities which were to form the Habsburg empire.

Peasant unrest in the Austrian Hereditary and Hungarian lands was similar, although the peasants primarily affected in Hungary in the last decades preceding the union of 1526 belonged to a higher order than the revolutionary peasants in Austria; in Bohemia similar social problems were tackled if not solved almost a century earlier.

Yet common problems do not necessarily make for common solutions. The conditions for the union of 1526–1527 were unfavorable because of external threats and internal resistance in the various units and because the social and cultural structures of the major historico-political entities were different. Political history, however, worked for integration. Historical developments in the two centuries following the union of 1526–1527 will be discussed in the next two chapters, social-cultural issues in Chapter IV. The mentioned major social and cultural differences in the hereditary and the newly gained Habsburg lands bode ill for the prospects of durability of the new union. The problem which we have to discuss in the following is, to what extent these impediments could be overcome by political association.

CHAPTER II

Turks and Protestants (1526-1648)

A. The beginnings of political integration

The succession of the Habsburgs to the crowns of Bohemia and Hungary-Croatia established merely the dynastic premises for the evolution of an eastern Central European empire. These premises were as yet feeble. Only in the German Alpine lands was their hereditary basis unchallenged, while in Hungary recognition of the king by the diet and in the Bohemian lands his formal election by the estates were necessary. Considering the political rifts inside Hungary, which followed the disaster of Mohács and the religious and social division within the lands of the Bohemian crown, one has to look for deeper reasons than succession pacts to explain the integration process toward the formation of an empire.

Four such reasons will be advanced here: First, the Turkish advance into Central Europe, which coincided with the Habsburg succession in Hungary, created common defense needs. They could be met in the long run only in an empire-like organization. Second, the fight between the rapidly spreading Reformation and the incipient and ultimately victorious Counter Reformation established a political bond between the Habsburg domains. These two issues have been mentioned before. Third, it is said that the hereditary lands and the new Habsburg crowns supplemented each other economically. Lastly, geographic conditions were claimed to be conducive to integration.

All these advanced reasons are controversial. The relatively most convincing one is the Turkish danger since the needs for defense against it were sound enough. Yet this is something rather different from the frequently proclaimed Austrian mission to defend Christianity against the

Ottoman onslaught. It is, of course, true that ideological reasons played a part, but primarily we face here just a common European defense policy against imperialist aggression. Austria's contribution to it was great, and particularly so in view of underhand French attempts to support her enemies, but by no means exclusive.

As for consequences of the Turkish wars, seen in the more modest frame of the Danube basin, the almost two centuries of Turkish inroads into Hungary, and particularly the first 150 years of them, had exacerbated previously existing differences between Hungary and the hereditary lands. Moreover, a number of new ones, clearly traceable until the end of the empire, were created by the impact of the Turkish wars.

The Counter Reformation established, indeed, common bonds between new and old Habsburg lands, but it could do so only at the price of humiliating and alienating the Czech people for centuries to come. Moreover a sharply divisive issue in Hungary and the Alpine lands surfaced. Consequences of all these developments, particularly those in the Bohemian lands, were apparent until 1918 and, indeed, beyond.

That the western and eastern Habsburg lands ideally complemented each other economically is frequently considered an axiom. Yet an axiom is based on impossibility of proof and on self-evidence. Only the first holds at least partly true for the Habsburg empire. The factor of self-evidence is entirely lacking. Not until the second half of the eighteenth century did the industrial economic structure of Bohemia begin to differ markedly from that of the hereditary lands. About the same time the difference between their mixed agricultural-industrial character and Hungarian agriculture became more conspicuous. Then only, and only in a limited way did the process of economic complementation between the historico-political units of the Habsburg lands gradually assume significance. Before the reign of Maria Theresa these structural differences in economic conditions were not distinctive enough to explain the integration of an empire on economic grounds. This applies in particular also to the Polish territories acquired by the empress.[1]

The argument that the Habsburg empire formed a natural geographic unit seems to be even weaker. The lands of Galicia-Bukovina in the northeast were almost completely separated from the bulk of the Habs-

[1] Oscár Jászi, *The Dissolution of the Habsburg Monarchy* (Chicago, 1929), pp. 185–212; Robert A. Kann, *Werden und Zerfall des Habsburgerreiches* (Graz, Vienna, Cologne, 1962), pp. 121–135, revised edition of Robert A. Kann, *The Habsburg Empire: A Study in Integration and Disintegration* (2nd ed. New York, 1973), pp. 94–106.

burg domains by the Carpathians. Dalmatia in the southeast, which covered most of the monarchy's coastal territories, was separated by the Karst mountains from Croatia and the Hungarian plains. Of the two principal rivers, the Danube led from the main routes of European traffic into the practically land-locked Black Sea. Navigation in several places, above all at the Iron Gate (Orsova) and at the delta was very cumbersome and demanded unloading of freight. The Elbe, originating in Bohemia, on the other hand, did indeed flow into a main center of European North Sea traffic. Yet only a short stretch of its course passed through Habsburg territory and the main volume of its traffic entered the river only after it had left Bohemia. The geographic unity between Alpine hereditary lands, mountain-girded Bohemia, and Hungarian plains was no greater than of any other major European power.[2]

All this does not suggest that the four factors cited above as generally advanced to explain the evolution of the Habsburg power lack entirely cohesive features. Undoubtedly traits of this kind have furthered integration to various degrees at various times. Yet not even combined, let alone separately, do they suffice to explain the rise of an empire, more diversified than any other in existence in modern times, in regard to ethnic, linguistic, and historic traditions. No comprehensive theory, why an empire emerged and dissolved is entirely convincing on the strength of post facto reasoning. But some personal issues help to make us see the missing links in the disparate factors discussed. To one of them, the personality of the first true ruler of the newly acquired Habsburg lands, we are now turning.

The introductory chapter mentioned Emperor Charles V's brother, Ferdinand (1503–1564) in regard to his status in the line of succession and acquisition of new lands. Emperor Maximilian I, as will be remembered, had envisaged that the Bohemian, Hungarian, and Croation crowns would accrue to the Habsburgs, by way of the Jagiellonian succession. The Jagiellon-Habsburg marriages were concluded, but the untimely death of King Louis II of Hungary in the battle of Mohács in 1526 turned dynastic speculation to a reality close at hand. It meant, at the same time, wide enlargement of Habsburg power but also its division.

At the time of the family pact of Worms of 1521 between Charles and Ferdinand, when the Habsburg succession in the East was not yet determined, the universality of the rule of Charles, since 1516 king of Castile and Aragon, and since 1519 emperor, was strictly maintained. According to that agreement, Ferdinand could have succeeded only to the then five

[2] Kann, *Werden und Zerfall des Habsburgerreiches,* pp. 27–29.

Lower Austrian duchies, Upper and Lower Austria, Styria, Carinthia, and Carniola. He would have remained a major vassal prince of the empire. The threefold crisis, which evolved in 1521, the beginnings of the Turkish advance beyond Belgrad into Hungary, the opening of the struggle between the houses of Habsburg and Bourbon, and the spread of the political impact of the Reformation, forced the young emperor to lighten his burden in the east and to make sure that his position in the west would be fortified at the same time. The consequence of these considerations was the treaty of Brussels of the following year, 1522, according to which Ferdinand succeeded now in all the lands, which later would be referred to as the Austrian lands, namely, in addition to the five Lower Austrian duchies, Tirol, the Vorlande, the temporary regency in Württemberg, and that for lifetime in the Alsace. On the other hand, Ferdinand, from now on his brother's viceroy in all German lands, had to renounce his claims to the Spanish-Burgundian inheritance. These partition treaties, which precede the birth of the male offspring of the two brothers —the future Philip II of Spain and Maximilian II—constitute the parting of the way between the Spanish and German Habsburg lines.[3] The acts of 1556 after the abdication of Charles, according to which Philip succeeded his father as king of Spain and its appendages and Ferdinand, his brother, as emperor, provided only the official confirmation.

An independent Habsburg state in Central Europe might conceivably have evolved under the terms of the pacts of Worms and Brussels, but such political structure could hardly have risen to great power if it had not encompassed the pending link of the whole Habsburg German inheritance with the three eastern Bohemian and Hungarian-Croatian crowns to which Ferdinand succeeded in 1526–1527. It is difficult to see how that peculiar body, a great power, multinational in its ethnic character and German-oriented by its western ties, could have developed under then existing conditions any other way, namely by the various marriage, inheritance, and partition treaties, which introduced a basically peaceful element in the difficult process of integration.

Under the over-all rule of Charles, the emperor king in whose—loosely knit—realms the sun never set, the center of gravity of Habsburg rule and Habsburg power was in the west. The same held still true for the second half of the sixteenth and the first half of the seventeenth century. Actually only the Peace of the Pyrenees between France and Spain in

[3] Adam Wandruszka, *Das Haus Habsburg* (Vienna, 1956), pp. 115 f.; Wilhelm Bauer, *Die Anfänge Ferdinands I* (Vienna, 1907), pp. 64–161; Helmut G. Koenigsberger, *The Habsburgs and Europe 1515–1660* (Ithaca, 1971), pp. 1–63.

1659 marked the decline of royal Spain so clearly that the German Habsburgs with their wide eastern affiliations became now truly equal partners in the family alliance. Yet a genuine supremacy of the younger German line was not recognized as long as the older Spanish one existed, that is, to the death of the last Spanish Habsburg, Charles II, in 1700.

It is important to keep these facts in mind, if one wants to understand the relationship between Ferdinand and his imperial brother and the relationship between the two empires in the west and east based on the family alliance. Ferdinand, superior in intelligence, administrative ability, and at the same time less prejudiced than his older brother, deferred to the emperor notwithstanding conflicts on many specific issues in his over-all policies. So did more than two centuries later another Habsburg, Leopold of Tuscany to Joseph II, whom he equaled in ability but surpassed in political prudence and common sense. Still a generation further, the able Archduke Charles yielded to his brother, the mediocre Emperor Francis I. The allegiance to the unity of the dynasty, no matter who represented it, was one of the foremost premises of the rise of Habsburg power, the subordination of the eastern problems to the western was another. Ferdinand's political deference to Charles—a man of strong character but of little wisdom—meant recognition of the strength of imperial-dynastic ties. It meant also that the gradually evolving integration with the incongruous parts of the eastern empire could take place off the main roads of European power politics between France and Spain, above all off the essentially sterile theater of struggle in Italy. This meant further that the seemingly insoluble conflict between emperor and Protestant princes in Germany had for some time only a fringe impact on the association between Alpine hereditary lands and those of the eastern crowns. Had it been otherwise Ferdinand could hardly have coped successfully with the enormous problems of his reign, the progress of the Protestant Reformation in the hereditary lands, the question of integration of the eastern Habsburg lands, the recognition of the Habsburg succession in Hungary, and the Turkish advance from Belgrad to the gates of Vienna. Subordination to Emperor Charles, linked at the same time to the endeavor to separate western and eastern problems, is a key to the understanding of Ferdinand's impressive efforts and respectable success.[4]

It would be impossible to recognize the early results of this cautious policy if Ferdinand had not given to his realms some internal cohesion by far-reaching administrative reforms. Outstanding in this respect was

[4] Bauer, *Die Anfänge Ferdinands I* pp. 189–238.

the establishment of the mentioned Aulic Council (Hofrat) as Court of Appeal and controlling administrative agency in the hereditary lands and in the empire where Ferdinand acted as regent for his imperial brother. In 1558 after he had succeeded as emperor in his own right, this body was transformed into the imperial Aulic Council (Reichshofrat). The General Court Chancery (Allgemeine Hofkanzlei) on the other hand became not merely a deliberative and advisory body, but an executive body. By implication it could supervise enforcement of the decisions of the Aulic Council and Secret Council. Under Maximilian I, the chambers for financial administration in Vienna and Innsbruck were set up partly according to administrative functions and partly on a territorial basis. When Ferdinand ruled as emperor in his own right they were divided and expanded in sections of the imperial and the Austrian hereditary lands.

Even more significant from the standpoint of integration were those new institutions which pertained to all of Ferdinand's realms including the new ones of the three eastern crowns. The most important one was the Secret Council (Geheimer Rat) set up in 1527. It became the supreme body for affairs of state (foreign and military), but also for financial matters deriving from the income from crown domains and sovereign prerogatives (regalia). The council exercised also jurisdiction in matters of domestic policies, either under the presidency of the emperor or, more often, of Ferdinand or his representative, the supreme chancellor or the master of the household. The Court Chamber (Hofkammer) was an administrative body with the most clearly established jurisdiction for the hereditary lands, for common agenda with the Holy Roman Empire, and in some degree also for the lands of the Bohemian and Hungarian crowns. This institution combined functions of a treasury and a ministry of economic administration entrusted with the supervision of the fiscal agencies in Vienna, Innsbruck, Prague, and Pozsony (Pressburg). Lastly, the Court War Council (Hofkriegsrat) was created, a collegiate body which served as a ministry of defense for the German and Austro-Bohemian-Hungarian Habsburg lands. The supervisory control of military operations, which this agency assumed later, was resented by Austria's most eminent generals such as Count Raimond Montecuccoli and Prince Eugene of Savoy.

These main offices do not represent a clearcut structure of an evolving Habsburg empire. Judicial and administrative functions, in particular in regard to the contested jurisdiction of the estates of various lands, were at least as much in conflict as those between the administrative agencies of the Holy Roman Empire, the Austro-German hereditary lands, and those of the eastern crowns. The administrative ties between Holy Roman Empire and Austro-German hereditary lands, which went largely back to the reforms of Ferdinand's grandfather Maximilian I, were still stronger than those with the newly acquired eastern realms. As for the bonds with the empire, the Aulic Council, and later the Imperial Aulic Council, represented at least an unequivocal relationship of common interests although issues of subordination or coordination remained in doubt. Matters were even more complex in relationship to the east. Hungarians were for all practical purposes not represented in the Secret Council. This fact was explained by the long Turkish occupation of the best part of Hungarian territories. Yet Hungarian objections, and to a somewhat lesser extent those of the Bohemian estates, impeded also the complete integration of the financial administration under the Court Chamber. The same was true for the relationship to the Court War Council.[5]

And yet the incongruity of common institutions between empire, hereditary lands, and the eastern crowns bears witness to the flexibility of Ferdinand's skillful statesmanship rather than to lack of efficiency. Loose, and in the beginnings in some ways almost accidental, as the relationship between hereditary lands and eastern lands seemed, it might have been strained if the sovereign had insisted on a greater degree of centralization. On the other hand, the nature of the gradually evolving ties between hereditary and eastern lands loosened also the relationship of the former to the empire. No clear constitutional actions, but the fact that the hereditary lands in their still indistinctive union with the eastern lands became too unyieldy to be a manageable part of the empire, explain the very gradual evolution of the new great power of the future.

It is difficult to say how far Ferdinand had planned all this and to what extent he followed merely the principle that politics represented the pursuit of the practically feasible. Yet the assumption that his regency and reign stood for more than government by flair is borne out by several factors. His well-planned religious and foreign policy, executed cautiously but determinedly under difficult conditions, rank foremost among them.

[5] Alphons Huber and Alphons Dopsch, *Österreichische Reichsgeschichte* (Vienna, 1901), pp. 180–232; Ernst C. Hellbling, *Österreichische Verfassungs- und Verwaltungsgeschichte* (Vienna, 1956), pp. 210–267. László Makkai, *Die Entstehung der gesellschaftlichen Basis des Absolutismus in den Ländern der österreichischen Habsburger* (Budapest, 1960), passim.

B. Sovereignty in the Austro-German and eastern Habsburg lands

The supreme power of a political entity is vested primarily in its sovereign right to conduct an independent foreign policy. Far-reaching autonomy in regard to domestic administration on the other hand is compatible with subordination to a superior governmental authority. Such relationship may be of a federal or quasi-federal character. Unless we deal with a confederation of independent states with common institutions between but not above them, such organization falls short off full sovereignty.[6] What was the status of the rising new Habsburg power in eastern Central Europe in this respect?

To recapitulate briefly the legal situation: Ferdinand, according to the family compact of Brussels in 1522, which amended the pact of Worms of the preceding year, had become ruler of all hereditary Austro-German lands. Furthermore, on the basis of the state treaties with the Jagiello kings, he succeeded in 1526–1527 to the crowns of Hungary-Croatia, and Bohemia. His succession was confirmed by the Bohemian estates but only by a part of the Hungarian ones. Yet in spite of this contested election Ferdinand was crowned in Hungary as in Bohemia.

The Hungarian challenge will be discussed later. At this point, we are concerned with the relationship of the new union to the empire and reign of Charles V. Ferdinand, though now a prince of the empire endowed with wider territories than any other, still owed allegiance to his brother, as emperor and as head of the Habsburg dynasty. In this respect, but also in consideration of the obligations of the princes to support the Roman emperor against foreign foes and domestic insurrection, he was legally no fully sovereign ruler. Moreover, on the basis of the Golden Bull of Emperor Charles IV which in 1356 confined the imperial elections to four temporal and three ecclesiastic princes, he was not even the full equal of the slate of electors, which did not include a Habsburg.

But in a roundabout way equal status with the electors, demanded already by Charles IV's son-in-law Duke Rudolf IV (the Founder) of Austria was brought about under Ferdinand, as a result of the peculiar relationship between the empire and the Bohemian crown. Whether the king of Bohemia was to be considered a prince of the empire like other German electoral princes was a controversial question until 1356. His

[6] See Robert A. Kann, "Federalism and the Federal State in History," and the literature quoted there in *Rapports, Comité International des Sciènces Historiques,* XII Congrès International des Sciènces Historiques, IV (Vienna, 1965), 33–48.

status as imperial prince did not follow necessarily from his participation in imperial elections and from the honor of acting as libationer at the imperial coronations, but was generally assumed, because both of Charles IV's sons, like their father, wore the crown of the empire as well as the Bohemian. Their Habsburg successor as German ruler, Albrecht II, almost a century before Ferdinand laid at least claim to the Bohemian crown and to the Bohemian-imperial association.[7] These constitutional developments raised the status of the king of Bohemia as genuine royalty in relations to the German princes.[8] When Ferdinand succeeded to the Bohemian crown in 1526, the old question of loyalty of a Bohemian ruler to the emperor was revived. Even though the Habsburg king of Bohemia did not participate in the imperial elections in any but a mere formal sense, and even that only by the so-called readmission after 1708,[9] a relationship of subordination of the Bohemian crown bearer to the Roman emperor had now come into existence. The electoral function which had been denied thus far to the powerful Habsburgs became accessible to them by the backdoor. More important, the character of the association between the emperor and the king of Bohemia was substantially changed when a ruler of Bohemia owed allegiance to an emperor who was simultaneously head of his house. When Ferdinand succeeded his brother as emperor in 1556, and the union of imperial and Bohemian crowns was established in the same person, an important precedent had been set. The Bohemian crown was now definitely subordinated to the imperial crown.

[7] On the relationship of the imperial crown to the Bohemian see James Bryce, *The Holy Roman Empire* (London, 1914), pp. 242 f., 265; Ferdinand Seibt, in Karl Bosl, ed. *Handbuch der Geschichte der böhmischen Länder,* I, pp. 391–407; Hellbling, *Österreichische Verfassungs- und Verwaltungsgeschichte,* pp. 156 ff., 225. S. H. Thomson,, *Czechoslovakia in European History* (Princeton, 1956), pp. 29 f., 42 f. See also Frederick G. Heymann, *George of Bohemia: King of Heretics* (Princeton, 1965), pp. 554–557.

[8] But in the long run this peculiar relationship restricted the freedom of the ruler of Bohemia since the lands of the Bohemian crown were now more closely tied to empire and emperor. Until the death of Albrecht II of Habsburg, king of Bohemia and Hungary and duly elected German king in 1438, the legal issue appeared to be dominant if not altogether settled. During the time of trouble after Albrecht's death, and particularly under the regency and subsequent reign of the Hussite King George of Podiebrady (1452–1471), the question of the Bohemian electoral status within the empire became hardly practical. The same held true under the reigns of his Jagiello successors. Both Jagiello kings, Vladislav II and Louis I (as king of Hungary the second of his name), were not challenged as sovereign rulers by the Habsburg emperors.

[9] Franz von Krones, *Handbuch der Geschichte Österreichs,* 4 vols. and index vol. (Berlin, 1880–1881), see IV, 79 f. See also Huber and Dopsch, *Österreichische Reichsgeschichte,* pp. 173–175.

This fact establishes a distinction between the relationship of the lands of the Bohemian and the Hungarian-Croatian crowns to emperor and empire. Frequently it has been held that only the separation of the latter domains from the bulk of the Habsburg lands by the impact of two centuries of Turkish wars explains their more autonomous development. But the historical associations between empire and Bohemian lands, which have no parallel in the Hungarian-Croatian orbit, must be considered also as a reason for a closer link between empire and Bohemian crown. More important, they help to understand the bonds between the Austro-German Alpine hereditary lands as part of the empire and those of the crown of St. Wenceslav.

Under Charles V these distinctions between German-affiliated and non-affiliated eastern lands of the Habsburgs were blurred because the regent of all of them owed allegiance to an emperor as head of the dynasty whose center of power was far to the west of Germany between Spain, Italy, and Flanders. This situation changed in mid-century. The separation between the Spanish-Italian line under Philip II and the German line under Ferdinand became manifest when Charles V abdicated in 1556.[10] As a symbol of the separation, the imperial title reverted now to the head of the Austrian Line.

Still the primacy of the western (Spanish) line outlasted the reign of Charles V. In matters of politics the center of gravity of Habsburg rule was its relation to the leading power of seventeenth-century Europe, France. In this relationship, Spain, even in its decline and in a passive way, was a more important factor than the lands of the German Habsburgs. Only the extinction of the Spanish line in 1700 gave the German Habsburgs, heretofore the junior partner in the family alliance, their chance to enter world politics.

C. Principles of foreign policy

The foreign policy of Ferdinand I and his successors to the middle of the seventeenth century has to be seen in the light of the facts discussed. For a generation after 1526 the new king was only the chief executive organ of the policies of his brother. Impressive as his powers were and independent as he showed himself in the pursuit of policies, their basic principles represented necessarily the spirit of Madrid and not of Vienna. After the reign of Charles V the Austrian Habsburgs still were bound to

[10] Krones, *Handbuch der Geschichte Österreichs,* III, 395–397; Hermann I. Bidermann, *Geschichte der österreichischen Gesamtstaatsidee 1526–1804* (Innsbruck, 1867), Section I. 1526–1705, pp. 26–36.

support Italian and French policies of Spain, and this at a time when they were faced by threats from the east. Even after the tide of fortunes turned against the Turks in 1699 with the peace of Karlowitz (Karlovic) Austrian policies were still largely dominated by western interests. When they could not be successfully defended in the War of the Spanish Succession, eastern expansion served as mere substitute for the western ambitions of Charles VI in Spain, Italy, and the vast colonial empire beyond the sea.

What is true for the wars against the Turks pertains also to the ideological and political power struggle against the Protestants. Ferdinand I was no less devout Catholic than Charles V. The same can be said for most of his successors until 1918 in regard to strictly religious attitudes as distinguished from state-Church relations. The German Habsburgs may not always have been obedient to the will of the Church in Rome, but their devotion to the Catholic faith could seldom be doubted. The Spanish Habsburgs under Charles V and Philip II tried to undo the Reformation as far as possible by fire and sword; the Austrian Habsburgs, up to the reign of Matthias I, attempted to take the wind out of the sails of Protestantism by compromise. Intolerance on the part of the Austrian Habsburgs rose only gradually in direct proportion to the decline of the Spanish power as the foremost fighting champion of the Counter Reformation.

In secular politics, Charles V focused on the fight for supremacy against the French Bourbons. Their mighty kingdom blocked the amalgamation of the lands of the Spanish crown with the Holy Roman Empire and the new eastern domains of the Habsburgs. Inasmuch as Italy became the forefield of the old power struggle between Habsburgs and Bourbons, the papacy became involved in it, in the sixteenth century, on the side of the weaker French. They represented less of the threat to the Church than Spain supported by the Habsburg power in the east. A ruler not as devout as Charles under such conditions might have veered from the orthodox Catholic line to a policy of expediency. He could have followed in the footsteps of Francis I of France who concluded the first formal alliance with the infidel Turks and supported the German Protestant princes in an underhand way as well. In the case of Charles, such actions by the French king and the shifty and, from the emperor's viewpoint, opportunistic foreign policy of the popes from Clement VII to Paul IV strengthened only his determination to make the Church a more effective instrument of imperial power against the Protestant German princes and Protestantism. The struggle against the French and Protestantism, as a challenge to imperial power and imperial faith were the basic tenets of

Charles' policy. To them may be added his resolve to curb a spirit of moral laxity and independence from imperial influence within the Church in Rome.

The struggle in the east against the Turkish advance meant to Charles undoubtedly an external threat to the faith but not perhaps to the same degree to which he saw an internal threat in Protestantism. The Turks represented mere diversionary tactics of infidelity which kept him from a final settling of accounts against heresy. True enough, the struggle against the Ottoman power meant also a chance to rally the German princes to a common purpose, but that did not mean reconciliation with Protestantism—it meant the hope that in the face of the danger abroad the heretic princes at home would return to the fold of emperor and Church. The Schmalkaldian religious war against the Protestant princes, from 1546 essentially to the Religious Peace of Augsburg in 1555, resulted from the emperor's recognition that the undoing of Protestantism had become illusionary. His abdication was the final consequence of this insight.

Ferdinand perceived the priorities of imperial policies in a different way. To him the Burgundian, and Flemish interests of his house and the possessions beyond the sea meant little in themselves, although they were important from the viewpoint of loyalty to the imperial brother and from that of the grandeur of the dynasty. The conflict with France appeared to him as diversionary an attack as the Turkish one to emperor Charles. The Ottoman Turkish advance, however, meant to him the clear and present danger of expulsion from his domains not only in Hungary, but in the hereditary lands as well; besides, if they should be lost to the infidels, there was little chance for him to establish his rule in Bohemia. As for the issue of Protestantism, where Charles obviously subordinated his political strategy largely to his religious convictions, Ferdinand followed on the whole an opposite course. Not less devout but less intolerant a Catholic than his older brother, he was ready to compromise with the Protestants even on such dogmatic questions as celibacy for priests or the cup for the laity. Ferdinand's resistance to the foremost threat against his rule, the Ottoman Turks, was to a greater extent based on needs for domestic tranquility than Charles' in his fight across western Europe.

In the light of these considerations, Ferdinand stayed out of the emperor's conflict with France and the Italian states, above all the papal states. Even in Germany he supported the emperor only as much as the threefold obligations as member of the Habsburg dynasty to its head, as prince of the empire to the emperor, and as elected Roman king and successor to the imperial throne demanded. Accordingly Ferdinand during the Schmalkaldian war exercised a restraining influence on the emperor. At the time of the treacherous attack of Moritz of Saxony in 1552 against Charles he even acted as intermediary. In the same sense he worked for the unsatisfactory compromise of the treaty of Passau of 1552 and its confirmation in the Religious Peace of Augsburg in 1555. Indeed, Ferdinand's moderating influence was apparent as early as the first session of the Council of Trent from 1545 to 1547.[11] This does not mean that the problem of Protestantism did not play an important part in the reign of Ferdinand and his sons. The following discussion of events in the hereditary and eastern lands will show that the contrary was true. Yet Ferdinand's moderate attitude toward his imperial brother's counterreformatory activities proves that his foreign policy was not nearly as much motivated by the Protestant than by the Ottoman Turkish danger. To its character, course, and consequences we now turn.

D. The Turkish wars

The problem of the Turkish wars in the sixteenth, and to a lesser degree the seventeenth and early eighteenth centuries, was that of two interrelated, but basically separate, issues: the struggle of the Habsburg dynasty for recognition in Hungary against the claims of native princes and the fight of the Habsburg power against the Turks. The second issue was one of international relations; the first was a Hungarian domestic issue, international only insofar as it helped Turkish conquest. At this point, however, we are concerned with the international aspects of the problem.

In November 1526 a royal diet elected John Zápolya, count of Zips and voiwode of Transylvania, king of Hungary. He was crowned at Székesfejérvár (Stuhlweißenburg). This anti-Habsburg action of the nobles—mostly lesser nobles—was not meant as an accommodation with the threatening Turkish power under Suleiman II, that had been victorious at Mohács two months before. More likely, the diet in these times of troubles wanted to rally around a national king. Such characterization could not apply to Ferdinand, referred to as the German king by the Magyars. He was elected on the grounds of the hardly popular marriage- and succession treaties with the Jagiellons a month later at Pozsony, and crowned in the following year 1527. Ferdinand, though

[11] Karl Brandi, *Kaiser Karl V,* 2 vols. (München, 1937–1941), see I, 359–361, 428–429; II, 184–186, 386–387. Franz von Bucholtz, *Geschichte der Regierung Ferdinands I,* 9 vols. (Graz, 1968), originally published 1831–1838, see Vol. VIII.

recognized by the diet of Buda, was in the main only supported by the western Hungarian *comitats* (counties). Yet his claims to the Bohemian and Austrian hereditary lands, but above all the German and Spanish connections of his house gave him in the end a decisive advantage. As for the interests of the Turks, accommodation with the national forces of Hungary in isolation was easier than with those of a Habsburg with his power connection. The price offered for this kind of accommodation by the Ottoman Turks was limited autonomy, granted to that part of Hungary separated most securely from imperialist Habsburg designs. Thus the Habsburg objective to incorporate the new eastern possessions into an empire could be thwarted. This explains why the easternmost part of the Hungarian domains, Transylvania, up to then in substance a geographic and social cultural entity, now became a political one under Turkish auspices.

Still, there was only an indirect connection between the renewed Turkish advance in 1528, when Suleiman demanded the evacuation of Hungary by the Habsburgs and the as yet undecisive struggle between Zápolya's and Ferdinand's forces. It was in its beginning of little direct consequence for the main Turkish threat to the Habsburg lands. This became evident when Suleiman after the conquest of Buda in 1529—to be under Turkish control for more than 150 years—laid siege to Vienna in the fall of the same year. This first siege of Vienna has not caught the imagination of Europe to the same extent as the second one of 1683, which in word and song has been pictured for generations as the salvation of Christian Europe from the threat of Mohammedan domination. Actually the delivery of Vienna by a brave garrison under the command of Count Niklas Salm in 1529 was probably a greater though less spectacular achievement than the liberation five generations later brought about primarily by the efforts of a rather large army of combined imperial and Polish forces. More important, the siege of 1683 represented a last powerful but isolated offensive at a time, when the tide of Turkish advance to the west had come by and large to a standstill. At the time of Suleiman's attack, on the other hand, the young and aggressive Ottoman power which had swept through Hungary operated in a cycle of spectacular success. Suleiman terminated the siege, unlike the situation in 1683, not because he was defeated by a superior relief force, but simply because losses in battle and casualties due to various plagues did not seem to be worth the price. Considering the fact that the imperial and Austrian forces did not follow the retreating and disorganized Turkish army beyond a relatively narrow fringe of northwestern and western Hungary, there is little reasons to assume that Suleiman could not have renewed the attack with stronger forces, within the next years. If he did not do so again after just one unsuccessful attempt in 1532 it was precisely because he did not deem the conquest of Vienna and a further advance into the Danube valley worth the effort. At a time when the center of gravity of Habsburg power was anchored between western Germany and Spain, Vienna was neither as economic base nor as status symbol a prize of the first order for a conqueror. Even the Danube valley rated only as mere glacis of German interests. In this respect the situation had changed substantially by 1683 when the German Habsburgs and their capital, and not the possessions of the Spanish crown, represented the first line of defense against French imperialism from the west as well as aggression from the east. In a nutshell: the primary and permanent Turkish designs were focused on the conquest and control of Hungary. Forays farther west under Suleiman were devices of temporary political and military expediency. The issue of the Turkish wars was not a fight for the control of Europe but of Hungary, and interrelated with it the effort to prevent the rise of a great Habsburg power in the east.

In 1532 the high tide of Suleiman's offensive power beyond the borders of Hungary had passed. In 1538 the fortunes in the struggle between Zápolya and Ferdinand for the crown of Hungary began to turn as well: Zápolya, in the secret pact of Nagyvárad advised by his astute diplomatic representative Marinuzzi (George Utiešenić), promised to give up his alliance with the Turks and to recognize the Habsburg succession in return for the recognition of his rule in Hungary east of the Tisza for his lifetime. Inasmuch as Ferdinand had little control over events in these parts of Hungary anyway, this was a small concession. It was presumably a major reason why Zápolya a year later, strengthened now in his international connections by the marriage to the Polish Jagiello princess Isabella, went back on the treaty. Yet the fact that it had to be concluded in the first place and had to be renewed in one form or another repeatedly, indicated that the Habsburg power in Hungary was on the rise.

For the time being the pact had little effect on the administration of the parts of Hungary not controlled by Habsburg. Except for the lands east of the Tisza and particularly Transylvania, endowed with administrative autonomy under national rulers, and a strong evolution of religious tolerance, the area was simply converted into a Turkish province with the center in Buda. Only the mountainous northwest with the Slovak mining towns and a small western strip partly settled by Germans remained under Habsburg control. In the region under direct Turkish rule protracted warfare took its toll among the native Magyar population in the south. It was gradually and largely replaced by Southern Slav immigrants from the Balkans. The zone north and northwest of Buda, but still south of the fringe under Habsburg control, suffered less from the wars. Here the peasant towns remained primarily populated by Magyars.

The Habsburg power for some time to come was more successful in negotiations than in frustrating military campaigns for the reconquest of central Hungary. A five-year armistice beginning 1547, although encumbered by a humiliating annual tribute to the sultan, allowed for consolidation of Ferdinand's forces, just at the critical time when the emperor was engaged in the military conflict with the Protestant princes. In 1551 after the Catholic forces in Germany were seemingly, though in the long run not actually, successful, Ferdinand negotiated a new agreement with Martinuzzi on behalf of Zápolya's widow and his infant son at Gyula-Fehárvár (Karlsburg). The pact acknowledged for the first time Ferdinand's right to rule throughout all of Hungary including Transylvania without reservations. Again the promises were broken, this time by the younger Zápolya who moved back to Transylvania. Nevertheless, the precedent of unrestricted recognition of the Habsburg succession in Hungary was established. The outlook seemed to be all the more favorable to Ferdinand as the conflict with the Turks shifted now into lower gear. In 1562 peace was established with the Turks on the basis of the status quo. It still included preservation of the annual humiliating "honorary" tribute.[12]

In 1564 Ferdinand died, and the next year Suleiman followed him to the grave. The death of both men had a bearing on the Eastern question. With the passing of the great sultan the main period of sixteenth-century Turkish imperialist aggression had come to a temporary end. Ferdinand, although not motivated by the urge of expansion but of defense of what he considered legitimate rights, was resolved to take possession of all the lands of the Hungarian crown. A conflict of long duration seemed inevitable. But Ferdinand's oldest son and successor, Maximilian II, took an indifferent attitude to the eastern question. Deeply interested in the reconciliation with Protestantism, and in the hour of his death in 1575 possibly a convert to the new faith himself, this man of peace was not

[12] Bucholtz, *ibid.*, vols. IV, V, VII; Eugen Csuday, *Die Geschichte Ungarns* (Vienna, 1900), 2nd revised ed., II, 5–49. Mathias Bernath, *Habsburg und die Anfänge der rumänischen Nationsbildung* (Leiden, 1972), pp. 3–20. Ladislas Makkai, *Histoire de Transylvanie* (Paris, 1946), pp. 131–138. Mihaly Bucsay, *Geschichte des Protestantismus in Ungarn* (Stuttgart, 1959), pp. 20 ff., 39 f., 58; on the situation in Transylvania see also Chapter IV, Section B:b of this study.

interested in the active pursuit of any war. Neither from the viewpoint of Habsburg succession in the east nor on ideological grounds—the grounds of a fighting Catholic Church rather than his own concept of a kind of universal Christianity—did the Turkish war in particular mean much to him. The peace of Adrianople of 1568 ended it.

In 1570 Maximilian dropped also claims to Transylvania in favor of the younger Zápolya, who was followed soon by a far more aggressive successor as prince of Transylvania, the able Stephen Báthory. In a royal election contested by the supporters of Emperor Maximilian II he became king of Poland in 1575. A forced, prestigious marriage with the daughter of the last surviving Jagiello ruler strengthened Báthory's hands against the Habsburgs in Hungary. After his death in 1586 various members of the Habsburg dynasty vied unsuccessfully for election to the Polish throne. Yet rule by a member of the powerful foreign dynasty was feared by the majority of the membership of the Sejm and thus the chance that the Habsburgs might become rulers of the Polish-Lithuanian realms passed for good.

Meanwhile the Habsburg position in Hungary which had been fought for with great efforts and some success by Ferdinand I weakened again.[13] Several reasons account for this decline. In 1576 Maximilian was followed by his oldest son, Rudolf II, politically one of the most ineffectual, though one of the most cultured Habsburg rulers. Almost immediately he became involved in the political and religious problems of a fighting Protestant revolution rather than a mere religious Reformation in Bohemia. Soon he was also challenged by ambitious members of the dynasty on the issue of counterreformatory policies. Burdened with difficulties he was unable to cope with, Rudolf felt he could not budge on the eastern question. When the Turks refused to honor any further the twice-renewed peace of Adrianople of 1568,[14] the emperor felt he had to accept the challenge. The new Turkish war from 1593 to 1606 was at least as unsuccessful for the imperial side as any previous one, largely because of the lack of ideological appeal of the new war but also because of the military incompetence of Rudolf's brother Matthias as commander in chief. Charles V, with the support of Ferdinand, had succeeded in establishing some

[13] Lászlo Makkai, in Ervin Pamlényi, ed., *Die Geschichte Ungarns,* (Budapest, 1971), Chapter III, pp. 131–149; Makkai, *Historie de Transylvanie,* pp. 176–181; Csuday, *Die Geschichte Ungarns,* II, 49–61; Eugen Horvath, *Geschichte Siebenbürgens* (Budapest, n.d.), pp. 51–80; Nicolae Iorga, *Histoire des Roumains et de leur Civilisation* (Paris, 1920), pp. 164–180; and by the same author *Histoire des Roumains et de la Romanité Orientale* (Bucarest, 1937), IV, 435–457.

[14] In 1584 and 1592.

measure of solidarity between Catholic and Protestant princes in the eastern campaigns. Rudolf failed completely in this respect. The Turkish war during his reign did neither delay nor modify the conflicts with the Protestant German princes, let alone with the aggressive Protestant estates in the Bohemian and Austro-German hereditary lands. It merely weakened the power of the regime further and made its inefficiency and lack of inner unity even within the ranks of the dynasty more obvious.

Except for the brief and sometimes exaggerated importance of the events of 1683 the time had passed when the war against the Turks could become a rallying cry for Christian Europe. Nevertheless, although the war taken as a whole was a failure, it had some short-range redeeming aspects. The Báthory princes, and with them the estates, primarily those from the comitats east of the Tisza, recognized now in principle imperial rule in Transylvania and the necessity of common action against the Turks. Yet these agreements arrived at after several crises between 1589 and 1605 were not lasting. In 1605, Stephan Bocskay was elected prince of Transylvania and a few weeks later was proclaimed prince of Hungary by a substantial part of the Hungarian estates. This title as well as the manner of his elevation ran counter to the precedents of Hungarian constitutional tradition. Yet the political constellation was unprecedented as well. Bocskay previously had been a champion of cooperation with the imperial forces. Realizing that a national kingdom would have to take a stand against the Habsburgs, he now reversed his policy. This, however, did not mean an outright pro-Turkish position but rather the attempt to establish a Hungary as a "third force" between Habsburgs and Crescent. The agreement of Vienna of 1606 between Matthias on behalf of his imperial brother and Bocskay acknowledged the latter's rule as prince of Transylvania with the addition of three Hungarian comitats and in exchange for a token of imperial suzerainty rather than sovereignty. Bocskay's ultimate aim—not just rule of Transylvania but establishment of a Hungary independent of both, imperial and Turkish rule—naturally was not discussed. The subsequent peace of Zsitvatorok with the High Portal still in the same year was based on the Vienna agreement. Apart from the recognition of Transylvania as almost independent power, it included the cession of some further formerly imperial territory to the Turks (Eger, Esztergom, and Kanisza), but at least the annual tribute was replaced by a one-time "honorary gift." Peace with the Turks, but not with the rebellious Christian anti-Habsburg forces east of the Tisza, was now established for a half century. Inasmuch as the Transylvanian rulers could challenge successfully imperial control of Hungary this meant that the imperial position in Hungary remained as precarious as ever. Yet this meant also that the one factor in the eastern power game that could have decisively obstructed Habsburg power in Central and Eastern European affairs in the coming decades, namely Ottoman power, remained neutral during the Thirty Years' War. The importance of this attitude, confirmed in a treaty of 1627 to be valid for 21 years, can hardly be overrated.[15]

While thus relations with the High Portal appeared to be fairly stabilized for many years to come, conditions in Transylvania remained still in flux, highly unsatisfactory to the interests of Habsburg power. After the sudden death of the outstanding leader Bocskay in 1607, Gabriel Báthory was elected prince of Transylvania by the estates and recognized by the Ottoman power. Archduke Matthias, since 1608 recognized as acting head of the dynasty, crowned king of Hungary within a few months, king of Bohemia in 1611, and emperor after the death of his brother in 1612, took up the war against Báthory. He did so without success. Of Matthias, one of the poorest of all Habsburg rulers, it may be said that he possessed all the faults of his brother Rudolf II, but none of his redeeming qualities of kindness and cultural interests. Not mentally deranged like his brother at the end of his life, but slow-witted and just as indecisive in his actions, first an opportunistic friend of Protestantism, and then an ardent but ineffective champion of the Counter Reformation, Matthias, an equally inept and unreliable personality, stumbled from one misfortune to the other. Saved seemingly by the bell of Báthory's assassination in 1613 he had as it turned out to cope with an even more formidable successor, Bethlen Gábor (Gabriel Bethlen). In the peace of Nagyszombat (Tyrnau) the emperor recognized him as prince of Transylvania, confirmed the right of the estates to free election of the prince in exchange for recognition of the union between Transylvania and Hungary, and the pledge of support against the Turks.

Both these concessions were under existing conditions chiefly of nominal value. The peace of Zsitvatorok of 1606 with the Turks was in the same year prolonged for twenty years and, all pledges to the contrary notwithstanding, Gábor had himself elected "prince of Hungary" at the diet of Pozsony in January 1620. The election as king, though without subsequent coronation, followed hardly six months later. This event takes

[15] Horvath, *Geschichte Siebenbürgens;* Constantin Daicoviciu and Miron Constantinescu, *Brève Histoire de la Transylvanie* (Bucarest, 1965), pp. 112–137; Robert W. Seton-Watson, *A History of the Roumanians* (Cambridge, 1963), pp. 50–116; Bernath, *Habsburg und die Anfänge der rumänischen Nationsbildung,* pp. 3–46.

us into the reign of Emperor Ferdinand II (1619–1637) and the first, Bohemian, phase of the Thirty Years' War. Gábor, as national Hungarian prince and champion of Protestantism, tried to make use of the new emperor's troubles to his own advantage. In his endeavors to help the beleaguered Czech Protestants he was foiled, however, by the invasion of Transylvania initiated by the devout Catholic king of Poland, Sigmund III Vasa, in the fall of 1619. Consequently, after the victory of the imperial forces in the battle of the White Mountain in November 1620, Bethlen Gábor was forced to agree to a compromise with the emperor in the peace of Nikolsburg (Mikulov). It secured him outside of Transylvania only the rule in several Hungarian comitats. In theory more important was the fact that the emperor recognized religious freedom and the estates' constitution in Hungary. As it turned out, imperial concessions in this respect were worth a little more, but not much more in Hungary than in Bohemia. Subsequently they were considered to have been made under duress. In a sense this was true, and because of the impact of Turkish power in Hungary it was duress of a more lasting kind.

On the other hand it is equally true that Bethlen was not more reliable as contracting partner than the emperor. In alliance with the Protestant princes and undoubtedly in collusion with the Turks he resumed his campaign against the imperial forces in northern Hungary in 1623. In the face of the increasingly critical situation in Germany the emperor was forced now to confirm the Nikolsburg agreement by the treaty of Vienna in 1624 and to confirm it again two years later after a new attack on Ferdinand's forces. Bethlen Gábor, undoubtedly a distinguished ruler of Hungary, died in 1629. Had he lived longer he might conceivably have intervened decisively in the supreme crisis of the war on the side of the Protestant powers. But his interests were exclusively focused on Hungarian affairs and his western policy was inconsistent and therefore such turn of events must be considered speculative. Certainly the decisive force in the east, the Turks, were as yet not interested in resumption of the war. Only by the alliance of George I Rákóczy, prince of Transylvania after 1629, with the French in 1643 (treaty of Gyula-Fehérvár renewed 1645 at Munkács) did the eastern question briefly again become part of the game of European great-power politics. Peace between the emperor and Rákóczy was established at Linz in 1645.[16]

[16] Horvath, *Geschichte Siebenbürgens,* pp. 81–100; Dominic C. Kosáry, *A History of Hungary* (Cleveland, 1941), pp. 92–130. Makkai, *Histoire de Transylvanie,* pp. 224–237; Seton-Watson, *A History of the Roumanians,* pp. 116–119; Bernath, *Habsburg und die Anfänge der rumänischen Nationsbildung,* pp. 21–23.

Up to that point the question of Habsburg rule in Hungary was held in abeyance and could not be decided before new clashes with the Turks on a large scale. Only in conjunction with their policies does the Transylvanian question assume significance in international relations. What was more important in this respect, the Habsburgs' claims to all the lands of the Hungarian crown were still maintained during the worst crisis of Habsburg rule, namely the Bohemian revolt, to which we now turn. One of the strongest integrating factors of Habsburg ascendancy in the domains of the eastern crowns pledged to the dynasty in 1526–1527 was, indeed, the stubborn resolve to maintain and to defend all allegedly legitimate claims even under the most adverse conditions.

E. The Thirty Years' War; Protestantism and the Habsburg cause

The Bohemian crisis led the Habsburgs straight into the Thirty Years' War. This means that the major international conflict of the seventeenth century, and perhaps altogether the major conflict in European history between the Crusades and the Napoleonic wars, started as a domestic affair within one of the Habsburg domains. There were two main reasons why a struggle focused on the Habsburg claims to rule in Bohemia established in 1526 led to an international conflagration. First, the outcome of the Bohemian revolt was bound to upset the precarious balance of the Religious Peace of Augsburg of 1555 between Protestant and Catholic princes and the emperor; his interests were closely related to those of the Catholic princes, but not identical with them. Secondly, there was a crisis of confidence between these three forces, which meant that any of them would take full advantage of the situation if and when the occasion would present itself. Because the imperial side was victorious in the first phase of the conflict, the Protestant princes took to arms to undo the new state of affairs. Yet they would undoubtedly have done nothing to restore imperial rights if the elector palatine, the new king of Bohemia, would have managed to keep himself in power in Prague.

In the context of the peculiar relationship between the Bohemian revolt and a major international conflagration the question has to be raised, whether the Thirty Years' War is altogether part of the history of the Habsburg lands in terms of the union of 1526–1527. In one sense it is. Apart from its religious and national aspects, the Bohemian crisis, like the Hungarian one, was an integration crisis. It shook to the core the evolving new eastern Habsburg empire in the lands of the former Jagiello crowns as in the ancient hereditary lands. This means a Habsburg empire crisis. In another sense it is not. Certainly all Habsburg lands from Spain to Hungary were affected by the war, but the same became true for the whole of western and central Europe outside of the rule of the Habsburgs. Bohemia as foremost cause, main theater, and principal sufferer, was most deeply involved. As for Hungary, only the Transylvanian question, largely in its denominational ramification, linked the country to the events of the west, whereas the Turkish domination meant that Hungary was shielded from the danger of becoming a main theater of war. The hereditary lands were on the whole spared these horrors, too, but they suffered from the general misery and from the lowering of living standards in the trail of the war. This was felt all the more deeply since there was a very short respite between the end of the Thirty Years' War and the resumption of hostilities with the Turks. But because in the Thirty Years' War Bohemia was a foremost victim, and in the coming conflicts with the High Portal the Hungarian lands as well, the economic and social status of the hereditary lands became relatively speaking more favorable. This was not a minor consequence of the great war and of its aftermath, the new Turkish advance in 1663 into western Hungary.

The new Turkish offensive was in part motivated by the weakening of the Habsburg position brought about by general exhaustion, and one may therefore conclude that the great war was of long-range consequence for the emperor's personal domains. As for the short-range effect of the war the situation looked different. With the exception of Bohemia for the short period between the defenestration of the royal governors and their secretary in 1618 and the battle of the White Mountain in 1620, the eastern Habsburg lands did not influence the military and political course of the war to the same extent as the empire, France, Spain, Denmark, Sweden, the United Netherlands, or even Electoral Saxony, Brandenburg, and Bavaria. Except for the so-called Bohemian period of the war, Ferdinand II and, after his death in 1637, his son Ferdinand III acted primarily not as rulers of the eastern Habsburg realms but as the heads of the empire to defend, fight for, and reestablish Catholic supremacy and with it that of their house. Naturally the hereditary power of the Habsburgs in Austria and subsequently in Bohemia and even Hungary, gave the emperor badly needed leverage in this conflict. Yet essentially the Thirty Years' War as ideological as well as great-power struggle was above all a conflict about the Holy Roman Empire. It is one of the major features and consequences of the war that the Habsburgs acted here primarily as emperors of the Holy Roman Empire, and only in the second place as rulers of their own hereditary and quasi-elective realms.

Due to the weakening of Emperor Ferdinand II's German position and the relative strengthening of his status in the hereditary lands and the eastern kingdoms, his, and even more so his successors', priorities were from now on reversed. In this sense the war represented indeed a dividing line not only in German history but also in that of the Habsburg lands up to 1648, and after 1648 until the dissolution of the Holy Roman Empire in 1806.

Just the same, there are numerous connections between the local prehistory of the war and its international implications. Concessions by the pro-Protestant Emperor Maximilian II to the Bohemian Protestants as early as 1575, particularly the appointment of so-called *defensores,* to represent the Protestants before the emperor strengthened the Reformation in Bohemia. Mainly the beginnings of the counterreformatory drive in the hereditary lands around 1580 laid the ground for the coming conflict. This situation was accentuated by the fact that Archduke Ferdinand in 1596 became sovereign in Inner Austria (Styria, Carinthia, Carniola, Istria, and Trieste).[17] With this accession the Counter Reformation secured a leader, nearly as incompetent as the then chief of the house, Emperor Rudolf II, as narrow-minded as his brother the future emperor Matthias, but more energetic and stubborn than either. If and when Ferdinand should succeed to the imperial crown, a decisive and disastrous showdown with the Reformation appeared inevitable. The possibility of diversionary activities against the Turks did not offer itself again. The unstable situation in Transylvania represented merely a political sideshow.

Even before Ferdinand was elevated to a wider sphere of power, the ambitious and equally intolerant duke of Bavaria, Maximilian, his cousin, began to destroy the precarious balance of the Religious Peace of Augsburg in the empire, when he occupied the Protestant free city of Donauwörth. The alliance between the Protestant estates representatives of Bohemia, Moravia, and the hereditary lands in conjunction with the Hungarian estates at Pozsony in February 1608 and confirmed in June was a response to Maximilian's action. Of greater importance on an international scale was the union of the Protestant German states and free cities in the same year. It was meant to be a defensive alliance against encroachments of the status quo by the duke of Bavaria.

In 1609 Protestantism continued its counter-offensive. The hard-pressed Rudolf II was forced to issue the famous Letter of Majesty, which granted freedom of conscience to all inhabitants of Bohemia, and to

[17] As ruler in Inner Austria the third of his name, as emperor the second.

lords, knights, and royal chartered towns free public exercise of religion and the right to erect places of public worship and denominational schools.[18] This concession meant an extension of Protestant rights of various denominations far beyond the provisions of the peace of Augsburg. Yet this accomplishment was made against the turn of the political tide. This tide was represented by the Catholic League of bishops, imperial cities, and estates under the leadership of the duke of Bavaria. The conflict about the Jülich-Cleve succession in west Germany saw the Protestant Union and the Catholic League almost ready for a showdown. The uncertain situation created by the assassination of Henry IV of France, in 1610, who had favored the Protestants on the issue of balance of power, prompted both sides to abstain from immediate hostilities. Accordingly they settled for a temporary compromise. The death of Rudolf II in 1612, shorn of practically all powers after 1610, and the succession of Matthias as emperor, distrusted by Catholics and Protestants almost alike, did not help to mitigate the tense atmosphere.

Neither did the action of general diets which were meant to represent all the lands involved in the union of 1526–1527. They were never fully representative of their constituencies. One held at Budweis (Budějovice) in Bohemia in 1614 refused the emperor help against Bethlen Gábor. A more comprehensive assembly convoked in Linz in the same year endorsed this position, largely out of fear to become involved in a new conflict with the Turks. A further meeting in Prague in 1615 was dominated by the demands of the Protestant Czech estates for wider autonomy. Imperial authority appeared to be feeble in all these instances.

The issue that actually led to the defenestration of 1618 in Prague and therewith to open revolt, was relatively minor, namely the question of erection or elimination of Protestant churches built by Protestant subjects on the estates of Catholic lords. The defenestration symbolized only the surface of a much farther reaching conflict. Two secret treaties of March and June 1617 between Ferdinand, then already clearly the heir apparent to the imperial throne, with Philip III of Spain prepared the ground for open conflict. In the first treaty Philip, in return for concessions in western central Italy (Finale and Piombino), and for transfer of imperial

[18] Issued for Bohemia in July 1609 and extended to Silesia the following month. See Ernst W. Zeeden, *Die Entstehung der Konfessionen: Grundlagen und Formen der Konfessionsbildung im Zeitalter der Glaubenskämpfe* (Munich, 1965), pp. 161–164; Count Franz von Lützow, *Bohemia,* revised by H. A. Pichler (London, 1939), pp. 223–237; Karl Brandi, *Deutsche Geschichte im Zeitalter der Reformation und Gegenreformation* (Munich, 1960), pp. 453–458; R. J. W. Evans, *Rudolf II and his World* (Oxford, 1973), pp. 43–115.

claims to the Alsace, pledged to be not a candidate for the soon to be expected imperial election. This left the field free for Ferdinand. The second treaty, a genuine succession pact, was even more specific. It recognized the right of Ferdinand as heir to the Habsburg eastern realms, even though Philip III was more closely related to Matthias than Ferdinand. This meant in effect the final and permanent separation of the Spanish from the German branch of the Habsburg dynasty.[19] These agreements became very practical, when Ferdinand elected and crowned king of Bohemia in 1617 and of Hungary in 1618, succeeded Matthias, who died in 1619, as emperor as well. The ruler, firmly resolved for the final showdown with the Reformation, had laid the groundwork for the European alliances with Spain and the Catholic League. Before his election as king of Bohemia in 1617 Ferdinand had expressly pledged adherence to the Letter of Majesty of Rudolf II, and thereby indicated that he was resolved to obtain his aims, if necessary by force.

The open Bohemian revolt which followed the defenestration, the establishment of an Estates Directory under Count Matthias Thurn as the government of the land, gave Ferdinand his chance. Undoubtedly, the Bohemian rebels, who had a good case in their protests against violation of the Letter of Majesty, lost their lawful standing when they turned to open revolt against the ruler to whom they had sworn allegiance. The condemnation of this action was in the beginnings of the conflict not restricted to Catholic Europe. The excessive imperial response, the concomitant spread of a revolutionary appeal still based in part on an issue of faith, but, above all, the threatening shift in the balance of power between Reformation and Counter Reformation changed these feelings within two years substantially.

The intransigence of Ferdinand's new course was revealed when he dismissed and confined Cardinal Khlesl, up to this time Matthias' and his own trusted political adviser and himself an ardent champion of counter-reformatory activities. Yet Khlesl, far superior in intelligence to Ferdinand —a modest compliment to be sure—for reasons of expediency had counseled compromise with Protestants in Bohemia and for this reason was

[19] A reservation, that the male lines of either branch would still precede the female of the other, remained without practical importance up to the extinction of the older Spanish line in 1700. See Gustav Turba, *Die Grundlagen der pragmatischen Sanktion,* Vol. II: *Die Hausgesetze* (Vienna, 1912), pp. 99–119; Grete Mecenseffy, "Habsburger im 17. Jahrhundert: Die Beziehungen der Höfe von Wien und Madrid während des dreißigjährigen Krieges," in *Archiv für österreichische Geschichte* (Vienna, 1955), Vol. 121:1, 4–10; Koenigsberger, *The Habsburgs and Europe 1515–1660*, pp. 219–231.

removed. His dismissal is one of the personal changes which has not found the attention in historiography it deserves. The cardinal's fall in 1618 may possibly have changed the course of history profoundly. Whether Khlesl could have prevented the Thirty Years' War is, of course, uncertain; but that Ferdinand's new, predominantly ideological policy, now deprived of any restraint, made a major conflagration inevitable is obvious.[20]

A discussion of the whole course of the Thirty Years' War would divert attention from the history of the new eastern Habsburg empire that came gradually into being. Its direct interests stood out chiefly in the earlier phases of the struggle; though they became less conspicuous, they did not disappear in the later ones either. Major events in this respect were the invalidation of Ferdinand's election as king of Bohemia in August 1619 by the estates, the following choice of the elector palatine Frederick, the "winter king," who had the additional support of revolting estates not only in Silesia but indirectly by the Protestants lords and knights in Lower- and above all Upper Austria. Ferdinand, certain of the benevolent attitude of the great Catholic powers—Spain and for the time being France as well—hoped for outside support if worst should come to worst. This in addition to his uncontested strong faith were the main reasons why he did not choose to yield in the face of the advance of Thurn's army close to the gates of Vienna and the impetuous demands of the Upper and Lower Austrian estates for a Letter of Majesty comparable to the one granted by Rudolf II. Ferdinand accordingly stood his ground in the summer and spring 1619 against the combined but not concerted attacks of the Bohemian forces under Thurn and the Hungarian forces under Bethlen Gábor. Lack of planning on the part of his enemies, reliance on the ultimate support of the great powers, and the offensive spirit of the head of the Catholic League, Maximilian of Bavaria, who invaded Upper Austria, helped the emperor. Important was also the military prowess of his commander in chief, Count Tilly, which turned the engagement between the imperial forces and those of the new king of Bohemia at the White Mountain, a few miles from Prague, into one of the most decisive victories ever obtained by Habsburg troops against an enemy.

[20] Krones, *Handbuch der Geschichte Österreichs,* III, 402–424; Lützow, *Bohemia,* pp. 253–265; Hans Sturmberger, *Aufstand in Böhmen: Der Benginn des dreißigjährigen Krieges* (Munich, 1959), pp. 7–34. Cecily V. Wedgwood, *The Thirty Years War* (London, 1944), pp. 76–82; Ernest Denis, *Fin de l'Indépendance Bohême* (Paris, 1890), II, 31–560.

Yet while the ominous political consequences of the battle were lasting, the military impact was of short duration. Its implications in this respect were superseded to a point already by the Danish intervention in the war in 1625 and certainly by the Swedish one in 1630. What remained as consequence until the end of the Habsburg empire was the permanent alienation of the Czechs. It originated with the cruel vengeance of the imperial authorities, the undoing of the Bohemian Reformation and national autonomy by force, and it culminated in the new Bohemian constitution of 1627 which reduced the country practically to a province. Long after the direct effects of these acts of repression had ceased and were, in the course of many generations, in part even righted by law, the indirect psychological ones remained.

Again it is necessary to distinguish between the direct and indirect impact of events. Even the spectacular rise of Wallenstein from a simple colonel in 1617 to commander in chief of all imperial forces (1625), his great success against the Danes and his indifferent one against the Swedes, his subsequent dismissal in 1630 and reappointment in 1631, have only indirect bearings on the foreign relations of the rising eastern Habsburg power. This pertains also to Wallenstein's deposition, outlawing, and legalized murder in 1634 on acount of his vacillating, and, from the imperial viewpoint, treasonable policies of secret negotiations with the Swedes. The motivations and counter-motivations of these doings by and against the great general are focused on imperial and not on Austrian, Bohemian, or Hungarian politics. Wallenstein's thinking and acting, or calculated nonacting, were in essence counter-moves against the Edict of Restitution of Ferdinand II in 1629. This act meant to undo the Protestant ascendancy in the empire after the peace of Augsburg in 1555. It ordered consequently the return of all the estates of the Church, secularized in the interim period, and the continued restriction of the provisions of Augsburg to Lutheran Protestants alone. These conditions were to be ever more strictly enforced. Yet all this made little difference for the Habsburg hereditary lands and those of the Bohemian crown where the Counter Reformation had reached its objectives against Lutherans and Calvinists alike for several years before the issuing of the Edict of Restitution of 1629. It made little difference either for the bulk of Hungarian territory under Ottoman control and of Transylvanian control under Bethlen Gábor and George Rákóczy.

The emperor had simply attempted to force German political and religious conditions as far as possible into step with those in his own lands. This meant as seen from a long-range viewpoint to bring them out of step with western European developments. Yet for a long time Ferdinand's repressive policies were as successful in his own realms as they had failed on the German and European level. This is one of the major tragedies of the history of the Habsburg lands, particularly in the cultural field. It is doubly tragic because conformism triumphed by strength of enforcement and not persuasion. Faith, however genuine but brought about by external pressures, carried the seeds of future intolerance and intellectual stagnation in many fields.[21]

The Edict of Restitution represented the high tide of Ferdinand's restoration politics. He lived long enough to see the results of the Swedish intervention of 1630 and the Swedish-French anti-imperial alliance of 1635. When he died in 1637 Catholic counterreformatory policies were succeessful in his own lands apart from Hungary, yet they had failed beyond his domains. Succeeded by a less stubborn and more peacefully inclined son, Ferdinand III (1637–1657), the personality of the new bearer of the Holy Roman crown added at least not to the difficulties, which had to be overcome, before general peace could be established. This peace, the Westphalian peace treaty of Münster and Osnabrück in 1648 did not affect the Habsburg lands directly to a greater degree than the war, if we except the devastations of Bohemia. True, the Habsburgs lost important southwest German domains (particularly in the Alsace and the Sundgau). Yet these domains in the Vorlande were not adjacent to the main body of the Habsburg lands. The modifications of the Edict of Restitution of 1629, in reverting to the state of ecclesiastic property in 1624[22] and the long overdue extension of the provisions of the peace of Augsburg to the Calvinist creed, were insignificant in territories where Protestants had been expelled and Protestantism had been driven underground altogether. More important from a political viewpoint was the fact that the sovereignty of the princes of the empire was extended. The right to conclude alliances among the German princes themselves as well as with foreign powers had to be recognized—save for covenants directed against emperor and empire. Numerous alliances, not excluding even the forbidden ones against emperor and empire, were concluded before the war. Still it meant something, particularly for the smaller princes, to have them legalized now to a point. Yet it meant nothing for the Habsburgs in their double capacity as bearers of the crown and mightiest princes of the empire. How could a Habsburg emperor who conspired against the

[21] See also Hans Sturmberger, *Kaiser Ferdinand II und das Problem des Absolutismus* (Munich, 1957), pp. 32–46.

[22] This specific provision did not apply to the hereditary lands.

empire be controlled, if he was by far the most powerful prince of the empire himself and ruler of wide territories beyond its boundaries? How could he be curbed as prince if he refused to apply these curbs as emperor? The old problem of *Quis custodiet custodem?* arose here in full force again.

We have noted already the obvious, namely that course and outcome of the war hurt Bohemia far more than the hereditary lands and thus improved the latter's relative status. This advantage—a partial advantage only—was, however, for some time offset by the general economic setback brought about by the war and the retarding cultural influence resulting from the victory of the Counter Reformation in the Habsburg lands. Apart from this, one of the most important consequences of the war for the Habsburg domains was the fact that the power of the ruler of the eastern Habsburg lands was ever increasingly based on his status as prince of the empire and not of emperor himself. A trend originating already after the great interregnum under Rudolf, the patron of Habsburg rule in the hereditary lands in the thirteenth century gained now renewed strength. This trend diverted the Habsburg power to some extent from German interests outside its hereditary domains, and therefore meant a strengthening of the bonds between the realms of the eastern empire in the making since 1526.

CHAPTER III

An Empire Evolves and Asserts Itself (1648–1748)

A. Common succession and common institutions

A great Austrian historian, Oswald Redlich, perceived the rise of the Habsburg empire to a genuine great-power position during the period from 1700 to 1740.[1] This interpretation is justified if power is measured by results: the position of the Habsburg power as it evolved from the conflagrations in western and Central Europe of the first half of the eighteenth century and from the spectacular though short-lived successes in the east throughout the first part of that period. But if we measure the rise of the Habsburg lands not by success but by determinant conditions and objectives we may antedate this period to the outcome of the Thirty Years' War.

Whether this war had weakened the Catholic cause on the whole may be controversial; that it had weakened the Holy Roman Empire is uncontested. Correspondingly, the power of a Habsburg emperor after 1648 had to rely more on his sovereignty in the Austrian hereditary lands and the lands of the Bohemian and Hungarian crowns, which he considered now as hereditary possessions as well. In regard to the Bohemian crown, Ferdinand II had fully succeeded in 1627: according to the Vernewerte Landesordnung the right of the estates to elect the king was forfeited and

[1] Oswald Redlich, *Das Werden einer Großmacht: Österreich 1700–1740* (Baden, 1938). H. I. Bidermann, *Geschichte der österreichischen Gesamtstaatsidee 1526–1804* (Innsbruck, 1867–1889), II, 8–27.

could be reestablished only if the royal house, male and female members alike, should become extinct.

After 1648 every major move of the emperor had to be based exclusively on the strength resulting from the rule in his hereditary lands and those of the eastern crowns. The success of this dynastic policy was not spectacular at least until 1683, but it was still the basic premise for the attainment of a great-power position. The legal foundations of this development were the provisions of the Westphalian peace treaty which pertain to the extension of the sovereign rights of the German princes in foreign relations. The political consequences became apparent in the first years after the reestablishment of peace. The decreased dependence of the princes on emperor and empire in international relations strengthened their position, yet this did not mean that their gain was the emperor's loss. Actually the first among the princes, the Habsburg ruler, gained most, because he became ever more independent from obligations to the other princes and from their concomitant interference in imperial matters. However, he secured this position not as emperor but as the most powerful prince in the empire and established thus a precedent for his peers.

Such increase in strength however, held not true in every respect. In 1653–1654 the imperial diet in Regensburg met for the last time as a genuine assembly of estates which could still be called a decision-making body. The new body, the permanent imperial diet (*Immerwährende Reichstag*), which opened in 1663 and remained, in theory, in continuous session until the end of the empire in 1806, was a mere deliberative assembly of representatives of princes, secular and ecclesiastic lords, and imperial cities. This does not mean that the empire as image in the realms of ideas and the imperial crown as prestige-forming institution had lost their significance, but does mean that the new diet gave little additional leverage to Habsburg power in imperial domestic matters.[2]

Another factor related to the rise of Habsburg power as distinguished from the dynasty's imperial position was political. The designs of Louis XIV of France in conjunction with the decline of Spain involved the Austrian Habsburgs increasingly in western European politics. The renewed conflict with the Turks represented a struggle for survival, that with the French one for supremacy in Europe as well. In this sense we

[2] Fritz Hartung, *Deutsche Verfassungsgeschichte vom 15. Jahrhundert bis zur Gegenwart* (Stuttgart, 1950), pp. 150–156; Heinrich Brunner and Ernst Heymann, *Grundriss der deutschen Rechtsgeschichte* (Munich, 1927), pp. 289–291; Adam Wolf, *Fürst Wenzel Lobkowitz,* (Vienna, 1869), pp. 51–104.

may consider the history of the Habsburg lands after 1648 as incipient evolution of the great-power position, even though the amalgamation of administrative institutions from 1648 to 1748 was meager in content and slow in speed. More important during this era was the gradual establishment of a common succession in the German and eastern Habsburg lands. This succession brought about a limited centralization of government, although as yet imperfectly reflected in common institutions.

The Habsburgs from the time of their succession to the Bohemian and Hungarian crowns had claimed hereditary rule there as much as in the hereditary lands themselves. This could be materialized in regard to the Bohemian crown after the battle of the White Mountain in 1620. In Hungary the same result was achieved only at the diet of Pozsony (Pressburg) in 1687 after decisive victories against the Turks were won. Yet here the rights of the estates for free election of the king had lapsed only in case the male line of the royal house would become extinct, since female succession was not recognized. In the hereditary realms of the Habsburg succession had remained uncontested. No election, or even assent of the estates in the Austro-German lands was necessary; but there were other weighty impediments to an uncontested succession.

The succession order, as it stood at the end of the reign of Ferdinand I and for two generations afterward, pertained to the dynasty as a whole and not to a generally recognized law of primogeniture, that is, succession by the closest male descendant. Inasmuch as the succession in the Bohemian and Hungarian lands approximated politically that in the hereditary lands we find here a major obstacle to the establishment of a unified empire, since the lands to be bequeathed did not automatically revert to individual persons.

When Ferdinand I died in 1564 the lands under the rule of the German (eastern) line of the Habsburgs were divided between his three sons according to the Hausordnung of 1554. Maximilian II, his eldest son and successor as emperor (1564–1576), became king in Bohemia and Hungary [3] and sovereign in Upper and Lower Austria. The second son inherited the rule in Tirol and in the southwest German Vorlande, the third Styria, Carinthia, Carniola, Gorizia, Trieste, and Istria. When the Tirolian line became extinct in 1595 its possessions were divided between the two others. Yet this was no final determination of the issue. Only in 1665 were all

[3] Recognized as king and future ruler in Bohemia already in 1549 and crowned as king of Hungary in 1563. Prior to the death of the ruling sovereign such acts of state, like in the Holy Roman empire, established, of course, only the right to succession not as yet the actual succession to the throne.

domains of the dynasty united in the same hand, that of the emperor. The principle of indivisibility of the Habsburg possessions under the emperor's hereditary rule and the sole and only succession by primogeniture, was established in the will of Ferdinand II in 1621.[4] Whatever the shortcomings of the narrow-minded Ferdinand were, he realized that a strictly regulated succession under the emperor as head of the house was important to give cohesion to his disparate lands. To achieve it by succession pacts seemed to be easier than by the development of common institutions.

Ferdinand II failed in institutions and succeeded only partly in a unified succession. One loophole in the latter could be plugged temporarily, when the Hungarian Reichstag of 1687 was forced to recognize the hereditary Habsburg succession in the male line. This meant, however, that the right of free elections of the king would still resort to the estates in case the male lines should become extinct. At the end of the seventeenth century this contingency had become a definite possibility for all Habsburg lands. The situation had become complicated by the death of the last Spanish Habsburg, King Charles II, in 1700 which led to thirteen years of major European conflagration and subsequent international crisis directly related to it at least until 1748. This international aspect of the succession problem will be discussed in the context of international relations.

At this point we are concerned with the impact of the question on the eastern Habsburg lands. Frequently one cause is singled out as main reason for the establishment of a unified succession system, namely the need to secure the succession of the oldest daughter of Emperor Charles VI, Maria Theresa, born in 1717. Actually, the whole problem except for its latest stages was unrelated to the issue of Charles VI's male or female descendancy.

As noted, the succession question became acute between the death of the last male Habsburg in Spain, King Charles II in 1700 and that of the last male German Habsburg, Emperor Charles VI in 1740. After it was decided in Vienna, that the younger son of Emperor Leopold, Archduke Charles, should claim the whole Spanish inheritance in defiance of the

[4] There are several equally valid interpretations of the principle of primogeniture. In the narrowest sense it would mean succession by the oldest son. Somewhat farther go the concepts of succession in a sideline. This means that in case there are no living direct heirs, the surviving oldest brother and his descendants, respectively, if there are no brothers, male first cousins and their sons etc. would qualify. This latter, wider concept of primogeniture was the one acknowledged in the will of Ferdinand. The even broader concept of female succession, if the male lines should become extinct was not recognized by the emperor. On the whole question see Gustav Turba, *Die Grundlagen der pragmatischen Sanktion, II*, 75–125.

will of Charles II of Spain a *pactum mutuae successionis* between the German line and the new Spanish line was established in some secrecy in 1703. Translated from the legal into the political sphere this meant that in case the German Habsburg claim to the Spanish inheritance could be successfully maintained against the French Bourbons, Emperor Leopold I (1657–1705) was willing to recognize the separation of the Spanish royal succession from the German (Austrian)-Hungarian-Bohemian imperial line. If, however, either of the two lines—the German now represented by Leopold's older son Joseph, the Spanish by his younger son Charles—should become extinct, either one was to be succeeded by the other. In no other case should Spain and the possessions of the German line be united under one scepter as they were under Charles V after 1518. Provisions concerning a possible new division of the eastern possessions were added in favor of Leopold's younger son, in case he should fail to succeed to the Spanish crown. Also the female succession after the male in Spain as well as in the Austrian hereditary lands was recognized.

These agreements, however, were conjectural in several respects. The attempts to establish a new Habsburg line in Spain failed; equally unforeseen, the contingency of compensation of the claimant to the Spanish crown, Leopold's younger son Charles by his older brother Joseph, did not arise. Emperor Joseph died in 1711, which meant that the German eastern inheritance reverted now to Charles, as Emperor Charles VI (1711–1740).[5]

In 1713, when Charles VI announced publicly before the chief dignitaries of his realms his intentions to establish a common order of succession for all Habsburg lands, the main issue of the war of the Spanish succession was practically settled. The rule over a much reduced Spanish empire would revert to Philip of Anjou (Philip V), a grandson of Louis XIV, and not to the new Habsburg emperor. Charles, largely on emotional grounds, refused to recognize this fact formally before 1720. Just the same, the issue was clear. A common order of succession in the Habsburg lands could no longer pertain to common or mutual succession pact in Spain and the German eastern orbit.

Charles wanted to establish the precedence of the succession of his own descendants before those of his deceased older brother Joseph. Charles at that time had every reason to hope for a male heir, and the question of the female succession was therefore as yet moot.[6] But the decisive question of the order of common succession for all Habsburg domains remained.

[5] Turba, II, 136–157.

[6] Actually Charles had a son Leopold, who was born and died in 1716, the year before Maria Theresa's birth.

Common institutions were most imperfect and expected to remain so; the succession question, therefore, was of overriding importance for the evolution of an adequately integrated Habsburg empire. In fact this issue retained its importance to the end of the empire. The great state acts, such as the proclamation of the Austrian empire of 1804 and the Austro-Hungarian Compromise of 1867 were anchored in the Pragmatic Sanction. Indeed, had the heir apparent, Archduke Francis Ferdinand, murdered in Sarajevo in June 1914, acceded to the throne, the interpretation of the Austrian and Hungarian version of the order of succession might have led to a new empire crisis.[7]

The passing of the Pragmatic Sanction had to be channeled through a cumbersome process of submission to the estates in the various Habsburg lands. The Austrian and Bohemian estates accepted the *Sanctio pragmatica lex perpetua valitura* in 1720, the Croatian in the following year. The latter declared their willingness to submit the act to the king of Hungary, but not to the kingdom of Hungary, a distinction, which in the era of revised Slavonic nationalism acquired significance.[8] More difficult were the negotiations with the Hungarian and Transylvanian estates, who in substance confirmed the legislation in 1722–1723. The hereditary succession as established by the diet of Pozsony of 1687 remained in force, but the requirement of a coronation oath to uphold Hungarian laws and liberties was further tightened.[9] The estates of the Austrian Netherlands and of Lombardy followed in 1724 and 1725. According to this legislation the male line was always to precede the female line, but the latter had now a right to succession in case no male heirs existed. In as much as the last child of Charles VI, a daughter, was not born until 1725, the question of female succession was even now far less a motivating factor for the whole legislation than the wish to establish the precedence of the

[7] According to the Hungarian version of the Pragmatic Sanction the offspring of the morganatic (non equal) marriage between Archduke Francis Ferdinand and Countess Sophie Chotek (later Duchess of Hohenberg) would have been entitled to succeed in Hungary, but not in Austria. Even though Francis Ferdinand renounced the rights to the succession of his descendants for Austria and Hungary—in both respects undoubtedly in good faith—the issue was not really settled. The assassination made, of course, any further speculations purely academic. See also Turba, ibid., I, 44–47, II, 251–257; and by the same author, *Die pragmatische Sanktion mit besonderer Berücksichtigung der Länder der Stephanskrone* (Vienna, 1906), pp. 28–31.

[8] The principle was embodied in the Croatian dietal declaration of 1712. See Stanko Guldescu, The *Croatian-Slavonian Kingdom 1526–1792* and Turba, *Die Grundlagen*, II, 402–403.

[9] See Heinrich Marczali, *Ungarisches Verfassungsrecht* (Tübingen, 1911), pp. 14–16, 58–63.

offspring of the ruling emperor. Yet this aim, too, was not nearly as important as the establishment of a common order of succession in all Habsburg lands as foundation of the new great power's gradual integration.

This, of course, was a long-range objective. The short-range goal, namely the incessant, but largely vain efforts by Charles VI to obtain recognition of this legislation by the European powers appeared more important. This problem dominated the European diplomatic and martial scene for decades. The dire consequences of the Pragmatic Sanction will have to be taken up at a later point. Here we note a domestic side effect, namely the required estates' cooperation to enact the succession legislation. Except for Hungary, Charles might well have been able to dispense with this cumbersome procedure. He probably could have put it through simply by imperial decree. If he did not choose to do so, the motivation was certainly not one of preference for representative government. The emperor just wanted to play it safe, and in foreign relations excessively so, according to most critics. In domestic matters this particular effect of the succession policy was not necessarily injurious to Austrian interests. In Bohemia it helped to modify the harsh policies introduced by Ferdinand II after the battle of the White Mountain. In the other Habsburg lands—not only in Hungary—the concept of separate historic-political entities was undoubtedly strengthened. Whether this could be considered a development for better or worse depends on the evaluation of estates' policies, which will be discussed in the following chapter.

At this point we will consider the process of administrative and legislative integration of the Habsburg lands, whose slow and inadequate development was a primary reason for the complexity of Charles' policy concerning the succession. It was handicapped by the ties of the hereditary lands to the empire and by the tradition of independence and the struggle for the preservation of autonomous institutions in the lands of the Bohemian and Hungarian crowns. In regard to the Bohemian realm the events following the battle of the White Mountain produced a measure of administrative amalgamation brought about by external force. As for the Croatian-Hungarian-Transylvanian orbit the opposite was true. The prolonged continuation of direct Turkish occupation or Turkish controlled autonomy estranged the institutional development of these lands further from Habsburg rule.

It is difficult to comprise this rule as yet under any other common denominator than the dynasty itself. Common administrative institutions changed little from the end of the reign of Ferdinand I to the beginnings of Maria Theresa's reforms, roughly at the end of the Austrian succession war in 1748. The Secret Council, the supreme agency dealing with important administrative matters, was considerably enlarged under Ferdinand II, and further expanded to an assembly of more than 60 councillors under Leopold I. This meant a transition from genuinely deliberative to largely honorary functions. The place of the Council was taken over now by the Secret Conference, which under Joseph I was narrowed further to an executive committee on foreign and military affairs, whereas judicial matters were left to the Secret Council, otherwise now a body of reduced significance

Likewise, the General Court Chancery lost in importance, when Ferdinand II assigned agenda of the hereditary lands and of the dynasty to the new Austrian Court Chancery. Altogether the division of the Austro-German eastern Habsburg realms after the death of Ferdinand I among his three sons led also to departmentalization of the functions of the Supreme War Council, and the financial affairs handled by the Court Chamber. Separate administrative bodies were created and revamped under Ferdinand II and Leopold I. Not until Joseph I was a measure of centralization reintroduced. The Austrian Court Chancery became now the supreme administrative agency under the direction of two court chancellors. Under Charles VI these changes were formalized. One section of the Chancery dealt now in essence with foreign and military affairs and those of the imperial house, the other with administrative and judicial matters. In these latter respects cognizance had to be taken in varying degrees of the Hungarian demands for separate administrative and judicial institutions. The Finance Conference had supervisory and policy-making functions but not directly administrative executive ones. Progress could be acknowledged here only in the fact, that the Court Chamber after 1713 was organized according to subject matter and not only to territorial requirements. Basic issues of taxation and recruiting of military forces were still handled separately in the individual lands. The same was true for the bulk of judicial agenda.[10]

To sum up: Integration of the Habsburg lands was blocked by long wars in the west and even longer ones in the east. Although the regimes of Turkish satellite princes or outright occupation by foreign troops were obstacles, the lack of progress in administrative integration after more than two centuries of joint Habsburg rule in the hereditary lands and

[10] Huber and Dopsch, *Österreichische Reichsgeschichte,* pp. 181–184, 186–191, 193–205; Hellbling, *Österreichische Verfassungs- und Verwaltungsgeschichte,* pp. 248–282.

those territories of the eastern crowns, not directly exposed to enemy attacks in east and west, was extraordinary. This can be understood only, if we realize the different traditions of the lands, and the divisive issues of reformatory and counterreformatory struggles.

The integration of the Habsburg realms cannot be judged by the evolution of common administrative institutions alone. Social and intellectual factors will be discussed in the following chapter. At this point we are concerned with the impact of common defense needs and evolving common political interests of the peoples under Habsburg rule. These needs and interests developed without the rulers paying appropriate heed to the consent of the governed, which had tragic consequences.

B. Resumption of the Turkish wars

The resumption of the Turkish wars in the third quarter of the seventeenth century cannot be attributed to the same kind of imperialist aggression that prevailed under Suleiman the Magnificent in the first and second quarter of the sixteenth century. The differences were of a twofold nature. First, the Turks remained remarkably quiet during the Thirty Years' War, when they would have had the advantage of French, Swedish, and German Protestant support, and when their advance would have been particularly dangerous to the imperial cause. This is not to say that the High Portal did not make use of the critical situation, which the Habsburg power faced in the west, to enhance the Turkish position in the Hungarian-Transylvanian orbit, but the Turkish moves are minor if compared with the Turkish offensives launched between 1526 and 1529. Turkish policy between 1663 (the beginnings of the first Turkish war of Leopold I) and 1683 (the turning of the tide in the east, the lifting of the second siege of Vienna) was not based on long-range Ottoman designs for further conquest in the west but on endeavours to maintain the Turkish position in Hungary that had lasted for nearly one and a half century.

Second, Suleiman II took advantage of the difficult imperial position brought about by the conflict between emperor and those German princes who supported the Reformation. Nevertheless this was a war entirely in its own right, which presumably would have been fought anyway, irrespective of the general European constellation. Only with the Franco-Turkish alliance of 1536, the first nonideological diplomatic alliance of its kind between a Christian and non-Christian empire, did the Turkish wars become part of the game of European power politics. Even then this was true only to a limited extent. The conflagrations in the east throughout the century, from the death of Suleiman II in 1566 to the outbreak of the first Turkish war under Leopold I in 1663, changed intermittently the structure of Turkish domination in Hungary and the sovereignty in Transylvania. Yet the extent of Turkish control throughout this period remained stable. The situation in the west during the Huguenot wars and those of the Fronde in France was too diffuse to allow for a concerted plan of cooperation between two great continental flanking powers.

When Louis XIV began to rule in his own right, all this changed even without the formal conclusion of a new alliance with the Turks. The struggle for a lineup of European powers under the leadership of France had begun. From now on, major decisions were bound to occur in the west. In this context, the Turkish wars represented a mere sideshow, serious enough for the Habsburg power, but a secondary theatre of operation just the same.

Because of the impact of these wars on the evolution of the Habsburg empire in international and domestic affairs, it is necessary to survey their conduct and results. They declined in importance only from 1718, after the peace of Passarowitz (Passarovic), to the end of the last Austro-Turkish war in 1791. By that time the Ottoman power had practically ceased to belong to the concert of European great powers. Yet for the two centuries when the Ottoman empire codetermined European affairs actively, the Turkish question has to be discussed on two levels: the relations between Ottoman and Habsburg power, and the impact of the Turkish wars on the eastern Habsburg realms. We will consider first the relationship between Ottoman and Habsburg power.

The motivations for the resumption of the Turkish wars in 1663—Turkish or imperial aggressive designs, autonomy of Transylvania, French threat in the west—may be contested as either individual or collective causes. Uncontested is the fact that these wars developed at least a limited feeling of cohesion between the Habsburg realms. This feeling could not have been brought about speedily in any other way than by fighting a power which was clearly different from all historical-political entities of the Habsburg lands. As a result, the Habsburg armed forces were forged into the strongest centripetal factor in the history of the evolving empire. In the battles in the Hungarian plains these forces had become a powerful, well-organized military instrument. It is here also, where the great Austrian military commanders rose to mastery of their profession. Yet only few of them were later able to use their eastern experience in the struggle against the French in the west.

This was hardly accidental. The Habsburg armies were trained to compete in the wide-open spaces of the plains with a strongly motivated and disciplined but technologically somewhat backward foe. They were not in step with military forces modernized by the reforms of Louis XIV under his great minister of war Louvois and his brilliant chief military engineer Vauban. Nevertheless, the second half of the seventeenth and the first two decades of the eighteenth century were the times when an Austrian generalship evolved, whose performance was never to be surpassed.

Of previous military leaders, Wallenstein in the Thirty Years' War was a man of brilliance as military organizer and in a diffuse way also as political general. Neither his predecessor, Count Johannes Tilly, nor his lieutenants Octavio, Prince (Count) Piccolomini and Count Matthias Gallas were more than competent field commanders, who showed neither the daring nor the ingenuity of Gustavus Adolphus or Condé. The Turkish war of 1663–1664, fought over the issue whether Transylvania should remain a Turkish satellite state, gave a new imperial general, Count Raimund Montecuccoli, a chance to show himself as organizer, tactician, and strategist. In the battle of St. Gotthard (1664) in western Hungary, close to the Styrian border, he performed brilliantly and prevented a Turkish invasion of the hereditary lands. Yet the unpredictable situation in the west, the unrest in Hungary and Transylvania, and the economic crisis in the empire and hereditary lands, forced Leopold I to conclude a rather unfavorable but under existing conditions warranted negotiated peace at Vasvár (Eisenburg) in 1664. It gave Nagyvárad (Grosswardein) and Érsekujvár (Neuhäusel) in east central Hungary to the Turks. Above all, Turkish suzerainty in Transylvania was preserved.

The Habsburg cause had received a setback at a time when foreign relations were relatively favorable for them. The emperor had the support of a contingent of imperial troops and even of a small corps of French troops, and yet the political results were dismal. The conspiracy against the imperial government in the parts of Hungary under Habsburg control in the following years and the change of relations with France from a pending to an active threat made the prospects of the Habsburg cause appear more critical than in 1683, when the second Turkish war began under Leopold I. It could not be foreseen twenty years earlier that it could be brought to an amazingly successful conclusion in 1699.

Leopold's position was indeed critical. The Turkish army, assembled in 1683 in Adrianople, was prepared for a major push against the west.

The alliance of the emperor with King John Sobieski of Poland did not assure him unequivocally of strong support and the same was true for the pacts with the western German imperial estates. Reliance on French nonintervention on the basis of Christian solidarity in a war against the infidels was questionable. Thus major odds were staked against the Habsburg emperor, when the war began.[11]

As noted in the introductory chapter, the Turkish advance to the gates of Vienna in the critical summer of 1683 posed presumably not the same decisive threat to Christian Europe, which had existed at the time of Charles Martel's victory against the Moslems at Tours in 732 or even Count Niklas Salm's defense of Vienna against Suleiman the Magnificent's attack in 1529. Still, the situation was serious enough, when the Turkish armies swept through Hungary in 1683. Vienna might have been taken, the emperor's armies and the incipient Habsburg eastern power could have been destroyed. The final showdown, not so much between Crescent and Cross, but between Near and Middle East and Western and Central Europe would have depended almost exclusively on the defensive power of France, to be supported possibly by the rising Russian empire under Peter the Great. Not the victory of the Cross, but maintenance of a politically viable Central and eastern Central Europe was the major consequence of this great war.

It is a measure of the emperor's curious mixture of tenacity, stubbornness, faith in adversity and, as it turned out, unrealistic harshness in victory that Leopold, like his grandfather Ferdinand II, accepted such major challenge against great odds. The siege of Vienna from July 14 to September 12, 1683 represents a heroic chapter in Austrian history. Credit should go to the citizenry under the mayor Andreas von Liebenberg, who did not live to see victory, the commander Count Rüdiger von Starhemberg, and the charitable but bigoted bishop (later cardinal) Count Kollonitsch. There is disagreement, whether chief credit for the relief of the city should go to the colorful and daring Polish King John Sobieski as at least honorary commander in chief or to the leader of the imperial forces, the emperor's brother-in-law, Duke Charles of Lorraine. The latter was as circumspect a commander as the grand vizier and leader of the Turkish forces Kara Mustapha was a negligent one.[12] Since Sobieski felt slighted

[11] Csuday, *Die Geschichte Ungarns,* II, 126–172; Kosáry, *A History of Hungary,* pp. 127–132. Bela Köpeczi, *La France et la Hongrie au début du XVIII siècle* (Budapest, 1971).

[12] On the siege of Vienna see Thomas M. Barker, *Double Eagle and Crescent: Vienna's Turkish Siege and its Historical Setting* (Albany N.Y., 1967) and Reinhold Lorenz, *Türkenjahr 1683* (Vienna, 1933); see also Otto Forst de Battaglia, *Jan*

by the emperor's subsequent disregard for his decisive contribution to victory, he withdrew to his home country in December 1683, and the architect of the later successful campaign in Hungary was Charles of Lorraine. Protected by an imperial armistice agreement with France (1684), the so-called Holy League with Poland and the Republic of Venice in the same year, and a reinsurance treaty against possible French attack with Brandenburg (1686), the Habsburg forces advanced successfully into central Hungary. In September 1686 heavily fortified Buda was taken by the Duke of Lorraine, and in 1687 a decisive victory was achieved in the field at Nágy-Harsany, close to the battlefield of Mohács of unblessed memories. With these two victories the back of the Turkish power in central Hungary was permanently broken. In 1688 imperial forces under the command of the elector of Bavaria, Max Emanuel, Leopold's son-in-law, supported by margrave Louis of Baden, took for the first time Belgrade, gate to the core area of the Ottoman empire and symbol of Turkish threats to the west. Yet the fact that the war was for a brief period carried into undisputed enemy territory, was of more than symbolic significance. This victory showed that the balance had turned in the east. It was to serve the emperor in good stead in the ever-threatening situation in the west.

The change in the Hungarian constitution brought about by the emperor's insistence at the diet of Pozsony in 1687–1688 and the establishment of an imperial protectorate in Transylvania some months later will be discussed in the following section. Yet it is necessary to state at this point that the great opportunities for genuine integration of the reconquered lands with the bulk of the Habsburg power in Central Europe were largely offset by Leopold's ruthless attempts to undo 150 years of history and to enforce a victory of the Counter Reformation in Hungary at a time when the intolerance of this movement had otherwise gradually abated in Central Europe.

During the war of the League of Augsburg (1689–1697), in which the emperor tried with a limited degree of success to stem the tide of French imperialist advance, the consequences of the failure to pacify Hungary became apparent. In 1689, Margrave Louis of Baden, Charles of Lorraine's successor, vainly advanced far into Serbia. Unrest in Transylvania commenced again. Belgrade was retaken by the Turks in 1690, but in 1691 Louis of Baden could still achieve a major victory at Szalankamen

Sobieski: König von Polen (Zürich, 1946) pp. 157–255 and Janusz Woliński, "König Johann Sobieski und die Schlacht bei Wien 1683," in *La Pologne, au XII Congrès International des Sciences Historiques à Vienne* (Warsaw, 1965), pp. 49–62.

(Slankamen) where the Tisza flows in the Danube. Yet in regard to the over-all pacification of Hungary, concessions to the Hungarian Serbs and the grant of a limited autonomy to Transylvania were of little avail. Whether cooperation with the Magyars would have been helpful, is an open question since no concessions were offered to them. In 1695 the imperial forces were defeated at Lugos in eastern Hungary. As a consequence of the military crisis the young French prince, Eugene of Savoy, who had distinguished himself in imperial service since 1683, obtained now command in Hungary. In the battle of Zenta, adjacent to the southern Tisza, Eugene won finally a decisive victory against the Turks. It freed Hungary except for the Banat of Temesvár, as agreed upon in the peace of Karlowitz (Karlócza, Karlovici) in 1699. Further Turkish concessions had to be made to Venice and Poland. Although the Turkish wars had not ended, and neither the territorial integrity nor the domestic pacification of the kingdom was assured, a permanent success had been scored. Never again could the Ottoman power single-handed threaten the existence of Habsburg power.[13]

With the physically unprepossessing French prince of Italian origin, Eugene of Savoy, a new brilliant figure enters the Austrian and soon the international scene. The greatest general ever to serve the interests of the Habsburgs, he also became one of the leading statesmen and patrons of arts—a personality who splendidly fitted the colorful frame of the Baroque era. Eugene, who came perhaps closer to the concept of an Habsburg empire-wide hero[14] than any other great Austrian, won his European reputation in the west in the war of the Spanish Succession (1701–1714). His popularity was based on his victories in the east. The years of revolutionary risings in Hungary from 1703 to 1711 saw his spectacular activities in the west. Yet after the termination of the war of the Spanish Succession with its brilliant victories and indifferent political outcome for the Habsburg cause, Austrian interests turned again eastward, and in 1716 a new Turkish war began.

The question of who started it is controversial. The High Portal, after the defeat at Zenta, appeared reluctant to intervene in the great European war of succession which began in 1701. Despite French prompting the Turks proceeded only cautiously and indirectly in Transylvania. Even in

[13] Krones, *Handbuch der Geschichte Österreichs,* III, 628–688; Oswald Redlich, *Weltmacht des Barock: Österreich in der Zeit Leopolds I* (Vienna, 1961), pp. 415–484; László Makkai in Ervin Pamlényi, ed. *Die Geschichte Ungarns,* Chapter III, pp. 193–195.

[14] Robert A. Kann, *The Habsburg Empire: A Study in Integration and Disintegration* (2nd ed. New York, 1973), pp. 178–180.

1716 they turned only against Austria's feeble ally Venice in Morea, an area in which the Habsburg power was not directly interested. Yet the frustrating results of the war in the west and the vistas of rich and easy conquests in the east made the emperor Charles VI decide that the moment for decisive action—nominally in support of Venice—had come. This last Turkish war under Prince Eugene's command has become the most popular chapter in the book of his many military victories. In particular the battle of Peterwardein (Pétervárad) in the summer of 1716 and the new conquest of Belgrade two years later, celebrated by the Prince Eugene song, rank highest. This war, the most clearly imperialistic one in its objectives, though not necessarily in its causes, ever fought by the Habsburg empire was essentially a sideshow of strength. It displayed the efficiency of the armed forces and the recently acquired prestige of a new great power. Yet neither were basic issues of survival at stake nor had the results of the war a more than transitory effect. The peace of Passarowitz of July, 1718, in conjunction with the peace of Rastatt with France in 1714, gave the Habsburg power its greatest extent. The Banat of Temesvár, Little Walachia (the southwestern part of Walachia) and the northern part of Bosnia and Serbia were added to the Habsburg realms. Yet, ironically, Morea, for whose retention by Venice the war was allegedly fought, remained in Turkish hands. Only small compensations were given to the republic: the islands of Corfu, Cerigo, and some Albanian coastal places. Might but not necessarily right had won.[15]

Might had won an inconclusive victory. Although Hungary's territorial identity under the Habsburg scepter had been assured, the great possibilities of getting a foothold in the eastern Mediterranean, obtaining control of the Danube principalities, and possibly gaining access to the Dardanelles, was lost. Charles VI had a strong sense for the exalted mission of the house of Habsburg. He saw this mission still clearly in the west, in the vain hope to become heir to the Spanish empire, now under Bourbon rule. As substitute for its loss, Charles concentrated his energies on the recognition of the Pragmatic Sanction by the European powers. This was understandable, though not wise. Yet his second aim to hold at all costs to the crumbs of this Spanish empire in Italy rather than focusing his attention on Austria's eastern position was, even from his limited point of view, neither understandable nor wise. The Emperor would have liked to hold on to the new territories in the east, but to do

[15] Redlich, *Das Werden . . .*, pp. 218–242; Krones, *Handbuch,* IV, 112–120. Max Braubach, *Prinx Eugen,* 5 vols., Vienna, 1963–1965), see I, 235–271, III, 293–379.

so and to conduct at the same time an expansive policy in the west would have taxed the Habsburg empire's strength beyond the breaking point. Faced by this dilemma Charles opted for the western position, but even here more in the sense of diplomatic than military preparation.

One of the consequences of this eastern foreign policy was the alliance with Russia in 1726. For the recognition of the Pragmatic Sanction by a power not primarily interested in the Austrian succession, anyway, the Habsburg emperor was now forced to pay an exorbitant price, namely his support of Russian policy of southeast European expansion. Russia was naturally pleased to accept inordinate concessions for the minor service of recognizing a state act of no consequence to her interests. Her claims were cashed in in 1737 when Austria, according to her treaty obligations with Russia, joined the new eastern ally in a war against Turkey. This war Austria did not want and was unable to fight because her armaments were neglected by then. The consequences of this most inglorious Austrian oriental war corresponded to this situation.[16]

Actually the handwriting had been on the wall since the poor Austrian military showing in the war of the Polish Succession (1733–1735). Here the aged Prince Eugene, who died in 1736, was no longer in full command of his great faculties. Even if he had been, the poor state of preparedness brought about by financial disarray and economic exhaustion, would have denied him victory. Thus the stage was set for the debacle: Little Walachia, northern Bosnia, and Serbia were lost in the peace of Belgrade in 1739. Besides, the Russian ally, who felt deserted by Austria, was resentful about this miserable outcome.[17]

Nevertheless, the result of Charles VI's second Turkish war, which after all did not infringe on the territorial integrity of Hungary, did not really touch vital territorial interests of Habsburg power. Yet feebly as the war was fought, it made it appear likely that Austria would continue to give priority to minor interests in Italy rather than major eastern potentialities. Above all, it showed that Austria's military power, as tested in the heydays of Eugene of Savoy's military glory, had become a thing of the past. The peace encouraged the enemies of Habsburg power and made it likely that a third war of succession[18] would promise rich spoils to all

[16] On the foreign policy of Charles VI, see also Max Braubach, *Versailles und Wien von Ludwig XIV. bis Kaunitz* (Bonn, 1952), pp. 7–359 passim; Redlich, *Das Werden . . .*, pp. 243–297. Köpeczi, *La France et la Hongrie.*

[17] Karl A. Roider, *The Reluctant Ally: Austria's Policy in the Austro-Turkish War 1737–1739* (Baton Rouge, 1972); Redlich, *Das Werden . . .*, pp. 298–319; Krones, *Handbuch*, IV, 137–144.

[18] The wars of the Spanish, Polish, and subsequently Austrian succession.

those who had recognized the Pragmatic Sanction with politically appropriate mental reservations.

Under Joseph II the Habsburg armies once more were called into the field against the Ottoman power, and again at the side of Russia (1788–1791). Maria Theresa's chancellor, Prince Kaunitz, by a skillful political operation, had succeeded to gain peacefully the Bukovina as aftermath of the Russo-Turkish war of 1771–1774. Joseph II on the other hand, like his grandfather forced as Russia's ally into an imperialist war not of his own choosing, failed to make measurable territorial gains, despite major military efforts.

The Austrians fought with indifferent success. Leopold II terminated the war after his older brother's death by the peace of Sistowa in 1791. Except for the annexation of Old Orsova it had to be concluded on the basis of the status quo, even though Austrian forces had occupied sizeable enemy territories. The reasons for this unsatisfactory outcome were varied: Leopold was faced by a revolutionary situation in Hungary and in the Austrian Netherlands; diplomatic friction with Prussia had to be smoothed over in the face of Russian dissatisfaction with an inevitable Austrian separate peace; the second partition of Poland was in the offing; above everything else, the great unknown, the development of the revolutionary situation in France, casts its shadows on the European scene. Leopold II was indeed prudent to cut losses and to agree to a meager compromise.

How right he was, was not realized until almost a century later, when Austrian occupation of Bosnia-Hercegovina in 1878 initiated a new active, and in the long run disastrous, stage of the Habsburg empire's Balkan policy. Its consequences for the empire and Europe would become more serious than the Turkish threats to the west in the sixteenth and seventeenth centuries, since they contributed directly to the gradual disintegration of the Habsburg empire. The Turkish wars, roughly in the period between the two sieges of Vienna, 1529–1683, played the converse and major part in the evolution and preservation of the great-power position of the empire. This has been indicated in the foregoing in regard of foreign and military policies. It will subsequently be discussed in regard to domestic policies.

C. Hungary, Transylvania, Croatia, and the Habsburg scepter

In a survey of events in the eastern Habsburg lands from mid-seventeenth to mid-eighteenth century, the impact of the Turkish wars is important even on the second, the civilian, level. In 1645 Prince George II

Rákóczi of Transylvania had issued a manifesto, in which he called on the Hungarian nation to fight the emperor. Yet such a fight would have involved the High Portal, too, which was not ready for a major showdown with the Habsburgs. Rákóczi could not have dared to initiate an avowed anti-imperial policy against Turkish advice, if he had not been promised the support of other powers—in this case by alliance treaties with Sweden and France, concluded in 1631. Yet even such understanding, renewed again in spring 1645, meant little at such a late stage of the Thirty Years' War, when Ferdinand III, Cardinal Mazarin (Richelieu's more moderate successor), and Chancellor Oxenstjerna of Sweden, were all heading for the great compromise of Münster and Osnabrück. It had become clear that French-Swedish assurances at this time represented not more than tactical manoeuvres to strengthen their position in the peace negotiations. Recognition of this state of affairs forced Rákóczi in the late summer of 1645 to the pacts of Rampersdorf and Linz with the emperor, according to which he had to give up the Franco-Swedish alliance in return for the recognition of his rule in seven east Hungarian comitats in addition to Transylvania. Considering the fact that Swedish and French support would be worth little, as soon as the general peace was signed, Rákóczi had struck a good bargain. Favorable to his cause was also the recognition of freedom of religion for the lands under his rule. It included the peasants and all those who previously had been forced to change their faith, which meant in practice change under counterreformatory duress. Only the general tiredness on the imperial side and the lack of readiness on the Turkish side to take advantage of this situation explains how the Transylvanian prince and Hungarian national leader could accomplish as much as he did.

The precarious peace of 1645 lasted for almost twenty years. It was strained considerably, when Rákóczi supported the Swedes against the Poles in the so-called first Northern War (1655–1660). In doing so he challenged the Habsburg-Polish alliance but at the same time the interests of his Turkish suzerain, who did not yet want to get involved in a war with the Habsburgs. This concern appeared justified. Rákóczi was deposed by the High Portal to avoid further involvements with the Habsburgs. Prudent Emperor Ferdinand III on his part had not responded in force to Rákóczi's repeated forrays into the parts of Hungary in imperial hands. While thus both powers wanted to avoid a confrontation, the election of an imperial candidate as prince of Transylvania, John Kemény, versus a Turkish appointee, Michael Apafy, led to a predictable clash. Both sides intervened in Transylvania, and the war began in 1663 under the new and inexperienced emperor Leopold, a year after one of the two contestants, Kemény, was killed in battle.

The war and the resulting peace of Vasvár, traced in the previous section, displeased the Hungarian nobility. The great nobles felt that their national leader, Count Nikolas Zrinyi (Zrinski), had not received the necessary support of the imperial commander Montecuccoli. Feeling was widespread that the emperor had fought the war to eliminate Hungarian constitutional government and to replace it by imperial absolutism after the fashion of the regime in Bohemia following the battle of the White Mountain. Hungary, as far as it had a voice, was alienated by the action on both sides, Habsburg and Ottoman power alike. Several additional factors, military requisitions, camping of German troops on Hungarian soil, counterreformatory activities, and the dependency on imperial foreign and defense policy added to the general dissatisfaction.

In this atmosphere Hungarian postwar conspiracy throve. It was led by men, who were undoubtedly Hungarian patriots after a fashion, including Zrinyi, the banus of Croatia (one of the rare personalities, who was acknowledged as national leader there as well as in Hungary),[19] his brother Peter, the Palatin Count Ferencz Wesselény, and the *Judex curiae* Count Ferencz Nádasdy. The weakness of these men was twofold: they identified Hungarian national interests largely with those of the national aristocracy and they were not strong enough to pursue a truly independent national policy. Thus they attempted to get Turkish and French support and thereby laid themselves open to the charge of high treason, compounded by the extension of the conspiracy to nobles in the hereditary lands (Count Hans Tattenbach in Styria and Count Karl Thurn in Goricia). The conspiracy was discovered, some of the leaders executed (Peter Zrinyi, Nádasdy, and Tattenbach among them); the life of Zrinyi's son-in-law, Ferencz Rákóczi I, was spared.

One of the consequences of the exposure of the great cabal was a wave of persecution of Protestants in Hungary, particularly in the northern mining towns. Pastors were convicted by special tribunals, in which Bishop Kollonitsch played an ignoble part. The pastors were not executed, but the choice of those convicted was between recantation and serving as galley slaves. Brutal measures of this kind may have been based on the counterreformatory tendencies at the imperial court under Jesuit influ-

[19] Great grandson of the former Banus Count Nikolas Zrinyi (Zrinski) who had died in the defense of Szigetvár against Suleiman II in 1566. Zrinyi is the Magyar, Zrinski the Croatian spelling of the name of the family.

ence. Yet they could not cover up the fact that Catholic as well as Protestant nobles participated about equally in the conspiracy.[20]

Taking a long-range view—which Leopold and his unenlightened advisers were least capable to take—the consequences of this policy were as disastrous for the imperial side as for the national Hungarian cause. The special interests of the revolutionary Hungarian noble conspirators may have obscured the fact, that they fought for a national Hungarian idea. The religious persecutions directed against nobles, free and unfree commoners alike, made this clear to everybody. So did the attempt to amalgamate the Hungarian administration with that in Vienna. The establishment of a royal gubernatorial office in Pozsony in 1673 was an inmportant step in this direction. Hungary was treated as conquered territory, and treated so without the semblance of justification that had existed in Bohemia after 1620—namely defeat after a general revolt. Yet a general revolutionary peasant force, the Kurucok,[21] emerged from these actions and remained at least as guerillas in being for a generation.

Their first prominent leader was a noble from Upper Hungary, Count Imre Thököly. He managed to obtain French and Polish support for a time, but Louis XIV did not consider it to his best interest to continue it after conclusion of the peace of Nijmwegen with the emperor in 1679. Thököly's manifesto to fight for a free Hungary did not prove entirely successful, but a detachment of imperial troops was defeated and the emperor, hard pressed in the east, agreed to suspend for the time being his policy of Hungarian "Gleichschaltung." At the diet of Sopron (Ödenburg) the ancient constitutional liberties were acknowledged, the office of Palatine restored, and religious freedom for the Protestants in the northern mining towns reestablished. This meant a notable though limited victory for the Hungarian cause, but Thököly reversed it to future defeat, when he openly joined the Turkish side at a time when the disastrous campaign, which led the Ottoman power to the gates of Vienna, was already under way. The emperor's ministers and generals, Lobkowitz, Caraffa, Montecuccoli foremost among them, who wanted to reduce Hungary to the status of a mere province, seemingly had proved their case.

The Hungarian nation had to pay the bill after the reconquest. By this

[20] Redlich, *Weltmacht des Barock* . . . , pp. 158–235; Lackó in E. Pamlényi, ed., "Die Geschichte Ungarns," pp. 190–198; Csuday, *Geschichte Ungarns,* II, 119–160. Bucsay, *Dic Geschichte des Protestantismus in Ungarn,* pp. 81–106; Wolf, *Lobkowitz* . . . pp. 236–334.

[21] The name derives either from the Latin crux (cross), the peasants revolting in the name of the cross, or from the Turkish khurudsch (the rebel).

conquest land was redistributed now through imperial commissions. Former owners, suspected of disloyalty or religious nonconformism, lost their estates, which were given to foreigners, mostly German nobles. Worse was in store for many burghers in northern cities, who lost their property and, after submission to torture, their lives.[22]

Considering the ruthless brutality of the bloody assizes of Eperjes of 1687, the results of the famous diet of Pozsony (Pressburg) in 1687–1688 have to be considered as relatively moderate. The hereditary succession of the Habsburgs had to be acknowledged and the right of resistance of the nobles according to the *Bulla Aurea* of 1222 was relinquished. Yet the coronation oath, repeated by the heir to the throne Joseph at his coronation, acknowledged the ancient liberties of the nation. Transylvania, however, remained separated from Hungary, even though religious freedom was recognized there in 1688 and free election of the prince promised after the death of Apafy's son.[23]

In 1690, the sultan recognized Count Thököly as Prince of Transylvania, and the emperor considered this enthronization as open challenge. In 1691, after the country was reconquered by the imperial forces, the *Diplomum Leopoldinum* acknowledged the special status of Transylvania under the emperor including recognition of the religious liberties of the three nations, Magyars, Szekels, and Saxons. Those of the underprivileged Roumanian Vlachs were added only after a fashion, provided they conformed under counterreformatory pressure to accommodation with a Uniate Church under papal jurisdiction by the end of the seventeenth century. After the son of Apafy, who had not yet come of age, was forced to abdicate and a separate Transylvanian court chancery was established in Vienna, the country was definitely considered as *corpus separatum* directly under the emperor and not as part of the Hungarian crown lands. These measures as well as the autonomy granted in 1690 to the Hungarian Serbs in the Voiwodina between Tisza and Danube, increased anew the dissatisfaction of the Magyar nobility.

Magyar nationalists on both sides of the Tisza waited only for the opportunity for new risings. They found it in the first critical years of the War of the Spanish Succession, when the French were ready to support revolt in Transylvania and the emperor's Protestant allies, the British

[22] Csuday, *Die Geschichte Ungarns,* II, 160–187; Redlich, *Weltmacht des Barock . . .*, pp. 414–440.

[23] Heinrich Marczali, *Ungarische Verfassungsgeschichte* (Tübingen, 1910), pp. 88–90; and by the same author and publisher *Ungarisches Verfassungsrecht* (1911), pp. 13–14. Bucsay, *Geschichte des Protestantismus . . .*, pp. 98–119.

and the Dutch, could be expected to be resentful of a brutal imperial policy of suppression. Thus the risks seemed to be limited, whichever way the dice may fall; still, they had to be taken.

In 1703, Prince Francis II Rákóczi issued a call to the nation to act and free the country from foreign oppression. This time the movement could count on strong support. Furthermore, not the question of Turkish versus Habsburg alignments was at issue but that of an independent, though as yet only in a rudimentary way democratic Hungary. The prince received some French aid. In this case he could certainly not be charged with an attempt to compromise the independence of Hungary, which could only be threatened directly by Turkish or Habsburg power. Still, Rákóczi in spite of short-lived military success particularly in Upper Hungary would have been well advised to seek a compromise with the enlightened new emperor Joseph (1705–1711). He yielded, however, to the pressure of the radicals.

The assembly of the Hungarian and Transylvanian insurrectionists at Ónod deposed the emperor as king of Hungary and with him the whole house of Habsburg. Joseph to his credit was still ready for a compromise and invited Rákóczi and his followers to participate in a new diet at Pozsony in 1708. Rákóczi refused and continued the civil war, though not for long. Defeated by an imperial army he was forced to flee to France. When his pleas for support were hardly listened to there, he left for Turkey, where he died in 1735. Neither Louis XIV nor the sultan had been willing to invest further in an apparent loser. Ind 1711, shortly after the death of Emperor Joseph, the leaders of the moderate wing of the revolutionary movement finally made peace with Charles VI at Szatmár. Hungarian and Translyvanian liberties within the frame of the agreements of 1687 and 1691 (diet of Pozsony and *Diplomum Leopoldinum*) were restored and a general amnesty issued. The national movement lacked military support, arms, and supplies for continued resistance, but the emperor too, after Britain had withdrawn from the War of the Spanish Succession, could ill afford to handle harshly a festering revolutionary situation in his backyard. Hence the compromise, which served the interests of both parties, but, from a long-range viewpoint, more the Hungarian cause that the imperial. The Rákóczi revolt had wide support not only of a privilege-conscious nobility, but also of burghers and of many peasants. Rákóczi took up the cause of religious freedom and that of the oppressed unfree peasantry, for Magyars and non-Magyars. He failed in regard to his major objectives, but his movement kept its demands alive. Its leaders in the next century represented socially still aristocracy and gentry, but they could no longer be associated primarily with the fight for the privileges of the national nobility, as was true of most of Rákóczi's peers. The first major break in this system of identification of class and national interest goes to Rákóczi's credit.

Even from a short-range viewpoint the position of the only temporarily retreating national movement had its advantages. Charles's desire to have the Hungarian diet consent to the Pragmatic Sanction made it advisable not to revert to a policy of renewed suppression, which might lead to revolution on a still larger scale. Throughout his reign and that of his daughter, Maria Theresa,—that means, for two generations—Hungarian national rights in the modest frame established at Szatmár had not been tampered with. This applied equally to taxation and defense organizations, and to a point also to the conduct of foreign affairs. Hungary could not go it alone but neither could the Habsburg emperors subordinate Hungary by force in an international situation fraught with dangers.[24]

The Hungarian autonomist objectives had distinct repercussions in Croatia-Slavonia. One factor was the common Croatian-Magyar experience of having been exposed to the Turkish holocaust. The eastern part of Croatia and Bosnia had been for most of the period of the Turkish wars under Ottoman domination. Attempts to seal off further Turkish invasions in the southwest by establishing a permanently policed military frontier go back to the early sixteenth century. They were fully materialized by 1578 and kept in being for three centuries. The Croatian military frontier represented a combination of military agricultural communities, who lived in small groups, the *zadrugas,* held together by a combination of family ties and military discipline. Similar defense zones existed south of the Banat of Temesvár and in southern Transylvania. In return for the grant of land by the government, the frontiersmen or *granicari* (*Grenzer*), who recognized the head of the family as their military superior, were called up for service at short order any time a Turkish attack threatened. These *granicari,* mostly Croatian or German in national origin, were thus directly subordinated to the centralized imperial military authority. This fact, accentuated by the provisions of the

[24] Csuday, *Die Geschichte Ungarns,* II, 187–211; Kosáry, *A History of Hungary,* pp. 131–137; Redlich, *Das Werden . . . ,* pp. 148–217; Marczali, *Ungarische Verfassungsgeschichte,* pp. 90–93; Marczali, *Ungarisches Verfassungsrecht,* pp. 14–15; Horvath, *Geschichte Siebenbürgens,* pp. 109–113. László Makkai, in E. Pamlényi, ed., *Die Geschichte Ungarns,* Chapter III, IV, pp. 175–206; Seton-Watson, *A History of the Roumanians,* pp. 116–125; Köpeczi, *La France et la Hongrie;* Mathias Bernath, *Habsburg und die Anfänge der rumänischen Nationsbildung,* Leiden, 1972, pp. 21–46.

peace of Karlowitz of 1699, was resented by the Croatian national nobility and frequently subject to complaint in the Croatian estates diet, the Sabor, where subordination under the national authorities was demanded.

With this, Croatian and Magyar opposition to imperial centralism merged for a time. In fact the Croatian diet as protest against the imperial centralizing policy had agreed as early as 1691 to send delegates to the Hungarian diet. The banus, the head of the Croatian government, joined in 1625 the Hungarian house of Magnates. The great defender of Szigetvár in 1566 against the overpowering armies of Suleiman II, Count Nikolas Zrinyi (Zrinski) the older, became now a joint Magyar and Croatian hero. The same, though to a lesser degree, was true for his great-grandsons, Nikolas and Peter, who both represented also the Croatian interests in the Hungarian conspiracy of the 1620s.

Yet Magyar and Croatian common interests were based only on the limited solidarity of the nobles and the common danger from the Turkish east. As soon as this threat ceased, the nobles' position became more precarious also. The Southern Slav problem in Croatia and in the Serb autonomous districts in Hungary assumed new and wider proportions.[25]

D. The struggle about the balance of power

The integration of the Habsburg lands into a moderately centralized empire was closely connected with the Turkish wars. They were primarily fought on territories which until 1918 remained part of the Habsburg monarchy. The simultaneous struggle in the west against France and her satellites represented a different situation. Few contested territories remained under the Habsburg scepter for a long time. Yet the primary reason for the wars in the west, whether this was clear to the leading statesmen or not, was not the conflict about the possessions of the Spanish crown but a quite different double objective: establishment of a recognized great-power position and the fight against the supremacy of France. This conflict assumed at times strange forms. The latter part of the seventeenth century and the eighteenth century before the French Revolution was the period of the wars of succession. The issues at stake were seemingly the dynastic interests to increase the power of individual sover-

[25] Rudolf Kiszling, *Die Kroaten* (Graz-Cologne, 1956), pp. 24–38; Günther E. Rothenberg, *The Austrian Military Border in Croatia, 1522–1747* (Urbana, 1960), pp. 52–100. Nikolaus von Preradovich, *Des Kaisers Grenzer* (Vienna, 1970), pp. 7–67; Kurt Wessely, *Die K. K. Militärgrenze. Beiträge zu ihrer Geschichte* (Vienna, 1973), pp. 29–94.

eigns on the basis of succession claims. To a point, these wars were indeed fought over the narrow interests of individual dynasties, Habsburgs, French and Spanish Bourbons, Wettins in Saxony and Poland, and Wittelsbachs in Bavaria. Yet the struggle was one for power, that had to be rationalized and in part even justified by reference to uncontested legal claims. Such claims to fight a just war over contested territories could be established most effectively on grounds of succession claims. Hence the wars of devolution and succession, which in the coming nineteenth century were to yield to wars over national issues, that is again largely ideological issues. Again these wars of the future camouflaged imperialist interests, as indeed had been true in part for the seemingly purely ideological religious wars of the past.

The fact that these European wars of the seventeenth and eighteenth centuries were not primarily ideological did not scale down the ferocity of warfare. A decline in emotional motivation was offset by the advance in military technology and improvements in communications. These advances made the conduct of operations in some respect less hard on the civilan population but in the effect on the combatant forces more deadly. Another difference from previous large-scale wars, was the greater flexibility of the alliance systems. Alliances between Catholic and Protestant powers, still rather novel during the Thirty Years' War, had become common occurrences, which meant that almost everybody could ally with anybody else, even with the Turks. Professional diplomacy thus got an uplift and enjoyed great influence.

In this continued diplomatic struggle Habsburg power was handicapped by almost a century (1657 to 1740) of two long reigns of narrow-minded rulers, Leopold I and Charles VI. Both were stubborn, of limited vision, and unable to decide. Leopold was more of a bigot than Charles; on the other hand, Leopold's intelligence and erudition was superior to that of his younger son. The brief reign of the able Joseph I was thus sandwiched between those of two incompetent rulers at the height of the war in the west and the Hungarian revolt in the east. There was little room for diplomatic manoeuvering as was frequently the case under Leopold and Charles. The latter's failings, however, were partly offset by the activities of the competent diplomats and generals referred to before. To these military commanders the name of Count Guido Starhemberg has to be added for the last years of the reign of Leopold and throughout the War of the Spanish Succession.

As for the diplomats, Count Max Trautmannsdorff, chief adviser and representative of Ferdinand III at the Westphalian peace negotiations, was a prudent statesman in foreign affairs and still active in Ferdinand III's reign. More controversial was the policy of Prince Wenzel Lobkowitz, the president of the Court War Council, who advocated the harsh course in Hungary, which alienated the Magyars in a critical period. He and another top adviser in foreign affairs, Prince (Count) Johann Weikart Auersperg, pursued a conciliatory policy toward France, which encouraged the young Louis XIV to further aggression. In the later part of the reign of Leopold I, Count Theodor Strattman and Count Dominik Anton Kaunitz proved to be skillful negotiators.

Truly outstanding were some of Leopold's ambassadors at a time, when the deficiency of communications resulted in wide ambassadorial power. Count Franz Eusebius Pötting, ambassador to Poland and Spain, was also personally close to Leopold; Count Wenzel Wratislaw, the ambassador to the Court of St. James, kept a difficult alliance system with England under Leopold and his two sons as long as possible on an even keel; Franz Baron Lisola brilliantly represented the emperor in Poland, Spain, and above all in the Netherlands. Lisola was one of the chief architects of the coming great alliance against France. In the later reign of Charles VI, Count Karl Friedrich Schönborn, the imperial court chancellor, brought the interests of the Holy Roman Empire and those of the Habsburg power more into line. Count Ludwig Philip Sinzendorf and Baron Johann Christoph Bartenstein—the latter not nominally but actually—were chief advisers in international relations during the reign of Charles VI. Both, particularly Bartenstein, the converted son of a Protestant minister, served also with distinction in the early reign of Maria Theresa.[26]

That the tide after 1718 turned against the Habsburgs was more the fault of the policies of Emperor Charles VI and his neglect of military reorganization than that of the diplomats. As for the generals, only Prince Eugene of Savoy exercised some influence in foreign affairs at the court. Although his military faculties in the last years before his death in 1736 were in decline, his advice not to yield the eastern interests to the Spanish preferences of the emperor was as sound as his distrust in the international guarantees for Maria Theresa's succession.

Leopold's early reign was largely occupied with counterreformatory activities and increased involvement in Hungarian-Transylvanian affairs, which threatened a confrontation with the Ottoman empire. Efforts to

[26] Redlich, *Weltmacht des Barock . . .*, pp. 56–71, 82–140, 211–217, 388–400.

undo the devastation of the Thirty Years' War, linked to a modest program of an elementary kind of mercantilism, played an important role too. There was little interest and as it seemed little need to worry about French policies in the west. Austria refrained from participation in the Franco-Spanish war on the side of Spain as might have been expected. The treaty of the Pyrenees of 1659 had no direct impact on territorial interests of the eastern Habsburg line but it weakened the position of the Habsburg dynasty as a whole since it was still considered as one house, divided in an older Spanish and a younger closely allied German branch. In Louis XIV's first war of Devolution of 1667–1668, Leopold according to a secret treaty with the French king managed to stay neutral. In this war, fought over the issue of Louis's claims to the Spanish Netherlands as dowry not only Habsburg dynastic, but also German imperial interests were at stake, because a French victory would have brought the French power closer to the gates of the Holy Roman Empire. Yet Leopold could rely on the English, Dutch, Swedish intervention, which forced Louis XIV in the peace of Aix la Chapelle to a meager compromise. Louis's second war (1672–1678), primarily directed against Holland, the core country of the alliance of 1667, affected the empire more closely, but again Leopold by a neutrality treaty with Louis in 1671 did not discourage aggression. Several facts eventually forced Leopold's irresolute hand: Louis's invasion of an imperial domain, the duchy of Lorraine, in 1670 had aroused some national feelings in the Germanies. The so-called great elector of Brandenburg, Frederick William I, supported Holland and urged Leopold to intervene in behalf of the Dutch States General although he concluded a separate peace with France as soon as imperial intervention was assured. This time Leopold could not hope that England would pull his chestnuts out of the fire. Louis had secured his position in this respect by the neutrality treaty of Dover (1670) with Charles II. Leopold however, was probably more influenced by unmistakable proof, that the king of France had his hand in the Hungarian conspiracy against the emperor. This and Lisola's advice led to Leopold's belated decision to intervene as head of the empire in 1674. Ill prepared for military action and conscious of the threat in the east, the results were significant enough to block a full-fledged success by Louis. In the treaties of Nijmwegen of 1678, Holland, subsequently a main bulwark against French advance, remained territorially intact. The rapidly declining Spanish empire, on the other hand, lost the French Comté and some places in the Spanish Netherlands. The emperor had to cede only Freiburg. Undistinguished in war and, after Lisola's untimely death in

1675, also in the peace negotiations, Leopold as other Habsburgs before and after him had at least preserved the chance to fight another day against France. It was not far in the offing.

Between 1680 and 1683 Louis set up the Chambers of Reunions, the courts of claims which were to validate Louis's demands to towns in the Alsace and Luxemburg as legally justified. The French occupation occurred almost simultaneously with the judgments of the courts. A full-fledged French invasion of the Spanish Netherlands and Lorraine followed in 1683, that of the territory of the archbishop of Trèves in 1684. Yet Leopold in the face of the second great Turkish war of his reign, which led Kara Mustapha's armies to the gates of Vienna in view of a still critical situation in the east, in 1684 concluded the armistice of Regensburg with France. France, in addition to Strassburg and Luxemburg, could keep all the new places occupied on the basis of the controversial Reunion decisions of French courts for twenty years. This agreement superseded an alliance with the western German estates of 1682 and another one of the same year with Holland, Sweden, and Spain to fight the Reunions and the invasions of the Spanish Netherlands. In exchange for a free hand in Hungary, Leopold had for the time being sacrificed his western to his eastern interests. This might be considered a matter of mere political expediency except for the fact that in doing so Leopold had violated his sworn obligations as emperor to protect the territorial integrity of the Holy Roman Empire.

True, resolute action in the west at this time would not only have interfered with the defense of the Habsburg eastern position but also with its potential expansion in the Orient. In this sense Leopold's decision was a devious, if unimpressive attempt to preserve the chances to fight at a later more opportune moment for Habsburg and imperial interests in the west, while for the time being accounts could be settled undisturbed by French intervention, in the east.[27]

Political and ideological orientation may be logically but not necessarily psychologically contradictory. The implicit imperial-French understanding was, to a point, motivated also by a feeling of Christian solidarity against the Mohammedan onslaught. Thus Louis XIV, even without formal agreement had refrained from attack against the emperor at the height of the Turkish advance in 1683. Yet the successful Habsburg campaign into Hungary changed all this. In 1688 Louis XIV started his third major war (1688–1697), commonly called the War of the League of Augsburg or the War of the Succession in the Palatinate. The first

[27] Redlich, ibid., pp. 77–151, 324–375; Braubach, *Versailles und Wien*, pp. 7–19.

designation refers to the preventive alliance against further French advance, formed by the emperor, the kings of Sweden, Spain, and the electors of Bavaria and Saxony. The term War of the Succession in the Palatinate pointed to Louis's questionable claims on behalf of his clever sister-in-law, Princess Liselotte, sister of the deceased elector Palatine.

In September 1688 Habsburg troops had occupied Belgrade, and in the following month Louis started the anticipated offensive into the Palatinate. The aim to check further imperial advances into the east was only a side effect of the French king's major design to establish predominance not only in western Europe, but in Central Europe, above all in Germany. Obviously this was a direct challenge to the empire, the emperor, and Habsburg power as well. Leopold pronounced the *Reichskrieg,* and a new, even grander alliance consisting of the members of the League of Augsburg, supplemented by England and Holland, came into being. The soul of this coalition was William III of Orange. His accession to the English throne, jointly with his wife Mary II (Stuart) after the Glorious Revolution of 1688 gave British participation a meaning which it never had had before in continental affairs beyond the French-Spanish orbit. Largely due to the preoccupation of Habsburg power in the east the war was on the Allied side fought only with indifferent success. The discord usually concomitant with the actions of a large coalition outweighed almost the advantage of the greater war potential on the Allied side.

In the peace of Ryswick (1697) Louis was forced to give up major portions of his previous conquests. The border fortresses between Spanish Netherlands and the States General, however, were to be manned by Dutch troops. Yet this concession on Louis's part was outweighed by retention of Alsace and Palatinate. Just the same, French aggression was blocked for the time being. The decline of Spain had become ever more obvious, far more so than the rise of Britain, which still suffered from the discord of the civil war and the Restoration period. Dutch power, the most consistent in its opposition to France, had been preserved, but it was too limited to be of decisive importance in a major European confrontation. The forces of the empire represented such conflicting interests that they were not fully effective. The emperor was far too deeply involved in the eastern war to act decisively in the west. Still, Leopold preserved his chance to intervene in the west if he could bring the war against the Turks to a successful conclusion. This was, indeed, the case when the peace of Karlowitz, which freed most of Hungary from the Turks, was signed in 1699.[28]

[28] Heinrich von Srbik, *Wein and Versailles, 1692–1697* (Munich, 1944).

A major reason for Louis XIV's anti-Habsburg policy and for Leopold's attempts to check it was the question of the Spanish succession. It might be compared to an undischarged time bomb, the explosion of which threatened the peace of Europe. This threat lasted throughout the period from the birth of the last Spanish Habsburg, the debilitated Charles II in 1661, to his death in 1700.[29]

It has been stated previously that the European conflicts about dynastic succession were primarily rationalizations of the struggles for the balance of power or against the supremacy of one continental power. This statement does not mean, that the European monarchs at a time when the divine-rights theory was still widely respected, considered dynastic wars as pretexts. The legal questions involved were controversial, and both Leopold and his cousin Louis XIV took their claim to the Spanish succession after the death of the childless king of Spain seriously, in a political and in a dynastic sense. Both rulers were married to daughters of Philip IV, Louis's consort from the first marriage, Leopold's from the second. The French king could claim that the renunciation of his wife to the succession was void, because the Spanish crown had never paid her duly pledged dowry. As older daughter of Philip IV her claims would precede those of the emperor's wife. Leopold, with somewhat better reason, could refer to mutual succession pacts between the Spanish and German Habsburg lines. Since Leopold's first consort had died in 1673, the only son of her daughter, married to the elector of Bavaria, would have been the most obvious successor to the Spanish inheritance as seen from the imperial dynastic viewpoint. Yet, due to the diplomatic cooperation between Bourbons and Wittelsbachs, French interests might have been accommodated, too. After the sudden death of the infant prince in 1699 the legal issue could be considered wide open.

Several attempts supported by the good offices of third powers in the interest of the balance of power in Europe were made to prevent the big Bourbon-Habsburg confrontation. Both Louis and Leopold proved to be equally unreasonable in their claims to gain the undivided Spanish inheritance for their houses. The opinion that Louis fought for French dominance and Leopold for the balance of power is true only insofar as the former did get his chance to make a stab for political leadership in Europe and the emperor did not. He certainly did not lack the intent.

[29] Charles II (1661–1700) was nominally king since the death of his father Philip IV in 1665. Until 1675 his mother Maria Anna governed as regent in his name, afterwards he was king in his own right and notwithstanding his incapacity he exercised a certain influence on the course of government. See also Reginald Trevor-Davies, *Spain in Decline 1621–1700* (London, 1957), pp. 109–140.

Efforts to arrive at partition treaties first in favor of the "kur prince" (son of the elector) of Bavaria as a third party with minor adjustments in favor of Austria and France had failed. Yet there was still hope for an eventual compromise. After the prince's death endeavors to arrive at an understanding sponsored by England and France came to naught. It would have left to Charles, Leopold's younger son, the bulk of the Spanish inheritance with Naples, Sicily, and Lorraine going to the Bourbon side. Leopold still refused to consent, because a condition of this agreement would have been a firm commitment that the Spanish and Austrian Habsburg lines should never be united. Irrational overbearing, however, was not confined to one side. When French diplomacy in Madrid finally won out it was precisely the same attitude on the part of Louis XIV, which led to the War of the Spanish Succession. When the dying king of Spain finally signed a will in favor of Louis's second grandson, Philip, Duke of Anjou, Louis refused to make a commitment concerning the permanent separation of the French and Spanish crowns. In this respect he followed a precedent set by his imperial cousin, Leopold I, concerning the relationship of the Austrian and Spanish Habsburg lines. Unlike Louis, however, Leopold was not confronted with the actual bequest of the undivided Spanish inheritance. The French king, aware of the fact that this comprehensive bequest would appeal to the Spanish pride better than any partition agreement in the interest of the balance of power, decided to take advantage of the situation. He deemed it no longer necessary to commit himself to the permanent separation of the French and Spanish crowns, however remote the contingency of union was. Therewith he provoked the great war, which the emperor probably would have brought about already, if his younger son, Charles, had been the sole beneficiary of the will.

There is, however, a political difference in the situation. The European powers on the strength of Louis's record in foreign and domestic policies had reason to believe that he had the power and ability to establish a genuine union between France and Spain. It was doubtful that Leopold had the political strength and administrative capacity to do the same in regard to two Habsburg empires.[30]

The great war, in which hostilities were opened in summer of 1701, was in two ways unique in the history of the Habsburg monarchy. First, it was the only war, in which not Austria's survival but her emergence as one of the leading continental powers was an issue. Even though her chances to become the predominant power on the continent of Europe

[30] Braubach, *Versailles und Wien,* pp. 7–27; Redlich, *Weltmacht des Barock . . .*, pp. 376–414.

may have been more remote than those of France, she was a more active agent in this great coalition war than ever before and afterward. Second, the War of the Spanish Succession showed Austria's military proficiency at its best. The commanders of her armies, Margrave Louis of Baden, Count Guido Starhemberg, and above all Prince Eugene of Savoy, gained victories on a general European scale, unrivaled in the Habsburgs' history.

The lineup of the two armed camps saw England and Holland, the chief Protestant powers, on the imperial side. It will always remain conjecture whether an earlier and more reasonable peace could have been achieved, if King William III, the ruler of both countries and chief architect of the alliance, had not died at the beginning of the war. The other principal allies of the emperor were the new elector of Hanover, the elector of Brandenburg, as well as (after 1701) the Holy Roman Empire as a whole. The participation of Brandenburg had to be bought by the emperor's consent to the elector's Frederick I coronation as king in Prussia, legally then no longer a Polish fief. Even though this elevation did not involve imperial territory, it accelerated the rise of Prussia-Brandenburg to a position where she could challenge Austrian leadership in Germany. Frederick's "promotion" was only one and not the decisive factor in this development.

France was supported by Max Emanuel, the ambitious elector of Bavaria, the emperor's son-in-law, whose imperial aspirations were encouraged by Louis XIV. The ecclesiastic elector of Cologne and the Dukes of Mantua and Savoy (Sardinia) likewise supported Louis, although Eugene's victories in Italy had already persuaded the latter to change sides in 1703. At that time Portugal also joined the alliance. While the Austro-British led coalition represented the greater war potential, Spain herself, the chief battle ground of the war, leaned definitely to the French claimant and disliked the Austrian archduke Charles.[31] It was widely believed that Louis's grandson would be better qualified to preserve the Spanish identity and great-power tradition than the Habsburg prince. Such beliefs were hardly based on the evaluation of characters. Both, the later king Philip V of Spain and Emperor Charles VI (as rival king of Spain Charles III) were mediocre personalities. It is more suggestive that Spanish public opinion—which could not be ignored entirely even in a country under autocratic rule—saw the German Habsburg linked to a variety of extraneous Central and eastern European interests, whereas the conversion of a French to a Spanish prince seemed to be simpler.

Until 1712, the military operations of the war, on the side of the grand

[31] Except for Catalonia. See also Krones, *Handbuch,* IV, 83–86.

alliance, were governed by the strategy of the two equally outstanding soldiers, the British John Churchill, Duke of Marlborough, and Eugene of Savoy. The two commanders scored a series of spectacular victories against an excellent slate of French generals, foremost among them Villars, Vendôme, and the great military engineer, Vauban. It must suffice here to refer to Eugene's victories in the northern Italian campaigns, Luzzara (1702) and Turin (1706). Joint victories by Eugene and Marlborough were fought in southern Germany at Höchstädt and Blenheim (1704). Chief credit for this later triumph, one of the most brilliant strategic surprise movements executed in the history of warfare, should go to Marlborough, who scored also at Ramillies (1706) in the Spanish Netherlands, and again jointly with Eugene at Oudenarde (1708) and Malplaquet (1709) in Flanders. In casualties this was the costliest battle on either side.[32]

Nevertheless, the peace negotiations which had begun in 1708 ended in failure. Louis by this time was ready to surrender the whole Spanish inheritance and let the victors divide the spoils with the lion's share to be going to Charles. The Allied demand that the French king should, beyond this, make a financial contribution to the Austro-British campaigns in Spain, and, if necessary, drive his grandson by force of arms from Spanish soil, has always been considered an example of ruthless arrogance and political blindness. Yet it must be added that the Allied demand was made not without reason though perhaps not with good reason. To dislodge Philip and invest the Austrian prince against the will of the majority of all strata of Spanish society was something the Allies had failed to achieve in seven years of warfare and were not likely to accomplish with French help either, which, of course, due to Louis's refusal they did not get. Still, they saw in the possibility of such support at least a chance to achieve their objective. Experience of the future proved that to fight the Spaniards on their own soil was a hopeless task. It proveed the futility of the great war altogether convincingly.

The rejection of the French peace offer indicated the turning of the tide in the fortunes of the warring parties. Several factors accounted for this. Religious differences strained the alliance. The pope, who frowned upon the Austro-British-Dutch coalition, gave his moral support to Philip. The British and Dutch in turn resented the suppression of the revolutionary movement in Hungary and Transylvania, inasmuch as counterreformatory tendencies against Protestants were involved there.

[32] Redlich, *Das Werden . . .*, pp. 1–93; John B. Wolf, *The Emergence of the Great Powers, 1685–1715* (New York, 1951), pp. 170–181.

The same issue was involved, when Charles XII of Sweden in the Great Northern War marched through Silesia to Saxony and supported the cause of the Silesian Protestants. Joseph I, the new emperor, yielded in the peace of Altranstädt of 1707 to Charles XII's intervention and had to relieve the king in his capacity as prince of the empire of all obligations to support the imperial war against France. Joseph had acted prudently, when by these sacrifices he managed to extricate himself from involvement in the eastern war with Russia and Poland. But he had done so largely because he depended on the good will of his Protestant Allies and this was hardly popular at the Austrian court. In the long run it did not help much to improve Austro-British relations either. The Whig party, which supported the war, was in decline in England. In 1710 it had to yield to a Tory government, which was in favor of peace. Its cause was strengthened by the fact that support of the Stuart pretender to the British throne on the part of Louis had now become academic. Marlborough, by order of the new Tory ministry, was restricted to defensive action and in 1711 relieved of his command altogether. England was well on the way to leave the alliance.

The reason usually given for this decision is the unexpected death of Emperor Joseph in 1711. This left one single Habsburg ruler, Charles, for both Spain, the empire and the eastern possessions of the house of Austria. France being weakened already, the resurrection of the empire of Charles V might at this point have disturbed the European balance of power even more seriously than a compromise with France. Actually, Leopold's *pactum mutuae successionis* of 1703, discussed at the beginning of this chapter, was no surprise to the state chancelleries of Europe. Everybody took it for granted, that the Habsburgs would claim the mutual succession, if the male line of either one of Leopold's sons should become extinct. The great coalition supported the Habsburg side, not because the Habsburgs could be trusted any more than the Bourbons never to attempt the union of the Spanish inheritance with their own lands. But such a dreaded union under the auspices of an administratively, economically, and culturally advanced state like France appeared more likely and dangerous than under the Habsburg scepter. The Habsburg power system looked now perhaps not much stronger than in 1702, but France was relatively weaker. Hence the change in the British-Dutch position concerning continuation of the great alliance, when Charles, the Habsburg pretender king of Spain, was elected emperor in 1711 after his brother's death. A stubborn man of limited ability had thus taken charge of the Austrian fortunes during the last phase of the war.

Charles's decision to continue the struggle single-handed after his major allies had concluded peace with France compounded the mistakes of his predecessors. In the treaty of Utrecht (April, 1713), Spain and the colonies were left to Philip, whose royal line had to give up any further claims to rule in France, unlikely as such contingency had been even before. Except for Minorca and Gibraltar, France and not Spain had to satisfy the colonial claims of Britain, the chief winner in the struggle. Holland received the right to garrison the barrier fortifications between the Spanish Netherlands and her own territories. With this right a major encumbrance was to be put upon the Habsburg claims to these territories. Yet it was Charles's fault alone, when his interests were not adequately represented in these negotiations.[33] The same was true when Sicily was given to Savoy and Sardinia was reserved for the emperor, even though the former island was almost contiguous to Naples, whose subsequent acquisition could be expected, whereas Sardinia was separated from Habsburg territory. Brandenburg-Prussia gained Neuchâtel and Guelders, in addition to international recognition of the royal title of her ruler; Portugal obtained frontier rectifications in the colonies. Major additional Austrian gains were thus foreclosed, while the Habsburgs continued the struggle. Moreover, Austria's former allies were now obliged to the sea powers and not to the emperor for their territorial gains.

The new emperor, Charles VI, carried on until 1714 with indifferent results, for which none of his generals was to blame. In March, 1714, France and Austria finally signed a peace treaty at Rastatt. In September, peace with the Holy Roman Empire was concluded at Baden in Switzerland. This treaty was essentially a mere confirmation of the agreement of Rastatt. Even though the imperial forces had by this time cleared out of Spain, Charles did not recognize reality and refused to make peace with King Philip V.

According to the terms of Rastatt, which could be almost fully envisaged at Utrecht, Austria received the Spanish Netherlands—that is, most present-day Belgium. The value of this acquisition, however, was restricted by the barrier treaties concluded with the Dutch (and the backing of Britain) in 1713, 1715, and 1718. It was humiliating that the Dutch could garrison the frontier fortifications in southern Belgium against France at Belgian—this meant practically Austrian—expense. More important was the provision that the Scheld river must be closed to ocean

[33] Count Philip Sinzendorf served merely as a kind of imperial observer at the peace conference. See also Max Braubach, *Prinz Eugen von Savoyen,* 5 vols. (Vienna, 1963–1965), III, 99–144.

trade.[34] In Italy, the emperor obtained Naples, Milan, Mantua, Sardinia, but not Sicily. Some of these scattered new domains were rich acquisitions, but also encumbrances, difficult to defend. These consequences of the war for Austria must be laid largely at the door of Charles's personal failings, in particular his inordinate dynastic pride. The outcome was disappointing.[35]

The main positive result was that the danger of a French-dominated Europe had passed. This outcome could have been achieveed at an earlier stage of the war, if not by a reasonable compromise even before its outbreak. The reestablishment of a Habsburg monarchy in Spain, even of a Spain deprived of many of its appendages and colonies might have enhanced the imperial position in the same way as the various French-Spanish Bourbon family compacts helped to strengthen prestige and security of France. Since Austria failed to achieve this aim, she lost the war as issue of political prestige, which counted for much at that time. It largely obscured the fact that the major objective of blocking the supremacy of France in Europe had been achieved. On the other hand, the acquisition of the Spanish Netherlands—not contiguous to the bulk of the Habsburg domains and by treaties curtailed in regard to their future economic development—was practically indefensible. Belgium could at most serve as compensatory object for later territorial barter. An attempt by Joseph II to exchange it for Bavaria, however, was understandably enough blocked by Frederick II of Prussia in 1785. Disregarding the merely transitory provisions of the peace of Campo Formio of 1797, in which the Austrian Netherlands and Lombardy were traded for the territory of the Republic of Venice, a final deal was made only at the Congress of Vienna. Austria received now the so-called Lombardo-Venetian kingdom in exchange for the Spanish Netherlands.

With this exchange Austria became further and more permanently involved in Italian affairs, a development which had not actually started but had been activated by the treaty of Rastatt. The kingdoms of Naples and Sardinia belonged to the poorest regions of Italy and were difficult to defend without sea power. Milan and Mantua had strategic value, the former also economic wealth. Yet here Habsburg power was to become involved in the centuries-old internal and external conflicts of the penin-

[34] Actually agreed for the first time in the Westphalian peace negotiations at Münster in 1648 between the representatives of Philip IV of Spain and those of the Dutch republic. The later barrier agreement specified the issue further.

[35] Redlich, *Das Werden* . . . pp. 93–147; John B. Wolf, *Toward a European Balance of Power, 1620–1715* (Chicago, 1970), pp. 156–196.

sula. Here, too, the lack of sea power prevented the development of these possessions to full economic advantage. The geographic position of Italy and political and economic interests of France, Spain, Britain, and for the time being Venice and Tuscany, made it impossible for the Habsburgs even to think of the unification of Italy under their scepter. All that could be done was to keep a hold on scattered possessions, which offered little benefits in the face of foreign competition and were exposed to attack by other powers. When the possessions in Italy were finally consolidated in 1814 no gain could be expected either. The rise of nationalism after the great French revolution made new Austrian policies stillborn from the new start.

Not all this could be foreseen in 1714. Yet the geographic and economic facts should have been clear. The unfortunate policy helped to create the notion of the nonhomogeneous unorganic empire almost from the time the great power was born. And such belief was largely due to Charles VI's unfortunate attempts to hold on to the illusion of a Spanish empire under Habsburg rule. As he saw it, any control of the shreds of Spanish territories in Europe, but particularly in Italy, left the door open to the realization of his dreams. They were persistently tied to the west and southwest. They largely ignored the east, where the development of a better integrated empire might still have been feasible.

E. Stalemate and decline

The first decades after 1740–1741 when new rulers ascended the throne in the Habsburg empire, Russia and Prussia initiated the era usually referred to in diplomatic history as that of the reversal of alliances. The new Austro-French and British-Prussian associations came into being step by step. In the transitional preceding period (1714–1740) no definite new lineup was recognizable. But it became clear that the old alliance systems had outlived their usefulness. For a generation they were replaced by new combinations based on expediency and devoid of any ideological foundation, not even that of loyalty to treaty obligations. Only after the War of the Austrian Succession (1740–1748) were the new alliances more stable. The seeds of the earlier instability resulted largely from the outcome of the War of the Spanish Succession as unsatisfactory for all continental parties. In particular also the power vacuum in continental Europe created by the gradual decline of France became a factor of international insecurity.

The ways of the new alliance systems were shifty, but some trends in Austrian policies are recognizable. In the first place, Charles VI had not given up hope to become king of Spain, and neither had King Philip V of Spain resigned himself to the loss of his Italian possessions; continued conflict was therefore inevitable. Secondly, the emperor was anxious to establish a unified order of succession. It became necessary to test its validity by assuring the succession of a female Habsburg, Charles VI's oldest daughter, Maria Theresa. The emperor believed this could be assured only by international guarantee from the European powers—at a price. As part of the price Austrian eastern policy became now increasingly obliged to conform to Russian interests. This development put brakes on the Habsburg empire's freedom of diplomatic movement.

For almost a century, until 1813–1814, the peace of Passarowitz in 1718, which terminated Charles VI's first Turkish war, was the last unqualified success of Habsburg arms and political power. In 1717 and 1718 Spain, with whom the emperor had refused to sign a peace treaty, occupied Sardinia and Sicily. The feeble response of the signatories of the treaty system of Utrecht, Rastatt, and Baden was the quadruple alliance of England, France, Holland, and Austria to maintain the provisions of the peace terms. In 1720 a compromise, the treaty of the Hague, terminated the conflict. Charles finally recognized the Bourbon rule in Spain, and in return an exchange of Sardina and Sicily took place between Savoy and Austria, after the islands were evacuated by Spain. With Sicily, Austria had thus gained another noncontiguous, hardly defensible territory. A Spanish secundogeniture in Parma, Piacenza, and Tuscany was promised to the second son of the King of Spain. Yet Spain had not done too well either. King Philip, intellectually hardly superior to his imperial colleague, was ready to pay a price for the Habsburg recognition of a loss which the emperor could not have recovered anyway. Furthermore, in the spring of 1725 a rather meaningless Austro-Spanish alliance in which Austria pledged to support Spain in her fight for the recovery of Gibraltar in exchange for the Spanish recognition of the Austrian Ostende Trade Company, founded between 1719 and 1722 for the trade with the East and West Indies and the coasts of Africa, did not serve the true interests of either power. Spain failed to regain Gibraltar, but Austria's pledge of help was a major step in the deterioration of relations with Britain. The British response was an alliance of 1725, for the maintenance of the European balance of power, with France, Holland, Prussia, Denmark, and Sweden. This treaty system was directed against the discontent of Spain and Austria, whose feeble colonial ambitions aroused British concern.

From that time on, Charles's foreign policy was ever more clearly directed to obtaining international guarantees for the recognition of his daughter's succession, although Prince Eugene advised that rearmament would be better than paper guarantees. Actually, both guarantees and armaments combined were entirely justified, but one could not replace the other. Had this been properly understood, an Austria strong in arms *and* guarantees would hardly have been challenged after the death of Charles VI in 1740.

In the fall of 1725 Charles succeeded in obtaining Spain's recognition of the Pragmatic Sanction in return for the emperor's promise to marry Maria Theresa and one of her sisters to the sons of Philip V. There was considerable imperial naïveté involved in this deal. Despite assurances, the Bourbons could have followed Louis XIV's earlier pattern to make later claims of devolution resulting from such marriage contracts. This contingency did not arise, however, since both England and Holland saw in these marriage projects a threat to the future European balance of power, which had been so precariously established at Utrecht. The king of Prussia, Frederick William I, was likewise opposed to this marriage plan for the Austrian heiress. He wished her to become the consort of a prince from a German house. Consequently, Charles as partial price for the British and Prussian recognition of the Pragmatic Sanction (in 1726 and 1731), withdrew his consent to the Spanish marriage of Maria Theresa. A partial price, indeed! Charles had to promise also to support the Prussian king's claim to the succession to the duchy of Berg. The friction caused by this pledge put an ominous strain on imperial-Prussian relations.[36]

Even more far-reaching were the concessions, which the emperor was forced to make to England for her consent to the female succession, although the island power had no primary interest in this question. The price for the British recognition of the Pragmatic Sanction was the dissolution of Charles VI's Trade Company. This move followed temporary suspension conceded in 1727.

To sum up the foregoing: The sweeping concessions laid future Austrian colonial aspirations to rest for all times. In principle Charles VI's Trade Company project was on of his few constructive ideas. The design, however, probably would not have succeeded because the Belgian base could hardly be defended by Austria. The difficulty of maintaining the company's headquarters and naval installations in a port across the British channel coast would presumably have increased the more the company would have prospered. To assume, however, that Charles was motivated by such long-term considerations would credit him with too

[36] Braubach, *Versailles und Wien*, pp. 105–185.

much foresight. His decision to abandon this interesting project was probably based primarily on his curious sense of values which rated an uncontested succession and the control of the genuine Italian appendages of the Spanish crown higher than other interests.[37]

When in 1726 Russia joined the tenuous Austro-Spanish alliance, Charles, as will be remembered, made another sacrifice in connection with the succession issue: the reorientation of Habsburg eastern policy in favor of Russia. Direct consequences of this shift were the disastrous outcome of the Turkish war of 1737–1739 and indirectly the unsatisfactory result of the last war against the Ottoman empire 1788–1791. These matters have been discussed briefly in the survey on the Turkish wars.

In 1732 other German states recognized the Pragmatic Sanction. Of significance were in particular the declarations of the electors. One of them was Frederick Augustus I of Saxony (as king of Poland Augustus II) whose son Frederick Augustus II was married to the first-born daughter of Charles VI's older brother, Emperor Joseph I. The other elector was Charles Albert of Bavaria, married to Joseph's younger daughter. Both princesses, who thus came from an older line of the dynasty than Maria Theresa, had duly renounced their claims to the succession when they were married. Neither the elector of Saxony, Augustus, who was in several ways indebted to Austria, nor that of Bavaria respected their consorts's disclaimers. In fact, Charles Albert of Bavaria's father had signed a secret treaty with France in 1714, according to which the French king pledged his support to Wittelsbach claims to the imperial title and lands of the Bohemian crown.[38] These Bavarian claims were to become an unpleasant surprise, to be revealed only after the emperor's death.

Frederick Augustus of Saxony demanded immediately and obtained a price for the recognition of the Pragmatic Sanction, though this did not prevent him to challenge Maria Theresa's succession in 1740. He asked for imperial support for his candidacy to the Polish crown when the throne became vacant in 1732.The majority of the Polish nobles supported Stanislas Lesczinski, the father-in-law of Louis XV, who once before (1704–1709) had been Polish king, and an undistinguished one at that. Neither did the candidate of the minority, Frederick Augustus of Saxony,

[37] Redlich, *Das Werden . . .* , pp. 255–271; Krones, *Handbuch,* IV, 120–137.

[38] Technically the Bavarian claims were not based on a refusal to recognize the Pragmatic Sanction but on a clause in the will of the Emperor Ferdinand I according to which the Wittelsbach dynasty would succeed after the male Habsburg line had become extinct. Yet this claim was evidently based on a forgery. Ferdinand's will referred to the extinction of all legitimate heirs that is those born in wedlock and not just male heirs. See also Krones, *Handbuch,* IV, 173–176.

surpass him in abilities as a ruler. Yet Frederick Augustus was Russia's candidate and thereby that of her ally Austria. Stanislas was supported by France. It was against Russian interests to have a king supported by a great power as well as by the majority of the Polish Sejm. Undoubtedly, Frederick Augustus, who had little backing in the country would be more dependent on the mighty Russian neighbor. For that reason Austria should have favored the French candidate. In that case Poland would not have become a Russian satellite, and France completely separated from Poland could have done little to sway the kingdom in the long run. A Russian predominance in Poland, on the other hand, might create difficulties at Austria's eastern borders.

Charles VI's reasoning, however, was different. In the first place, in relation to Russia he could no longer act as a free agent. Secondly, the Bourbons were still the traditional enemies of the Habsburgs, and imperial support of the elector of Saxony would add another signature to the parchment collection guaranteeing the Pragmatic Sanction. Thus, Charles entered the Polish War of Succession (1733–1735) on the Saxon-Russian side, that is, from the viewpoint of genuine Austrian interests, on the wrong side.

The results of this war for the Habsburgs were equally disappointing in a military and diplomatic sense. Neither the army nor its more than seventy-year-old commander Eugene of Savoy could be compared with the armed forces and their leadership in the War of the Spanish Succession and the first Turkish war fought in Charles's reign. The Russians let the Austrians do most of the fighting. The Rhine army under Eugene's command barely held its own and could not prevent the conquest of Lorraine by the French under Marshal Villars. Spain and Savoy, who saw their chance in Italy, gave the emperor a lesson concerning the reliability of treaty obligations. Worse could be expected after his death since the poor state of the Austrian military establishment had now been fully revealed to the world.

The Austrians lost most of their Italian possessions to the French-Spanish-Savoyan military forces. Villars, Eugene of Savoy's old counterpart, took Milan, and the Spanish occupied Naples and Sicily. The hostilities ended in 1735, but a formal peace treaty was not signed until November 1738 in Vienna. According to its terms Frederick Augustus of Saxony was recognized as King Augustus III of Poland, Stanislas Lesczinski was retired as duke of Lorraine (actually only Upper Lorraine) to be yielded by the young sovereign of the duchy, Francis Stephan. After the death of the aged Stanislas, Lorraine, legally still imperial land, was to become part of France.[39] After the expected extinction of the Medici dynasty in Tuscany, Francis Stephan, now a landless prince, was to succeed there as ruler with the seat of residence in Florence. This was considered to be a meager substitute for Lorraine, but an added compensation of considerable prestige and political significance was the marriage to the emperor's heiress, Archduchess Maria Theresa, in 1736. As a pleasant by product, this diplomatically arranged deal became one of the rare princely love marriages in history.[40]

If Francis thus did not fare too badly, Austria did. Naples and Sicily were ceded to a Spanish secundogeniture in Italy under the second son of Philip V. Parma and Piacenza were in turn given to Austria. Together with Tuscany, where Francis and Maria Theresa ruled after 1736, these principalities would become secundo- and tertio-genitures for their offspring. The French pledge to recognize the Pragmatic Sanction, supposedly a major concession, had to be considered as worthless. The establishment of the Saxon King in Poland, though brought about largely by Austrian military efforts and territorial sacrifices, served mainly Russian interests. Naples and Sicily, although poorly developed, were strategically and perhaps also economically more promising domains than Parma and Piacenza. Even now the Austrian possessions in Italy, though closer to the hereditary lands than Naples and Sicily, did not represent a homogeneous and fully contiguous territory adjacent to the hereditary lands. It might have been conceivable to establish a new trading company in southern Italian territory. The only major Tuscanese port, Livorno, faced the Tyrrhenian sea, whereas Habsburg commercial trade by sea pointed toward the Levant. This meant that Austrian dreams to become a sea power beyond the almost landlocked Adriatic Sea had come to an end within less than twenty years after they were born. They followed thus the termination of colonial aspirations, brought about by the previous dissolution of the Trading Company in Ostende.

The Habsburgs had gained no shred of security for all their sacrifices. On the contrary, the poor showing in the War of the Polish Succession, compounded by the defeat and ensuing territorial losses in Charles's second Turkish war (1737–1739), put Europe on notice that a second empire might soon be put on the auction block to be parceled out to the

[39] Upper Lorraine, in substance the territory around Metz and Nancy, still retained representation at the imperial Reichstag in Regensburg. This ambiguous status was a contributory cause to the war of the First Coalition against France in 1792.

[40] Braubach, *Versailles und Wien,* pp. 186–275; Redlich, *Das Werden . . . ,* pp. 277–287; Wladyslaw Konopzyński, *The Cambridge History of Poland* (Cambridge, 1951), II, chapt. 1, 25–32.

highest bidders. The rapid accumulation of territories between 1713 and 1718 and the almost equally speedy losses between 1737 and 1739 seemed to confirm the experience that a soap bubble busts all the more easily the more rapidly it is blown up.

F. The great-power position is tested

Charles VI died on October 20, 1740, and within less than two months the great struggle known in history as the War of the Austrian Succession (1740–1748) had begun with its first installment: the invasion of Silesia by the new king of Prussia, Frederick II. Neither the specific conflict between Austria and Prussia nor the character of Maria Theresa's momentous reign, which was initiated by the war, will be discussed in this section. The War of the Austrian Succession will be perceived as the end of the era of the evolution of Austria as a great power. The reign of Maria Theresa belongs to a new one, discussed in Chapter V.

Maria Theresa's succession was challenged at once by Bavaria, Saxony, and Spain, whose rulers made claims to the succession in all Habsburg lands, by the elector of Bavaria on the strength of his marriage to a daughter of Joseph I and Ferdinand I's alleged will. This former issue was now raised also by the elector of Saxony and new king of Poland. The Spanish crown considered itself heir to the succession treaties between the two main branches of the Habsburg dynasty. None of these demands had a legal foundation. Prussia did not challenge the succession, but merely demanded the cession of Silesia. Frederick II himself did not take the legal grounds on which this request was made too seriously. Neither was there much substance to the initial claims of Savoy to all or part of the duchy of Milan. What counted in the territorial aspects of this war, one of the most widespread in history before World War I, was not the comprehensiveness of the individual claims but the total political impact of the claimants and the seriousness of their purpose to enforce their dubious demands.

The attempts to bring about the dismemberment of the Habsburg empire were fully backed and largely initiated by France, which hoped in the beginning to get rid of her major European rival without direct military intervention. Of the other powers, England, Holland, and Russia could not be considered openly favoring Austria, yet they had a common interest in preventing a complete upset of the balance of power in Europe. Of general political claims to the succession, those of Bavaria had to be taken most seriously, not on account of the military strength of the country, but because France used her demands as the most convenient handle to bring about Austria's disintegration. Spain and Saxony hoped to fish in troubled waters but they never really expected to become heirs to all Austrian lands. Savoy's limited and brief intervention depended on the involvement of others; Prussia's success directed at limited objectives was primarily due to the military proficiency of her army.

A major diplomatic event of the war was the alliance of Nymphenburg of May, 1741, between France, Spain, and Bavaria, in which France pledged to support the claims of the two other powers. The fact that these claims in their comprehensiveness were actually mutually exclusive, shows convincingly that this phase of European history was more antithetic to ideological issues than almost any period of the past after the early Middle Ages. What counted more than anything else in Austria's disfavor was the French promise to support the Bavarian elector Charles Albert as candidate for the crown of the Holy Roman empire. Only a week after the Nymphenburg agreement France concluded a treaty with Bavaria and Prussia, according to which Prussia's conquest of Lower Silesia, initiated already in December of 1740 and completed by October of 1741, was recognized. In turn, Frederick of Prussia undertook the obligation to support the imperial claims of the elector of Bavaria. Charles Albert was to receive also Bohemia and a major part of the hereditary lands. In August, 1741, another treaty of support was concluded between France and Saxony, Austria's former ally. In November, an additional pact of mutual assistance and guarantee of conquests was concluded between Bavaria and Prussia.

The more often the same issues are confirmed by treaty obligations, the less is observance of each specific agreement to be trusted. In October, 1741, Maria Theresa and Frederick II had concluded the secret pact of Klein-Schnellendorf, according to which Austria after the unfavorable outcome of the first campaign was forced to cede Lower Silesia to Prussia and Prussia in turn promised to desist from further attack. With this pact Frederick managed to doublecross friend and foe alike. The ruler of Bavaria, elected emperor in January, 1742, at the time when he was crowned in February in Frankfurt, was practically a prince without land. The Austrians had occupied a part of Bavaria including the capital Munich. By December, 1742, the Bavarians were forced also to evacuate Bohemia, which they had occupied only a few months before with French help. In accordance with the changing fortunes of the war Sardinia-Savoy in return for the promise of the Milanese territory west of the Ticino reversed her position, and her noble king joined now the Austrian side. Yet a new setback was in store for Maria Theresa. Frederick, contrary to the convention of Klein-Schnellendorf, had resumed the war; Austria after further defeats had to cede not only Lower but also Upper Silesia to Prussia in June and July, 1742 (preliminary peace of Breslau and permanent peace of Berlin).[41] Against all Austrian expectations this turned out to be in the end a permanent cession.

Yet, not everything was lost for Austria. In September, 1743, England, Sardina, and Austria pledged a concerted effort to drive the Spanish armies out of central and northern Italy. A firm French-Spanish alliance followed as response. Saxony, scared now by the unexepected Prussian military success, reverted to the more predictable Austrian side. To even up the score, France in May, 1744, officially declared war on Austria and England. This move formalized merely a state of hostilities which in camouflaged manner had commenced after the death of Charles VI. The old British fear of the Bourbon French-Spanish family alliance with its inherent threat to the balance of power in Europe now worked clearly in favor of Austria.

Meanwhile Frederick II, worried that Austria might be almost ready for a recovery of Silesia, concluded a new alliance with France, whose trust he had violated by the peace of Berlin. In August, 1744, Frederick marched through Saxony—the Belgium of the second half of the eighteenth century—into Bohemia. After severe, costly, but largely indecisive fighting, peace was concluded at Dresden on Christmas day 1745. Frederick maintained what he had gotten in the first Silesian war, but dropped plans for further conquests in Bohemia, which were beyond his reach. He also recognized Francis of Lorraine as emperor, whose election had taken place in September 1745 after Charles (Albert) VII's death had ended his unhappy reign in January of the same year.

The election of Francis, undistinguished as he was as emperor of the decaying Holy Roman Empire, restored prestige to the house of Austria. Since Maria Theresa as a woman was legally barred from accession to the imperial throne of the Holy Roman Empire in her own right, this meant for all practical, though not legal, purposes that the Habsburg dynasty under the new heading House of Habsburg-Lorraine would continue to bear the imperial title. The weakness of the empire notwithstanding, this meant further that Austria in the future would not be deprived of the force of nearly a millennium of imperial tradition. The nominal chief challenger, Bavaria, through the son of Charles Albert, acknowledged now in the peace of Füssen April, 1745, the Pragmatic Sanction. Maria Theresa, heretofore known as queen of Bohemia and Hungary,

[41] Austria, however, kept Teschen, Troppau and Jägerndorf.

and now officially empress consort, was from now on referred to as empress or empress-queen, a title which not in law but in practice corresponded to the majesty of her position and personality.

The war continued for a time in full fury, and spread even further. The French and British battled each other not only in the Austrian Netherlands, where the French won the spectacular victory at Fontenoy in May, 1745, but also in North America and India. The final determination of most of the colonial issues was not made until the peace of Paris in 1763. Yet as far as the Austrian War of Succession was concerned, the main issue could be considered as settled. Maria Theresa's succession was hardly any longer in doubt after 1745. Still, the war in western Italy continued with indifferent results; by 1746 the Spanish-French troops withdrew, but they managed to stay in the Austrian Netherlands and made even forays into Holland. But a defensive Austrian-Russian alliance of June, 1746, directed against a potential new Prussian attack, protected the Habsburgs from their militarily most formidable foe.

The peace treaty of Aix la Chapelle, in which Count (later Prince) Anton Wenzel Kaunitz-Rietberg, the future state chancellor, showed his superb skill as Austria's chief negotiator, was concluded in October, 1748. In addition to the loss of Silesia, the Habsburgs had to cede Parma, Piacenza, and Guastalla to the third son of Philip of Spain. Parma was to return to Austria, in case the Spanish line should become extinct as it actually occurred after the French Revolution. Savoy's gain of the Milanese territories west of the Ticino was confirmed. The Spanish Netherlands, under existing conditions more an encumbrance than a source of power, were returned to Austria. The basic issue over which the war, in a sense the first world war, was fought, Maria Theresa's succession according to the Pragmatic Sanction, was accepted by all parties. So was the Habsburg-Lorraine imperial title in the Holy Roman Empire. Austria's losses in Italy may be considered as negligible, but that of Silesia, had far-reaching consequences for Austria's position in Germany and even for the future development of the national problems in the Habsburg monarchy. These issues will be discussed in different contexts in chapters V and VII. Maria Theresa did not yet write off Silesia. The loss in political prestige was made up by the fact that the Habsburg empire had survived concerted attacks and not been reduced like Spain in 1713–1714 to a secondary power, or like Poland in 1735 to a Russian puppet state.

The pacification of Hungary secured in 1711 was still effective. When

Maria Theresa appeared in summer, 1741, before the Hungarian estates at Pozsony they pledged their support and asked only for relatively minor concessions on the issue of tax exemption. The military assistance of the Hungarian estates' forces, the so-called estates insurrection, did not amount to much help, but the fact that the estates did not exploit the actual situation of the courageous young queen to renewed revolutionary advantage, cemented the stability of her rule. The Bohemian estates however, conscious of their abject reduction in political status after the Battle of the White Mountain, gave Charles Albert of Bavaria in 1741–1742 considerable support, but they accepted the reestablishment of Habsburg rule without revolutionary action. Bavarian overlordship seemed just as far, if not farther, removed from their national aspirations than the Habsburg scepter.

The defensive success of Habsburg power in the War of the Austrian Succession was not the result of particular military brilliance. Austria had great generals under Leopold I, Joseph I, and the earlier part of the reign of Charles VI, and respectable ones later in the Seven Years' War. The supreme commander in the War of the Austrian Succession, Charles of Lorraine, Maria Theresa's brother-in-law, on the other hand, was a man of more than ordinary incompetence, whose poor showing impaired also the performance of better Austrian generals such as counts Khevenhüller and Traun. No brilliant military feat was connected with the outcome of the war.

Yet if looked at in isolation from other events, the survival of Habsburg's power, a far less homogeneous empire than even Spain at the beginning of the century, could be considered almost a miracle. It was a tremendous phenomenon which refutes the simplistic notion that this new empire was an artificial contraption, incapable to withstand the blowing of a great storm. International and even Austrian historiography have still not fully acknowledged that the divisive first great test of Austria's cohesive strength as great power was not the victory of the Counter Reformation, nor the relief of Vienna from the second Turkish siege, nor the dismemberment of the Spanish empire. It was rather the largely disconnected and diffuse War of the Austrian Succession. The siege of Vienna in 1683 could hardly have led at that time to a lasting Turkish victory, and the other events mentioned here brought about as many disadvantages as assets to the Austrian cause. The defensive victory in the War of the Austrian Succession, on the other hand, proved to the world that this new empire despite its shortcomings was bound to survive.[42]

[42] Walter L. Dorn, *Competition for Empire, 1740–1763* (New York, 1940), pp. 122–177; Braubach, *Versailles und Wien,* pp. 276–396; Alfred von Arneth,

This amazing outcome of the war was partly due to the fact, that the envisaged results of dismemberment did not, for any of the historico-political entities of the empire, hold expectations worth suffering and fighting for. Prospects such as control of Bohemia by Bavaria, Hungary by the Turks, or Belgium by France, did not inspire people to national risings. Yet with due caution we may suggest here, that the recognition of more positive values than the mere passive issues of choice between greater or lesser evils contributed to the successful test of the Habsburg empire's staying power. Factors of this kind are to be found in the socio-cultural field as much as in legal-political bonds. Some of them will be discussed in the following chapter.

Geschichte Maria Theresias, 10 vols. (Vienna, 1863–1879), see I–III; Robert A. Kann, *The Habsburg Empire: A Study in Integration and Disintegration* (2nd ed. New York, 1973), pp. 30–32.

CHAPTER IV

Late Renaissance and Baroque Age in the Habsburg Lands (1526-1740)

A. Over-all issues

It is impossible to comprise the social and cultural history of the Habsburg domains from the second quarter of the sixteenth to the middle of the eighteenth century under one comprehensive concept. In accordance with the terminology of European cultural history, late Renaissance, humanism, possibly mannerism in the fine arts, and certainly Baroque and Rococo would represent movements of nearly equal significance. So would be references to the age of the great philosophical systems in strictly intellectual history, the era of mercantilism or princely absolutism in the sociopolitical field or Reformation and Counter Reformation in the religious one. Most of these problems, currents, and conflicts are applicable to aspects of the history of the rising Habsburg empire as they would be to that of any other western or Central European power. Yet although such concepts are not equally relevant to all these powers, the impact of several of them appears to be more incongruous in the history of the Habsburg empire than in that of many other countries.

Why so? The Renaissance reached the Habsburg lands only at the end of the fifteenth century. Before it could spread widely from the centers of courtly culture to urban bourgeois civilization it was diverted from its course by the austerity and the radicalism of the incipient Reformation. In the Habsburg lands it became engaged in a particularly bitter struggle with the Counter Reformation, which lasted more than a century. The Turkish wars were followed in the east by a delayed-action counter-reformatory period, after Hungary was freed from the Turks as late as the last decades of the seventeenth and the first of the eighteenth centuries.

In the course of the overall struggle, states rights and the spread of representative government to burghers and peasants were thoroughly checked by princely absolutism. Yet while its rise in the political sphere can be observed equally well in seventeenth-century France, the corresponding change in social structure to a kind of state capitalism played a more limited role in the Habsburg lands. Mercantilism did exist but not an age of mercantilism. This was partly due to the differences in social and cultural structure between hereditary and Bohemian lands, but particularly those of the Hungarian crown.

These realms did not experience an age of great philosophical systems and of outstanding scientific discoveries. The ideas of Hobbes, Locke, Descartes, Spinoza, Leibniz found little repercussions in seventeenth- and early-eighteenth-century thinking of the Habsburg domains. The situation was somewhat different in the sciences where outstanding achievements did exist though rather as isolated feats than as part of continuous trends.

As for the arts, literature was not strongly influenced by the predominant intellectual accomplishments of the west and north. Music in the seventeenth century, apart from folksongs, was largely under the sway of the Italian opera. Strong Italian and later also French influence was experienced also in painting, sculpture, and architecture. Many talents were trained and inspired in these fields. The Habsburg empire established here a commanding position in the seventeenth and early eighteenth century. In accordance with the dominant ideas of time and place, emphasis on the grandiose and spectacular—particularly in architecture—were characteristic. These schemes and concepts of the age of the victorious Counter Reformation could be put to life in the frame of absolute government, stimulated and colored further by the pattern of courtly secular and upper ecclesiastic culture.

Such development was impeded by slow economic progress but strengthened by the urge for ideological conformity, which furthered the fine arts as much as it fettered the evolution and exchange of secular ideas in the humanities. All this falls into place under the concept of the Austrian Baroque. Unlike parallel movements in the west, it did not extend its desires for comprehensiveness to great deductive systems and models of thought. It was concerned, though frequently on a high plane, with impressions of the senses and emotions.

This Baroque era was introduced by a late Renaissance period in which the rise of the towns and the struggle of the unfree peasants was crushed in the confrontation of two great, but almost equally intolerant ideological systems, Reformation and Counter Reformation. It was succeeded by a brief and neither in Austrian arts nor literature particularly significant Rococo period. The real heir of the Austrian Baroque is the Enlightenment, with a more puritan style of arts. Its consequences are in reverse proportions to its brief hold in the Habsburg lands.

Thus, if we speak in this chapter broadly of the Baroque age, we have to make chronological allowance for a last phase of the Renaissance, a brief transition period of mannerism in its beginnings, and a still tender rise of rationalism at its end in the Rococo period. Besides, we have to recognize trends within the Austrian Baroque itself. They are reflected in different ways in the three political main units discussed here, the Austro-German hereditary lands, the lands of the Bohemian crown, and in the sixteenth and seventeenth centuries the lands of the Hungarian crown. Conditions in all three units differed from each other, but those in Hungary were even more at variance with patterns in the Austrian and Bohemian lands than dissimiliarities between the two latter realms.

Yet there were also common concepts and trends, which made an impact on all political entities. Disregarding here matters of foreign policy, discussed in the previous chapter, four of these trends were all pervasive: the struggle between Reformation and Counter Reformation, the conflict between estates and princely absolutism, the economic development under the influence of the ideas of an elementary type of mercantilism, and the influence of Baroque arts in general.

Of these four main trends the first plays an important role in the history of all three Habsburg domains, though in Hungary, as a result of the Turkish occupation, at a later time than in the hereditary and the Bohemian lands. The collision between princely absolutism and estates power in the sixteenth century was all-pervasive, but in the seventeenth century and in particular in the later seventeenth century important only in Hungary where the Counter Reformation in political terms never succeeded to the same degree as in the west and north. Mercantilism and industrialization played a more important part in the hereditary and Bohemian lands than in rural Hungary. Baroque art pertains again to all Habsburg lands.

B. Reformation and Counter Reformation

In the sixteenth and seventeenth centuries the Church in the Habsburg lands had to face religious and political struggles. The former aspect resulted from a conflict between two spiritual trends: the late medieval reform movement within the Church from which Protestantism developed, and the response to it which in the second quarter of the sixteenth century changed into a Catholic reform movement within the Church. The latter is generally referred to as the Catholic Reformation and should be considered as truly religious counterpart to Protestantism. Accompanying and following the religious dispute was a conflict between the political and social forces, which backed the Reformation and those which fought it. This long-lasting confrontation between imperial and princely authorities, Catholic and Protestant nobles, bishops and pastors, towns and occasionally peasants against vested feudal interests on both sides, is properly referred to as the fight between Reformation and Counter Reformation.[1]

The following pages will primarily discuss the political aspects of the struggle. Yet this conflict, which lasted more than a century, is not the only one which the Church had to face. Less dramatic in early modern times but of even longer duration and most difficult to solve was the struggle between Church and state power. In the context of this study this means conflict between institutions within a Catholic empire, even after the religious confrontation had abated. Here we face the remnants of the medieval conflict between pope and emperor, as expressed in the symbols of the two-swords theory.[2]

In political terms we have to refer to such issues as the century-old struggle concerning the promulgation of papal bulls and diocesan encyclicals with or without the consent of princely sovereigns; further, all questions of ecclesiastic investiture and those of privileged clerical jurisdiction for the priesthood, embargo of money shipments to Rome, and clerical taxation. Most of these problems represented in changed form continuous themes from the Middle Ages well into the latter part of the nineteenth century. Yet they have a specific relationship to the Protestant Reformation inasmuch as the Church in the late fifteenth and early

[1] A clear distinction between the political nature of the Counter Reformation and the predominantly ideological one of the Catholic Reformation is possible, but the same semantic distinction between the religious and political aspects of the Protestant Reformation is difficult to make. The earlier concept of the Reformation comprises both the religious and political aspects of the movement, whereas that of Protestants and Protestantism—not introduced until the second imperial diet of Speyer in 1529—refers primarily to the religious issue. Since the concept of Reformation, which without qualifying adjective always refers to the *Protestant* Reformation, comprises religious and political aspects, it is advisable to state always in what context the term is used.

[2] For an over-all discussion of the Austrian situation in political terms, see Robert A. Kann, *The Problem of Restoration* (Berkeley and Los Angeles, 1968), pp. 231–278.

sixteenth centuries was in a state of crisis pertaining equally to questions of ecclesiastic authority and the controversial mores of individual higher ecclesiastics. This Church, harassed in several ways in all Habsburg lands, could fight the Reformation only with the support, indeed the direction of, the crown. Thus the *placetum regis* for the promulgation of papal bulls was a continuous unresolved issue of policy in the era under discussion from Ferdinand I to Maria Theresa. The supervision of universities according to standards of religious conformity, the visitations of churches and monasteries, indeed the establishment of government-controlled monastic councils were introduced by Ferdinand I and continued by his successors. To strengthen the princely position, the visitations of monasteries and convents by foreign generals of orders and foreign provincials were forbidden.

Yet it was neither a particularly harsh nor unyielding ruler, who had initiated this policy. Ferdinand I had approached Pope Pius IV with the request to grant the Cup to the Laity in his lands. He had been willing to accept the marriage of ecclesiastics. Here was a sovereign to whom the unity of the faith, not unlike the views of Melanchton on the side of the Protestant Reformation, meant more than the issue of Church regiment, Church liturgy, and the unflexible interpretation of dogmas. Naturally he was concerned not only with the unity of faith under the tiara, but even more with that under the scepter. This concern accounts for the fact that the sternest measures of suppression and persecution were directed against the Anabaptists and later Calvinists, of whom the first threatened the social order and the latter the political order by denying the emperor what was to be the emperor's.

This is not to say that Ferdinand either as ruler of the hereditary lands and those of the eastern crowns ever condoned less radical forms of Protestantism. Yet his attitude toward the Reformation war primarily motivated by the specter of rebellion of the Protestant German princes against the emperor, whereas his brother Charles V was at least equally strongly moved by religious considerations.[3]

The question arises, who should be considered as Protestant in terms of conditions in the sixteenth-century Habsburg domains. Fully reliable evaluations are not possible. Apart from differences in liturgy in the main units of the Habsburg lands, Protestant interpretations emphasize that the majority of the noble estates, lords, and knights became adherents of reformatory doctrines and that the same can be said in many instances

[3] See Franz von Bucholtz, *Geschichte der Regierung Ferdinands I,* 9 vols. (Graz, 1968), VIII.

also for town representatives. Catholic interpretations can counter with some right that deductions drawn from social elites to the population as a whole are dubious. Besides, in the Habsburg lands, unlike in southern and central Germany, the nobles, not the towns, were the chief champions of Protestantism. These nobles were primarily concerned with the issue of estates rights against princely absolutism and less directly with questions of creed.

Still, the lords, and particularly the lower nobility, were the most vocal, fairly independent political force in the sixteenth century. The high clergy matched them in power, but they could not express their opinions freely. The towns were frequently not strong enough to act independently from the nobles, and the same was true for the peasants. There religious revolt and social revolt against the liege lord was even more inextricably intertwined than was the issue of faith and estates rights within the Protestant nobility.

The Reformation in the lands under the Habsburg scepter made enormous progress between the fifteen twenties and fifteen forties. It was then somewhat curbed as consequence of the Schmalkaldian war in Germany (1546–1547) and its aftermath. Its spread, however, was consolidated again and perhaps even strengthened under the rule of Ferdinand's eldest son Maximilian II (1564–1576), who will be remembered as the Habsburg ruler friendliest to Protestantism and, according to some interpretations, at his deathbed even converted to Protestantism.[4] During the reign of his son, Rudolf II (1576–1602), the Counter Reformation had decidedly gained the upper hand, local reformatory successes in Bohemia notwithstanding. Throughout the last years of Rudolf's increasingly contested reign and during that of the first years of his brother, Matthias (1612–1619), the Protestant estates in the hereditary and Bohemian lands took advantage of the fratricidal conflict within the dynasty. This led only to short-range success, brought about by external events. No genuine new religious transformation reoccurred. At the end of Matthias' reign and during that of Ferdinand II (1619–1637) the Counter Reformation won in a literal sense a smashing victory. Yet before it, for two generations the

[4] Maximilian's loyalty to the faith was questioned by his father Ferdinand I and his royal cousin Philip II of Spain, but Maximilian himself consistently denied it. Confirmed seems to be only the fact that he refused Extreme Unction on his deathbed. See Karl Brandi, *Deutsche Reformation und Gegenreformation,* 2 vols. (Leipzig, 1927), II, 60 f. Matthias Koch, *Quellen zur Geschichte des Kaisers Maximilian* (Leipzig, 1857–1861), II, 92–100. Franz von Krones, *Handbuch der Geschichte Österreichs* (Berlin, 1889), III, 266 ff. See also Viktor Bibl, *Zur Frage der religiösen Haltung Kaiser Maximilians II* (Vienna, 1917), pp. 3–102 passim.

Protestants shared political power and held a monopoly in regard to a measure of free expression of public opinion. Both these sources of strength were heavily contested; nevertheless, they exercised considerable impact for two generations.

Beyond these general considerations for all Habsburg realms, allowance has to be made for specific conditions in the hereditary lands and those of the eastern crowns. In every one of them at least one basic element was different. Protestantism in the hereditary lands was greatly influenced by the fact, that the sixteenth-century Reformation had started from Germany and thus no language barrier impeded its early spread. In Bohemia, on the other hand, the Reformation could claim far longer antecedents going back to the Hussite movement in the fifteeenth century which in turn was influenced by Wyclif's ideas and actions in the fourteenth. In Hungary the main clash between Reformation and Counter Reformation occurred much later because of one and a half century of Turkish occupation. When the showdown took place the outcome was predetermined.

a) THE HEREDITARY LANDS

In the hereditary lands relative moderation on the part of estates and Church was a distinct factor for two generations.[5] This attitude changed first radically in Inner Austria, when the later emperor Ferdinand II began his rule as archduke in his hereditary domains in 1596. Similar changes occurred in Vorderösterreich even in the 1580's, whereas the counterreformatory measures in Upper and Lower Austria introduced by the Emperor Rudolf II met stiffer resistance among nobles, some towns,

[5] The introductory chapter referred to the organization of the hereditary lands under Emperor Maximilian I. At the end of Ferdinand's I reign in 1564 a division of the inheritance of long lasting significance took place between his three sons. According to Ferdinand's will, his oldest son and successor as emperor Maximilian II, king of Hungary, Croatia, and Bohemia secured the archduchies above and below the Enns, referred until to-day as Upper and Lower Austria. There terms, however, are neither identical nor even similar to the concept of Lower and Upper Austria as established in the administrative reforms of Maximilian I. The second son, Ferdinand, inherited Tyrol, Vorarlberg, and the Habsburg possessions in south and western Germany (Vorlande). The whole complex of lands was generally referred to as Vorderösterreich. The third son, Charles, obtained Styria, Carinthia, Carniola, Gorizia, Trieste, and Istria (Inner Austria). Only by 1665 did all three ruling lines merge permanently in the imperial line. See also Alfons Huber and Alfons Dopsch, *Österreichische Reichsgeschichte* (Vienna, 1901), pp. 170–180. Friedrich Walter, *Österreichische Verfassungs- und Verwaltungsgeschichte* (Vienna-Graz-Cologne, 1972), pp. 54–61.

and, particularly in Upper Austria, the peasants.[6] At the time of his accession in 1578 the noble estates in Upper and Lower Austria had obtained the right of free religious exercise according to the Augsburg creed in castles, houses, and domains as well as in the churches under their inherited patronage. Within these limits Protestant education was at least tolerated. In substance, these rights either expressly granted or at least not directly interfered with liberties secured in the other two parts of the tripartite hereditary lands. They were, however, never formally extended to towns, markets, let alone villages. Yet the Protestant peasants benefited indirectly from the extension of the rights of lords and knights to their subjects. This extension stood for an adaption of the principle of the peace of Augsburg *cuius regio eius religio* to the feudal order, but did not imply formal recognition of religious freedom of the commoners. Relatively best off in this respect seemed to be urban Protestants. They could share in the religious services and educational facilities of the schools held in adjacent castles. Since they were financially stronger and naturally more concerned with educational problems than the unfree peasants they could even in some places establish religious and educational institutions on their own grounds. These, however, never had unchallenged legal standing.

In fact, the victory of the Counter Reformation in Vorder and Inner Austria commenced with the move against Protestant establishments in towns and markets. It shifted from the closing of schools to the eviction of so-called agitators and step by step to large-scale expulsion of peasants, who were faced with the choice of forced reconversion or forced emigration. Protestant nobles, originally the spearheads of the movement, had failed to give the peasants sufficient support when they rose equally for social and religious reasons.[7] The heroic peasant revolt in Upper Austria between 1624 and 1627 is a striking example. Shortly afterward, the Counter

[6] The terms Upper and Lower Austria will be used from here on in the modern sense, that means the archduchies above and below the Enns (Ober- and Niederösterreich) rather than in terms of the reforms of Maximilian I, that is: Lower Austria including modern Upper Austria, Styria, Carinthia, and Carniola; Upper Austria including Tyrol,Windisch March, Istria, Trieste, Gorizia, Vorarlberg, as well as the German Vorlande (Vorderösterreich).

[7] See Grete Mecenseffy, *Geschichte des Protestantismus in Österreich* (Graz-Cologne, 1956), pp. 50–108; Josef Wodka, *Kirche in Österreich* (Vienna, 1959), pp. 195–240; Paul Dedic, "Der Protestantismus in der Steiermark im Zeitalter der Reformation und Gegenreformation" (Leipzig, 1930), 48:2, 1–204 passim; and as background reading Johann Loserth, *Die Reformation und Gegenreformation in den innerösterreichischen Ländern im XVI. Jahrhundert* (Stuttgart, 1898).

Reformation flushed by transitory military success in the Thirty Years' War reached its political peak with the Edict of Restitution of 1629, which was meant to undo the strongholds of the Reformation, gained after the peace of Augsburg. Ironically, Ferdinand II owed this rashly exploited victory to the strategy of the commander in chief of his forces, Wallenstein, who was personally indifferent to the religious aspects of the struggle.[8]

Altogether the success of the Counter Reformation in the hereditary lands was only in small parts due to the helplessness of feeble rulers like Rudolf II and his brother Matthias, who vacillated between suppression and appeasement of the estates. Neither could a bigot like Ferdinand II claim much credit. The fate of the Reformation and the course of the Counter Reformation were largely determined by the outcome of the Huguenot wars in France, the predominance of Spain in south and southwestern Europe, and the isolationist policies of James I in England. The Habsburgs in the hereditary lands influenced more the content of the counterreformatory program than its political course. In this respect the impact of the events in Bohemia, which gradually were to lead to the foreign intervention of the powers involved in the Thirty Years' War, and the events in Hungary, which had been brought about by foreign (Turkish) intervention, were important.

b) THE LANDS OF THE BOHEMIAN CROWN

The situation in the lands of the Bohemian crown was different because of the religious heretic and social revolutionary indoctrination, which at the time of the triumph of the Counter Reformation had a history of two centuries behind it. The fires of the Hussite wars had been extinguished in the 1430's, but the idea of the national kingdom, which embraced that of a national Church had been alive as recently as the reign of George of Poděbrady in the late fifteenth century and the first Jagiello kings in the early sixteenth century. In the Bohemian lands, the notion of a restriction of religious and religious educational freedom did not exist—unlike the situation in the hereditary lands.

Three main reformatory trends prevailed under Habsburg rule in Bohemia up to the catastrophe of the White Mountain in 1620: the Utraquist movement, representing the moderate turn of the Hussite movement in the later fifteenth and sixteenth centuries; the Unity of the Bohemian

[8] See Hans Sturmberger, *Georg Erasmus Tschernembl: Ein Beitrag zur Geschichte der Gegenreformation und des Landes ob der Enns* (Graz-Cologne, 1953), pp. 261–365.

Brethren, the somewhat mellowed heirs to the radical Taborite ideas; and the Lutherans. Only the latter can strictly speaking be referred to as Protestants. Still, the Bohemian Brethren approved, like the Utraquists, of Communion in both kinds,[9] and also of the completely, free lay ministry without control by higher authority, the renunciation of material ecclesiastic power, and the affirmation of the rights and duties of Christianity to reform society. In the sixteenth century this last demand could no longer be taken literally, let alone enforced. Yet the moderate Utraquists had also modified the notion of the unrestricted lay ministry. The austerity of the ways of life of the ministry was still endorsed, but the social reform idea was dropped. This is the basic difference between the so-called Articles of Prague of 1420, which represented the creed of the Unity of Bohemian Brethern and the *Compactata* arrived as compromise solution at the Council of Constance in 1436–1437 to which the Utraquists adhered henceforward.

Early Lutheranism, because of its Hussite antecedents and Luther's dynamic reformism up to his return to Wittenberg in 1522, appeared to the Czech Reformation closer to the "Unity" than to the Utraquists. Luther for a time responded to this interpretation, and in the second quarter of the sixteenth century Czech-German cooperation was closer than before or afterward. The battered Hussite reform movement had received a new impetus, which was to be disappointed later, due to Czech concern regarding the national issue, ostensibly threatened in the long run by a German-directed reformatory movement. Therefore Calvinism appeared more congenial to the Reformation in the Bohemian lands. Ferdinand I, however, who feared a prospective alliance, if not merger, between the Utraquist and Lutheran movements tried to conciliate the Utraquists. He seemed to be willing to recognize the *Compactata,* if such move would return moderate Utraquism to the Church. The Council of Trent and Charles V's victory in the Schmalkaldian war prevented the success of this statesmanlike design. Indeed, a new wave of persecution against the Bohemian Brethren followed, in the course of

[9] The term Utraquists refers to the doctrine of Communion in both kinds, which means the Cup for the Laity, and therefore pertained equally to Bohemian Brethren and moderates. Yet, particularly in sixteen-century developments Utraquism in regard to the Eucharist had become the core of the doctrine of the moderates, whereas it stood only for one of the demands of the radicals. This seems to be the historical, though not logical interpretation, why the term Utraquists is generally used for the moderates. See also Friedrich G. Heymann, *John Žižka and the Hussite Revolution* (Princeton, 1955), pp. 602–606. See also Ferdinand Seibt in K. Bosl, ed., *Handbuch der Geschichte der böhmischen Länder,* I, 546–558.

which their bishop Johannes Augusta was imprisoned and tortured. The Jesuits were now called to Bohemia and gained a stronghold in higher education in the Clementinum in Prague. Bishop Peter Canisius (1521–1597),[10] proved himself here as effective an agent of the Counter Reformation as he had been previously in southern Germany and Austria.

Augusta's hope to reconcile Bohemian Brethren and Lutheranism failed as did a more far-reaching compromise plan under the new emperor Maximilian II to merge both creeds with Utraquism. The new *Confessio Bohemica* was rejected. Not so much the question of religious creed but the conservatism of the Utraquist nobles prevented this last chance of merger. By the institution of *Defensores*—granted obligingly by the sympathetic emperor Maximilian II—the nobles in the Bohemian estates were now to control the religious establishment.[11] A new rapprochement between the Utraquists in the upper strata of the national society and the Catholic Church seemed to be in the offing. But the Bohemian Brethren, the remnants of the social revolutionary movement of old, were increasingly suppressed.

Matters came to a head under the new feeble Emperor Rudolf II. The purely religious question moved increasingly into the background, that of Utraquist estates rights versus the imperial administration, rose to the fore. The new war against the Turks and feuds within the dynasty (above all between Rudolf and his brother Matthias) weakened the imperial cause and strengthened the estates party. It benefited also from the increasingly apparent national rift between Lutheranism and so-called Old-Utraquism, which leaned toward a reconciliation with the Church. Yet the more important Neo-Utraquism fully retained its relationship to Lutheran doctrines. Only against this background is it possible to understand Emperor Rudolf II's Letter of Majesty of July, 1609, in which he recognized the *Confessio Bohemica.* It pertained mainly to Utraquists, but also to Lutherans and former Bohemian Brethren. The estates obtained Church and school control on the highest educational level. The right to build churches and schools was, indeed, granted to Protestants on the some footing as to Catholics. The Defensores were now to become a workable institution. The victory of the estates party over the crown was far-reaching, though not complete.

In one way the Letter of Majesty was the product of imperial weakness

[10] Canonized in 1925.

[11] The *Defensores* were to be public secular officials entrusted with the representation and defense of Protestant-Utraquist Church autonomy. The institution was, however, not fully put into practice by the emperor and repudiated after his death by his successor. See also Robert W. Seton-Watson, *History of the Czechs and Slovaks* (Hamden, 1965), pp. 96–110.

and aristocratic overbearing. Yet inasmuch as it granted religious freedom to townspeople and peasants (the latter not just as retainers of the lords and knights but in their own right), it was also a document of liberty of conscience, though one of short duration. It was actually not the Letter itself, but the agreement of the same day between the Catholic and Protestant estates concerning the right to build churches and schools which led to the break with the government. It culminated in the fateful defenestration of Prague in 1618. The fact that in this case Protestant rights were violated by Ferdinand of Styria (soon to be Emperor Ferdinand II), and the violent response of the Protestant estates are less significant than the showdown between the retreating Reformation, the rising demands for national autonomy of an aristocratic republican establishment, and the victoriously advancing Counter Reformation. The effect on the political organization of the lands of the Bohemian crown after the battle of the White Mountain will be discussed in Section D of this chapter, in the context of princely absolutism and estates rights.

Culturally the policy of forced reconversion of heretics or expulsion had far-reaching effects. Jesuits, jointly with other orders, were now in complete control of higher education and exclusively of the great University of Prague. Yet neither the forced emigration of possibly as many as 40,000 families, including many of the high nobility and substantial strata of the well-educated burghers in the towns, nor the widespread burning of books and manuscripts had as decisive an impact on the future as alleged by the new emperor's courtiers and ecclesiastic advisers.[12] Why this was so can best be seen in a brief comparative analysis of the struggle between Reformation and Counter Reformation in the three main units of Habsburg rule. A discussion of the first of them, the lands of the Hungarian crown follows.

c) THE LANDS OF THE HUNGARIAN CROWN

The problem of the Reformation in the Hungarian lands is closely tied to the Turkish occupation. By and large the Ottoman power was indifferent to the religious conflict in itself but its interests were affected by the political angle of the problem. The Catholic position was identified with the hereditary enemy, the Habsburgs, the Protestant position largely with that of the Transylvanian satellite principality and, beginning with the last quarter of the seventeenth century, with underhand support by the French ally in the west. The High Portal considered the enemies of its enemies to be friends.

The Reformation struck Hungary chiefly as consequence of Luther's

[12] Hermann Münch, *Böhmische Tragödie* (Braunschweig, 1949), pp. 77–87, 123.

movement in Germany. Considering the slow speed of communication this meant that its effect almost coincided with the Habsburg accession in Hungary in 1526. The spread of Lutheranism created resentment against German influence, even though the Habsburgs were as firmly opposed to the Reformation in Hungary as anywhere else. Yet Ferdinand I and Maximilian II tried at least to diminish opposition in the relatively small part of Hungary under their control by similar concessions to those offered in the hereditary lands and in Bohemia. Furthermore, the cruel *cuius regio eius religio* principle was applied in Hungary only by analogy in a limited number of towns.

On the other hand the peace of Vienna of June, 1606, concluded between the representatives of Emperor Rudolf II's brother Matthias and Prince Stephan Bocskay forced the imperial side to recognition of far-reaching religious freedom in Hungary for high and low nobility and free towns and markets; the religious affiliation of the unfree peasants was still tied to that of the lords. Transylvania, for most of the sixteenth and seventeenth century under Turkish suzerainty, had become largely Protestant by the sixteenth century and remained in this respect under Ottoman overlordship substantially undisturbed. Altogether the Reformation east of the Tisza river had great success with a minimum of accompanying violence.

In this respect the Transylvanian situation was particularly instructive in view of the existence there of three recognized political nations (Magyars, Szekels,[13] and since the middle of the twelfth century Germans, called Saxons as *pars pro toto*) and four creeds (Catholicism, Lutheranism, Calvinism, and after the 1560's Unitarianism). The large Roumanian part of the unfree peasant population did not share in the political and religious rights and liberties accrued in the course of time to the "three-nation state" or, more correctly, the "three-privileged-nations state." The three nations, aligned by defensive alliances against the Turks in the fifteenth century, continued to live peacefully together as long as outside political interests and eventually the built-in ethnic and social inequalities of the domestic situation did not interfere.

Hungary before the reconquest of Buda in 1686 was not affected to the same degree as Bohemia by a victory of the Counter Reformation by direct military confrontation. The Counter Reformation in Hungary in its early stages was influenced by the more persuasive cultural endeavors of

[13] The Szekels were a Magyar-speaking tribe and later completely identified with the Magyars. Whether there existed once a basic ethnic difference between Magyars and Szekels has never been unequivocally established.

Péter Pázmány (1570–1637), eminent primas of Hungary, teacher, writer, and founder of the University at Nagyszombat (Tyrnau).[14] This Jesuit father, a convert from Calvinism in his youth, was in a way the counterpart of Peter Canisius, the Jesuit missionary in the hereditary and Bohemian lands, but had a wider and stronger cultural appeal. Partly this may have been due to his greater moderation. Up to the middle of the seventeenth century, religious conditions in Hungary were on a more even keel than in other Habsburg realms. The complete victory of the Catholic cause in the hereditary and Bohemian lands in general and the ideological fallout of the Magyar nobles' revolt under the leadership of Count Francis Wesselênyi and counts Miklos and Peter Zrinyi between 1666 and 1669 helped to change all this. Counterreformatory activities under the particularly intolerant bishop of Neutra and later cardinal primas of Hungary, Count Leopold Kollonitsch (1631–1707), were instrumental here. Forced conversions, wholesale confiscation of property of heretics, and the cruel sentences given to Protestant ministers in the northern mining towns complement the portrait of the man, who because of his brave conduct during the siege of Vienna by the Turks in 1683, was hailed as great humanitarian in Austria.

Yet even if Kollonitsch had not been a leader in religious intolerance in the 1670's, the reconquest of Hungary in the 1680's culminating in the capture of Buda in 1686 would have altered the picture. Count Caprara's ruthless military administration combined features of a harsh military occupation, persecution of Protestants, and strongly partisan actions in favor of German officers and nobles now to be endowed with the estates of heretics. Protestantism survived, but mainly and publicly in the eighteenth century in the lands east of the Tisza, in particular in Transylvania, whose religious liberties had to be sanctioned after the reconquest by Leopold I in 1691. The recognition was part of the price to be paid in installments for the liberation of the bulk of Hungary by the peace of Karlócza (Karlowitz) in 1699. Another part were the privileges of 1690–1691 granted to the Greek Orthodox Serbs in reconquered Hungary. These conversions represented early examples of cultural autonomy in the religious educational field. Religious tolerance shown to Carpatho-Ukrainians (Ruthenians), on the other hand, had to be paid for by recognition of Uniate churches with separate ritual but under the suprème jurisdiction of the Roman Catholic primate in Esztergom (Gran). Still complete Gleichschaltung under the Catholic Church, comparable with the one now prevailing in the Bohemian and hereditary lands, did not

[14] Transferred to Budapest as Péter Pázmány University in 1777.

exist in Hungary. There the ancient constitutional tradition remained still very much alive.[15]

Differences in the impact of the Counter Reformation on all three political units, the hereditary lands, and those of the Bohemian and Hungarian crowns, were substantial. Similar was, however, the fact, that there were highly detrimental effects in all three cases, though they were quite divergent in nature. In the hereditary lands harsh measures were taken, particularly in Upper Austria and Inner Austria, where forced emigrations of many thousands took place. Yet neither was the nobility decimated nor the social structure of town life radically changed. After all the Counter Reformation in the hereditary lands was victorious by means of mission, supported by police action but not by large scale violence. The autonomous forces of nobles and towns were in substance pressured to conform; they were not actually crushed. Furthermore, neither estates autonomy nor urban civilization, which was chiefly affected by the Counter Reformation had been developed to the same levels as in Bohemia. The chief and far reaching consequences of reformatory pressure consisted not so much in the memories of the injuries done but in those to be avoided by a cultivation of conformism and expediency. This factor had a long lasting, highly detrimental effect on Austrian cultural and particularly intellectual life. The attitude of what does not hurt me is not my business, so prevalent and obvious in the period between the Congress of Vienna and the revolution of 1848—to take only one outstanding example—was indirectly still a consequence of the unwholesome counterreformatory experience. Judged by various incidents in the hereditary lands in the sixteenth and early seventeenth centuries it is true, that a victory of the Protestant Reformation may not have heralded a more tolerant age. Yet since this victory did not occur, this argument has to be ruled out.

Apart from immediate sufferings, the terrible consequences of imperial counterreformatory revenge and action after the battle of the White Mountain resulted in a delay of at least two centuries in regard to economic, political and cultural developments. Yet delay means neither destruction nor even lesser accomplishments on the part of the counterreformatory Habsburgs if one takes a long-range view. The opposite may be true. The era of suppression which affected Bohemia, Moravia, and in

[15] Denis Sinor, *History of Hungary* (London, 1959), pp. 184–209; Eugen Csuday, *Die Geschichte Ungarns,* 2 vols. (Vienna, 1900), II, 61–71, 187–206; Mihaly Bucsay, *Geschichte des Protestantismus in Ungarn* (Stuttgart, 1959), pp. 20–122.

part Silesia, strengthened the consciousness of national identity. It helped to heal the rift, created and deepened in two centuries of social-religious strife. The glorious achievements of the Slavic Renaissance in Bohemia at the beginnings of the nineteenth century were the payoff of the suppression in the seventeenth.

True, suppression did not help to reconcile the national struggle in Bohemia, which permeated increasingly the nineteenth century and the subsequent history of Czech-German relationship. This struggle became apparent during the Hussite wars and, though modified under the influence of early Lutheranism, became apparent again under the Protestant estates reign after 1609. The impact of German officials and particularly of foreign nobles as heirs to the confiscated estates after 1620 aggravated matters. Yet, again taking a long range view, these issues could hardly have been reconciled even under different circumstances. The Counter Reformation may have had an exacerbating influence on national strife in the lands of the Bohemian crown but hardly a decisive one.

In the long run, the lands of the Hungarian crown were least affected by the impact of the Counter Reformation, introduced by the military policies of the Habsburg armies in seventeenth-century Hungary. The rise of Calvinism in eastern Hungary and in particular in Transylvania as a symbol of inveterate Magyarism, equally free from bonds to the Roman Church and the previously noted Germanizing influence of Lutheranism, was witness to this. Protestantism in Hungary did not have a tradition of revolutionary social and antinational programs behind it. The social issues of peasants versus lords were not primarily focused on the religious question. Neither was this true for the living though socially unrepresentative constitutional tradition of the country. Less than in Bohemia and in the hereditary lands was the estates program interrelated to Protestantism. Here again, largely because of the Turkish wars, overriding issues of a different nature prevented a deep split along religious lines. The national issues in Hungary, grave as they were and graver as they became, are less deeply connected with the religious issue than in other component parts of the Habsburg empire.

C. Socioeconomic trends

The Habsburg lands in sixteenth-century Europe represented the paradigm of a rural feudal economy, somewhat modified by mining of precious metals in the western parts of Inner Austria, northwestern and central Bohemia, and northeastern Hungary. The same territorial qualifications hold roughly true for industrial development. The evolution of crafts and trades in early modern Europe was interrelated to an advanced urban culture. In the Habsburg realms this evolution pertained more to Bohemia and Silesia than to the hereditary lands and Hungary. These generalizations, however, apply to conditions in the lands of the Bohemian and Hungarian crowns only as long as they did not become theatres of drawn-out wars—the Thirty Year's War here, the Turkish wars there. The devastations brought about by them and the delay in economic development caused by them, explain, in part, why the impact of the seventeenth-century mercantilist policies was more strongly felt in the hereditary lands. Their consequences could become fully conspicuous only in territories which were spared the direct ravages of the conflagrations. Yet it would be rash to deduce that the new doctrines and their application changed the economic picture radically even there.

The following discussion will therefore have to concentrate on the lands not under foreign occupation of long duration. Only there was it possible gradually to move away from a predominantly feudal economy, primitive in its technological aspects and unjust in its economic distribution. This development pertains above all to the operation of a governmental financial administration, which could collect taxes and spend them (however unwisely and unjustly) but not entirely in the service of a feudal political establishment.

a) FINANCIAL ADMINISTRATION

The general structure of the financial administration in the Habsburg lands was traced briefly in Chapter II in connection with Ferdinand I's reforms. The chief income of the crown in the hereditary lands derived from the regalia such as mint, mining rights, tolls, and custom duties. In addition, there were the returns from the public domains and town taxes, all administered by the Court Chambers. Furthermore, the sovereign summoned the estates of the various lands to approve extraordinary taxes, particularly in wartime, the so-called contributions (*Contributionen*). A land tax, based on the income from estates (*Herrengülten*) was collected from the domains of the lords. As early as under Maximilian I's reign however, the incidence of this tax was generally shifted from the lords to the peasants. This means that some of the most oppressive burdens of the peasants were imposed still indirectly, but in the course of the sixteenth century directly levied obligations became the rule.

Excise taxes on drinks, salt, beef, leather, chalk, bricks, luxury articles such as laces or tobacco—the latter after the seventeenth century a state monopoly [16]—were imposed on everybody. Again, the lords were able to unload a major part of this obligation on the peasants. Towns and markets were not given this opportunity.

Taxes collected in the lands of the Bohemian crown were considerably higher than in the hereditary lands. This was, before the Thirty Years' War, primarily due to the greater prosperity of the towns in Bohemia and Silesia. Bohemia derived also considerable prosperity from the mining of precious ores, particularly silver. After 1620 the severely restricted political power of the estates in these lands could not redress the imbalance of taxation to the disadvantage of Bohemia and Moravia.[17] The government in Vienna never admitted the rather obvious punitive intent. Yet the new foreign noble soldiers of fortune who after the battle of the White Mountain had dispossessed the national nobility, could afford stiff taxation, because exploitation of the peasants had become now particularly ruthless and hence profitable under the emperor's partisans. The lot of the unfree peasants from the Hussite wars to 1620 had hardly been much better than in the hereditary lands, but it now became definitely worse.

It is difficult to compare the situation in the Hungarian lands, even those free from Turkish occupation, with those in the socially more closely associated hereditary and Bohemian lands. In Hungary the right of the parliament (royal diet) to pass on taxation was more firmly rooted in the coronation diploma and the estates rights, as anchored in the Hungarian code of public law, the *opus triparitum juris consuetudinarii in cycli regni Hungariae* of Istvan Verböcziy of 1514. In Hungary the Court Chamber[18] was in theory subordinated to Vienna. Yet Hungarian taxes, apart from the military administration after 1686, and even then only for a short time, were not used for imperial objectives beyond the borders of the country. Even within the country, royal attempts in the seventeenth and early eighteenth centuries to bypass the Reichstag by a selected committee of high dignitaries were curbed by a law of 1715. All things considered, contributions granted by the Hungarian diets to the

[16] In Austrian terms—still in force today—only the state is entitled to raise tobacco plants, manufacture tobacco, and to sell such manufactured products processed in governmental plants.

[17] For a comparison of tax structure and yield in the hereditary lands and those of the Bohemian crown in the sixteenth and seventeenth centuries see particularly Huber and Dopsch, *Österreichische Reichsgeschichte,* pp. 211–213. See also as background reading Ferdinand Tremel, *Der Frühkapitalismus in Innerösterreich* (Graz, 1954), pp. 96–147.

[18] Henry Marczali, *Ungarische Verfassungsgeschichte* (Tübingen, 1910), pp. 65–67. After the fall of Buda to the Turks in 1541 the Court Chamber was transferred to Pozsony (Pressburg).

royal treasury, unlike conditions in the hereditary and Bohemian lands, did not even in part accrue to common objectives of the over-all Habsburg power. Tax exemptions of the nobles were actually abolished under King Matthias Corvinus, although the unloading of taxes levied on the nobles upon their unfree peasants existed there as in the other Habsburg lands. Moreover, because of the changing fortunes of the Turkish wars, peasants were frequently subjected to Turkish and Habsburg tax collections in rapid succession.

Important for the financial structure of all Habsburg lands was the mining of ores, primarily silver and copper. The mines of the Erzgebirge in northwestern Bohemia, in Central and southern Bohemia, in the High and Low Tatra of Hungary in present-day Slovakia, and at an earlier time in Tyrol played an important role. Gold-mining, as for instance in Rauris (Salzburg), was never of major significance. After the middle of the sixteenth century the returns from the silver mines began to decline and the financial crisis brought about by the ravages of the Thirty Years' War led to a general debasing of coins.

Yet the easy-money situation, which enabled the great southern-German banking houses of the Fuggers and Welsers to finance the administration and counterreformatory wars of Charles V, had come to an end by the second half of the sixteenth century, long before the outbreak of the Thirty Years' War. Here the colonial policy of the Spanish world empire, which led to its financial bankruptcy, weakened and partly destroyed also the financial market for the German Habsburgs in favor of the rising French economic power.

b) AGRICULTURE

The chief burdens of the spreading economic crisis were carried by the peasants, even though they still lived largely outside of a money economy. Throughout the sixteenth century the lords in the hereditary and Bohemian lands strained to enlarge their personal holdings by buying peasant lands or expelling the tenant-owners as refractory. Furthermore, uncultivated lands increasingly accrued to the lords by law. The expulsions or forced emigrations in the wake of the Counter Reformation in Inner Austria and Salzburg in the last decades before the Thirty Years' War had likewise an at least indirect effect in the same direction. The number of peasants obliged to robot in the personal services of the lords decreased thereby, but the service obligations levied now on smaller numbers became even harsher. Somewhat better in this respect were conditions in the western hereditary lands, in Tyrol and Vorarlberg, where most peasants were personally free or enjoyed unrestricted freedom of movement. Yet even here the peasants revolted under Michael Gaismair's leadership at the end of the first quarter of the sixteenth century. As in Salzburg, Styria, and Carniola, they were eventually put down by military force.

In the Bohemian lands living conditions of the peasants under the rule of the noble estates had deteriorated in the last decades preceding the great war. The redistribution of the land of the Bohemian nobility among foreign—German, Italian or even Spanish—nobles, after 1620, changed not so much institutions as expectations. Chances for reform in regard to the excesses of personal services, restriction of freedom of movement, exorbitant charges for the use of the lord's pastures, and sweeping patrimonial jurisdiction had ceased in prostrated Bohemia for a long time to come.[19] The outlook in this respect in the hereditary lands was no better. Leopold I and his sons, Joseph I and Charles VI, had tried in a stumbling way to curb at least the most oppressive excesses of the robot system, because they further impaired the output of an agricultural system which was backward by western and central European standards. Long lists of the specific duties of the peasants were drawn up. They were not meant to lighten the heavy burden directly, but they should at least prevent exploitation beyond the letter of the law. However, the lords insisted successfully that saving clauses be inserted into these patents. They were to allow for unspecified additional duties referred to in the feudal contract, and pertained to so-called emergency situations to be invoked at the pleasure of the lord. These clauses, of course, added mockery to injury.[20]

In the lands of the Hungarian crown, the situation could be considered better only in one respect: more reasonable expectations for change. The peasant risings in the 1510's, 1520's, 1570's, and 1630's in German (Styrian), Slovene, and some Croatian areas had accomplished as little as the serious ones in Bohemia in 1680. They all were cruelly suppressed. In Hungary the peasant revolts were tied to the objective of national freedom. The risings of the Kurucoks under the leadership of

[19] Josef Macek, *Der Tiroler Bauernkrieg und Michael Gaismair* (Berlin, 1965), pp. 128–431; Ferdinand Tremel, *Wirtschafts- und Sozialgeschichte Österreichs* (Vienna, 1969), pp. 132–148; Karl Grünberg, *Die Bauernbefreiung in Böhmen, Mähren und Schlesien* (Leipzig, 1894), I, 1–16.

[20] Tremel, *Wirtschafts- und Sozialgeschichte Österreichs,* pp. 232–245; Franz M. Mayer, *Geschichte Österreichs mit besonderer Rücksicht auf das Kulturleben* (Vienna, 1909, 3rd ed.), pp. 292–303; see also as background reading Otto Brunner, *Land und Herrschaft: Grundfragen der territorialen Verfassungsgeschichte Österreichs im Mittelalter* (Vienna, 1959, 4th revised ed.), pp. 240–356.

Francis Rákóczy II culminating in the revolutionary Hungarian-Transylvanian diet of Ónod of 1707 led to defeat in the peace of Szatmár of 1711, spelling disaster for the cause of unfree peasants in reconquered Hungary and Transylvania. Yet the belief that the freedom of the Hungarian nation was anchored in that of the Hungarian peasantry was indelibly tied to these risings. A free Hungary, in whatever blurred form, meant a free peasantry.[21] The same idea had not taken hold to the same degree in the Bohemian and hereditary lands.

c) CRAFTS AND INDUSTRY

Until mercantilism began to make its influence felt in the last quarter of the seventeenth century crafts were controlled by the guild system. Particularly in Inner Austria counterreformatory screenings tightened these procedures. The government did not begin until the end of the seventeenth century to exercise greater influence on guild regulations. Yet in the era under discussion it did not succeed to do more than to loosen up slightly the *numerus clausus* policy of the craft guilds. Under Charles VI the establishment of new guilds was brought under governmental control.

The one major and permanently active industrial establishment in the hereditary lands, hardware manufacturing in Styria and Carinthia, based primarily on the rich Styrian iron-ore mines, received too little attention at the time of the silver boom. Wool weaving was practiced purely domestically on a small scale. The manufactured merchandise of highly skilled craftsmen such as those of silversmiths, jewelers, producers of leather-goods and of various textile fabrics developed only slowly, partly because the wars of the sixteenth century had blocked the eastern markets and the wars of the early seventeenth the western as well. Moreover, before the impact of mercantilism, court and aristocracy obtained luxury articles mostly from abroad, first from Italy and Germany, later also from France.

Bohemian and Silesian textile industries developed in the sixteenth and at the beginning of the seventeenth centuries on a larger scale than in the hereditary lands. The same was true for the glass industry. Its products included, what might be called in modern times, costume jewelry, that is, manufacturing of semiprecious stones in Bohemia. Lace industry there and linen industry in Silesia were significant. This remarkable industrial development was not greatly impaired during the first half of

[21] See Zsigmond P. Pach, *Die ungarische Agrarentwicklung im 16.–17. Jahrhundert* (Budapest, 1964), pp. 39–93.

the Thirty Years' War, as long as Wallenstein was in command. He supplied his army primarily from Bohemian resources and drew on the Bohemian luxury industry for his and his retainers' ambitious designs. After his fall and under the impact of devastations of the Bohemian and Silesian countryside industries declined.

In Hungary the threefold impact of Turkish misadministration in central Hungary, the direct war damages, and the reduction of returns from the north Hungarian ore mines blocked potentialities for substantial industrial developments. Domestic industry on a small scale and the mining of precious ores continued during this period relatively undisturbed in Transylvania.[22]

d) MERCANTILISM

Economic standstill, if not retrogression, changed to some extent under the influence of mercantilism, which made its influence felt in the Habsburg lands relatively late. It would be far too much to state, that mercantile influence amounted to a change as comprehensive as that of Prussian economy under the soldier king Frederick William I—to take a model of comparison in Central Europe.

The relatively modest achievements of this Austrian type of mercantilism are generally associated with the activities of three meritorious reformers from southern and western Germany, Johann Joachim Becher, Wilhelm von Schroeder, and his brother-in-law Philip Wilhelm von Hörnigk.[23] Becher, son of a Protestant minister, may be credited with the establishment of a commercial college in Vienna, a first among commercial administrative agencies in Central Europe. In the 1660's and 1670's, he also introduced silk industry in Lower Austria and the institution of a Kunst- und Werkhaus in Vienna for the training in crafts by foreign masters outside the fetters of guild restrictions. A planned Oriental company was meant to establish some trade relations with the Levant, an objective hampered by the critical nature of relations to the High Portal. The company folded up after a few years. Plans to establish a wool factory in Linz in Upper Austria proved to be even more disappointing.[24]

[22] Mayer, *Geschichte Österreichs,* II, 312–355; Tremel, *Wirtschafts- und Sozialgeschichte,* pp. 112–280.

[23] Louise Sommer, *Die österreichischen Kameralisten in dogmengeschichtlicher Darstellung* (Vienna, 1920), I, 43–56, 87–95.

[24] See Herbert Hassinger, *Johann Joachim Becher* (Vienna, 1951), pp. 138–204. Becher's project concerning the Oriental Trade Company, however, was revised under Charles VI.

Wilhelm von Schroeder may be considered as Becher's hardly more fortunate successor. Because of governmental stumbling blocks, he was unable to extend Becher's modest reforms to northeastern Hungary. The Kunst- und Werkhaus did not succeed under his management any better than under Becher's; it folded up in the early 1680's. Governmental reluctance to invite foreign teachers of crafts of Protestant affiliation played a part here. It is true, that the administration during the later part of Leopold I's reign and the reigns of his sons frequently tacitly tolerated limited activities of German Protestant businessmen in Vienna. But immigration of large numbers of skilled foreign Protestant workers and teachers in crafts was not approved. Nevertheless, at least the theoretical contributions of Schroeder to the new political sciences of cameralism with particular emphasis on public finance had some long-range effect.

Literary achievements are also associated with the third significant Austrian mercantilist, Philip Wilhelm von Hörnigk, whose economic treatise *Österreich über alles, wenn es nur will* of 1684 may be considered as a first in patriotic Austro-German economic literature. The stirring title of this book has to this very day been used to foment a kind of Austrian nationalism, but never met with much success. This catechism of a comprehensive Austrian mercantilism and reformism in agriculture, mining, and industry did not recognize existing limitations. Apart from religious intolerance, strict protectionism hampered the rudimentary pilot projects. Austrian industry could have benefited indirectly from the import of foreign goods for a time, which might have stimulated consumer demand and would have helped to establish the need for large-scale industrial enterprises. But the second step, protectionism, was taken before the first, the raising of standards and with them genuine wants.

In fact, late-seventeenth and early-eighteenth century western Europe under the influence of incipient physiocratic doctrines began to modify mercantilism by populationist doctrines. According to them a skilled domestic labor force was the chief asset of the economic strength of a country. In this respect the Habsburg lands lagged far behind western Europe, particularly because of the ill effects of religious intolerance and foreign wars. They had hurt the most promising industries, glass and textiles in Bohemia, and because of restrictions on exports also the ore industry in the hereditary lands.

Added to this must be the government's failure to establish a stable banking system, which could be kept under some control of the public domain. The government in the late sixteenth century had failed in its cooperation with the great banking houses of the Fuggers and Welsers.

It is a paradox of Austrian public life, that despite the frantic persecution of the Jews under Leopold's reign as scapegoats for war and pestilence (expulsions from Vienna of 1669–1670), Jews were called to finance the imperial wars of the early eighteenth century, and some accepted. Their activities ended in bankruptcy as did the stumbling efforts of Charles VI to establish government-controlled banks. Here not even the popular scapegoat device worked. It became clear that the Austrian government, despite efforts of the mercantilist reformers, had not yet grasped the rudimentary skill of operating within a predetermined budget.[25]

As noted before, the failure of the reign of Charles VI, the chief mercantilist among the Habsburg rulers, was tied to the controversial consequences in the west and southwest of the War of the Spanish Succession. Neither the northern Belgian nor the southern Italian position could be fully used and the latter not even be held as base for future colonial and commercial naval expansion. Yet at least port facilities in Trieste and communications between the Adriatic ports and the Alpine lands were improved and foreign trade encouraged to a limited degree. This was at least modest success. The economic achievements of Maria Theresa's reign were based on the recognition of her father's failures.

D. Estates and princely absolutism

In the sixteenth century the Habsburg lands were to a wide extent under estates control, and the noble estates in turn were then largely dominated by Protestantism. The defeat of Protestant Reformation by the Counter Reformation meant consequently also the defeat of the Protestant estates and estates power. The victor, who moved into the vacuum, partly by default and partly by action, was princely absolutism in the hereditary and Bohemian lands. Hungary and her institutions, anchored in a different tradition and for more than a century subjected to warfare and foreign domination, charted a somewhat dissimilar course.

a) estates participation in government

Estates government did not stand for democratic government, but it did stand for some kind of representative government based on narrow group interests. Taking an over-all profile on conditions in the hereditary lands as a sample and disregarding variations in individual political domains, the situation presented itself about as follows: The four basic estates were first the prelates (ecclesiastic or spiritual lords), secondly

[25] Robert A. Kann, *A Study in Austrian Intellectual History* (2nd ed. New York, 1973), pp. 26–34.

secular lords, thirdly knights (lower nobility), and lastly princely towns and markets. In Tyrol, communities of free peasants represented the fourth estate, whereas lords and lower nobility were joined in the same curia. In other lands, commoners were only represented in the estate of towns and markets. This curia usually enjoyed less influence than the ecclesiastic and noble estates, from whose midst the officers of the diets were selected. At the time of a new sovereign's accession, all estates, in return for their pledge of loyalty, received confirmation and at times extensions of their rights and privileges. These consisted in principle in the approval of taxation, the consent to the quota of soldiers to be recruited in individual lands, and beyond that a flexible control of the princely budget. Furthermore the estates had the right to petition the prince (to present grievances) and to ask for changes, usually brought about by tedious negotiations. The estates reached the summit of their power during the reign of Ferdinand I, maintained it, intermittent conflicts notwithstanding, throughout the reigns of the following rulers, but lost most of their power under the principal counterreformatory emperor Ferdinand II. Even before he reached the summit of his power, throughout this whole century from 1526 to 1620 (the battle of the White Mountain) estates power was limited in several respects. The prince could collect regalia and levy excise taxes frequently without estates consent. Of course, large-scale warfare, such as that against the Turks, could not be fought as long as the estates controlled—and generally impeded—the raising of substantial armed forces. This power of control led to frequent bypassing of estates consent.[26]

Throughout the sixteenth century, the power of the estates in the Bohemian lands was greater than in the hereditary lands, inasmuch as the first semi-hereditary Habsburg ruler there, Ferdinand I, owed his election to the Bohemian estates. His successors up to the promulgation of the oppressive constitution of 1627 likewise had to go through an electoral procedure before the coronation in St. Vitus Cathedral on Hradčany hill in Prague. Technically this meant acceptance as king by the estates rather than formal election. Privileges and rights to be recognized by the kings before the battle of the White Mountain included the restriction of appointment of royal dignitaries to natives, judgment of these officials by

[26] Brunner, *Land und Herrschaft,* pp. 394–440; Henry E. Strakosch, *State Absolutism and the Rule of Law* (Sydney, 1967), pp. 19–21; Huber and Dopsch, *Österreichische Reichsgeschichte,* pp. 212–217; see also Francis L. Carsten, *Princes and Parliaments in Germany from the Fifteenth to the Eighteenth Century* (Oxford, 1963), pp. 422–444; Eugen Heischmann, *Die Anfänge des stehenden Heeres in Österreich* (Vienna, 1925), pp. 135–181.

their peers, and appointment of a member of the national nobility as regent in the king's absence. These rights lapsed according to the Vernewerte Landesordnung imposed by the conqueror Ferdinand II in 1627, until such time as the royal Habsburg line—male as well as female—would become extinct, an occurrence, which, incidentally, has not taken place to this day.

According to the different social stratification, the town representatives in the Bohemian estates carried more weight than in the hereditary lands. Their activities, however, as much of the estates' power altogether, became practically meaningless after 1627. It was not unlimited previously either, to be sure. The right to convoke the diet rested traditionally with the sovereign, as in the hereditary lands, and the way to reject royal financial demands meant in practice ignoring them for a time rather than formally rejecting them. Yet when skillfully handled the whole taxation system before 1627 was still under stricter dietal control in Bohemia than in the hereditary lands. Afterward these rights were taken away from the Bohemian and Moravian diets. Yet previously the diets in Moravia as well as Silesia—the latter only indirectly affected by the counterreformatory reversal of previous privileges—enjoyed about the same status as the Bohemian diet in regard to financial matters.

After the victory of the Counter Reformation, general diets of all Bohemian lands met only rarely, and not often before. The chief estates power rested in the individual diets of Bohemia, Moravia, and Silesia (the last-mentioned composed of several provincial assemblies). The margravates of Upper and Lower Lusatia, previously part of the Bohemian realms, were in the course of the Thirty Years War ceded to Saxony. The general diets of all Bohemian lands had in practice hardly ever more significance than the three so-called general diets of all Habsburg lands, 1530 in Linz (without participation of the Bohemian estates), 1541 in Prague (neither the southwestern German Vorlande nor the lands of the Hungarian crown were represented then), and 1614 again in Linz (with little Hungarian and no Bohemian participation).[27]

As for Hungary, princely absolutism did not develop fully before the end of the seventeenth century, partly because of the constitutional tradition of the country, dating back to the Bulla Aurea of 1222 and partly because of the Turkish wars. Even afterward, except for the era 1849–1860, absolutism was never as fully in command as subsequently in the

[27] Huber and Dopsch, *Österreichische Reichsgeschichte,* pp. 217–222; Ernst C. Hellbling, *Österreichische Verfassungs- und Verwaltungsgeschichte* (Vienna, 1956), pp. 246–249, 262–264.

hereditary and Bohemian lands. Yet the position of the diet versus the king even before the Counter Reformation was stronger than in the other Habsburg realms. Moreover, the center of gravity of estates participation in the legislative process rested here in the lower curia. The Hungarian diet was composed of only two such curias, those of the magnates and the so-called estates. The former, under the chairmanship of the palatine, a kind of viceroy, consisted of the prelates under the leadership of the primate, the archbishop of Esztergom, the aristocracy, the banus of Croatia, the other highest dignitaries of the kingdom, and the top officials of the *comitats* (counties with considerable local autonomy). Members of the estates curia were the lower nobility, the representatives of the chartered royal towns, and some judicial and ecclesiastic officials, the latter mainly abbots and members of diocesan chapters. The diet, as in the other Habsburg lands, could be convoked only by the king—only in exceptional cases by the palatine as his representative. Yet here it was a tradition that this parliamentary body should meet in general every two years. At the time of constitutional decline in the eighteenth and early nineteenth centuries this custom fell into desuetude, yet even then the diet remained a significant political factor. It could discuss royal propositions as well as estates grievances. Both curias had to agree on motions, in particular the approval of extraordinary taxation, but the principal legislation had to originate in the Lower House, a feature unparalleled in the diets of other lands under Habsburg rule.

Matters changed in 1687 after the reconquest of Buda. As noted before, the diet of Pozsony of 1687–1688 had to consent to the relinquishment of its right of royal election and had to acquiesce in the hereditary succession of the dynasty. Furthermore, the nobles had to sacrifice their ancient right of resistance to what they considered unlawful royal legislation. This, however, was a more symbolic than actual decline of status. The powers of the diet remained still substantial. The king was no longer elected by this body, but he had to uphold the major part of the ancient liberties in a coronation oath. Election of the palatine, (a highly important office in the absence of the king), approval of extraordinary taxation, and passage of the quota of recruits, remained prerogatives of the diet. In fact, all royal bills, citizenship questions, and the granting of the charters of royal towns still required the sanction of the diet. Royal attempts to circumvent it by resort to the convocation of smaller royal councils, were not lacking, particularly in the eighteenth century, but they never succeeded for any length of time. In the eighteenth century, the geographical position of Hungary in face of the Turkish danger was still too precarious to allow the Habsburgs to procede against the country, the way they had done a century earlier against Bohemia. The reign of Joseph II provided an object lesson. In the nineteenth century, fear of Russian intervention took the place of concern about Ottoman power. Above all, the bitter experience of the Hungarian war of independence of 1848–1849 still had to be learned.[28]

E. Administration

Although the estates in the Habsburg lands were legislative or legislative consultative bodies of sorts, early modern times did not recognize a strict division between administrative and judicial institutions of government. Ferdinand I, however, acknowledged such a division by approximation in the hereditary lands. Final decisions were rendered by officials of both types of agencies jointly. As pointed out in Chapter I, neither were imperial institutions, those of all Habsburg lands and those of the hereditary lands alone, strictly separated. Yet, beginnings to that effect were made during the reign of that great administrator and organizer among the Habsburg rulers, Ferdinand I. Highest officials in the individual lands were now the *Landeshauptleute,* who presided also in the curia of the secular lords in the diets. Thus they served as connecting links between princely and estates functions. The high officials included many nobles, but also some learned lawyers. In the princely towns and markets commoners played the decisive role. Town councils were elected by a narrow group of propertied burghers. Members of the inner council and the mayor were usually elected, subject to confirmation by the government. The town judges, however, were appointed by the prince. Altogether town administration was partly elective and partly appointive, but generally under princely supervision. A special constitution for Vienna granted by Ferdinand I provided for the appointment of the mayor by the sovereign from a slate of elected councillors. An appointed princely representative participated in the deliberations of the city council.[29]

Before the Vernwerte Landesordnung of 1627, the chief official in Bohemia (the *Oberst Burggraf*), held wider power than any appointee in the hereditary lands. The king had to consult the estates before appointment. The highest officials held lifetime tenure—they could not be dismissed by the sovereign. They had to take an oath of loyalty to king

[28] Marczali, *Ungarische Verfassungsgeschichte,* pp. 67–104; Marczali, *Ungarisches Verfassungsrecht,* pp. 78–84.

[29] Huber and Dopsch, *Österreichische Reichsgeschichte,* pp. 180–184; Hellbling, *Österreichische Verfassungs- und Verwaltungsgeschichte,* pp. 246–249.

and estates. The Bohemian administration was more clearly separated from the imperial one than the government in the hereditary lands. Moravia and Silesia likewise enjoyed autonomous administrations. In Moravia conditions changed with the defeat at the White Mountain as in Bohemia. The autonomous administration in Silesia, however, in which the governor was at the same time the head of the estates of the great nobles was only indirectly affected.

An effect of the victory of the counterreformatory upset in Bohemia—and similarly in Moravia—on the administrative level was the change in the position of the Oberst Burggraf, who from now on became solely responsible to the sovereign. The estates lost their right to share in appointive powers altogether and lifetime tenure of offices was abolished. Major governmental agencies were transferred from Prague to Vienna. Changes on the administrative level were thus even more oppressive than in the legislative sphere.[30]

In Hungary, Ferdinand I established general administration, financial administration, and a court chancery as separate agencies. He and his successors tried to avoid the installment of palatines, who in the king's absence might usurp too much power. Frequently a kind of palatine deputy or a prince of the Church served in the palatine's stead although with more restricted powers. Yet much of this governmental structure could not be put into practice during the Turkish wars. Only in 1722–1723 was a new type of administration by royal appointment set up in Pozsony, the seat of the diet. The gubernatorial council communicated with the king through the Court Chancery in Vienna. The lower administrative comitat organization remained basically unchanged. The same held true for the limited autonomy of the royal towns. In Croatia-Slavonia the banus was head of the government and, in addition to supreme judicial functions, also in charge of defense matters. His position remained subordinated, however, to the administration in Pozsony and the Hungarian Court Chancery in Vienna.[31]

Outside of the banus' jurisdiction, and in fact of that of the Hungarian government, were the military frontier districts, the Croatian district to the Adriatic, the Slavonian district between the left bank of the Sava and the confluence of Tisza and Danube, and farther east, the

[30] Huber and Dopsch, *Österreichische Reichsgeschichte,* pp. 217–222; Hellbling, *Österreichische Verfassungs- und Verwaltungsgeschichte,* pp. 233–237; Münch, *Böhmische Tragödie,* pp. 79–87.

[31] Huber and Dopsch, *Österreichische Reichsgeschichte,* pp. 222–224; Hellbling, *Österreichische Verfassungs- und Verwaltungsgeschichte,* pp. 237–239.

Banat of Temesvar. Transylvania, after the Turkish wars, had separate royal governors and a financial administration of its own; it was also represented by a separate Court Chancery in Vienna.[32]

F. Judicial system

In the hereditary lands, minor civil and criminal cases were under the patrimonial jurisdiction of the lords of the manor. Town courts had about the same kind of jurisdiction for the burghers unless they had the legal power to render judgment in major criminal cases as well (the so-called *Blutbann*). *Landgerichte* dealt with such cases in towns which did not have the Blutbann. They also adjudicated major criminal cases in the countryside leaving minor offenses to the jurisdiction of the noble estate owners. Major civil cases among unfree peasants on the estates of the lords could become hardly practical. The so-called *Landrecht*, composed of members of the noble estates, was the court which had jurisdiction over secular nobles and prelates; the affairs of ordinary priests were conducted by ecclesiastic courts. Appeals from courts of the first instance were acted upon by the administration after special permission for new hearings had been granted. Here the only semi-independent court system ended in a dead alley. Special commercial courts and even a (regular) commercial court and an independent court of appeal in commercial matters were established by Charles VI. These, however, were still the exceptions to the rule.[33]

In Bohemia there existed a so-called major Landrecht as court for the privileged noble estates, which sat in important cases under the chairmanship of the king, regularly under that of his chief representative, the Oberst Burggraf. A particularly reprehensible feature of the Bohemian judicial system was the power of several hundred lords to exercise not only patrimonial jurisdiction as in the hereditary lands in minor cases, but to command the Blutbann. The life of the peasants was in practice and by law at the mercy of the liege lord. This state of affairs lasted until 1765, in the reign of Maria Theresa.[34]

In Hungary, the Hungarian judicial system was organized best, although here, too, the two chief evils of justice in early modern times prevailed: the medieval relic of at least partial symbiosis of justice and

[32] Günther Erich Rothenberg, *The Austrian Military Border in Croatia: 1522–1747* (Urbana, 1960), pp. 27–123; Guldescu, *The Croatian-Slavonian Kingdom 1526–1792*, pp. 59–183.

[33] Brunner, *Land und Herrschaft*, pp. 363–387.

[34] Hellbling, *Österreichische Verfassungs- und Verwaltungsgeschichte*, pp. 234–235.

administration and the class character of the court system with its privileges for prelates, nobles, and occasionally free burghers. Just the same, the organization of the Hungarian system was superior to that in the hereditary lands and in Bohemia. Patrimonial courts of the magnates, town and market courts, and comitat courts resembled institutions in other Habsburg lands. Here, too, particularly on the higher level, judges were at the same time administrative officials. Here, too, nobles had their own privileged jurisdiction. Hungary had a better developed system of appeals. The supreme court (the royal curia) consisted of two sections. The one, the septemviral section, composed of the seven highest dignitaries of the country under the chairmanship of the palatine and in his absence the *judex curiae* (the supreme judge), was the highest instance in the country. The other, the royal tablet, composed of professional judges, magnates, and prelates, decided major cases in first instance, but was otherwise in general the court of appeal for all cases acted upon in lower courts. In Croatia, the banus presided in a court of similar composition. Transylvania had a separate court system.[35]

G. Defense system

A factor of highest importance in the evolution of the Habsburg power was, of course, the development of an adequate defense system. The overall administrative organization under the Court War Council (Hofkriegsrat) set up in mid-sixteenth century were traced in Chapter I. The Turkish wars had made it clear that an estates army based on contingents approved by individual lands in ever varying numbers and for limited length of service—usually measured by weeks or months—could not cope with the major tasks confronting Habsburg power. Ferdinand I, at the end of his reign, laid the keystone to a permanent army, as yet only a force of 9,000 men. The expansion of the military-frontier system led to further increases of these forces throughout the seventeenth century. Yet before sweeping changes could be made, the emperor had to go through the harrowing experience of a large-scale mercenary system as it worked for a time successfully under Wallenstein's command between 1625 and 1634.[36] The drawbacks, however, became apparent soon enough. The system put the emperor at the mercy of a brilliant condottiere type of general. Other commanders of mercenary forces had been less dangerous but also less successful. Not until the second half of the century was a stand-

[35] Marczali, *Ungarisches Verfassungsrecht*, pp. 120–122.

[36] Heischmann, *Die Anfänge des stehenden Heeres in Österreich*, pp. 181–224; Oskar Regele, *Der österreichische Hofkriegsrat* (Vienna, 1949), pp. 15–20.

ing army established by much trial and error. Montecuccoli and Eugene of Savoy deserve chief credit for a new system, which established definite professional standards for officers and noncommissioned officers, whereas previously regimental commanders had sold commissions to the highest bidder at their discretion, at least in regard to the lower ranks. To a limited extent a permanent supply system was established now. This did not prevent armies to live off the land, but curbed at least the outrages of individual soldiers and small units.

The estates "contribution" system of passing on quotas of recruits to be drafted was not abandoned in the hereditary lands before Maria Theresa's reign, but it lost in importance. In Bohemia, however, the constitution of 1627, as a consequence of the defeat, transferred the estates power in these matters to the sovereign. In Hungary the diet did not admit until 1715 that armed forces sponsored by the estates, the so-called "insurrection," could not cope with the Ottoman military threat. If the diet had not submitted long before to the operation of imperial armies —to the estates foreign ones—on Hungarian soil, the country could never have been freed from Turkish occupation. Yet the diet did not like to attach the force of law to an emergency situation. The age-old conflict of Hungarian statehood, that the country wanted to go it alone and had not sufficient strength to do it, made itself painfully felt. Furthermore, apart from the manpower and training problem, the fortification system within the Military Borders could not be financed by the Hungarian crown. Here, centralization in theory stole a march on centralization in practice. Otherwise Habsburg power could never had risen to the heights it reached in the eighteenth century.[37]

H. Church-state relations

Another important field where state power advanced faster in practice than in theory was that of relations to the Church. The victory of the Counter Reformation signified an outright ideological victory of the Church only in some areas, especially education. In the political sphere the new situation meant that the ascendancy of the Church over forces of the Reformation was largely state-sponsored and state-controlled. Ferdinand I in his efforts to check misconduct within the clergy had earlier established partly secular and partly ecclesiastic commissions for the visitation and inspection of monasteries and churches. He ordered further that monastic property should be sold only with governmental approval. This system continued under Maximilian II. Even under Rudolf II, who

[37] See note 32.

was more obliging to the papal power, the promulgation of papal bulls was forbidden without princely approval. The visitation commissions continued their work. Nor did the devout Ferdinand II yield any princely prerogatives and Ferdinand III even proscribed the visitation of monastic establishments by foreign generals of orders. Conflicts concerning ecclesiastic property should from now on be decided by secular courts. Leopold I introduced the important principle of reviewing the judgments of ecclesiastic courts by secular ones. He also prohibited the sale of secular estates to ecclesiastics. Charles VI then determined that appeals in ecclesiastic matters in which the secular power took a primary interest, should go from the consistories to the government and not to the Holy See.

These measures illustrate that the assertion of princely prerogatives of sovereignty and state power versus the autonomy of the Church existed long before the rise of Josephinism in the second half of the eighteenth century. In many ways this princely attitude was a part of the heritage of the medieval contest between papal and imperial power. Personal faith and, indeed, devoutness of individual Habsburg rulers had nothing to do with their determination to remain masters in what they considered to be their own house.[38]

It is difficult to draw a general conclusion at this point concerning the struggle between estates power and princely absolutism. No doubt the estates, in particular the powerful secular lords and knights, stood primarily for their own interests. They fought state power in their defense and not—save in a limited sense in the religious sphere—in the interest of wider social contexts, let alone society as a whole. In socioeconomic, in particular financial matters there was little difference between the interests of ecclesiastic princes and secular lords and knights, including the Protestants. The representatives of towns and markets were no more concerned with the common good than the other estates, and to the extent that they were, they had less power than the other estates to do much about it.

The reforms of the enlightened eighteenth century could never have come to pass, if the estates with their specific interests would have remained firmly in the saddle. History does not recognize a straight development from estates regimes to democracy. In between interposed are despotic and enlightened absolutism. There is no rigid line between an estates system and absolute government. Louis XIV, the Great Elector,

[38] Josef Wodka, *Kirche in Österreich* (Vienna, 1959), pp. 241–285; Ernst Tomek, *Kirchengeschichte Österreichs* (Innsbruck, 1959), III, 22–111.

the Soldier King, and Peter the Great, belonged to both; the Habsburgs, from the time when estates influence came to an end to the early reign of Maria Theresa, belonged rather to the first group as so-called absolute —though not ruthless—despots.

No streak of cruelty promoted the actions even of Ferdinand II, but there was still little concern for the public welfare evident, even in the feeble mercantilistic experiences under his grandson and great grandson Leopold I and Charles VI. On the other hand, the estates regime contributed little to a more prosperous and socially more balanced society. Princely absolutism did not replace an effective system; it merely filled a vacuum, but did not fill it well. It is difficult to see absolutism in Austria as a connecting link to the Enlightenment.

Perhaps the one genuine merit of the estates establishment in the Habsburg lands rested in the fact that it represented modest beginnings of a more pluralistic society. In this sense the Habsburg regime of the seventeenth and early eighteenth centuries may be credited for not wiping out this system entirely, although it had the power to do so in Bohemia and to some extent in the hereditary lands and Hungary after 1686. The preservation of the estates institution—lame-duck estates orders though they became outside of Hungary—did not represent even a small step toward democratic society but meant, in some way, the image of a pluralistic society.[39]

I. Cultural evolution

The discussion of two basic points has to precede the survey presented in this section on culture and those of a similar nature in following chapters. "Culture" is a practically all-inclusive term. It penetrates all activities of society. It is inherent as much in the conduct of foreign and domestic policies as in the arts and sciences. If one confines a survey of cultural trends primarily to them it is not because cultural developments are more striking there than in the realms of government, but because government is traditionally perceived within a closely definable sphere whereas other pursuits within a society which transcend the course of concerted actions in the public domain are left in a vacuum. They are then conveniently summarized under "cultural developments." This study follows established patterns in this respect, not because culture is what is left if one separates it from governmental actions or economic-social movements, but because literature, music, the fine arts, and scholarly

[39] See also Carsten, *Princes and Parliaments in Germany,* pp. 13–24, 60–68 and Fritz Hartung, *Deutsche Verfassungsgeschichte* (Stuttgart, 1950), pp. 84–94.

disciplines of all kinds represent, indeed, specific aspects of the over-all culture of a society. These are the pursuits of activities, trends which emerge largely as the products of individual motion and not of collective action, whether directed by orders from above or by consent of the governed. Here only the will and consent of the individual are the issue. Education, which in parts is an arm of the governmental structure, offers the means to develop these individual endeavours. While it might well be discussed in the context of the governmental structure—and will be referred to as such in regard to later stages of history, when public education became prevalent—its relationship to the creative contributions of the individual is considered here particularly important. Hence the brief survey of education in this section, even though its impact on the strengthening of individual endeavors had a rather unwitting stimulating effect for most of the era under discussion.

There is a second point to be considered concerning culture. It has been touched upon in the introduction to this study and is repeated here, namely that a single volume dealing with the history of a far-flung empire and its diverse peoples in four centuries offers no opportunity to list even by name the most important cultural contributions. If one were to try it, the reader would be presented by a directory of names with little meaning. On the other hand, the smaller the number of names presented, the more arbitrary and controversial would be the selection. To be caught in this bind seems almost inevitable.

The purpose of this study is different from presenting a wider or narrower selection of outstanding cultural contributions. Our principal purpose is briefly to discuss trends, and only in the second place the works of individuals. Names of outstanding men and their achievements will be adduced only to illustrate these trends. This means that in specific cases our selection will have to be focussed primarily on characteristic features and only in the second place on the greatness of achievement. The number of specific references will be limited further by the resolve to list none whose significance will not be discussed, however briefly. Thus a comprehensiveness of names will have to yield to an attempt of selectiveness in depth. Even here the limitations of space should be obvious.

a) LOWER AND ADVANCED EDUCATION

The Reformation furthered to some degree general elementary education. A substantial number of schools in the hereditary lands offered instruction in the three R's. In many places, among others in Vienna, these schools were sponsored by the Protestant estates, but in some crownlands elementary education in the vernacular language of instruction was partly sponsored by the sovereign. In the Bohemian lands the estates exercised greater influence on education than in the hereditary lands. In Hungary elementary schooling was under the control of either the Church (parish schools) or of town councils. Protestant schools were particularly concerned with more advanced education. Yet in none of the Habsburg lands can one speak of a broad sixteenth-century trend toward general education. The mighty impetus toward broadening and deepening of instruction was associated in one way with the upgrading of the vernacular language and in another with the desire for better training of the middle classes apart from the strictly professional requirements of Church, law, and academic teaching. This points to reforms at the intermediate level, and here the Reformation and, as consequence and response to it, the Counter Reformation were quite successful.

The distinction between intermediate and elementary education is relatively clear. Admission to the former was reserved for the propertied classes. The chief subject, generally also the language of instruction, was Latin as was the vernacular in the elementary schools. The Protestant estates, nobles and burghers alike, deserved credit for the establishment of estates schools in Lower Austria, and particularly in Upper Austria, but also in Styria, Carinthia, and Carniola. Limitations were obvious: instruction in history was meager, the sciences were still practically ignored, and the vernacular language not sufficiently cultivated; but at least grammar and Latin were emphasized. Thorough religious instruction was stressed. In Bohemia and Moravia such Latin schools were more numerous and existed even in small towns and markets, which means that they transmitted education to the sons of the middle class, irrespective of a specific professional training. In Hungary a similar type of schools existed in western and northwestern Hungary, particularly in the mining towns. Most of these schools developed in the course of the second half of Ferdinand I's and Maximilian II's reign.[40]

The Counter Reformation changed the situation. At the end of Ferdinand I's reign the Jesuits under the leadership of the eminent missionary and court preacher (Saint) Peter Canisius gained a foothold at the University of Vienna. By the end of the century Jesuit gymnasiums or colleges existed in the major cities of the hereditary lands, above all in Graz, but also in Innsbruck, Linz, Salzburg, and other cities. Similar was the situation in Bohemia, particularly in Prague, where the outstanding

[40] Eduard Winter, *Frühaufklärung* (Berlin, 1966), pp. 107–117; Mayer, *Geschichte Österreichs,* II, 355–359.

Jesuit gymnasium, the Clementinum, became already under Ferdinand I's sponsorship the competitor of the Carolinum, the university established in 1348 by Charles IV as the first in Central Europe. Numerous other Jesuit colleges were established throughout Bohemia and Moravia, usually subdivided in two sections with separate dormitories for nobles and commoners. In Hungary Nagyszombat (Tyrnau, Trnava) in Slovakian territory, the birthplace of the first permanent university, became the center of Jesuit higher education.[41] Jesuit instruction at the beginnings of the Counter Reformation was not superior to the earlier estates schools. In fact, the Jesuit institutions neglected instruction in the vernacular languages even more than the Protestant estates schools had done. Their teaching of Latin, to them not a means of understanding the classics but mainly the teachings of the medieval Church, was on a lower level, too. The feeble traces of a somewhat more diverse Renaissance spirit were eradicated by these schools. At the height of seventeenth-century Baroque culture, the form, though not the spirit, of Jesuit education became more secular. Cultivation of dramatics and more interest in the classics on aesthetic grounds developed, Greek was now frequently taught, and of modern languages Italian was introduced. As far as the teaching of skills was concerned, it would be difficult to place one type of schools above the other. The Protestant schools contained, however, the seeds of a general liberal education as did later the Catholic Benedictine and Piarist gymnasiums. In some disciplines, the Jesuit schools, which in numbers and impact exceeded other higher Catholic educational establishments, were supreme. Yet these institutions were run primarily in the service of the *ecclesia militans* and this held just as much true for the education of secular nobles as for that of the clergy.

It is not easy to separate gymnasiums or colleges distinctly from university education in the modern sense. Graz in Inner Austria became a regular Jesuit university in the 1580's and remained for the next decades an intellectual center of the Counter Reformation in the hereditary lands. The fourteenth-century university of Vienna (founded 1365) came under full Jesuit control only a generation after the university of Graz. The university of Salzburg was founded as a Jesuit institution in the 1620's and the university of Innsbruck in the 1670's. After the battle of the White Mountain, the Carolinum in Prague was forced to merge with the Jesuit Clementinum. Since the university of Olomouc (Olmütz) in

[41] A university was actually established as early as 1367 in Pécs (Fünfkirchen), but it did not survive the Turkish wars. See also Johann Andritsch ed., *Ungarische Geisteswelt* (Baden-Baden, 1960), pp. 90–99.

Moravia had become a Jesuit institution half a century before, higher education in the hereditary lands and Bohemia came fully under Jesuit control in the seventeenth century. Nagyszombat, founded by Peter Pazmány, the thoroughly cultured leader of the Catholic Reformation and Counter Reformation in Hungary, became the corresponding Jesuit university in Hungary in 1637. Several Jesuit gymnasiums were established also in Transylvania.

It would be an oversimplification to say that education under Jesuit counterreformatory direction meant in itself a deterioration of higher learning. Neither the record of scholarly achievements in sixteenth-century universities before the Jesuit ascendancy nor that in estates-sponsored schools could be considered outstanding or free from prejudices. In generally inadequate systems of education, differences as to specifics may not be decisive. Still, sixteenth-century education up to the victory of the Counter Reformation had moved haltingly and perhaps even largely unintentionally in the direction of a pluralistic culture. This trend was now radically reversed.[42]

b) THE SCIENCES

Beyond the fact of this reversal it is difficult to assess scholarship in institutions of higher learning in the late sixteenth and seventeenth centuries. The connection between scholarly achievements and universities was tenuous. Universities were centers of professional training, but only to a limited degree, if any, also of research. Often outstanding scholars of lasting fame had either no or only a transitory university connection. The point can be illustrated best in regard to the sciences. Largely neglected in the sixteenth and even the seventeenth centuries, they were represented nevertheless by some men of genius whose achievements surpassed with few exceptions those in what would be referred to today as the social sciences and humanities. The strange genius of Paracelsus (Theophrastus Hohenheim; 1494–1541), largely by speculation but partly also by practical experience, arrived at deductions which stimulated medical thought in several respects, including psychosomatic notions, but he had no university connection. The great Danish court astronomer of Rudolf II in Prague, Tycho de Brahe (1546–1601) likewise had no association with any institution of higher learning. His assistant and successor as court astronomer in Prague, Johannes Kepler (1571–1630), was probably the greatest scientific genius in Central Europe between Copernicus and

[42] Mayer, *Geschichte Österreichs,* II, 359–386; Richard Meister, *Entwicklung und Reform des österreichischen Studienwesens* (Vienna, 1963), I, 11–19.

Leibniz. The lifework of the founder of the laws of planetary movement, as far as it pertains to the hereditary and Bohemian lands, is indicative of the influence of the Counter Reformation on higher learning and of the social status of the scholar in general. In the 1590's Kepler taught for a few years at a secondary school, the gymnasium in Graz. Rising Jesuit influence and insinuations of heretic tendencies raised against him made it highly advisable to leave Styria for Prague, where he was protected not so much by a more liberal spirit as by Rudolf II's personal interest in astrology. Thus the successor of Tycho de Brahe had to move again after the emperor's death, this time to Linz in Upper Austria, where for a time he taught at the estates school. By then it was no longer under Protestant influence. The Counter Reformation was on the rise. Thus, Kepler at the beginning of the Thirty Years' War, terrified by inquisitory proceedings against his old mother in Württemberg, moved again to Bohemia and from there to Silesia off the mainroads of the theater of military and counterreformatory operations. Here he enjoyed the patronage of Wallenstein. After he had declined a professorship at the University of Rostock, he moved to Regensburg (Ratisbone). There he intended to complain to the imperial diet about various wrongs done to him. Before he could do so, his tormented life came to an end in 1630. Kepler and his family were undoubtedly harrassed by the Counter Reformation in the hereditary lands as well as in Bohemia. However, Emperor Rudolf II, who was interested not only in astrology but also in astronomy, and his successor Matthias in regard to calendar reform availed themselves of Kepler's counsel. Even the zealot Ferdinand II, despite Kepler's dubious religious loyalty, did not repudiate his services entirely. Rudolf II and Wallenstein, his main protectors, were both concerned with astrology as was, indeed, Kepler himself. Yet he was not only consulted as astrologer, but also as astronomer and mathematician. Both services were in demand. Kepler could be protected even as scientist by the counterreformatory emperors as long as he stayed within his place in the service of the court and not of the estates, and as long as his scholarly activities were confined to astronomy and mathematics, and not to their philosophical implications. Yet the tragedy in Kepler's life did not directly evolve from difficulties he had encountered as teacher, but as citizen suspected of heretic proclivities in a world of intolerance. Of the hardships and humiliations he had to endure, the restrictions of his teachings were easiest to bear. In fact he himself turned down a teaching position in the Protestant north, which might have offered him protection from counterreformatory zeal but only a very meagre income, manifold tedious teaching obligations and no social prestige. Kepler's fate within the scientific life of his time is neither that of the hero nor quite that of the martyr, but of the genius, for whom the social and intellectual conditions of his time and place proved to be intolerable.[43]

c) SOCIAL SCIENCES AND HUMANITIES

Conditions that applied to the great scientists were applicable to usually far lesser lights in the social sciences and humanities. After the brief era of the courtly Renaissance around Maximilian I, briefly referred to in Chapter I, the scholarly discipline most productive in returns was a kind of sociography or descriptive ethnic-political historiography. Among the scholars in the field were the Tyrolean seventeenth-century geographer, Georg Vischer, a proficient cartographer, and his fellow-countryman Matthias Burglechner who was interested also in statistics. The most outstanding of the sociographers was Johann Weigand von Valvasor, who in the second half of the seventeenth century published several weighty, quite accurate and readable works on the history of Carniola, the duchy situated at the southern fringe of the hereditary lands. His writings were sponsored by the estates of Carniola. These works are more important as specimens of the interest opened up by this approach than as sources of information. Neither Valvasor nor the court historian of Ferdinand I, Wolfgang Lazius, or of Joseph I, Hans Jakob Wagner von Wagenfels (the author of the *Ehrenruff Teutschlands, der Teutschen und ihres Reiches*) had an academic connection. Their works were anchored in the interest and endorsement of the public authorities, whether representative in the estates meaning of the term or princely authoritarian. Favored by the latter were also the distinguished cameralists Becher, Schröder, Hörnigk mentioned in Section C of this chapter. A place between cameralism,[44] sociography, and belles lettres was held by the seventeenth-century Upper Austrian Protestant nobleman, Wolf Helmhard von Hohberg, who settled in Lower Austria and wrote there his famous *Georgica curiosa* or *Adeliges*

[43] Mayer, *Geschichte Österreichs,* II, 377–378; Carl J. Friedrich, *The Age of the Baroque: 1610–1660* (New York, 1952), pp. 107–111. Herbert Butterfield, *The Origins of Modern Science: 1300–1801* (New York, 1962), pp. 69–78. Eduard Winter, *Barock, Absolutismus und Aufklärung in der Donaumonarchie* (Vienna, 1971), pp. 26 f., 144 ff. R. J. W. Evans, *Rudolf II and his World: A Study in Intellectual History* (New York, 1972).

[44] Cameralism can best be described rather than defined as a synthesis of economic policy under mercantilist and later physiocratic auspices with doctrines of public law, particularly public finance and comparative government. See Sommer, *Die österreichischen Kameralisten,* pp. 1–19.

Land und Feldleben, an original and charming work on the conditions and attractions of country life on a noble estate.[45]

In general conditions concerning scholarly production were similar in the Bohemian lands, although here the severe setback resulting from the defeat at the beginnings of the Thirty Years' War, helps to explain the cultural lag better than that in the hereditary lands. A Catholic priest, Václav Hájek of Libočan, another court historian of Ferdinand I, wrote a Bohemian chronicle up to the accession of the emperor as king of Bohemia, at points quite colorful, in other respects an undistinguished piece of pseudo-historical writing. No more can be said for the work of his contemporary, the bishop of Olomouc Joannes Dubravius, author of a Bohemian history which covers also the beginnings of the Turkish war under Suleiman the Magnificent. More distinguished were the works of the previously mentioned seventeenth-century Jesuit Bohuslav Balbin, written after the battle of the White Mountain. We are indebted to Balbin for a brief, in essence political history of Bohemia and—more important—a literary history of the country. These works were written in the darkest days of the country until Hitler's infamous assault and were subject to the conformism of the Counter Reformation. They stand in lieu of many valuable writings destroyed by the fury of contemporary witchhunts and they attest to the continuation of intellectual activities under trying external conditions. The merits of Balbin were significant, indeed.

Naturally they pale in significance in comparison to those of Jan Amos Komenský (Comenius), born 1592 in Nivnice Moravia, died 1671 in Amsterdam. Comenius, preacher and later bishop of the Bohemian Brethren, studied in Germany in his youth and later gained experiences in exile in Poland and western Europe, particularly in England and in the country, noblest in its hospitality to victims of intolerance, Holland. Yet the substance of his lifework was deeply anchored in his Moravian home grounds. His often underrated theological writings, particularly the *Emendatio rerum humanorum,* are markedly devoid of the intolerance of his time. The *Magna didactica,* the great work of educational theory and practice, published in exile, is based on empiricism. Comenius heralds the victory of the coming Enlightenment over the pedagogy of scholas-

[45] Otto Brunner, *Adeliges Landleben und europäischer Geist: Leben und Werk Helmhards von Hohberg, 1612–1688* (Salzburg, 1959); Kann, *A Study in Austrian Intellectual History,* pp. 34–47; Anna Coreth, *Österreichische Geschichtsschreibung in der Barockzeit (1620–1740)* (Vienna, 1957), passim; Winter, *Barock, Absolutismus und Aufklärung in der Donaumonarchie,* pp. 21–32.

ticism. He was undoubtedly the greatest of the political emigrés from the impact of the Counter Reformation in Central Europe, one of the greatest men of all times who ever fled oppression. Other distinguished refugees were Pavel Skála ze Zhoře from Plzeň, the author of a comprehensive Bohemian Church history and Pavel Stránský, who wrote a kind of Bohemian sociography, the *res publica Bojema,* not unlike in character from the works of Valvasor. The former found asylum in Saxony, the latter in Poland.[46]

More closely focused on political history is the voluminous *Historiarum de rebus Hungaricis libri,* written in the later sixteenth and early seventeenth centuries by the Magyar Nicolas Istuanffy (1538–1615). The work begins with the death of Corvinus and ends with the resumption of the Turkish wars under Rudolf II and Matthias; it was continued, after his death, in Magyar. Istuanffy, like Lazius and Wagner, was for a time court historian. The able man of strong counterreformatory tendencies also held high public office in Hungary. This type of official was only rarely interested in academic affiliations which offered in general a rather inferior social status.[47] Emigrés and dissenters were barred even from such modest positions.

Conditions for the rise of creative scholarship in the Habsburg lands were usually unfavorable. Some achievements were respectable and some were original and creative, but the affiliation of creative thinkers with institutions of higher learning was tenuous. The intellectual bonds to the west and north, to the Hobbes and Locke, Bodin and Descartes, Althusius and Pufendorf or Spinoza were practically nonexistent. Not before the heights of the Enlightenment did the Habsburgs establish a scholarly "Anschluss" to the western world.

[46] Hanuš Jelinek, *Histoire de la Literature Tchèque: Des Origines à 1850* (Paris, 1933) I, 163–218. A. N. Pypin and V. D. Spasović, *Geschichte der slawischen Literaturen* (Leipzig, 1884), II:2, 160–171; Seton-Watson, *History of the Czechs and Slovaks,* pp. 125–129. Jan Machal in P. Hinneberg, ed., *Die osteuropäischen Literaturen* (Leipzig, 1908), pp. 184–89. Winter, *Barock, Absolutismus und Aufklärung in der Donaumonarchie,* pp. 33–56.

[47] The mentioned Wolfgang Lazius—one of the few exceptions to the rule—held, however, simultaneously positions as court historian of Emperor Ferdinand I and professor at the University of Vienna. Istuanffy, although strongly associated with counterreformatory tendencies, was court historian under Maximilian II, the most tolerant among the sixteenth- and seventeenth-century Habsburg rulers. See also Johann H. Schwicker, *Geschichte der ungarischen Literatur* (Leipzig, 1888), pp. 78–85, 113–130, 178–186; Winter, *Barock, Absolutismus und Aufklärung in der Donaumonarchie,* pp. 57–77.

d) LITERATURE

There is no rigid line of demarcation between the social sciences, humanities, and general literature. A major part of literature (apart from folklore) was didactic. Didactics in sixteenth- and seventeenth-century terms meant—dependent on the political setting—promotion of the ideas of Reformation, Catholic Reformation, and Counter Reformation. It is not intended here to discuss theological writings in general. What should be emphasized, however, is the not sufficiently recognized fact, that the translation of the Scriptures into the vernacular languages was of decisive significance in the further literary development of German, the Slavic languages, Magyar, and Roumanian. Luther's fundamental work of translating the Testaments into German was paralleled in this respect by that of Jan Blahoslav among Czechs, of Primož Trubar and Jurij Dalmatin among the forgotten of the forgotten Slavic people, the Slovenes, of Gaspar Heltai among the Magyars, and of Michael Tordassi, who translated Heltai's version into Roumanian. These significant literary efforts were undertaken within about half a century after Luther's pioneer work in the Central European orbit. Luther's literary accomplishments have found fully adequate recognition, but other translations may have meant something even more basic for Slovenes or Roumanians than for Germans, Czechs, or Magyars. To Slovenes and Roumanians the translations represented in large measure the creation of new literary languages. To the Germans they meant the transformation of an existing one. The issue with Czechs and Magyars was primarily the elevation of language to a higher plane of semantics. This need for literary upgrading was at the time greatly in demand among the nations with a political history of their own.

As for the German orbit, this impact of the purification of language was more pronounced in the north and west than in the hereditary lands. There literature was far removed from the golden age, which it did not reach until the second quarter of the nineteenth century. Few outstanding individuals in the Austro-German sphere set their marks on the literature of the period; this does not mean that their contributions were insignificant. Much of the community spirit of the late medieval art prevailed, where the artist fades behind the work. This pertains to many of the ecclesiastic folksongs, the cooperative enterprise of the Meistersinger in the guilds, and to the plays performed in Jesuit institutions of higher learning—dramas, comedies, operas, and even ballet, frequently all rolled into one dramatic performance. Topics were taken from the Bible, the lives of the saints and martyrs, from mythology, and occasionally from Roman and medieval history. Objective of this education in dramatics was primarily to give self-confidence and poise to those students who should make their way in the world. Naturally entertainment was one purpose too.

The latter was undoubtedly the chief objective of the popular comedy, the Hanswurst or harlequine shows, which at the end of the seventeenth century followed patterns of the Italian comedia dell'arte, but developed soon a style of its own. Within less than a century the wit and charm of these late flowers of the Baroque and Rococo spirit had to yield to the rationalism of humorless enlightened reformers. The plays of the outstanding comedians in the early eighteenth century, such as Gottfried Prehauser and Joseph Stranitzky, were only sketched in regard to plot, whereas the text was largely improvised, hence much of this literature is lost to us. It contained some mild social criticism tolerated by the government—possibly as a subconscious outlet for a spirit of opposition. By the end of the Baroque period the counterreformatory spirit had relaxed to a point where popular entertainment became legitimate. Furthermore it became obvious and has been obvious in Austria even since, that satire and social criticism without humor, sometimes even slapstick, could not be effective.[48]

This factor is the key to the understanding of the most prominent and most original literary figure of the Baroque era in the hereditary lands, the Augustinian father and later court preacher in Vienna, Abraham a Sancta Clara, who was born as Ulrich Megerle in Kreheinstetten, Swabia, 1644 and died in Vienna, 1709. The preacher's tracts, sermons, exhortations, fables, anecdotes, sometimes incorporated in a novel-like frame, fill many volumes. They follow the satirical patterns of the counterreformatory preachers in late seventeenth-century Austria. Abraham a Sancta Clara surpasses them, however, in his colorful and witty criticism of the fabric of society and in his unparalleled command of a language of puns, alliterations, similes, and sometimes compulsive loquaciousness. Frightening in contrast are his vehement diatribes against Protestants, Turks, Jews, and conceivable dissenters of all kinds. No superstition or prejudice is read out of court by the intolerant zeal of the brilliant preacher. His

[48] See Johann W. Nagl, Jakob Zeidler, Eduard Castle, *Deutsch-österreichische Literaturgeschichte* (Vienna, various editions), 2 vols. See I, section 2, II, section 1; Josef Nadler, *Österreichische Literaturgeschichte* (Linz, 1943), pp. 94–168.

wit is a deadly weapon in the service of the militant Church, but also—despite his criticism of ridiculous customs and menial sins—in defense of established society.

Abraham also established the tradition, characteristic for a long time to come, to place intellectual gifts in the service of a passionate anti-intellectualism, which helped to separate Austria further from the west. Even if one makes the necessary allowance for the spirit of time and place, and in particular Abraham's intention to plead a great cause, the consequences of this glorification of bias and unreason are deplorable. The literary gourmet of today may enjoy Abraham's works, but the reader, including the one to whom Abraham's cause means much, will regret his unwholesome, powerful, and lasting influence on Austrian intellectual life.[49]

Unlike conditions in the hereditary lands, the century from the accession of Ferdinand I to the battle of the White Mountain is frequently referred to as a golden age of Czech literature. Such characterization pertains less to individual contributions but to the symbiosis between the spirit of the community of the Bohemian Brethren and that of late humanism. The mentioned Jan Blahoslav and Comenius represent both these trends—Blahoslav primarily the spirit of the Brethren, Comenius that of a reformed humanism. Daniel Adam of Valeslavín (1546–1599) furthered historical and literary endeavors as sociographer, translator, and compiler of dictionaries of the Czech language. This court historian of Rudolf II was affiliated also with the University of Prague, a rare combination. Balbin's efforts to repair the damages done to Czech culture and its further development after 1620 have been mentioned. He was supported by the Moravian historiographer Thomas Pešina of Cechorod (1629–1680).[50]

Among the ethnically and linguistically closely related Slovaks in northern Hungary and Moravia, were some authors of Protestant church hymnals, impressive in their melancholic sentiments. Ján Silván in the late sixteenth century and the preacher George Tranoscus (Tranovský) in the early seventeenth century distinguished themselves in the development of ecclesiastic Protestant lyrics. Linguistics which played such an important part in the Slavic renaissance in the late eighteenth and early nineteenth

[49] Kann, *A Study in Austrian Intellectual History*, pp. 50–115.

[50] Pypin and Spasović, *Geschichte der slawischen Literaturen*, II:2, 144–177; František Chudoba, *A Short Survey of Czech Literature* (New York, 1969), pp. 30–67. Dmitry Cizevsky, *Outline of Comparative Slavic Literatures: Survey of Slavic Civilization* (Boston, 1952), pp. 56–69. Paul Diels, *Geschichte der slawischen Literaturen* (Wiesbaden, 1963), pp. 212–214.

century had been important among the Slovaks in the early eighteenth century. Matthias Bél (1684–1741) was a notable historian-geographer and linguist; he revised the Bible translation of the Bohemian Brethren. Paul Doležal was also a prominent linguist at about the same time, whose contributions were equally significant for the development of the Slovak and the Czech languages.[51]

As for the Magyars, the Turkish advance and the long occupation impeded literary development even more than the Counter Reformation did in the Bohemian lands. The latter diverted intellectual life in Bohemia and Moravia, the Turkish occupation destroyed it physically to a large extent, in Hungary. On the other hand, although the Turkish wars prevented the growth and spread of literary achievements, they exercised no influence on the intellectual trends behind them. At the end of the seventeenth century, when the Counter Reformation triumphed in Hungary, the first currents of the Enlightenment were felt. Of the Hungarian humanists who in the unoccupied territories were only indirectly affected by the Ottoman advance, Péter Bornemisza (1535–1585) was the most important social critic and linguist of his time. Gáspár Károli translated the Bible into Magyar; it was published in 1590. Distinguished poets at that time were Sebestyén Tinódi Lantos (about 1505–1556), famous through his ballads and the lyric Bálint Balassi. He fell in the Turkish wars.

Two seventeenth-century personalities, a Protestant and a Catholic, distinguished themselves in the further advancement of the Magyar literary language and its cultural relationship to the west. Albert Scenczi Molnár (1574–1634) was a translator of English and French literature into Magyar. This widely traveled Calvinist composed also a Latin-Magyar dictionary and a Magyar grammar in Latin. Cardinal Peter Pázmány (1570–1637) has been mentioned as religious leader of the Hungarian Catholic Reformation and Counter Reformation and founder of the University in Nagyszombat (Trnava); equal is his significance as linguist. His sermons, theological writings, and the translation of Thomas a Kempis' Imitation of Christ were unparalleled masterpieces of prose. The epic poet of chivalry from the Zrínyi family of legendary heroic fame, Count Miklos Zrínyi (1620–1664) glorified the deeds of the nation under the leadership of his ancestor, the defender of Szigetvár, against Suleiman the Magnificent. At about the same time, Janos Cseri von Apaczá, a Calvinist in Transylvania (1625–1659) compiled a Hungarian encyclopedia which took

[51] Pypin and Spasović, *Geschichte der slawischen Literaturen,* pp. 307–314; see also Ludwig von Gogolák, *Beiträge zur Geschichte des slowakischen Volkes* (Munich, 1963), I, 55–179.

full cognizance of western philosophic and scientific developments. This was a feature unparalleled in the contemporary literature of any other people under Habsburg rule, save for the works of the exiles. Just as original was this young Cartesian's pioneer struggle for the replacement of Latin by Magyar as language of instruction in higher education. Hungarian theatrical culture, very much alive in the High Renaissance, was also cultivated in autonomous Transylvania at a time when the Turkish advance brought these activities to a halt in Hungary proper. In the later seventeenth century, the Jesuit drama was introduced in the wake of the reconquering Habsburg armies.[52]

Concerning the Southern Slavs, Serbs and Serbian literature in the strict sense of the term played only a minor part within the confines of the empire in the late seventeenth and early eighteenth century. This situation began to change in mid-eighteenth century in the course of the swiftly evolving Enlightenment and the following Slavic renaissance. The educational and ecclesiastic autonomy granted by Leopold I in 1690–1691 facilitated this development.

Instruction in German as well as Latin was offered, particularly in the secondary education under ecclesiastic control.[53] Croatian literature in Dalmatia was enriched by incentives deriving from Italian and Latin writings, but in another sense it was impeded because development of writings in Croatian idioms was delayed by the interest of the intelligentsia in Latin and the literary works of the Italian Renaissance. Still, progress was substantial, and in the sixteenth century perhaps more so than in the seventeenth, the century of continuous warfare. Lyrical poetry was widely cultivated in the sixteenth century and flourished under Petár Hektorović from Hvar. From the same Dalmatian island came the writer of secular plays, Hanibal Lucić, whose work represented a significant change from the ecclesiastic dramatics of other sixteenth-century writers. The best-known literary figure of the seventeenth century was perhaps Ivan Gundulić (1589–1638), the creator of national epical literature whose main topics were the wars of Christianity against the infidels. Gundulić was also a lyrical poet of distinction. Count F. C. Frankopan was one of the as yet rare literary representatives from northern Croatia. He participated in the aristocratic conspiracy against the emperor in 1671 like his brother-in-law and fellow political martyr, Peter Zrinyi. Like Zrinyi,

[52] Schwicker, *Geschichte der ungarischen Literatur,* pp. 121–186; Andritsch, ed., *Ungarische Geisteswelt,* pp. 99–108.

[53] Wendel, *Der Kampf der Südslawen um Freiheit und Einheit,* pp. 65–67; Emile Picot, *Les Serbes de la Hongrie* (Prague, 1873), pp. 76–98.

Frankopan was also a lyric of great emotional power. The same was true of Nikola Dordić, a generation later.[54]

As for the Slovenes, the great influence of the Reformation and its ecclesiastic literature on the development of the Slovene literary language has been noted. The literary development rested on a promising but still weak foundation, hence the Counter Reformation caused a particularly severe setback. Missionary and other didactic literature, not comparable to the linguistic pioneer work of Primož Turbar (1508–1586) and his student Jurij Dalmatin (1517–1589) in the Protestant phase of Slovene literature, did exist, but more widely recognized writings, such as those by Valvasor, were written largely in German. Slovene literary evolution had to wait for the day of the Slavic renaissance.[55]

Among the Roumanians in Transylvania, Archbishop Nicolas Olachus of Roumanian stock (1493–1568) was a distinguished humanist and friend of Erasmus of Rotterdam. In the 1540's, a catechism in Roumanian was published. In the first half of the seventeenth century a translation of the New Testament and some other writings came out in Transylvania. Apparently the Rákócsy regent of Transylvania, Prince George II, tolerated such enterprises because they served as means to shield the Vlachs from Slavic-Orthodox influences. Nevertheless, considering the extent to which the Vlachs were discriminated against Germans and Magyars, this was a remarkable achievement. Until well into the eighteenth century the language of the educated remained primarily Latin, German, and increasingly French. The establishment of a Magyar Calvinist university at Clui (Kolozsvár, Klausenburg), which might have become a genuine Roumanian national university, folded in 1603 after two decades.[56]

e) MUSIC

For two centuries, from Ferdinand I to Charles VI, music enjoyed the support of the Habsburg rulers to a greater degree than literature. They

[54] Franjo Trogrančić, "Literature 1400–1835," in Francis H. Eterovich and Christopher Spalatin, eds., *Croatia: Land, People, Culture* (Toronto, 1964–1970), II, 180–214; Pypin and Spasović, *Geschichte der slawischen Literaturen*, I, 217–267; see also Nicola Andrić, "Ergänzung zur croatischen Literaturgeschichte," in [Crownprince Rudolf], *Die österreichisch-ungarische Monarchie*, Vol. *Croatia-Slavonia*, pp. 128–134.

[55] Anton Slodnjak, *Geschichte der slowenischen Literatur* (Berlin, 1958), pp. 49–80; Pypin and Spasović, *Geschichte der slawischen Literaturen*, I, 374–380.

[56] Constantin Daicoviciu and Miron Constantinescu, *Brève Histoire de la Transylvanie* (Bucarest, 1965), pp. 111–112, 133–137. Matthias Bernath, *Habsburg und die Anfänge der rumänischen Nationsbildung* (Leiden, 1972), pp. 63–143. Ladislas Makkai, *Histoire de Transylvanie* (Paris, 1946), pp. 166–175.

cultivated particularly ecclesiastic choral music, and since Leopold I also the grand Baroque opera in Italian style. Leopold, the most musical of the Habsburg rulers, spent vast sums of money in its support, despite the chronic economic crisis of his regime. In an artistic sense, more important than the pompous Italian operas performed under Leopold were the operas composed by Charles VI's court composer, Pietro Metastasio (1698–1782), who distinguished himself also as writer of oratorios and cantatas, well into the reign of Maria Theresa. Highly significant in Charles VI's time was the work of the Styrian Johann Joseph Fux, a musical theorist. Performances of Baroque music depended more on princely patronage than publication of literature. This patronage was forthcoming, though applied frequently to the ostentatious rather than the profound.

In the Bohemian lands as in the hereditary lands folk music was of great originality and appeal. Yet the Counter Reformation did not offer to orchestral music and operas in the defeated lands the same princely patronage as in Austria. Furthermore many excellent musicians emigrated after 1620. The patronage of the great Bohemian aristocratic families did not make itself felt strongly before the eighteenth century.

In Hungary, the national aristocracy, more deeply rooted in the soil than the new knights of fortune in Bohemia, were willing and able to sponsor art even in the stormy seventeenth century. The collection of Hungarian tunes, the *Cantus Catholici,* could be published in 1651. Prince Pal Esterházy, the editor of the *Harmonia caelestis,* was a sponsor, collector, a composer, and theorist of notable skill and erudition.[57]

f) FINE ARTS

During the sixteenth and seventeenth centuries the development of the fine arts in the Habsburg lands was colorful, diverse, and in several ways highly original. Some dominant principles stand out. The peoples in these lands had and still have great innate artistic abilities and inclinations. The possibility of expressing them freely in literature was hampered during the age of ideological warfare and at the height of the Counter Reformation almost completely strangled. But in architecture, painting, and sculpture the issue of freedom of expression was only indirectly affected by strictures imposed by the Counter Reformation. Fine arts apparently served as outlets for artists and their public, when expressions of thought in spoken and written word were controlled or suppressed.

[57] See for instance Paul Lang, *Music in Western Civilization* (New York, 1941), pp. 387–408, 456–459, 553–567, 955–956; Ottokar Hostinský, "Musik in Böhmen," in [Crownprince Rudolf], *Die österreichisch-ungarische Monarchie,* Vol. *Böhmen,* II, 8–20; András Pernye, in *Ungarn* (Budapest, 1966), pp. 386–389; Fedor Kabalin, "Music," in F. Eterovich, C. Spalatin, eds., *Croatia,* I, 280–282.

Yet architecture, painting, and sculpture were also affected by the social conditions of the age. They required to the greatest extent the patronage of sovereigns, government, Church, and aristocracy—the "establishment." The formative artists, above all the architects, also depended on the maintenance of law and order, but only in conjunction with the absence of oppressive police supervision and punitive taxation. In both respects the hereditary lands were in a relatively more advantageous position than the Bohemian lands. Worst off were the lands of the Hungarian crown during the Turkish occupation and the following wars. Not until the eighteenth century did Hungary as a whole have opportunities for an evolution of the fine arts, which in the sixteenth and seventeenth centuries could develop only in areas not subject to direct Turkish occupation.

g) RENAISSANCE AND BAROQUE

The two great styles of arts of the sixteenth and seventeenth centuries were Renaissance and Baroque.[58] Renaissance style lends itself well to the sentiments of all strata of society including the aristocracy. Above all it is the expression of the prestige of the postmedieval urban patriciate and middle class, as it arose in Italy in the fourteenth and fifteenth centuries and in Germany in the late fifteenth and sixteenth centuries. In Germany and in the Habsburg lands Renaissance represented primarily estates and city power, the antithesis of political feudalism and princely absolutism. These forces, as discussed previously, shared in the hereditary lands power only for a relatively brief and strongly contested period. Consequently the impact of this style is less marked there than that of Baroque, the grandiose expression of the twofold triumph of Counter Reformation and princely absolutism. The Baroque signifies the rise and expansion of a secular power, able to reinstall and at the same time to control the revival of the Catholic Church. In that sense the Baroque is more a secular than an ecclesiastic style, or rather a style that reveals the impact of secularism on the ecclesia militans. Nevertheless, in the hereditary lands most of the proudest ecclesiastic buildings were created in the Baroque style. It is not a style that expresses the dignified austerity of an independent puritan citizenry in the towns, as represented primarily by the guilds; these had to take a back seat throughout the long era of Baroque artistic triumph. Yet, though in the background, the artistic expressions of an urban bourgeois style, as evidenced for instance in the market squares of many

[58] In a brief study of this kind, "mannerism" will not be considered as a separate style, but rather as a mere transitional phase between late Renaissance and early Baroque, but closer to the latter.

smaller towns, were not lost to posterity and offered great potentialities for the future.

The Renaissance reached the hereditary lands relatively late, that is, not much before the middle of the sixteenth century. The estate structure was less developed there than in the Bohemian or Hungarian domains, hence its monuments were primarily palaces and renovated Gothic castles, and only a few town halls or patrician urban houses. The Italian influence is prevalent in the sixteenth-century Schallaburg castle south of the Danube in Lower Austria. The Habsburg castle of Ambras in Tyrol stands for the Renaissance transformation of the original Gothic style. The imposing palace of the princely house of Porcia in Spittal in Carinthia by Scamozzi is another outstanding example of the aristocratic variant of the Renaissance in Austria. Notable also is the tomb of Emperor Maximilian I in the Court Church in Innsbruck. Estates' strength, on the other hand, is represented in the diet building in Graz, Styria. Vienna has comparatively few Renaissance buildings. No ambitious building program could develop under the duress of the Turkish wars raging at times close to the walls of the city. In the intervals the pressures of the struggle between burghers and sovereign, Reformation and Counter Reformation, contributed further to the loss of the modest prosperity and relative security which the city had enjoyed during the late Gothic era, which gave Vienna and Austria some of its greatest works of art. But only the Baroque style offered the city the opportunity to display the splendor due to the center of a rising great power.

The Austrian Baroque era began in the early seventeenth century and reached its summit at the beginning of the eighteenth. Yet it outlasted the reign of Charles VI, followed by a very brief Rococo epilogue. Baroque in the hereditary lands was distinctly a style of imperial, aristocratic, and monastic ecclesiastic grandeur. The influence of Italian architecture on the Austrian Renaissance was strong, on the Baroque even stronger. Baroque's first heralds were Santino Solari, architect of the noble cathedral in Salzburg, and Carlo Carlone, designer of several churches in Vienna. Because of the narrowness of an essentially still medieval city such churches sometimes have a modest façade incongruously contrasting with the splendor of interior decoration. Two generations later Domenico Martinelli was an outstanding architect of palaces of the aristocracy of the realm. In their garden palaces outside the city walls, space limitations did not have to be considered. The façades of the new palaces were now no less striking than the interiors. Later native Austrian architects, though still trained in Italy, became the most celebrated creators of Baroque art. Johann Bernhard Fischer von Erlach the elder (Graz 1656–Vienna 1723) and Johann Lukas von Hildebrandt (Genova 1660–Vienna 1750) became the unrivaled standard bearers of the new style. The former designed the church of St. Charles Borromäus (the most monumental Baroque church in Vienna), the central parts of the rebuilt Hofburg, and the new Schönbrunn palace (completed by Nicolas Pacassi). Graz and particularly Prague are some of the cities which show other monuments of his genius. Hildebrandt was more graceful though less monumental in his designs. He became the architect of elegant Baroque palaces, including Eugene of Savoy's garden residence, the Belvedere, one of the most beautiful specimens of the new style in the German orbit.

Hildebrandt designed also the monastery of Göttweig. It ranks with Jakob Prandtauer's sublime Melk and St. Florian, and Mungenast's Seitenstetten and Zwettl among the proudest monuments of the Austrian ecclesiastic Baroque. Here a curious phenomenon strikes the observer. Reference has sometimes been made to the "building craze" (*Bauwut*) of the great ecclesiastic and secular noble sponsors of Baroque architecture, who favored huge designs for incongruously more modest needs. The phenomenon repeats similar though less ostentatious discrepancies in the Italian Renaissance. Rising prosperity after a long war period, the unrestricted power of princely absolutism, symbolism for the victory of the Counter Reformation, the desire to copy the splendor of Louis XIV, and a new feeling of self-assertive pride, played their part. Nevertheless, it is still hard to explain why and how a score of huge monasteries, particularly in Lower and Upper Austria were built in thinly populated wooded areas. Some of these beautiful structures with façades of several hundred yards length are separated from each other by a distance of less than ten miles and few by as much as fifty. Rivalry between various orders, especially Benedictines, Premonstratensians, Augustinians, and Cistercensians, does not explain sufficiently the missionary economic and political pressures at work to establish these tremendous structures. Were the efforts, which made these constructions possible, meant to be also signs of penance for feelings of guilt, perhaps as counterweight for an exhibitionism of pride? Did they signify a gravitation of the Church to the orders, at a time when the bishops had to withstand governmental pressure? Every answer raises new questions.[59]

In the Bohemian lands, the perhaps greatest work of the Renaissance was another Belvedere palace built in Prague by the Italian architect Paolo della Stella for Ferdinand I's consort in mid-sixteenth century.

[59] See Ludwig Baldass, Rupert Feuchtmüller, Wilhelm Mrazek, *Renaissance in Österreich* (Vienna, 1966); Bruno Grimschitz, *Wiener Barockpaläste* (Vienna, 1944); Alfred Schnerich, *Wiens Kirchen und Kapellen* (Vienna, 1921).

Italian influence was just as strong in Bohemian Renaissance architecture as in the hereditary lands. A counterpart to the castle of Ambras in Tyrol with its Gothic core and Renaissance renovation is the Schwarzenberg palace of Krumlov (Krumau) in southwestern Bohemia. Otherwise, corresponding to the greater influence of a prosperous urban burgher class in sixteenth-century Bohemia and in part of Moravia, there was also greater influence of Renaissance architecture on this urban culture as exemplified by the town halls in Plzeň, Olomuc and other places. Altogether, corresponding to the different social-political structure Renaissance art was richer in Bohemia than in the hereditary lands.

Baroque architecture in Bohemia and again to some extent in Moravia was as splendid as in Austria. In view of the long history of revolution and war in the country this in itself was a major accomplishment. The early influence of Italian masters, such as Carlo Loragho and Martin Antonio da Porta was later equaled by that of the Germans Christoph Dientzenhofer and his son Kilian Ignaz. Prague abounds in sublime Baroque churches and in great palaces of the aristocracy that had risen in power after 1620, the families of Silva Tarouca, Clam-Gallas, Schönborn, Lobkowitz, Thun, and others. The architecture of the palaces of the aristocracy is as characteristic for Bohemia and Moravia as the monastic architecture in the hereditary lands. The association of the rise of the Baroque with the destruction of the old nobility and the influx of the alien new one helps to explain also why the new style in the Bohemian lands was more strongly related to foreign influence than in the hereditary lands. Yet genuine national artists such as the late Baroque sculptor Ferdinand Prokop (Brockhoff) made a great contribution as did his Lower Austrian contemporary, Raphael Donner. Nevertheless, although Baroque paintings and sculptures are colorful, decorative, and impressive, they are in general not on a par with architecture. There is truth in the saying *saxa loquntur,* the stones bear witness for an inventive and ingenious spirit, where counterreformatory absolutism had blocked the free exchange of ideas.[60]

Mentioned should be also the great art collections of Ferdinand of Tyrol in Ambras, Rudolf II in Prague, and the distinguished connoisseur Archduke Leopold Wilhelm, brother of Ferdinand III in Brussels.[61] They

[60] Oskar Schürer, *Prag: Kultur, Kunst, Geschichte* (Munich, 1935, 5th ed.); Jaromir Neumann, *Das böhmische Barock* (Vienna, 1971); on the sponsor of Baroque architecture in Bohemia, Count Sporck, see Heinrich Benedikt, *Franz Anton Graf von Sporck* (Vienna, 1923).

[61] This collection represents the nucleus of the art gallery in the Kunsthistorisches Museum in Vienna.

pertain to arms, sculpture, jewelry, and Renaissance and Baroque paintings. Such collections required more genuine feelings for art than expertise does today.

Art collections played a significant part also in the Hungarian Renaissance, which had reached its summit at the court of King Matthias Corvinus (1443–90). The great treasures of Italian paintings and sculpture and the priceless library of the king with its precious manuscripts were scattered and destroyed during the Turkish wars. Some monuments of ecclesiastic architecture, particularly in Esztergom (Gran), Pécs (Fünfkirchen), and Gyulafehérvár (Alba Julia) were preserved as was the Rákóczy castle in Sárospatak.

The rise of Baroque architecture was impeded primarily by the Turkish wars, but the slow development of urbanization was also a factor. In the northwestern Slovak section of Hungary, which was spared the Turkish occupation, the Jesuit college and Baroque cathedral of Nagyszombat (Trnava) designed by Pietro Spasso, rose in the early seventeenth century. Yet the building of this grand church as well as the rebuilding of the cathedral of Györ (Raab) were at that time rather exceptions. Hungarian Baroque could develop more freely only after the reconquest of the country between 1683 and 1699. Even then it was hampered by the burdens of military occupation. Some Baroque palaces, such as that of the Esterházys in Eisentadt (Kismarton) and Buda, were built and the royal palace in Buda was in fact reconstructed in the new style, somewhat earlier than those in Vienna and Prague. Yet at the time when Hungary was completely freed from the Turks, the monuments of the great Hungarian Renaissance period were largely destroyed and the Baroque style in the west had nearly passed its peak. Despite notable exceptions, particularly in Buda, Baroque achitecture in Hungary was not on a par with that in the hereditary and Bohemian lands.[62]

Still, all things considered, Baroque art, as shiny facet of the counterreformatory experience, forges an impressive bond between the three main units of the lands under Habsburg rule. In every one of them the new style expresses the experience of the senses as substitute for those of the intellect. In every one of them the new style expresses the political and religious triumphs of the era.

[62] Lajos Neméth, in *Ungarn* (Budapest, 1966), pp. 361–367; Gustav Keleti, "Malerei und Plastik," in [Crownprince Rudolf], *Die österreichisch-ungarische Monarchie,* Vol. *Ungarn,* III, 413–418. See also Ruža Bajurin, "Architecture, Sculpture, and Painting," in Francis H. Eterovich and Christopher Spalatin, eds., *Croatia,* I, 322 f., 329 f., 336 f.

CHAPTER V

An Empire Reasserts Itself (1740-1815)

A. Foreign policy (1740–1792)

The account of Austrian foreign policy in Chapter III led to the end of the War of the Austrian Succession, the peace treaty of Aix la Chapelle in 1748. The outcome proved that the new Habsburg power could withstand the concerted attack of a major European coalition, which would either have partitioned Austria or reduced it to a secondary state. Austria was faced by the same threats to which Spain succumbed a generation before and Poland half a century afterward. The new empire could avoid either fate and remained a major force within the concert of Europe for more than a century. For another two generations, until 1918, it could not quite continue to maintain the rank of a first-rate power in fact, but did so in name and with it retained much of the prestige and the paraphernalia of a great power with considerable area and population.

Within two generations after the War of the Austrian Succession, the Habsburg empire had to face another crisis in the revolutionary and Napoleonic eras, which threatened her with reduction to a satellite state of the Napoleonic empire. Again Austria weathered a serious crisis.

One reason why Austria survived was the personality of her rulers. For thirty of the hectic seventy-five years from 1740 to 1815, Austria was involved in wars, most of them of decisive importance for Habsburg power. Yet it was not her military leadership, which proved to be of particular benefit during this period. Only two generals, Laudon during the Third Silesian War and the archduke Charles during the first part of the Napoleonic war period, could be considered outstanding soldiers. But Laudon was never commander-in-chief, and the archduke, hemmed in by the superior genius of Napoleon and the inferior jealousy of his petty imperial brother Francis, lacked the good fortune without which no great commander can succeed. If the asset of masters of strategy was thus not on the side of Austria, she could still claim a major advantage. During the first part of the period (1740–1815) under discussion here, the rulers of Austria were three personalities of above-average qualifications: Maria Theresa (1740–1780), her son Joseph II (1780–1790), and his brother Leopold II (1790–1792). Of these three, the mother, from an intellectual viewpoint, was more limited than the sons, which has to be understood, however, in a relative sense. Born and raised in the late Baroque and early Rococo eras, the empress never felt at home in the intellectual sphere of the Enlightenment; she could overcome inherited prejudices only slowly and partly. Yet she had a practical mind, sound perception, a warm heart, and resolution. What is perhaps most important for a ruler, she was ready to acknowledge the mental superiority of some of her advisers and knew how to yield gracefully to a superior mind.

Her oldest son, Joseph II, whose relations to the mother were not without warmth but always difficult, failed in this respect, although and perhaps because he was intellectually superior to Maria Theresa. This most controversial of all Habsburg rulers has generally been charged with precipitate, all-too-sweeping reforms, derived from lack of respect for traditions and the psychological resistance of people and an administrative apparatus in a still semifeudal and in many ways nonhomogeneous empire. Such oversimplifications are usually based on a short-range outlook and a conservative philosophy. Whichever way one evaluates Joseph II's hectic reign, there is certainly room for abundant criticism. A ruler whose philosophy of government and corresponding actions anticipated much of the reforms undertaken in Central and western Europe in the two generations after his death cannot be dismissed as a failure although he cannot be extolled as an unqualified success. Quite a few conflicts resulting from his precipitate actions and the frequently irrational response to them could be straightened out in the all-too-short reign of his brother Leopold. It was the latter's personal tragedy that, although he could adjust some old problems, he died too soon to solve the new overpowering one, namely to keep Austria and perhaps with her Europe out of more than two decades of almost continuous warfare.

Of these three distinguished rulers Maria Theresa had the gift to project her personality well across the domestic and international scene. She enjoyed the support of advisers whose philosophy of government differed from her own. Joseph II, on the other hand, as noted above, could not establish rapport with the same advisers, although most of them were in spirit closer to him than to the empress. More important, he could not gain, in his lifetime the support of the broad strata of the people, the prospective beneficiaries of his reforms. Yet if one judges him not by the response to his actions by his contemporaries but by his image in later generations, he made a stronger impact on Austrian history than any of his successors and most of his predecessors. Retrospectively he appeared not even devoid of charismatic leadership. Leopold II, more pragmatic in intelligence and stronger in administrative abilities than Joseph, lacked this dramatic quality. He could lead but not inspire, yet he exceeded in ability and performance any Habsburg ruler from Ferdinand I to Charles the last (1916–1918) almost four centuries later.

The three rulers will have to be referred to frequently in the following pages. At this point in the discussion of Austrian foreign policy its engineers and executors should be introduced. Throughout the whole century from the peace of Aix la Chapelle in 1748 to the revolution of 1848 Austria had the strange fortune of having only two men in charge of her external affairs for more than three-quarters of that time, each for 39 years. Prince Wenzel Anton Kaunitz-Rietberg (1711–1794) was court and state chancellor from 1753–1792 and Prince Clemens Lothar Metternich (1773–1859) was in charge of foreign affairs from 1809 to 1848 and state chancellor from 1821 to 1848. Disregarding Metternich's frequently alleged evil influence on domestic affairs, which is usually overrated, the long tenure of these two men in foreign affairs turned out to be a good fortune for the Habsburg empire. It gave to its conduct in international relations the benefits of continuity, experience, consistency, tempered by pragmatism, and accentuated sometimes by brilliance. All these factors combined outweighed undisputed serious shortcomings as to breadth and depth of social outlook.

Kaunitz, unlike Metternich, was almost exclusively concerned with the conduct of foreign affairs. He had accumulated a rich diplomatic experience at the imperial diet in Regensburg, in diplomatic missions in Rome, Florence, Turin, Brussels, as delegate at the peace conference of Aix la Chapelle, and as ambassador to France (1750–1753), when Maria Theresa appointed him court and state chancellor. Kaunitz is generally considered the chief architect of the reversal of alliances in eighteenth-century Europe. France, the traditional enemy of Austria, became her ally, England her traditional friend the partner of Prussia, and Russia, previously a benevolent associate of English and Austrian policy, became the fighting ally of the Habsburgs. The reasons for the regroupment between 1753 and 1757 were manifold. French-English colonial rivalries in North America, English concern with Prussia's potential threat to Hanover as well as that of Russia to East Prussia, played a part, as did English-Russian commercial conflicts. Besides, the continental conservative powers feared the ambitious Prussian upstart King Frederick II; and personal considerations of the religious bond between the sovereigns of the two foremost Catholic powers and hatred of the established rulers against the cynical and unreliable Prussian king were also significant.

Among all these collisions of interests, the Austrian-Prussian conflict was probably not even the most important one. With the benefit of hindsight it is easy to see now that the outcome of the British-French struggle in North America settled by the peace of Paris of February of 1763 was of more lasting importance in world history than the war in Central Europe. What made the Austro-Prussian Seven Years' War the core issue of a conflict that involved five major powers, the Holy Roman Empire, and two continents as theatres of war, was something else than just the fight about a province, however rich. Consistency and seriousness of purpose on the Habsburg side were greater than those of any other of her allies or opponents. To Maria Theresa, Frederick II of Prussia was not just an adversary but the enemy, who had wronged her twice between 1740 and 1745 and had betrayed his obligations as prince of the empire to the memory of her father and to the future imperial mantle of her husband. In the succession war, other German princes, such as the electors of Bavaria and Saxony, had taken hostile stands against her but these were relatively minor conflicts and family quarrels, which could be patched up. But the fight against the ambitions of the great atheist and heretic shook all that was sacred in Europe, in Maria Theresa's eyes. She never forgave England the conclusion of the treaty of Westminister with Frederick in May of 1756, although this was actually no more than a nonaggression pact. England too had been a heretic power to Maria Theresa. Though the empress-queen was aware of the contingencies of Austria's great-power position, the war appeared to her, as the only one among European rulers of the time, as primarily an ideological conflict.

Nothing was further from Kaunitz's interpretation. The connoisseur and admirer of the French Enlightenment brought about a reconciliation of the conservative European powers according to terms highly favorable to the Habsburgs. A cession of Belgian territory to the French sphere of interests should take place but only after the reconquest of Silesia and after, if possible, the partition of Prussia was secured.[1] This would have given to Habsburg power the primacy in continental Europe, which she had not possessed after the reign of Charles V.

Habsburg's armed forces in this struggle, in contrast to the conditions at the time of the War of the Austrian Succession, had undergone comprehensive reforms. In the intervening years regular manoeuvres were held and the officers' training was improved by the establishment of military schools, especially the Military Academy in Wiener Neustadt and the Engineering Academy in Vienna. The Military Frontiers from which many of Austria's finest soldiers came, were reorganized. The artillery was made more formidable under the direction of Prince Wenzel Liechtenstein. The inadequate system of enlistments on the basis of estates approval of manpower quota by individual lands was now changed to a system of regular conscription by order of the central authorities according to needs. Basically the Austrian military system, as it continued to exist for more than one and a half centuries, was created under Maria Theresa, and it stood its test in critical times to come.

Yet Habsburg's forces fought most of the time with indifferent success. Frederick II had started the war—from a military viewpoint one of the few genuinely preventive ones in history—in August, 1756, by the invasion of Saxony, before the Grand Alliance was quite ready. Austrian victories, such as Hochkirch (1757) and Kolin (1758) under Count Daun and Kunersdorf (1759) under Laudon, in between Frederick's triumphs, were not of lasting strategic significance. Even the brief occupation of Berlin by Austrian cavalry forces in October, 1757, amounted to nothing more than a fleeting prestige success.

In comparison, Frederick's victories, though frequently likewise transitory, resounded as triumphs through a world, which sympathized with the underdog. His victories at Lobositz (1756) on Saxon territory, Prague and Gross Jägerndorf (1757) in Silesia, and above all Rossbach (then on Bohemian territory, also 1757) rated higher than the Austrian achievements. It did not matter that this success was scored against inferior French military forces and the feeble army of the Holy Roman Empire raised against the Prussian king as declared aggressor.[2] Europe became excited by the

[1] On the complex negotiations concerning the planned cession of the Austrian Netherlands, in part to the French satellite Prince Conti and in part outright to France, see Alfred von Arneth, *Geschichte Maria Theresias,* 10 vols. (Vienna, 1870–1879), IV, 390–397, V, 24–38.

[2] The Reichstag of Regensburg at the behest of Francis von Lorraine, the emperor and husband of Maria Theresa, branded Frederick as aggressor primarily on ac-

sensational war news; startling indeed, were the later Prussian victories at Zorndorf (1758) against the Russians, and Leuthen (1757), Liegnitz and Torgau (1760) against the Austrians.

Frederick had the advantage of the inner line of defense, and of the habitual jealousies within the coalition formed against him. Finally, his military genius was a major asset.

It is a commonplace conclusion that Frederick still would have lost had it not been for the windfall of the death of the Tsarina Elizabeth in January, 1762. It led almost immediately to the truce with Russia under the new tsar and admirer of Frederick, Peter III. In May of the same year, a few weeks before the new tsar's overthrow by his consort (Catherine II), he concluded a separate peace with Frederick II on the basis of the status quo. Russia's insufficient interest in the pursuit of the struggle had in fact been a weak link in the coalition from its start. Even weaker was the alliance with France in which military unpreparedness and incompetence of leadership played a major part. As for the expected French interests in the stakes Kaunitz had indeed overplayed his hand, which became apparent, when the Austrians failed to dislodge Frederick from Silesia. Accordingly, they did not cede their Belgian possessions. Thereupon in October 1762 the French withdrew from the war, to whose pursuit they had contributed little before. The French and Russian governments had participated in a large-scale, long-drawn-out war that ran so much counter to public opinion that it seemed in the long run hardly bearable even in the prerevolutionary eighteenth century. The age of reason, even under absolutism, apparently could not stand unlimited losses for problematical and limited benefits.

In an era where armies rarely exceeded 100,000 men because neither communication nor supply systems could handle much larger numbers, the higher population figures of the Habsburg empire as compared to Prussia were not decisive. As for territory, the smallness of Prussia was actually an asset in view of Frederick's strategy, which was offensive only in a military but defensive in a political sense. It had a single objective—to hold its own. Yet, after all this is said, the question still remains why a Habsburg empire superior in every kind of resource could not singlehanded bring the war against Prussia to a successful conclusion. The suggested answer is threefold. First, the Habsburg monarchy still suffered from the economic mismanagement under Maria Theresa's predecessors,

count of his invasion of Saxony and declared on behalf of the empire war against him (Reichskrieg).

whereas Frederick II had inherited a well organized economy. Second, the Maria Theresan administrative reforms had not been completed and certainly not succeeded to a degree that would bid well for a concerted war effort for years to come. Third, international relations had changed: Since the war had failed to strengthen the position of Russia, France, Sweden, or for that matter of any of the German princes, who feebly supported the alliance, an Austrian victory would have offset the balance of power. There was little reason to assume that Europe would have allowed Habsburg power to weaken Prussia seriously—let alone to destroy her—provided she would have been able to do so. The peace of Hubertusburg of February 15, 1763, concluded just five days after the more important peace of Paris between France and England, comprised these main provisions. Prussia would keep Silesia with the exception of the small southern part, that is precisely within the confines established at the peace of Dresden in December, 1745. Saxony was restored, and Frederick agreed to have the vote of Brandenburg in a future imperial election cast for Joseph. Consequently the following month he was elected in Frankfurt as Roman king and heir to his father as emperor. Emperor Francis, Maria Theresa's consort, died unexpectedly in August 1765, hence Joseph succeeded him sooner than expected. Unlike his father he became also coregent in the Habsburg domains. Had it not been for the Prussian approval, Joseph's succession as Holy Roman emperor would probably have had to be secured with some further concessions to Prussia. In this respect Frederick's consent to Joseph's election in the peace treaty had meaning.

Yet in substance Prussia's retention of Silesia represented, of course, a defensive victory of major proportions. It impressed contemporary Europe as much as posterity ever since. Though the extent of Frederick's spectacular success should not be minimized, in German and Austrian historiography it is frequently seen in distorted proportions. It is widely held that the struggle for the supremacy in Germany, to use Heinrich Friedjung's terms, began there and then and continued until it was resolved by the Prussian victory at Königgrätz in 1866. To a point this opinion is correct, but only to a point. By 1763 an all-out victory of Austria ending with the partition of Prussia had become impossible. Even if Austria had regained Silesia it would not have meant the end of Prussia and the end of the struggle for the supremacy in Germany. The conflict presumably would have continued in different form and at a different speed, but continued it would have.

More controversial is another viewpoint frequently argued, namely that the outcome of the Seven Years' War—taking a long-range view—had doomed the leadership of the Germans as the dominant national group in the Habsburg empire. Since reduction of the number and the economic strength of Germans in relative terms—so the argument goes—impaired Austria's position, Maria Theresa was forced to look for compensation in Polish, Ruthenian, and Roumanian territories. With this policy the possibility of Germanizing the non-German peoples within the Habsburg monarchy was lost. Austria was to become permanently a multinational empire, which eventually led to its dissolution.

This is an argument *post hoc propter hoc*. The loss of the fertile Silesian principalities, endowed with rich mineral resources and advanced industrial establishments, undoubtedly weakened the Habsburg empire, apart from the serious decline in political prestige. Yet the loss of Silesia by itself did not represent a major shift in the national composition of Habsburg power, which comprised at the beginnings of the Seven Years' War, exclusive of Belgium and Milan, fifteen million people. Fewer than one and a half million of them were inhabitants of Silesia and a sizable proportion of them was of Polish nationality. The acquisition of Galicia in the first partition of Poland in 1772 changed the ethnic composition of the Habsburg monarchy, but it would be an oversimplification to assume that Austria's participation in the partition was primarily dependent on the outcome of the Silesian wars.

These are the facts. When Joseph became emperor of the Holy Roman Empire and coregent of the Habsburg lands in 1765, the foreign policy of the monarchy became undoubtedly more dynamic and ambitious, though the empress and Kaunitz still controlled the brakes. Austria's and Prussia's interests as shown in the first meeting between Frederick II and Joseph in Neisse in Silesia in 1770 were focused on Russia's expansion in eastern Europe in general, and the Black Sea region and her sway over Poland in particular. Actually the Habsburg empire did not play a very restrained part at that time. A few weeks before the entrevue at Neisse Austrian troops had occupied the Zips district[3] as prelude of more sweeping territorial changes to come. This move preceded the Russo-Polish understanding concerning the first partition of Poland and in particular the Prussian occupation of northwestern Polish territories (West Prussia) by about three years. The occupation of the Zips had morally weakened the Aus-

[3] Legally, the Zips comitat, on the northern fringe of Slovak territory belonged to Hungary, but at the time of the Austrian occupation it was, according to the terms of the treaty of Lublin of 1412, for an undetermined period mortgaged to the Polish crown.

trian position, the Russo-Polish agreement did so politically. Now it had become impossible for Austria to hold back. The alternative would have been up to that point either an undivided Poland as Russian satellite or a partition between Russia and Prussia only. Either solution would have meant a considerable shift of the balance of power to the disadvantage of the Habsburg empire. Predictably, Maria Theresa yielded to the entreaties of Kaunitz and Joseph. Since Austria could not change the course of events, Frederick's prediction that the empress would pray and weep but eventually take, thus came fully true. All things considered the Habsburg empire complied with the standard course of prerevolutionary eighteenth-century power politics. The consequences, however, were far reaching. There was, first, the over-all effect of undermining international relations by an act of concerted piracy by three major powers while Europe watched passively. This first Munich helped much, in an ideological sense, to ease the way for later conquests by threat rather than use of violence.

Second, the domestic aspects of the partition were important. They must be seen in context with the acquisition of the Bukovina from Turkey in 1775, which connected Transylvania with Galicia. The cession of this land of mixed Ruthenian and Roumanian population was extorted from Turkey as price of Austrian mediation in the peace of Kuchuk-Kainarji between Russia and the High Portal in 1774. By taking Turkey's side cautiously and preventing a Russian annexation of the Danube principalities, Austria had actually defended her interests more successfully than some eighty years later during the Crimean war. The Habsburg monarchy, furthermore, could cash in on her diplomatic intervention and be paid by Turkey for an action which was as much in her own interest as in that of the declining Ottoman empire. This was perhaps the most successful single move in Kaunitz's foreign policy.

Third, the acquisition of Galicia, roughly within the confines reestablished at the Congress of Vienna in 1815, substantially changed the ethnic composition of the Habsburg monarchy. Austria was presented with the problems of territories north and northeast of the Carpathian mountain ranges, which in geographical terms were separated from the bulk of the empire. More important, however, were the social aspects of the problem. A population of inferior economic status was incorporated in the monarchy. Although the potentialities of its development were great, they were never made fully used, to the end of the empire in 1918. The annexation of Galicia, seen again in conjunction with the acquisition of Bukovina, added also formidable national problems to those gradually developing in the monarchy. Apart from the fact that now the German position was really weakened, the Galician Poles were part of a great nation with a powerful tradition of cultural-political independence. The ensuing problems could be adjusted to a degree but never solved within the confines of the Habsburg monarchy. There were other issues as well. With the acquisition of Galicia, the Habsburg monarchy inherited the national struggle between Poles and the Ruthenian branch of the Ukrainian people in the eastern part of the new crownland.[4] The social position of the Ruthenians was and remained poorer than even that of the poor Polish peasants. This inferiority extended also to political status. Unlike the Galician Poles, the Ruthenians were devoid of a class of aristocratic and minor noble landowners. Some strength, it is true, was added to the unsatisfactory Ruthenian situation in Galicia through the acquisition of Bukovina with a population of more than two-fifths Ruthenians. They had lived within the Hungarian southern ranges of the Carpathians (after 1918 called Carpato-Ukraine) ever after the thirteenth century. They had not represented a significant national problem. This came into existence only with the incorporation of substantial Ruthenian minorities in Galicia and Bukovina.

What was true concerning the emergence of a Ruthenian-Ukrainian problem applied to a lesser degree to a Roumanian. The position of the Transylvanian Vlachs was strengthened by the incorporation of the more than one-third Roumanian population in Bukovina. This in turn was bound to have an effect on relations between the national groups in Transylvania. The specter of a formidable national problem in conjunction with a social one—the absorption of peoples of different socioeconomic levels—was on the rise.

The ensuing German policy of Joseph II, reluctantly tolerated by Maria Theresa but supported by Kaunitz, has to be seen in the context of these events. As noted before, the outcome of the Silesian wars had not yet substantially affected Austria's German position. The acquisitions of Zips (1769), Galicia (1772), and Bukovina (1775) undoubtedly did. Yet the war of the Bavarian Succession (1778–1779) did not result directly from Austria's defeat in the Seven Years' War nor for that matter from any clear recognition of the national problems created by the acquisition of Slavic territory in the east in conjunction with the loss of predominantly German Silesia. Joseph II and Kaunitz followed rather a more sweeping and consistent but unwise Habsburg policy, namely that annexations in

[4] The Ruthenians (the name is a latinization of Russians) are understood here as the most western branch of the Ukrainian people, settled in the main in eastern Galicia but in part also in northeastern Hungary.

the east were all right but that they counted less than any territorial gains in the west. To Leopold I the French invasion of the Alsace was more important than the Turkish one of Hungary, to Charles VI the status of Parma, Piacenza, and Guastalla as crumbs of the desired and lost Spanish inheritance counted more than the possibilities of sweeping conquests in the Balkans. Joseph II, more sophisticated but also more ambitious than his grandfather and great-grandfather, did not underrate the significance of Austria's position in the east but believed, in accordance with the European value system of the time, that the Habsburg German position counted more. Yet Joseph did not wish to make a mere compensatory choice; he wanted to expand in east and west as well.

When the ruling main line of the house of Wittelsbach in Bavaria expired, Joseph on the strength of an agreement with the head of the secondary Palatine line claimed Bavaria for his house and sent troops across the Austrian borders. As to be expected, Frederick II opposed this expedition. It was not quite in the cards though, that Maria Theresa would restrict the Austrian action as much as she could. After some indifferent fighting in Bohemia, where dysentery and cholera took a greater toll than bullets, the war, much against Joseph's wishes, was ended by the compromise of the peace of Teschen in May 1779. It gave Austria the Innviertel between Inn and Salzach and enlarged thus western Upper Austria, but the major objective, the acquisition of Bavaria was not achieved. Joseph believed that Maria Theresa, by agreeing to this meager compromise, had abandoned him in the face of the enemy. Actually it is doubtful whether the young emperor and coregent could have secured a military victory over Frederick even in his decline. It is practically certain that he would never have been put in the position to take advantage of such a victory. The fact that peace was achieved through the "good" offices of France and Russia meant they would never have agreed to a clear-cut Austrian predominance in Germany.

Such change in the balance of power in favor of Austria is indeed, what the Austrian succession in Bavaria would have meant. The stakes were high and for that reason Joseph made another attempt to reach his goal five years after the death of the empress. This time he acted in a more circumspect way. He proposed not an outright Austrian aggrandizement but the exchange of the Austrian Netherlands for Bavaria. It would have meant the barter of an indefensible strategic position and in some respects also an economic liability for a great territorial and political gain, adjacent to the monarchy. Naturally Prussia opposed Joseph's policy again. This time Frederick's countermove was based on stronger foundations than power politics. A league of princes (Fürstenbund) was sponsored by Prussia and joined by Saxony, Hanover, and later by Mayence, Baden, Hesse-Cassel, and Thuringian, and other smaller German states. This association stood indeed on justifiable grounds when it opposed the domination of Germany by one power.

It is difficult to find many examples in history, how the foreign policy of a brilliant ruler, not a ruthless dictator, but a humane and rational man failed not just in some instances, but in almost all respects. This example is provided by the events in the decade 1780–1790, when Joseph governed in his own right. In international relations he still made clumsy use of the old devices of power politics, which alienated friend and foe alike. If his foreign policy had succeeded he would undoubtedly have been an enlightened ruler in the conquered territories; but foreign policy is not judged by ifs.

The offer to trade the Austrian Netherlands for Bavaria was in part promoted by Joseph II's resentment concerning the fetters imposed by the treaties of Utrecht and Rastatt of 1713–1714; namely the closing of the Scheldt river and hence of the port of Antwerp by the Dutch, and the Dutch right to man the Flemish barrier fortresses against France at Austrian expenses. Between 1781 and 1784 Joseph unilaterally revoked these politically humiliating and economically detrimental restrictions. Yet by 1785 he was forced to draw back in the face of vigorous Dutch protests supported by France. To a large extent this failure of an ill-prepared and ill-executed policy was at the bottom of the Belgian revolt in 1789.

As pointed out in Chapter III, Joseph was even more unfortunate in his Balkan policy. In the Turkish war of 1788–1791, into which Austria was drawn as Russia's ally, she had much to lose and little to gain as noted earlier. Much in prestige, resources, and manpower she did indeed lose until Leopold II, Joseph's successor, by the separate peace of Sistowa in August 1791 extricated Austria by a meager compromise. This peace caused Catherine II's misgivings. She felt to be let down by her ally, a resentment which in part caused the Habsburg empire's exclusion from the second partition of Poland in 1793.

The new emperor, Leopold II, could not have acted differently in the east. Within the Habsburg borders he found Hungary and Belgium in open uproar. The war against Turkey was going badly, the German princes distrusted Joseph and Kaunitz, and the French revolutionary crisis loomed as rapidly increasing danger on the horizon. Leopold's domestic policy is easier to judge than his foreign policy. In the former sphere his intention to preserve and gradually to extend the enlightened reforms is clear. In foreign politics most of his designs failed to materialize. This failure can largely be explained by the emperor's sudden death in March 1792. But there is also the added problem of his complex and introvert character, which makes evaluations of some of his designs difficult.

This much seems clear: the emperor wanted to have his political fences in Central and eastern Europe mended in the face of an expanding crisis in the west. This policy meant peace with Turkey in the southeast, an understanding with Prussia and Russia concerning Poland and, increasingly important, one with Prussia in regard to the French danger. As for Poland, the emperor's primary aim was to preserve Austria's gain by preventing an alliance of the two other partitioning powers against the third. He also wanted genuinely to support reform in Poland and thereby strengthen the country. This wish tied in with his enlightened domestic philosophy, but it would also serve its purpose in foreign affairs. In the face of the expanding crisis in the west, Russia and possibly also Prussia would be the chief—and as it turned out indeed to be the only—beneficiaries of a further partition of Poland brought about under the pretext of domestic unrest in the kingdom. This the emperor tried, unsuccessfully, to prevent.

Leopold's major concern was the French crisis. Like other enlightened rationalists he had observed developments in France in 1789 on the whole with sympathy. His feelings in that respect were not primarily influenced by the fact that his youngest sister, Marie Antoinette, was the consort of Louis XVI. He approved of Louis XVI's acceptance of the radically revised French constitution in September 1791 and considered still at this late point peaceful relations with France desirable and feasible. He did so because he basically believed in the philosophy and stability of the constitutional monarchy. Yet he did not dismiss from his calculation the possibility of dangerous developments. He had cleared the deck of most contested issues, suppression of the Belgian revolution, termination of the Turkish war, and mutual guarantee of the Austro-Prussian gains in the first partition of Poland by the agreement of Reichenbach in July, 1790. While all these weighty problems were in the foreground, the basic idea behind was to remove friction between the Central European powers to make a joint policy in regard to France possible. For Leopold this meant, if at all feasible, a peaceful policy.

Pressures mounted, however. The French Constituent Assembly seized the estates of great nobles in the Alsace, who had claims to imperial jurisdiction and protection. Treves and Koblenz became centers of French emigré activities under the leadership of Louis XVI's youngest brother, the Count of Artois, the proverbial political Kiebitzer, for whom stakes were never too high. Leopold kept these emigré activities under strict control and counseled his sister in Paris in their secret correspondence, that the king should take his new constitutional obligations seriously. Yet although the emperor looked with concern at the radicalization of conditions in France, he was resolved that if it should come to a conflict of unpredictable consequences, Austria must not go it alone. He considered the possibility of a joint warning of the European powers to France and came to an understanding with Frederick William II of Prussia at Pillnitz in Saxony in August, 1791, according to which the French crisis was declared to be a European concern. Yet only with British and Russian support would Austria and Prussia intervene. This qualification was well founded. It was clear that Britain wanted to stay out of a continental war and that Russia preferred to fish in the troubled waters of Poland, while her western neighbors were engaged in the struggle with France. This constellation served as additional reason for the emperor to preserve peace as long as possible. Even the alliance concluded with Prussia in February of 1792 was of an only slightly camouflaged defensive nature; it was meant to be a measured response to what the new French Legislative Assembly saw as provocation. According to its demands the emperor was to recognize the alliance of 1756 as still valid, even though conditions had changed radically. That Leopold wished for peace is certain. To what length he would have gone to preserve it, we will never know. He died on March 1, 1792, and within six weeks the French Assembly forced Louis XVI to declare war on the emperor's son and successor, Francis II (Francis I as Austrian emperor). Two months later, Prussia joined the war as Austria's ally. Again, it is uncertain whether Francis could have avoided this war; that he did not try as hard as his father to avoid it is a fact. More than twenty years of warfare followed, in which Austria fought not only the revolution but the remaining traces of the Enlightenment as well.

In August, 1792, the old state chancellor Kaunitz resigned in the face of the breakdown of his western policy. His concept of association with France had indeed never been fortunate, though he could, of course, not predict in 1756 the revolutionary course after 1788. What he could have foreseen, however, was that Austrian fortunes were tied to that of a declining power. Neither she nor France had much to gain from an association, which involved either party in problems alien to her main interests. The French Enlightenment, with which Kaunitz, Joseph, and Leopold sympathized, did not extend its influence in the political sphere, where Habsburg power had become tied to a brittle French absolutism. In the east, Austria had made admittedly remarkable though morally dubious gains in the second half of Maria Theresa's reign. Success in prerevolutionary eighteenth-century terms turned out, however, to become liabilities in the nineteenth. On the other hand, Austria's position in Germany was as yet by no means desperate although it remained contested. All in all, the Habsburg empire had retained its great-power position, which had been so severely tried between 1740 and 1748. Because of the unpredictable course of events it appeared as secure now as half a century earlier.[5]

B. The Reform era

Enlightened reforms in Austria stretch from the beginnings of Maria Theresa's to the end of Leopold II's reign (1740–1792). Under Leopold's successor Francis the reforms came soon to an end, primarily because a new period of armed conflagrations on a large scale had started. As the war of the first coalition against France in 1792 assumed from the start on the part of Austria and Prussia an ideological character hostile to the French Revolution, this meant also the rapid transition to a conservative and, indeed, soon a reactionary era.

Frequently the reform period is divided into two distinct periods. First, the Maria Theresan era, strictly pragmatic in character and adverse to the principles of a radical enlightened "superstructure." Then the era of Joseph II, a period of doctrinaire zeal, which, though not revolutionary, led to a countermovement in opposition to previous imperial actions. Leopold's subsequent brief reign of two years is frequently understood as an appendix to that of Joseph. According to such view its chief purpose was an effort to undo the damage brought about by Joseph's unwise haste.[6] Actually, Leopold's administration represented a sincere effort to save the substance of the reform legislation by modification on specific

[5] Good presentations of foreign policy are: Arneth, *Geschichte Maria Theresias,* in particular vols. I–VI, VIII, X; Hugo Hantsch, *Die Geschichte Österreichs* (Graz, various editions), Vol. II. In the context of general European policies, see Walter L. Dorn, *Competition for Empire, 1740–1763* (New York, 1963), Leo Gershoy, *From Despotism to Revolution, 1763–1789* (New York, 1944), and Albert Sorel, *The Eastern Question in the Eighteenth Century* (London, 1898), translated from the French, which covers the period from 1756 to 1776.

[6] See for instance Hantsch, *Die Geschichte Österreichs,* II, 256 f. Adam Wolf and Hans Zwiedinek-Südenhorst, *Österreich unter Maria Theresia, Joseph II, und Leopold II* (Berlin, 1884) pp. 326–329. Both authors argue their case well.

points. Retreat from an advanced position was to serve only as temporary means to prevent outright repeal. Resumption of reforms under more favorable conditions was indeed hoped for.

Such an interpretation is somewhat simplistic. In the first place it is difficult to see a clear distinction between the reigns of Maria Theresa and Joseph. During the war period from 1756 to 1763, reforms which were actively pursued during the brief spell of peace after the War of the Austrian Succession had come to a halt. When they were resumed Joseph had become coregent (in 1765) and while the empress still reserved final decisions for herself, he exercised considerable influence in foreign affairs, defense, legal matters, and to some extent also state-church relations. Yet beyond this Joseph was the chief counsellor of the empress on all political matters and his influence on the administration was unmistakable. After 1780 it became, of course, decisive. Yet, in questions of reforms Maria Theresa had not only listened to the often peremptory advice of Joseph, but also to the more diplomatic but equally enlightened counsel of her second son, Leopold, grandduke of Tuscany. It is often assumed, that Leopold, after he succeeded his brother, did nothing but withdraw cautiously from Joseph's extreme positions. This does not seem to be the full truth. Leopold did not merely intend to check the dangers of domestic revolution. After this was done, various plans of his indicate that he wanted to continue the reforms, an objective stopped only by his sudden death. Thus neither can Joseph's and Leopold's reigns be separated from each other nor Joseph's from Maria Theresa's. Therefore the whole reform era from Maria Theresa to Leopold is treated here as a whole.

The anti-ideological pragmatism of the Maria Theresan era was not only due to the conservative character and the religious devoutness of the empress. Austria's isolation from the intellectual evolution in the west played an important part. Maria Theresa probably could not have taken a position more in line with the political theories of the Enlightenment if she had wanted to; that she did not even want to is another matter. Pragmatic reforms seemed to be the order of the day in most major western and northern countries. It was a course favored also by domestic developments. After the peace of Szatmár of 1711 between king (emperor) Joseph I and the insurrectionist forces under Prince Francis Rákóczy II, the revolts in Hungary had come to an end for a time, although the wounds reopened so cruelly in the lands of the Bohemian crown in 1620 had never healed. Still, more than a century after the era of violent suppression, time had done much to take out the sting of the painful recollections of the past. Furthermore, despite Maria Theresa's intolerance, the era of the Counter Reformation had definitely passed and the time was ripe for reforms in the antiquated Habsburg empire. Besides, several factors which up to Maria Theresa's reign had impeded them had declined in significance. This meant greater possibilities for more centralization and integration than at any time after the administrative reforms of Ferdinand I in the sixteenth century. An efficient but basically conservative ruler like Maria Theresa could be expected to take a measured advantage of these possibilities.

a) THE PERSONALITIES

At this point a brief survey of the chief administrators and advisors of the three enlightened rulers is appropriate. Maria Theresa, some poor appointments notwithstanding, came out better here than her sons. Irrespective of her personal preferences she selected competent men, even though their political philosophy was on major issues opposed to that of the empress. It is evidence of her personal eminence, that she listened to the advice of men which differed frequently from her own convictions. This attitude applied equally to administrative and ideological matters. Joseph II, on the other hand, took far less well to advice, but where he did it was still that of the prominent advisers of his mother. It was one of his personal limitations to be neither a patient nor particularly tolerant recipient of counsel that might conflict with his own views. Consequently his administration attracted fewer outstanding men than that of the empress, partly in spite but also partly because of the fact, that he was undoubtedly a highly controversial leader himself. Leopold II, on the other hand, was like the imperial mother, more tolerant of the views of others. His reign was too brief to enable him to select a competent administrative staff and brain trust of his own. Yet Leopold like Joseph benefited from the slate of Maria Theresa's advisers.

It has been mentioned earlier that Maria Theresa's armies were never commanded by brilliant military men. One of her generals, her brother-in-law Charles of Lorraine, in the first and second Silesian war proved to be a disaster. Count Leopold Daun (1705–1766) commander in chief during the Seven Years' War,—a *cunctator,* but not a great one—was at best competent. There were some able generals of secondary rank in the field, such as Counts Otto Traun and Ludwig Andreas Khevenhüller during the first war period of the empress' reign, and the ablest of them Baron Ernst Gideon Laudon, during the second. He still served, though without any fault of his own unsuccessfully, in Joseph's Turkish war.

While Austria did not have the benefit of outstanding commanders in chief, she had able military organizers, such as Prince Wenzel Liechtenstein who improved the Austrian artillery and Count Moritz Lacy, who drew his lessons from the experiences of the Seven Years' War.

In the domestic field the score of administrators was better. Four supreme chancellors of the United Court Chancery of the hereditary lands, and after 1760 of the Bohemian lands, Count Friedrich Wilhelm Haugwitz (1700–1765), Count Rudolf Chotek (1707–1771), Count Friedrich Hatzfeld (1718–1793) and Count Heinrich Blümegen (1715–1788), were consecutively from 1753 to 1782 in charge of supreme administrative-financial, and in part also military and judicial matters. Before their appointment to the Court Chancery they had served in various administrative fields. Haugwitz deserves probably chief credit for the conversion of Austrian government from an estates-type structure to one partly based on a civil service system. This change applies almost equally to general administration, tax reform, and the underlying principles of the new recruiting system. Chotek was an experienced financial administrator. Hatzfeld a conservative bureaucrat, little affected by the aura of the Enlightenment, furthered, however, the centralization of the administration. Blümegen was a cautious enlightened reformer, particularly in the judicial sphere.

In education, the minister of state Count Anton Pergen and the Silesian canon Johann Ignaz Felbiger, the creator of the elementary educational reforms, distinguished themselves in the second half of the empress' reign.

Many gifted personalities from various walks of life and antecedents served officially only in secondary positions but were actually the brain trust behind the reform movement. Gerhard van Swieten (1700–1772) from the Netherlands, Maria Theresa's personal physician, was a circumspect, indeed brilliant advisor on higher education, censorship, state-church relations, particularly in regard to the sensitive problems relating to the expulsion of the Jesuits. Like Kaunitz, van Swieten represented the influence of the Enlightenment, in its moderate reform aspects. The same held true for the state councillor Tobias Philip von Gebler (1726–1786) a Protestant convert involved as much in cultural agenda as in the reforms of lord-peasant relations. Three professors of law played a major part in initiating judicial reforms, Paul Josef Riegger in regulating state-church relations, Karl Anton von Martini in reforming the civil law, and most important Joseph von Sonnenfels (1737–1817). Sonnenfels, descendant of a rabbinical family and converted in his childhood, was the gadfly and promoter of various major and minor reforms from the training of government officials, new economic populationist policies, revision of the police organization, humanization of criminal law and procedure, to the purification and supposed elevation of dramatic literature from the popular to the classical style. Sometimes excessive, often dogmatic, querulous, and vain, his comprehensive lifework was that of a great man. As much as Maria Theresa disagreed at times with his proposals and those of other reformers, she listened, learned, rarely rejected outright, and usually compromised. The results were uneven but often respectable and in regard to several issues admirable. Much of what has been transmitted to posterity as the Josephin reforms goes back to the initial efforts during the reign of the empress.[7]

C. Feudalism versus centralism in the Reform era

a) administration

The overriding issue and impact of the Maria Theresan reform period was the gradual ascendancy of the centralized government over the basically still feudal estates institutions. It was not a complete victory, particularly not in Hungary, yet it was lasting. The fact that the centralization process destroyed largely the power of the estates but by deliberate caution on the part of the government left the superstructure itself intact, may be one reason that major reforms survived in substance the reaction that followed the reign of Leopold II.

To be sure, curtailment of estates power increased in principle the strength of absolutism, and a despotic absolutism could benefit from this change as much as an enlightened one. In early nineteenth-century practice, however, things looked differently. The estates stood for specific group interests of the upper structure of society. Centralized absolutism, even of the most narrow-minded kind, such as that prevailing during the reign of Francis I (1792–1835),[8] was forced to establish at least a common denominator of these interests in the diverse Habsburg lands. Thereby the social outlook of the regime widened, particularly under pressure of external conditions, although it widened by necessity rather than by

[7] See also Friedrich Walter, *Männer um Maria Theresia* (Vienna, 1951); Frank D. Brechka, *Gerhard van Swieten and his World* (The Hague, 1970); on Joseph von Sonnenfels, see Karl Heinz Osterloh, *Joseph von Sonnenfels und die österreichische Reformbewegung im Zeitalter des aufgeklärten Absolutismus* (Hamburg, 1970). Robert A. Kann, *A Study in Austrian Intellectual History* (2nd ed. New York, 1973), pp. 146–258.

[8] Francis, as Holy Roman emperor, the second of his name, (1792–1806) and as Austrian emperor the first (1804–1835), will be consistently referred to from here on as Francis I.

virtue. Throughout the half century of the government of enlightened absolutism in Austria one might go further and admit that its political philosophy did not merely represent the common denominator of upper-class claims. It was bound to widen concern with the social strata whose interests had to be considered to some extent.

The rise of centralization during the reform era makes separate discussion of the lands of the Bohemian crown in the social administrative field hardly practical. Even the discussion of those of the Hungarian crown as separate entity is no longer justified in several major respects. It is characteristic for the era of the Austrian Enlightenment and the following conservative period under Francis I that the significance of the concepts of the separate historico-political entities of the Habsburg lands was in decline and the new one of ethnic-national political units not yet distinctly on the rise. Historiography has to accommodate itself to these facts, however, only in domestic policies in the widest sense. In that of cultural-intellectual achievements, specific national endeavors will be discussed in Chapter VII.

The basic reason why the estates system was drastically restricted under Maria Theresa's reign, was the defense needs in expectation of and throughout the long war periods. It became intolerable for the establishment, that the conduct of wars which threatened the existence of the monarchy would be dependent on the drafting of limited quotas of recruits at the mercy of the good will of the individual estates in various crownlands. The narrow self-interest of the noble estates controlled also the pursestrings in regard to military equipment and supplies. In most of the hereditary and in the Bohemian lands the empress, strongly supported by Haugwitz, succeeded after 1748 without difficulty to obtain estates approval for the raising of recruit quotas for a ten-year period (decennial recess). Within this period the ceiling of manpower needed and the appropriations necessary for their equipment were to be determined by the central government and not by the estates.[9]

Equally important as the political-military aspects of the innovations were the financial ones. The government was forced to tax the noble estates without exemptions and to charge those of the Church correspondingly. While burghers in towns and peasants still paid a relatively higher

[9] In some crownlands such as Styria, Carniola, Gorizia, the estates refused, however, to grant these rights to the administration for a longer period than for three years at a time. Yet the government obtained without much difficulty renewals of these so-called recesses from the estates in the individual lands. Only in one, Carinthia, was it necessary to introduce the new order by decree without estates endorsement.

land or ground tax than the nobles, a complete unloading of these taxes on the impoverished lower classes would naturally have yielded lesser results. These levies did not meet the governmental needs in any case and had to be supplemented by a kind of personal income tax, whose incidence was slightly more equitable than the old head taxes had been. Excise taxes on consumer goods and inheritance taxes (in lieu of which the Church had to pay an equivalent) likewise changed the social picture slightly in favor of the peasants and urban burghers.

These radical innovations outside of Hungary broke the back of estates power, and Maria Theresa saw no reason to alienate the first two estates further by doing away with the frame of the estates structure as well. In fact, in 1775 she established a new estates diet in Galicia, though by this time the bow to tradition represented no more than an empty shell of former power. In this respect, even Joseph II pushed the reforms in the hereditary and Bohemian lands further in form rather than in content. Whereas previously the highest officials were frequently members of the noble estates as well as of the evolving civil-service system, they represented now only the latter. The estates rights concerning approval of taxation were now eliminated by law, while they previously had been suspended by recesses. Under Leopold II the status of the diets, as it had existed under the empress' reign in the 1760's, was restored after cumbersome negotiations.

The centralization of the administration proceeded by trial and error. In the early stages of the reform the financial administration was separated from the general one, but after 1748 merged with it more solidly than before. On the other hand, the judicial administration was only in the supreme instance, not on the intermediate level, set clearly apart from the general administration. Definite progress can be seen in the division of the Court Chancery in 1742 in a Court and State Chancery concerned primarily with the conduct of foreign affairs and an Austrian Court Chancery entrusted with the domestic administration on the highest level. Only the council of state consisting of three aristocrats, three members of the lower nobility, and three professional expects (under Joseph four), stood above all these agencies inasmuch as the State Council represented all Habsburg lands including Hungary. On the other hand, the council served only as advisory body, although an influential one. Otherwise only the Commerce Directory, newly established in 1753, acted as agency for all Habsburg lands. Originally it was associated with the directory in *publicis et cameralibus,* in which the administration of the Austrian hereditary and Bohemian lands and also most of the financial agenda of the Court Chamber established by Ferdinand I were merged. They were separated again from the political administration with the establishment of the Bohemian-Austrian Court Chancery, an administrative body which served for almost a century until 1848. Under Joseph II, the supreme—and excessive—centralizer, a new merger of political and financial administration took place. Yet it hardly outlasted his reign. Under the following regimes the previous separation was restored.

The general administration in the crownlands was improved also. The so-called Representations and Chambers, after 1762 referred to as *gubernia,* were in control of political, financial, and military agenda under the direction of the Court Chancery in Vienna. Commercial affairs were directly subordinated to the Commerce Directory in the capital. The administration of justice on this intermediate crownland level was still perceived as branch, though a distinct one, of the over-all political administration. Again, top officials of the estates were at the same time officials of the administration. By way of this double capacity the gulf between central administration and estates government was smoothed over, though not basically changed. Under Joseph several gubernia were merged but this amalgamation, which ran counter to tradition, was rescinded after his death.

Chief motivation for all these reforms was greater efficiency of government. The humanitarian factor, so important in the evaluation of enlightened government, was secondary. But in the administrative reforms on the town and village level, the strengthening and protection of the rights of the underprivileged became a direct issue. Limitations of previous town economy meant here in the first place curtailment of the powers of the noble estates, the narrow self-interests of the guilds, and in the villages curbing of the arbitrary and ruthless patrimonial jurisdiction of the lords. The gubernia were to supervise town administration. Elected syndici and town clerks in chartered princely towns now required governmental approval, dependent on qualifications. The powers of the guilds to control economic expansion were curbed and the anachronistic prerogatives of the towns to take care of their own defense needs were abolished. Urban judicial autonomy was restricted. All these urban agenda came now under the control of the district offices (*Kreisämter*) which in turn were subordinated to the gubernia. These important and salutary innovations were strengthened and expanded under Joseph II, when practically the whole administration on the level of local government came under the control of the district offices. The emperor supplemented the reforms in an important way by ordering that the elected mayors, vice mayors, and town counsellors needed government approval in regard to their qualification and that magistrates and syndici had to come from the civil service rank.

Conspicuously absent under existing conditions was the democratic element in this new order. Elective office at that time meant election on the basis of a cast system. Only the municipality legislation introduced by Count Franz Stadion in 1849, but not permanently enforced until 1862, added at least in part the missing and decisive democratic element.[10]

b) JUDICIAL SPHERE

Less conspicuous were the efforts and consequently the success of the Maria Theresan regime in the judicial sphere. On the highest level of the *Oberste Justizstelle* in Vienna, the bench was divided into several regional panels, whose composition took cognizance of regional selection of judges. Otherwise the chief merit of the modest reforms was the drastic restriction of the patrimonial courts of the liege lords. Also hundreds of town courts, which exercized the *Blutbann* (the right to judge capital cases, in which a death sentence could be passed), lost this sinister priviledge. The reform intended to staff fewer courts with better qualified judges, who could curb the arbitrariness and harshness excercised previously by many courts of the first instance. The over-all objective of improvement of justice was only partly reached under Maria Theresa. But the specific aim of checking the judicial power of the liege lords within the over-all revision of lord-peasant relations, came close to realization under Joseph's reign.

Even though the emperor as champion of streamlined reforms was not sold on the idea of separation of administration and justice, he reluctantly yielded to the advice of prominent lawyers on this point. In general, progress under his regime in this area was superior to that of Maria Theresa. This characterization of progress pertained equally to the appointment of qualified judges, to the regular system of appeal in civil litigation from magistrate courts to the *Landrecht* (appellate level), and to the oberste Justizstelle as supreme court in Vienna. The number of

[10] Arneth, *Geschichte Maria Theresias,* Vols. IV, VII, IX, X; Eugen Guglia, *Maria Theresia: Ihr Leben und ihre Regierung,* 2 vols. (Munich, 1917), see I, pt. II, 313–340, II, pt. III, 1–59; Paul von Mitrofanov, *Joseph II,* 2 vols. (Vienna, 1910), I, 235–346; Adam Wandruszka, *Leopold II,* 2 vols. (Vienna, 1963–1965), II, 312–342; Huber and Dopsch, *Österreichische Reichsgeschichte,* pp. 246–259, 267–272, 386–388; Hellbling, *Österreichische Verfassungs- und Verwaltungsgeschichte,* pp. 287–294, 302–308, 318–323; Kann, *A Study in Austrian Intellectual History,* pp. 136–145.

courts in criminal jurisdiction was further reduced to one in each administrative district and one court of appeal in each crownland. This last wholesome part of the reform was partly undone after the emperor's death.

The chief difference between government in the judicial sphere under Maria Theresa and her sons pertains primarily not to judicial administration but to legislative codification. Maria Theresa did not take much interest in legal matters in general, which she considered beyond her full understanding. As for criminal law where the spirit of the Enlightenment in many countries came clearly into the open, she was opposed to changes not based on pragmatic expediency but on ideology. Consequently the legislative record of the Maria Theresan era in this sphere was deficient. Legislative commissions for the reform of civil law, criminal law, and procedure were set up in the middle period of the empress' reign. Yet the first, over-lengthy, but piecemeal drafts of a code of civil law were rejected by the ruler and the completion of new ones not strongly encouraged. Only in commercial law and the registry of transfer of lands was some progress made. Orders of criminal procedure in the Bohemian lands were amalgamated but the legislative main work of the empress' reign, the *Constitutio Criminalis Maria Theresiana* of 1769, despite the efforts of competent advisers, still closely resembled the spirit of the Carolina of Emperor Charles V in the sixteenth century.[11] In its time the Carolina was a progressive code; a new one based on similar principles after two centuries appeared anachronistic from the start. True, the system of government prosecution in matters of public interest was enlarged, but the inquisitory principle, in which prosecutor, counsel for the defense, and judge were all merged into one, was still basically preserved. All the barbarities of various kinds of capital and other physical punishment, based on torture as means of obtaining confessions, were preserved, contrary to the pleas of the reformers. Maria Theresa's objections to the abolition of torture were supported by the archbishop of Vienna, Cardinal Count Christoph Anton Migazzi. Finally, Court Chancellor Count Johann Chotek and Vice Chancellor Count Leopold Kolowrat-Krakowsky yielded to the chief advocate of the movement for elimination of torture and limitation of capital punishment, Joseph von Sonnenfels, who had the backing of the coregent Emperor Joseph and the qualified one of the supreme chancellor Count Heinrich Cajetan Blümegen. They did not win out against a reluctantly yielding empress

[11] Both codifications were meant to pertain to procedure, yet they both comprised a great deal of substantive law.

until 1776. The fact that Maria Theresa only slowly followed humanitarian reforms introduced already in Denmark and several German states including Prussia, was not due to any innate cruelty of her character but to her inability to comprehend the new thought that proof would be more convincing if based on a combination of testimony by witnesses and circumstantial evidence than primarily on extorted confessions.

This modern notion was, of course, fully within the intellectual grasp of Joseph who introduced a new order of criminal procedure in 1788, in line with the reforms wrested from the empress in 1776. Yet if Joseph was a humanitarian, he was one of a strictly utilitarian nature and his Code of Substantive Criminal Law of 1787, which did away with capital punishment substituted for it life sentences of hard labor of the most cruel kind like pulling ships or treading mills to give the government the benefit of a wretched criminal's toil. On the other hand, the egalitarian character of the new code with emphasis on humiliating punishment for crimes committed by nobles did much to break the class character of Austrian justice. An order of civil procedure, initiated under Maria Theresa, which left more initiative to the litigants than before, was introduced between 1782 and 1784; an order on procedure in cases of bankruptcy followed.

Joseph did not live long enough to see the enactment of the drafts of the planned Austrian code of civil law. This comprehensive codification, considered to this day the crowning masterpiece of Austrian judicial legislation, was not promulgated until 1811. Yet a marriage law, which reverted jurisdiction from ecclesiastic to civil courts and a new inheritance law were introduced in Joseph's time. So was in 1786 at least the first part of the Austrian civil code dealing with the personal status of the individual. None of these legislative works pertained to Hungary. Joseph's legislative reform for the hereditary and Bohemian lands and Galicia represented, despite some shortcomings, a proud and enduring achievement.[12]

c) REFORM IN THE NEW PROVINCES

Another undeniable achievement of Maria Theresa's and Joseph's reigns pertained to Galicia and Bukovina, whose administrations were merged with the Austrian-Bohemian court chancery in 1787 after a short-lived Galician court chancery had been dissolved. Not until 1849 was a separate

[12] Henry E. Strakosch, *State Absolutism and the Rule of Law: The struggle for Codification of Civil Law in Austria 1753–1811* (Sydney, 1967), pp. 1–163; Osterloh, *Joseph von Sonnenfels*, pp. 165–199; Kann, *A Study in Austrian Intellectual History*, pp. 181–189.

crownland administration permanently established in the Bukovina. Both, Maria Theresa and Joseph, but particularly the latter, tried to raise the Galician economy to the modest level of the neighboring Habsburg lands. Protection against the excesses of *robot* (personal labor for the lords) was granted to all peasants; immigrants were exempted. Immigration of peasants, particularly from south Germany was encouraged. They were granted tax exemption for a number of years and freedom from military service for their sons, received building material, and were allowed premiums for agricultural improvements. The settlement of craftsmen from other lands was also encouraged, and the internal customs duties for imports of (usually inferior) agricultural products from Galicia to the neighboring Bohemian lands abolished. Similar measures were provided for the peasantry in Bukovina, though here, unlike in Galicia, the great latifundia owners were not Polish nobles. The Uniate Church with her orthodox liturgy but Roman Catholic affiliation held most of the land. The Habsburg policy in Galicia and Bukovina to support the Uniate Church and her educational institutions and to a lesser degree the Greek Orthodox Church for the benefit of the Ruthenian Ukrainian population in the new eastern territories cannot be classified simply as *divide et impera* policy between Poles and Ruthenians. But undoubtedly the Austrian administration was aware that the Poles in the period between first and second partition presented a serious national and political problem, an issue that could not be found as yet in the relations to the Ruthenians.[13]

D. ECONOMIC POLICIES

The regime under the direction of the empire-wide Commerce Directory, established as early as 1741, pursued a mercantilist commercial and industrial policy, revised and somewhat refined by the doctrines of populationism. According to these theories, the wealth of the state rested primarily in its skilled labor force. It would be instrumental in achieving the old mercantilist aim of a big export surplus balance of trade, though in a more sophisticated sense than had previously been the case. Skilled labor was now considered a value in itself like previously bullion. Under Maria Theresa these objectives were pursued, partly by a system of high protective tariffs, partly by the prohibition of the import of luxury goods and an embargo on the export of various raw materials. A number of internal custom lines were abolished, but those between Hungary and

[13] Arneth, *Geschichte Maria Theresias,* X, 76–101; Mitrofanov, *Joseph II,* I, 252–268.

the hereditary lands, the Bohemian and the hereditary lands, and the Bohemian lands and Galicia[14] remained in force. The plans of the state council to put a completely unified empire-wide customs system into operation were never enacted. But after 1774 the crude embargo policies in regard to foreign manufactured goods were modified. They had killed domestic initiative and could do little to support an as yet still insignificant manufacturing output.

A sliding and more sophisticated system of customs replaced the previous regulations. Private and public tolls and internal customs lines, except those between Hungary and the hereditary lands, were now gradually abolished. Improvements of roads and of navigation on major water ways and expansion of the port of Trieste helped to further domestic trade. Under Joseph's harsh regime the government fell back on the straight prohibition of imports of many manufactured goods, not only luxury goods. Export premiums were now given to domestic manufacturers. Maria Theresa as well as Joseph believed in the validity of populationist theories, advocated in Austria above all by Sonnenfels.[15] Yet here the progress from theory to practice in a domestic economy with limited industrial output, a restricted interior market and a powerful tradition of crafts guilds, was limited. True, Maria Theresa modified the compulsory character of the guild system with its *numerus clausus* on apprentices and journeymen and Joseph lifted it in regard to some crafts such as textile weaving and metal works. Printing became now a free trade. Yet "free" under the Josephin system meant basically only the lifting of the *numerus clausus,* not of labor regulations (*Handwerksartikel*), which in their way were as restrictive as the compulsory regulations of the old guild system. In one respect, however, Joseph's attitude proved to be amazingly liberal in the classical economic sense of the term. Although a champion of state control in all branches of administration, he believed in private industrial enterprise as superior to government-operated plants. In practice, however, governmental controls were strong.

The results of all these changes were notable but not sweeping. The

[14] With the exception of the import of agricultural goods from Galicia to the Bohemian and Moravian lands noted in Section C: c.

[15] See particularly his *Grundsätze der Polizei- Handlungs- und Finanzwissenschaft* (Vienna, 1765). See further, "XXXX Sätze über die Bevölkerung" (first published Vienna, 1764), "Von dem Zusammenflusse" and "Von der Theuerung in grossen Städten." These three essays are published in Joseph von Sonnenfels, *Gesammelte Werke* (Vienna, 1787), Vol. X. Osterloh, *Joseph von Sonnenfels,* pp. 29–123; see also Kann, *A Study in Austrian Intellectual History,* pp. 174–181.

loss of Silesia included that of a blooming textile industry. It was to some extent compensated by the expansion of textile industry in Bohemia, Lower and Upper Austria. A new and prospering branch of the manufacture of fabrics was introduced into the western-most Alpine crownland, Vorarlberg. Glass industry continued to prosper in Bohemia, iron mining in Styria, lead mining in Carinthia, and mercury mining in Carniola. Laces, leather articles, and jewelry were produced in Vienna; in quality they rated high, in output they affected the national economy relatively little.

In the east industrial production was even more limited. Hungary had not recovered from the economic consequences of the long Turkish occupation. Here industrial output, apart from the mining industry in the north, was without practical significance in volume, though in regard to some textile and metal work respectable in quality. Basically Hungary was not a full-fledged economic partner of the hereditary and Bohemian lands but a source of raw materials imported at low cost. This achievement was brought about by the use of labor, cheaper even than that toiling in the west.[16]

E. Josephinism

The three fields of reforms discussed in this and the following sections—ecclesiastic issues, lord-peasant relations, and education—are ideologically more significant for the evaluation of the reform era than the administrative, judicial, or economic reforms. This statement pertains as much to the Maria Theresan as to the Josephin reforms because in all these fields important changes were initiated under the empress often supported, but more often prompted and rushed by the coregent. For this reason they are generally perceived as the core of the political program of Joseph II and, beyond that, as the political concept of Josephinism, which has played a major part in the history of the Habsburg empire ever since. At the outset of this survey of reforms in three fields, the concept is therefore briefly discussed, with emphasis on the problem rather than its initiator.

Josephinism in its beginnings represented the genuine reform spirit, in regard to content as sweeping as possible and brought about at the greatest

16 Gustav Otruba, *Die Wirtschaftspolitik Maria Theresias* (Vienna, 1963); Tremel, *Wirtschafts- und Sozialgeschichte,* pp. 230–318; Herbert Hassinger, *Der Außenhandel der Habsburgermonarchie in der zweiten Hälfte des 18. Jahrhunderts* and by the same author *Der Stand der Manufakturen in den deutschen Erbländern der Habsburgermonarchie am Ende des 18. Jahrhunderts,* pp. 61–98, 110–176, both in Friedrich Lütge, ed., *Die wirtschaftliche Situation in Deutschland und Österreich um die Wende vom 18. zum 19. Jahrhundert* (Stuttgart, 1964).

political speed regardless of opposition, in particular from conservative-traditional quarters. Both these aspects, scope and impetuosity, rooted in the tragic zeal of a man conscious of the precious little time at his disposal, got lost in the later evolution of the Josephin ideology. Josephinism froze into a political philosophy of rigid principles, lacking dynamic change and momentum. At the center of the original philosophy was the system of the enlightened police state: everything for the people nothing by the people. This principle, however, requires elaboration and qualification. First, it is to be understood in utilitarian-social terms. Second, it put a burden of enforceable cooperation on the people. The system required hard work, dedication, and the development of all skills which the individual potentially could acquire. This does not mean that this individual should forego initiative in the social-economic sphere. The emperor was opposed to a state industrial establishment and, though more in principle than in practice, favored private economy. This feature of Josephinism has survived though it is not generally associated with the emperor's ideas.

The eagerness of Josephinism to study, experiment with, and apply new ideas must not lead to the fallacious conclusion, that the political frame of such readiness was flexible. It was rigid and uncompromising. The notion that Joseph, had he lived to observe the French Revolution in full swing, might have endorsed democratic ideas, would be naïve. The core of the Josephin philosophy is the notion that only one man can rule and govern and that all those entrusted with the manifold tasks of government should receive their authority from him. This conviction was based probably more on personal experience with the narrow estates interests, the conservatism of his mother, and the court party than on abstract principles. Just the same, this concept of integral absolutism is also at the core of Joseph's fight for supremacy of the state against Church power. It had nothing to do with anticlericalism in the established sense. Recent research by Ferdinand Maass revealed that Joseph seriously entertained the idea of establishing an Austrian state church,[17] but this plan did not mean to the emperor a playing down of religion but rather the contrary: that its profound ideological importance required close association with and supervision by the state. Centralism was a means to that effect in this as in all other fields.

Posterity has preserved the concept of Josephinism in this respect in a somewhat modified form but has changed it in regard to Church-state relations. With the introduction of representative government in the

[17] See Ferdinand Maass, "Das Werk des Hofrat Heinke, 1768–1790," Vol. III of the author's *Der Josephinismus* (Vienna, 1956), pp. 3–137 passim.

Habsburg empire, which in its first phase was brought about primarily by liberal endeavors, it came inevitably to a confrontation between a Church opposed to liberalism, and liberal forces hostile to the ideological impact of the Church. Since Josephinism had also been opposed to Church power, a strange *quid hoc propter hoc* occurred. As F. Valjavec points out, "Vulgär Josephinismus" identified Josephinism with liberalism and anti-clericalism.[18] Liberalism needed an ally, popular in the Austrian tradition. The emperor, controversial in his lifetime but extolled as the champion of the people in the era of an absolutism without social and intellectual interests after his death, served this purpose. This historical error occurred probably in good faith, but it was an error of monumental proportions nevertheless and it has distorted the picture of Josephinism ever since.

More complex than the identification of Josephinism with liberal anti-clericalism was its association with liberalism in another field: nationalism. Between the 1840's and 1870's, the liberalism which exercised great—though for some time merely underground—influence in Austria was primarily German-directed. The German liberals perceived Joseph as a liberal of German national tendencies. This may be characterized as over-simplification but not necessarily as distortion. The Maria Theresan administration used German as the internal language of government outside of Hungary, where it remained Latin. No nationalist significance can be attached to this practice, which was only meant to be an adaptation of various customs. Italian and French had been widely used in the top circles of government of previous reigns well beyond the conduct of diplomatic affairs. In Maria Theresa's government, no purpose beyond that of expediency existed in the handling of the language question. This applied equally to the hereditary, the Bohemian lands, and Galicia and Bukovina.

When Joseph issued the notorious language decree of 1784, according to which officials in the lands of the Hungarian crown had to officiate in German instead of Latin he was in part motivated by expediency. The emperor was deeply convinced that the German language of administration and instruction served the best interests of all of his subjects irrespec-

[18] Fritz Valjavec, *Der Josephinismus: Zur geistigen Entwicklung Österreichs im achtzehnten und neunzehnten Jahrhundert* (Vienna, 1945, 2nd revised ed.), pp. 141–144. See also Kann, *A Study in Austrian Intellectual History*, pp. 136–145, 249–250. Eduard Winter, *Der Josephinismus und seine Geschichte* (Brünn, 1943), a left wing interpretation; and Ferdinand Maass, *Der Frühjosephinismus* (Vienna, 1969), a conservative one. See further, Paul Bernard, *Jesuits and Jacobins: Enlightenment and Enlightened Despotism in Austria* (Urbana, 1971).

tive of their nationality. Yet he held to that view not only because the knowledge of German among the educated classes was more widespread than any other save possibly Latin,[19] he believed also that German culture was superior to any other. As much as Joseph strove to learn about it and to further this culture in history, the social and the applied sciences, in education, and on the stage, as little did he know about the incipient Slavic renaissance and the Magyar literature of the Enlightenment. Joseph, in this sense, was at least a moderate nationalist and the ancestor not only of the German-directed centralistic administration of the era of Francis Joseph (1848–1916), but also of German claims for cultural predominance.

The primary factor in the evaluation of Josephinism is the state concept itself. The tradition of the Austrian bureaucratic state was Josephin in its demand for complete loyalty to an empire rooted in a German foundation. Josephin was also the tradition of tolerance toward minorities of religious or national affiliations. And yet the emperor's original intention was misunderstood here. When he issued the famous Edict of Tolerance (*Toleranzpatent*) of 1781 which abolished most of the discrimination against Protestants and the lesser ones against the Greek Orthodox, he had a different objective. To him the measures taken against discrimination meant the first step toward complete equality. For that reason he wanted minorities to be protected, whether he respected them as he did the Protestants or disdained them as he did the Jews. Nevertheless, he wanted to raise their standards after his fashion by legislation similar to the Tolerance Edict. To him, equality under the law to be decreed and enforced by an absolute government was not a matter of sentiment but of utilitarian rationalism. To the extent that this rationalism ran in many respects counter to the feelings of the majority of his subjects, the absolute character of government had to be strengthened. This applies equally to the egalitarian trend in his emancipation legislation for the peasants, where he had to face not the opposition of the majority of the people but the sentiments of the powerful upper-class structure of society. This

[19] No reliable statistics are available on this point. Yet it can be assumed that knowledge of German, as the language of communication among the better educated classes in the hereditary and Bohemian lands and in part of Galicia was wider than Latin. The knowledge of Latin, the language of the Church, of science, and in part of law, exceeded undoubtedly that of French, the language of diplomacy. Otherwise French was rather the language of high society than that of the broader group of well-educated people in the non-German Habsburg lands. These two strata overlapped only to some extent. Requirements to use German were to some degree prescribed also in Italian possessions of the Habsburgs.

striving for equality as a broad base of a rigid absolutism constitutes the basic difference between Joseph's and Maria Theresa's philosophy of government. The latter in the field of social relations was concerned only with gradualism, that is, a strengthening of the relative position of the lower classes. This ideology was opposed to the egalitarian character of Josephinism. It stood for equal and equally limited rights, both to be subordinated to supreme power. Egalitarianism and absolutism may have been a strange mixture even in the eighteenth century; in the nineteenth century, in the era of constitutional government, it appeared paradox. Just the same, it is the decisive factor, which differentiates the idea of Josephinism from that of mere adherence to the German-directed, centralized bureaucratic state.

F. Church-state relations

If we now return to the problems of Church-state relations throughout the reform era from 1740 to 1792 we have to remind ourselves that the issue in relation to the Catholic Church was primarily one of state control, secondly of centralism. Concerning the other denominations we are confronted by a different aspect of Josephinism, not yet found in Maria Theresan government: equality of men under absolute enlightened government.

If one keeps these guiding principles in mind it is easy to see that the main reforms concerning strictly ecclesiastic matters of the Catholic Church were initiated under the devout empress Maria Theresa. This means of course, that an antireligious motivation can be ruled out during her reign. The Josephin reforms were focused primarily on the status of nonCatholics, and on the monastic institutions. The first issue was only indirectly related to the position of the Catholic Church; as for monastic problems, new policies had already been initiated under the empress. Only in the relatively minor but sensitive area of liturgy did the emperor open up a new approach for a brief period.

The ecclesiastic policies of Maria Theresa like those of other devout Habsburgs, such as Ferdinand II, Leopold I, and her father, Charles VI, were based on the primacy of government control in Church-state relations, though not of Church organization. Added to this, under the empress, were economic considerations of the mercantilist era, further strengthened by populationist ideas. This meant prohibition of the export of bullion to Rome and prevention of such exports by state control of financial transactions of the Church. Measures of this kind had been decreed and at times enforced in the century-old struggle between medieval papacy and Christian rulers; new was now the government's concern, based on the neomercantilist populationist doctrines, not to divert skills from the production process by which the state was to profit. This meant specifically manpower that might be absorbed by religious orders and monastic establishments.

As for state control of the Church, the empress prohibited visitations of regular dioceses by apostolic delegates. Specifically also the inspection of monasteries by foreign generals of orders or their representatives was in disfavor. Under Joseph, bonds to the main establishment of orders abroad were severed. The approval of the sovereign for promulgation of papal encyclicals or diocesan exhortatory pronouncements pertaining to other than religious matters was required. Regulations demanding approval of the investiture of bishops and of the grant of prebends to canons in diocesan chapters by the sovereign were enforced. Clerical jurisdiction over priests in nonecclesiastic matters and of laymen altogether, was abolished. Civic consequences of excommunimations were no longer considered to be automatic but required now governmental approval. Much of this legislation had historic precedents, new was the vigorous enforcement. Reform consisted thus largely in methods, not in principles.

On the other hand, the dissolution of the Jesuit order, which followed that in Catholic countries such as France, Spain, Portugal, and Naples and above all the decree of dissolution by Pope Clement XIV in 1773, can hardly be considered part of the reform legislation. Here the empress ignored Kaunitz's warnings concerning the unwholesome political influence of the Jesuits as long as she could, that is until Pope Clement's decision had left her no choice. Part of the property of the order was now to serve the needs of secular education, part of it had to be spent for the wants of the former members of the order and the clergy in general. Many functions of the Jesuits in higher education were now taken over by Piarists, Benedictines, and other orders.

The empress yielded somewhat in lifting of censorship for enlightened literature on ecclesiastic matters. But she continued to reject the so-called Febronian doctrines (promoted by the auxiliary bishop of Treves, Nikolaus Hontheim),[20] which advocated a Catholic State Church independent from Rome. In doctrinal matters and those of Church organization, Maria Theresa followed the advise of the conservative archbishop of Vienna, Cardinal Count Migazzi, but she overruled him often when

[20] He wrote under the pseudonym Justinus Febronius: hence Febronianism. On Febronianism in Austria see Ernst Tomek, *Kirchengeschichte Österreichs* (Innsbruck, 1959), III, 356–362.

economic interests of the state were affected.[21] In this respect the weakening of Church power resulted from the tax reforms after 1748, which abolished the tax exemptions of the Church like those of nobility. Undoubtedly fiscal needs, unrelated to anticlerical intents, were decisive. Consequently the government in the early 1750's assumed the control, though not the administration of the property of the Church, above all of her vast land holdings. Under the influence of Joseph as coregent two decades later, the acquisition of land by the Church was made altogether dependent on governmental approval. Again in line with neomercantilist-populationist doctrines, the number of religious holidays, in which production ceased, was restricted. The taking of permanent monastic vows before the age of twenty-four was forbidden. The joining of monastic orders and convents was discouraged to prevent inroads into the labor force.

The empress reluctantly approved of these policies. The area where she was most stubborn and where her record was really dismal, was not strictly religious or ecclesiastic matters but the treatment of Protestants and Jews. In this respect Maria Theresa's position was more backward than that of her father and similar to that of her grandfather, the music-loving Leopold I, who yielding to popular superstitions and pressures had expelled the Jews from Vienna in 1670, an operation which did not keep him from continued efforts to do business with Jewish bankers.

Maria Theresa, more than a century after the Counter Reformation had run its course, did neither shrink from missionary activities among Protestants in remote Alpine valleys, deportation of several hundreds of them as late as the 1770's, and denial of graduation to Protestants at the University of Vienna until the last years of her reign. If she gave in, unwillingly and piecemeal, in these respects it was only due to a limited recognition that oppressive measures had proved to be totally ineffective.[22]

As for the Jews, the empress had inherited all existing prejudices and acquired some additional ones. Main rationalization for actions against the Jews was the charge of disloyal attitude at the time of the Bavarian-French occupation of Prague during the War of the Austrian Succession, a conduct that in essence did not differ from that of the nobility, burghers, and peasants. The response of the Bohemian population to the foreign occupation had proved that the counterreformatory suppression was not

[21] See Cölestin Wolfsgruber, *Christoph Anton Cardinal Migazzi* (Ravensburg, 1897, 2nd ed.), pp. 254–336.

[22] Grete Mecenseffy, *Geschichte des Protestantismus in Österreich* (Graz-Cologne, 1956), pp. 190–207.

yet forgotten; that of the Jews showed the reaction to a particular harsh kind of discrimination. Moving in the direction of least resistance, the empress ordered the expulsion of the Jewish population of 20,000 from Prague. Then, in an irate response to the protests of the magistracy of Prague and of the Bohemian estates, she ordered the expulsion of the Jews from all of Bohemia and of the major cities in Moravia. A camouflaged sabotage of the empress' orders on the part of the local authorities, based less on humanitarian than on economic considerations, forced Maria Theresa finally to backtrack on the expulsions except for those carried out in Prague already. But heavy indemnities were imposed on all Bohemian Jews. Their designation as "voluntary donations" added insult to injury.[23] It would be an oversimplification of the character portrait of the empress to say that this course of action betrayed cruelty and backwardness in an otherwise humane ruler, yet it would be just as erroneous to excuse such action by simple reference to the spirit of the times. Maria Theresa's treatment of religious minorities was not only contrary to the spirit of incipient enlightened reformists, but here the empress lacked the minimum of understanding, which some of her predecessors had shown even at the height of the Counter Reformation. This holds true for the attitude of Ferdinand I, Maximilian II, and even Rudolf II toward the Protestants, and of Ferdinand II and Ferdinand III toward the Jews. Maria Theresa's extreme bigotry was, indeed, a highly personal feature, somewhat out of step with the mores of the times, a trait which mars an otherwise attractive character in history. This conclusion must be reached, although she discriminated little against the Greek Orthodox Ruthenians in Galicia and Bukovina, and the Serbs in Hungary, who enjoyed religious freedom and for a long time also a measure of church autonomy granted by Leopold I.[24]

[23] Numerous Bohemian nobles who had paid homage to the elector of Bavaria were only censured by a brief banishment from the court in Prague and only a few outright rebels were punished. On the other hand some villages were destroyed, whose peasants had taken the proclamation of the new sovereign (Charles Albert of Bavaria, as king of Bohemia Charles V, as emperor Charles VII) seriously, that servitude would be abolished, if they would rise against their Habsburg queen. See in particular Arneth, *Geschichte Maria Theresias,* II, 220–249, 511–515; IV, 42–54, 510–511.

[24] Between 1786 and 1849 the Bukovina was administered as part of Galicia and not as separate crownland. Inasmuch as the Orthodox Ruthenians in Galicia and Bukovina and the Orthodox Vlachs (Roumanians) in Transylvania, were in their overwhelming majority unfree peasants, the question of religious discrimination for political reasons became hardly practical. As for the Serbs in Hungary the political motive to curb a Magyar insurrectionist spirit, played probably a major part.

Joseph's continuation of that specific policy was in line with his general attitude toward religious dissenters, identified for all times with the Edict of Tolerance of 1781. It secured near-equality to the Protestants and allowed even the conversion of individuals (though not of communities) from Catholicism to Protestantism. Such permission did not pertain to the Jews. However, by special legislation, not included in the Tolerance Patent, they were allowed now to settle in communities previously out of bounds for them. Numerous trades were opened to them and they were even admitted to university studies. On the other hand, they were forced to abandon various traditional customs and had to undergo a superficial Germanization process. This strange mixture of despotism and humanitarianism was characteristic for the Josephin administration. It did not discredit the emperor that he initiated these reforms, not because he respected the Jews as he did the Protestants, but because he considered their previous ways of life damaging to society.[25]

As for state control of the Church, Joseph's administration followed, accelerated, and strengthened the Maria Theresan reforms. In 1782, a governmental so-called spiritual court commission was charged with ecclesiastic matters, save purely religious ones. Joseph's attempt to simplify the liturgy following the pattern of Protestant Puritan austerity might well be interpreted as interference in matters of faith. These changes in a venerable ceremonial created more resentment than more far-reaching substantive innovations. Ecclesiastic legislation was now restricted to members of the clergy. Jurisdiction in marriage questions was fully transferred to the state. Likewise diocesan seminaries became now state institutions and parish districts were equated with administrative ones.

Joseph's reform considered generally as the most radical in Church matters was the elimination of monasteries, whose members spent a merely contemplative religious life. This meant the dissolution of some seven hundred monasteries and convents in the Habsburg lands, roughly one-third of all such institutions. The remaining ones were those engaged in education, caring for the sick, agriculture, and various trades. The income of the sequestered monasteries and convents was administered by the so-called Religious Fund (Religionsfond) and used to maintain and enlarge the number of parishes. For two centuries this fund, enlarged by other contributions, remained the keystone in the governmental system

[25] See Charles H. O'Brien, *Ideas of Religious Toleration at the Time of Joseph II: A Study of the Enlightenment among Catholics in Austria* (Philadelphia, 1969), passim. Paul von Mitrofanov, *Joseph II: Seine politische und kulturelle Tätigkeit* (Vienna, 1910), Part II, 711–727; Bernard, *Jesuits and Jacobins*, pp. 52–73.

of state-directed Church support. Again, Joseph's monastic legislation which helped also to put the remaining institutions on firmer economic foundations was primarily based on populationist theories.[26]

Although the emperor contemplated the establishment of an independent Austrian State Church, such long-range considerations hardly motivated his immediate actions. The independence of the Austrian Church was assured without a formal break with Rome, which might have had unpredictable consequences. Whatever Joseph's motivations, they strengthened the prestige of the Church in the coming European revolutionary period. They helped later to prevent complete popular identification of the Church with the coming era of reaction. In essence, the Josephin Church reforms were bound to stay, and when Leopold II, Joseph's prudent successor, retracted the changes in the liturgy and the governmental control of seminaries, he managed by these relatively small concessions to save the bulk of the reforms for the stormy times to come.[27]

G. Education

As for educational reforms, Maria Theresa deserves more credit than the more learned emperor. Both the empress and her son had reservations concerning the value of higher education, though not for the same reasons. Maria Theresa was opposed to the revolutionary influence of enlightened ideas; Joseph, in an empire of relatively low social technological standards, was like Peter the Great of Russia two generations before him, opposed to educational developments which in pursuit of uncontrolled free research would deviate from utilitarian vocational goals for the training of administrators and professional men. Even in regard to elementary schools for the children of soldiers in the military camps, Joseph objected to institutions which might undermine military discipline. He supported general education only to the extent that the material benefits for society were demonstrable.

In this respect the empress was less rigid as long as educational reforms would not affect the traditional sense of values of her subjects. This danger appeared remote in regard to elementary and intermediate education for the masses, more likely in secondary education for the higher classes, and quite risky in university education. Consequently Maria Theresa's educational reforms were effective on the lower level, of mixed signifi-

[26] Mitrofanov, *Joseph II,* Part II, 666–799 passim; Maass, *Der Josephinismus,* Vol. II, "Entfaltung und Krise des Josephinismus 1770–1790," pp. 63–126; Tomek, *Kirchengeschichte Österreichs,* II, 388–410.

[27] Mitrofanov, *Joseph II,* Part II, 799–801; Maass, *Der Josephinismus,* Vol. IV, "Der Spätjosephinismus, 1790–1820," pp. 3–26; O'Brien, *Ideas of Religious Toleration,* pp. 38–50.

cance on the intermediate one, and rather insignificant on the university plane.

Chief credit for the reforms of elementary and general intermediate schools deserves the prelate from Prussian Silesia, Johann Andreas Felbiger, who was called into Austrian governmental service in 1774. In a few years he accomplished much against considerable odds. Felbiger's reforms pertained to the hereditary and Bohemian lands, generally for schools with German language of instruction. They introduced three types of institutions, the one-year "trivial" (elementary) schools, at the parish seats in the country, which practically meant in all small towns, markets, and larger villages. Instruction was provided in the "trivium," reading, writing, and arithmetic. Attendance in general, was compulsory. Unlike in Prussia, the teaching staffs were not retired noncommissioned officers, but teachers trained in state institutions. A main school (Hauptschule) was established in every district at the seat of the district office. Here history, geometry, drawing, some more advanced instruction in German, and some vocational training was added. In the capitals of the individual crownlands "Normal Schools," which served as terminal schools for the urban middle-class children and also teachers' training institutions for elementary education were added. In no sense, however, could they be called institutions of higher learning. Education even to this limited extent was not free. It was financed only in part by the income of the sequestered Jesuit estates, liege lords, parish districts, and communities. But a small tuition was charged, and textbooks had to be paid for by the parents. These costs did not add to the popularity of the new school system, whose relative merits were not generally recognized.

As for higher education, the dissolution of the Jesuit order would have offered the government the opportunity to take over monastic institutions of higher learning and to introduce a modernized secular curriculum. These were, indeed, the plans of Maria Theresa's able minister of state in charge of educational reforms, Count Anton Pergen. Yet such ideas ran counter to the empress' philosophy. The monastic gymnasiums were merely transferred from Jesuit control to that of other, though generally more tolerant orders. The curriculum with its emphasis on the classical languages and religious instruction was somewhat expanded in favor of ancient and medieval history, geography, some mathematics, and German literature, but hardly any science.[28]

In university education, definite progress was primarily made in the

[28] See Eugen Guglia, *Maria Theresia: Ihr Leben und ihre Regierung* (Munich, 1917), II, 74–91; Arneth, *Geschichte Maria Theresias,* IX, 225–260; Brechka, *Gerhard van Swieten and his World,* pp. 111–146.

faculty of medicine in Vienna under the influence of van Swieten. Some distinguished appointments were made to the law school in Vienna, from which the earlier discussed judicial reforms reaped considerable benefits. Some scientists in astronomy, botany, and chemistry were appointed to newly established chairs. Improvements by occasional appointments here and there were still spotty and uncoordinated. Moreover, even limited progress was stopped, if not reversed, in the coming Franciscan era of reaction.[29]

Exceptions to Maria Theresa's policy of limiting the advancement of higher education were some special schools of higher professional training. The Maria Theresan Academy in Vienna, the famous Theresianum, established in 1749 for the training of young nobles for higher administrative positions in government has been mentioned. Other institutions were the Military Academy in Wiener Neustadt (1752) for the training of officers, the Oriental Academy in Vienna (1754) for the cultivation of political and commercial interrelations to the Near and Middle East, and the Commercial Academy in Vienna in 1770. Their purpose was to increase the efficiency of government, not to broaden and deepen its educational base. If anything the contrary was true: the ruling class should be better equipped to govern and command. Wider participation of lower social strata in the affairs of the state was not desired.

The same was by and large true for early Josephinism. Although Joseph increased the number of elementary schools and converted some gymnasiums into state schools, these benefits were offset by his dissolution of a greater number of such schools, because he could see little value in the old curricula and only a limited need for the training of future university students. In fact he reduced the universities of Graz and Innsbruck in status, because governmental needs could be met by those in Prague and Vienna. Like the empress, he opposed the appointment of distinguished scholars from Germany, not because their ideas were revolutionary as the empress feared, but because their maintenance would have cost too much. Strictly professional training within the country—studies abroad were forbidden by the empress for political and by the emperor for economic reasons—were conducted with prescribed text books and with no encouragement for nonapplied research.[30]

Censorship under Joseph was substantially modified as far as it pertained to cricitism of the government. The exaggerated campaign against

[29] Arneth, *Geschichte Maria Theresias,* IX, 156–224.

[30] Mitrofanov, *Joseph II,* Part II, 802–826; Bernard, *Jesuits and Jacobins,* pp. 168–178.

indecency hotly pursued by Maria Theresan censorship in belles lettres ceased as did the suppression of criticism of some religious institutions. Gottfried van Swieten, the son of Maria Theresa's enlightened adviser became the chief official instrumental in this respect. Now, however, though no longer under the label of censorship but of various other administrative licensing devices, the printing and therefore dissemination of doctrines not essential to governmental objectives was made difficult, if not impossible. Neither was there any progress in this respect during the brief reign of Leopold. While government control of educational institutions was somewhat loosened, censorship was tightened again and increasingly so under the following long reign of Francis I. Yet even before that time—and this is indeed a dark spot in the Josephin philosophy—utilitarianism had proved almost as stiff an impediment to intellectual freedom as conservative traditionalism.[31]

H. The peasant question

Maria Theresa's and Joseph's agricultural reforms were complex. Maria Theresa's policies were introduced step by step at different times in different territories. Depending on the greater or lesser opposition of the lords they differend also in content. Equally important, clear-cut legal concepts which would serve as precedent did not exist in this most important field of legislation. No doubt, obfuscation on the part of the noble estates was intended, yet the same was only in part true for the government. The failure to grapple successfully with the problem by the empress' three predecessors was more due to incompetence of their legal advisers than to ill intent. At the time of Maria Theresa's accession it was generally recognized that an empire with a predominantly rural population could not prosper, if social conditions of the peasants were miserable. The path from recognition of this simple fact to reform, however, was extremely difficult, because the main pillars of the throne, such as the landed aristocracy and to a substantial part the Church, were vehemently opposed to reforms at their expense.[32]

Basically, the peasants fall into two groups: tenants or dominicalists, who had a contractual relationship with the lord, which did not exclude, however, personal services; and rusticalists, a larger group, consisting of the hereditary unfree peasants settled on the lords' estates. Again broadly

[31] Mitrofanov, *Joseph II,* Part II, 826–832; Oskar Sashegy, *Zensur und Geistesfreiheit unter Joseph II* (Budapest, 1958), pp. 15–52, 153–176; see further, Hermann Gnau, *Die Zensur unter Joseph II* (Strassburg, 1910) and Kurt Strasser, *Die Wiener Presse in der josephinischen Zeit* (Wien, 1962).

[32] Arneth, *Geschichte Maria Theresias,* IX, 339–381.

speaking, the distinction in the status of these two groups was that between mere *Unterthänigkeit* and *Leibeigenschaft.* The distinction in English terms, approximating that between lord-subject relationship and lord-serf relationship is easy to comprehend in theory but before the Josephin abolition of Leibeigenschaft in 1781 in the Bohemian-hereditary lands and Galicia, and in 1786 in Hungary it was rather blurred in practice.[33] Before this legislation the situation was highly complex. The lord, even in his relationship to the "free" tenant represented the full authority of local government as he did indeed in a restricted sense even under Joseph and afterward until the revolution of 1848–1849. From this dependency followed the subordination of the tenants to the lords in administrative and judicial matters. In both respects this power was greatly restricted under the empress and even more so under her older son. Personal services of the tenant to the lord were an indirect consequence of the lord-tenant relationship. This obligation derived mainly from the fact that the lord had the whip hand because the manorial contract with the tenant could be terminated at the lord's pleasure. This particular oppressive device could not be used against the serf, whose relationship to the lord was permanent and hereditary. Here, however, other social and administrative pressures, such as special service obligations and exorbitant dues for facilities provided by the manorial estate, could be used at the discretion of the lords. Although the tenant was thus more insecure than the serf, he was in other respects in a better position, because, on the basis of a mere subject relationship (in distinction to serfdom) he had the freedom of movement and the freedom of marriage for himself and his children outside of the estate without consent of the lord. Finally, he and his son had the right to learn a craft without the lord's consent. Yet although the so-called free tenant had these rights in principle, he did not always have them in practice. They did not include even in theory, as was noted before, general exemption from personal services to the lord. Yet tenant rights implied at least that personal services were limited.

By and large Maria Theresa was prepared to grant to all her peasant subjects by approximation the status of the free tenant, endowed with freedom of movement, freedom of marriage without the lord's consent, freedom of occupation, but definitely not freedom from personal service for the lord as long as the peasant held manorial land. Were it otherwise, the empress held, the difference between lord and subject would disappear and anarchy would result. How much she was in earnest about this is

[33] By this time serfdom had practically ceased to exist in the Austrian hereditary lands.

shown by her response to the actions of those peasants in Bohemia who in return for a promise of abolition of serfdom in 1742 had paid homage to Charles Albert of Bavaria. Their villages were destroyed and one of the leaders of the movement was executed.[34]

Yet the empress wanted sincerely to restrict or modify serfdom, and, where she could (as in the crown domains), to change to mere Unterthänigkeit. She persisted in the struggle for these objectives all through her reign. Immediately after the end of the War of the Austrian Succession and in line with the tax reforms, a clear determination of the extent of peasant and manorial land was made for the first time. This in itself helped to check further arbitrary seizures of land by the lords. Patrimonial jurisdiction was restricted and gradually was brought under the control of the new district offices. The arbitrary fees imposed by the lords, as noted above, were not abolished but at least standardized. A so-called governmental, urbarial commission (that is, one dealing with lord-peasant relations) was set up to control excesses of the robot system. Between 1766 and 1775 restrictions had been enacted in Austrian Silesia, Moravia, Styria, and Carniola. Opposition of the lords was strong, but nowhere as obstructionist and vehement as in Bohemia, where the aristocracy, foremost among them the descendants of the counterreformatory soldiers of fortune endowed with the land of the old national nobility, exercised a reign of gross and often bloody abuse. Peasant revolts were suppressed and the leaders severely punished. It speaks for Maria Theresa that these riots did not spur her to further suppression but to action against the Bohemian lords. The Robot Patent of 1775 elaborated by further legislation of 1777 and 1778 restricted robot to a period of between one and three days weekly, usually the latter. Even this maximum of half of the peasants' working time, which allowed them hardly to till their own land, represented a considerable improvement over the previous situation. Actually the empress and the coregent found it difficult to enforce even the three days outer limit.[35]

In 1766 Maria Theresa succeeded in Hungary by a decree to have feudal dues determined. A regular system of appeal from patrimonial jurisdiction to the comitats courts was introduced and freedom of movement for the unfree peasants established. The large-scale government-

[34] See also note 23.

[35] Guglia, *Maria Theresia,* II, 347–357; William E. Wright, *Serf, Seigneur and Sovereign: Agrarian Reform in Eighteenth Century Bohemia* (Minneapolis, 1966), pp. 38–70; Edith M. Link, *The Emancipation of the Austrian Peasant 1740–1748* (New York, 1949), passim.

sponsored immigration of South Germans was helpful here; they were mostly Suebian peasants, who moved into the southeastern areas of Hungary, which appeared largely deserted after the Turkish wars. The concessions granted to these immigrants in terms of free land, cattle, building material, and tax exemption for ten years, made it necessary to alleviate the lot of the whole Hungarian peasantry at least to some extent. Compensatory concessions to the nobility were by implication the incorporation of the Banat of Temesvár (previously part of the Military Frontier) and of Fiume (Rijeka) as a free city into the constitutional frame of Hungary.[36]

The first phase of Joseph's agricultural policy represented a badly needed continuation of the Maria Theresa's reforms. The *Unterthanenpatent* of September, 1781, and legislation in November of the same year, had abolished serfdom formally in the Bohemian lands. Inasmuch as the decree referred to conversion of the status of the peasants in the hereditary lands and Galicia, this implied also the formal not merely the practical elimination of serfdom there. Formal abolition of serfdom in Hungary followed in 1785.[37] The patent of 1781 introduced also a constructive system of arbitration, first by the district office as administrative agency and, if its efforts failed, by regular judicial litigation between lords and peasants. In such proceeding, the peasants were represented by a governmental lawyer. Patrimonial jurisdiction in criminal affairs was now permanently restricted to petty crime.

Other aspects of the Josephin legislation were more controversial. In the first place, the land tax imposed on the peasants to the amount of about 30 per cent of their meager earnings—if community taxes were added even more—was still far too high. Secondly, the personal services for the lord were not abolished, though the restrictions on them were strictly enforced. Conversion of robot into monetary payments was encouraged by the government. The last step in this direction was the tax and urbarial regulation of 1789, according to which all personal services were to be converted to monetary payments of 17 per cent of over-all revenue to the lord, about 13 to the government, both together roughly amounting to the compensation for two working days. This last reform measure was rejected with almost equal fervor by lords and by peasants—for whose benefit it was intended. The peasants' violent resistance in

[36] Béla K. Király, *Hungary in the late Eighteenth Century* (New York, 1969), pp. 13–65; Henry Marczali, *Hungary in the Eighteenth Century* (Cambridge, 1910), pp. 204–211.

[37] Wright, *Serf, Seigneur and Sovereign*, pp. 71–150; Mitrofanov, *Joseph II*, Part II, 621–623; Marczali, *Hungary in the Eighteenth Century*, pp. 170–195.

Hungary is easily understood, if one considers that a rural economy, largely dependent on barter could not at the command of government be immediately converted into a money economy. The precipitate action drove many peasants into bankruptcy and desperation.[38]

No blame is to be attached to the emperor's intentions but his policies, based on an erroneous appraisal of the peasants' economic potentialities, lacked rational foresight. This criticism is not to be confounded with the cliché that Joseph should have acted more slowly. He knew that after his death there was not much chance that the reforms would be completed, and perhaps not even continued. In fact even the well-meaning and intelligent Leopold II was forced to restore the Maria Theresan tax system of the peasants and the regulations of her robot patent of 1775. Thus it is questionable whether Joheph should have acted at a more deliberate speed, but he might have abolished the personal service obligations altogether and replaced them by an installment plan of annual payments partly carried by the peasants and partly by the government. Thus the lords would have been indemnified for the use of the land, and the economic freedom of the peasants could have been established without ruinous obligations in cash payments at short order. It took the experience of half a century and a major revolution before these principles were enacted in 1848–1849. They were fully materialized only by additional legislation in 1853 and 1862. As it was, a good part of the Josephin agricultural policy went to shambles with other efforts of his tragic and noble reign. Yet success for the agricultural reforms even half a century later, at the time of the revolution of 1848, would have been inconceivable without his earlier endeavors.

I. Hungary and the End of the First Reform Era

Some facts about conditions in Hungary have to be added. In conjunction with other points they should explain more clearly why the reform period ended. The Hungarian estates system, confirmed solemnly by the empress in the War of the Austrian Succession, survived her reign in substance unchanged. All the more passionate was the national reaction—not confined to the upper classes—to the Josephin reforms after 1780. Social change and administrative reforms were substantial but appeared tolerable because they did not touch on the main interests of the establishment and on the traditions of the whole country. An important factor, relevant to all political and social innovation, were the conse-

[38] Mitrofanov, *Joseph II,* Part II, 586–621; Wright, *Serf, Seigneur and Sovereign,* pp. 112–164; Link, *The Emancipation of the Austrian Peasant,* pp. 139–151.

quences of the Turkish wars. Decline in the native Magyar population in southern Hungary by more or less forced emigration during the almost two-century-long period of the Turkish wars had been made up to a good part by immigration of Southern Slavs into southern Hungary; the same was true for Roumanian immigrations into Transylvania. The new settlements were welcome to the Habsburg administration, which considered the Magyar nobility as the primary source of political dissatisfaction in the Hungarian realms. Correspondingly Magyar immigration from western Hungary into the newly liberated lands was not encouraged. Instead, the government in Vienna, in particular after the establishment of a colonization committee in Vienna in 1766, urged immigration of peasants from southwestern Germany to whom land, livestock, and tax exemptions were offered. Besides, many estates, vacated during the Turkish wars by their former owners, were awarded to foreign, mostly German officers and nobles. The agricultural structure, therefore, in which the lower nobility had previously played a dominant part, changed now in favor of the big aristocratic landowners. More important for future political developments in Hungary proper, Croatia, and Transylvania, the numbers and weight of the non-Magyar population rose.

The change in the social structure is one reason why tax reforms like those in the hereditary and Bohemian lands could not be carried out in Hungary. The tax exemptions of the nobility, in which the big estates owners played a more prominent part now, remained untouched. This tax structure in turn hampered Hungarian industrial development. The Hungarian budget was separated from that of the other Habsburg lands, hence the government in Vienna had a good excuse to consider Hungary chiefly as cheap source of raw materials and agricultural labor. The Hungarian textile, silk, metal, and ore-mining industries, did not receive support comparable to that in Austria and the Bohemian lands.

The Hungarian education situation, however, was not very different from that in other Habsburg domains. Higher and intermediate education for the privileged classes (gymnasiums) was primarily under Jesuit control. After the dissolution of the Jesuit order and under the influence of the Hungarian Enlightenment, particularly strong in the east among the Protestants, reforms were initiated in the last years of the empress' reign. Elementary education was placed under government control. This meant that schools and public health care were improved on the village level. In intermediate schools instruction in French began to gain against Latin. In state-Church relations the empress pursued the same course in Hungary as in her other lands. She upheld the autonomy of the Orthodox and Uniate churches in contrast to her anti-Protestant policies. Yet the educational autonomy of the Serb settlements under the direction of the Orthodox clergy (as distinguished from religious autonomy) had to yield to state control.

In 1765–1767 Maria Theresa made an effort to improve the lot of the Hungarian peasants by decrees specifying the duties of the peasants to the lords. The freedom of movement and the choice of occupation for the peasants' children were introduced, provided the peasant had met his obligations to the lord. Considering the established interests of the Hungarian noble landowners, Maria Theresa could not hope for approval of such measures by the Reichstag—if she had called it into session. She refused to do so after 1764.[39]

She managed nevertheless to avoid a major collision with the ecclesiastic dignitaries and secular nobles represented in the Reichstag. She dissolved the administrative agency in Vienna, which controlled the Serb territories in Hungary. Moreover, as noted before, in 1777–1778 the Banat of Temesvár and the free city of Fiume (Rijeka) were incorporated into Hungary. Also the court commission concerning agenda of Transylvania, the Banat, and Illyria—the archaic and vague Roman terminology for the territory between Adriatic and northwestern Greece—was abolished in 1777. Its authority had been limited, but the elimination complied with the wishes of Magyar nobles.

Such measures, pleasing to the Magyar establishment, enabled Maria Theresa to put through others of a more controversial nature. The territorial autonomy of Transylvania was strengthened by full supreme governmental control of the grand principality under a Transylvanian court chancery in Vienna. Furthermore, the Military Frontiers—with the exception of the Banat of Temesvár—remained exempt from Hungarian estates control. The empress' policy to move into Hungary with her reforms, but not to move faster than in the hereditary and Bohemian lands, had thus proved successful.[40]

Maria Theresa's limited success, but still success, was achieved because she had confined her reform program. Joseph's limited but substantial failure in Hungary, was due to the attempt to disregard such re-

[39] Király, *Hungary in the late Eighteenth Century,* pp. 51–73 passim; Marczali, *Hungary in the Eighteenth Century,* pp. 170–195; Franz Krones, *Ungarn unter Maria Theresia und Joseph II, 1740–1790* (Graz, 1871), pp. 71–90; Lászlo Makkai in Ervin Pamlényi, ed., *Die Geschichte Ungarns* (Budapest, 1971), Chapter IV, pp. 218–235.

[40] Arneth, *Geschichte Maria Theresias,* X, 122–158; Makkai in Ervin Pamlényi, ed., *Die Geschichte Ungarns,* Chapter IV, pp. 227–235.

strictions. The emperor who refused to be crowned king of Hungary, because such historic ceremony would run counter to the desired goal of a unitary centralized empire, also did away with the ancient medieval comitat organization of the country. He replaced it by a division in ten adminstration districts under royal commissioners. This tragic Josephin reform curtailed the power of the local nobility and destroyed the potentialities of developing the comitat autonomy in a democratic sense. Less controversial were his reforms of the judicial organization. A regular sequence of appeals from the district courts to the courts of appeal and the supreme court—the Septemviral table—was organized. Buda became the permanent center of the judicial as well as the administrative system. Croatia and Transylvania retained a separate court system under the jurisdiction of the supreme court in Buda. The emperor also initiated two other salutary measures: the retention of the comitat courts below the district courts and the elimination of patrimonial jurisdiction in criminal affairs. The former measure preserved an important branch of local government close to the people, the latter abolished one of the most flagrant sources of class justice. Yet neither of these reforms survived Joseph's reign.

Of momentous significance, because of lasting importance at least in a technical sense, was the abolition of serfdom in Transylvania and Hungary between 1783 and 1785 and its conversion into a mere lord-subject relationship. These regulations abolished the restrictions on marriage, movement, and choice of occupation, but retained the obligation to personal service as in the other Habsburg lands. Conversion of these services into cash payments proved even more difficult in Hungary with its almost exclusively agricultural economy than in the hereditary and Bohemian lands. Indeed, the whole reform legislation was misunderstood. Opposition of the noble landowners could be fully expected, but that of the peasantry, particularly in Transylvania, caught the emperor unprepared. Seen from a long-range point of view it should not have come as a surprise. Restrictions on long-standing abuses kindle demands for their complete abolition. The Hungarian, and particularly the "Vlachs," the Roumanian peasants in Transylvania, could hardly be expected to understand the fine distinction between personal services resulting from serfdom and those from a tenant status as yet unknown to them.[41]

This lack of understanding was one reason for the revolutionary peas-

[41] Király, *Hungary in the late Eighteenth Century,* pp. 217–218; Daicoviciu and Constantinescu, *Brève Histoire de la Transylvanie,* pp. 141–166; Ladislas Makkai, *Histoire de la Transylvanie* (Paris, 1946), pp. 270–280.

ant risings which spread from Transylvania to Hungary proper. Another was the large-scale military conscription in preparation of the Russo-Austrian war against the Ottoman empire. The government ignored the traditional dietal and local patrimontial rights to pass upon the military quota. Besides, a greater number of Hungarians were recruited than during the Silesian wars of the previous reign. The new system of military conscription which in part was meant to protect the peasants against the arbitrary recruiting system of the diet hurt them in its first application more than the traditional order. Rumors spread that military service meant also abolition of personal services. Although the rumors were without substance, peasants generally believed them, which added fuel to fire or discontent.

Emperor Joseph had no time to bring his ecclesiastic policy in Hungary as thoroughly in line with his reforms in the hereditary and the Bohemian lands, as he might have wished. The dissolution of the Jesuit order had a direct influence, and the Edict of Tolerance and the monastic legislation in Austria, a strong and lasting indirect influence on conditions in Hungary. The visit of Pope Pius VI to the emperor in Vienna in 1782 thus pertained nearly as much to Hungarian as to Austrian and Bohemian conditions. Yet the papal intervention in favor of the status quo was of as little avail here as there.[42] As for education, the language decree of 1784 which required Hungarian public officials to officiate in German within three years would have less affected—if it had been put through—government on the intermediate and higher levels than the administrative institutions on the comitat level. There bureaucratic control was new, and this control exercised in German in the administrative as well as the judicial sphere appeared truly revolutionary. Directly this decree of fateful importance did not mean a restriction of Magyar but of Latin as language of governmental communication.[43] Indirectly, and in its long-range effect this act opened the pandora box of multinational discontent in Hungary. The psychological blunder of ordering the transfer of the Holy Hungarian crown to Vienna at about the same time needlessly incensed public opinion further.

Joseph undoubtedly intended his language legislation primarily as an expediency for a centralistic system. Secondarily, however, he believed by

[42] Marczali, *Hungary in the Eighteenth Century,* pp. 269–300; Krones, *Ungarn unter Maria Theresia und Joseph II,* pp. 107–110.

[43] Confidential communication on the highest level of government between Vienna, Buda, and Pressburg (Pozsony) had been transacted throughout the whole reform period in either German or French and without opposition.

implication in the superiority of German social and cultural institutions and assumed their entrenchment by law would work to the benefit of all his subjects. Such a philosophy was in line with the rationalistic premises of enlightened absolutism. It is also true that the emperor's language legislation, if we consider the mere linguistic, so to speak technical, problem, might have been workable. But this was hardly the decisive factor. Joseph was aware of the potential opposition not only of Magyars, but also of Croats and Vlachs, but he underestimated its significance. He did not realize that the language issue on psychological grounds was a spark in a powder keg. Naturally the emperor did not realize that his language policy was bound to fail in a political sense. In fact, with the benefit of hindsight one can assume that the national conflict would have come into the open in any case, in the near future. Joseph may have accelerated its outbreak by a few years. But the Magyars who represented after all somewhat more than half of the population of the kingdom as a whole would hardly have permanently accepted the Latin language of administration of the privileged nobility. It is equally improbable that gentler tactics on Joseph's part could have led to the gradual replacement of Latin by German. National questions in the multinational state can be compromised by expediency with greater or lesser skill for some time, but to assume that by some ingenious device they can be solved is an illusion.

The language decree created a wave of public indignation in Hungary against German customs and institutions in general and correspondingly an upsurge in national sentiments. These began to express themselves among the educated in Magyar, rather than in German, French, or Latin. Centers of resistance were the towns, yet the rural population became increasingly concerned, too. Here the opposition to the conversion of personal services into cash payments when no cash was available, the new methods of recruiting, and the seizure of grain for the armed forces in the following years fed the opposition. It abated only when the language decree was rescinded, shortly before the emperor's death and before it had been put fully into effect.[44]

Thus the main impact of the language decree was not the short-range opposition to a transitory measure but the lasting influence on the rise of nationalism, in particular in regard to the Croats and Vlachs. The

[44] François Fejtö, *Un Habsbourg Revolutionnaire: Joseph II, Portrait d'un Despote Éclairé* (Paris, 1953), pp. 262–267; Krones, *Ungarn unter Maria Theresia und Joseph II*, pp. 23–45; Lászlo Makkai and Istvan Barta in Ervin Pamlényi, ed., *Die Geschichte Ungarns*, Chapters IV, V, pp. 235–245.

language issue came to the fore here as a twofold movement, which merged soon in the same stream of resistance against the government. The support of Latin by the Croatian estates was directed less against German than against Magyar nationalism. With keen insight, they expected Magyarization to follow Joseph's Germanization. Opposition against Protestantism, primarily that of the Suabians in the Banat and that of Suabians and Saxons in Transylvania and in the Military Frontier districts, was only partly based on religious grounds and largely directed against German penetration in the South Slav territories. South Slav nationalism was not yet strong enough to represent its own case. It had to fight on the forefield of related issues, Catholicism versus Protestantism, Latin versus German, which meant actually Croatian versus Magyar nationalism. The general objectives of nationalism had become fairly clear by this time, though its specific targets had not yet been crystalized with equal precision.

In Transylvania, on the other hand, the century-old tradition of the three-nation state had led to more direct confrontations between the imperial government and the national forces. Throughout the reform era we observe here a steady increase of the Roumanian (Vlach) population, particularly because of immigration from the Danube principalities and a corresponding relative decline of Magyars and "Saxons" (Germans). Joseph had granted citizenship to the Vlach serfs, yet recognition as a fourth nation of equal legal standing with Magyars, Saxons,[45] and Szekels was still denied. The fact that limited concessions often are more irritating than none, referred to in the context of the peasant riots of 1784, is borne out by events in Transylvania. The merger of the Transylvanian court chancery with the Hungarian and the de facto abolition of the three-nation state did not diminish dissatisfaction among the Magyars, and ignited resentment among the Saxons. The emperor saw in the Saxons an anachronistic national group, whose public funds were now sequestered.[46]

The last phase of the Josephin reform regime in Hungary and its brief aftermath under Leopold II has to be perceived in conjunction with the crisis in Belgium. Joseph's anticlerical legislation in Belgium, similar to

[45] As noted before, the term Saxons in Transylvania in modern history stands for Germans in general and no longer specifically for Saxons.

[46] Henry Marczali, *Ungarische Verfassungsgeschichte* (Tübingen, 1910), pp. 113–116; Eugen Horvath, *Die Geschichte Siebenbürgens* (Budapest, n.d.), pp. 109–130; Daicoviciu and Constantinescu, *Brève Histoire de la Transylvanie*, pp. 156–161; Makkai, *Histoire de la Transylvanie*, pp. 280 f.

his legislation in Austria, had alienated a powerful clergy, though the imperial policy in this respect had apparently the tacit support of the urban middle class. Yet Joseph's further attempts to centralize in violation of the established rights of the provincial estates in Belgium caused general resentment among opponents and adherents of an enlightened policy. The emperor's readiness to barter the Austrian Netherlands for Bavaria was well remembered and did not endear him to either party. That he was forced to yield to the Dutch in the question of the encumbrances imposed by the peace of Utrecht concerning the barrier fortresses and the shipping on the Scheldt river, did not increase respect for him either. An open revolt supported more or less openly by the Dutch and underhand by Prussia was the popular reaction. An imperial offer to withdraw the offensive legislation came too late. In November, 1789, the estates of Flanders declared that the emperor had forfeited his claim to rule in Belgium. The imperial governor, Duke Albert of Saxony-Teschen, the emperor's brother-in-law, and the limited armed forces at his disposal were forced to leave the country. Reconquest, while the Austrian army was engaged in a sterile war against the Turks, was out of the question. Only after an armistice with the Ottoman empire was signed, and a general understanding with Prussia had been reached, could Leopold II restore the Austrian regime in Belgium on the basis of the status before Joseph's accession. The price for this understanding and a general termination of clandestine Prussian support of insurrectionist movements in the Habsburg empire, particularly in Hungary, was the renunciation of conquests in the east.

The Belgian crisis had glaringly revealed the weakness of the imperial power structure. The language decrees in Hungary had a long-range demoralizing effect on the country, and conscription and requisition of grain for the army fighting an unpopular war against Turkey had an immediately explosive effect.

The authorities could not cope with the violent response to these measures. By the end of January, 1790, Joseph then a dying man had to withdraw most of the reforms, save for the abolition of serfdom, the Tolerance Edict, and the monastic legislation. Even now he refused to convoke the Hungarian royal diet. He took his retrogressive measures only because of the danger of a Prussian-supported general insurrection in Hungary. The possibility of an overthrow of the dynasty and the establishment of a German prince as king of Hungary and satellite of the Prussian ruler seemed real. Joseph was equally loyal to the traditions of his house and to his commitment to the welfare of his peoples. He wanted to see the succession of his brother Leopold, grand duke of Tuscany, secured, in whom he saw a faithful and able executor of his ideas. Desperately sick, he called Leopold to his bedside to transmit to him the inheritance. But when Leopold arrived in Vienna on March 12, 1790, Joseph's tragic and noble reign had already come to its end. The great emperor had died, in deep desperation, on February 20.

The brief reign of his successor was no less tragic though not quite so dramatic. He was fully, indeed in some ways better, equipped than Joseph to expand and entrench the reform policies. Leopold was widely experienced as ruler in Tuscany, highly knowledgeable, with a judicial temper, although he lacked the older brother's dynamic energy accentuated in his image. This appeal strengthened Joseph's position in posterity, but it was no help in the specific crises which an enlightened sovereign of his rare kind had to face. Leopold's first task was to check open revolt at the price of some retreat on the domestic front. Considering his record as regent and the advice frequently rendered to mother and brother, there is no doubt that after he had successfully accomplished his immediate aim, he would have liked to continue the reform policy pursued by him so ably during his twenty-five-year reign in Tuscany. Before he could start with this second and to him presumably more important task, he died suddenly on March 1, 1792, to leave the execution of his plans to an unequal successor.

Leopold's first objective was to restore peace and order in Hungary. To that effect he called the diet into session and after long and tedious negotiations reached a compromise in 1791. Hungary was recognized again as separate country, though—with minor differences—subject to the same order of succession as the other Habsburg lands. Legislation was to be enacted jointly by king and parliament. Government by royal decree was made unlawful. In particular, the program of taxation had to be approved by the Reichstag, which was to be called into session at least every third year. Legal equality of Protestantism was recognized, and Latin was restored as the official language of communication. In response to Joseph's Germanization policy, Magyar was now to be taught in all schools. Serfdom was not restored but the conversion of personal services into monetary payments, withdrawn already by Joseph in extremis, lapsed until 1848. By and large, the status of the peasant in all Habsburg lands corresponded now to Maria Theresa's legislation of 1767.[47]

Leopold's success in his negotiations with parliament was partly based on a *divide et impera* policy between Magyars and the other Hungarian

[47] Wandruszka, *Leopold II*, see II, 273–290.

nationalities. In this sense he restored the Transylvanian three-nation state and the Transylvanian court chancery. An Illyrian court chancery primarily for the benefit of the Hungarian Serbs was established in 1791, but dissolved by Leopold's successor the following year.[48]

Leopold's concessions did not go far enough to initiate a reorganization of Hungary on a multinational basis but they sufficed to warn the diet that the new emperor was not entirely at the mercy of Magyarism. All this was done with circumspection and frequently in a roundabout way as fitted Leopold's temperament. The same attitude is shown also in his ambiguous attitude toward the radical republican aspects of the late Hungarian enlightenment, which frightened king and nobility alike. In fighting it Leopold saw nothing wrong in using an agent-provocateur system.[49] Although he was less than frank in his methods of government and not always choosy in his means, there is no reason to doubt the idealistic objectives of his reign.

In all major respects his merits were great. He established external—though highly precarious—peace and secured internal law and order. In the domestic field he came to an understanding with the establishment without abandoning Maria Theresa's reform legislation. Under prevailing conditions, this was an outstanding achievement. In fact he had preserved a substantial part of the Josephin reforms as well, in particular in state-church relations, administrative and judicial organization, and protection of the right of the peasant in litigations. Certainly the principles of the reforms were kept alive. Thus, the reform era ended in retreat but not in defeat. It was beyond Leopold's control that this "temporary" retreat continued after his death for two generations.

J. Foreign policy (1792–1815)

Throughout the war period which had begun with the war of the First Coalition against France in April, 1792, and ended with Napoleon's debacle at Waterloo in June, 1815, the Habsburg empire was the most consistent and, throughout much of the period, also the most persistent continental opponent of France. In this respect it hardly ever had outstanding military leadership and only after the war of 1809 competent diplomacy. Until the end of the war of the Second Coalition in 1801,

[48] An Illyrian court deputation, basically with the same functions, had been established by Maria Theresa, but abolished by Joseph.

[49] Wandruszka, *Leopold II*, II, 279–280; Denis Silagi, *Jakobiner in der Habsburger Monarchie* (Vienna, 1962), pp. 65–117; Ernst Wangermann, *From Joseph II to the Jakobin Trials* (Oxford, 1959), pp. 61–65; Király, *Hungary in the late Eighteenth Century*, pp. 196–197; Bernard, *Jesuits and Jacobins*, pp. 155–167.

Habsburg policy reflected Austria's determined stand against what appeared to the government still as revolutionary development in France. As result of the peace of Utrecht and the position of the Habsburg ruler as Holy Roman emperor, Austria during this whole period in its outlying possessions and appendages in southwestern Germany, in northern and central Italy and Belgium was more directly involved in a confrontation with French territorial interests than either Prussia or Russia. After this period and particularly after Napoleon's proclamation as French emperor in 1804, when the revolutionary scare had been laid to rest, the territorial aspects of the conflict became more strongly apparent. Now the issue was mainly a struggle for the balance of power in which Austria in the midst of the continent had high stakes, namely either survival as a great power or further existence as a middle-sized French satellite state.

The direction of the foreign relations of the Habsburg monarchy was at all times under the supreme authority of the new emperor Francis I (1767–1835), as Holy Roman emperor during the first part of his reign Francis II.[50] In moral and intellectual stature he was very different from his father and uncle. This did not immediately indicate a completely different philosophy. Francis had been raised in Tuscany in the atmosphere of the enlightened government of the then grand duke Leopold. He spent the latter part of Joseph's reign either at the seat of the emperor's government or as observer in the eastern theater of war. His hard taskmaster thoroughly indoctrinated him with the principles and practice of Josephin reformism. During the first years of his long reign of forty-three years he apparently seemed resolved to follow its patterns. But he was too small in intellectual attainment to comprehend the French Revolution in any other way than as a regime of terror and anarchy, whose traces must be wiped off the earth.

The regime of the Convention in France and the execution of king and queen in 1793, which he perceived exclusively in personal terms of regicide of a fellow sovereign and his consort (his aunt Queen Marie Antoinette), shocked him deeply. Another experience, the discovery of so-called Jacobin conspiracies in Budapest, with ramifications extending to Vienna and Graz, strengthened him in the belief that only a stern conservative and in many respects reactionary absolutism could prevent a regime of revolutionary terror in his empire. Actually the Jacobin conspiracy headed by the Hungarian Abbé Martinovic was a small-scale enterprise of relatively few intellectuals, suppressed with harsh measures

[50] See note 7 in this chapter.

in 1794–1795. A system of police spies and agents provocateurs, an unfortunate inheritance of Emperor Leopold, had led to the discovery of the plot. Francis took its lessons as he understood them to heart.[51] This meant that his personality from now on increasingly reflected the negative features of his two predecessors' absolutism but few of their outstanding qualities. Francis was as secretive and in some ways as insincere as his father and as authoritarian as his uncle. He lacked the genius, the basic humanitarian motivation of the uncle, the sophisticated expert knowledge and the skill of the father. Mediocre in ability but not stupid, he was, like most small men, suspicious of new ideas, that is, suspicious of advisers with original thoughts. Incapable to grasp complex ideas, vengeful against opponents, and petty in dealing with counsellors in particular those of great ability, he did not lack charm and superficial cordiality in personal contacts with his subjects. Neither did he lack shrewdness nor at times bureaucratic industry. Of the Josephin philosophy he retained the full belief in absolute government, in particular in regard to state-church relations and in his negative attitude toward the estates system. However, he dropped the last shreds of enlightened sentiments within a few years. Although this ruler had no respect for brilliance, he did not interfere with the work of competent civil servants, as long as he could be sure of their conservative leaning and bureaucratic habits. Brilliance of any kind, even of a highly conservative character was suspect to him, since it might turn into unpredictable directions. He asked for quiet conformism and not for public articulate approval.

This assessment is not contradicted by the fact that Francis drew on the support of brilliant men such as counts Johann Philip Stadion and Metternich, Friedrich von Gentz and Adam Müller. Stadion fell out of grace within a few years; Gentz and Müller were tolerated as subordinates of Francis' chief adviser Metternich; Metternich himself attracted Francis by strength of his devious and successful methods rather than by the brilliance of his concepts, whose pursuit was frequently misunderstood by the sovereign.

As for the conduct of foreign affairs, the young emperor parted with Kaunitz as early as the summer of 1792. The octagenarian was not yet convinced that an attempt at reconciliation with France was beyond

[51] Silagi, *Jakobiner in der Habsburger Monarchie,* pp. 128–131; Wangermann, *From Joseph II to the Jakobin Trials,* pp. 133–167; Bernard, *Jesuits and Jacobins,* pp. 155–167. On the relationship of Francis to Joseph II and Leopold II see Walter C. Langsam, *Francis the Good: The Education of an Emperor, 1768–1792* (New York, 1949), pp. 55–107. On the education of Francis see also Walther Tritsch, *Franz von Österreich* (Mährisch Ostrau, 1937), pp. 21–112.

reach, whereas he looked at the alliance with Prussia, the traditional enemy for half a century, with misgivings. Kaunitz' successor, Baron Johann Thugut, born as a commoner and never elevated to Kaunitz' high position in a formal sense, had rich diplomatic experience in eastern affairs. He shared Kaunitz' suspicions of Russia and Prussia, yet these feelings were overshadowed by his passionate anti-French sentiments. A champion of all-out antirevolutionary war, he had to quit in 1800 to make a more flexible policy possible. Formally Thugut was subordinated to Count Johann Cobenzl, who resigned, however, in 1793 because Austria's exclusion from the second partition of Poland displeased the emperor. He served later as ambassador to France. His abler cousin, Count Johann Ludwig Cobenzl, became his and Thugut's successor and was in charge of foreign affairs between 1801 and 1805. He had to share the responsibilities of office with the emperor's old "Ajo" (that is, chief tutor and master of his household as crownprince) Count Franz Colloredo, a man of little experience in foreign affairs. After Austria's defeat in the war of the Third Coalition, both he and Cobenzl resigned, yet during their tenure the switch from primarily antirevolutionary war to primarily pro-balance-of-power conflict had taken place. Count Johann Ludwig Cobenzl's successor as foreign minister from 1805 to 1809 was Count Johann Philip Stadion. Previously ambassador to the court in St. Petersburg Stadion was a man of outstanding gifts, perhaps the foremost diplomat in imperial Austrian history; he wanted to conduct a foreign policy, in this case a German-oriented foreign policy, in line with public opinion. However, he proved to be not in line with it but ahead of public opinion.[52] After Austria's defeat in the war of 1809 he was forced to leave his position to then Count Clemens Wenzel Metternich (1773–1859), former minister to Dresden and from 1806 to 1808 ambassador to Napoleon's court. In 1821 Metternich, prince since 1813, became court and state chancellor and was not only in charge of foreign affairs, but at least nominally of the whole administration until his forced resignation on the eve of the March revolution of 1848. Metternich's merits in foreign affairs and his deficiencies in domestic policies will be considered later. He put his mark on European history during a tenure of office of nearly forty years more clearly and in some ways more lastingly than any other Austrian statesman either before or after him.

As for military problems, modernization and reorganization of the armed forces had been an objective high on Joseph II's list of priorities, but short of fulfillment. Leopold, a ruler less interested in military affairs

[52] Hellmuth Rössler, *Graf Johann Philipp Stadion* (Vienna, 1966), I, 225–255.

than his brother had neither the chance nor the wish for sweeping changes in this respect. A few weeks after the accession of Francis the empire was plunged into war and now it was too late for orderly peace-time military reorganization. The troops lacked modern equipment, unity of command, and frequently proper motivation. The leadership up to the war of 1809 was with one exception poor and afterward mediocre. This exception was represented by one of the younger brothers of the emperor, Archduke Charles (1771–1847), a popular member of the imperial house and a knowledgeable and dedicated soldier. Even this true leader and strategist was no match for Napoleon's military genius. He could have accomplished more than he did, but the emperor, jealous of a close relative superior in ability and popularity, gave him only incomplete authority. This hampered all his campaigns beginning in December 1795 and including his tenure as commander in chief from 1806 to 1809. The war of that year terminated for all practical purposes his military career.[53] Although fortune denied Charles conspicuous success he improved the tactical training of the troops, and the education of the officers corps. His successor as commander in chief in the wars from 1813 to 1815, Prince Karl Schwarzenberg, a better military diplomat than soldier and his abler chief of staff, Count Joseph Radetzky, destined to a future spectacular military career in Italy, reaped the benefit of the archduke's reforms.

When the French Constituent Assembly forced the unhappy King Louis XVI on April 20, 1792, to declare war on Austria, this action sealed only a foregone conclusion on both sides by this time. It is certain that revolutionary France wanted to forestall armed intervention by a counter-revolutionary alliance. It is not so certain that Emperor Leopold, who concluded the military alliance with Prussia three weeks before his death, could have prevented the showdown. Yet when the French government demanded voiding of the Austro-Prussian alliance and Austrian demobilization, and the new emperor Francis asked for restoration of the sequestered estates of Alsatian aristocrats and for the return of Avignon to the pope, war became inevitable. Prussia joined the war only in June, 1792. Its conduct on the side of the Allies was hampered from the beginnings by poor motivation of the armies against the revolutionary elan of the French. The better French leadership played also its part against

[53] He held only nominal command as governor of the fortress of Mainz in 1815. See also Viktor Bibl, *Erzherzog Karl* (Vienna, 1962), pp. 226–242. On the relationship between the emperor and his brother, see Manfred Rauchensteiner, *Kaiser Franz und Erzherzog Carl* (Munich, 1972).

the indifferent Austro-Prussian command, headed by the duke of Brunswick. His manifesto of July, 1793, threatened the French people with destruction of the capital and terrible retribution against leading revolutionaries, if the life of the royal couple should be threatened. The duke with this act of political lunacy sealed not only the fate of the king, but made the counterrevolutionary character of the war obvious to every last doubter in France.

Yet if the duke's action revealed misguided zeal on the Allied side, a reverse spirit of ideological indifference was shown by the Russian-Prussian understanding concerning the Polish question. Emperor Leopold would have been willing to preserve the territorial integrity of Poland rapidly striving for enlightened reform within the restricted boundaries of 1772. Prussia, in violation of her treaty with Poland, wished to gain the area around the mouth of the Vistula with Danzig as well as Poznán. Prussia prepared herself for a possible confrontation in the east by stalling her war efforts in the west. Thereby she blocked Catherine II's aims of taking over Poland while the Central European powers were engaged in the west. Prussia's direct betrayal of Poland—supposedly her ally—and indirectly of the Austrian military alliance spiked such designs. Russia and Prussia proceeded with the second partition, while Austria had to stand on the sideline. Under Emperor Leopold II such abstention might have been intentional because the Habsburg empire would have wanted to become the friend of a reformed Poland. Under Francis, Austria's isolated stand was simply due to the fact that she had missed the boat in the new landgrab. Cobenzl, held responsible for this diplomatic defeat, was replaced by Thugut. Neither did France, the former traditional ally of a conservative Poland, and the hoped-for ally of a liberalized one, distinguish herself under the regime of the Convention in this sordid affair. The French government hoped by nonintervention in the Polish cause to appease Russia, a restraint understandable under political duress, but regrettable. Actually the sacrifice of Poland merely delayed Russian intervention, but as the war of the Second Coalition and, indeed, any kind of appeasement show, did not permanently prevent it.[54]

The Austrians with only limited Prussian support fought between 1793 and 1795 in Holland, Belgium, and on the left bank of the Rhine. In the fall of 1794 they had to withdraw to the right bank. The declaration of war on the part of the Holy Roman Empire and of Spain against France (March and April, 1793) changed matters little. Even the British

[54] William F. Reddaway in *Cambridge History of Poland* (Cambridge, 1951), II, 137–153; Sorel, *The Eastern Question*, pp. 264–266.

entry into the war in February, 1793, had only relatively little immediate effect. The British engaged some French troops in Holland and although the country could not be held by the Allies, this intervention gave them a breathing spell. When Archduke Charles assumed command in December, 1795, he forced a French withdrawal across the Rhine.

At this point two major new factors turned the fortunes of war decisively against Austria: the Prussian withdrawal from the war, closely related to the third and final partition of Poland, and the appearance of the young general Bonaparte in northern Italy. This strategy changed a secondary theater of war to the decisive battle ground. The revolutionary rising in Poland in 1794 under Kośziuszko's leadership was crushed by Russian and Prussian military forces. With this victory the conservative powers considered truncated but potentially revolutionary Poland to be doomed.

Doubt existed, however, concerning the question of who would get the lion's share in the final partition. Prussia, as the still smallest of the three powers felt again that she had to keep her hands free for the final barter in the east. With the fall of Robespierre in July, 1794, the revolutionary tide in France seemed to have turned anyway and thus Frederick William II, a cynical but shrewd politician, was ready for peace in the west. In April, 1795, the separate peace of Basel between Prussia and France was concluded. Saxony, Hanover, and Hesse-Cassel also dropped out. France pledged to evacuate the right bank of the Rhine and, according to a secret clause, Prussia would receive compensations by seizure of ecclesiastic principalities, in case the left bank should be subsequently annexed by France. Both sides considered the annexation a foregone conclusion, and in view of the peculiar political morale of the German princes in their complete separation from the spirit of German nationalism they were not disappointed. A speculation banking at the same time on French military prowess and land-grabbing greed of the German princes could indeed not fail. Frederick William II had also correctly foreseen the course of the Polish partition question. By a treaty of January, 1795, Austria had come to an understanding with Russia with the objective of excluding Prussia from participation in the planned third partition as Austria had been excluded in 1793. The peace of Basel foiled this plan. Prussia's armed strength was ready to force participation in the new partition, if necessary. In fact she gained the center of Poland including the capital Warsaw. Russia obtained Lithuania and part of Volynia, Austria an extension of western Galicia far to the north almost to the gates of

Warsaw.[55] She had little chance of developing these territories, which she lost again permanently in the peace of Schönbrunn in 1809. Her political prestige was certainly not enhanced by this transaction, but, more important, even limited Prussian support in the war against France—blocked by the Polish deal—might have prevented the catastrophe in the south.

The Austrian government perhaps wrongly believed that France was still in the throes of a domestic revolution but it was right insofar as the revolutionary designs in international relations had not yet ceased. The war was continued in the west with varying but not catastrophic results. Yet within a year, from March, 1796, to March, 1797, Napoleon Bonaparte unrolled the whole Austrian front in the south and his army, after spectacular successes (Arcole, November, 1796, and Rivoli, January, 1797), crossed the Austrian Alps and in western Styria came within 100 miles of Vienna in April, 1797. It was impossible to continue the war in the west and there was little chance now to defend even the capital. An armistice was concluded in Leoben in April, 1797, followed by the formal peace of Campo Formio of October 17, 1797.

Austria had to cede Belgium and Lombardy to France; the Austrian tertiogeniture, the duchy of Modena, had to be merged with the French satellite Cisalpine republic; the Habsburg duke of Modena was to be indemnified with the Austrian possessions in the Breisgau. Thus this part of the treaty could be considered a family affair. A more important, more cynical, though not exactly voluntary, deal on the part of Francis as Holy Roman emperor, was the secret agreement to the cession of the left bank of the Rhine in return for not yet clearly defined indemnifications of Austria. The openly agreed compensation for the immediate Austrian losses (mainly Belgium and Lombardy) was the cession of the eastern part of the Venetian republic, up to the Adige, including Venice, Istria, and Dalmatia.

The results of the peace treaty from the point of view of power politics could have been worse for Austria. Belgium, particularly after the insurrection of 1789, had little value for Austria and could not be defended under existing conditions. The same was true for Lombardy, though its strategic value was greater. With the territory of Venice east of the Adige (including Dalmatia) the Habsburg empire gained a wide area contiguous to its meager maritime possessions and as such, as it seemed then, doubly valuable. On the other hand, partition of the ancient republic be-

[55] Marian Kukiel in *Cambridge History of Poland* (Cambridge, 1951), II, 154–176.

tween Austria and the Cisalpine republic, a French satellite, was as cynical as the partition of Poland. This deal and the soon to be revealed arrangement about the Rhineland lowered Austria's political prestige even more than the military setback during the Italian campaign. This evaluation does not take into account the future serious implications in regard to the national question, which were to evolve in this politically sensitive area.

Emperor Francis, within five years, had contributed greatly to the weakening of the empire and had compromised the prestige of the house of Habsburg which in several ways had been strengthened by his three predecessors.

The peace of Campo Formio had settled nothing except confirmed that France was still a growing and dynamic power, whose nationalistic fervor continued to exercise considerable drawing power beyond her frontiers. This was shown by the establishment of the Roman and Helvetian satellite republics in March, 1798. In particular the abolition of the secular power of the pope created considerable resentment in Austria. Practically more important than the reduction of the status of the papacy were the results of the negotiations of the Congress of Rastatt (December, 1797, to April, 1799) in which France cashed in on the secret Austrian and Prussian agreements concerning her annexation of the left bank of the Rhine, which became now a reality. The subsequent wrangling between German states concerning the compensation resulting from the secularization of the ecclesiastic principalities weakened the empire further. The French drive and the fear on the part of the European powers of its by now more alleged than true revolutionary character made a further showdown in the near future inevitable.

The war of the Second Coalition against France was popular among the Austro-Germans as manifested by a demonstration against the French embassy in Vienna in the spring of 1798. Of the two leading powers in the new grand coalition, Great Britain was primarily concerned with the French expansion into the Netherlands, Russia later with France's threat in the Mediterranean focused on Malta; Naples, Portugal, and the Ottoman empire joined the alliance. The war began in December, 1798, but Austria did not get directly involved until March, 1799, when France, as preventive move in a clearly predictable conflict, declared war on her. Its first phase coincided roughly with Napoleon Bonaparte's Egyptian campaign. The second began practically with his coup d'état after the return from Egypt in November of 1799, and his subsequent invasion of Italy, after his army had crossed the Great St. Bernhard pass in May of 1800.

The campaigns up to that point had been fought with varying success in the northern Rhineland, Switzerland, and Italy. Beside the archduke Charles another commander, the colorful and experienced Russian field marshal Alexander Suvórov distinguished himself. Yet the unpredictable tsar Paul I recalled the Russian troops in December, 1799, because of Russian worries about British objectives, Austrian inefficiency, and the hope for a profitable understanding with France in the east. Russia's defection helped Bonaparte's further military success. His great victories in Italy, culminating in the battle of Marengo in June of 1800 led also to the collapse of the south German front, where General Jean Victor Moreau commanded, perhaps the ablest of Napoleon's lieutenants. Austria had to ask for an armistice. Peace was concluded at Luneville in France in February, 1801. It was agreed to by the Holy Roman empire or rather by now its remnants the following month. Actually the treaty affected the dying empire more directly than Austria. The revisions of the peace of Campo Formio, agreed at the Congress of Rastatt, concerning the territories left of the Rhine and in a general way the compensations of the German princes on the right bank of the river were determined and confirmed. Prussia, this time a *tertius gaudens,* benefited from these arrangements. Habsburg power was weakened in this treaty by the surrender of the emperor's position as guardian of the integrity of the Holy Roman Empire.

Austria herself had to recognize the French conquests in the Netherlands, Switzerland, and Italy. Tuscany, heretofore ruled by a Habsburg grand duke, was in substance converted into the French satellite kingdom of Etruria. In 1803, the former grand duke obtained Salzburg and parts of several south German bishoprics as compensations. Considering the extent of Austria's military defeat she had been treated rather leniently again, a fact to be explained by Bonaparte's chief concern with England and Russia. Austria's estimate of Napoleon as her chief enemy was never reciprocated by him.

A direct consequence of the defeat was Thugut's dismissal, which preceded even the conclusion of the peace treaty. He was blamed for his intransigent policy against France and replaced by the somewhat more flexible counts Johann Ludwig Cobenzl and Franz Colloredo. Archduke Charles as president of the antiquated Court War Council was now entrusted with the introduction of military reforms, whose beneficial effects however, could hardly have been felt in the war of the Third Coalition of 1805. In fact, aware that organizational shortcomings could not be corrected within a few years, and worried about the precipitate outbreak of a new war crisis, the archduke resigned in 1804. His warnings remained unheeded, when the following year Austria plunged ill-prepared into a new conflagration. Preceding these events were the protracted and unedifying negotiations of the Reichshauptdeputation of 1802–1803, the conference of the representatives of the princes of the Holy Roman Empire whose agreement, the notorious *Reichsdeputationshauptschluss* of February, 1803, determined the new territorial organization of the empire, after the left bank of the Rhine had been surrendered to France. The compensatory settlement of the claims of deprived princes was supposed to be an internal affair of the Holy Roman Empire. Actually it was regulated by Napoleon and his foreign minister, Charles Maurice de Talleyrand. Since Salzburg, the Breisgau, and part of the bishopric of Passau had been awarded to the grand duke of Tuscany and the duke of Modena, who had lost their principalities in Italy, Austria's sphere of influence was reduced by this deal, although she was in part compensated by the acquisition of the ecclesiastic principalities of Brixen and Trento south of the Brenner pass.

Over-all, the empire, and therewith Austria, were not hurt so much by the enlargement of Prussia, Bavaria, Württemberg, Baden, Hanover, and other German states, but by the fact that these transactions had taken place by French intervention rather than by imperial decision. The elimination of the ecclesiatic principalities and the reduction of the number of free imperial cities, which in principle, though not necessarily in practice, might have stood for progressive reform thus represented in the eyes of public opinion a national humiliation endorsed by a powerless emperor. On December 2, 1804, when Napoleon, under papal auspices, crowned himself emperor of the French, the signs were clearly on the wall: The dissolution of the Holy Roman Empire was fast approaching and Habsburg power would be reduced again to an association of diverse principalities—a kingdom of Bohemia, deprived of its proud historic tradition, an obstreperous Hungarian kingdom, and Italian possessions brought only recently and by barter under the rule of the dynasty. The cohesive and in part constructive efforts of three centuries might be lost in the face of the threat from the West. In this situation, more critical than the one in 1526, when the precarious new union of the Austro-German-Bohemian-Hungarian lands was backed by the vigor and wealth of a rising Spanish empire, Francis decided to forestall the danger of pending disintegration.

If he could not restore the cohesion of Habsburg power by military force he hoped to save it by political devices. On August 14, 1804, he proclaimed himself emperor of a newly established Austrian empire. The charters, rights, and privileges of his lands, in the first place Hungary, should not be impaired by this declaration made to a conference of Austrian dignitaries. A unilateral act of this kind had neither the authority of genuine constitutional government nor the tradition of the thousand-year-old Holy Roman Empire behind it. Moreover it was legally doubtful whether the emperor could on his own initiative join imperial territory—the hereditary and Bohemian lands—to a new empire. Yet considering French pressure and the egoistic policies of the German princes, the imperial action had as much justification as the Pragmatic Sanction promoted by Francis' great-grandfather Charles VI. The proclamation of 1804 could no more prevent further collisions with France and German princes than the Pragmatic Sanction could prevent the War of the Austrian Succession, but at least it did not have to be paid for in political concessions to other countries. Thus, to a limited degree, it served the purpose of preserving the image of Habsburg power.[56]

Austria's participation in the war of the Third Coalition against France did not. True, she had concluded an alliance with Russia in November, 1804, and had gained some further protection by joining a Russo-British alliance system in August, 1805. Furthermore, open conflict could probably not have been avoided after Napoleon at about the same time had demanded the withdrawal of Austrian troops from Venetian and Tyrolian territories. Yet there may have been a possibility, that the war for which Austria was not yet ready could have been put off until Prussia would join the alliance. The course of action taken ruled out the practicability of Prussian participation, which would have been essential for military success.

In early September hostilities began. This time the archduke Charles, whose criticism had dismayed the emperor, was given only a minor command in Italy, commander in chief in Germany was General Karl Mack von Leiberich. One of the poorest military leaders in Austrian history, he was court-martialed after the war for lack of fighting spirit, when he capitulated at Ulm in Württemberg.[57] Considering the formidable coalition of French, southern, and western German states under Napoleon's leadership and the cautious strategy of the Russian commander Prince Kutuzov, even a better man would not have succeeded

[56] See Robert A. Kann, *Das Nationalitätenproblem der Habsburgermonarchie* (Graz-Cologne, 1964) and the literature cited there, I, 25–30, 346–349; Josef Redlich, *Das österreichische Staats- und Reichsproblem* (Leipzig, 1920), I, 42–45.

[57] Mack was reprieved later and in 1819 restored to his former rank. The emperor, always harsh in questions of too independent a judgment by subordinates, showed much understanding for incompetence.

in the long run where Mack had failed. The allied armies in Germany were soon in steady retreat. Northern Italy had to be evacuated, but the troops withdrawn there to defend Vienna came too late. The French entered the capital on November 13 after a campaign of barely three months. Napoleon, received by the Viennese population more as a celebrity than as an enemy, established his headquarters at Schönbrunn palace. His spectacular triumph did not yet mean the end of the war. In the three emperors' battle of Austerlitz in Moravia, fought December 2, on the first anniversary of Napoleon's coronation, he routed in one morning the joint Austrian and Russian armies. The defeat seems to have been more due to the precipitate action of Tsar Alexander than to the hesitation of Emperor Francis. The Russians under Kutuzov's leadership managed a retreat to their home base in fairly good order, but the Austrians were completely routed and had to sue for an immediate armistice. Three weeks later they had to accept the peace terms dictated by Napoleon at Pressburg (Pozsony). This time the peace was harsh. Austria had to cede the Venetian territories gained at the peace of Campo Formio, which made her practically a landlocked country. Napoleon was recognized as king of Italy. Yet more humiliating and painful were the terms which at the French emperor's command had to be conceded to his German satellites. Bavaria and Württemberg were raised to kingdoms. Together with the grand duchy of Baden they were to share the spoils of the Austrian Vorlande in southwestern Germany. Bavaria, furthermore, secured Tyrol, Vorarlberg, the territories of the rich western bishoprics Burgau, Eichstädt, Lindau, Passau, and the southern part of Brixen and Trento. The acquisition of Salzburg and Berchtesgaden by Austria represented only a pitiable compensation for her formidable losses in the German-speaking southwest. Austria had ceased to be a great power but, unlike Prussia after her downfall less than a year later, she retained at least her independence in domestic affairs. Compared with Britain and Russia, Habsburg's European power position had become critical.[58]

Nevertheless, some changes in domestic policies signified possibilities of change for the better. Archduke Charles and the emperor's youngest brother, the relatively progressive John, were entrusted now with the continuation of military reform. Count Johann Philip Stadion, previously ambassador to St. Petersburg, was appointed minister of foreign affairs. Whether Stadion's policy served the best interest of Austria is doubtful, but he and the emperor's two brothers now in important positions introduced a broader outlook than the outstanding Austrian civil servants

[58] See Rudolfine von Oer, *Der Friede von Pressburg* (Münster, 1965).

under Maria Theresa. All three looked for the support of "public opinion," which, considering the tradition of the Habsburg monarchy, its affiliation with the Holy Roman Empire, and the elimination of Prussia as active factor in Central European politics, meant to them German public opinion. They believed it was Austria's mission to rally the German nation in the struggle against Napoleon, to them the dictatorial apostle of violence in external affairs, but no longer as previously pictured the threat and herald of revolution. A somewhat more liberal spirit, though one tinged distinctly with German nationalist overtones, governed Austria for the next four years.[59]

To a point this spirit was a reaction to the consequences of the peace of Pressburg, which gradually revealed themselves in their full seriousness. In July, 1806, Napoleon established the Confederation of the Rhine, comprising the major states in western and southern Germany, not including of course Austria and Prussia. Other princes in central Germany joined the confederation subsequently. The proclamation of the princes denounced the Holy Roman Empire and requested Francis to abdicate as Roman emperor. On August 6, 1806, he was forced to oblige. It is a moot point to discuss, whether the abdication of the emperor meant legally also the dissolution of the empire, because no statute or tradition existed that governed the process of dissolution.[60] The empire had come to an end permanently because the German Confederation of 1815, the so-called Second Empire of 1871, and Hitler's shameful Third Reich, represented no revival but very different concepts. The end of the empire also meant that irrespective of future developments the Habsburgs were deprived of an ancient and proud association which linked them to the core of western political and religious tradition. Of ever greater psychological impact than the establishment of the French-dominated satellite Confederation of the Rhine was the crushing defeat of Prussia in October, 1806, in less than a month and against only feeble resistance. The pride of German nationalism was deeply wounded, the demand for domestic reform was now openly raised, and the desire for termination of appeasement of the foreign conqueror expressed more secretly but even more passionately. Inevitable submission to Napoleon's demand of 1808 that Austria join in the Continental Blockade of England strengthened this desire.

[59] Rössler, *Graf Johann Philipp Stadion,* II, 13–73.

[60] Ernst R. Huber, *Deutsche Verfassungsgeschichte seit 1789* (Stuttgart, 1957), I, 62–74; Fritz Hartung, *Deutsche Verfassungsgeschichte* (Stuttgart, 1950), pp. 162–169.

An indirect but clear Austrian response to the situation was the establishment of a national militia in 1808–1809 which expanded Maria Theresa's military system to a limited general conscription. The direct appeal to Austrian patriotism on which the new institution was based, met an encouraging response. Yet neither Stadion nor the archdukes had learned their lesson in full. They believed that a people's army would do as well as the French one in and after 1792, but they did not understand that the French success was due not only to military reforms but to the influence of a broad social revolution.

Illusions, however, are understandable in a severe political crisis. Austria was now undoubtedly the last hope of German patriots, though hardly that of non-Germanic national groups within the Habsburg empire. The English counteractions against the Continental Blockade and the Spanish guerrilla warfare encouraged underhand resistance against the French throughout Europe. Still, the understanding between Napoleon and Tsar Alexander, and the Russian advice in Berlin against precipitate action were unmistakable warning signs. They remained unheeded. Habsburg power took the big jump, too soon and again not adequately prepared.

The Austrian war manifesto of March 25, 1809, written by Stadion's brilliant public-relations officer Friedrich von Gentz, appealed to the German nation as to the Austrian people. The manifesto urged their rise against the French emperor. Under existing conditions of centuries-old absolutism throughout the Germanies these invocations were bound to fail. Although they had some effect on German intellectuals, particularly on the academic youth, these groups did not represent the comprehensive concept of a German political nation. Yet even if such a concept had existed under the rule of the princes of the Confederation of the Rhine, it would hardly have meant political reality. In Austria the appeal to the German nation undoubtedly had a deep effect on the people in the hereditary lands, who felt they were fighting this time a war not in the rearguard but in the forefront of continental interests. No such immediate effects were visible in the other Habsburg lands, and the war did not last long enough to test their reaction.

The war began with a prearranged rising of gallant Tyrolian peasants against the hateful Bavarian satellite regime on the very day of the Austrian declaration of war on April 9, 1809. A southern army under Archduke John, an enlightened prince sympathetic to popular causes, but not an experienced general, fought the French first with some success in Italy. Yet within a few weeks this army was called back to relieve the critical situation of the main forces. A second Austrian army made a successful foray against Warsaw in the north. The main purpose of this offensive, to encourage Prussia to join the Austrian cause, failed. When Russia as Napoleon's nominal ally sent an army to Galicia, the Austrians were forced to retreat. Archduke Charles, as commander in chief and commander of the main army, lost his first engagements in southern Germany. No successful resistance could be offered in Upper Austria either, and within five weeks after the opening of hostilities Napoleon entered Vienna. In view of the bitter Austrian resistance, the new occupation was much harsher than that in 1805.

The Austrians fought on. On May 21, 1809, the archduke attacked the French army at Aspern on the left bank of the Danube opposite Vienna. After a savage battle Napoleon was forced to retreat to the Lobau, an island between the Danube and one of its arms. Whether lack of daring on the part of the archduke or exhaustion of his troops and the terrible losses inflicted by the enemy prevented him from following and routing the defeated army in its precarious camping position between the waters is uncertain. A great opportunity may have been lost. Even so, the victory of Aspern electrified Germany and stands throughout the centuries as a lasting testimony of Austrian military prowess under adverse conditions. In a sense it was Austria's "finest hour."

Its immediate military effect was lost like that of the efforts of the Tyrolian insurrectionists under Andreas Hofer's gallant leadership. On July 5 and 6 another hard, but this time decisive, battle was fought at Wagram less than twenty miles from Aspern. Archduke John's army did not arrive in time and Archduke Charles ordered the retreat of his forces prematurely. The Austrian government, formerly anxious to start the war, now acted with undue haste in the conclusion of an armistice at Znaim (Znoijmo) on July 12. The Austrians might possibly have received better terms if they had not done so, though victory was now definitely beyond their grasp. The peace imposed upon the Habsburg empire was very severe, though again in view of Napoleon's ulterior design not as cruel as the treatment of Prussia at Tilsit.

Austria had to cede Salzburg, Berchtesgaden, part of Upper Austria, and Vorarlberg to Bavaria, but "revolutionary" Tyrol seemed not to be safe under undivided control. The eastern part came now under French-Illyrian, the southern under French-Italian jurisdiction. The Tyrolian peasants were abandoned completely by the Austrian government, and their leader, Andreas Hofer, was court-martialed by the French and shot as insurrectionist in February, 1810. He has remained a Tyrolian national hero to this day. Cracow and western Galicia had to be ceded nominally to the grand duchy of Warsaw, with the king of Saxony as grand duke. Actually this meant cession to France, because Saxony never got into possession. Part of eastern Galicia was given to the tsar, with the intention of driving a wedge between Austria and Russia. This intention, however, failed; fear of French imperialism overshadowed the issue.

Extremely painful was the loss of the Austrian "Illyrian" Southern Slav territories to French rule, as it happened under an able and skillful administration by Marshall Auguste Frédéric Louis Marmont as viceroy. This cession pertained to the southern parts of Carinthia, Carniola, the eastern Tyrolian Puster valley, Friuli, Trieste, Istria, Dalmatia, as well as Fiume (Rijeka) and western Croatia as Hungarian contributions to the surrender. The Habsburg empire was now completely landlocked. Yet these humiliating losses including a heavy indemnity, still left the bulk of the hereditary lands, and fully the Bohemian and most of the Hungarian realms intact. Austria, though no longer a great power continued to be a viable state, and the potentialities for future rise were still open. It was clear that these potentialities could not be exercised now in pursuit of a German course in Austria. Archduke Charles resigned as commander in chief and so did Count Stadion as minister of foreign affairs. On October 8, less than a week before the signing of the peace treaty of Schönbrunn, Count Metternich was appointed minister of foreign affairs, and a new chapter in the history of Austrian foreign and soon also domestic relations began.

This brilliant, skillful, and personally attractive diplomat came from the Rhineland, where his father had belonged to the sovereign (*reichsunmittelbar*) Rhenish aristocracy whose domains were expropriated during the French Revolution. Raised in hatred and fear of revolutionary government of any kind Metternich was not anti-French on national grounds, nor did he see the situation in 1809 as comparable to that in 1792. To him Napoleon represented the overwhelming power that threatened the foundations of the old order. Yet if Napoleon's ambitious designs could be curbed Metternich did not see him necessarily as an enemy but, on the contrary, as the bulwark against new revolutions, as the man who had succeeded to restore order in France.

There is another point which in view of Metternich's controversial domestic policies after 1815 has frequently been overlooked. Metternich was in his youth indoctrinated with the spirit of the French enlightenment as distinguished from its Josephin utilitarian Austrian brand. He was not adverse to all French domestic reforms, in particular not in regard to state-church relations. Above all, the puritan spirit of Josephinism was completely alien to him.

Metternich was concerned that Austria needed a breathing spell to recover from the losses of four grievous wars, to be ready to fight another day, if the situation should present itself. It was clear to him that this recovery could never be brought about in open opposition to France but only by devious ways of limited cooperation. If then the opportunity for a new grand alliance should arise Austria should not jump into the fray as in previous wars bearing the brunt of the attack. She should rather wait until a favorable bid was made to her. In that way her great power position could be secured by the pen even before it was assured by the sword. Metternich was essentially a pragmatist, although he liked to consider himself the creator of a political system. Yet although his plans were clear in principle he was ready to adjust them to the situation as it would present itself.[61]

He did not have to wait long. Napoleon, anxious to have an heir, whom he could not expect from Josephine Beauharnais, divorced the empress. The new consort should be the daughter of one of the great European dynasties to strengthen the hold of the Bonapartes on the throne of France by the bonds of an artificial legitimacy. After having been repudiated in a roundabout way by the tsar who was unwilling to agree to Napoleon's marriage with Alexander's youngest sister, Napoleon turned to Emperor Francis and asked for the hand of his oldest daughter Maria Louise.

The decision between acceptance or rejection represented a difficult political problem quite apart from the issue of dynastic pride. The marriage might put a heavy strain on Austrian public opinion. Could the people be asked to welcome or even to tolerate such an association just a year after they had been exhorted to fight a holy national war against the foreign conqueror? Metternich, the cool rationalist and profound sceptic concerning any expression of public opinion, thought the opportunity to reconcile Napoleon was well worth the risk of alienating public opinion. As it turned out, he had no reason to worry. The marriage amused the Viennese greatly and met little opposition in the crownlands. Accordingly, Maria Louise a princess who lacked charm, brains, and character, was married to Napoleon in April, 1810. A year later the unfortunate heir, dubbed solemnly king of Rome, was born.[62]

[61] Heinrich von Srbik, *Metternich: Der Staatsmann und Mensch* (Munich, 1925), I, 1–128; Enno Kraehe, *Metternich's German Policy: The Contest with Napoleon, 1799–1814* (Princeton, 1963), I, 58–118.

[62] Srbik, *Metternich,* I, 129–141; Kraehe, *Metternich's German Policy,* I, 128–130.

It was high time to be prepared for a new crisis. Austria had hardly gone through the state bankruptcy of 1811 when the threatening French-Russian showdown cast its shadow. Austria was even forced to contribute an auxiliary corps of 30,000 men to Napoleon's Russian campaign of 1812. These troops under Prince Karl Schwarzenberg followed secret directions from Vienna and managed to stay out of major engagements with the nominal enemy and potential ally. After the French breakdown, an armistice with Russia was secured in January, 1813. Nobody doubted that the real foe was Napoleonic France and that Austria had to prepare for "the day." According to Metternich's designs it had not yet come.

When a hesitating Frederick William III of Prussia had to yield to public opinion and to declare war on France in March, 1813, Austria stood on the sidelines and offered only "armed mediation," on behalf of the warring parties, which meant on behalf of the anti-French coalition. Napoleon was asked to evacuate the right bank of the Rhine, to abolish the grand duchy of Warsaw, and to return the conquests imposed by the peace of Schönnbrunn in 1809. Metternich, who played for time, certainly did not expect that the French emperor, after he had won several victories over the combined Prusso-Russian forces and before Austria had fired a single shot, would agree to such demands. Yet Napoleon, severely shaken by the frightful losses of the Russian campaign, agreed to an armistice, which he later characterized as the greatest mistake of his career. Meanwhile Austria, on June 27, 1813, concluded the agreement of Reichenbach with Russia, Prussia, and Sweden. According to it she would join the grand alliance with these powers and Britain if Napoleon would reject the mediation offer by the end of the armistice (July 20, but due to Metternich's efforts prolonged until August 10).

On June 26 Napoleon and Metternich met in Dresden. In this conference the Austrian offer was rejected, though this rejection was not confirmed until the termination of the armistice in August. Napoleon, consistently from his point of view, declared that he as the son of fortune could not accept defeat like the legitimate rulers—and the Austrian offer meant, indeed, acceptance of defeat. Metternich knew this, of course, as well as Napoleon. Austria's entry into the war was then a foregone conclusion, though, according to Metternich's designs Napoleon's complete downfall was presumably not considered inevitable at that time.[63]

On August 12, 1813, Austria joined the allied cause. The commander

[63] For Metternich's account of this conversation see Prince Richard Metternich Winneburg, ed., *Aus Metternichs nachgelassenen Papieren* (Vienna, 1880), II, 461–463.

of the Austrian army, Prince Charles Schwarzenberg, operating from Bohemian headquarters, was at the same time commander in chief of all allied forces. His competent chief of staff was Count Radetzky. It was a measure of Metternich's skill that he had maneuvered Austria into this leading position, though her contribution of manpower was considerably below that of Prussia and Russia (Prussia 162,000 men, Russia 184,000 Austria 128,000). Schwarzenberg, a tactful coordinator of the military coalition was not an outstanding general and several setbacks occurred within the next two months. Yet at the decisive battle of Leipzig (the so-called Battle of Nations) from October 16 to 19, the allied superiority in numbers combined with the reversal of allegiance of Napoleon's allies, the princes of the Confederation of the Rhine, was overpowering. Napoleon whose armies had suffered irretrievable losses was forced to retreat across the Rhine into France.

Now the diplomats went into action, and Metternich played a dominant role. On December 1 Napoleon was offered the natural boundaries of France (Rhine, Alps, Pyrenees). He rejected, and the war continued. We do not know whether the propositions were meant seriously or whether Metternich, the originator of the proposal, wanted to expose Napoleon as unrepentent aggressor so that the continuation of the war in France appeared fully justified in the eyes of the public. Metternich, a facile and sometimes loquacious writer, did not express himself on this important point in his voluminous memoirs. Yet there is good reason to assume that he would not have put up the plan against stiff Russian and particularly Prussian opposion, had he discounted its acceptance from the start. It is more likely that he played it both ways. Should Napoleon reject the plan, continuation of the war in French territory would appear justified in the eyes of the public. Should he accept, however, a Napoleonic regime would guarantee the necessary strength and efficiency to curb the possibilities of future revolutions in France. A Bourbon restoration would of course readily offer such guarantee. The big question was whether a Bourbon king would be strong enough to honor a commitment of this kind. Much in Metternich's rationalist philosophy seems to support the notion that at that time he put more trust in Napoleonic ruthless strength than in the staying power of the restored ancient regime. On the other hand, Napoleon's position as son-in-law of Emperor Francis hardly played a role in Metternich's or even Francis' considerations. Dynastic solidarity did not extend to an upstart, who was now clearly out of luck.[64]

[64] Srbik, *Metternich,* I, 163–182; Kraehe, *Metternich's German Policy,* I, 313–326.

Following Napoleon's rejection, the war was carried into France after Christmas 1813. Now the Austrian forces were superior in numbers but not in leadership. Strategists consider the spring campaign of 1814, when Napoleon was outnumbered four to one, as one of his most brilliant campaigns. Schwarzenberg, a slow and undecisive general, was no match for Napoleon's lightening attacks; the Russians and Prussians did not do very much better. The final victory was simply due to the exhaustion of the French army and a change in strategy directed toward engagements with Napoleon's subleaders and a march on the capital rather than battles with the main army under his command. The Allies entered Paris on May 31, 1814, which meant the end of the Napoleonic empire.

Irrespective of allied military ineptitude, Napoleon's end had been a foregone conclusion for a long time. The treaty of Chaumont signed March 9, 1814, by Austria, Great Britain, Prussia, and Russia had established that the Allies would conclude peace not separately but only jointly. The French meanwhile had lost control of Italy, Holland, and —by summer, 1814—of all Austrian Southern Slav territories.

There is no question that in Paris Talleyrand influenced the tsar concerning the restoration of the Bourbons, which as seen from the French viewpoint would assure the frontiers of 1792. There is much reason to speculate that Metternich for a time still considered the continued association with the Bonapartic system as a better guarantee of law and order than the Bourbon restoration. The conflict about the selection of an appropriate French government, however, came never into the open. The tsar accepted Talleyrand's advice and the French Senate yielded to the counsel of prudence but certainly not to popular enthusiasm. Accordingly, on April 6, the count of Provence was proclaimed king of France, two days after Napoleon's forced abdication at Fontainebleau. His honorable banishment to Elba, as whose sovereign he was recognized, followed. The Allies, on May 30, concluded a peace with France (first treaty of Paris). Metternich played a decisive part in the conclusion of this covenant, which for all times will have to be considered as model of restraint in victory. The new French frontiers in the east were in fact somewhat more favorable than those of 1792, before the beginning of the war period.

On September 18, 1814, the great peace congress, whose task it was to settle international and particularly territorial relations between all participants of the wars of the revolutionary and Napoleonic period, convened in Vienna. The final agreements were signed on June 9, 1815, even before the adventure of Napoleon's comeback attempt—the Hundred Days regime—had ended in the disaster of Waterloo (June 18, 1815).

The end of the Napoleonic regime could be considered as permanent by spring, 1814; the events between the return from Elba and the banishment to St. Helena were no more than a gripping historic episode, significant only because it restored allied unity at a critical moment. As far as Austria's position was concerned, the return of her territories ceded to Bavaria in 1805 had been agreed upon earlier by a special convention in June, 1814. In July, the Southern Slav territories were also reoccupied by Austrian troops. This preceded the opening of the Congress of Vienna.

Nevertheless, the Congress whose diplomatic conferences were presided over by Metternich was significant for the Habsburgs. Even the choice of the place added to their newly regained prestige. Yet except for the German question Austria at the Congress was primarily concerned with the general European balance of power, rather than with specific boundary questions, which Metternich could frequently settle in bilateral negotiations.

A discussion of the general settlement would go beyond the objective of this study. An evaluation of the position of such eminent statesmen as Castlereagh and Wellington for Britain, Talleyrand for France, Hardenberg and Wilhelm von Humboldt for Prussia, Nesselrode and Capo D'Istria for Russia to mention only a few outstanding names, is only indirectly relevant. This applies also to the sovereigns present at the Congress, of whom the obtuse Frederick William III of Prussia and in particular the bright but volatile tsar disturbed rather than helped negotiations. The emperor Francis on the other hand left Metternich and his right hand man Gentz, the secretary of the Congress, much discretionary power.

An understanding of the Austrian position within the general European situation but without specific discussions of the over-all European territorial problems, requires a recognition of the principles that guided the peace-making. Metternich pursued them within possible limits with diplomatic flexibility but without dogmatism. As generally known, these principles were legitimacy, restoration of the prerevolutionary status if possible, adequate compensation if necessary, and balance of power between the great European states as imperative. Austrian policies can be developed from these tenets.[65]

[65] Sir Charles Webster, *The Congress of Vienna,* (New York, 1963), pp. 164–167. See Guglielmo Ferrero, *The Principles of Power* (New York, 1942), pp. 21–28, and

Thus, it was a foregone conclusion that the Habsburgs had a claim to get the territories back that they had lost after 1791. The claim was to be modified, however, by the experience gained since the War of the Spanish Succession that noncontiguous areas, however valuable otherwise, would be difficult to defend and thus might become sources of international friction. Recognition of this fact meant the renunciation of the claim to Belgium. Repossession and defense of the Vorlande in southwestern Germany did not seem to be advisable either. Approval of the partition of these lands between the three major southern German states, Bavaria, Württemberg, and Baden, however, bade well for cordial relations with all of them and the possibility of Austrian leadership in the German south. In the northeast, eastern Galicia was returned to Austria, but the parts of Poland received in the third partition became part of so-called Congress Poland, the truncated Polish satellite kingdom under the rule of the tsar. Cracow was recognized as a city republic under the protection of the three partitioning powers of 1772 and 1796. Austria, then, lost poorly developed territories, which had been under her rule for only a few years. They would have been difficult to defend against Russia, that appeared on the rapid rise to become the foremost continental power, whose cooperation Austria needed in many ways. Recuperation of the spoils of 1796 thus did not prove practical and was superseded by the principle of adequate compensation. Unfortunately it was exercised according to the views of seventeenth- and eighteenth-century statecraft, that territorial acquisitions in the west accounted for more than many times larger ones in the east.

Yet while renunciation of former Austrian territories appeared sensible under existing conditions, acquisition of compensatory territories raised formidable long-range problems. Austria's fully restored great-power position was now to rest largely in her regained as well as her new Italian possessions. A Lombardo-Venetian kingdom including the Swiss Veltlin Valley, Tuscany, and Modena as appendages under Habsburg archdukes were involved in this deal. Such appendages came into play in the disposition of the three north-central Italian duchies Piacenza, Parma, and Guastalla, which were given to the emperor's daughter (Napoleon's consort) Maria Louise, who had left her husband

---

by the same author *The Reconstruction of Europe* (New York, 1941), pp. 47–61, 195–216. Sir Harold Nicolson, *The Congress of Vienna* (New York, 1946), pp. 257–264. Karl Griewank, *Der Wiener Kongress und die Neuordnung Europas* (Leipzig, 1942), pp. 111–146.

as soon as his fall appeared inevitable.[66] Napoleon's son, the former "King of Rome," now reduced to a modest duke of Reichstadt (an imperial domain in Bohemia), was barred from the succession and lived from now on as a semiprisoner in the gilded cage of Schönbrunn, where he died in 1832. Both, the emperor and Metternich, had hoped to quash the revival of Bonapartism. Metternich lived long enough to see this illusion shattered after the revolution of 1848. In regard to the over-all pacification of Italy the failure of Metternich's policy became apparent with the return of Napoleon from Elba, when his brother-in-law Murat, the satellite king of Naples, revolted against the new Italian order, even before the Congress act was signed. The insurrection was quelled by Austrian armed forces, the gallant Murat shot, and the kingdom of the two Sicilies handed over to the hated Italian Bourbons, despised by everybody except the staunch adherents of feudal pre-1789 Europe. Actually Metternich himself belonged to those who were soon to hold the regime in contempt, which reentered now the Italian scene with increased inefficiency and feebleness but compensatory cruelty. Unmistakable warnings were on the wall in the Murat revolt, which was more nationalist than Bonapartist.

The moral foundations of Metternich's Italian policy have to be understood if not defended by his concern for the balance of power. He saw no other ways of maintaining it than by bringing Lombardy with feeble, Venice with hardly any, and the north-central Italian duchies with brittle dynastic bonds under the Austrian roof. Here at least almost territorial contiguity and the possibility of military defense existed, if as Metternich saw it, the Habsburg empire continued to be a great power. In view of the concessions he was willing to make in the German question he felt he had to insist on the Italian acquisitions and restitutions of former status in the face of national resentment.

Metternich believed he could appease it in the German theater, if he maintained the over-all Austrian power position by insisting on the control of north-central and northeastern Italy regardless of popular opposition. In doing so the ultimately and inevitably played in the hands of nationalism and national liberalism. Whether this policy was erroneous

[66] Parma and Guastalla were to revert after Maria Louise's death (in 1847) to a sideline of the Bourbons, whereas Piacenza was to remain within the Austro-Italian political system.

Concerning the nationalist issue, see Hannah A. Strauss, *The Attitude of the Congress of Vienna towards Nationalism in Germany, Italy and Poland* (New York, 1949), pp. 85–122.

also from a short-range viewpoint depends on the opinion whether delaying actions in an indefensible position make sense or not. Metternich may indeed have treated Italy as a merely geographic concept, a fact for which he was justly criticized especially because he understood that Italy meant something else.[67]

The core of Metternich's policy was the German question. When he agreed to the admission of France into the inner councils of the deliberations of the Congress, he did so to counteract the threat of a Russian-backed Prussian hegemony in Germany. When in January, 1815, he signed a secret alliance with Britain and France against Russia and Prussia he did not do so to block a Russian solution of the Polish question and a Prussian solution of the Saxon question. This would have meant in the case of Poland the affiliation of the whole country with Russia and in that of Saxony its complete incorporation into Prussia. Metternich was not even predominantly concerned with the balance of power in these instances. His attention was focused again on the overall German question. This meant to him that the Germanies must be protected from the control by one power, Prussia backed by Russia. When he stood for German unity rather than union he took this issue more seriously than his stand against German liberalism and constitutional government.

To achieve unity Metternich and the emperor made important concessions, including the provisions of the second peace of Paris in November, 1815. Despite the agreed upon occupation of northern France by allied troops for five years—as it turned out actually only three—and despite the imposition of a war indemnity and the change from the frontiers of 1792 to those of 1790, the terms were still moderate. Austria might have done better in southwest Germany, if she had concurred in Prussia's demands for a harsh peace. Yet the price would have been agreement to a further Prussian aggrandizement and a further step toward her threatening hegemony in Germany.

The Habsburg empire could also have sabotaged the tsar's personal favorite project, the conclusion of the Holy Alliance of September 1815, whose ideological and political significance is often underrated. It pledged the adherence of the signatory sovereigns to the principles of Christian patriarchic government in international as well as domestic affairs. The implied endorsement of intervention by the conservative powers in the

[67] Sir Charles Webster, *The Congress of Vienna,* pp. 142–147; Sir Harold Nicolson, *The Congress of Vienna,* pp. 182–195; Griewank, *Der Wiener Kongress,* pp. 236–240.

affairs of other countries kept England from participating. The more subtly injected anti-Catholic character and the great weight carried by Russia made the pope withhold his support. Austria might have done likewise and would have secured for herself greater freedom of action. Yet again in view of the further course of Austro-Prussian rivalry in regard to the German question, Metternich acquiesced.[68]

Proof of this policy was the charter of the German Confederation[69] signed on June 8, 1815, the day before the Congress adjourned and supplemented by the Viennese terminal act of May 15, 1820. The new association of thirty-nine sovereign states (four of them free cities) represented in its greatly reduced number of members as compared with those in the Holy Roman Empire an adaption to more modern conditions. Basically an alliance against foreign foes, the Confederation became an instrument of mutual defense against revolutionary activities within member states. Indirectly this provided also for the possibility of intervention of major states in the affairs of smaller ones. Constitutional guarantees were reduced to the establishment of the ancient feudal estates diets, travesties of genuine representative government and greater impediments to social reforms than the government of enlightened absolutism. The confederal diet, in permanent session in Frankfurt am Main, was to consist of two houses: (1) the ordinary assembly, in which most states, including the two great powers Austria and Prussia, had only one vote each (only some of the smaller ones had to cast a joint vote); and (2) the plenary assembly, in which the number of votes were weighted slightly in favor of the larger states. Inasmuch as the change of the basic laws of the Confederation required unanimity, this kind of organization meant little more than a courteous deference to the principle of sovereignty of the small states. Essentially also a prestige matter was the politically meaningless permanent presidency of Austria in the proceedings of the Confederation. This provision hurt Prussian sensibilities but added nothing to Austria's power. Austria and Prussia combined were the controlling forces in the Confederation, a fact strengthened further by the terminal act of 1820. Apart from the right of confederal intervention in a domestic crisis of member states, the indissolubility of the association, which

[68] Henry A. Kissinger, *A World Restored* (Boston, 1957), pp. 175–190.

[69] Literature in English refers usually to the association as German or Germanic federation and to its assembly as federal diet. Actually the organization was an example of a confederation, that is, a union of sovereign states, where common institutions—above all the confederal assembly and the confederate council—represented interstate relations and agencies. They did not form a federal government, to which the individual states were subordinated.

prohibited voluntary withdrawal, guaranteed the firm hold of the great powers. The membership of foreign states with their German possessions (Holland in regard to Luxemburg, Denmark to Holstein, England to Hanover) complicated the external relations of the Confederation.

In regard to Austria, two factors were significant, which disturbed the internal order of the association. The first was, that the Habsburg empire belonged only with those of her territories to the organization that had been part of the Holy Roman Empire. This included the hereditary lands, the Bohemian lands, Goricia, Trieste, parts of Istria, and a small part of western Galicia. In other words for the Austrian domains the membership in the German Confederation was based on historic and not on ethnic affiliation. The second disturbing factor, which derived from the first one, was that the alliance function of the Confederation did not extend to Hungary, the major part of the Polish-Ruthenian territories, and the Lombardo-Venetian kingdom. Austria might thus become involved in a war with Russia over Polish-Ruthenian territories, and with France over Italian areas without guarantee of support from the Confederation. In such a war, part of a national group—Italians or Poles—might have to fight in the service of the Confederation and part against it, a factor inherent in the structure of the multinational empire.

Disadvantages, in fact contradictory disadvantages, of Austria's membership in the Confederation were thus obvious. Yet the Habsburgs, largely for the sake not only of heading off the national and potentially democratic revolutionary movements, but also of an understanding with Prussia, dropped any claims for restoration of the ancient Holy Roman Empire. The proud heritage of the traditional Habsburg association with its crown was neither renounced for selfless reasons nor purely in the interests of power politics. The relationship to Prussia, to the Confederation as a whole, and to the tradition of the Holy Roman Empire, represented the ambiguous character of a power exposed to Germanic, Slavic, Magyar, and Italian crosscurrents. Considering the complexity of this relationship no solution could serve as anything better than an expedient. That of the German Confederation, which helped to assure peace in Central Europe for a generation, was far from ideal but considering the many possibilities of armed conflict not the worst either. The unromantic, reactionary and—an unusual combination—at the same time antitraditional character of the new organization tempts students of its history to overlook these facts.[70]

[70] Ferrero, *The Reconstruction of Europe*, pp. 217–241; Griewank, *Der Wiener Kongress*, pp. 207–233; Robert A. Kann, *The Problem of Restoration* (Berkeley, 1968), pp. 362–370; Huber, *Deutsche Verfassungsgeschichte seit 1789*, I, 475–563.

Concerning Austria's over-all situation Metternich had made far-reaching concessions in 1815 to the principles of legitimacy and restoration in the German and Italian sphere. On the other hand, by a limited application of the device of adequate compensations and adjustments he had even aggravated the situation by creating an essentially unhistoric Lombardo-Venetian kingdom and an equally unhistoric, though somewhat less controversial, German Confederation. He had thus created a system of neoconservatism, that could not appeal to the power of tradition. In this sense he was the scion of the Enlightenment. But he had in an admittedly imperfect way secured in this manner the preservation of peace for some time, that is peace at a price of suppression of popular liberties and delay of essential social reforms. Yet Metternich had to some extent modernized the new association of German states and he had made Austria a territorially contiguous power at the price of some justifiable territorial losses. To accomplish these ends he had to ignore nationalism rather than fight it. Had a man of his standards tried to cope with it, such undertaking might have brought about disaster in its beginnings as it did in the end. It cannot be held against Metternich that he failed to jump over his own shadow—either from the viewpoint of his character or of his rationalism in terms of time and place.

As for the last principle of Metternich's foreign policy, establishment and maintenance of the balance of power, his success was far-reaching and doubly impressive, considering that he began his operations in 1809 from the position of a defeated state. By competing with England, sparing France, curbing Prussia, and subtly blocking Russia, Metternich under trying conditions had, indeed, in substance worked successfully for peace. He continued to do so for a generation to come.

K. Domestic administration of Francis I (1792–1815)

The reign of Francis I can be divided into the war period from 1792 to 1815[71] and the subsequent twenty years of peace. The latter led undistinguishably, except for the change from a mediocre to a mentally disabled ruler (Ferdinand, the Benign, 1835–1848), to the revolution of 1848. Permanent economic and social changes took place during the peace period and will be covered in the following chapter. Since intellectual trends during the Franciscan era will be treated separately, the discussion in this section can be brief.

As noted before, the domestic reign of Francis did not begin with a renunciation of the aims of Josephinism but rather as a continuation of its objectives of further centralization, true to form but entirely lacking

[71] Only in 1812 technically against Russia and not against France.

the spirit of the reform era. We mentioned the shock effect of the radical executions in France and the discovery of the so-called Jacobin conspiracies in Budapest, Vienna, and Graz, leading to numerous arrests in 1794 and several executions and barbarous jail sentences the following year. The political activities of those participating in the plot were limited, but the scare raised by the social composition of these groups was considerable. The involvement of respectable government officials of fairly high rank, professors, burghers of means, let alone the subversive priest Martinovic, filled the emperor's narrow mind with fear. The fact that most conspirators happened to be freemasons, which had little to do with their Jacobin affiliations, made him feel that anything not in the limelight of public inspection was suspicious. Public discussion of controversial questions was not acceptable to the regime. Emperor Francis neither requested nor even welcomed support of his policies. Its acceptance would have implied recognition of the importance of public opinion. This in turn might eventually have led to recognition of public criticism. The sovereign asked for quiet obedience, the motto of his system of government. Added to this attitude was his fear that because difficult problems went over his head, his advisers might disregard his orders. This fear forced him to decide frequently important matters without proper consultation with his advisers, because he felt unable to cope with their arguments. Thus we face a strangely contradictory system of sometimes precipitate but usually vacillating and often inconsistent decisions.

As noted, Francis' regime moved in the beginning in the direction of strict centralization including Hungarian, Belgian, and Italian affairs. Yet in 1793 the financial agenda and the government of the Belgian and Italian domains were again separated from the over-all administration. In 1801 political, financial, and even judicial agenda were merged anew on the highest level. Maria Theresa's State Council was dissolved and replaced by a so-called Conference Ministry in three departments (foreign affairs, armed forces, interior). In 1808 the emperor reversed himself once more—the Conference Ministry was dissolved and the State Council restored.

More permanent were changes introduced in 1802. The United Court Chancery was now entrusted with German, Bohemian, Galician, and Italian affairs. The judicial administration was separated again from the political administration and the financial and commercial affairs were given over to an empire-wide court chamber. The State Council operated now in four sections (general administration, judicial affairs, military, and financial agenda). At least one member of every one of these four sections was to be a Hungarian. Above the State Council was the Conference Council entrusted with agenda that could not be disposed of by the State Council. Yet none of these collegiate bodies could be blamed for imperfect operation. The emperor consulted frequently with individual members rather than with the whole body. Often he failed to inform an adviser, that he had asked somebody else to deal with one of the adviser's affairs.[72]

In 1813 a separate minister of finance was appointed. After the emperor's death a state conference under the chairmanship of the emperor's brother, Archduke Louis, two other archdukes, Metternich, and the minister of state, Count Anton Kolowrat, was established to handle affairs on behalf of the mentally retarded successor, Ferdinand.

The estates structure as it had been restored under Emperor Leopold II remained in substance unchanged, which meant a policy of ignoring the estates rather than fighting them. Even the bow to the estates constitutions embedded in the Charter of the German Confederation did not change this. In this respect the centralist trend initiated by Maria Theresa was continued, except for Hungary. Here the diet, a body somewhat more representative than a mere estates assembly, was regularly summoned to pass on governmental requests for taxation and conscription. A conflict with the diet in 1811–1812, however, concerning the demand for recognition of the state bankruptcy and its devaluation of money led to continued prorogations until 1825, when efforts to have the coronation of Ferdinand secured made reconciliation with the diet necessary. From now on the Hungarian diet was convened regularly again, not so the Translylvanian, which met only twice during Francis' reign.[73] Absolutism, dominant throughout his regime, was even more firmly in the saddle during the years of peace after 1815 when the impact of public dissatisfaction seemed less dangerous. This trend pertained also to the administration on the local level in Austria, where the remaining urban elective offices were gradually changed to appointive ones.

More positive should be the evaluation of the judicial administration, where the separation of justice from administration was now generally recognized, in the lower courts as well as in the two instances of the

[72] Huber and Dopsch, *Österreichische Reichsgeschichte* pp. 302–323; Ernst C Hellbling, *Österreichische Verfassungs- und Verwaltungsgeschichte* (Vienna, 1956), pp. 323–330; Friedrich Walter, *Österreichische Verfassungs- und Verwaltungsgeschichte* (Vienna-Cologne-Graz, 1972), pp. 118–138.

[73] Marczali, *Ungarische Verfassungsgeschichte,* pp. 125–129.

courts of appeal. Patrimonial jurisdiction was further restricted, not so much for humanitarian reasons but to uphold the principles of absolute central government.

The few outstanding achievements of Franciscan government are two of three major legislative works, new codes of civil procedure, criminal law, and civil law. Between 1796 and 1816 the code on civil procedure had been introduced in several crownlands and the Lombardo-Venetian kingdom, but it was never recognized in all Habsburg lands outside of Hungary.[74] With its cumbersome written procedure this code did not represent a marked improvement over that of 1781. The Code of Criminal Law of 1803 initiated by Emperor Leopold II, but strongly influenced by earlier Josephin legislation, has frequently been unfairly criticized. Changed by several piecemeal revisions and one major one in 1852, it is in essence still in force, though about to be replaced while these lines are written. No code of criminal law can do justice to social changes brought about in the course of five generations. Imperative as the needs for a new code are today as indeed they have been for almost a century, the old one was a remarkable, sophisticated legislative achievement in its theoretical aspects concerning the responsibility of the individual. It was surpassed, however, by the general civil code of 1811, drafted by a commission under the chairmanship of Franz von Zeiller and tested first in Galicia. Here the Josephin legislative drafts were of primary importance. The revisions of the Code of Criminal Law never succeeded in bringing it up to date but those of the Code of Civil Law have accomplished just that. This code has thus become the crowning achievement of Austrian legislative efforts. With only one major revision some fifty years ago it has stood the test of time to this day and is still recognized as the greatest legislative work in the judicial sphere in the German language orbit. At the same time it is a monument of Austrian culture, not fully recognized outside the legal sphere. Emperor Francis deserves at least the negative credit that he did not wreck this work. More deserving of praise are Joseph II and the members of the codification commissions whose efforts succeeded in bringing about a synthesis between principles of natural law, enlightened etatism, and legal tradition. The high standards of this code and that of criminal law are illustrated by the clear language of these instruments. In this respect they surpassed previous as well as future codifications. The correlation with the evolution of classicism in German literature is noteworthy.[75]

[74] None of these codifications in the judicial sphere pertained to Hungary.

[75] See Strakosch, *State Absolutism and the Rule of Law,* pp. 152–217; Ernst Swoboda, *Franz von Zeiller* (Graz, 1931).

Military reforms under the influence of Archduke Charles and Count Stadion have been referred to. The chief problem, even more important than the badly needed reorganization of the army itself, was that of raising military forces sufficient in numbers for the major engagements ahead. Two seemingly conflicting trends in the administration which, however, were meant to serve this purpose became apparent. Beginning with the year 1795, service exemptions were gradually restricted though by 1827 they still applied for instance to nobles, government officials, physicians, students, peasants who had to cultivate larger farms, and sons who supported their parents. At the same time, to make the service less intolerable, life-term obligations were reduced in 1802 in the hereditary lands to commitments ranging from 10 to 14 years, and by 1845 in the Habsburg lands outside of Hungary altogether to 8 years, in Hungary in 1839–1840 to 10 years.

In the course of the reforms inititated in 1802, military justice was improved and the cruel military discipline somewhat modified. These reforms, though on a smaller scale than those introduced by Scharnhorst, Gneisenau, and Boyen in Prussia, actually preceded them. One complicating factor different from Prussia was the lack of popular appeal of military service after 1813; but the establishment of a national militia in the wars of 1809 and 1813, joined by volunteers, offset the impact of the manpower crisis during a most critical period of Austrian history. On the other hand, the success of the militia system at that time obscured the seriousness of the manpower problem for many years.[76]

The peasant population in Austria did not only bear the hardship of long-time military service. The conversion of personal services to the lords into monetary dues initiated so unsuccessfully by Joseph, was after 1797 left entirely to "free" agreements between lord and subject. In Hungary similar legislation was introduced during the last years of Francis' reign. In conjunction with the decrees issued by Leopold II this meant for all practical purposes a full retreat to conditions during the second half of Maria Theresa's reign, rather than an effort to improve on the Josephin legislation.

In one sphere, state-church relations, Emperor Francis seemed to be pleased with Joseph's legislation: complete state control, though in contrast to its administration under the great emperor one lacking all social considerations. Changes within the Church in a more conservative direction were encouraged under governmental control. Marriage legislation remained under jurisdiction of the state, but the state incorporated the principles of ecclesiastic law into state legislation—the one inevitable,

[76] Rössler, *Graf Johann Philipp Stadion,* I, 233–235, 263–267.

glaring weakness of the Civil Code of 1811. Thus divorce of Catholic marriages was prohibited—a Catholic to be defined as somebody who, irrespective of his later persuasion, was born into the faith. Influence of the Church on elementary and intermediate education—again under state supervision—was strengthened. The monastic legislation of the Josephin era was somewhat loosened.[77] Young men and women were allowed now to join orders at the age of twenty-one. The papal decision to restore the Jesuit Order led to its readmission in Austria and although its influence became substantial again, the order never regained the powers there it had held before its dissolution. The establishment of the Redemptorist congregation (Liguorian Order in Austria) under the influence of its outstanding member Clemens Maria Hofbauer (later sainted) did not succeed fully in strengthening social-welfare interests within the Church in his lifetime.[78]

The narrow approach of the official Church in Austria to educational and social problems (see Chapter VI. E) did not mean impoverishment of the faith. Outside of the sphere of state-church relations contemporary Catholic intellectual life injected interesting and frequently constructive new ideas into society at large.

The same cannot be said wherever state and Church intervened officially. There was some improvement in the purely administrative aspects of elementary education, but this was offset by the fact, that parish priests and ecclesiastic deans were now entrusted by the state with the full supervision of education in their districts. The number of advanced institutions in secondary education increased somewhat. But here again clerical control was on the rise and censorship was tightened. Moderate progress could be seen, however, in the establishment of technical colleges of university rank in Prague (1812) and Vienna (1815), none in the universities themselves. This does not exclude, of course, outstanding scholarly achievements of specific individuals.[79]

Technological progress in industry during the protracted war period of the first half of Francis' regime was slow, even though the best-developed Austrian industry, textile manufacture, in the Bohemian lands and in Lower Austria benefited from the Continental Blockade, when English competition was eliminated for a time. The initial development of sugar

[77] Josef Wodka, *Kirche in Österreich* (Vienna, 1959), pp. 312–320; Anton Weiss, *Geschichte der österreichischen Volksschule 1792–1848* (Graz, 1964), Vol. II.

[78] Rudolf Till, *Hofbauer und sein Kreis* (Vienna, 1951), pp. 59–77.

[79] Richard Meister, *Entwicklung und Reform des österreichischen Studienwesens* (Vienna, 1963), I, 44–53.

refineries benefited also from the restriction of imports, and the Bohemian glass industry, a true quality industry, progressed. Yet the chief impediment of large-scale industrial progress was the lack of governmental and private capital, brought about by the prolonged financial crisis of the war period and the first years afterward. Apart from the exorbitant costs of the war, mismanagement played a part. Austrian high dignitaries involved in domestic administration, such as Archduke Charles and Count Stadion had only a limited understanding of financial affairs and of the relationship of a sound economy to the war effort. The ablest administrator in this domain, Count Franz Saurau, the president of the Lower Austrian gubernium, had only a territorially restricted jurisdiction, and Emperor Francis' top financial adviser after 1809, and technically speaking his first minister of finance, Count Joseph Wallis, proved to be a poor administrator and an even worse consultant. Inflation had existed in Austria throughout the reign of Joseph II. Great military expenditures could not be covered by the disappointing results of agricultural and industrial reforms. The public debt at the beginning of the reign of Leopold II amounted to 375 million guilders in government bonds. Only after 1796 did they have to be accepted, however, as payment in lieu of cash. At that time paper money was introduced officially as legal tender.

The situation soon worsened. By 1809 coins were hoarded. Even copper coins disappeared from circulation. The public debt had risen to nearly 700 million guilders and was to rise further. Private credit was unobtainable. In March, 1811, a decree signed by the emperor a month before it was published, declared in effect state bankruptcy. The value of the paper guilder, officially the full equivalent of the silver coin, amounted in effect (that is, in private trade) only to one-twelfth. But the decree reduced the banknotes merely to one-fifth of their nominal value. Moreover, the secret of the governmental transaction was badly kept, and speculation profited widely before the official announcement. A governmental promise that henceforth no more paper money would be printed could not be kept.[80] In fact, the wars of 1813–1814 were fully financed by recourse to inflationary measures, which increased the public debt further. Only the establishment of an Austrian National Bank in 1816, which coincided roughly with the end of the war and the termination of the concomitant expenditures gradually stabilized the situation. The influx

[80] Johanna Kraft, *Die Finanzreform des Grafen Wallis und der Staatsbankerott von 1811* (Graz, 1927); Anton Springer, *Geschichte Österreichs seit dem Wiener Frieden 1809* (Leipzig, 1863), I, 139–278; Viktor Bibl, *Der Zerfall Österreichs* (Vienna, 1922), Vol. I, Kaiser Franz und sein Erbe, 194–202.

of the French war indemnity imposed in 1815 helped to ease conditions.[81] Chief sufferers from the devaluation and the continued price rise during the wars were, of course, employees with fixed incomes. But independent craftsmen and small merchants were also hurt by the increase of food prices as were peasants by that of manufactured goods. In other words, the lower middle class and daily wage earners suffered most.

The state bankruptcy in itself may have been necessary, but the way it was initiated by insufficient measures and defended by false promises turned it into a failure also in a psychological sense. A wide credibility gap was created between the Austrian people and their government, which did not make for ready acceptance of the sacrifices.

The first part of the Franciscan reign had ended with a limited but impressive success in the arena of international relations. In the domestic-economic field it had proved to be a failure, camouflaged by continued stress on the hardships of war. The second part of the reign, though under less external strain, revealed also gradually that the insufficiency of government could be explained but not excused by reference to events beyond its control.

[81] Rössler, *Graf Johann Philipp Stadion,* II, 149–220.

CHAPTER VI

Standstill, Decline and Stabilization (1815-1879)

The span of two generations from the Congress of Vienna to the conclusion of the Austro-German alliance covers a fairly homogeneous period but its beginnings and end mark considerable change. In 1814–1815 the Habsburg empire was reestablished as a great European power, although its restored influence was more due to its central position in the balance between east and west than to a great military potential. Second in strength only to Russia and Britain at the beginning of the new era, at its end Austria had to yield also to the second German empire, and in global respects to France. Her great-power status after the conclusion of the alliance of 1879, according to which she had to operate under the umbrella of Germany's strength, was more nominal than real. In domestic policies these sixty-odd years present the transition from absolutism to constitutional government, a transition with several ups and downs, but on the whole leading to remarkable results. Fairly clear were also the characteristics of the era in intellectual history. It comprised romanticism, the Slavic renaissance, the rise and decline of a new liberalism, and the dawn of an integral nationalism. These and other intellectual trends, however, did not occur among all Habsburg peoples at the same time and under the same social conditions. Therefore, these complex problems of ideological change are discussed separately in Chapter VII.

A. Foreign policy (1815–1879)

It is easier to trace a continuous course of Austrian history in international relations than in any other field. Without losing sight of the decisive impact of domestic developments on foreign affairs, it is still possible to survey them in their entirety and discuss concomitant internal politics later.

The loss of Austria's Italian and German position is a dominant theme. Both were influenced by the break with Russia, brought about by the Crimean War. This rift was never healed and was still a cause of the unfortunate position in which Austria found herself when World War I broke out in 1914. Yet it is true also, that all these reversals, which became fully manifest only with the outcome of the Crimean War, could not have had such an adverse impact on the Habsburg monarchy, if the congressional system of 1815, so ingeniously designed by Metternich and Castlereagh, would not have shown serious cracks within less than a decade and almost complete paralysis by 1830.

It might be said that Metternich, advanced to the position of state chancellor in 1821, was as controlling agent though never as "coachman of Europe," as the shallow phrase goes, in command of the machinery of the Concert of Europe until 1822. This means during the brief period, when one can speak of a system of government by international conferences. In 1818 at the conference of Aix la Chapelle, the occupation of northern France by the four allied powers was terminated in substance and France as fifth great power was readmitted to the Concert of Europe, irrespective of the continuation of the wartime quadruple alliance between Austria, Britain, Prussia, and Russia. Under the Bourbons the readmission of France strengthened undoubtedly the conservative system. What seemed even more important, the weaker and less aggressive western flank of Europe was braced against Russia and Prussia.

The second and third conferences at Troppau in 1819 and at Laibach (Ljubljana) in 1820 proved how necessary the strengthening of the system was from the standpoint of Metternich's policy. At Troppau the great powers agreed in principle to check the revolutionary movements in Spain, Portugal, and the kingdom of the two Sicilies. At Laibach, in January, 1821, the Austrian armed intervention against the popular insurrection in Naples was actually decided upon against the counsel but not against the open dissent of the British and French governments. Austrian troops restored order in Naples as well as in Piedmont, where Torino was occupied. Neither of these interventions had to cope with significant armed resistance, yet by openly aligning Austrian interests with the shameful despotism of the Italian Bourbons, repugnant even to Metternich, Habsburg power began to present itself to moderately enlightened and liberal Europe as the jailer of Italian national liberties. The Austrian government could probably in the long run not have avoided the confrontation with the Italian national movement if it wanted to hold on to the territories secured in 1814–1815, but Austria might conceivably have defended her Italian position in a spirit of conciliation and concession. Such an attitude would not have solved the problem but it might have blunted the fierce hatred of progressive forces, not only in Italy but all throughout Europe. This factor made its influence felt in all aspects of Austrian international relations in the coming decades.

Not lack of skill on Metternich's part, but the impossibility to restore Austria's great-power rank without strengthening the untenable Italian position at the Congress of Vienna were responsible for this turn of events. The Congress of Verona in 1822, which agreed upon the French intervention in support of the Spanish Bourbon regime in France, a hardly less disgraceful one than that in Naples, did not concern Austrian interests as directly as the Italian national movement. Yet in as much as this decision led to the British breakaway from the congressional system of foreign intervention in the domestic affairs of other states, the long-range effect of the French massive military action in Spain proved to be even more unfavorable to Austrian conservative interests than the intervention in Italy. The withdrawal of Britain meant that the congressional system had proved to be unworkable by now. British isolationism became now, if not a fact, a probability. Consequently, Russia's rising inordinate strength among the continental powers made a mockery of the balance-of-power idea. This fact was put to the test in the Greek revolution and war of independence from 1821 to 1830. Metternich, to whom legitimacy meant more than alleged Christian principles of government, had prevailed with difficulty on Tsar Alexander I not to intervene openly on behalf of the Greek independence movement against the Ottoman empire. He might even have succeeded in this respect also with Alexander's harsher successor Nicholas I, if he had had to deal with the impact of Russian imperialism alone which hoped to establish an orthodox satellite regime in the Balkans. Metternich's failure to curb Russian designs was primarily due to the Russian-British agreement of 1826 which made it clear that the two great flanking powers of Europe had resolved in part to share and in part to divide an eastern Mediterranean sphere of influence. In any case, the preservation of the status quo of 1814–1815 meant no longer anything to them and was discarded. Thus the renunciation of the congressional system by the mightiest conservative empire, unimpeded by the leading naval power, preceded the proclamation of full Greek independence. Yet this was not the only event of the year 1830 which unhinged the Metternich system.[1]

The July revolution of that dramatic year in France which replaced the pseudo-constitutional Bourbon monarchy with the pseudo-parliamentary Orléans monarchy represented another patent defeat for Metternich's policy. As it turned out, the Orléans regime of Louis Philippe proved to be less liberal than Metternich had feared originally and the tricolor under the Orléans was hardly more revolutionary than the lily banner under the Bourbons. And yet Metternich, and again from his point of view rightly, was afraid of the precedent generating impact of the situation.[2] This was indeed manifested by the separation of Belgium from Holland just a month later, by the Polish revolution suppressed only the following year, and by new risings in central Italy which required Austrian military intervention.

To Metternich the revolutionary impact of Carbonari underground activities and a much publicized Mazzinian Young Italy movement, paralleled by a wave of liberal pro-Hellenic and pro-Polish sentiments throughout Europe, would have seemed less dangerous if he still could have dared to cooperate fully with Russia. Yet in the critical July days of 1830, confronted with the prospect of allowing Russian military intervention in France, which would have entailed the marching through and perhaps even stationing of Russian troops in the territories of the German Confederation, he submitted to the lesser evil of the recognition of the Orléans monarchy. A system, afraid more of the protection by its own guardians than by the activities of its enemies, had defeated itself.

Yet it had not defeated itself completely. The German question permitted still and required a measure of cooperation by the eastern powers. "Das Hemd ist näher als der Rock." In other words cooperation in the German orbit, as a center of the Habsburg power position, was more important for Austria and Prussia, than the struggle for the economic and political supremacy in the Germanies. The same applied to Russia. At the stage of political conditions between 1815 and 1848 the ruling system in the Habsburg empire could be damaged and weakened by revolts in Italy and the east. It could be destroyed, however, by revolutionary movements in Germany. The same was true for Prussia. Both tsars, Alexander I and Nicholas I, acted accordingly.

[1] Nicholas C. Irby, *European Pentarchy and the Congress of Vienna* (Ithaca, 1971), passim. John A. R. Marriot, *The Eastern Question* (Oxford, 1951), pp. 193–224; Heinrich von Srbik, *Metternich: Der Staatsmann und Mensch* (Munich, 1925), I, 629–655.

[2] Ibid., I, 645–682. George H. F. Berkeley, *Italy in the Making*, 3 vols. (Cambridge, 1932–1940), see Vol. I.

The Metternich regime, in particular under the influence of the state chancellor's most influential counsellor in German affairs, Gentz, had viewed with concern the radical national and, to a point, liberal demonstration of German youth at the Wartburg festivities of 1817. The assassination of the playwright August von Kotzebue—allegedly, but not in the real meaning of the term, a police spy in the service of the Russian government—by a romantic nationalist student, Karl Sand, in March, 1819, seemed to confirm these fears. Considering the limited extent and as yet limited appeal of the *Burschenschaften,* the short-range impact of this movement was not great, its long-range effect, particularly on the events of 1848, is arguable, but the inordinately severe response of the Metternich system against transgression of German intellectual life was certain.

Metternich took the initiative in the proceedings of the Carlsbad Congress (August 6–31, 1819) which concerned itself largely with the police supervision of intellectual, particularly academic activities. Actually Austria with her only modestly developed university system and public cultural activities, was in this respect far less directly affected than several other member states of the German Confederation represented at the conference such as Prussia, Bavaria, Hanover, Saxony, Württemberg, Baden, Nassau, and Saxony-Weimar. Moreover, Metternich himself insisted on cooperation with the tsar, even though Russia had only an ideological-political and no legal stake in the situation. The Carlsbad Decrees, approved under Austro-Prussian pressure by the Bundestag in Frankfurt the following month by unanimous vote, provided in substance for strict governmental university control, prohibition of all student associations, in particular the Burschenschaften, strict censorship of publications, above all of brochures and pamphlets, and the establishment of a confederal central investigation commission of subversive activities in Mayence, entrusted also with the task of blacklisting politically suspicious persons. Valid originally for only five years, the Carlsbad Decrees, at the behest of Austria and Prussia, were obligingly renewed for an indefinite period in 1824 and voided only under pressure during the March revolution of 1848. These joint efforts to defend the German Confederation and indirectly also the Habsburg territories to the east against a coming revolution, were in some degree instrumental in fermenting internal unrest among intellectuals, though this unrest stirred up Prussia and central Germany north of the Main more than the relative quietism in the Catholic south and particularly in the Austro-German hereditary lands.

The necessity for political cooperation of the ruling regimes explains also why the Prussian efforts for a German customs union, excluding Austria, were so successful and the failure of the Habsburg policies to check them so spectacular. Prussian economic policy was in part prompted and in part helped by the fact that the industrial revolution had made greater progress in Germany than in Austria. The advantages of a customs union, initiated by Prussia as early as 1819, appeared more conspicuous to the German member states of the Confederation than to the Austrian statesmen. Metternich's feeble efforts to delay a German economic union, which easily might become a political one to the detriment of Austria, were unsuccessful, in part also because he wanted to avoid a political showdown with Prussia as long as the political philosophy of the Prussian government was agreeable to him. Political considerations preceded economic ones. Accordingly his means of checking the Prussian designs were ineffective. A South German customs union, consisting of Bavaria and Württemberg and a large Central German union of Saxony, Hanover, Kurhessen, and the Thuringian states, both concluded in 1828, were favored by Austria. Just the same, most members joined the *Deutsche Zollverein,* which became a reality on January 1, 1834. It comprised most states of the Confederation except for Austria, Baden, the Hansa cities, Nassau, and Mecklenburg. Altogether, this union comprised 23,000,000 people and in part territories with high cultural and economic standards. It is not too much to say, that the materialization of the Zollverein stood for a preliminary decision, that the coming political struggle for the supremacy in Germany would result in the victory of Prussia. No matter how reactionary the Prussian regime under Frederick William III and Frederick William IV was, no matter how brutal—indeed more brutal than in Austria—the persecutions of the "demagogues" were, the German nation associated the idea of German unification with a reformed and liberalized Prussia and not with a predominantly agricultural and predominantly non-Germanic Habsburg empire.[3]

The question arises whether the death of Emperor Francis in 1835 changed matters for better or worse. The replacement of a petty tyrant by a feeble-minded successor, the new emperor Ferdinand, dubbed "the Benign," changed little. The absurdly excessive application of the principle of legitimacy adhered to by Francis and Metternich, namely the succession of an incapacitated man because he was the next heir to the throne, damaged the system itself. On the other hand, the intellectual equipment of the second prince in the line of succession, Archduke Francis Charles, the father of the future emperor Francis Joseph, was not impressive

[3] Theodore J. Hamerow, *Restoration, Revolution, Reaction: Economics and Politics in Germany, 1815–1871* (Princeton, 1966), pp. 10–16; Heinrich von Srbik, *Deutsche Einheit: Idee und Wirklichkeit vom heiligen Reich bis Königgrätz* (Munich, 1963), I, 257–283.

either. In this sense the State Conference established in 1836, nominally to assist but actually to replace the emperor, could hardly do worse and in some respect might have done better than a Ferdinand or Francis Charles who would have had free reign. The conference was presided over by Emperor Francis' most undistinguished brother, Archduke Louis. Francis Charles added little lustre to it, while the only gifted and by character strongest scions of the imperial house, archdukes Charles and John, were excluded by the will of the late emperor. Decisive influence in council was held by Metternich and by Count Anton Kolowrat, since 1826 conference minister and in charge of financial and of over-all domestic policies. Thus in internal policies it is perhaps more correct to speak for the last two decades of the restoration period of a Kolowrat regime rather than a Metternich regime. Yet the philosophy of the restoration system in external and the police system in internal affairs was associated with Metternich all over Europe. In any case, two statesmen of stature were the leading members of the state conference. Metternich, though he had passed the peak of his success, was still considered a man of foremost experience in foreign affairs. Kolowrat, a more capable administrator, had at least a limited understanding for the problems of nationalism in its conservative and traditional historical-political pattern.[4]

In 1833, at the entrevue of Münchengrätz in Bohemia the old emperor Francis had received the solemn promise of the tsar, that he would support the antirevolutionary policies conducted in the name of the debilitated heir. Considering Nicholas' sentiments of conservative chivalry there was no reason to doubt the seriousness of this pledge. There was complete cooperation in the settlement of the Turkish-Egyptian crisis of 1840 and in the conclusion of the Dardanelles treaty the following year, which closed the Straits in peacetime to the men of war of all nations. Yet these were matters of no immediate concern to the Habsburgs. A better test of still harmonious relations with Russia was the incorporation of the Free City State of Cracow in 1846 into Austrian territory, which, following the Polish insurrection in Galicia, took place with the full endorsement of the two other partitioning powers of old. The Polish Piedmont seemed to be destroyed. Equally important for Austria, the incorporation, combined with the conspicuous factor of Russian and Prussian intolerance against their Polish subjects, helped to give a relatively moderate Habsburg Polish policy the chance of smooth sailing for a long time.[5]

[4] Eduard Winter, *Romantismus, Restauration und Frühliberalismus im österreichischen Vormärz* (Vienna, 1968), pp. 206–211; Srbik, *Metternich,* II, 8–24.

[5] Hanns Schlitter, *Aus Österreichs Vormärz* (Vienna, 1920), I, Galizien und Krakau, 19–34.

The revolution of 1848–1849, as far as domestic policies are concerned, was of supreme importance for the Habsburg empire. The same is not fully true for foreign affairs, which changed the anticipated course of international relations only in regard to the German question and only intermittently for some years. Yet the German question was as much and perhaps even more an issue of domestic as of foreign policy and has to be viewed from both angles. Only the latter will be reviewed at this point.

On March 13, 1848, unrest in Vienna was fermented by students, young professional men, mostly representatives of the better-educated citizenry. These liberal forces found support from the workers in the suburbs. Their initial success might have remained illusory had it not been for the transitory backing by moderate, even conservative reformers, whose influence reached at least briefly members of the imperial house such as the archduchess Sophie, mother of the heir presumptive Francis Joseph and the archduke John, youngest brother of Emperor Francis. These conservative circles, more influential than the unorganized liberals, forced the resignation of Metternich. They and particularly the intriguing archduchess did not do so because they disagreed with the principles of his foreign policy and even less so because they sympathized with revolutionary activities. They simply believed that evolutionary moderate reforms of the estates system, as proposed by the able and sincere former Tyrolian estates member, Victor von Andrian-Werburg, and his ideological friend, the artillery captain (later general) Karl Moering, might help to contain a potentially dangerous revolutionary situation. Above all, they concurred that the name of Metternich served as European cliché symbol of reaction and hostility to reforms, even though the conduct of foreign policy had only an indirect and not immediately apparent connection with the revolutionary events. This is the principal reason why Metternich had to go, and it serves also as explanation of the fact that his downfall could unbalance foreign relations for a time but not basically change them. Metternich's enemies at the court who were in principle enemies of the revolution as well, would probably have reconsidered their attack against the chancellor's shaky position, had they foreseen the course of revolutionary events just for a week.

Actually Austria's foreign relations were not primarily determined by the conservative or liberal domestic regime of individual powers but by the change or threat of change of the European equilibrium in general. As seen from the vantage point of foreign policy, this is the explanation why the turmoil of the events of the liberal revolution returned relations to the revolutionary Germanies and Italy to the status quo, whereas those to an ideological ally like tsarist Russia permanently changed the European picture of international relations.

The revolutionary period in Austrian domestic policies ended in a larger sense neither with the dissolution of the Austrian Reichstag of Kremsier in March 1849 nor even with the surrender of the Hungarian insurrectionists in August, 1849, at Világos, but with the official reestablishment of absolutism throughout the empire by decree (New Year's Eve Patent of 1851). This event almost coincides with the termination of the crisis in foreign policy, the so-called Prussian Capitulation of Olmütz (Olomouc) to Austria's ultimatum in November, 1850.

During the revolutionary period we have to focus our attention in regard to foreign policy on three main theaters. First the revolution in Italy and the invasion of Lombardy by the Sardinian army; second the revolution (later the war of independence) in Hungary, although this extreme crisis concerns us at this point only so far as it forced the Austrian government in May, 1849, to make the humiliating demand for Russian military support; third the struggle about and around the German issue. Events in all three theaters were, of course, to some extent interrelated. Even though Russian military help was requested at a time when the intervention of Piedmont-Sardinia had been repulsed already, the Habsburg armies save for the Italian crisis would probaly have been able to put down the Hungarian insurrection so speedily and decisively that Russian intervention would not have become necessary.[6] The conflict about and around the German issue, which goes back as far as the Silesian wars between Frederick II and Maria Theresa, would have come about regardless of the Italian and Hungarian confrontations, yet here too Austria could have acted sooner and more energetically against Prussian claims, if it had not been for the divisionary events in other theaters of action. Finally, the Austrian dependency on Russian support in the Hungarian crisis foreclosed the possibilities of a more flexible course in German affairs, which might have been frowned upon by the last despotic ruler in the old style European sense, Tsar Nicholas I.

We begin with the revolutionary events in Italy. Disorders and public demonstrations against the hated Austrian regime in Brescia, Milan, and Padua had preceded the outbreak of the revolution in Vienna by several months. Following the signal of Metternich's downfall, the revolution started in earnest on March 17 in Venice, where Daniel Manin, an inveterate liberal foe of Austrian rule and early champion of Italian unifica-

[6] On the background history of the Russian intervention see Elisabeth Andics, *Das Bündnis Habsburg-Romanow* (Budapest, 1963), pp. 7–105.

tion, proclaimed a republican government. The following day the revolution spread to Milan, the center of Austrian administration and economic and cultural activities in the Italian territories. On March 25 the army of King Charles Albert of Piedmont-Sardinia invaded Lombardy. He had himself proclaimed king of Upper Italy in June. The Sardinian invasion would not have posed a major military threat, except for the fact that the Habsburg empire had to be prepared for other risings in its far-flung realms. Just as serious was the fact that the Italian national movement found active support throughout the peninsula and strong sympathies in France. On the other hand the Italians were the one enemy whom the Austrian forces fought consistently with military success. The Austrians were well experienced in this arena, and strong fortifications, particularly the so-called quadrilateral fortresses to the south of Lake Garda, served their purpose well. The aged commander in chief, Count Joseph Radetzky, chief of staff of Prince Charles Schwarzenberg in the battle of Leipzig in 1813, was an experienced soldier. His quarter master general and chief of staff, Baron Heinrich Hess, was likewise a capable officer. The military efficiency of the Sardinian-Piedmontese troops was not on a par with their strong motivation and individual bravery in many instances. The same observation was true for the Italian performance in 1859, 1866, and 1915–1918. In August, 1848, the Sardinians were defeated, after the Austrians had scored a decisive victory at Custozza on July 25. The duchies Modena and Parma were freed too as seen from the Austrian viewpoint or submitted to renewed oppression as seen from the Italian. On August 9, 1848, Charles Albert was forced to evacuate the territories under direct Austrian rule or protectorate and an armistice was signed. Yet in January, 1849, a new revolt began in Tuscany. It followed the outbreak of the revolution in Hungary on a large scale by a few weeks. When the conflagration spread there further, Charles Albert made another try and invaded Lombardy in March, 1849 again. A week later, defeated by Radetzky at Novara, he abdicated in favor of his son, Victor Emmanuel II, who immediately concluded an armistice with Austria.[7] Peace was signed with the assistance of British mediation on August 6, 1849. Piedmont-Sardinia was obliged to pay an indemnity of 75 million francs, but she could at least maintain the territorial status quo. Two weeks later the republican regime in Venice came to an end. Manin fled to France, and the Austrians repossessed the city and province.

One consequence of the Italian risings was the ineffectiveness of the

[7] Oskar Regele, *Feldmarschall Radetzky* (Vienna, 1957), pp. 233–320; Berkeley, see III, 97–394.

Austrian campaign in Hungary which eventually made Russian assistance and the concomitant dependence on the tsar inevitable. The incompetence of the Austrian commander in Hungary, Prince Alfred Windischgrätz, played its part.

As for long-range effects of the Italian campaigns, northern Italy and the duchies would hardly ever have acquiesced to Austrian rule. The war escalated Italian rejection of foreign domination to passionate nationalism, although Austria had fought a defensive war against Sardinia and had only answered force with measured force. Harder to defend were internal measures of suppression in the Lombardo-Venetian kingdom. General Alexander von Haynau, "the butcher of Brescia," who besmirched the reputation of a centuries-old military tradition, a champion of hangings and floggings of male and female Italian patriots, was longer remembered than an often heavy-handed but on the whole remarkably clean Austrian administration in Italy.[8]

An issue more central to the Habsburg empire was its position in the German Confederation. The Italian question touched upon the Habsburgs' continued existence as great power, mainly as affected by access to the eastern shores of the Adriatic sea and not yet by other territorial issues. The German question, on the other hand, was interlocked with Austria's survival up to the dark days of her dissolution in 1918.

Seen at this point only from the angle of international relations, the situation presented itself as follows: The so-called *Vorparlament,* the preliminary assembly of the representatives of the German peoples, a self-appointed body of German estates members, met in Frankfurt after previous discussions in Heidelberg. The objective was arrangement for the establishment of a constituent German national assembly to be elected by a democratic franchise. This assembly was joined after a few days by a handful of Austrian delegates, who like most of the five-hundred members, were either enlightened conservatives, such as Victor v. Andrian-Werburg, or moderate liberals like Franz Schuselka and the poet Count Anton Alexander Auersperg (as writer Anastasius Grün). While at the beginning of the revolution the fate of the old order in Vienna and Berlin hung in the balance, this semiofficial body could exercise sufficient pressure on the confederal diet to repeal the Carlsbad Decrees and to do away with concomitant police machinery of enforcement in Mainz (Mayence). It was a feature of tragic irony that the subsequently elected National As-

[8] See Friedrich Walter, "Von Windischgrätz über Welden zu Haynau" in F. Walter and H. Steinacker, *Die Nationalitätenfrage im alten Ungarn und die Südostpolitik Wiens* (Munich, 1959), pp. 115–161.

sembly never managed to acquire the same influence as its predecessor,[9] which, constitutionally, was entirely unrepresentative.

As in the dramatic overture to a grand opera, some leitmotifs of Austria's relations to the Germanies were heard already in these preliminary proceedings. The great Czech historian Francis Palacký (1798–1876), in an open letter of April 11, 1848, declined Czech participation in the Vorparlament and by inference in that of the coming National Assembly as well. In an official sense Palacký was not a representative of the Czech people, yet in a spiritual sense he was, indeed, the spokesman for the Slavic peoples who had settled in territories within the confines of the German Confederation, above all the Czechs in the Bohemian lands, but also the Slovenes in Carniola, southern Styria, and the northern part of the Austrian Littoral. In a wider sense Palacký could be considered as a voice, not only of a revived Austrian Slavism, but of all non-Germanic peoples of an actually existing but not recognized multinational empire, tied to the superstructure of a German political framework. Palacký denied legal bonds of the lands of the Bohemian crown to the Holy Roman Empire and subsequently the German Confederation. With this argument he stood on strong moral and national but questionable legal and historical grounds. Even less convincing was the argumentation of the conservative Czech leader that an association of German-directed principalities would not work and that a republican system in its place would lead to the disintegration of the Habsburg empire. Whether such deductions held some truth or not, they were based on conjecture. Decisive, however, was Palacký's third argument, that a viable Habsburg empire must become a true multinational association of peoples of equal rights. Freed from the pressures of German nationalism within its borders as well as from outside it would become a bulwark against Russian expansionism toward the west. Neither accommodation with the other member states of the German Confederation nor a peaceful and friendly relationship with Russia, however, was outruled in this powerful appeal.[10]

Coming from the representative of a people that had been politically disarmed for more than two centuries, the Palacký letter could not have had profound repercussions if it had not fitted in with some of the burning issues raised in the freely elected Frankfurt Constituent Assembly. It met for the first time in St. Paul's Church on May 18, 1848, with 115 Austrians in a membership of about 560 representatives.

[9] Robert A. Kann, *Das Nationalitätenproblem der Habsburgermonarchie* (Graz-Cologne, 1964), I, 72–87, 369–372.
[10] Ibid., I, 171–174, 412.

The issues, which the Frankfurt parliament had to face, were in many ways overlapping with those of the Austrian revolution. Yet endeavors to establish a federal democratic organization, the question of a hereditary or elective imperial head or possibly even republican presidential constitutional pattern were of concern to the entire membership of the German Confederation. The same held true for the basic question of procedure namely to solve any of these crucial problems through a legislature that had no executive arm at its service. The sovereign states, even though in the throes of the revolution, held out against subordination under a fictitious central government for all German entities. This meant further that with the eventual victory of the old establishment in the individual states after the revolution, the dream that a democratic German legislature could be cemented by an over-all democratic executive force across a hoped-for German empire would come to an end. This, indeed, was the case hardly a year after the revolution had begun.

These were the main issues which concerned the Habsburg empire specifically while the struggle continued: First, the basic question of democratization of government; inasmuch as German intellectual life, particularly in the German west exercised its influence on Austria in this direction, this was undoubtedly a major factor which strengthened the revolutionary forces in the Habsburg monarchy for a time.

Second, there was the struggle for the supremacy in Germany between Austria and Prussia, revived in a period of political instability and only transitory establishment of a genuine constitutional pattern. This constitutional aspect of the German question had considerable influence on public opinion but little direct impact on the course of action throughout the revolution. Negotiations in this respect were conducted primarily on the Austrian and Prussian cabinet levels. They threatened for a brief time to escalate into military confrontation, but this collision (actually as it turned out not more than a political episode) was primarily not the direct consequence of the revolution but due to the ruthless and daring policy of one man. This was the Austrian prime minister from November 1848 to his death in 1852, Prince Felix Schwarzenberg. He was officer and diplomat by training, by accomplishment rather a political gambler and in any case a statesman of spectacular but only transitory success. Seen from the long-range point of view he was a brilliant failure. His predecessors in charge of foreign affairs from March, 1848 (the fall of Metternich), to November, 1849, General Count Karl Ficquelmont, Baron Franz Pillersdorf, an able administrator in domestic affairs, and barons Anton Doblhoff and Johann Wessenberg, had done little to force the issue of the Austrian-Prussian showdown. Deeply involved in the internal crisis, in addition to the war against Italy and the revolution in Hungary, they played a temporizing game. As it turned out this was a wiser policy than Schwarzenberg's vabanque policy.[11]

This, however, was not possible in regard to the third and main issue, which involved not just the cabinets but appealed to the emotions of the educated strata in Germany and Austria and, as Palacký's letter indicated, was to arouse Slavic interests as well. The question of the relationship of the Austrian empire to the Germanies, be it in the frame of a revised confederation or of a new federation of one kind or another, was the first issue of genuine popular appeal in Austrian foreign policy between the war of 1809 and the war against Serbia more than a century later. This powerful impact was primarily due to the fact, that this question, though in its technicalities primarily one of international relations, was in its cultural and emotional sense very much an issue of home-grown national interests.[12]

In terms of the stillborn Frankfurt Constitution of May 28, 1849 (Articles 2 and 3), this meant that the non-German parts of the Habsburg empire were required to have separate constitutions and administrations. Otherwise Austria could not join the new German empire even with the Austro-German hereditary lands alone. In other words, and with specific regard to the Habsburg monarchy, this meant, that the government of the German lands under Habsburg rule could be associated with the non-German Habsburg lands by way of a mere personal union only. The fact alone that the bearer of the crown in the hereditary lands would happen to be the same person as the ruler of all other Habsburg domains would tie entirely separate governments to each other. By clear intention of the Frankfurt Assembly this would imply the end of the Habsburg empire in its traditional sense.

It meant also in substance that a basic issue, dormant since 1815, had come to life now and was to remain so for a century: the *grossdeutsch* idea of a German empire with the inclusion of German Austria versus a *klein-deutsch* program, which barred its incorporation and would thus preempt German leadership for Prussia.[13] The *grossdeutsch* idea presented the

[11] Srbik, *Deutsche Einheit,* II, 123–142; Kann, *Nationalitätenproblem,* II, 70–72, 321–322; Rudolf Kissling, *Fürst Felix zu Schwarzenberg* (Graz-Cologne, 1952), pp. 206–227.

[12] Srbik, *Deutsche Einheit,* I, 315–365.

[13] The terms *grossdeutsch* and *kleindeutsch* are not translated here, since the translation into English would attach to *grossdeutsch* an inaccurate nationalist

wishes, indeed aspirations, of the Austrian liberals and moderate conservatives, deputies such as Eugen Megerle von Mühlfeld, Anton von Schmerling, Karl Giskra, Franz von Sommaruga, and somewhat to the left Moritz Hartmann. Only a few other Austrians in Frankfurt, like Victor von Andrian-Werburg and Karl Moering would have been ready, if necessary, to sacrifice the German affiliation in favor of a strong fully independent Austria. Yet the liberals believed that the German association and Austria's independence as great power were compatible. The adherents of the *kleindeutsch* program found little support among the Austrian delegation. Outside of Austria proponents of this concept were about equally divided between adherents of a Prussian supremacy as objective per se and those who believed that affiliation with Austria stood for reaction, symbolized by the bygone Metternich system. Although German intellectuals across the border were much larger in number and often more radical than their Austrian compatriots, it is difficult to see in practical terms a basic ideological distinction between Metternich's and Francis' conservatism and that of Frederick William III and the false neoromanticism of his mentally unbalanced son and successor, Frederick William IV. Yet the existence of such distinction belongs to the mythology of the revolution and has been nurtured ever since, in particular by Heinrich von Treitschke's influence on German historiography. Actually only the radical democratic Left which stood for the homogeneous German national state and a liberalism equally opposed to Austrian and Prussian reaction, can be credited with full consistency in this respect. On the other hand, the liberal Left at Frankfurt cannot be exonerated from a spirit of integral nationalism in regard to the Germans in Schleswig-Holstein under Danish rule. The other side of the coin of German national sensitivity was the oppressive treatment of the Poles in the Prussian east.[14]

Highlight of the struggle in Frankfurt was the election of the enlightened conservative Archduke John on June 29, 1848, as regent of the hopefully but not actually emerging new Germany. After Emperor Ferdinand and his entourage had left Vienna, the hotbed of revolution, for the safer Innsbruck, this prince of noble intention had been for a few weeks regent in Austria. His election to the more conspicuous but actually less important honor of regent of the new Germany after the assembly had

slant and to *kleindeutsch* a touch of diminution not generally associated with the way the term is understood in German.

[14] Srbik, *Deutsche Einheit*, I, 366–403; Sir Lewis B. Namier, *The Revolution of the Intellectuals* (London, 1944), pp. 43–65.

declared the confederal diet dissolved (June, 1848) was to herald the permanence of Austro-German affiliations and German and Austro-German constitutional development.

The seeming victory of the National Assembly over the confederal forces of old proved empty. The archduke's position was untenable from the start; he had no executive forces at his disposal to bring about the progress of German democratization. Yet even if this situation could have been remedied, progress was not likely under his auspices. John was neither a German, Austro-German, or simply Austrian liberal, but simply an enlightened Austrian conservative prince. Moreover, he was not endowed with political skill. His unquestioned sympathies for German unification could hardly serve as substitute. Accordingly the archduke's regency proved to be a failure, though more due to the force of circumstances than to his own inefficiency. For this reason the Reich ministry appointed by the new regent exercised hardly more power than a cabinet of puppets although its members were distinguished men. One of the abler Austrian statesmen, Anton von Schmerling, for a few weeks speaker of the Assembly, served in it first as minister of the interior and of foreign affairs, and from September to December, 1848, as prime minister. Then, disillusioned by the forced political impotence of his position, he resigned and returned to Vienna.[15]

Yet, though Schmerling had little power, his appointment proved that the Austrian government, despite its difficulties in Italy and Hungary, was not ready to withdraw from its German position and was not willing to yield to Prussia. Thus Schmerling and his like-minded Austrian colleagues could at least claim credit that the draft of the new German constitution, whose discussion began in October moved in the direction of a *grossdeutsch* compromise, acceptable to Austria.

But the decisive move even in this respect had little to do with the speeches and interventions of the Austrian parliamentary delegation in Frankfurt. More important was the appointment of the new Austrian prime minister, Schwarzenberg, on November 21, 1848, in Olmütz (Olomuc), the temporary refuge and residence of Emperor Ferdinand.

The domestic activities of Schwarzenberg will be discussed in the following section. Here we are concerned with his foreign policy, which was only the reverse of the same coin; namely the resolve to make Austria the leading Central European power, indeed super power, and to do this by

[15] Viktor Theiss, *Erzherzog Johann* (Graz, 1950), pp. 80–88; Anton von Arneth, *Anton Ritter von Schmerling* (Vienna, 1895), pp. 160–183.

transforming her semifeudal conservative tradition into a more efficient, centralized, revamped neoconservatism. The Austro-Prussian struggle for supremacy in Germany offered Schwarzenberg a convenient handle to camouflage his imperialism behind a false front of an alleged *grossdeutsch* ideology.[16]

The neoconservatives around Schwarzenberg scored a success within a few days, which greatly enhanced the influence of the prime minister. On December 2, 1848, Emperor Ferdinand was induced to abdicate in favor of his hardly eighteen-year-old nephew Francis Joseph, the head of the Habsburg monarchy for the next sixty-eight years, almost to its end. His accession was an important event. Brought about chiefly by the endeavors of his mother, Archduchess Sophie, who induced her intellectually mediocre husband Francis Charles, the emperor's brother, to renounce his own claims to the throne, the transition meant that the old forces of traditional feudalism represented by the incompetent commander in chief in Hungary, Fieldmarshal Prince Alfred Windischgrätz, lost much of their power to the more energetic and daring neoconservatives around Schwarzenberg. The youth of eighteen faced by a bewildering and complex new situation yielded in the beginnings of his reign to Schwarzenberg's overpowering personality. After Schwarzenberg's death, no man was in the position to exercise a similar influence on the emperor.[17]

Confronted by the war of independence in Hungary,[18] Schwarzenberg played for time in regard to the threatening confrontation with Prussia. First he wanted to bring his own house in order—in his ruthless fashion. In March, 1849, he dissolved the Austrian Reichstag of Kremsier, proving to the world and in particular to the Germanies that the period of revolutionary advance had come to a definite halt. By implication this meant also a future tougher stand not only in relation to Prussia but also in regard

[16] See also Henry C. Meyer, *Mitteleuropa* (The Hague, 1955), pp. 8–11; Jacques Droz, *L'Europe Centrale* (Paris, 1960), pp. 77–92; Kissling, *Fürst Felix zu Schwarzenberg*, pp. 119–166.

[17] Josef Redlich, *Kaiser Franz Joseph von Österreich* (Berlin, 1928), pp. 37–50; Egon Cesare Conte Corti, *Vom Kind zum Kaiser* (Salzburg, 1950), pp. 313–344.

[18] It is appropriate to comprehend the events in Hungary beginning with the royal sanctioning of the revised Hungarian constitution of April 11, 1848, as Hungarian revolution until the surrender at Világos on August 13, 1849. Yet within this revolution the phase beginning with the proclamation of the Hungarian republic in Debreczin April 14, 1849, is properly understood as the Hungarian war of independence. A distinction, on the other hand, according to which the war of independence followed the revolution is in line with Hungarian political views but not with the constitutional doctrine of the Habsburg empire, which could not recognize unilateral secession.

to Austria's further participation in the Frankfurt Assembly and indeed to representative government in any German state.

After the Frankfurt Assembly had elected Friedrich Wilhelm IV of Prussia German emperor, and before he had rejected the crown, Schwarzenberg accordingly recalled the Austrian delegation from Frankfurt. This move was designed to wreck the National Assembly rather than to prevent acceptance of the election by the romantic Prussian king, who was ready to yield to his imperial nephew Francis Joseph, in whom he saw the heir of the Holy Roman emperors. Schwarzenberg's tactics were successful: the Assembly never recovered from this recall. In June, 1849, after the Prussian deputies were likewise withdrawn by their government, the rump assembly moved to Stuttgart where it hoped against hope to have a better chance of withstanding the pressure of the rising forces of the counterrevolution. Here a glorious enterprise found an unglorious end by simple police action of the Württemberg government. By mid-June the dream of a democratic German empire was laid to rest. The noble constitution of March 28, 1849, remained its monument—on paper.

Schwarzenberg had successfully scuttled the Assembly, but in another respect he was only seemingly successful. On May 1, 1849, Francis Joseph met Tsar Nicholas in Warsaw. The tsar, the representative of the feudal imperialism of old and therefore a strong champion of monarchical solidarity, was much taken by the zeal and seriousness of the youthful Francis Joseph. He granted the latter's request for armed support in Hungary, issued on Schwarzenberg's behest. Nicholas had good political reasons to accommodate Francis Joseph, above all fear of the spread of the Hungarian uprisings to Congress Poland. Yet as he himself saw it, this armed intervention was primarily an act of political generosity, and Francis Joseph, as we know from his correspondence with the tsar, considered it as such. The emperor felt humiliated by the necessity to accept such favor. To be sure, Francis Joseph's anti-Russian position during the Crimean war was not primarily a response to this resentment, but undoubtedly he felt it to be necessary to prove that Austria could conduct an independent foreign policy even against Russia. There is little doubt either that Nicholas would have felt less enraged by Francis Joseph's political strategy then, if the despotic tsar could not have perceived it as ingratitude. Austria's call for intervention had made her lose face in the eyes of the world and Francis Joseph's belated response had the same effect in the eyes of the tsar and his successors.[19]

Thus the request for the Russian intervention was a fateful, though

[19] Andics, *Das Bündnis Habsburg-Romanow*, pp. 160–191.

from the emperor's and Schwarzenberg's conservative point of view, inevitable step. The fact that the military alliance with Russia was directed against a liberal revolution in Francis Joseph's own realms alienated German liberalism deeply and perhaps irrevocably from the Austrian establishment. It meant in turn that Austria became increasingly dependent on the good graces of the tsar in the German question too. This was bound to strengthen Schwarzenberg's resolve to veer increasingly to the absolutist Right, to which even the conservatism of the Prussian government appeared suspect of constitutional democratic proclivities.

From here on the Austrian-Prussian rivalry moves into the sphere of competing imperialist interests directed and controlled exclusively on the cabinet level. As long as Austria was involved in the Hungarian war of independence and during the following months of pacification Prussia had the upper hand. In September, 1849, Schwarzenberg had to agree to an "interim" German central power in which Austria and Prussia were to be equally represented. Archduke John, who could possibly be rated as trump card on the Austrian side, relinquished his shallow powers as regent. With Saxony and Hanover leaning to the Prussian side, and the southern kingdoms charting a more independent course, the advantage was Prussia's. In the Prussian union scheme culminating in the Erfurt parliament, planned since fall, 1849, and convoked in March, 1850, Prussia pressed these advantages. A so-called inner union under Prussian leadership was to be formed. Austria was to remain outside of this federation, but to be affiliated with it loosely by a special alliance resembling the frame of the old Confederation. The Habsburgs, however, with the backing of the tsar pressured the four German kingdoms apart from Prussia, namely Bavaria, Hanover, Saxony, and Württemberg, to abandon the union scheme and to join Austria's efforts to reestablish the Confederation in Frankfurt. Since the Erfurt union scheme would have been based on St. Paul's constitution of March, 1849, whereas the Confederation represented simply the revival of the institutions of 1815, this meant, indeed, return to unrestricted reaction. By September, 1849, Schwarzenberg, over Prussia's protest, succeeded in reopening the Confederal Assembly in Frankfurt. In October he and the emperor assured themselves of the backing of the southern kingdoms, and in November, in a new entrevue in Warsaw, of the support of the tsar. Nicholas I put more faith in Austrian absolutism than in the limited constitutionalism of his Prussian brother-in-law.[20]

The Austrian prime minister was now ready for the showdown with Prussia. The issue itself, confederal armed intervention on behalf of the

[20] Srbik, *Deutsche Einheit,* I, 404–436; II, 17–55.

reactionary elector of Hessen-Kassel against his subjects who were injured in their constitutional rights, was of secondary importance. Yet Schwarzenberg had picked his ground for the contest well. The Austrian-Bavarian confederal forces represented the spirit and the program of the restoration era, the opposing Prussian forces certainly not those of liberalism, but at least of limited constitutionalism. Schwarzenberg in an ultimatum demanded the withdrawal of Prussian troops from northern Hesse and the Prussian government, anxious to avoid a showdown with an Austria supported behind the scenes by Russia, acceded. In the so-called punctation of Olmütz (Olomouc) of November 29, 1850, the Prussian government yielded. Moreover, after protracted negotiations it conceded the reestablishment of the Confederation according to the terms of 1815, supplemented in 1820. By May, 1850, the old Confederate Assembly was in operation again.[21] The complex Schleswig-Holstein question was settled, though not permanently, by the London Protocol of May, 1852, signed by the five great powers of Europe. At issue was that the duchies of Schleswig and Holstein, both largely German in character and the latter also a part of the German Confederation, might continue to be ruled by the king of Denmark but must in no way be integrated into Denmark. It was one of the few questions where the nationalism of the *grossdeutsch* German Left in the Frankfurt National Assembly of 1848–1849, Prussian expansionism, and Austrian neoconservatism could see eye to eye on common policies—as long as direct interests were not immediately involved. The agreement of the powers, led by Russia and Great Britain, was that the separation of the duchies from Denmark was put off for the time being. As it turned out, the opening of the issue hardly a decade later was used by Prussia first by appeal to national sentiments to wrest the duchies from the Danish crown, in cooperation with Austria. The second step was then to use the ensuing conflict over their administration not only as a means to get control over the whole area but also in a formal showdown with the Habsburg empire to establish Prussian supremacy in Germany. Here indeed one could speak of small causes leading to great effects.[22]

The decisions of the London Conference were taken after a change of personnel in the Austrian foreign office had taken place. On April 5, 1852, Prince Schwarzenberg had died suddenly. As foreign minister he was

[21] Ibid.; Heinrich Friedjung, *Österreich von 1848–1860* (Stuttgart, 1912, 2nd ed.), II:1, 1–51, 66–91.

[22] Veit Valentin, *Geschichte der deutschen Revolution von 1848–1849* (Berlin, 1931), II, 337–347.

replaced by Count Carl Ferdinand Buol-Schauenstein (1852–1859), an experienced diplomat, less inclined than Schwarzenberg to take an aggressive stance. Schwarzenberg's death was an important event in Austrian history. Yet except for the fact that he was the last minister whose directives Francis Joseph followed without hesitation, his impact on foreign policies represented only a dramatic historical episode. He was, indeed, within more than a century, the first statesman, who had forced Prussia to yield, but with little benefit to Austria. The capitulation of Olmütz (Olomuc), the term used by Prussian historiography, proved to be an empty prestige success, which rankled the nationalist leaders of the Prussian establishment. The desire to avenge Olmütz drove Wilhelm I, Bismarck, Moltke, and Roon to the battlefields of Königgrätz. In his larger objectives, the entry of the entire Habsburg empire into the Confederation or at least into a German-Austrian customs union, Schwarzenberg had failed. His oppressive domestic policies had earned Austria the ill will of the west and, as it turned out after his death, they had not gained her the permanent support of the east either. True enough, Schwarzenberg had restored Austria's power position as it had existed before 1848, but it began to crumble only seven years after his death. He could hardly have prevented the loss of the Austrian position in Italy and Germany, though he might conceivably have delayed it.

The reason why he presumably would have failed like his successors rests in his domestic policies, to be discussed in Section D of this chapter. Suffice it here to say that by introducing a new absolutism after 1848 Austria fell more out of step with European developments west of Russia than at any time after 1815. A regime whose course ran contrary to the currents of European public opinion, could not continue to hold the position it had held before 1848.

Unfavorable events began to cast their shadow in 1852 and 1853. In December, 1851, Louis Bonaparte had transformed his presidency into a dictatorship, and a year later he proclaimed himself French emperor. Now a new element of instability had come into play in European power politics. One of the devices of restored Bonapartism was the encouragement of Italian nationalism and irredentist activities against Habsburg rule in Italy. Napoleon III failed to appease the French liberals with these opportunistic policies, but he could stir up trouble for the Austrian government. A revolt in Milan in February, 1853, had to be put down by force.

The immediate crisis, however, began in the east. Tsar Nicholas' true foreign policy concerning the control of the Straits, which led to the Crimean war, is not fully clear to this day. There is no question though, that the demand to exercise a protectorate over the Orthodox churches in the Ottoman empire would have been a means of reducing Turkey to a Russian vassal state. This was unacceptable to Britain, and also for France—more for prestige reasons than on account of political interests. More directly involved were the interests of the Habsburg monarchy, when Russian troops moved into the Danube principalities in July, 1853, allegedly to hold them as pawn for further negotiations. Actually this step represented the threat of a permanent occupation which would have doubled the length of the common frontier between Austria and Russia. Austrian efforts to check this danger by an offer to mediate between Russia and the other European powers, of whom only Prussia played a cautious waiting game, failed because of Russian intransigence. Furthermore, the tsar went back on a promise given to the Austrian and Prussian sovereigns to refrain from crossing the Danube in exchange for their declarations of neutrality. A new Russo-Turkish war began in October, 1853; in March of the following year the Russians crossed the Danube. The French and British declarations of war against Russia followed a few days later. Austria and Prussia had meanwhile come to a secret understanding that they would resist by force if Russia would attempt to annex the Danube principalities. However, Russia could easily circumvent a formal annexation by an interminable occupation similar to the Austrian occupation of Bosnia in 1878. Accordingly, in June 1854, Austria demanded the evacuation of the principalities by Russian troops. At the same time her minister of foreign affairs, Count Buol, secured from the Turkish government permission for Austrian forces to occupy the principalities after the Russian withdrawal for the duration of the crisis. The tsar now wanted to make the best of a bad bargain and tried to obtain an Austrian guarantee for the termination of hostilities on the part of Russia's enemies in exchange for the recall of Russian forces from the principalities.

The Austrian government could never have exercised sufficient pressure on the western powers to make such a guarantee workable, even if it had wanted to. That it did, however, is doubtful. Events took now their course. Confronted by the large-scale Allied preparations for Black Sea naval operations, the tsar had to evacuate the principalities, which were occupied by Austrian troops after Russia rejected the so-called Vienna four-point terms. They amounted to an abandonment of the Russian designs against Turkey (including control of the Dardanelles) and an implied guarantee for the Turkish sovereign rights in Serbia and the Danube principalities.

The escalation of the conflict between major European powers followed.

In September, 1854, British and French troups began the siege of Sebastopol. In soldiers killed it was to become one of the costliest military operations of the nineteenth century. The Russian casualties alone exceeded 100,000. After the occupation of the principalities, which had irreparably damaged Austro-Russian relations, it was only logical that the Habsburg monarchy joined the western alliance in December, 1854. According to its terms Austria was to defend the principalities and agree to territorial changes requested there by the western Allies in subsequent peace negotiations. In return, the Allies pledged support against a Russian attack on Austria and guaranted further the inviolability of the Habsburg possessions in Italy for the duration of the war. Strange as the need of such assurance of legally uncontestable rights may appear, its reasons became apparent when Sardinia-Piedmont in January, 1855, joined the anti-Russian alliance and contributed 15,000 men to the expeditionary forces fighting on the Crimean peninsula. Sardinia had no dispute with Russia; her motivation of the unprecedented action of sacrificing Italian troops on foreign battlefields was to force the western Allies at least morally to support future claims of Italian nationalism against the Austrian rule in the kingdom of Lombardy-Venetia.

With the fall of Sebastopol in mid-December, 1855, the war was practically over. Nicholas I had died a month before this crowning injury to his pride. His son and heir, Alexander II, attributed the death of his father to his anguish about Austria's attitude which had made this humiliation possible. In the peace negotiations of Paris, February–March, 1855, Sardinia was admitted to the conference over Austria's protests. Great as the differences were between victorious and defeated powers, it seemed that both sides were united in strong feelings against the Habsburg monarchy; on the part of the western Allies, as oppressor of Italians and Magyars, on the part of Russia as traitor to the cause of European conservatism. Here resentment against the Austrian ingratitude for the supposedly selfless tsarist help in 1849 accentuated national feelings beyond the establishment.

The terms of the treaty of Paris, however, gave the Habsburg monarchy some satisfaction by barring Russian control of the Danube principalities. They were placed under the guarantee of the great powers. The mouth of the Danube and a strip of Bessarabia were ceded to Turkey. Other provisions, such as the neutralization of the Black Sea, the maintenance of the Strait Convention of 1841, and the denial of the fraudulent Russian claim for protection of adherents of the Orthodox faith in the Ottoman empire involved Austrian interests to a lesser extent. Nevertheless the consequences of the Crimean crisis for Habsburg interests were long lasting and, as it turned out, irrevocably unfavorable. Austria had prevented her encirclement by Russia in the southeast, yet at the price of permanent enmity. England became morally bound not to intervene on Austria's behalf in case of a new war of liberation in Italy. France, beyond such moral commitment, became soon obliged to come to the support of Sardinia in case of an Austrian attack. Prussia skillfully had stayed out of the conflict and could be sure that in a new Austro-Prussian conflict about supremacy in Germany, Russia would to the very last no longer support the Habsburg empire.

Could Austria have avoided these consequences? Diplomatic historians have frequently made the point that she fell between two chairs because she could not decide whether to go all out in armed support of the western powers or become an ally or at least a friendly neutral on the Russian side. However, the calamitous outcome of the crisis was not due to any particular blunder of Austrian diplomacy, but to the insoluble dilemma which the multinational empire under absolutist rule had to face. Undoubtedly Slavic Russia, in which Panslav tendencies and Panslav lures across the border had begun to stir, was potentially the most dangerous enemy of a power, half of whose population were Slavs. From this point of view Austria should have thrown her lot more energetically to the western side. Yet this side was at the same time, despite Bonapartist Caesarism in domestic matters, the champion of representative government and of national unification. Above all, the west was in several ways heir to the traditions of 1789. Russia stood for the principles of the Austrian police state of Metternich, Schwarzenberg, and his successor Bach. An Austria permanently allied to the western powers could never have maintained her system of absolutism. Yet if she wanted to change it, the loss of the Italian provinces was a foregone conclusion, and a new national revolution of much larger scale might be in the offing. An alliance with Russia, on the other hand, would have made the Habsburg empire the junior partner of a despotism that could always control Austria by the whiphand of Panslavist agitation. This did not exclude the possiblity that this greatly feared force might at an opportune time make common cause with the policies of western national liberalism.

Habsburg Austria had indeed to face an insoluble dilemma. She could not coordinate her long-range interests as a great power with those of a gigantic and imperialist eastern police state. Yet at the same time she felt that western liberalism threatened the durability of her domestic structure. This dilemma between equally contradictory internal and foreign policy interests in an empire ill adapted to the political and social changes of the second half of the nineteenth century was at the core of the crisis, which was heightened with the Crimean war.[23]

The first spectacular consequence of the Crimean crisis was the heating up of the situation in Italy. Several factors strained the situation further. The Sardinian government obtained with the appointment of Count Camillo Cavour as prime minister a far-sighted, resolute, and yet cautious leader, who was able without much fanfare to prepare his country for war and to gain the confidence of the western powers. At the same time the more intemperate nationalist agitation in the south by the followers of Giuseppe Garibaldi put pressure on the more moderate nationalists in the north. Napoleon III became more anxious to regain the favor of the liberals. The attempt of the misguided nationalist Italian youth Felice Orsini to assassinate Napoleon in January, 1858, strengthened his resolve. At the secret meeting of the French emperor with Cavour in Plombières in July, 1858, Napoleon agreed to support Sardinia-Piedmont in a war to gain Lombardy-Venetia. Other designs to create an Italian federation of four component units: in addition to the Upper Italian (Sardinian) kingdom, a central Italian kingdom, the Papal States, and the kingdom of Naples and Sicily, did affect Austria at least indirectly. The alliance was formalized in December, 1858, after Russia's benevolent attitude had been assured. Its operation, however, as a safety measure demanded by Napoleon III, was made contingent on an overt act of aggression by Austria against Sardinia.

While these proceedings were secret, Austria had ample reason to move cautiously. At the diplomatic New Year's reception of 1859 in Paris, the French emperor had issued a hardly veiled warning concerning the coming crisis to the Austrian ambassador Hübner. A few days later the king of Sardinia, Victor Emanuel II, in an address from the throne to the Piedmontese chamber declared that the cries of anguish of the oppressed provinces would not remain unheeded. Passionate nationalist propaganda was unloosened and open military preparations of troops by Sardinia were followed by Austrian countermeasures. At the same time Napoleon III, vacillating as usual, assured the Austrian government that he sup-

[23] Heinrich Friedjung, *Der Krimkrieg und die österreichische Politik* (Stuttgart, 1907), pp. 3–194 passim; Josef Redlich, *Kaiser Franz Joseph* (Berlin, 1928), pp. 119–171; Paul W. Schroeder, "Austria and the Danubian Principalities" in *Central European History,* II:3 (1969), 216–236; and by the same author, *Austria, Great Britain and the Crimean War* (Ithaca, 1972), pp. 41–284; Bernhard Unckel, *Österreich und der Krimkrieg* (Lübeck, 1969), pp. 15–32, 190–217, 239–295; and Winfrid Baumgart, *Der Frieden von Paris 1856* (Munich, 1972), passim.

ported only a defensive action on the part of Sardinia. Since the situation called for diplomatic circumspection on Austria's part, it was a blunder of her foreign minister, Count Buol, to present the Sardinian government on April 23 with a formal ultimatum to disarm within three days. When Sardinia declined, the Austrian forces crossed the Ticino into Piedmont and the *casus foederis* with France, which Cavour had tried to bring about by underhand provocations of the Austrian government, was now thrown into his lap by an obliging enemy. On the very day of the Austrian invasion the French declaration of war followed. Buol's precipitate action—worse than his performance during the Crimean war—was fully backed by the emperor, who was to follow up this first ultimatum close to the beginnings of his reign with an even more disastrous one at its end. The self-deception brought about by a system of absolutism can explain the first action, the temporary elimination of parliament, in part, the second.

Austria's military preparations for this war and the conduct of operations were not better than her diplomatic activities. Count Francis Gyulay, a procrastinator, who delayed action against the relatively weak Sardinian army until the French forces appeared on the scene, was one of the most incapable commanders in Austria's long military history. He could not even claim that he had to fight a better led or equipped foe. The French and Sardinian forces benefited from the Austrian blunders. Gyulay did not accept battle until after the French had joined the Sardinians. He preferred to fight the combined armed forces on his own grounds. After a brief advance, he withdrew behind the Ticino and was defeated at Magenta on June 4. A week later the eighty-six-year-old Metternich died in desperation about Austria's political future. Whatever may be said about his policies, he would not have fallen into the French-Sardinian trap as his successor Count Buol.

In May, Francis Joseph had replaced the unlucky Buol by Count Johann Bernhard Rechberg, an experienced diplomat in German affairs. Now the emperor discharged also Gyulay and assumed the functions of commander in chief himself, apparently with the idea that imperial prestige could compensate for the lack of military experience. However, at the battle of Solferino on June 24, with terrible losses on both sides, the Austrians were defeated, although they could withdraw in good order. Only one general had fulfilled all expectations, the subcommander of the right wing of the Austrian forces, Ludwig von Benedek. He stood his ground well against the Sardinian attacks. In tragic irony, this performance was one reason why in 1866 he was entrusted with the command against the Prussian armies, in which he failed.

Francis Joseph, shocked by the catastrophe, to which he had been an eyewitness, might have been able to continue the war with German confederal (that is, mainly Prussian) support, if he had been ready to recognize Prince Regent Wilhelm of Prussia as commander in chief of the confederal forces. As the emperor saw it, such concession would have been tantamount to a surrender of the supremacy in Germany to Prussia. Rather than accepting this political "humiliation" Francis Joseph was ready to come to terms with Napoleon in the entrevue of Villafranca on July 11, 1859. The French emperor, not anxious to risk Prussian intervention, offered moderate terms. Austria was to cede the best part of Lombardy, but not Venetia to Napoleon III, who in turn was to hand over the province to the Sardinians. This transaction was to cater to the French emperor's pride and soften Austrian humiliation, but it infuriated Italian nationalists who felt betrayed already because Napoleon had gone back on half of his promise, the liberation of Venetia. To have to accept Lombardy, for which Italian blood had been shed, as handout from Napoleon III exacerbated these feelings further. Yet at the peace of Zürich of November 10, 1859, the preliminary terms were sanctioned and Sardinia could feel comforted because the Austrian appendage states, Tuscany, Modena, and Parma, which had driven out their princes, confirmed this action by plebiscites. Accordingly, their territories as well as that of Romagna were merged with Sardinia. Only now, by the treaty of Torino of March, 1860, could Napoleon III collect his own reward from Piedmont-Sardinia, namely Nice and Savoy.[24]

The Austrian hold in Italy had become untenable, as even Francis Joseph was to realize within a few years. It might have been wise to cede Venetia jointly with Lombardy, a decision which could have helped to forestall the more critical situation of 1866. The most spectacular proof of the bankruptcy of a system of absolute government is indeed military defeat. It was possible to camouflage the diplomatic setback in the Crimean crisis, not so the military debacle of 1859. Austria's prestige was deeply hurt by the outcome of the war. Yet her great-power position, though weakened, remained still uncontested. The features of oppression, inefficiency, and some corruption which the defeat revealed to the public, led almost immediately to the restriction and gradually to the abolition

[24] Bolton King, *A History of Italian Unification from 1814–1867,* 2 vols. (New York, 1967), see II, 45–81.

of absolute government in favor of constitutionalism. If these long overdue changes had been delayed further, the consequences might have been even worse for Austria than those of the showdown on the German question in 1866. In this sense the outcome of the war of 1859 offset to some degree the losses. It led to defeat but it helped to save the monarchy from unmitigated disaster a few years later.[25]

After the termination of another phase of the Italian crisis, the German question moved into the center of the political stage. The accession of Wilhelm I, in 1858 as regent and in 1861 as king in his own right in place of his brother Friedrich Wilhelm IV who had suffered a stroke, changed the political picture. Wilhelm was quite narrow-minded and intellectually inferior to his idle and garrulous older brother. Yet he was a well-disciplined soldier. Like Maria Theresa and unlike Francis Joseph, he knew how to accept advice of those of superior qualifications, of counts Helmuth Moltke and Albrecht Roon in the military field and in the political of Otto von Bismarck, who became his prime minister in 1862. Bismarck's appointment made it clear, that the struggle for German supremacy would have to be solved in favor of Prussia, perhaps not necessarily as he put it in a speech to a committee of the Chamber of Deputies in September, 1862, by "blood and iron" but, if necessary, by force. Bismarck's first move to block continuation and enhancement of the Austrian position in Germany by a limited revision of the Confederal charter led to the refusal of the king of Prussia to attend the *Fürstentag* at Frankfurt in August, 1863. According to Francis Joseph's invitation this convention of princes was to introduce some very moderate reforms under Austrian sponsorship, namely a Confederal directory under Austrian chairmanship and the convocation of a new Confederal legislative assembly elected by the individual diets. Such as assembly meant mostly estates diets, hence the concession to the liberals was minor and due to Bismarck's sabotage of the proceedings abortive in any case. It was easy for Bismarck to top the Austrian proposals in 1866 by more sweeping but more meaningless proposals for Confederal reforms based on general franchise, whose rejection by Austria was a foregone conclusion.

The Schleswig-Holstein question, from the Austrian viewpoint, was

[25] Charles W. Hallberg, *Franz Joseph and Napoleon III, 1852–1864: A Study of Austro-French Relations* (New York, 1955), pp. 138–229; Carl J. Burckhardt, *Briefe des Staatskanzlers Fürsten Metternich-Winneburg an den österreichischen Minister des allerhöchsten Hauses und des Äussern, Grafen Buol-Schauenstein* (Munich, 1934), pp. 225–233; William R. Thayer, *The Life and Times of Cavour* (Boston, 1914), II, 1–117.

the overture to the decision in the struggle for supremacy in Germany. It was to delay rather than to prevent the showdown and was meant not to upset the existing precarious balance of power. Prussia used the question of the separation of the duchies from Denmark as a means of getting into a favorable position for the coming conflict with the Habsburg empire; besides, she had a direct interest to get control of the duchies herself. The Austrian objective, on the other hand, was merely to prevent a Prussian predominance in Germany.

War was declared when Denmark, in January, 1864, rejected the joint Austro-Prussian ultimatum demanding that the kingdom rescind a new constitution which for all practical purposes would incorporate Schleswig into Denmark. Confederal troops—in fact only Austro-Prussian troops—entered Holstein. Although the legal issue was doubtful on either side and protracted diplomatic negotiations had preceded the invasion, Europe saw the military operation as an action of two big conservative powers suspected of imperialistic designs against a small, more liberal country. The fact that Austrian interests were less involved than those of Prussia made Austria look worse, because the German national-liberal sentiments that supported the Prussian cause, did not extend to Austria. Little Denmark was bound to be defeated. The king of Denmark was forced to cede his rights to Schleswig-Holstein and to the smaller duchy of Lauenburg to the two great German powers (peace of Vienna of October 30, 1864), which administered them first by provisional joint administration. Recognition of the fact that the Austrian policy had played into Bismarck's hands to obtain eventually exclusive Prussian control of the duchies persuaded Emperor Francis Joseph to replace Count Rechberg by Count Alexander Mensdorff-Pouilly, a general with only limited diplomatic experience. Actually from the death of Schwarzenberg to the end of the Austro-Prussian war of 1866 Francis Joseph acted more or less as his own foreign minister, and only when the disastrous results of his policies in the conflict with Prussia became fully obvious to him, did he give his future ministers of foreign affairs a somewhat freer rein.

The immediate conflict was papered over by the Gastein Convention of August 14, 1865, according to which Lauenburg was sold to Prussia, whereas Schleswig-Holstein remained in principle a joint Austro-Prussian condominium. The northern duchy, Schleswig, was to be administered by Prussia, the southern, Holstein, which was contiguous to Prussia, by Austria under General Ludwig von Gablenz.

Soon a renewed crisis loomed on the political horizon. Napoleon III, who as a prophet of yesterday, was convinced that Austria would be the winner in a conflict with Prussia, in October, 1865, promised Bismarck at Biarritz French neutrality in case of war. Bismarck meanwhile used alleged Austrian interference with Prussian interests in the duchies to protest to the government in Vienna, which, as expected, rejected these complaints as mere pretexts for more serious Prussian aggressive designs. In early 1866 Prussia concluded an alliance with the new kingdom of Italy, proclaimed in 1861. The objective was a common war against Austria within three months, which should secure the Venetian province for Italy. The terminal date for the outbreak of the conflict was set.[26]

The issue of Venetia, though a mere sideshow, represented one of the strangest episodes of diplomatic history, in which the trends of modern nationalism mingled with medieval concepts of chivalry. In spring, 1866, the Austrian governmnet was convinced that the position in Venetia was as untenable as it previously had been in Lombardy. Nevertheless, an Italian offer made before the conclusion of the alliance with Prussia, to pay an indemnity for the cession of the province, was rejected as insulting. Just the same, within a few days before the outbreak of the war, Austria and France signed a notable neutrality agreement. Both powers concurred that the temporal jurisdiction of the pope in Rome must be preserved and protected against the threat of Italian nationalism. Indemnities for the deposed Habsburg rulers in the appendages (Modena, Tuscany, Parma) were assented to by France. Above all, Austria gave an assurance that French agreement would be secured in case a victorious Habsburg power wanted to make territorial changes in Germany which would upset the European balance of power. In the light of coming events this last point certainly looks strange, but there was a more startling one concerning the contested Venetian territory. Austria, win or lose, would oblige herself to cede Venetia to Napoleon III, who in turn would hand the province over to Italy. This willingness was in part due to an understandable wish to avoid a two-front war, against Prussia in the north and Italy in the south; but in part it was also due to the belated recognition that the retention of the province against the united will of the population and the upcoming Italian neighbor represented in the long run a hopeless proposition. To use Napoleon as the perhaps none too honest broker in this deal was meant to strengthen his position in the Italian sphere and at the same time to influence him in favor of Aus-

[26] King, *A History of Italian Unification,* II, 281–290; Heinrich Friedjung, *Der Kampf um die Vorherrschaft in Deutschland, 1859—1866* (Stuttgart, 1897–1898), I, 67–128; Srbik, *Deutsche Einheit,* IV, 118–291.

tria in the crisis with Prussia. Italy felt, however, that this proposal hurt her national pride as much as outright cession to Italy would have injured the feudal mentality of the Austrian establishment. Accordingly negotiations were broken off and Italy declared war on Austria less than a week after the beginning of Austro-Prussian hostilities. The Italian military showing was even poorer than the Sardinian in the wars of 1848 and 1859. Although the main Austrian forces were engaged against Prussia in the north, an army under Archduke Albrecht won easily at Custozza on June 24, the place of a previous Austrian victory in 1848. Hardly a month later the small Austrian navy under Tegethoff's command in a brilliant engagement near Lissa off the Dalmatian coast routed an Italian naval force, whose fighting spirit was not equal to its superiority in tonnage and firing power. Further feeble Italian efforts to gain territory to the north and northeast of the Venetian province in the Trentino and the Littoral failed. Peace was concluded in Vienna on October 3. Venice, ceded to Napoleon III immediately after the defeat at Königgrätz, now had to be yielded to Italy directly and the Italian kingdom was *de jure* recognized by Austria. Thus the victory which the Italians had failed to win on the battlefield was secured at the conference table.[27]

Several conclusions can be drawn from these proceedings. First, the decision on both sides to fight a war over a matter of national prestige, although Austria and Italy in substance agreed on the outcome beforehand, represented a moral low in international relations. Thousands were killed for the sake of "chivalry" of two military establishments. Second, the Italians resented Napoleon's attempt to intervene as cheap benefactor without risk, yet they were dissatisfied also that the Prussian ally had not helped them to gain the Trentino to the north of Venice. According to the terms of the alliance treaty Prussia was indeed not obliged to contribute to this objective. Bismarck did not feel it was to be to her interest that Austria should be weakened further.

The question may be asked, whether a far-seeing Austrian policy might not have done better to relinquish the Trentino and the northwestern strip of the Littoral voluntarily. At this particular time after a spectacular military showing in the south such concession might have been interpreted as evidence of wisdom rather than weakness. In that case Italy might have become a dependable neutral rather than a second permanent and major foe, who—a later meaningless alliance notwithstanding—at the critical time was almost bound to become an outright enemy. Such

[27] Richard Blaas, *Tentativi di approccio per la cessione del Veneto* (Venice, 1967), passim. Friedjung, *Der Kampf um die Vorherrschaft*, I, 212–251.

a concession to Italy in time could have changed the course of history in and after 1914. On the other hand, it was the tragedy of the multinational empire that one wisely executed conciliatory step in regard to one national group would have prompted demands by others.

As for the conflict between Austria and Prussia, Bismarck, in April of 1866 had already introduced a motion for reform of the Confederal diet which included election of members of the Assembly by general male franchise. The plan was designed to be rejected by Austria. Bismarck, had he not been sure of this, would not have introduced the motion which intended to win the support of genuine German liberalism on the side of the false one put forward by him. Meanwhile the conflict about the administration of the duchies continued, and when the Austrian governor of Holstein, General Gablenz, summoned the provincial diet, Bismarck declared this to be a breach of the Gastein convention and ordered Prussian troops into Holstein. Austria now convoked the Confederal diet in Frankfurt, charged Prussia with violation of the charter of the Confederation and demanded Confederal execution against Prussia. The diet approved the Austrian motion, whereupon Prussia declared the Confederation to be dissolved. Against strong Prussian pressure all major states of the Confederation stood by Austria motivated undoubtedly by fear of Prussian imperialism rather than the trappings of Bismarck's sham liberalism. The hostilities began with the Prussian invasion of Hanover, Saxony, and Kurhesse, all then Austria's allies.

Could it therefore be said then that Austria had Germany on her side in the coming showdown? Hardly. Military support of the Austrian cause by the German states was meager, except for the contributions by Saxony and the initial ones by Hanover. Moreover the southern and central German states acted not out of sympathy with Austrian policies and even less so with her philosophy of government, but out of fear of Prussian military expansionism. The Prussian strategy, brilliantly designed by the chief of staff, Moltke, and well prepared by Minister of War Roon's reorganization of the army, called for a three-pronged attack on Bohemia. After the invading armies had converged in central Bohemia, the Austrian forces should be forced to accept a decisive battle. This was the way it was planned and so it happened.

The Austrian commander in chief, Ludwig von Benedek, was one of those mediocre strategists, who could be forced to follow the ruts drawn by a superior foe. Much ink has been spilled about the appointment and tragic fate of this man, who was pressed to accept a difficult assignment, to which he was not qualified by experience or strategic ability. Evidently the emperor felt that a conceivable military disaster in the north would reflect on the crown, if Archduke Albrecht, Benedek's senior in rank, would be given the command in the north.

However, Benedek's insufficiency was only one cause for the military catastrophe. The Austrian general staff, and particularly Benedek's personal staff, failed completely, and the Prussian army was better organized, better led, and better equipped. Its use of the needle gun with its superior and faster firing power was a major item in the balance sheet. Before the battle of Königgrätz, Benedek, after his subcommanders had been defeated, repeatedly urged the emperor to conclude preace rather than risk a major confrontation. Francis Joseph appealing to military chivalry used indirect but strong pressure on Benedek to accept battle in unfavorable terrain. Another commander would hardly have done much better. Even if Benedek had been ordered to retreat rather than having been pushed into battle, it is difficult to see, how the Austrians could have blocked a Prussian victory.[28]

In this sense the frequently voiced assertion that the bloody battle of Königgrätz, fought on July 4, 1866, was a decisive battle in world history, is correct only to the extent that Austria's rout smashed the backbone of her military resistance and led within weeks to what amounted to capitulation—a defeat of far-reaching consequences. Yet this defeat was not brought about so much by a military turn of events at Königgrätz, where the Austrians fought as well as the Prussians. Königgrätz merely confirmed a course of history, inevitably brought about by the accumulated effects of the national revolutions of 1848–1849: Schwarzenberg's provocative policy against Prussia, the Crimean and Austro-Sardinian crisis, the oppressive policies in Italy, and the insensitivity of neoabsolutism and pseudo-constitutionalism to public opinion.

The shaken and disorganized Austrian troops retreated to the vicinity of Vienna. The replacement of Benedek by Archduke Albrecht and transfer of major contingents of his southern army to the north changed little. Moreover, a Prussian-equipped Hungarian legion of insurgents under the revolutionary General Klapka had entered Slovakian territory in Hungary. Although unsuccessful in non-Magyar regions, this force posed a threat in terms of potential national disintegration.

Undoubtedly the victorious Prussians had to face some risks. Napoleon

[28] Gordon A. Craig, *The Battle of Königgrätz* (Philadelphia, 1964); Wilhelm Schüssler, *Königgrätz, 1866* (Munich, 1958), pp. 15–24; Heinrich Friedjung, ed., *Benedeks nachgelassene Papiere* (Dresden, 1904), pp. 352–404; Friedjung, *Der Kampf um die Vorherrschaft,* II, 179–263.

III had been intimidated by the Austrian disaster. The possibility of French intervention on behalf of Austria remained a potential threat to Prussia, despite Bismarck's skillful diplomatic maneuverings. Only speedy conclusion of an armistice with Austria could check it. There were also the typical dangers for armies in the field—cholera and dysentery. Finally, a last stand of the Austrian troops reenforced by the southern army presented at least some uncertainty. Bismarck had reason to conclude an armistice and a preliminary peace treaty with Austria. The terms of this agreement, signed on July 26 at Nikolsburg in southern Moravia, were confirmed by the peace of Prague, less than a month later.

Bismarck had to overcome considerable resistance of his king, whose intellectual horizon did not transcend much that of a drill sergeant. Consequently he wished for substantial annexations of Austrian territory, whereas the prime minister intended to offer rather generous terms. The king yielded and Bismarck had his way. Fram all we know, he did not as yet have a future alliance in mind but wanted to keep all possibilities open.

These were the results: Austria recognized the dissolution of the German Confederation and approved in advance the new organization of Germany. This included the establishment of a North German federation under Prussian leadership and the annexation by Prussia of Kurhesse, Hanover, Nassau, Frankfurt and the controversial duchies Schleswig and Holstein. A minor though humiliating indemnity of 20,000,000 Talers was to be paid by Austria. On the other hand she was able to secure the territorial integrity of her most faithful ally, Saxony.

The outcome of the war was of lasting and in several respects decisive significance. As for domestic policies, it was widely felt that the new debacle was still the consequence of the neoabsolutist mismanagement and its too slow transformation after 1859. Here the defeat of Austria promoted the establishment of genuine constitutional government. Even greater were the consequences in foreign affairs. The two defeats in 1859 and 1866 had reduced Austria from a genuine great power to a nominal one. Never again was she to rise in status. More important, the coming defeat of France in the Franco-Prussian war of 1870–1871, the permanent strained relations with Russia and in a sense also with Italy, made it clear that Germany was the only genuine potential ally of Austria. Yet an alliance with Germany meant that she would be the senior partner, to whose basic policies Austria would have to agree. The most basic of these was the notion that Germans and Magyars must be the dominant national groups in the Habsburg empire, as the only reliable bulwark against Slav advances toward the west. This ruled out the possibility of sweeping national reforms.[29]

These facts dawned only gradually on Emperor Francis Joseph and the leading Austrian statesmen. Their first reaction in the years following the defeat of 1866 was to look for the possibility of revenge against Prussia, and when that possibility vanished on the battlefield of Sedan, to seek compensation of the losses in the east. This meant expansion in the Balkans, involvement in conflicts with Turkey, and most important, a new source of friction with Russia, which finally led to the crisis of the first World War. Here, too, the connection with the fatal war of 1866 is apparent because an aggressive, militaristic state like Prussia might obtain the leadership of Germany, but never, in the age of nationalism, of a multinational empire. Recognition of this simple fact lies at the root of the Austrian decline.

In October, 1866, Francis Joseph accepted the resignation of Count Mensdorff-Pouilly and entrusted foreign affairs to the former Saxon prime minister, Baron(later Count) Ferdinand Beust, a shrewd but unequal opponent of Bismarck's policy. His assignment was, if possible, to initiate a new anti-Prussian combination, if not alliance, which should undo what never could be undone. One of the major means to that effect was seen in domestic reorganization. This meant full reconciliation with Hungary, embodied in the Compromise of 1867, henceforth the constitutional frame of the empire, to be discussed in Section E. In foreign policy the first aim was to arrive at an understanding with Napoleon III. The Salzburg entrevue of August, 1867, between Francis Joseph and the French emperor was officially a visit of condolence on the occasion of the execution of Francis Joseph's brother Maximilian of Mexico in Queretaro. He had been prompted by Napoleon to engage in the trans-Atlantic adventure but had been abandoned by him later. French fears of involvement in a conflict with the United States were understandable in political terms. Just the same, Napoleon's attitude looked cynical as seen from a dynastic angle.

Napoleon's past Mexican policy, however, was not the reason for the failure of the two emperors to come to terms. Francis Joseph, never too fond of his brother, certainly could overcome feelings of resentment

[29] Srbik, *Deutsche Einheit,* IV, 366–466; Friedjung, *Der Kampf um die Vorherrschaft,* II, 470–518; Adam Wandruszka, *Schicksalsjahr, 1866* (Graz, 1966), pp. 175–203. F. R. Bridge, *From Sadowa to Sarajevo: The Foreign Policy of Austria-Hungary 1866–1914* (London, 1972), pp. 11–29.

against the upstart Bonaparte, but neither he nor Napoleon dared to take the big anti-Prussian jump. Later attempts to bring Italy into negotiations for an Austro-French-Italian alliance against Prussia never reached a stage of serious discussions. The cautious preliminary Austrian decision in favor of neutrality taken by a crown council on the eve of the outbreak of the war of 1870–1871 became permanent when the Bonapartist empire fell within six weeks under the shattering blows of the German attack. Whatever happened from now on in the war, a republican France was, for reasons of domestic policy, hardly a feasible ally for the Habsburg empire. Francis Joseph changed his course accordingly and dismissed Beust in November, 1871. His place was taken by Count Julius Andrássy, Magyar rebel in 1848–1849, subsequently proscribed émigré, sentenced in absentia to be hanged, but rehabilitated and appointed Hungarian prime minister in 1867. Andrássy, one of the architects of the Austro-Hungarian Compromise, was committed to the principle of German-Magyar predominance in the Habsburg monarchy. Consequently he was a supporter of amicable relations with Germany. He wanted to bring Austria into such combination as equal partner, and this was the main reason for the unfortunate Oriental policy of this attractive, courageous, and in many ways capable man.[30]

First, however, an attempt by Bismarck was made to establish a European order directed by the three eastern empires on the basis of the principle of monarchic solidarity. In 1894, with the conclusion of the Franco-Russian alliance directed against both central powers, these efforts ended in definite failure. But long before, in fact within a few years after 1871, the failure of Bismarck's endeavors became apparent. The so-called Three Emperors' League of 1873 consisted in a military convention between Russia and the new German empire of 1871 to which mere consultation and vague cooperation pacts between Russia and Austria were added. Germany gained the advantage of at least benevolent Austro-Russian neutrality in the event of a French attack—unlikely as it might have been for some time. For Austria and Russia only a common front against international revolutionary activities on the extreme Left were easily feasible. Yet common actions against such true or alleged danger did hardly require a formal pact.

The real test of the agreement would have been Austro-Russian cooperation in case of a crisis in the east—as it were in the Balkans. In 1875

[30] For an over-all evaluation of Andrássy with emphasis on his services as diplomat see Eduard von Wertheimer, *Graf Julius Andrássy und seine Zeit,* 3 vols. (Stuttgart, 1910–1913), see III, 340–368.

revolts against the oppressive Turkish regime started in Bosnia-Hercegovina. The Serbs supported the insurrections and Russia gave at least indirect support to risings in the eastern Balkans. A new Russian advance in this area appeared to be in the offing. Negotiations between the leading Austrian and Russian statesmen (Andrássy and Gorchakov) and subsequently between the sovereigns Francis Joseph and Alexander II in the summer of 1876 led to the so-called Reichstadt agreement, formalized by the second treaty of Budapest (January, 1877): Austria pledged her neutrality in a Russo-Turkish conflict and Russia waived objection to an Austrian occupation of Bosnia-Hercegovina.

The ensuing new Russo-Turkish war of 1877–1878 alarmed Europe, particularly Great Britain and Austria. The Ottoman empire's resistance was stronger than expected but its eventual defeat inevitable. In the preliminary peace of St. Stefano of March, 1878, Serbia, Montenegro, and Roumania were to sever their tenuous bonds to Turkey. The High Portal was also to agree to the creation of a Greater Bulgaria extending from the Black Sea to the Aegean Sea, to be occupied for several years by Russian troops. Even thereafter the new Bulgaria was to be a Russian vassal state. By this arrangement Russia would gain free passage for her naval forces through the Dardanelles and military predominance in the Balkans. The first objective was intolerable for Britain, the second for Austria. Their joint protests led to the convocation of the Congress of Berlin under Bismarck's chairmanship in June, 1878. When the Congress adjourned in mid-July Russian advances were restricted on all fronts. In particular a territorially considerably reduced Bulgaria was confined now to a northern principality tributary to Turkey, whereas the southeastern part (East Roumelia) was given merely separate administration as a Turkish province. Thus a potential Russian satellite state was cut down to size. As for Austria, the signatories of the Congress act (that is, the great powers and Turkey), granted Austria the right to occupy and fully administer Bosnia and Hercegovina for an undetermined period. Furthermore the powers conceded military occupation of the Sanjak of Novibazar, a small wooded strip of territory between Serbia and Montenegro. In a secret agreement between Austria and the Ottoman empire, the Turks were assured that the occupation was meant to be provisional in character but indefinite in time. The sovereignty of the sultan should continue in principle though not in practice. This meant sweeping occupational rights but not formal annexation, which would have required the approval of the signatory powers of the Congress act.

This outcome of the congressional decisions was of mixed value for the Habsburg monarchy. Russia's dissatisfaction continued, though it was extended now from Austria to Germany. The fact that Andrássy resigned himself to mere occupation and did not insist on annexation, which might have been achieved with the approval of the great powers (though not with that of Turkey) was to create difficulties in the future. The garrisoning of the Sanjak, probably indefensible in case of war, was to be a further mortgage on relations with Serbia and Montenegro, while the conceivable benefits were truly minor.

Yet annexation or occupation of Bosnia-Hercegovina or mere military garrisoning in the Sanjak were secondary questions. The basic issue was the justification of Austrian military and political expansion in the Balkans. Three arguments could be advanced for the Austrian Balkan policy. One, never openly admitted but clear from further actions was that of economic penetration of southeastern Europe; this was difficult to achieve, dangerous to put through, but from the point of the Habsburg monarchy's interests, not unreasonable. Two, prestige, although the involvement in a hornets nest of conflicting Balkan interests was hardly likely to improve the Austrian position. Finally (and this was officially said), the danger of having the hinterland of Dalmatia controlled by a hostile country. This meant potentially Serbia rather than Turkey. However, the Habsburg monarchy was strong enough to take care of her interests in Dalmatia without acquisition of new territories.

Whatever the case in favor of occupation or annexation might have been, disadvantages and dangers outweighed the problematical advantages. Clearly the Southern Slav problem would become more serious with the acquisition of additional Southern Slav, largely Serb, territory. The precarious balance of national alignments established by the Austro-Hungarian Compromise would be upset and the unfortunate device of actually permanent but legally provisional occupation was to challenge the demands of rising Southern Slav and later to some degree also Turkish nationalism. It could be expected that the occupation would strain Austro-Russian relations further, meaning, in turn, greater dependency on German protection. This last point was indeed the first major direct international consequence of the occupation.[31]

[31] William L. Langer, *European Alliances and Alignments 1871–1890* (New York, 1938), pp. 121–170; Allan J. P. Taylor; *The Struggle for Mastery in Europe 1848–1918* (Oxford, 1957), pp. 228–254; L. von Südland, *Die südslawische Frage und der Weltkrieg* (Vienna, 1918), pp. 484–514; Bridge, *From Sadowa to Sarajevo*, pp. 81–102.

There were others. The occupation proved to be not a pushover. The costly military campaign put a strain on relations with the High Portal and Serbia at the same time. This was partly obscured by the fact that the Serbian king Milan was sustained by Austrian subsidies. Furthermore, Magyar nationalists but particularly German liberals saw in the occupation a dangerous upsetting of the balance of Slavic peoples against Germans and Magyars. It was primarily this fact which led to the downfall of the German liberal regime in Cisleithanian Austria and its replacement by a Slavic dominated conservative coalition. This meant not only the end of the problematical rule of German liberalism in the Habsburg empire but of political liberalism in general in the western half of the monarchy until the end.

In foreign relations, the Bosnian affair, as well as the German mediator role at the Congress of Berlin, strained German-Russian relations, as noted above, and led thus indirectly to the Austro-German alliance of October, 1879. Bismarck at this time was isolated. Consequently the terms of the alliance, which pledged the contracting parties to come to each other's support, if attacked by Russia single-handed, but by France only, if that power was supported by Russia, seemed to be favorable to Austria. On paper, her obligations were more limited than those of Germany. Actually a single-handed attack by France on Germany was a purely academic contingency. Bismarck was interested in preventing a dissolution of the Habsburg monarchy, from which Russia would have benefited more than Germany. From that point of view the alliance had indeed advantages for Austria. On the other hand, it should have become clear that the Habsburg monarchy as ally of Germany would become involved in a future Franco-Russian two-front war against Germany, whose outbreak Bismarck's genius could delay but not prevent. In addition, the reliance on a superior German ally barred forever the possibility for a comprehensive settlement of the nationality questions in the Habsburg monarchy, if such a chance still existed. Premise for the alliance was Austro-German and Magyar predominance in the empire. The alliance meant further that as long as Germany had the upper hand Austria would have to play the second role to German interests as "brilliant second" as William II put it at the time of the first Morocco crisis. On the other hand, if Austria should be given a freer rein in international relations then the danger of involvement in a major war with Russia and her potential allies resulting from a Balkan crisis might become ever more likely.

It could be held, against this line of reasoning, that the continuation of the alliance secured for the Danube peoples limited freedom for half a century, which they would not have enjoyed under the tsarist boot. Yet the freedom was limited, the dependency on Germany great and the danger of a major war even greater. Thus the alliance resulting in part from the Bosnian occupation represented a mixed blessing. Whether it could help to preserve constitutional government under peaceful conditions or whether it would involve the Danube monarchy in major wars would largely depend on the complexities of the national question in conjunction with the level of statesmanship of the future architects of Austrian foreign policy.[32]

B. Domestic affairs from 1815 to the revolution of 1848–1849

The twenty years of peace of the Franciscan administration after the end of the Napoleonic wars and their continuation during the reign of Ferdinand the Benign until 1848 may still be considered as apolitical in character. No parties, no pressure groups substantially influenced the course of government. It is true that after the revolution, from 1849 to 1860, we face a restoration of absolutist government. But a restored system is always different from the original system. The lessons of the revolution of 1848–1849 may never have been learned by the ruling forces of Austrian society but neither were they forgotten.

If we say that absolutism between 1815 and 1848 was still in full control, we have to qualify this statement in two respects. First, the changes brought about by the reform period in Hungary from 1825 to 1848, although not representing popular sovereignty in an organized manner, are in some respects a transition to a more modern social order. Second, the rumbling of nationalism among all the empire's national groups heralded new problems, new constellations of powers, and new conflicts. And yet momentous as nationalism was to become before 1848 it was expressed primarily in the ideological sphere, less so politically and socially. Thus the Restoration period and pre-March era were still becalmed in the political sphere.[33]

[32] Langer, *European Alliances,* pp. 171–216; Sidney B. Fay, *The Origins of the World War* (New York, 1928), 2 vols., I, pp. 59–70; Taylor, *The Struggle for Mastery in Europe,* pp. 255–264; Robert A. Kann, in Ludovit Holotik and Anton Vantuch, eds., *Der österreichisch-ungarische Ausgleich 1867* (Bratislava, 1971), pp. 24–44.

[33] In this study we perceive the Restoration period as the era from 1815 to the death of Francis I in 1835, and the pre-March era from here on to the outbreak of the revolution in 1848. See also Robert A. Kann, *The Problem of Restoration* (Berkeley, 1968), pp. 94–103.

a) ADMINISTRATIVE-JUDICIAL SPHERE

The second half of the Franciscan reign in domestic affairs was more stable than the first with its many, but unprincipled attempts to reshuffle the organization of government. After 1815 the police played an increasingly pervasive part, which rightly gave the new system the trademark "police state." Actually it was not entirely new. The police system had been introduced under Joseph II by Count Johann Anton Pergen to control actions initiated by the Josephin bureaucracy. The police certainly also reported the political attitude of individuals to the regime. Yet by and large it was still a security force and one of its main tasks was to enforce the reform legislation. In other words, in a devious way the police were to support a progressive philosophy of government. Under Francis, and particularly after 1815, the chief objective and task of the police, under its new chief, Count Joseph Sedlnitzky (as president of the police and censorship agency from 1817 to 1848) was to check the spread of even faintly liberal ideas, that meant, potentially revolutionary ideas. This task required a strict system of censorship. Loyalty stood for complete submission to political and social repression. Some Franciscan bureaucrats, like Count Franz Anton Kolowrat, a friend of the estates system in its restricted Maria Theresan sense, particularly in the Bohemian lands, was mildly opposed to this, yet Sedlnitzky's policies, backed by Metternich, prevailed until the revolution of 1848.[34]

The estates rights remained extremely limited; new estates constitutions for Tyrol, Carniola, and Galicia restricted estates powers to the right of petition and some very limited participation in the collection and allocation of tax money. Financial administration was separated from over-all political administration, and the General Court Chamber was restored as main financial agency. Karl Friedrich von Kübeck (1780–1855), one of the ablest bureaucrats under three emperors, established this new organization. The Franciscan government never fully overcame the consequences of the great financial crisis of 1811, which in turn was mainly the natural result of the war period. The establishment of the Austrian Nationalbank in 1816 and the government's reliance on support of private financiers (such as Rothschild, Arnstein, Eskeles) helped, however, to prevent new economic disasters. A modernization of the land tax on a broader basis introduced for the first time truly comprehensive records of all cultivated lands in the country and of all leases in town houses. An

[34] Julius Marx, *Die österreichische Zensur im Vormärz* (Vienna, 1959), pp. 11–24, 36–64.

indirect tax imposed in 1829 on the transportation of foodstuff beyond town and provincial limits was unfair and unpopular.

As for provincial organization, the separate administration of Lombardy-Venetia was to be divided into two gubernia in Milan and Venice. The Illyrian provinces, ceded to France in 1809, were reincorporated into Austria as two gubernia, one with the center of administration in Ljubljana and one in Trieste. The latter included the small part of Croatia on the right bank of the Sava and Fiume (Rijeka). Both, however, after some years were returned to Hungarian administration.

With the rising reaction after 1815, the influence of the ecclesiastic spirit of the strictest conservative observance became increasingly strong. Undoubtedly it conflicted with the lively intellectual contributions and interchange among the Catholic Romantics around Adam Müller, Josef von Pilat, Friedrich Schlegel, and Emanuel Veith. The social-oriented Christian doctrines of the previously mentioned Clemens Maria Hofbauer (1751–1820, sainted in 1909), who represented the Redemptorist (Liguorian) congregation in the early Restoration period in Austria had little immediate but considerable long-range influence on the charitable aspects of Church policy. On the other hand, the readmission of the Jesuit Order in 1814, restored to good graces by the Holy See, stood for the spirit of the *ecclesia militans.* All things considered a strange conversion, though not yet elimination, of Josephinism in state-Church relations, had taken place. The government never again relinquished its control of ecclesiastic matters but it used the Church as an arm of government to promote and enforce its policies. This practice pertained in particular to the supervision of secondary education for the intellectual and social elite. Here the state with the authoritative advice of the higher clergy reserved for itself the right to prescribe textbooks and academic curricula not only in the secular schools but also in the diocesan seminaries, even though they had been formally restored to episcopal control. The establishment of an Austrian Academy in 1847 was only an isolated instance of intellectual activities outside clerical control.[35]

A slight tendency toward liberalization in the governmental process could be seen only in two areas. In the judicial sphere patrimonial jurisdiction was further restricted, partly because it had become impossible to reintroduce it in the German Alpine and Southern Slav territories, which between 1805 and 1813 had been under Bavarian and French administra-

[35] Rudolf Till, *Hofbauer und sein Kreis* (Vienna, 1951), pp. 9–94; Winter, *Romantismus,* pp. 27–55, 125–143; Edward Hosp, *Kirche in Österreich im Vormärz, 1815–1850* (Vienna, 1971), pp. 15–21, 249–359.

tions; but partly also, because the safeguards of individual rights introduced by the Josephin legislation for the peasants, made continuation of this jurisdiction cumbersome and expensive for the lords.

In the military sphere the needs of the war period had led to a gradual extension of service obligations and corresponding reduction of exemptions from service. As discussed (Chapt. V/K), this policy was carried over into the era of peace after 1815. To make service obligations less hateful general modifications took place, however, in the 1840s. Conditions remained severe enough and yet these modifications, linked to gradual mitigations of the harsh and degrading military discipline, proved again that even an absolute government could not entirely ignore public opinion.[36]

b) ECONOMICS

Gradual economic development in Austria during this period was characterized more by changing technological conditions than by planned policies. It was neither rapid nor comprehensive enough to be regarded as industrial or agrarian revolution in western European terms. The tariff policy of the government remained unsuccessful and unimaginative. Barred from participation in the German *Zollverein* of 1833, the regime failed to establish an effective countersystem in Germany or even a comprehensive customs union of the Habsburg lands. Hungarian opposition represented the chief impediment. Thus a protective tariff system in regard to foreign countries continued, alongside one of lower so-called preferential internal customs. A cumbersome order of trade organization in the non-Hungarian lands hampered industrial progress. It consisted in a largely arbitrary division between so-called commercial trades controlled by the Court Chamber and police trades supervised by the Court Chancery. The former trades were meant to satisfy needs beyond the local demands and included manufacturing in industrial plants; the latter were primarily to serve local needs. To compound the complexity, another division existed between establishments controlled by guild regulations and "free crafts," a misleading term because they were subject to cumbersome government regulations.

Some industrial progress was made just the same. The textile industry in the German-Austrian and particularly in the Bohemian lands, the silk

[36] Henry A. Strakosch, *State Absolutism and the Rule of Law: The Struggle for Codification of Civil Law in Austria 1753–1811* (Sydney, 1967), pp. 181–194; Huber and Dopsch, *Österreichische Reichsgeschichte,* pp. 310–321; Herbert Matis, *Österreichs Wirtschaft 1848–1918* (Berlin, 1972), pp. 22–30.

industry in Lombardy, and some modest industrial establishments in Hungary (textiles, sugar refineries, distilleries) expanded. The iron and steel mining and processing industry in Witkowitz in Moravia and in northern Styria made substantial progress. Dye manufacturing was introduced in Lower Austria. Renowned for its quality was the glass industry in Bohemia and the manufacturing of leather goods in Lower Austria, particularly in Vienna.

Working conditions in the crafts were dismal. Teenage apprentices were delivered to the mercies of often cruel, greedy, but also impoverished masters. In the industrial plants a fourteen-hour working day was the rule, reduced to twelve hours in 1839 for children under twelve. In these respects Austria did neither worse nor better than industrially more advanced countries.

As to communications, the government supported the establishment of the Austrian Danube Steamship Company in 1829, and in 1836 the Austrian Lloyd, the main steamship company on the high seas, with headquarters in Trieste. Austria also pioneered on the Continent the introduction of railroads. Between 1825 and 1827 a railroad, though not yet steam-operated, was opened between Budweis (Budějovice) in Bohemia and Linz in Upper Austria; after 1836 a very short stretch of the future Northern Railway route (Floridsdorf to Deutsch-Wagram) was operated by steam locomotives. The canal waterway system of communications in the Austro-German-Bohemian orbit was improved. In all, there was some moderate progress but the fact that it was not accompanied by social legislation led to serious disturbances in Vienna, Prague, Plžen (Pilsen), and other places during the economic crisis between 1845 and 1848. They heralded worse troubles to come.[37]

c) THE SITUATION IN HUNGARY

During this period of artificial centralization Hungary requires a separate discussion—not so much on constitutional grounds, but because of independent intellectual and social currents, and in the pre-March period already distinct political actions. In 1848 Hungary including Croatia

[37] See Mayer-Kaindl-Pirchegger, *Geschichte und Kulturleben Österreichs,* 5th revised edition by A. Klein (Vienna, 1965), pp. 36–42, 78–97. Kristina M. Fink, *Die österreichisch-ungarische Monarchie als Wirtschaftsgemeinschaft* (Munich, 1968), pp. 9–19; Julius Marx, *Die wirtschaftlichen Ursachen der Revolution von 1848 in Östrreich* (Graz-Cologne, 1965), pp. 9–167 passim; Nachum T. Gross, "Die Stellung der Habsburgermonarchie in der Weltwirtschaft" in Adam Wandruszka and Peter Urbanitsch eds., *Die Habsburgermonarchie 1848–1918* (Wien, 1973–), vol. I, Die wirtschaftliche Entwicklung, pp. 1–28.

had a population of nearly 12 million, a figure almost doubled in 1918. The future capital, Pest, had 50,000 inhabitants in 1848, and 2 million a century later.[38] In this agricultural society the migrations of Serbs from the south, Slovaks from Bohemia and Moravia in the west, Jews and Ruthenians in substantial numbers from Galicia and Bukovina, and hundreds of thousands of Roumanians from Walachia into Transylvania, created a social structure, which first endangered and then overturned the Magyar majority in the country. Taking a long-range view, Magyar nationalism could, however, haltingly drop prejudices and privileges deriving from the specific ethnic distinction between the Ugro-Finnish Magyars, the Slavic, German, and the partly Mediterranean Roumanian peoples. It could never bow to the gradual reversal of nationality statistics and its social consequences to the disadvantage of the master race.

For the time being social pressures were equal to the national ones. The tax exemption of the nobility, not abolished until the revolution of 1848, meant that some 700,000 landowners, mostly in the middle-income brackets were tax exempted. This, rather than the privileged status of the aristocratic landowners which until the Maria Theresan period paralleled those in Bohemia, was the most characteristic feature of the Hungarian social system. The freedom of the peasants to own lands and purchase their full unrestricted personal freedom was not established until the diet of 1840. Peasant rebellions were bound to occur frequently, particularly during and after the great plague (cholera) of 1831–1832.[39]

National tension was piled on the social stresses and here the non-Magyar nationalities were second-class citizens even compared with the underprivileged Magyar peasants. Slovaks, Roumanians, and Ruthenians had no political or territorial organization. The Roumanians in Transylvania did not have equal status with the Magyars, Szekels, and Germans, in Hungary proper only the Serbs enjoyed a limited autonomy. Thus by a process of elimination the language conflict, never fully put to rest again after the reign of Joseph II, evolved first between Magyars and

[38] Pressburg (Pozsony) was the city where until 1848 the Hungarian diet usually convened and where the kings were crowned. It was, however, not the official capital. Beginning with the thirteenth century, Buda (Ofen) could be considered the major royal residence. Pest, on the left bank of the Danube, across from Buda, became the seat of government in 1848. In 1872, Buda and Pest merged and the new Budapest became the official capital of Hungary. The last two coronations took place there.

[39] Kann, *Das Nationalitätenproblem,* I, 117–122 and the literature quoted ibid. 389–392; Dominic C. Kosáry, *A History of Hungary* (Cleveland, 1941), pp. 138–184; Istvan Barta in Ervin Pamlényi, ed., *Die Geschichte Ungarns* (Budapest, 1971), V, 241–298, see in particular VII, 287–291.

Croatians, of whom a large part in the south and east lived within the Military Frontier organization. Only "Civil" or "Banal Croatia" (the territory under the jurisdiction of the banus) in the northwest formed a distinct social structure of political significance. Even though subordinated to the Hungarian crown and limited within its geographical confines, the political importance of Civil Croatia was strengthened by the neighboring Military Frontier of the same ethnic composition and tradition.

The Hungarian diet of 1830 had passed legislation according to which government officials and lawyers must be able to officiate in Hungarian, which up to then was only taught as second language in schools. Higher education was based almost exclusively on Latin and secondly on German—a policy in the interest of the Vienna government. Latin or Croatian was ruled out even as secondary official language by the Magyar nationalists, who at the diet of 1844 managed to put through a law that required the teaching of Magyar in secondary Croatian schools. More important were new laws which made immigration into Hungary including Croatia dependent on the knowledge of Magyar and made the Magyar language instead of Latin the official language of communication between Hungary proper and Croatia. This meant in substance that the ancient kingdom should be considered as *partes adnexae,* that is, mere provinces of Hungary with a very limited degree of autonomy rather than as *regna socia,* allied kingdoms, the terms according to which Croatia-Slavonia had entered the union of 1527 with its separate *sabor* (diet) and *banus* (governor), appointed by the Hungarian king.[40]

The ideological repercussions of such problems will be discussed in the following section in regard to all national groups. At this point we are only concerned with the political struggle in Hungary, which can be understood as the conflict between the enlightened conservative reformers represented by Count Stephan Széchenyi (1791–1860) and the radical, socially progressive nationalists by Louis Kossuth (1802–1894).

Széchenyi, even by his opponent Kossuth referred to as the greatest Hungarian, stood for evolutionary changes, first economically and then perhaps, but only in agreement within the Austrian government, politically according to the principles of English constitutional government.

[40] Jules Szekfü, *État et Nation* (Paris, 1945), pp. 11–103; Rudolf Kissling, *Die Kroaten* (Graz-Cologne, 1956), pp. 57–61; Stanko Guldescu, "Croatian Political History 1526–1918," in Francis H. Eterovich and Christopher Spalatin, eds., *Croatia: Land, People, Culture* (Toronto, 1964–1970), II, 38–40; Kann, *Nationalitätenproblem,* I, 246–259, 439–441.

His efforts to achieve reforms were only to a small part successful. Yet the foundation of the Hungarian Academy, the establishment of the National Casino as a kind of debating society primarily for the national aristocracy, the beginning of the regulation of the Danube and Tisza rivers, and Széchenyi's fight against the law of entail of landed property were impressive achievements under existing conditions. Such endeavors were supported by enlightened nobles like Baron Nicholas de Wesselényi, counts Aurel Dessewffy and Antony Szécsen and by leading members of the gentry such as Joseph von Eötvös and Francis Deák. Eötvös, the champion of Hungarian administrative reorganization, became later one of the most original promoters of empire reform. Francis Deák, an outstanding constitutional lawyer and moderate parliamentarian of wide popularity, was in later years to become the great old man of Hungarian politics.

Kossuth, on the other hand, the young, fiery provincial lawyer from the Slovakian region wanted to force several issues at the same time: the full emancipation of the Hungarian peasants, the recognition of Magyar as the national language throughout greater Hungary including Croatia and Transylvania, the transformation of the relationship to Austria to a kind of confederal association, and the establishment of a separate Hungarian customs territory. Széchenyi either refrained from demands which could not be put through in an evolutionary manner, that is, could not be put through at all, or he compromised, as in the Hungarian tariff question, in favor of the customs union with Austria.[41] Kossuth's brilliant dialectics and powerful, to some extent demagogic mass appeal, which was displayed in the dietal deliberations of 1832–1836, 1837–1840, and 1847–1848,[42] further alerted Magyar nationalism.

Although Széchenyi's success was more passive and less conspicuous, it was effective because his cautious reform policy prevented the break with Austria. If he had had his way, the liberal members of the diet of 1847 would have settled peacefully for a compromise on such demands as a lower house of parliament elected by general male franchise, govern-

[41] George Barany, *Stephen Szécheny and the Awakening of Hungarian Nationalism, 1791–1841* (Princeton, 1968), pp. 135–317; Johann Weber, *Eötvös und die ungarische Nationalitätenfrage* (Munich, 1966), pp. 104–154; Bela Király, "The Young Ferenc Deák and the Problem of the Serfs," *Südostforschungen,* XIX (1970), 91–127; Kann, *Nationalitätenproblem,* I, 117–122, 389–392.

[42] The king called no diets into session between 1812 and 1825 and this *ex lex* situation would have been continued had Francis not been anxious to secure recognition of the succession of his incapacitated son Ferdinand as crowned king of Hungary.

ment responsible to parliament, free press, and abolition of all tax exemptions. This was indeed a relatively enlightened approach on the part of the gentry majority of the diet, whereas the claim for unqualified incorporation of Transylvania into Hungary could be considered controversial from the viewpoint of liberal principles. However, this program, until March, 1848, the maximum of the obtainable, was soon superseded by the revolutionary events.

d) RISE OF THE PROBLEM OF NATIONALISM

In this section we are concerned with a brief analysis of a transitional stage of nationalist development. The new and important cultural contributions of the champions of the Slavic renaissance and changes in the nationalist ideologies within other groups will be discussed in Chapter VII. Here we start from the assumption that what frequently is referred to as "the emergence of the national (or nationalist) problem" or "the awakening of nationalism" goes back further in history than to the seminal ideas of Rousseau, Herder, or Schlözer in the transition period from late Enlightenment to early romanticism. What occurred in those decades is the crystallization of concepts while the phenomena of nationalism themselves can be traced back to the beginnings of modern times and in some cases to the Middle Ages. True enough, the so-called Slavic renaissance —roughly from the last quarter of the eighteenth century to the second quarter of the nineteenth—strengthened a sense of national consciousness among several national groups, but this era did not create these feelings.

Here an important distinction is suggestive. There were first national groups with a political history based on the tradition of medieval social stratification within the confines of the Habsburg empire (Croats, Czechs, Italians, Germans, Magyars, and Poles). They possessed a strong sense of national identity and consciousness. Secondly, such consciousness cannot be denied to the so-called national groups without history either, which for centuries were deprived by foreign overlords of autonomous political development. Consequently they could not take advantage of the mixed blessings of a nationally conscious nobility, gentry, and urban burgher class. The fact that such national groups as the Roumanians, Ruthenians, Serbs, Slovaks, Slovenes, had no independent political history and tradition of a separate social feudal structure within the borders of the Habsburg realms does not mean that they lacked history. Independent political national history of a national group—in terms of this study within the Habsburg empire—and national consciousness of such a group refer to separate concepts. If the first is present, the second is also, but if the first is lacking there is still a probability that national consciousness exists.[43]

What does this mean in terms of the transitional era under discussion here? Nationalism up to the beginning of the restoration period had at some time played an important role among some national groups within their domestic order as well as in their relationship to the empire. Now largely under the influence of the Slavic cultural renaissance and, concomitant with it, with the recognition of the ethnic factor, nationalism began to become a political problem for all national groups whereas previously it had been one only for some. It changed to *a,* if not *the* empire-wide chief problem. This became fully apparent in the political confrontations of the revolution of 1848–1849. Yet much occurred or began to occur in the preceding Restoration and pre-March period which heralded the metamorphosis of the national problem into the most pervasive of all problems of the multinational empire.

To begin with, the *grossdeutsch-kleindeutsch* issue was discussed briefly in Section A of this chapter in the context of foreign, especially Austrian-Prussian, relations. Of more immediate impact within Austria between 1815 and 1848 were the efforts to modernize the estates system as counterweight against the centralism of an oppressive absolutism. The former member of the Tyrolean estates, Victor von Andrian-Werburg (1813–1858) and the artillery captain Karl Moering (1810–1870), both mentioned in the discussion of St. Paul's Assembly in Frankfurt, played an important part. They were distinguished writers, who promoted the idea of an Austrian estates central assembly to be convened in Vienna. They also wanted to bring the peasants of the crownlands into this estates structure, and they further advocated communal autonomy. All this should have modified both absolutism and centralism in a rather limited

[43] The author, in line with his previous discussions of the problem, confines the validity of the concept of nations or national groups with independent political history to the area of the Habsburg empire. No nation in a wider sense lacks history altogether and all five national groups referred to here as lacking an independent political history within the confines of the Danube monarchy identified themselves throughout various phases of the Middle Ages with national political associations, though frequently of a mere tribal character. None of them, however, had a political center in the Habsburg empire prior to the 19th century as understood in the terms of this study. This modification separates the concept, as used here, from the Marxian interpretation of the concept of nations with and without history. See Kann, *Nationalitätenproblem,* I, 44–56, 359–362. For a contrary Marxian opinion see Franz Zwitter, "Die nationalen Fragen in der österreichisch-ungarischen Monarchie (1900–1914)," in Fritz Klein and Peter Hanák, eds., *Die nationale Frage in der österreichischungarischen Monarchie* (Budapest, 1966), pp. 11–28.

political and social sense. In effect such proposals in national terms meant a continuation of a qualified system of German-directed centralism. It was hoped that relatively minor changes of political institutions would meet the demands of other national groups halfway and in time and thus keep the ruling system viable with modest adjustments. Francis Schuselka (1811–1886), another St. Paul's deputy, more volatile in his views than either Andrian-Werburg or Moering but an equally versatile writer, had a better insight in the seriousness of the national problems, though he proposed no better solutions. A determined opponent of national and political oppression, he believed in the ideological superiority of German liberalism. Like many German political writers from the radical Left to the extreme Right he also feared the impact of substantial Slavic opposition. The assumption that the administrative separation of Galicia from the bulk of the empire, in conjunction with a more liberal domestic regime, would help matters in general seemed to be more reasonable than the ideas of the champions of the estates' reforms.[44]

The ideological rift among the Magyars between the enlightened conservatives or moderate liberals around Széchenyi and the spokesmen for a young Hungary in the Mazzinian national pattern behind Kossuth has been surveyed in the preceding section. Equally important and politically equally advanced, though subject to more stringent government controls, were propositions among the Czechs in the Bohemian lands. Here several basic concepts at cross purposes with each other were meant to check generally recognized grievances. Public opinion found the continued rule of German-directed centralism increasingly oppressive and unendurable. A widely supported device to check this situation was the cautiously camouflaged demand for Czech political dominance according to the medieval concepts of the Bohemian *Staatsrecht* with a view to eventual outright Czech-German separation. This program, however, was perceived as a terminal goal. As understood by the enlightened conservatives, represented later by the Old Czech party, the program stood for the prevalent political view from the pre-March period roughly to the Austro-Hungarian Compromise of 1867. It was reflected in several ways, first as that of the territorial aristocracy in the crownlands in juxtaposition to the court aristocracy in Vienna, secondly as that of a large sector of the educated upper middle class. But primarily it stood for the views and interests of the houses of Colloredo, Liechtenstein, Clam Gallas, Clam Martinic, Silva-Tarouca, Lützow, Thun, and Schwarzenberg among other aristocratic families who had settled in the Bohemia lands after 1620. In

[44] Kann, *Nationalitätenproblem,* I, 63–72, 365–368.

substance, they had never become Czech nationalists, but they were and remained in favor of strengthened estates rights in the lands of the Bohemian crown. Count Joseph M. Thun and the historian Palacký could be considered in the pre-March period spokesmen for these views, though Palacký outgrew such narrow constitutional philosophy. It is true, however, that he never accepted a more comprehensive social plan.

The political philosophy of the moderate Bohemian reformers overlapped at some point with Panslav ideas. Insofar as they expressed the desire for a political union of all Slavic nations as equal partners—as proposed during the revolution by Bakunin—they were hardly more practical than the somewhat mystic concept of a cultural Panslav association under Russian leadership advocated by the romantic Slovak writer Jan Kollár. More feasible though not more popular appeared the notion of a Russian-directed and dominated Panslavism, against which Palacký took a stand in his famous letter to the Frankfurt Assembly to be discussed below. Politically more farsighted than either the Panslavs or the adherents of the Bohemian *Staatsrecht* was a young Czech liberal writer and journalist, Karel Havliček (1821–1856) and an enlightened conservative, capable Bohemian aristocrat, Count Leo Thun (1811–1888). Havliček, the first great Czech journalist, who fought under pre-March absolutism for his cause in the thinly disguised role of a reporter of conditions in Ireland and China, came closest to the idea of a separate democratic Czech political nation, freed from Habsburg absolutism, but protected also from tsarist-dominated Panslavism. Thun, governor of Bohemia in 1848 and an outstanding Austrian minister of education for the following eleven years, saw the best solution for the Czech demands in the gradual achievement of equality with the Germans by bilingualism in mixed territories. This measure, as it turned out, would have indeed greatly benefited the Czechs against German intransigence and arrogant refusal to learn the language of a small Slavic nation. Thun's further-reaching notions that Austria would have to develop multinational parties, based on common political-social interests, which might take precedence over the national ones, were advocated shortly after the revolution. They came too late but at the same time also too early. At any rate, they were not heeded.[45]

[45] Hermann Münch, *Böhmische Tragödie* (Braunschweig, 1949), pp. 88–189; Richard Plaschka, "Das böhmische Staatrecht in tschechischer Sicht," in Ernst Birke and Kurt Oberdorffer, eds., *Das böhmische Staatsrecht in den deutsch-tschechischen Auseinandersetzungen des 19. und 20. Jahrhunderts* (Marburg, 1960), pp. 1–14; Hans Raupach, *Der tschechische Frühnationalismus* (Darmstadt, 1967), pp. 90–137; Barbara Kohák Kimmel, "Karel Havliček and the Czech Press before 1848," in Peter Brock and H. Gordon Skilling, eds., *The Czech Renaissance of the*

Regarding the Poles, the concept of a restoration in terms of the romantic Polish émigrés in the west, the resurrection of a free, independent, and liberal Poland remained very much alive. It was promoted in particular in the free city state of Cracow, established at the borders of western Galicia in 1815. From then until the incorporation of the city into Austria in 1846, Cracow was to serve as a kind of temporary Piedmont, a center from which endeavors for the restoration of a free undivided Poland radiated. In the pre-March period, the Poles under Prussian administration and, until the end of the reign of Tsar Alexander I, those under Russian rule were treated somewhat better than those under the Metternich system in Austria.[46] The frustrated revolution of 1830–1831 in Congress Poland, however, changed conditions in the Russian sphere for the worse. This lead to a shift of the revolutionary activities to Austrian soil, where police suppression was not quite as brutal as under the tyrannical Tsar Nicholas. "Young Poland" in Austria, among whose leaders a subsequently moderate Austrian speaker of parliament, Francis Smolka, and a future imperial Austrian minister, Florian Ziemialkowski, were to be found, was active, though not very successful. For once the Polish aristocracy in Galicia and its gentry clientele, the Szlachta, belonged to the most oppressive landlords in the Habsburg domains, second to none in Bohemia and Hungary. Furthermore the Austrian government, particularly under the enlightened governor of Galicia and later minister of interior Count Francis Stadion, had introduced at least some beneficial agricultural and administrative reforms and curtailment of patrimonial jurisdiction. The Galician peasants—Polish and Ruthenians alike—considered their own lords as worse enemies than the government in Vienna and the provincial administration in Lemberg (Lwów, L'viv). The Polish peasant revolt in 1846 in central and west Galicia—the Ruthenians in the east remained relatively quiet—represented thus primarily a social rather than a national rising against the lords, who happened to be Poles. Strictly nationalist revolutionary activities at that time were almost negligible, though they gave the Austrian government the pretext to annex Cracow. Belated Austrian military intervention indicated clearly that Vienna was willing to play the Ruthenians against the Poles. This devious and belated

---

Nineteenth Century (Toronto, 1970), pp. 113–130; Kann, *Nationalitätenproblem*, I, 149–166, 405–410. On the Palacký letter to the Frankfurt Assembly see ibid., I, 171–174, 412.

[46] Alexander was the close friend of Prince Adam Georg Czartoryski, the enlightened Polish patriot and reformer. See also Marian Kukiel, *Czartoryski and European Unity, 1770–1861* (Princeton, 1955), pp. 102–139.

military intervention taught the Polish landlords a lesson. They realized gradually that the solution of the Polish question could be initiated only among the Poles of all three partitioning powers at the same time. Before this hour of All-Polish liberation would strike, the interests of the Polish lords and their clientele called for accommodation with, not revolution against, the Austrian government. This would give the Polish people in Galicia a measure of national rights and at the same time keep the social privileges of the lords untouched. Such was the situation in Galicia at the beginning of the revolution of 1848.[47]

As for the Croats, the conflict with the Magyars, but not some of its consequences, has been noted in the previous section. The conflict stimulated two opposing trends: the assertion of Croatian estates autonomy, based on the social interests of aristocracy and gentry, and a sudden rise of a comprehensive Southern Slav nationalism and cultural if not political unionism. Undoubtedly the concept of ancient Illyrism of the western Southern Slav peoples, advanced under the liberal French administration, helped this development. It was furthered also underhand by the Metternich-Kolowrat administration, who saw here the possibility to establish a counterweight to Magyar nationalism. The journalist and writer Ljudevit Gaj (1809–1871), unimpeded by the government in Vienna, was active to advance these ideas. He promoted the notion of a common Southern Slav "Illyrian" literary language, which for the sake of Southern Slav union should be assimilated to the patterns of the rather obscure south Dalmatian Štokavian idiom rather than to Gaj's native Croatian. In many ways Gaj's endeavors could be compared with those of Havlíček's political journalism among the Czechs. Yet unlike Havlíček, Gaj, despite his cultural merits, always appeared in a political twilight through his cooperation with the pre-March government in Vienna. The interest of the government to balance an at that time still moderate cultural Southern Slav nationalism against the Magyar radicals was obvious.

The regime in Vienna apparently saw little danger in Southern Slav union activities. But Kossuth, who was alert to potentially radical ideas, particularly those he considered hostile to Magyar national interests, saw farther. To him Illyrism,[48] the cultural national movement of the western Catholic Southern Slavs under Croatian leadership, presented a more

[47] Schlitter, *Aus Österreichs Vormärz: Galizien und Krakau,* pp. 54–71; Wilhelm Feldman, *Geschichte der politischen Ideen in Polen seit dessen Teilungen* (Osnabrück, 1964), pp. 123–140; Kann, *Nationalitätenproblem,* I, 214–224, 427–432.

[48] Illyricum was the Roman province adjacent to the eastern shores of the Adriatic sea. Illyrians were the native people there, presumably of Celtic origin settled throughout the northwestern Balkans.

serious threat to Magyar nationalism than Croatian demands for estates autonomy. One reason why Vienna did not take this Illyrism seriously may have been the fact that the greatest Slavic contemporary linguist, the Slovene Bartholomäus Kopitar (1780–1844), advocated another southern Slav union idea, namely the concept of the Catholic Southern Slavs under the Habsburg scepter as balance against Russian-directed Panslavism. Under the dynamic bishop of Djakovo, Josip J. Strossmayer (1815–1905), these notions changed in time into a more radical, less Habsburg-oriented, direction.[49]

Concerning the Italians, the history of Italian nineteenth-century nationalism and the clear-cut language frontier between Italians and Germans at Salurn in Tyrol help to explain why accommodations, such as the administrative division of Tyrol into a German and Italian part amounted to merely temporary arrangements. No ideological scheme which promoted a permanent solution of the Italian problem within the Habsburg empire was ever taken seriously. This held true even for the Austrian Littoral where the Italians never held an absolute majority in a nationally homogeneous area as in the Trentino but only a relative one followed closely by Croatian and Slovene minorities. Here, too, plans for multinational reorganization were only temporary, although the autonomy of the port city of Trieste was recognized in practice since the times of Charles VI. The autonomous political administration was anchored also in special legislation of 1818, 1849, and finally of 1867 (semi-crownland status).

Such concessions did not change public opinion or ideological concepts, holding that, like the Polish question in a restored Poland, Italian nationalism could only be settled in a united Italy. The time for such grand solutions was uncertain in either case, but the European power constellation seemed to favor the Italians.[50]

More complex was the situation for some national groups without independent political history in the Habsburg empire. As for the Slovaks, the Reformation in Bohemia, particularly in its later stages under the

[49] On Illyrism see: Hermann Wendel, *Der Kampf der Südslawen um Freiheit und Einheit* (Frankfurt, 1925), pp. 113–140, 189–227; Alfred von Fischel, *Der Panslawismus bis zum Weltkrieg* (Stuttgart, 1919), pp. 130–148; Kann, *Nationalitätenproblem,* I, 246–258, 439–442; K. B. K. (initials only), "Literature from the Illyrian Movement to Realism, 1835–1895," in Francis H. Eterovich and Christopher Spalatin, eds., *Croatia,* I, 242–251 and Guldescu, ibid., II, 38–40. Kopitar as loyal citizen could even become director of the National Library (Hofbibliothek) in Vienna, then an unheard-of distinction for a Slovene.

[50] Hans Kramer, *Österreich und das Risorgimento* (Vienna, 1963), pp. 9–52; Kann, *Nationalitätenproblem,* I, 265–267, 443–445.

influence of Lutheranism, was identified in Slovak territory with the concept of a Czecho-Slovak political, cultural, and particularly linguistic union. The dissatisfaction, which this estrangement from the idea of straight Slovak national identity created, was used by the Counter Reformation, especially the Jesuits, to recreate the concept of a separate Slovak cultural and linguistic character. In the eighteenth century Father Bernolák on the Catholic side and in the early nineteenth century the cultural reformers Joseph Hurban, Michael Hodža, and L'udovit Štúr on the Protestant side, made each in their own way, new efforts to establish such Slovak national image. They were supported by the Catholic romantic poet Ján Hollý. We also find at that time endeavors by Slovaks of strong pro-Czech tendencies, Ján Kollár and Pavel J. Šafařík, to reestablish the old Czecho-Slovak union idea. However, in the Restoration period their attempts were unsuccessful. The major Slovak cultural trends moved in the direction of a separate national concept and here the Protestant influence was stronger than the Catholic. The political progress of the Slovaks toward autonomy was hampered by the fact that the nobility and part of the upper middle class had become magyarized, but cultural progress indicated that a political program was developing as well.[51]

The Serbs in Hungary were granted cultural and religious autonomy in the late seventeenth century, as discussed in Chapter *IV*:B. In the course of time Magyarism succeeded in restricting the autonomy to the religious sphere. Somewhat better was the situation in the Military Frontiers area to the south, and this discrepancy was one reason for the violent confrontations between Serbs and Magyars during the revolution. Another was that the Serb cultural renaissance during the pre-March period had its center in the Habsburg empire. The great Serbian poet and linguist Vuk Karadžić (1787–1864), widely celebrated also in the German-language orbit, serves as example. Cultural activities strengthened the Serb national pride and political consciousness.[52]

The Austrian Slovenes, the smallest of the Slavic national groups in the Habsburg empire and the one farthest removed from a potential po-

[51] Ludwig von Gogolák, *Beiträge zur Geschichte des slowakischen Volkes.* II: *Die slowakische nationale Frage in der Reformepoche Ungarns (1790–1848)* (Munich, 1969), pp. 11–240; Theodor G. Locher, *Die nationale Differenzierung und Integrierung der Slowaken und Tschechen in ihrem geschichtlichen Verlauf bis 1848* (Haarlem, 1931), pp. 139–187. Kann, *Nationalitätenproblem,* I, 274–280, 447–449.

[52] Wendel, *Der Kampf der Südslawen,* pp. 141–188; Fischel, *Der Panslawismus,* pp. 148–155; Emile Picot, *Les Serbes de Hongrie* (Paris, 1873), pp. 172–217; Duncan Wilson, *The Life and Times of Vuk S. Karadžić* (Oxford, 1970), pp. 294–313; Kann, *Nationalitätenproblem,* I, 286–289, 451–454.

litical autonomy, encountered little difficulties in their cultural life during the Restoration period. Politically they were not taken seriously; culturally as the example of Kopitar shows, they even found some support in Vienna, because the concept of a Catholic Austro-Slavism suited the interests of the government. But also outspoken German liberals such as Count Anton Alexander Auersperg (as poet Anastasius Grün) [53] strongly supported Slovene cultural activities, particularly in the language field. These peaceful conditions were to change when the Slovenes formulated a political program of their own in 1848.[54]

Peculiar was the situation among the Ruthenians. The conversion of many of them to the Uniate church under papal jurisdiction in Galicia and northern Hungary, established by the union of Brest Litowsk of 1596, separated them from their brethren in the Bukovina (until 1775 under Turkish rule) and from the Russian Ukrainians. In the cultural sense the Ruthenians could be considered as a separate branch of the Ukrainian people. The religious difference among them was of paramount importance in the development of national consciousness, as religion is important to many oppressed people where it is the only outlet for the creation of cultural programs. A Polish drive to convert the Ruthenian peasants to the Roman-Catholic Church, the Church of their oppressors, was understandably not very successful. Only the Ruthenian noble landlords merged almost imperceptibly with their Polish fellow aristocrats.

The program for a definite Ruthenian cultural identity based on langauge was promoted primarily within the Uniate Church and to a point supported by the Austrian government, which considered the Ruthenian peasants as loyal and the Polish nobility, gentry, and intellectuals as potential revolutionaries. Within the Uniate Church two trends were in conflict with each other, one which stressed the common bonds with the Orthodox Ukrainians in Russia and another western-oriented, which favored the development of a modernized Ruthenian literary language. No clear victory of either trend (Old and Young Ruthenians), both directed by Church organizations, was as yet discernible in 1848. But both stressed the necessity for the recognition of the Ruthenian language in the administration of eastern Galicia and for an educational system of their own.[55]

[53] The Auerspergs owned large estates in Carniola, particularly in the then German-language island of Gottschee.

[54] Bogumil Vošnjak, *A Bulwark against Germany* (London, 1917), pp. 66–82; Fischel, *Der Panslawismus,* pp. 125–130; Kann, *Nationalitätenproblem, I,* 299–303, 457–458.

[55] Boris Krupnyckyj, *Geschichte der Ukraine von den Anfängen bis zum Jahre 1917* (Wiesbaden, 1963), pp. 246–252; Schlitter, *Aus Österreichs Vormärz,* pp.

In the development of Roumanian nationalism, the establishment of a Uniate Church in Transylvania by the end of the seventeenth century and the example of the three-nation state of Magyars, Szekels, and Saxons (Germans) which gave their groups on the same territory a wide degree of political and cultural autonomy were important factors. The Roumanians (Vlachs) had secured a very limited recognition of their national rights under Joseph II. Francis I tried to appease the Magyars in the face of a strong Roumanian immigration from the Danube principalities. The national program called for full equality with the status of the other three nationalities in Transylvania, in other words the conversion from the three- to four-nation state. Further claims, though not yet fully crystallized, were for political union with their conationals in the Bukovina and the Banat of Temesvár. In this latter region the Roumanian national status was inferior even to that in Transylvania.[56]

By 1848 political activism and political programs among the eleven national groups of the empire had not developed and could not develop to the same cultural, let alone political level. Yet national consciousness among these groups had evolved to a degree that sufficed to be converted into political action if and when a revolutionary situation would offer the opportunity.

C. The revolution of 1848–1849

The revolution in the Habsburg empire took place in several theaters and on several levels. All were interrelated. This factor can never be fully shown in a historical presentation, which cannot tell all at the same time. There was a liberal constitutional revolution, a social (mainly agrarian) revolution, and—most significant for the Habsburg realms—a number of national revolutions.

Besides, the impact of foreign relations on the domestic situation opened up new revolutionary situations. Thus the Austro-Prussian rivalry was closely related to the German revolution and particularly to the events at

---

58–71; Ivan Žeguc, *Die nationalpolitischen Bestrebungen der Karpato-Ruthenen* (Wiesbaden, 1965), pp. 11–19; Fischel, *Der Panslawismus,* pp. 155–160; Kann, *Nationalitätenproblem,* I, 322–327, 466–468.

[56] Constantin Daicoviciu and Miron Constantinescu, *Brève Histoire de la Transylvanie* (Bucharest, 1965), pp. 179–193; Cornelia Bodea, *The Romanians' Struggle for Unification 1834–1849* (Bucarest, 1970); Vasile Maciu, *Mouvements Nationaux et Sociaux Roumains au XIXe Siècle* (Bucarest, 1971), pp. 40–101; Eugen Horváth, *Die Geschichte Siebenbürgens* (Budapest, n.d.), pp. 57–69, 77–80, 130–135; Carl Göllner, *Die Siebenbürger Sachsen in den Revolutionsjahren 1848–1849* (Bucharest, 1967), passim; Kann, *Nationalitätenproblem,* I, 309–314; 460–464.

St. Paul's Assembly in Frankfurt, while the war against Piedmont-Sardinia cannot be separated from the revolution in the Lombardo-Venetian kingdom. Finally, the Russian intervention in the war of independence in Hungary tied this passionate struggle to the realm of foreign relations.

The revolution in the Habsburg empire flared up in some places, then quieted down to move to other scenes, to break out again in the old place. There is no center nor continuity in the revolutionary events, even faintly similar to those of the French Revolution of 1789. Thus the Habsburg revolutions had no unity of action and no unity of problems and attempted solutions.

Many events led to the tense atmosphere in the early March days of 1848 in Vienna. The impact of the French February revolution, the unrest in Lombardy-Venetia, the radical liberal agitation at the Hungarian Reichstag in Pozsony and the preparations for the elections of a German National Assembly in Frankfurt, all tied to a prolonged economic urban crisis, served as background of the situation. Petitions of a liberal character, promoted primarily by professional men and students, were circulated between March 6 and 12. Demands for freedom of the press, jury trials, civil rights, abolition of religious discrimination, academic freedom, full emancipation of the peasants, and above all constitutional representative government were revolutionary by Austrian standards of the pre-March period. Most of these requests expressed the interests of the urban educated middle class. On March 13, their representatives were the first who clashed with military forces in front of the Lower Austrian diet. Students were the first victims of the confrontation. Yet more casualties, altogether about fifty, occurred, when the workers in the suburbs became involved and the armed forces under the command of Archduke Albrecht acted with increasing force and decreasing restraint against the underprivileged masses. The same evening Metternich was forced to resign. More or less enlightened conservatives hoped that his fall, not unwelcome to a court party centered on the archduchess Sophie, would put an end to the commotion. As events turned out, it was only the signal for its spread.

The crown permitted the establishment of a national guard of the citizenry. A more dynamic legion of academic youth supplemented it and spurred the guard to action. Freedom of the press was granted also and a liberal constitution promised for the near future. A new cabinet under the chairmanship of Count Franz Anton Kolowrat, with General Count Karl Ficquelmont (Foreign Affairs), Count Theodor Latour (Defense), Baron Karl Kübeck (Finances), and Baron Franz Pillersdorf (Interior) was to make arrangements for the transition to constitutional government. Everyone of these five men represented to some degree the old regime, though Kolowrat, as seen from a historic-traditional viewpoint, had shown more understanding for national aspirations than Metternich. Kübeck was a moderately enlightened bureaucrat, and only Pillersdorf, though by no means a liberal, seemed to welcome his assigned task to prepare constitutional reforms. Kolowrat, who seemed too closely associated with the Metternich regime, was forced to resign within a few weeks and Ficquelmont, his successor, closely linked to Metternich's pro-Russian policy, had to follow him soon. Pillersdorf now became prime minister in early May, and this meant that the crown began to take the revolution more seriously, though still not seriously enough.

A preliminary constitution was decreed at the end of April. It established a bicameral system, which was to share legislative powers with the emperor. Yet the franchise was severely restricted and daily and weekly wage earners, that meant practically all laborers were excluded. Furthermore the characterization of the constitution as "octroy"—that is, as privilege granted by the crown rather than as the accomplishment of a constituent assembly—created widespread resentment. As it occurred so often in the history of the Habsburg monarchy, a seemingly far-reaching concession had become largely meaningless, because it offered too little and came too late. And yet, Pillersdorf would not have been permitted to issue even this imperfect constitution, if events on many fronts had not carried bewilderment and fear into the highest ranks of government and the court, that is, primarily the feeble-minded emperor's uncles, his brother, and the most resolute personality in the imperial house, Ferdinand's sister-in-law, the Archduchess Sophie, mother of the future emperor Francis Joseph.[57]

Three days after Metternich's fall the opposition of the Hungarian diet, backed by a genuine majority, had demanded the establishment of a national government, responsible to a parliament to be elected by general male franchise. Legislation in the future was to require countersignature of the ministry. Tax exemptions for the noble landowners were to be abolished, freedom of the press to be granted, and—a blow to minority rights—Transylvania to be fully reincorporated into Hungary. Nevertheless the liberal provisions, particularly those that eliminated discrimination against the peasants in regard to taxation, outweighed the oppressive na-

[57] Joseph A. von Helfert, *Geschichte der österreichischen Revolution* (Freiburg, 1907), I, 237–477 passim; Rudolf Kissling, *Die Revolution im Kaisertum Österreich* (Vienna, 1948), pp. 39–62.

ationalistic measures. The crown denied two demands: one for the establishment of a national army subordinated to the national Hungarian government, the other for the initiation of a national budget, entirely separated from the imperial financial administration and tax policy. On March 22 the national ministry under the chairmanship of an enlightened, by no means radical aristocrat, Count Louis Batthiány, took office. Other members of the cabinet were Kossuth (Finances), Széchenyi (Public Works), Deák (Justice), and Eötvös (Public Instruction). To reconcile Croatian feelings of resentment against the far-reaching concessions to the Magyars, the emperor appointed a nationalist Croatian officer, Josef Jelacić de Bužim, as banus of Croatia. Meanwhile the Sardinian invasion of Lombardy had begun, the provisional National Assembly in Frankfurt had met, and Palacký had denounced Czech participation in the proceedings of the German Confederation. Czech nationalism in Prague, at the beginning of the revolution interested mainly in constitutional government and recognition of equality with the Germans, had renewed its old demand: the reestablishment of the union of the three lands of the Bohemian crown, in which the Czech people could claim a predominant role. The previous demands had been raised mainly by a vociferous, liberal minority but the newly revived ones also had the full support of a respected middle and upper middle urban burgher class, above all that of the powerful Bohemian aristocracy. Spring riots in Cracow and Lwów organized by Polish liberals complicated the situation further. Yet as it turned out, but could not easily be predicted at the time, the memories of the frustrated revolution of 1846 capped soon the revolutionary Polish activities.[58]

To return to events in Vienna: National guards (chiefly middle-class burghers), workers, and students demanded now stormily the withdrawal of the octroyed constitution and convocation of a constitutional national assembly. The establishment of a revolutionary security committee under the leadership of a young physician, Dr. Adolf Fischhof, a brave man and great political talent, followed. Even before this happened, the imperial court, mindful of the fate of Louis XVI, who in the beginning of the

[58] Helfert, *Geschichte der österreichischen Revolution* see in particular I, pp. 231–286, 431–449 for events in Hungary, 286–291 in Galicia. As for the situation in Prague and Vienna see Friedrich Prinz, *Prag und Wien 1848: Probleme der nationalen und sozialen Revolution im Spiegel der Ministerratsprotokolle* (Munich, 1968), pp. 76–105; Stanley Z. Pech, *The Czech Revolution of 1848* (Chapel Hill, 1969), pp. 47–78; Ivan D. Udalzow, *Aufzeichnungen über die Geschichte des nationalen und politischen Kampfes in Böhmen im Jahre 1848* (Berlin, 1953), pp. 43–86.

French revolution had practically become a prisoner in his own capital, left Vienna for Innsbruck. In July the radicals within the security committee forced the resignation of Pillersdorf. A ministry under Wessenberg, a moderate diplomat under the Metternich regime, followed after an interim regime of a few days. Dignitaries in the restoration era had often served for more years than the new men for days. The new cabinet was undistinguished, except for the minister of justice, Dr. Alexander Bach, a young lawyer, who had been a liberal at the beginning of the revolution, but with remarkable flair foresaw the turning of the tide and moved gradually into safer, moderate, and later conservative waters. He was to become the Fouché of the revolution, although one without the cruelty of his more formidable predecessor.

Meanwhile the Constituent Assembly had been duly elected and was convoked by the temporary regent, the emperor's uncle, Archduke John. As to be expected, due to the narrow franchise and therefore limited interest of the population in the elections, the political persuasion of the Austrian Reichstag of 383 deputies, of which the peasants represented more than one quarter, ranged in substance from moderate conservative to moderate liberal, with few radicals to the right and left. Experience in an entirely new political situation is often of far less value than under ordinary conditions. Just like the French Constituent Assembly of 1789, this new body confronted by entirely new problems turned out to be far more capable than one might have had reason to expect. Only days after the convocation of the Reichstag in mid-July 1848, legislation to abolish the personal service obligation of the peasants was introduced by the young Silesian deputy Hans Kudlich. An aggravated agrarian crisis, largely due to continued poor harvests, had been in existence since 1845. Its impact helped to have the Kudlich proposals passed in early September. The enactment of these laws which required determination of an indemnity for the lords, had to wait for the postrevolutionary era. Yet the impact of what has passed into history as the Austrian peasant emancipation by the revolutionary Reichstag was so great that even the coming neo-absolutist regime could not evade the duty to put it, with some changes, into effect. Meanwhile the Reichstag busied itself with the drafting of a permanent constitution which should take care of the manifold national problems of the empire.[59]

[59] Helfert, *Geschichte der österreichischen Revolution,* II, 244–269; R. John Rath, *The Viennese Revolution of 1848* (Austin, 1957), pp. 179–316; Max Bach, *Geschichte der Wiener Revolution im Jahre 1848* (Vienna, 1898), pp. 575–677; Friedrich Prinz, *Hans Kudlich* (Munich, 1962), pp. 86–107; Marx, *Die wirtschaftlichen Ursachen der Revolution von 1848,* pp. 123–162.

The events of spring and summer proved that they required indeed highest priority. Non-Magyar national groups in Hungary, Croats and Serbs in the Banat, Roumanians in Transylvania, rose against the intransigence and in some instances the blind zeal of Magyar nationalism. It was largely inspired by Kossuth who only in exile began to understand that the national discrimination which the non-Magyar peasant in Hungary had to face aggravated the social discrimination, which he shared with his Magyar countrymen. Particularly violent were the clashes with the Serbs, who saw their old and to-be-hoped-for enlarged autonomy trampled under. In May, the Transylvanian Roumanians protested at Blay against the incorporation of Transylvania into Hungary and asked at the same time for the conversion of the principality into a four-nation state. In September, they demanded the outright separation from Hungary and direct subordination under the administration in Vienna. The Slovaks, on the other hand, in an improvised popular assembly at Liptovský Sväty Mikuláš appeared satisfied with autonomy within Hungary, provided it would secure them the use of their language in administration and education. Similar demands were raised by the Ruthenians in Galicia, who requested the administrative separation of east and west Galicia. Pillersdorf promised to meet these claims, but nothing was done. The demands of the Carpatho-Ruthenians in Hungary for autonomy were ignored by Magyar nationalism. They were the most forgotten of the forgotten people. Interesting were the requests of the small Slovene national group spread over six Austrian crownlands. As the first national group they asked for autonomy within a territory whose boundaries should be drawn along ethnic and not historic-political lines. This latter alternative would not make sense in a nation whose status as historical-political entity had never existed in Austria. Recognition as ethnic group, more in practice than by law, became now the order of the day.[60]

Although the government could accomplish little in these matters as long as the revolutionary situation was in flux, even efforts toward reform were made only by the new legislative branch of government and not by the executive. Promptings to act were not lacking. On June 2 the international Slav Congress convened in Prague under the chairmanship of Palacký. Most of the outstanding leaders of the Slavic national groups in the Habsburg empire but few from abroad were present. Congress Poland could send only émigré delegates, mostly from Paris, which impaired the representative character of the Congress. Besides, the Poles

[60] Kann, *Nationalitätenproblem,* I, 72–87, 122–124, 166–174, 224–225, 245–254, 279–280, 289–290, 303–305, 313–315, 326–329; II, 13–15.

and others could offer no solution on Austrian territory that would have challenged the territorial integrity of the Habsburg monarchy. The mere discussion of such questions would have invited the charge of treason.

Still, the results of the Prague proceedings were impressive. If they had not been ignored by a narrow-minded and unimaginative government they could have been constructive. Thus the possibility of a Polish-Ruthenian compromise in Galicia which would have created a bilingual province with adequate representation of the Ruthenian minority (actually a majority in eastern Galicia) was seriously entertained. The possibility of a merger with the Hungarian Carpatho-Ukrainians was left open. Ruthenians and Slovenes, both widely scattered national groups without political history in the Habsburg empire, asked thus for ethnic solutions, whereas Slovaks and Serbs who lived in more homogeneous territories would have been satisfied with local autonomy within Hungary. Of the national groups with political history the Croatians demanded the recognition of the Triune kingdom, including Austrian-administered Dalmatia, as a separate political entity within the empire as a whole rather than within Hungary. Liberal and conservative Czechs agreed on the demands for the union of the lands of the Bohemian crown under a representative constitution. The national groups represented at the Congress professed in general terms the spiritual union of all Slavic peoples and in more specific ones in the Habsburg empire the right to full equality with Germans and Magyars. The federalization of the empire, by and large still along historic-political lines, was recommended.

Relatively minor clashes between Czech nationalists and imperial troops gave the commanding general, Prince Alfred Windischgrätz no more adept as a statesman than as a military commander, the pretext to dissolve the Congress by military force.[61] A great hope went down with this dissolution. The next Slav Congress, now dubbed Panslav Congress, was to meet in Moscow in 1867 in an atmosphere far less favorable for the preservation of the Habsburg monarchy.[62]

Meanwhile the crisis in Hungary heightened. On July 2 the Palatine Archduke Stephan opened the newly elected Reichstag. It was the first and only one in a century to be elected by a truly democratic franchise. Its first

[61] The tragic death of Windischgraetz's consort by a stray bullet during a relatively minor revolutionary riot in Prague at that time exacerbated the situation further.

[62] Hans Kohn, *Pan-Slavism* (New York, 1960), pp. 69–101; Fischel, *Der Panslawismus,* pp. 261–295; Pech, *The Czech Revolution of 1848,* pp. 123–166; Udalzow, *Aufzeichnungen,* pp. 86–122, 223–226; Kann, *Nationalitätenproblem,* II, 15–20, 308–310.

legislative actions were taken in defiance of the imperial administration. The establishment of a separate Hungarian (Honved) army, a separate budget, and separate currency bills were voted in. The imperial government accepted the challenge and sent armed forces under Jelačić across the Sava river into Hungary. The violent struggle between Magyars and Serbs embittered the Croatian commander. General civil war appeared imminent. Prime minister Count Batthyány neither could nor wished to deal with such a situation and resigned. The hero of the radicals, Louis Kossuth, took over now. Since the Palatine resigned also a few days later and was not replaced, Kossuth's position became a semi-dictorship. The Reichstag did not dare to oppose him, the more the crisis sharpened. Unfortunate incidents, typical of a tense situation, were not lacking. Thus Magyar fury against the armed invasion led to the lynching of the imperial commander in Budapest, Count Lamberg, by a mob.

The imperial government responded by invalidating the Reichstag legislation, which had not been sanctioned by the emperor. A state of siege was declared in Hungary. General Jelačić was given wider powers including the takeover of the civil administration in Hungary. The Reichstag declared itself in permanent session, the imperial manifesto as void; Jelačić was branded a traitor. With these actions on both sides the revolution in Hungary had moved to a stage beyond peaceful reconciliation; but the legitimacy of the crown was as yet not directly challenged.[63]

The revolutionary events in Hungary had an impact on the neighboring hereditary lands; conversely, unrest there encouraged the leaders of the Magyar revolution. In Vienna, dissatisfaction increased with the seemingly, but not actually slow progress of the Austrian Reichstag legislation, the continuing economic crisis, and various underhand efforts by the government to regain control for the reactionary forces of old. The minister of defense, Count Latour, was assailed for oppressive activities of the old establishment.

In early October a grenadier battalion of the Viennese garrison, ordered to march into Hungary, mutinied. Clashes followed between regular and insurrectionist troops, supported by students and workers. A mob entered the Ministry of War, attacked and lynched the old Count Latour, and strung up the mutilated body on a lamppost in the street. The authorities used this atrocity as symbol of revolutionary barbarism and as justification for acts of cruelty on the imperial side. Emperor Ferdinand and the court, who had returned to Vienna in the relatively quiet days of August, now left Vienna again, this time for Olmütz (Olomuc), a small town in east-

[63] Kissling, *Die Revolution,* I, 161–173.

tern Moravia, as the temporary seat of government. Ferdinand was not destined to return as emperor.

Within a matter of days a regular insurrection developed in Vienna against the military forces of Windischgrätz who moved from the north toward the rebellious city and against Jelačić whose Croatian troops approached the city from the east. Inside Vienna the revolutionaries gained the upper hand. They were commanded by the Polish émigré rebel General Joseph Bem who had participated in the risings of 1830–1831 against the tzarist government. The October revolution was characterized by the fact that the driving forces behind it were not middle-class intellectuals, professors at St. Paul's Assembly in Frankfurt, or enlightened political journalists but the industrial workers. Until the rising of the Paris Commune in 1871 it was the most clear-cut workers' revolution, and had an enormous, though short-lived impact on the sagging revolution in Germany. Nobody, whether he sympathizes with the ill-planned and largely irrational rising or not, can read the poem "Wien" (Vienna) written in the hectic days by the German revolutionary poet Ferdinand Freiligrath without being moved by its tragic revolutionary fervor.

> Wenn wir noch knien könnten, wir lägen auf den Knien;
> Wenn wir noch beten könnten, wir beteten für Wien!
> . . . Wozu noch betend winseln? Ihr Männer ins Gewehr,
> Heut ballt man nur die Hände, man faltet sie nicht mehr!
> . . . Ein riesig Schilderheben, ein Ringen wild und kühn—
> Das ist zur Weltgeschichte das rechte Flehn für Wien.[64]

Freiligrath's plea that the Germans should rise in support of the Austrian revolution fell on deaf ears and the seemingly more justified hope that Magyar revolutionary forces could succeed in lifting the siege of Vienna by imperial troops failed likewise. On October 30 the troops entered the city to hoist the banner of a military dictatorship. Bem managed to flee but Messenhauser, an artillery officer of the Viennese garrison who had refused to turn his guns against the people, was executed like some radicals, among them Robert Blum, a deputy of the Frankfurt Assembly

[64] From Ferdinand Freiligrath's poem "Wien," written in early November, 1848. In translation approximately:

> If we could still be kneeling, we would be on our knees;
> if we could still be praying, for Vienna were our pleas.
> Don't whimper now in prayer! Men, grab your guns, resist!
> Don't fold hands any longer and clench an angry fist.
> Raise in this giant struggle your shields defiantly:
> This is the Vienna prayer in world history.

(Translated by Max Knight)

and therefore legally immune from court-martial proceedings. A long dark night settled over Vienna, which, as in 1805 at the time of the first French occupation, adjusted all too readily to the changed conditions.[65]

The capture of Vienna by imperial troops meant in effect the end of revolutionary action outside of Hungary, though not yet the full victory of the counterrevolution, which in Austria was not to come in full force until early spring in 1849. Yet important steps to that effect were already taken in the fall of 1848. At the height of the Vienna October risings, the Reichstag, following the counsels of the government, decided to move to Kremsier (Kroměříž), the summer residence of the archbishop of Olmütz. While deliberations in Vienna at the height of the Viennese revolutionary risings were difficult, this action, as it became apparent within a few months, amounted to an abdication of the legislature as an independent branch of government. The Reichstag reopened the session at Kremsier on November 22, 1848, and continued there its legislative work, in particular on the draft of a permanent constitution. It was not openly threatened as yet, but it became clear that the Kremsier Assembly had become quite isolated from the turn of revolutionary events, which was determined henceforward exclusively by the Austrian and Prussian executive forces. It was a genuine Austrian tragedy, that the Kremsier parliament, at the time when it was engaged in its most constructive work, did not realize that its legislation would be condemned to futility by an authoritarian government. The responsibility for this rested in the first place with the crown and the imperial administration, yet the Reichstag cannot be absolved entirely for its naïveté or studied blindness, by which it surrendered its freedom of action to a determined, only thinly camouflaged counterrevolutionary government. Certainly the lesson of the first revolutionary phase of the events of 1789 was not learned.

On November 21, Prince Felix Schwarzenberg, diplomat and general, and by his antecedents an adventurer and political gambler, was appointed prime minister and the distinguished Count Franz Stadion minister of the interior. The following summer the sick Stadion was replaced by the former radical liberal and by now ultraconservative Alexander Bach, who in the meantime had held the less important office of minister of justice. With his new position he yielded the old one to Anton von Schmerling. Other members of the cabinet were Karl Friedrich von Bruck, minister of commerce, and in later years minister of finance, an imaginative person of *grossdeutsch* tendencies, who like most of Schwarzenberg's ministers

[65] Bach, *Geschichte der Wiener Revolution*, pp. 725–855; Rath, *The Viennese Revolution*, pp. 317–346.

took constitutional-legal "niceties" not too seriously. Krauss and Thinnfeld, the new ministers of finance and agriculture, were experienced bureaucrats and Count Leo Thun, who became the following summer minister of public instruction, was an outstanding talent. Nevertheless, the often-quoted remark by the British ambassador that this was a cabinet of prime ministers seems exaggerated praise. Schwarzenberg was an ingenious and resolute man but a dilettante; Stadion was an eminent administrator but had passed the high tide of his usefulness; Bach was a capable man whose defects of character were commensurate with his talents; Thun was the best man.[66]

The new prime minister did not show his hand immediately. He prevaricated in his dealings with the Reichstag with the excuse that definite steps concerning the new constitution could be taken only if and when the situation in Germany had been clarified. His first major decision was taken in conjunction with the Archduchess Sophie, namely to induce Emperor Ferdinand to abdicate in favor of his eighteen-year-old nephew Archduke Francis. The transfer of the crown took place on December 2.

The new emperor added to the name Francis, under which he was known in his family circle, Joseph, as a bow to enlightened Josephinism. This was meant to please the liberals. Yet the symbolic significance rested not so so much in the double name but in the fact that Francis, the name of the arch-reactionary dull grandfather came first and that of the enlightened brilliant great-great uncle second. This mixture and this rank of values was characteristic for Francis Joseph's sixty-eight-year reign.[67]

Of the young emperor's long line of prime ministers and leading statesmen, Schwarzenberg was probably the most daring and, taking a short-range view, the most successful. No wonder that Francis Joseph trusted him as hardly any other adviser afterward, a trust to be rewarded with mixed blessings. The first advice which Schwarzenberg gave his teenage sovereign, who was in danger to be influenced from many quarters, was rather suggestive. He counseled Francis Joseph never to discuss with his ministers any matter that did not strictly belong to their jurisdiction. This practice would protect the emperor from intrigues, hearsay, and any undue kind of influence. Francis Joseph's unimaginative personality did

[66] For a brief account on Schwarzenberg see Kann, *Nationalitätenproblem,* II, 72–75, on Bach, 86–89, on Bruck, 76–80, on Stadion, 63–69, on Thun, I, 159–162; II, 70–72. See further, Rudolf Kissling and Adolf Schwarzenberg *Prince Felix zu Schwarzenberg* (New York, 1946); Richard Charmatz, *Minister Freiherr von Bruck* (Leipzig, 1916); Christoph Thienen-Adlerflycht, *Graf Leo Thun im Vormärz* (Graz-Cologne, 1957); on Stadion see also note 67.

[67] Friedjung, *Österreich von 1848–1860,* I, 92–118.

not take this advice with a grain of salt but literally. Throughout his long reign he protected himself not only from undue and malicious underhand influences but also from any counsels by men whose vision and knowledge transcended the powers entrusted to them by their office. Sincere, dedicated, and always conscious of his duties, but lacking ideas of his own and unwilling to accept nonprofessional advice by others, sure of his values, but vacillating in his course of action, Francis Joseph's talents and achievements were never more than mediocre. This was perhaps more than could be said for the emperor's grandfather. On the other hand, unlike Francis, luck was never on his side. The one redeeming value of Francis Joseph's reign, a value which became ever more clear in his old age, was the impact of the combination of a colorless personality with great merits of industry, sense of duty, and integrity. This synthesis served better as a unifying symbol of imperial rule than the greater talents of a more colorful man could ever have.

Schwarzenberg showed his hand ever more clearly and brutally. His intransigent and imperialist stand on the German question, which represented in essence the compromise between a *grossdeutsch* and a Great Austrian solution, either one under Austrian-centralistic and conservative leadership, has been discussed in the previous section as far as it pertained to Germany. Concerning the domestic situation, Schwarzenberg sprung a surprise on the Reichstag of Kremsier and, indeed, anybody concerned with Austrian constitutional government. On March 4, 1849, the inexperienced young emperor sanctioned on his advice a new constitution drafted by Stadion and decreed (octroyed) on March 7. The same day the Reichstag was dissolved, and a number of deputies who had not taken care of their personal safety in time were arrested and imprisoned under various pretexts. None of the excuses could camouflage the flagrant violation of constitutional rights. Francis Joseph who lent his name unwittingly to this action by Schwarzenberg, could not be expected to see through Machiavellian tactics whose long-range effects, apart from the moral implications, proved to be unfortunate for the future of the empire. In any case Francis Joseph appeared in a dubious light. His eminent, though arch-conservative teachers Metternich and Rauscher (the later cardinal-archbishop of Vienna), undoubtedly would never have exposed his prestige the way the cynical Schwarzenberg did. The arrests put also an undeserved black mark beside the name of Stadion, who, when he drafted the so-called March constitution, believed that it would eventually become the law of the land; it did not. On the other hand neither he nor the emperor could have any doubt about Schwarzenberg's intentions to delay its operation for some time, when the octroyed constitution—frequently referred to as the Stadion constitution—received imperial sanction.

Before we survey this document, it is necessary to discuss the basic features of the draft of the Kremsier constitution by outstanding members of the freely elected parliament of the Austrian peoples. This draft was unanimously approved by the constitutional committee of the Reichstag. It would without doubt within days have been accepted as the constitution of the Habsburg empire had Schwarzenberg not dissolved the Reichstag. In fact it was dissolved at this time to deprive the document of the supreme authority to be conveyed by the sanction of an overwhelming majority of the representatives of the Austrian peoples. The deficiency of this charter of liberties, the noblest in Austrian history, represented also an act of wisdom on the part of the Reichstag. It refused to draw up constitutional provisions for Hungary, while the war of independence raged across the Leitha river. The justified conclusion of the deputies was that settlement of this conflagration by compromise would also make a constitutional compromise with Hungary possible. It could be incorporated then into the Kremsier constitution. If on the other hand radical Kossuthism should win, Hungary would be separated permanently from the empire or if—a more likely contingency—Schwarzenberg and Windischgrätz should crush the Magyar revolution by force of arms, it would be precipitate to draw up constitutional provisions in advance for the national groups in Hungary.

Chief credit for the Kremsier draft belongs to two committees, the general on the constitutional chart and the specific on civil rights. Conspicuously distinguished were the contributions of the Czech enlightened conservatives Palacký and Rieger, the Czech liberal Pinkas, the Polish liberals Smolka (later the speaker of the Reichstag), the German liberals Fischhof, Löhner, and Schuselka, the German moderates Cajetan Mayer, Brestel, Lasser, the German conservative Helfert, the Slovene Kavčič, the Italian Gobbi, and others. The final draft represented a compromise between centralism as proposed by most of the Germans and federalism (either along ethnic or historic-traditional lines) as favored by most of the Slavic representatives. Some capable deputies represented originally the ethnic position (Kavčič, Palacký, Fischhof), moved then to the historic traditional one (Rieger, Pinkas), and agreed finally on a semi-centralistic compromise (Mayer, Brestel, Hein, and eventually Palacký). This was the outcome: A bicameral legislation was to be elected by a relatively liberal, though not yet general male franchise. The upper chamber should represent the crownlands, whose boundaries were to be left unchanged. An ingenious compromise between federalism and centralism provided that the nationally mixed crownlands should be subdivided into homogeneous districts, whose representatives were added to the crownland delegations in the upper chamber. Thus the traditional political entities were preserved and yet a national organization on the lower administrative level was provided. It was to serve the interest of the national minorities in the multinational crownlands. Courts of national arbitration were to supplement this organization. On the lowest administrative level, a far-reaching autonomy was to be granted to the communities; on the highest level, parliament was to decide legislative matters. The crown was to have only a suspensive veto.

The Kremsier constitution carried all the positive and negative features of a compromise between federalism and centralism. Some problems, such as those of the scattered minorities, which did not fit into the territorial district organization, were left unsolved. More sophisticated solutions might have been feasible. Yet the basic achievement of Kremsier was not the legal quality of the constitution, but the fact, that it represented the will of the people. The representatives' work was not done for eternity and new attempts of solutions would probably have been necessary in the future. In any case, a multilateral agreement once achieved by an Austrian parliament would have represented a powerful constructive precedent for future democratic solutions. This precedent was never established, and the solutions which might have been based on it, did not occur. Reaction had destroyed a great opportunity.[68]

This defeat for constitutional government is only seemingly obscured by the fact that Stadion's constitution, though more conservative than the mildly liberal Kremsier draft, was a well-drawn document, in some respects more consistent than the Kremsier charter, since it did not have to be based on a compromise. It therefore could be comprehensive in a territorial sense and could include Hungarian affairs within its scope. This was hardly an asset, however, because Stadion in regard to Hungary had to move in a political vacuum, a dilemma which the Kremsier men had prudently avoided.

The property census of the franchise system in the new constitution was

[68] Josef Redlich, *Das österreichische Staats- und Reichsproblem* (Leipzig, 1920–1926), I, 220–323; Kann, *Nationalitätenproblem,* II, 19–45, 310–316; Paula Geist-Lányi, *Das Nationalitätenproblem auf dem Reichstag zu Kremsier 1848–1849* (Munich, 1920), pp. 55–203; Peter Burian, *Die Nationalitäten in Cisleithanien und das Wahlrecht der Märzrevolution 1848/49* (Graz-Cologne, 1962), pp. 175–214. See further Anton Springer, ed., *Protokolle des Verfassungsausschusses im österreichischen Reichstage 1848–1849* (Leipzig, 1885) and Alfred Fischel, ed., *Die Protokolle des Verfassungsausschusses über die Grundrechte* (Vienna, 1912).

stiffer, the tenure of the legislation longer, the imperial veto absolute. The national district organization was left intact, but the crownland autonomy reduced as was the federal element in the organization of the upper chamber. Regarding Hungary, the unity of the kingdom was preserved in principle, but balanced by autonomy for Croatia-Slavonia including Fiume and a separate status for Transylvania, which should bring equality to all national groups. Autonomous rights were also to be secured to the Serbs in the Vojvodina. A supplement to the constitution was a communal law, decreed ten days after the octroy of the constitution. It promised communal autonomy after the Kremsier fashion "the free municipality in the free state" in this case in the unfree one. This was the only part of the March legislation which was enacted, though on a permanent basis not before 1860. Altogether constitutional life under the Stadion constitution might have been as feasible as under the Kremsier draft, if it had not been "octroyed" from above and if Hungarian agreement rather than enforcement after military defeat could have been secured. But the Hungarian question was not solved. Yet an agreement under the Kremsier constitution would have stood a better chance than under the Stadion octroy. The Stadion constitution did not lack limited democratic features, though the concessions to the nationalities in Hungary were hardly issued for the sake of national justice but as punishment for the Magyars. In any case, Schwarzenberg, though not Stadion himself, considered this constitution as a meaningless scrap of paper, at the time it received imperial sanction.[69]

Meanwhile the Magyars by mid-December, 1848, refused to recognize the new emperor as their king, because he was not crowned with the crown of St. Stephen and obviously could not be crowned in Hungary any longer. This defiance against the regime and the crown itself is usually considered as the beginning of the decisive phase of the revolution or of the war of independence. Kossuth had worked for this break with Austria from the beginning of the revolution.

In early January, 1849, Windischgrätz's army took Budapest while Kossuth with the government moved to the east to Debreczen. Fighting continued with increased fury but with fluctuating success. Windischgrätz was an indifferent commander and the Magyar revolutionary generals, above all Görgey and Klapka skillfully took advantage of this fact. They

[69] Friedjung, *Österreich von 1848–1860,* pp. 255–291; Redlich, *Das österreichische Staats- und Reichsproblem,* I, 323–382; Kann, *Nationalitätenproblem,* II, 63–69, 320–321. See also Jiři Klabouch, *Die Gemeindeselbstverwaltung in Österreich 1848–1968* (Vienna, 1968), pp. 36–63.

were helped also by the renewed outbreak of hostilities between Austria and Sardinia in March, 1849. On the other hand the Magyar cause was not only in a military but also in a psychological sense hurt by the infighting against the Serbs in the Banat and the Saxons and Roumanians in Transylvania. Magyar victories in these struggles were dearly paid for by immediate consequences of internal discord as well as by the hatred evoked and continued until 1918 by the oppressed national groups. By April, however, the fortunes of war against the Austrian main forces had turned decidely in favor of the Magyars. On April 14 the assembly at Debreczen declared the dynasty of Habsburg-Lorraine deposed. Hungary was proclaimed a republic under Kossuth as governor with semidictatorial powers. The same day the emperor relieved Windischgrätz of his command.

Again, the action taken by the Hungarian Reichstag at the initiative of Kossuth had become in evitable, because the situation had developed in a way that made compromise impossible. Yet if this was so then it should have been clear to the revolutionary Hungarian government, that monarchical Europe would not stand idly by and see the Habsburg monarchy fall prey to revolution at a time of booming counterrevolutionary success in France and Germany. Russian intervention, agreed upon in May, 1849, had indeed become inevitable, if the Austrian government could not handle the situation alone. This contingency had now arisen. It does not take hindsight to come to these conclusions and the fact that Kossuth failed to draw them, belies his qualities as statesman.[70] A great orator and journalist, a man of brilliant ideas and qualities of charismatic leadership, this fierce patriot lacked the abilities required by a head of state in critical times. If he had had them he would have removed himself from the scene at an earlier time, possibly in the fall of 1848, to give a new leadership the chance for a compromise. That he failed to do so was the result of the strength and weakness inherent in singleness of purpose—in Kossuth's case charismatic leadership linked with inability to put himself in his opponents' position.[71]

[70] The anticipated Russian intervention was before the formal agreement widely demanded and discussed in Austrian conservative circles. Neither could Russian military preparations be kept secret. See Andics, *Das Bündnis Habsburg-Romanow,* pp. 160–191; Cecil Marcus Knatchbull-Hugessen, *The Political Evolution of the Hungarian Nation* (London, 1908), II, 80–81, 124–127; Barta in Ervin Pamlényi, ed., *Die Geschichte Ungarns,* V, 311–334.

[71] See Kosáry, *A History of Hungary,* pp. 219–249; Eugen Csuday, *Geschichte der Ungarn,* 2nd revised edition (Budapest, 1900), II, 429–467; Knatchbull-Hugessen, *The Political Evolution,* II, 121–190; Friedjung, *Österreich von 1848 bis 1860,* I, 201–235; see further Andritsch, ed., *Ungarische Geisteswelt,* 170–190.

The Russian intervention sealed the fate of the Hungarian revolution and in a wider sense that of Hungary. Fighting continued, however, until August, 1849. Discord between the Magyar leaders, particularly Kossuth and Görgey, accelerated disintegration. On August 13, Görgey surrendered his army to a Russian general at Világos, while Kossuth's fled to Turkey. Magyar nationalism has always and rightly approved of Kossuth's action to escape the Austrian gallows, while it has unjustly denounced Görgey for his justified decision to end useless slaughter. If Görgey can possibly be criticized, it is just for the fact, that as a nationalist he preferred to surrender to the Russians rather than to what he considered to be the Austrian oppressors. This action hardened Vienna's resolve to mete out terrible retribution for the revolution, although it is by no means certain that a more diplomatic action on the part of Görgey could have avoided it.

To the enduring shame of the Schwarzenberg government even the intervention of the tsar for the brave Hungarian commanders was rejected except for Görgey. He was confined to Klagenfurt, but nine Hungarian high officers were hanged, four others were shot.[72] Even the formerly moderate prime minister, Count Batthiány, was shot. The executions of the thirteen generals took place by explicit order of Schwarzenberg, but imprisonment of 2,000 officers and civilian patriots was ordered by General Haynau, Austrian commander during the final stages of the campaign in Hungary and later military governor of the prostrate country. As noted before, he had recommended himself for this assignment by his actions during the risings in Brescia in summer of 1848, when he had revolutionaries hanged and women flogged. The name "Hyena of Brescia" introduced him to revolutionary Hungary.

The action of the Schwarzenberg government and its henchmen stands in contrast to Grant's generous attitude toward the officers of the South after the surrender at Appomattox in the American Civil War. Schwarzenberg managed to unite English, French, German, and even Russian feelings in common revulsion against him and Haynau, who was publicly insulted during his subsequent "good will" visits to Brussels and London.[73] Strangely even modern historiography sometimes extols Haynau as a brilliant statesman.

The surrender at Világos means the end of the revolution in the Habsburg empire, which had run its course in Germany several weeks

[72] The officers who surrendered to the Russians were hung, the others shot. Altogether more than a hundred further executions took place within the next weeks.

[73] Andics, *Das Bündnis Habsburg-Romanow*, pp. 177–183.

before. The events that happened later should properly be considered as part of the neoabsolutistic period.

What were the permanent positive effects of the revolution? As for the national question they were few. Since the neoabsolutist regime represented a course of enforced German-directed centralism, the Germans were unjustly blamed by the other nationalities for the oppressive character of the government, from which the German liberals suffered as much as anybody else. The frustrated hatred of the defeated Magyar people was obvious. As for the Czechs, the revolution had done nothing to meet their constitutional demands; but the regime did not want to hurt the feelings of the powerful Bohemian aristocracy, hence moderate concessions were made to Czech national rights, particularly in education under the guidance of the able new minister of instruction, Count Leo Thun. The outcome of the revolution had given an opening to the moderate and conservative Czech nationalists, later organized in the Old Czech party. The Poles were not worse off than before, since they realized that cooperation with the Austrian government was preferable to isolated revolutionary action before the day of resurrection of Poland had struck. Its coming would depend on a change of world not just Austrian politics. This line of thought suited the Polish conservatives, who were closest to power. Few promises of the Austrian government to the Croats were kept, and a Croatian allegedly said to a Magyar: We received as reward what you got as punishment. The position of Croatian conservatism had been strengthened for a time, that of Southern Slav unionism, seen at short range, had weakened. Modest beneficiaries of the revolution were the Serbs, whose autonomy in the Vojvodina beyond the religious sphere, jointly with that of Roumanian and German minorities, was recognized for a time. Yet the governmental purpose was not to help the Serbs for their own sake but to hurt the Magyars. The autonomy of the Vojvodina was rescinded after 1860 when the negotiations with the Magyars got under way. Slovaks and Slovenes had to return to the *status quo ante* revolution, but an imperial patent of 1850 promised the Ruthenians in Galicia equality with the Poles. Some improvement on the administrative level took place and the same held true for the Carpatho-Ruthenian comitats in northern Hungary. But the concessions to the Hungarian Ruthenians fell victim to the Austro-Hungarian Compromise of 1867 and those to the Ruthenians in Galicia to the limited administrative autonomy granted to the crownland in 1868—and that meant a Polish-dominated Galicia. The Roumanians obtained actually nothing; the desired direct subordination of Transylvania under the imperial administration in

Vienna now meant in effect subordination under the absolutist regime—not with equal rights but with an equal lack of rights with other Transylvanian groups. In 1863 the Roumanians were officially recognized as fourth Translyvanian national group of equal standing, but the Compromise with Hungary and the reincorporation of the country under Magyar rule soon ended this transitory success. Less than a decade after 1867 the last remainders of the three-nation state in Translyvania were eliminated by the Magyar administration.

Thus the national achievements of the revolution were extremely meager, and if balanced against the degree of illusions destroyed and resentment created far more negative than positive. Yet the impetus given to the development of national political life, even through so short a period as the revolutionary one, was not in vain. It left its indelible traces. The political developments after 1867 would have been inconceivable without the vivid memories of 1848.

In the social sphere the revolution scored a success with the emancipation of the peasants in Austria and the roughly corresponding legislation in Hungary. As noted before, the fact that the neoabsolutist regime was forced to be the executor of the revolutionary agricultural legislation proved how widely these long overdue reforms were supported by public opinion. The revolution, on the other hand, did not leave any legislative traces in industrial organization and labor relations. Still, here too, the fact that industrial labor in Austria had for the first time played an active role was not entirely forgotten.

In the constitutional field absolutism after 1848 was even more stringent and for a time more effective than before the revolution. The main residue of the revolutionary era was equality before the law—though more in principle than in practice, and in regard to the Jews for some years not even in principle. Even Stadion's communal legislation did not become the law of the land until after the termination of the neoabsolutist period. Some rudiments of the Kremsier constitution, especially Article 21 dealing with national rights, were revived in slightly changed form in the Austrian Constitutional Law 142 of December, 1867, in the famous Article 19. Yet it could be said also with the same right that legislation by emergency decree on the part of the crown was passed on by the Stadion constitution to the December constitutional laws of 1867.[74]

The impact of the revolution on Austrian constitutional life after 1866 did not depend on such odds and ends. The political forces of an era, which forge its laws may use the pattern and traditions of a previous

[74] Kann, *Nationalitätenproblem,* II, 137–139.

one, but they do not necessarily need them. The meaning of the revolution as a whole is something more important. Political, social, and national changes which have once reached a higher stage may be temporarily stopped and even reversed for a time, but they cannot be wiped out from memory. When the opportunity strikes for new dynamic changes, a permanent return to the prerevolutionary situation becomes impossible. At least new changes have to include and advance the revolutionary experience of the past. This, for better or worse, is the significance of the Austrian revolution of 1848–1849.

D. Neoabsolutism

Neoabsolutism began in Austria with the dissolution of the Reichstag of Kremsier in the early March days of 1849, in Hungary with the capitulation of Világos in August of the same year.[75] The termination of the era is usually associated with the convocation of the enlarged Reichsrat in July, 1860. It did not represent as yet the return to constitutional government, but at least the realization that some, however halting steps in that direction were necessary. The complete failure of the regime in international relations, which became increasingly obvious after Schwarzenberg's death on April 5, 1852, but could hardly have been prevented by him in the long run, has been discussed. In domestic affairs the verdict is not quite so negative. The evaluation heard at the time, that the administration was run by a standing army of soldiers, a kneeling one of those praying in church to be acceptable to the government, and a crawling one of informers, seems unduly harsh. Yet this bitter joke illustrates the gross unpopularity of the regime, which was not modified by the fact that Schwarzenberg's successor in fact though not in name, Alexander Bach, was as administrator superior to Schwarzenberg. At the same time, because of his brief revolutionary past, he was generally rated an opportunist and turncoat and was hated more than Schwarzenberg. An aristocrat could be forgiven his conservative views and even his cruel actions to a point, as long as he was favored by political success. It was different with a commoner of liberal antecedents, even though Schwarzenberg's reckless daring, ruthlessness, and cavalier lack of concern regarding the consequences of his actions, were more responsible for the bankruptcy of the regime than Bach's opportunism. Opportunism is generally rated a

[75] The last Magyar resistance, however, ended only with the surrender of the garrison of the fortress of Komorn under the command of General Klapka on September 27, 1849.

more contemptible quality than recklessness and some believe it is even more reprehensible than cruelty. The notion that Bach may have changed his views out of conviction was dismissed by public opinion because his conversion to conservatism was of great benefit to his career. But in any case, Schwarzenberg was dead and Bach alive and thus it is clear that irrespective of his merits as administrator and promoter of economic reforms he became the chief target of criticism and hatred. As for the over-all evaluation of the period, a philosophy restored after a revolution, however brief, is different from the prerevolutionary order. Progress and setbacks will have to be considered not just in comparison with the achievements and setbacks of the old regime. In this respect neoabsolutism came out quite well, but in comparison with the revolution the situation appeared different, though not necessarily all bad.

The most influential personalities of the period, apart from Bach and Schwarzenberg, were in the emperor's entourage: his mother, the domineering archduchess Sophie, and his older cousin, the conservative archduke Albrecht, since 1860 governor of Hungary. The incapable and scheming chief aide de camp of the emperor, Count Ludwig Grünne, who sat with the cabinet, carried weight in military affairs. The minister of police, the widely feared Baron Johann Kempen-Fichtenstamm, had much authority. Francis Joseph's former teacher and ecclesiastic adviser, Joseph Othmar von Rauscher, became archbishop of Vienna in 1853, cardinal in 1855. This priest of the strictest observance understood well how to extend the influence of the Church even beyond the powerful position it had regained under Emperor Francis.[76] Of the cabinet members, Schmerling, though increasingly conservative himself, became disappointed with the reactionary course and resigned as minister of justice in 1851. Thun, who joined the cabinet in 1849, stayed throughout the whole period until 1860.[77] Bruck was minister of commerce until 1851 and minister of finance from 1855 to 1860, when he committed suicide because he was unjustly suspected of malfeasance in office.[78] These three men were undoubtedly the ablest of Schwarzenberg's and Bach's collaborators.

After Schwarzenberg's death Bach became leading minister but was never appointed prime minister. This may have been due in part to Francis Joseph's loyalty to Schwarzenberg's memory and in part to the personality of Bach, to whose past the emperor never became quite reconciled.

[76] See Friedjung, *Österreich von 1848–1860,* II, 473–480.
[77] Ibid., II, 480–503.
[78] Charmatz, *Bruck,* pp. 109–153.

A word about the emperor's family might at this point be in order. His relationship to his more liberal and more gifted brother Maximilian, the future emperor of Mexico, was always strained. Maximilian's position as commander of the Austrian navy did not satisfy him and his subsequent assignment as governor general of the Lombardo-Venetian kingdom from 1857 to 1859 did not please the emperor, who considered his brother too liberal. In 1854, the rather lonely Francis Joseph married his first cousin Elizabeth of Bavaria, from a dynasty many times related to the Habsburgs by marriage. The beautiful and romantic empress, a fascinating and unorthodox personality, was not interested in politics, but was to play a notable part in the reconciliation with Hungary.

The Schwarzenberg-Bach administrations, but particularly the latter, established the pattern of the over-all political organization of the Habsburg empire. The administration of the crownlands was in the hands of the provincial governors, who received their instructions from the minister of interior. The Kreis (county) organization of the by now faint memories of Kremsier and of Stadion's March constitution was for a time preserved in a limited sense, though later restricted to the judicial sphere.

As for Hungary, Croatia-Slavonia with Fiume, Translyvania (including a part of the southeastern Military Frontiers), the Vojvodina, and the Banat of Temesvár, were administratively separated from the country. The remaining trunk was divided into five districts under the over-all direction of the governor general in Budapest.

The judicial organization corresponded by and large to that in effect until 1918. Several modifications, however, are necessary. The revolutionary achievement of jury trials was abolished at the end of 1851 and with this went, consistently from the standpoint of the regime, the publicity of trials altogether. Furthermore the separation of justice and administration was eliminated on the lowest level of district office and magistrate courts. Patrimonial jurisdiction was not compatible with a system of not feudal but bureaucratic centralistic absolutism, which governed now the Habsburg lands. Yet this achievement of Josephinism did not mean protection for the rights of the individual under now existing conditions. An infamous aspect of the merger of administration and justice on the lowest level was the introduction of corporal punishment by police authority in the Austrian lands in 1854. This was not only a method to enforce obedience but also a device to coordinate Austrian bureaucracy with traditional Hungarian feudal institutions. The pseudolegal foundation of measures of this kind was the Sylvester Patent (New Year's Eve) of 1851, which formally invalidated the never-enacted March constitution of Stadion. Absolutism had now become official. Even though the issuance of the Patent implied a flagrant breach of an imperial assurance of constitutional government, it was perhaps preferable to the hypocritical references to a paper constitution. The only part of the Stadion legislation in terms of constitutional government that had been enacted, the communal autonomy, was voided. It was revised only in the constitutional era.

An improved organization of the register of real estate and a revision of the Code of Criminal Law of 1803, introduced in 1852, represented technical improvements. The enactment of a code of craft guild regulations with some protection of the workers followed the fall of Bach by four months. Yet his administration undoubtedly deserves the credit for its partly successful attempt to organize the conflicting Austrian policies in this respect. The problem was not entirely solved until 1973.

The true spirit of the regime was embodied in the reorganization of church-state relations, which represented an expansion of the Franciscan distortion of Josephinism, the operation of the Church as powerful arm of the state. Substantially as a result of the Concordat of 1855 the Church assumed also functions of its own, which went beyond those under her control after the reigns of Leopold I and his sons. All this was largely Rauscher's work. Bach cooperated with him primarily because a political system so flagrantly out of step with the spirit of the times needed at least one strong ideological ally; this ally by a process of elimination could only be the Church. The jurisdiction of the bishops was considerably extended by legislation of 1850. Their control of the clergy including canonical trials became now almost unlimited, and their administration of the seminaries was no longer under state control. Elimination of previous restrictions in regard to liturgical questions and ecclesiastic communications with Rome was, however, legitimate.

Otherwise the spirit of intolerance paralyzed intellectual life. New restrictions were placed on the civic status of the Jews in regard to the acquisition of landed property. This was the bill presented by the state to the Jews for their allegedly inordinate participation in the revolutionary activities. The legal status of the Protestants was not directly affected, but the ban on employment of non-Catholics as teachers in Catholic schools hurt them more than the Jews.

The Concordat of 1855, primarily Rauscher's work, went beyond the previous concessions to the Church. The Catholic Church as administrator of the state religion now secured autonomy to a degree no longer compatible with even the most flexible interpretation of Josephinism. The

Church did not only strengthen her position in previously contested areas of relations to the state, but gained control of additional areas. Marriage legislation for Catholics, which meant anybody baptized as Catholic irrespective of later changes in denominational status, had always been based on the principles of Canon law. Now something new was added. Jurisdiction in matrimonial questions was transferred from secular to ecclesiastic courts. The papacy regained also a barely restricted right to establish new bishoprics and parishes, which helped to enforce the expanded clerical jurisdiction. Above all, the new ecclesiastic rights pertained to education. The Church was now not only in control of religious instruction but was empowered to see to it, that teaching in any secular discipline (languages, history, science), must not be in conflict with the tenets of religious instruction. The Church also assumed the right of censorship of literature potentially dangerous to youth and the faithful altogether. Austria was thus thrown back into the era of the Counter Reformation in its most intransigent form. The difference was, however, that the religious policies of the Counter Reformation, though divisive in character, had powerful, possibly majority support of the population. The new policy was backed largely by police informers—to the detriment of the state and the truly faithful, that is, in the last analysis to the Church herself.[79]

It is remarkable that this spirit of intolerance did not hurt higher education as seriously as might have been expected. In fact, important reforms were put through in this era. Chief credit was due to the outstanding personality of the minister of education Count Leo Thun and his able collaborators Hermann Bonitz and Franz Exner. Thun, though a rigid conservative, managed to steer an independent course. Thus he succeeded not only in preserving previous modest standards but in improving them in several respects. He must be credited with the basic reorganization of higher secondary education, the curriculum of the Austrian classical *Gymnasium* and the new *Realschule* (higher secondary school with emphasis on modern languages, mathematics, and sciences).[80] Thun managed also—under existing prejudices a notable achievement—to pro-

[79] Erika Weinzierl-Fischer, *Die österreichischen Konkordate von 1855 und 1933* (Vienna, 1960), pp. 26–81; Winter, *Revolution, Neoabsolutismus und Liberalismus,* pp. 86–101.

[80] *Gymnasiums* and *Realschulen,* though most of them public schools, offered instruction only to those who had passed an entrance examination. They also charged tuition. Only graduates of these schools were admitted to universities. The tuition-free general secondary schools (*Bürgerschulen*), who admitted all graduates of grade schools, did not offer this privilege.

tect academic freedom in the universities to some extent and to appoint also some objective scholars of high reputation. Neither the university organization nor particularly that of the gymnasiums—fine schools, but with an overemphasis on the cultivation of classical languages—have fully stood the test of time. In some respect they have stood it too well since what appeared progressive in Thun's times would have required considerable adjustments in the following decades. These revisions were not forthcoming. His reforms were primarily focused on higher and intermediate higher education, not on general compulsory instruction, but this emphasis could be understood as counterweight against prevailing intolerance on the higher cultural level. By administrative actions and informally Thun also secured the right of various nationalities to have at least elementary instruction taught in the language of the majority of the population of individual communities.[81]

Improved were also the military regulations including the service obligations. The ancient institution of the Court War Council had to yield finally to the Ministry of War which in turn was merged with the High Command of the Army. The general service obligation of the citizenry was further extended and the method of selection for actual induction—from now on by lot—was made more equitable than before. The service obligation itself, harsh as it continued to be, was limited to eight years with two additional years in the army reserve. In equipment, modernization of training (especially of staff officers), emphasis on the outmoded cavalry rather than infantry, the army had fallen back behind those of other powers. These deficencies played an important role in the outcome of the wars of 1859 and 1866; the Austrian main armies in both wars were led by generals not fully up to the requirements of their task. Whether the results of both campaigns were not also due to the unpopularity or political weakness of the Austrian position is difficult to determine.

The regime did relatively best in the socioeconomic field; here absolutism had possibilities of imposing its will rather than balancing opposing interests, which a less autocratic regime would have lacked. Obviously this must not be understood as defense of a system, whose outlook never transcended the barriers of narrow class interests.

81 Hans Lentze, *Die Universitätsreform des Ministers Graf Leo Thun-Hohenstein* (Vienna, 1962), pp. 28–294 passim; Richard Meister, *Entwicklung und Reform des österreichischen Schulwesens* (Vienna, 1963), I, 77–255 passim. On Thun's background see Christoph Thienen-Adlerflycht, *Graf Leo Thun im Vormärz* (Graz-Vienna-Cologne, 1967). See also Robert A. Kann, "Hochschule und Politik im österreichischen Verfassungsstaat" in E. Botz, H. Hautmann, H. Konrad eds., *Festschrift für Karl Stadler* (Wien, 1974), pp. 507 ff.

Frequently the regime is credited with the exemplary manner in which the emancipation of the peasants was enacted. This is true with qualifications. The Austrian as well as the Hungarian emancipatory peasant legislation had provided that indemnities be paid to the previous owners of the land. But only the Hungarian legislation stated that the government should pay for it and the Bach administration did not accept this position in full. It burdened the peasant with one-third of the indemnities to be paid for the abolishment of personal services, payments in kind servitudes, tithes, etc. One-third was to be paid by the government (in Austria the crownland administrations) and one-third, indirectly, by the former owners of the land. The indemnities to the lords were to be rendered in twenty annual installments with 5 percent interest. This settlement did not correspond to the more liberal intentions of the emancipatory legislation of the Reichstag in September of 1848. On the other hand, the Bach administration acted at least with efficiency and deliberate speed. Unlike the peasants in Prussia and Russia the peasants in Austria did not have to pay for their obligation with parts of their meager landholdings. By the mid-1850's the complex legislation had been enacted with efficiency.[82]

In 1850–1851 the Austro-Hungarian interstate customs lines were abolished and the Habsburg monarchy for the first time, became a unified customs territory. Credit for this was due largely to the minister of commerce von Bruck, who actually had farther-reaching designs. He promoted the idea of a great Austro-German and possibly also Italian customs union, an association that Schwarzenberg had desired in political terms. Reality fell short off these plans, but tariffs between Austria and the member states of the German customs union could be reduced and a favorable customs treaty with Prussia was concluded in 1853.[83] For the first time Austria could deviate from her narrow protective tariff policy because after 1848 some beneficial effects of the industrial revolution had penetrated at least the western part of the monarchy. Austrian metallurgical and textile industries, to mention only two main industries, had be-

[82] Friedjung, *Österreich von 1848–1860,* I, 333–367; Tremel, *Wirtschafts- und Sozialgeschichte Österreichs,* pp. 321–324; Christoph Stölzl, *Die Ära Bach in Böhmen* (Munich, 1972), passim; Friedrich Walter, "Kaiser Franz Josephs Ungarnpolitik in der Zeit seines Neoabsolutismus," in Theodor Mayer, ed., *Der österreichisch-ungarische Ausgleich von 1867* (Munich, 1968), pp. 125–135.

[83] Charmatz, *Bruck,* pp. 107–124; Droz, *L'Europe Centrale,* pp. 92–99; Fink, *Die österreichisch-ungarische Monarchie als Wirtschaftsgemeinschaft,* pp. 19–25; Herbert Matis, "Leitlinien der österreichischen Wirtschaftspolitik" in A. Wandruszka and P. Urbanitsch eds., *Die Habsburgermonarchie,* I., pp. 29–67, and ibid. Eduard März and Karl Socher, "Währung und Banken in Cisleithanien", pp. 323–337.

come competitive on the European markets, and the same was true for various manufactured luxury goods. The protectionist policy deemed vital to Maria Theresa, Joseph II, and Francis was no longer necessary in the same sense, if it ever was before. Communications had also been improved. Much admired was the Semmering railway route opened in 1854, the first main railway in Europe that passed through mountainous territory. Hardly practical in its design as seen from the viewpoint of an observer today, this route with its beautiful views was a symbol of newly won Austrian engineering skill.

Unified and improved was also the taxation system. A general land tax, a rent tax on urban premises, and, a true first, a general income tax were initiated. Indirect taxes were reduced. The regulation of the tax system was followed by that of the currency. In 1858 a unified silver currency, the guilder (florin) containing sixty Kreutzers, was introduced.[84]

Most economic reforms meant greater efficiency rather than social concern focused on economic inequality. In the relationship between management and industrial labor, difficulties were in fact on the increase. The industrial sector moved more into the foreground of Austrian economic problems, and a still poorly industrialized country was ill-equipped to deal with the expanding problem of management-labor-relations and working conditions. Besides, Austrian economic progress was considerable only if compared with the situation of the pre-March era. In relation to western Europe and Germany it was very modest. Nevertheless, centralized bureaucratic absolutism, despite its class character, in an economic sense had proved superior to the semifeudal system of the prerevolutionary era.

At the same time this absolutism acted more recklessly in foreign affairs. We discussed the way in which it fell into the trap of accepting a studied Piedmontese provocation in the spring of 1859. The war proved to be the system's undoing. Actually Bach could not be blamed at all for the poor military leadership, and only to a limited degree for the inadequacy of military preparations. Yet in a wider sense the unpopularity of Austrian absolutism throughout Europe was largely responsible for the defeat. In August, 1859, Bach was dimissed and Grünne and Kempen, the most hated symbols of the oppressive regime, followed him into retirement. Neither Count Johann Rechberg, the new chairman of the

[84] Friedjung, *Österreich von 1848–1860,* I, 292–322; Heinrich Benedikt, *Die wirtschaftliche Entwicklung in der Franz Joseph Zeit* (Vienna, 1958), pp. 11–55; Eduard März, *Österreichische Industrie und Bankenpolitik in der Zeit Franz Joseph I.* (Vienna, 1965), pp. 48–94.

ministerial council and successor of Buol as minister of foreign affairs, nor Bach's direct replacement as minister of the interior, the Polish count Agenor Goluchowski, the experienced governor of Galicia, had the same influence that Bach had held for almost a decade.

On March 5, 1860, the emperor announced that the Reichsrat, an advisory council of six Austrian and two Hungarian dignitaries, established in 1851, should be considerably enlarged. New members should be archdukes, high secular and ecclesiastic office holders. Large landed property was strongly represented by these men. They were to hold lifetime appointments. There was also to be a second group of thirty-eight members, the representatives of the lands, most of whom also represented large landed property, appointed for six-year terms and selected by the emperor from a list of candidates submitted by the estates diets. They included six Magyars, two Croats, and two Serbs. The whole body was to serve in an advisory capacity, primarily in regard to financial agenda, but it should also deliberate—at the emperor's pleasure—on further and possibly more far-reaching constitutional changes. This and the as yet merely academic resolve to restore the administrative unity of Hungary and the appointment of some Magyar and Slavic advisers were mere straws in the wind. The enlarged Reichsrat presided by the fairly liberal Archduke Rainer was in fact a mere mockery of a constitutional body. And yet its convocation made it clear that absolutism had come to the end of the road and was forced to adjust to the ever more clearly perceptible underground rumblings pressing for change. To be sure, in terms of the regime's interests it should be as small as possible. On the basis of the experience of 1848 it became soon clear that such change could not be held within the confines of a modified absolutism. The events of 1859–1860 did not establish a constitutional system, yet they made the bankruptcy of the existing regime obvious. A system committed to the principle of equality before the law for everybody had proved that it stood for inequality—though not equal inequality—for the overwhelming majority of the peoples of the Habsburg empire.

E. Transition to constitutional government (1860–1867)

The enlarged Reichsrat in session from May to September, 1860, proved to the government that the token moves in to the direction of constitutional government had not met liberal expectations; even moderate conservatives were disappointed. Archduke Rainer, the president of the enlarged Reichsrat, supported limited liberal reforms within a centralistic system, and the emperor's former teacher, Cardinal Rauscher, just backed centralism without any liberal trimmings. Yet centralistic absolutism and liberalism had that much in common that they both worked for institutions pertinent to the empire as a whole. The tide was running now in favor of constitutional government and hence centralistic tendencies favored moderately liberal government, irrespective of the government's reluctance.

The more strongly entrenched conservative supporters of historic-traditional federalism, on the other hand, requested wider autonomy for the historic political entities or, more correctly, for the aristocratic leadership within these entities. The principal spokesman for these views in the cabinet was the Polish minister of interior, Count Goluchowski; the leading minister, Count Rechberg, exercised little influence beyond the sphere of foreign affairs. Since the feudal conservatives could still mute the voices of Czech and Magyar liberalism—though with declining efficiency—the resulting constitutional compromise, the octroyed constitution of October 20, 1860 (commonly referred to as October Diploma), leaned heavily in the direction of conservative federalism.

The October Diploma conceded to the Reichsrat, basically still the sham body of March of the same year, participation in legislation as enumerated in the charter. Such participation pertained to economic and financial matters and, apart from the required consent to taxation, only in an advisory capacity. Moreover, legislation had to be shared with diets in which the influence of the usually aristocratic owners of large estates, bishops, and chambers of trade and commerce in the urban sphere were meant to be predominant. The hundred members of the Reichsrat were largely dietal representatives who represented primarily the social groups referred to above. Illustrative is the Styrian diet, one example of several: It consisted of two bishops, four other clerics, twelve big estates owners, ten town representatives, two representatives of chambers of trade and commerce, and twelve of rural communities.[85] This was not all. The crown, which had the prerogative to appoint the members of the Reichsrat, reserved for itself the right to screen the dietal nominations before selection. Significant in this strange kind of constitution was also the built-in plan for a smaller assembly—the narrower Reichsrat—for the affairs of the western part of the empire. This arrangement pointed indeed toward a new approach to the Hungarian problem.

In Hungary opposition against the absolutist regime and the suppression of the historic rights of the divided country united Magyars more than the centralists and federalists in Austria. Moderate conservative aristo-

[85] See on the composition of the diets Richard Charmatz, *Österreichs innere Geschichte von 1848–1907*, 2 vols. (Leipzig, 1909–1911), second edition II, 46 ff.; Kann, *Nationalitätenproblem*, II, 110–111.

crats like counts Anton Szécsen, Emil Dessewffy, and Paul Somssich, with whom the crown hoped to cooperate, could not bring about reconciliation. The following of Francis Deák, the only statesman of the generation of 1848, increased. Without compromising himself he had not fallen entirely from the graces of the government. Major concessions seemed to be in order. The hated archduke Albrecht was recalled from Buda as governor general and replaced by the Magyar General Benedek, equally faithful to the crown as the archduke, but not tainted with the oppressive measures of military occupation. The separate Hungarian-Transylvanian court chancery was to be restored and a supreme court for Hungary was to be reestablished together with the old pre-1848 comitat constitution. Above all the Reichstag was to be reconvened on the basis of a membership equal before the law. This over-all principle of civil equality, as it existed now at least in theory in the Austrian statute books, was (together with the emancipation of the peasants) the main, though still largely academic, achievement of the revolution. It could no longer be fully ignored in Hungary either. Magyar conservatives were displeased and liberals dissatisfied. Still these were important promises for the future.

In Austria one could not even speak of promises at that time, save for the enforcement of Stadion's communal legislation, which led to elections on the communal level in November 1860. The feudal federalist spirit of the October Diploma was as backward as the centralistic spirit of the Bach regime and less efficient. With the still existing censorship, opposition could be expressed only by passive rejection. Goluchowski's schemes had failed and in December, 1860, he was replaced by Schmerling, whose prominent position at St. Paul's Assembly in 1848 was gratefully remembered by the liberals; the conservative centralists respected him as an only moderately liberal member in the Schwarzenberg cabinet. He had the reputation as man of integrity, able bureaucrat, and strongly profiled representative of the concept of German-directed, though not German-national, centralism. On February 4 the emperor appointed his cousin, Archduke Rainer, prime minister. Whereas Schmerling was to be spokesman and chief executive officer of the government, the association with an imperial prince meant that the crown hoped to reap popularity from this unusual combination never to be repeated in imperial Austrian history.[86]

[86] Redlich, *Das österreichische Staats- und Reichsproblem,* I, 460–671; Josef Ulbrich, *Das österreichische Staatsrecht* (Tübingen, 1909), pp. 46–49; Henry Marczali, *Ungarische Verfassungsgeschichte* (Tübingen, 1910), pp. 155–157; Kann, *Nationalitätenproblem,* II, 107–114, 323–331.

Schmerling is generally credited with the draft of the February Patent promulgated on February 26, 1861, which was meant to supplement the October Diploma but actually changed it fundamentally. The real intellectual father of the Patent, however, was a relatively minor government official, Hans von Perthaler, an even more pronounced conservative and traditionalist than his chief Schmerling.

The new constitution established a bicameral system. The Reichsrat was to be divided into a House of Lords, consisting of two groups, hereditary aristocratic members and members with life-time tenure, to be appointed by the crown. Some of the latter were to be high ecclesiastic and secular dignitaries who would serve ex officio. Most life-time members were to be personalities of particular distinction in politics and various cultural activities—as the crown judged these distinctions. The House of Representatives was to consist of about 300 members, elected by the estates diets of the individual crownlands. That meant that they were to represent still the old curias of great landowners, urban and rural communities, and chambers of trade and commerce. Actually the interests of commerce and industry, that is, of the urban middle and upper middle classes were to be somewhat better represented than in the October Diploma. Governmental gerrymandering favored the great landowners and the Germans—in line with Schmerling's and Perthaler's political philosophy. To bring these desired objectives about, the franchise was narrowly restricted by property qualifications. Individual votes in some districts weighed five times as much as in others. The Patent recognized originally neither the principle of ministerial responsibility nor parliamentary immunity. An emergency paragraph empowered the government to issue laws while the parliament was not in session, without any requirement for subsequent approval. Yet this parliament, unlike the chamber of the October Diploma, had at least the power of legislative initiative and the right to pass the annual budget. It was significant that a merely academic plenum should deal with the affairs of the empire as a whole, while a narrower and more workable Reichsrat would be concerned with those exclusive of Hungary, Croatia, Transylvania, and Venetia. This arrangement pointed in the direction of the future dualistic compromise, the permanent and final constitutional frame of the empire.

The February Patent was a poor representative constitution in which, to quote Orwell, everybody was equal but some more equal than others, but unlike the October Diploma it was a representative constitution of sorts nevertheless. Elections actually took place and the Reichsrat convened in May, 1861, in Vienna, though it was boycotted by Magyars,

Croatians, and Italians from the start and opposed generally as too centralistic and partly as too liberal by Czechs, Poles, Serbs, and Slovenes. With few exceptions, these Slavic members of parliament were conservatives who for national and social reasons were opposed to the traditional centralism of the German liberals. This discrepancy in German and Slavic political ideologies represented partly also differences in degrees of urbanization, partly it was due to manipulations of conflicting interests by the government, which worked more smoothly in rural than in urban districts. It favored centralism but was unwilling to buy its frequent corollary, liberalism. The still unsettled problem of Hungary's constitutional status prevented adequate operation of the new system in any case.[87]

The Hungarian parliament, not yet on equal footing with the Reichsrat in Vienna, convened in Pest, in April, 1861. Deák demanded recognition of the Hungarian constitution of April, 1848. As will be remembered, provisions in this document for a separate Hungarian budget, and the use of Hungarian forces only with the approval of the Hungarian government and legislature, had never been approved by the administration in Vienna. Yet the crown, apart from these particularly controversial issues, still adhered to the convenient reactionary philosophy that rebellious Magyar Hungary had forfeited its constitution. A new one would have to be based on imperial pleasure and not on historic rights. Consequently the Hungarian diet was dissolved in August, 1861. And while the Croats demanded complete separation from Hungary in a somewhat controversial law passed by the Sabor in November, 1861, this did not mean as in previous times that they endorsed the imperial policy in Vienna. They were opposed to a government that refused to grant the union of Dalmatia with the triune kingdom.[88]

Frustrated by the chronic Slavic dissatisfaction, the German liberal

[87] Redlich, *Das österreichische Staats- und Reichsproblem,* I, 715–814; Ulbrich, *Das österreichische Staatsrecht,* pp. 49–52; Kann, *Nationalitätenproblem,* II, 123–132; Josef A. Tzöbl, "Vorgeschichte des österreichisch-ungarischen Ausgleichs 1713–1867," in Peter Berger, ed., *Der österreichisch-ungarische Ausgleich von 1867: Vorgeschichte und Wirkungen* (Vienna, 1967), pp. 9–32; Otto Brunner, "Der österreichisch-ungarische Ausgleich von 1867 und seine geschichtlichen Grundlagen," in Theodor Mayer, ed., *Der österreichisch-ungarische Ausgleich von 1867* (Munich, 1968), pp. 15–24.

[88] Marczali, *Ungarische Verfassungsgeschichte,* pp. 157–162; [Francis Deák] *Deáks Adress-Entwurf und das Staatsrecht Österreichs* (Vienna, 1861), pp. 1–80 passim. Wenzel Lustkandl, *Abhandlungen aus dem österreichischen Staatsrecht über das Manifest . . . vom 20. September 1861 und die beiden Adressen des kaiserlichen ungarischen Landtages von 1861* (Vienna, 1866); Guldescu in F. H. Eterovich and C. Spalatin, eds., *Croatia,* II, 40–47; Gustav Steinbach *Franz Deák* (Vienna, 1888), pp. 34–37.

disappointment with the lack of legislative action, and the even more serious Magyar discontent, the cabinet Rainer-Schmerling resigned. In July, 1865, it was replaced by a cabinet under Count Richard Belcredi, who attempted to establish a modified conservative federal system. Such course was acceptable to the Czech and Polish feudals, a handful of Magyar aristocrats represented by Count Moritz Esterházy in the cabinet, and some German conservatives. But these groups had become increasingly unrepresentative themselves. Belcredi's task was bound to end in failure even sooner than that of Schmerling; the accentuation of the crisis in relations with Prussia after 1684 played its part.

The highlight of Belcredi's government was the suspension of the unworkable constitution in September, 1865. This did not mean a premeditated return to absolutism. In some respects the Belcredi regime was more liberal than that of the nominal German liberal Schmerling, for instance in regard to the operation of censorship. The suppression of the constitution meant primarily that the speedy reconciliation with Hungary —badly required in the face of the threatening war with Prussia—could not be brought about in terms of the February Patent. The crown might have welcomed a long-term perpetuation of the suspension of the constitution, but that was another question. It was not to be. Francis Joseph as a goodwill gesture had visited Budapest earlier, in the summer of 1865, and had consented to the reincorporation of Transylvania into Hungary. This was a major, and from the point of national justice unfair concession, but it opened the way for new negotiations with the Magyar leaders. In December, 1865, the king-emperor reopened the Hungarian diet and now negotiations with a select committee of the diet got seriously under way after validity of the Hungarian constitution of 1848 was recognized by the crown, as far as it could be sanctioned at that time. The theory of forfeiture of constitutional rights as punishment for rebellion was thus finally laid to rest.

Deák and Count Gyula Andrássy were to be the chief Hungarian negotiators. However, before the solution of the Austro-Prussian conflict a settlement appeared unlikely. The crown, which believed in victory over Prussia, hoped for a better bargaining position after the end of hostilities, and the Hungarian negotiators, though loyal to the monarchy, expected an improvement of theirs from a reverse outcome of the war. History proved them to be right.

The consequences of the war proved several other things as well. The crown could at best hope for a settlement on the terms demanded by Hungary before the outbreak of the war. This meant primarily recognition of a Hungarian state of at least equal constitutional standing with the other Habsburg lands. It had become clear, also, that genuine constitutional government was now an equally pressing necessity in the western part of the empire. The disastrous defeat by Prussia in 1866 was still linked to the failure of the absolutist Bach regime. Belcredi was not the man to bring the difficult changes about, which required above all an accommodation between Germans and Slavs in Austria, Magyars, Slavs, and Roumanians in Hungary, and Magyars and Germans in an empire-wide conflict. He resigned in February, 1867. His concept of an Austrian federation of five historic political entities, a German-Alpine, Magyar-Hungarian, Bohemian-Moravian, Polish-Ruthenian, and Southern Slav (Belcredi's so-called pentarchy), was not taken seriously as feasible political objective.[89]

His successor was Baron (later Count) Beust, formerly prime minister of Saxony and since October, 1866, minister of foreign affairs. In June, 1867, the title Reichskanzler was conferred on him, which was meant to preserve the appearance rather than the reality of a joint Austro-Hungarian chief executive. The title had become meaningless by agreement on the Austro-Hungarian Compromise in March, 1867. The Compromise, accordingly, was passed by the Hungarian parliament and was sanctioned by the emperor as king of Hungary in June of the same year. Chiefly instrumental in the agreement was, next to Deák and Beust, Count Andrássy. Appointed Hungarian prime minister in February, 1867, he was destined also to become Beust's successor as minister of foreign affairs in November, 1871. Beust himself lacked Andrássy's appeal. He was appointed minister of foreign affairs on account of Saxony's loyalty to Austria in 1866 and in the unjustified belief that his somewhat devious shrewdness could match Bismarck's abilities, in case a still-hoped-for Austro-French alliance could be brought about. As for his more immediate task in the negotiations leading to the Compromise and subsequently the Austrian constitutional settlement, it was hoped that a foreigner would encounter less opposition and a Protestant courtier might possibly be more amenable to the Catholic viewpoint than an enlightened conservative Catholic aristocrat.[90]

These assumptions were believed in and transmitted to the emperor by the new minister of the interior, Count Taaffe, a confidant of long standing. But they were just too intricate to be workable. What counted more than Beust's diplomatic skill, even more than the popular appeal

[89] Kann, *Nationalitätenproblem*, II, 132–139, 335–336.

[90] Andritsch ed., *Ungarische Geisteuswelt*, pp. 203–211; on Deák see Redlich, *Das österreichische Staats- und Reichsproblem*, II, 503–508; on Beust ibid., pp. 521–523.

which he lacked, was credibility and sincerity, both absent in the character of this complex man. These shortcomings counted more in Hungary than in Austria, where Beust's support of the Austro-German centralistic position could be taken for granted within the limits of the practically obtainable objectives. In Hungary, however, neither Deák's integrity, Andrássy's dexterity, the popularity of both men, nor the good will of the king-emperor Francis Joseph might have sufficed, if it had not been for the mediation of the queen-empress Elizabeth, who struck a chord in the chivalrous hearts of the Magyar gentry.

These were the main terms of the Compromise, henceforward the basic constitutional frame of the Austro-Hungarian monarchy up to the time of its dissolution.[91] The premise of the Compromise was the association of two independent states of equal rights, which shared a common ruler, as emperor in Austria, as king in Hungary. These dual states—hence the term Dualism used in the Compromise—had also other common features. The Compromise, therefore, represented not merely a personal union but a real union (a *Realunion*). What in practice amounted to a constitution for the Habsburg empire was strictly speaking a treaty between two in major respects sovereign states—but by no means in all. Nevertheless, in view of the restrictions of the sovereignty of each state, the Compromise was not an international treaty. It was not a federation or confederation either. There was no state above the two member states as in a federation nor were they fully sovereign as in a confederation. Neither were the Austrian and Hungarian versions of the Compromise embedded in the constitutional laws of both states completely alike. In other words, the Compromise represented a political structure *sui generis*. Not in a strictly legal but in a figurative way it is thus still permissible to speak of a Habsburg empire.

Agenda common to both states were foreign affairs, defense, and common finances. Concerning defense, however, the determination of the quota of recruits in each state, operation of general conscription, civil legislation connected with it, and organization of national militias were left to the two states. The language of command in the armed forces was to be German, an issue which, as the Magyars saw it, impaired their status of equality. Common finances were to be considered those that pertained to joint institutions, that is, primarily foreign affairs and

[91] The official term Austro-Hungarian monarchy was introduced in 1868, but in later years, when the interpretation and operation of the Compromise moved increasingly in the direction of Hungarian semiseparatist tendencies, the term Austria-Hungary was used. This implied clearly that there was no federal structure above the dual states.

defense matters. These joint expenditures were to be determined by agreement between the parliaments of both states every ten years.

Also the determination of the share in common expenditures was left to this settlement every ten years. The quota agreed upon by the dual governments in 1867 required Hungary to pay 30 percent of these costs. Throughout the history of the Compromise it never rose above 36.4 percent, that is, far less than would have been appropriate on the basis of Hungary's economic resources and potential.

Subject to regulation every ten years were some matters administered separately by Austria and Hungary, but according to common principles. These included customs—in practice the continuation of the customs union—currency regulations, and problems of railway communications passing through both states. Whereas the cabinets of each state had to submit legislation and in particular the budget to their respective parliaments, the three joint ministers, of foreign affairs, defense, and joint finances, had to deal with two executive committees of both parliaments, the so-called Delegations, which met once a year alternately in Vienna and Budapest, but communicated with each other only in writing. The Magyars requested this cumbersome operation to dispell any doubt that no parliament existed above the Hungarian and Austrian legislatures. Finally, the three joint ministers and the Austrian and Hungarian prime ministers under the chairmanship of the minister of foreign affairs, formed the joint ministerial council. This institution gave the two governments indirectly a share in the conduct of foreign and other joint affairs.

Among the divergencies between the Hungarian and Austrian versions of the Compromise and its interpretation, most important was the fact that the Hungarian was rooted in the Pragmatic Sanction and the assurances that the validity of the Compromise was dependent on constitutional government in Austria. The former provision pointed to a difference in the question of common succession, which might have arisen if the heir apparent Francis Ferdinand, assassinated in 1914 at Sarajevo, would have succeeded Francis Joseph. In that case his offspring from an unequal marriage would not have been eligible to rule in Austria but would have qualified in Hungary.[92] More serious was the issue concerning the preservation of constitutional government in Austria. It could be easily understood that the Hungarian constitution would have been threatened if absolutism would have been reintroduced in Austria. Yet according to Magyar constitutional interpretation this did not mean just existence of representative constitutional government in Austria but

[92] The oath of renunciation for his offspring in both states taken by the archduke in 1900 was to prevent such contingency.

existence of the specific constitutional laws introduced shortly afterward in December, 1867, in Austria. According to them, Austria, like Hungary, should be a unitary state and not a federal structure, which was to grant all national groups as political entities and not merely as individuals equal rights. Any change in that direction in Austria would impair also the Magyar predominance in Hungary. An imperial manifesto of mid-October, 1918, which promised the conversion of the western part of the empire into a multinational federation, gave the Hungarian parliament the legally and politically equally unjustified pretext to declare the Compromise beyond the further existence of the personal union as terminated. At the stage of the game of pending dissolution of the empire this made little difference, yet it was of great importance that this arbitrary Magyar interpretation of the Compromise was one of the chief reasons, that blocked a comprehensive solution of the national problem in the Habsburg monarchy after 1867, that means possibly still in good time.

Another problem was that five national groups, Croatians, Germans, Roumanians, Ruthenians, and Serbs lived in both parts of the dual monarchy and only a sweeping solution introduced for the whole empire could have regulated their national affairs. This, however, was barred by the Compromise.[93] There were other weak points. The ten-year compromise within the Compromise tested anew the coherence, indeed, the viability of the monarchy every decade. Usually these periodical agreements had to be made possible by new Austrian concessions to Hungarian demands for expansion of sovereign rights. Besides Austrian conributions to the common expenditures, roughly almost in a proportion of two to one, were inordinate. In an economic sense it has sometimes been said that the Austro-Hungarian protective customs system for industrial goods served the interests of Austrian industry and big business as did subsequently the protective customs on agricultural products serve the Hungarian aristocratic big landowners. Yet these were merely the indirect consequences of the Austro-Hungarian association rather than the direct results of the Compromise legislation. Hungarian industrialization proceded just the same. Although the necessity of the ten-year compromise created economic and political difficulties, none were critical. They were after all overcome, though not without difficulties,[94] the last time in 1917, in the midst of the World War crisis.

[93] There were also Italians in Hungarian Fiume, Magyars in the Austrian Bukovina, and Slovaks in Moravia. However, these groups were small.

[94] Between 1897 and 1907 it was necessary to resort in specific instances to emergency legislation by decree. This was anchored in the Compromise and the Austrian constitutional law, but not in the Hungarian constitution. See also

The Compromise did not terminate German predominance over other nationalities in the western part of the monarchy. It merely yielded in Hungary to a pronounced Magyar overlordship over the non-Magyar national groups, which could not be shaken except by revolution. The privileged position of two national groups, Germans and Magyars, over nine others represented a greater problem than the division of the empire in two states as such. Of these two states Hungary, the lands under the Holy Crown of St. Stephen, stood for national disequilibrium and indeed national injustice, particularly in regard to Roumanians, Ruthenians, Serbs, Slovaks, but also Germans and Croats. On the other hand, in a political sense the country represented a homogeneous historical entity with a constitutional tradition reaching far back into the beginning of medieval times. The same cannot be said for the western part of the Danube monarchy, which was composed of several historical units, but did not merge them to a larger one. This larger unit, associated with the concept of Austria in public opinion, was the Habsburg empire as a whole. Apart from this, the Alpine hereditary lands, the small core lands of the Habsburgs and the preceding dynasty, the Babenbergs, are still understood as "Austria" in a narrower sense. The notion of the western part of the Habsburg empire plus Galicia and Bukovina in the east, on the other hand, did not strike a chord in anybody's mind. The common bond between these lands as distinguished from the historical entities of which Austria in the terms of the Compromise was composed, such as hereditary lands, lands of the Bohemian crown, and so on, was the mere fact that these were the Habsburg lands outside of Hungary. Of these seventeen crownlands Galicia and Tyrol for instance were historically no closer to each other than Hungary to Bohemia or Transylvania to Carniola. The official name now given to this area—grotesque in its lack of historical appeal and tradition—was "the kingdoms and lands represented in the Reichsrat." No wonder that a somewhat greater tolerance in the handling of the national question in the west could not make up for this lack of historical cohesion. The venerable historic concept of Austria was applied for convenience's sake, to this unhistorical political conglomerate.[95]

But although the political and economic bonds worked not too smoothly

---

August Gmeiner, *Grundzüge der Verfassung Ungarns* (Nagyszeben-Hermannstadt, 1909), pp. 138–152.

[95] Redlich, *Das österreichische Staats- und Reichsproblem,* II, 523–680; Ivan Zolger, *Der staatsrechtliche Ausgleich zwischen Österreich und Ungarn* (Leipzig, 1912), passim. Ulbrich, *Das österreichische Staatsrecht,* pp. 101–137; Marczali, *Ungarisches Verfassungsrecht,* pp. 173–229; Kann, *Nationalitätenproblem,* I, 30–39, 345–354.

in the Compromise, they worked after all because the western and eastern parts of the monarchy complemented each other to a limited extent.[96] By no means was Austria primarily an industrial and Hungary a purely agricultural country. Both dual states were predominantly rural in character, though Hungary more so than Austria. Industrial progress in Hungary after 1867 could well compare with that in Austria. Thus economic complementation existed only to a point.

More important were the common interests in foreign relations. Had it not been for the Compromise, the empire would probably have disintegrated sooner because of the attraction of Panslavism for the Slavic peoples; they represented nearly half of the Habsburg monarchy's population, and after the annexation of Bosnia-Hercegovina more than half. Panslavism was primarily directed by authoritarian, if not despotic, ideologies in tsarist Russia. A showdown between Austria and Russia would probably have led to the empire's dismemberment, from which Russia would have benefited more than Germany, which presumably would have gained only the Alpine lands. The Slavic peoples, and possibly also the Magyars, would have come under the tsarist heel. The fact that the German and Magyars were the privileged peoples in the dual monarchy, although inequitable, made the Austro-German alliance of 1879 possible that blocked the threat of Russian tsarism and gave the empire the chance for further peaceful development and possibly evolutionary adaptation to more modern national and social conditions. Although this chance was partly missed by 1914, nevertheless between 1867 and 1914 Austria-Hungary had profited from nearly a half century of peaceful evolution. Pan-Germanism, though in some ways even more aggressive than Panslavism, could not rule in Austria because its numerical base was too small. Nor did it have to. Germany became the leading partner in the alliance, largely because of the German-Magyar predominance in the Habsburg monarchy, but, equally important, because the sovereignty of the Habsburg monarchy and its representative institutions had to be respected, since German annexation of Habsburg territories was out of the question. Had Bismarck acted otherwise, had he tried to rule Austria-Hungary rather than to have it ruled by the German-Magyar coalition within the monarchy, the Habsburg empire would have disintegrated sooner and to the chief benefit of tsarist Russia. On the other hand, the preservation of the monarchy and its territorial integrity for a half century

[96] See also Chapter II, Section A. Further, Robert A. Kann, *The Habsburg Empire: A Study in Integration and Disintegration* (2nd ed. New York, 1973), pp. 13 f., 102 f.

to come implied respect for its constitutional institutions, limited national rights for the Slavs in Austria, and at least the chance of securing them in Hungary. All these factors helped to maintain the Compromise.

It was not a perfect solution. German imperialism and militarism threatened. Yet Austria was shielded from them, partly by the nature of the Compromise and partly by the hope that reasonable men would remain at the steering wheel of Austro-German foreign relations. Eventually, the hope proved to be illusionary because of the tensions and finally conflagrations in the age of imperialism. Yet the final crisis was still a long way off and, allowing for appropriate reforms, not necessarily inevitable. The Compromise gave the Danube peoples the chance to live for nearly two generations peacefully and work hopefully for a longer lasting accommodation. That this hope failed eventually was not primarily because of deficiencies of the Compromise.[97]

The Compromise agreed upon in Hungary in March, 1867, had yet to be passed upon by an Austrian parliament. Approval was a foregone conclusion after the crown had surmounted the more difficult Hungarian barrier. Still, it was not an easy matter. The Czechs, feudals and liberals alike, felt they had been sold down the river, and the Poles likewise resented the new development. The great old man of heretofore loyal Czech nationalism, Francis Palacký, participated now in the Panslav Congress, assembled in Moscow in May, 1867, a gathering more hostile to Austrian interests than the Slav congress in Prague nineteen years before. It was clear that the crown could bring about the passage of the Compromise legislation only with full German support, but this support was to be had only for a price: constitutional laws which conformed to the wishes of the German liberals in regard to civil liberties as well as the preservation of the German privileged position in Austria.

The new Austrian parliament which convened in May, 1867, had a two-third German liberal majority versus federalist-clerical opposition, largely consisting of Slav deputies. Only the manipulating of dietal elections, still based on the unjust provisions of the February Patent, brought the result desired and expected by the crown. The first of the

[97] Robert A. Kann, "The Austro-Hungarian Compromise of 1867 in Retrospect, Causes and Effects," in Ludovit Holotík, ed., *Der österreichisch-ungarische Ausgleich 1867* (Bratislava, 1971), pp. 24–44. (Proceedings of the International Conference in Bratislava, 1967.) See also Peter Hanák, "Die bürgerliche Umgestaltung der Habsburger Monarchie und der Ausgleich von 1867," in Ervin Pamlényi, ed., *Social Economic Research in the History of East Central Europe* (Budapest, 1970), pp. 191–231.

five constitutional laws of December, 1867[98] on the jurisdiction of the legislation (Statute 141 of 1867) provided for a bicameral legislation, House of Lords and House of Deputies, the latter until 1873 still selected from the diets. The legislative powers of parliament were wider than in the narrow enumeration in the February Patent. Parliamentary immunity was fully granted. The big catch in this law, however, was embodied in Article 14, which gave cabinet and crown the power of temporary emergency legislation when the Reichsrat was not assembled. This legislation had to be submitted subsequently to parliament for approval, but since the crown in case of adjournment or dissolution of parliament could bring about the opportunity for the issuance of emegency decrees, this proviso meant a serious impairment of the legislative process. It was used frequently by subsequent ministries.

The second law, which offered a catalogue of the basic rights of the citizens was liberal except for the article pertaining to national rights. Yet it was impaired by the provision that the most important civil rights could be temporarily and locally suspended.

The most important provision in this law (Statute 142 of 1867), article 19 dealing with the national problem, was taken with some changes from the Kremsier draft (article 21). There, however, it was part of a more comprehensive approach to the problem.

> Art. 19
> All ethnic groups (*Volksstämme*) in the state have equal rights and every ethnic group has the inviolable right to preserve and cultivate its nationality and language.
>
> The equality of all languages customary in the crownlands (*landesübliche Sprachen*) are recognized in schools, government agencies, and public life.
>
> In the lands inhabited by several ethnic groups, the public schools shall be organized in a way that every ethnic group receives the necessary funds for training in its own language without being compelled to learn the second language of any land.

The liberalism of this famous article was more seeming than real. According to the letter of the law the ethnic groups were not recognized as corporate bodies with a right to representation. Only the interpretation of the supreme Austrian courts later made halting steps in that direction.

[98] These five constitutional laws comprised jointly what may be called the Austrian Cisleithanian constitution, though the word "constitution" was not used. This strange omission represented a kind of unofficial compromise of its own with the crown.

National rights accrued only to the individual citizen, who had great difficulties to assert them in public life. Furthermore, the equality of all national languages, guaranteed in the second paragraph, was indirectly invalidated in the third. Only if every child would have been required to learn two languages could real equality in this respect have been achieved. As it were the Germans were neither required nor in general willing to learn the languages of a smaller Slavic national group. The non-German peoples, on the other hand, had no chance to get ahead in public life, unless they learned German. Thus this article helped to enhance the German position.

A third bill established an imperial court (*Reichsgericht*) to safeguard the rights of the individual. Although this was a beneficial institution, it could not acknowledge what would have required an express statement by law: recognition of national groups as corporate bodies of public law. The fourth bill, on judicial power, recognized the separation of powers in the classical sense in a clear and satisfactory manner. But the fifth bill, on executive power, revealed another important limitation of the constitution. It provided for impeachment proceedings against the ministers of state in case of unconstitutional conduct in office. Yet the law did not introduce the more important principle, that the cabinet as well as individual ministers needed the confidence of the majority of parliament. In other words the executive could be recalled only in the event of unlawful conduct, but otherwise only the emperor's confidence was required. Ministers were appointed and requested to resign at his pleasure. They could enter office and continue to hold it in the face of an expression of nonconfidence by the majority of parliament. Since a legislative program could not be put through without the support of the majority of parliament, a cabinet would frequently resign if it did not enjoy the confidence of parliament, even though it was not legally forced to do so. On the other hand, by use of the emergency article 14 (law 141) in the bill on the jurisdiction of the legislature, a cabinet could for some time govern without the support of parliament and defy its will. The combination of an article which allowed for emergency legislation if parliament was not in session, and the absence of a requirement to resign if the cabinet did not enjoy the confidence of parliament, was, apart from the insufficient recognition of national rights, the most severe weakness of the new Austrian constitution.[99]

[99] There was a sixth constitutional law too which pertained to the common Austrian-Hungarian institutions according to the compromise legislation. A similar, though, as stated, not identical bill, was part of the Hungarian constitutional

Yet with all their shortcomings, compounded by the undemocratic franchise legislation referred to before, the December laws of 1867 stood for a representative constitution superior to the sham legislation of 1860–1861.[100] In conjunction with the constitution of Hungary, not unlike the English one a complex body of diverse laws and traditions from the Bulla Aurea of 1222 to the constitutional laws of 1848 and 1867, representative government through bicameral legislation, separation of powers, and an independent judiciary were assured there too. An unsatisfactory franchise legislation, worse in Hungary and remedied in Austria only in the course of the years, existed in both countries as did other insufficiencies in regard to the limitations of parliamentary power.[101] Hungarian constitutional life nevertheless rested on stronger foundations than the Austrian since it could look back on a centuries-old historic tradition. Perhaps for that same reason Austrian constitutional conditions, less strictly welded to the past, might have been more amenable to evolutionary change. Yet in neither state was the letter of constitutional law as important as its interpretation in political practice throughout half a century. Incongruity between the laws on the statute books and their application in administrative practice existed in both states, though more flagrantly in Hungary.

In spite of all shortcomings, possibilities for peaceful evolution in the direction of democratic government existed in both states. Francis Joseph was crowned king of Hungary in the nineteenth year of his reign (June, 1867) as symbol of reconciliation with the Magyar nation. The first joint ministers, headed by Beust as nominal imperial chancellor in charge of foreign affairs, were appointed in December, 1867. This occurred only days after the passage of the Austrian constitutional laws by the support of a large German liberal majority. The Habsburg empire had

---

legislation. (Hungarian const. law XII.) See Gmeiner, *Grundzüge der Verfassung Ungarns,* pp. 59–66; Gerald Stourzh, "Die Gleichberechtigung der Nationalitäten und die österreichische Dezemberverfassung," in Peter Berger, ed., *Der österreichisch-ungarische Ausgleich von 1867: Vorgeschichte und Wirkungen* (Vienna, 1967), pp. 186–218.

[100] Ulbrich, *Das österreichische Staatsrecht,* pp. 138–233; Kann, *Nationalitätenproblem,* II, 132–149, 334–339.

[101] The Hungarian electoral law of 1848 was revised in 1879 and 1881 but remained, with particular regard to administrative practice, unsatisfactory from the point of view of national and social justice. For a survey of the Hungarian constitutional status as of 1867, see Marczali, *Ungarisches Verfassungsrecht,* pp. 50–172 and Gmeiner, *Grundzüge der Verfassung Ungarns,* passim. See also Steinbach, *Franz Deák,* pp. 67–78; Laszló Katus, "La Couche Dirigeante de la Politique Hongroise et la Question de Nationalités à l'Époque du Compromis Austro-Hongrois de 1867," in Ludovit Holotík and Anton Valtuch, eds., *Der österreichisch-ungarische Ausgleich* (Bratislava, 1971), pp. 670–682.

entered the last phase of an uneasy existence. The outlook for its future was sober, but there was no reason to abandon hope entirely.

F. Domestic affairs (1860–1879)

a) economic development

The political reconciliation with Hungary more than the terms of the Compromise legislation itself accentuated the discrepancy of economic interests between the dual states. In the 1850's Austrian policy, largely under the influence of the *grossdeutsch* ideology of the minister von Bruck,[102] favored accommodation of tariffs with the German customs union. This policy, based on the Austro-Prussian commercial treaty of 1853, worked well because Austrian industry could compete with Prussian manufacture in some fields, particularly textiles, and several of the major German states needed imports of Austrian textile products. In 1862, however, Prussia granted France the most-favored-nation clause which weakened the Austrian position. The improvement of the Prussian position in regard to the manufacturing of textiles and in the metallurgical, chemical, and arms industry in the 1860's made further arrangements difficult. The political conflict sharpened between 1862 and 1867 and abated gradually in the following years. It was aggravated in several respects by the economic fallout of the Austro-Hungarian Compromise of 1867. The Hungarian economic interests in the 1860's and 1870's, or more correctly those of the big landowners, who represented them primarily, were not much different from those of the neoabsolutist era, but now demands of the Magyar establishment carried much greater weight than previously. They strongly favored free trade, because the relatively modest Hungarian industrial interests did not get tariff protection. This policy was to change to some extent after the 1870's. In the era under discussion demands of industry had to yield to agrarian interests. A free-trade policy facilitated the possibilities of Hungarian grain and cattle exports abroad, in particular to Germany. Austrian industry, on the other hand, in the face of strong German competition, felt to be in need of protective traiffs, whereas Austrian agriculture which had to play second string in their export policy, was not strong enough to balance industrial-commercial requirements and to counterbalance Hungarian demands. The Austro-Hungarian customs policy in the late 1860's and the 1870's

[102] Minister of Commerce, November, 1848 to May, 1851; Minister of Finance, March, 1855 to April, 1860, when Bruck committed suicide because he was unjustly suspected of corruption. See also Richard Charmatz, *Minister Freiherr von Bruck* (Leipzig, 1916), pp. 107–153.

therefore accommodated primarily the interests of the aristocratic owners of big estates in Hungary, even though they collided to some degree with Austrian industrial-commercial objectives. Not until the late 1870's when Germany and Russia moved in the direction of protective tariffs did Austria-Hungary initiate a modest protective tariff policy in regard to industrial goods: the so-called autonomous Austro-Hungarian customs tariff of 1878, was enacted on January 1, 1879. Hungarian agrarian interests remained still prevalent but in consideration of Hungarian rather than Austrian industrial progress not as markedly as before.

Austrian grain exports declined in the late 1860's and 1870's largely because of powerful Hungarian competition but also because of the heavy debts of the small- and middle-seized peasants incurred by Bach's rural emancipation policy. Owners of large estates were on the whole better equipped to benefit from an agricultural amelioration policy. Of particular significance was the strong advance in the sugar-beet industry, from which raising of beef cattle benefited as well. The foundation of the Austrian agricultural university in Vienna in 1872 and the elevation of the veterinary academy in Vienna to university rank were likewise instrumental to this effect. Nevertheless, Austrian agriculture, which still employed about three-fifths of the working population, had not improved its standing in comparison with Hungary and Germany.

The chief advancement took place in industry, commerce, communications, and private banking. This rise in the face of a heavy public debt of two and a half billion guilders was so rapid that it led to the great stock market crash of May, 1873. This boom-and-bust cycle was also embarrassing because it followed so soon the opening of the great Viennese world exhibition in April, 1873. The corruption which the crash revealed, compromised the minister of commerce Anton von Banhans, the director general of the new Galician railway Viktor Ofenheim von Ponteuxin, and the prominent German liberal parliamentary leader and former minister of the interior Dr. Karl Giskra. The crash was not so much the consequence of the action of individuals, as of overconfidence, resulting from blind faith in the blessings of a free-trade policy and corresponding widespread financial overcommitments and speculations. The crisis of industrial and financial overexpansion in 1873 resulted in higher interest rates and underemployment throughout the decade.[103]

Industrial progress during the period could compete with western European and German developments in regard to standards, but not to

[103] Oscar Jászi, *The Dissolution of the Habsburg Monarchy* (Chicago, 1929), pp. 194–239.

volume. Within Austria, the lands of the Bohemian crown strengthened their leading position in textile, machine and glass industries, and in breweries. Metallurgical and chemical industries and mining expanded. Textile, shoe, metallurgical industries and beet-sugar productions in Moravia, mining and iron foundries in Silesia were significant. Two main industrial areas were situated in the Alpine lands. One expanded in Styria and Carinthia where iron foundries, lead mining, and metallurgical industries went back to late medieval times. The others were in Lower Austria including Vienna. Here too, as in Bohemia, chemical, textile, and machine industries were important. In Vienna the well-established manufacturing of articles of high-class craftsmanship in leather-goods, furniture, and china prospered. All these industries and crafts had been in existence in the mercantilist era but now they were decidedly on the upswing. Of considerable importance was also the operation of oil wells in Galicia.

The railway net was expanded. The railroad across the Brenner pass was opened in 1868. The Danube steamship company could increase its activities and the Austrian Lloyd became a state-supported major company in commercial navigation overseas. Remarkable as this development was in absolute terms, it fell still somewhat behind industrial progress in western countries. One chief reason for this were the limitations of the domestic markets, especially the lower standards of living of the peasants and the sometimes even lower ones of the industrial workers; the latter did not gain a (restricted) right to establish trade unions and to strike until 1869 and 1870.[104]

Hungary, where more than two-thirds of the population were engaged in agricultural work, found an open market for its big grain surplus in Austria, as noted above. Grain could also be exported to Germany before the new protective tariff system came into force there. The beneficiaries however, were mainly the owners of big and middle-sized estates. The standards of the agricultural workers were even lower than those of their counterparts in Austria.

Considering the poor state of industry in the era of suppression during the neoabsolutist era, there was relatively more progress in Hungary than

[104] Benedikt, *Die wirtschaftliche Entwicklung*, pp. 34–121; März, *Österreichische Industrie*, pp. 95–212; Adolf Beer, *Der Staatshaushalt Österreich-Ungarns seit 1868* (Prague, 1881), pp. 64–398; Tremel, *Wirtschafts- und Sozialgeschichte Österreichs*, pp. 319–372; Matis, *Österreichs Wirtschaft 1848–1918*, pp. 128–341; Mayer-Kaindl-Pirchegger, *Geschichte und Kulturleben Österreichs*, III, 270–288; Robert A. Kann, *Werden und Zerfall des Habsburgerreiches* (Graz-Cologne, 1960), pp. 80–83, 121–124.

in Austria. Cotton and woolen goods, beet-sugar industry, breweries, agricultural machinery, and above all flour milling by steam mills advanced. Mining and iron foundries expanded further. The previously poor railway net developed fast, though it was hampered by strategic considerations and national rivalries with Austria. Railway routes were traced as far as possible from the Austrian borders. In view of the joint defense system this made little sense; the Hungarian veto against the construction of a badly needed railway from Austrian Dalmatia[105] to Zagreb (Agram), and Budapest was even more absurd. The Croatians in both states of the dual monarchy were thus equally unjustly punished. Yet the blow aimed at the economic development of an Austrian crownland with predominantly Croatian population, in a wider sense hurt also Austro-Hungarian economic development as a whole, particularly commercial shipping. Despite such vagaries of a nationalist economy, Hungarian industrial production increased and the balance of trade in the period under discussion became active.

In relative terms, economic progress in Hungary, freed from the chains of neoabsolutism, was greater than in Austria. From the point of view of distribution of the national wealth, conditions remained even more unsatisfactory than in the western half of the empire.[106]

b) EVOLUTION OF POLITICAL PARTY LIFE AND AGGRAVATION OF THE PROBLEM OF NATIONALISM

The introduction of representative constitutional government in both states, deficient though it was, brought about the evolution of a political party life, which despite much ensuing conflict injected a wholesome pluralistic feature into public life. To be sure the beneficial aspects of these innovations were partly offset by the fact that Austrian political institutions never quite succeeded in establishing permanent party structures across common social and cultural interests of the Austrian peoples rather than by national affiliation. This national affiliation remained the rallying force around which national organizations developed. Even the

[105] Claimed by Hungary as historically a part of the triune kingdom of Croatia-Slavonia-Dalmatia.

[106] Laszló Katus, "Economic Growth in Hungary during the Age of Dualism," in Ervin Pamlényi, ed., *Social Economic Research in the History of East Central Europe* (Budapest, 1970), pp. 35–127; Alexander von Matlekovits, *Das Königreich Ungarn volkswirtschaftlich und statistisch dargestellt,* 2 vols. (Leipzig, 1910), see I, 186–206, II, 1–340, 455–498; Kann, *Werden und Zerfall des Habsburgerreiches,* pp. 83–88, 124–135; Peter Hanák, "Hungary in the Austro-Hungarian Monarchy: Preponderance or Dependency?" in *Austrian History Yearbook,* III:1 (1969), 266–284. Guillaume Vautier, *La Hongrie Économique* (Paris, 1893), pp. 55–483 passim.

Social Democrats, by definition fully international, succumbed in the end to the pressure of national separatism. If this problem did not seem to exist in Hungary, the reason was only that as late as 1914 the Magyars who (exclusive of Croatia) represented 54 percent of the population, held 405 parliamentary seats, all other national groups combined only 8 seats.[107]

A discussion of the development of parliamentary life in Austria is also made difficult because names and composition of parliamentary clubs changed repeatedly and these clubs frequently represented not adherents of a common political philosophy but rather diverse groups bound together by a mere solidarity of tactical interests. Only radical fringe groups remained outside of these combinations. Moreover, only the electoral reform of 1873 introduced direct elections of parliament; therefore, members up to that time were merely representatives of the anachronistic estates diets which represented chiefly the interests of the big landowners, the propertied upper middle and middle class, the Church, and a sprinkling of the rural communities. Accordingly the parliamentary elections of 1870—actually still dietal elections—changed little. Even the electoral reform of 1873, a progressive one under existing conditions, meant only the extension of the franchise to a mere 6 percent of the adult male population, the overwhelming majority being still barred by stiff property qualifications.

In these first direct elections, held in 1873 shortly after the great crash, the Liberals—mostly Germans—retained their majority. This liberal so-called Left comprising the German Liberals, the somewhat less moderate Progressive Club, and some splinter groups, held about 160 seats, the big estates owners, including a considerable number of Czechs, some 50 seats, as did the Polish opposition on the Right. The German Clericals, Southern Slavs, and Moravian Czechs controlled about 40 seats. Thus from a national point of view most Slavs—with exception of the Ruthenian anti-Polish opposition—were on the Right. This coloration, however, indicated in no way basic Slavic conservative preferences but merely the inequitable peculiarities of the franchise system. The electoral districts were drawn in a

[107] This statement does not include the Croatian deputies in the Hungarian parliament, who according to the terms of the Croatian autonomy participated as delegates of the Croatian Sabor in the deliberations of the Hungarian parliament, but only on matters of joint Hungarian-Croatian interests, as spelled out by law (the Hungarian-Croatian Compromise of 1868). See also Branko M. Pešelj, "Der ungarisch-kroatische Ausgleich vom Jahre 1868," in Peter Berger, ed., *Der österreichisch-ungarische Ausgleich von 1867* (Vienna, 1967), pp. 169–185; Guldescu, in Francis H. Eterovich and Christopher Spalatin, eds., *Croatia,* II, 47–50. Kann, *Nationalitätenproblem* I, 131–132, 398.

way that gave liberal majorities a chance only in predominantly urban districts, whereas in the rural ones the big landowners were sure to gain safe parliamentary seats. Only to the extent that the rural population was in general more conservative than the urban one and the Slavs were more strongly represented in the rural constituencies, can one perceive an ideological difference in the Slavic and German vote.

The elections of 1879 were held under the still noticeable long-range effect of the crash of 1873 and the greater political involvement of the middle and underprivileged classes of the Slavis peoples. They reduced the German liberal majority to an association of parliamentary groups which was about evenly balanced against the Slavic groups and the German conservatives, altogether some 140 German Liberals and Progressives against about 55 German Conservatives, roughly the same number of Czech and Polish deputies, and some 40 members of parliament without definite political affiliation. Most of them however, supported, the Slavic deputies. They became now the core of a new majority. It was not to the same degree conservative as their predecessors in the parliament of 1873.

In reviewing the whole period of parliamentary life from 1867 to 1879 the German Liberals (in 1881 organized as the so-called United Left) were the real state party of Austria. The term Left as applied to them appears to many interpreters as anachronistic, even absurd because the German Liberals represented largely industry, the chambers of commerce, and high finance; their record on economic issues came often close to a laissez-faire spirit, blind to many social problems of the time. However, these Liberals represented also professional people, the well-educated urban middle and upper middle class, largely the bureaucracy, and altogether the strata of society that wanted to confine the Church to the religious sphere and improved Austrian education. A number of excellent men, including Rudolf Brestel as minister of finance and Johann Nepomuk Berger, a lawyer and likewise member of liberal cabinets, had begun their parliamentary career in the Reichstag of Kremsier. Leopold v.Hasner, professor of economics and subsequently prime minister, Julius v.Glaser, professor of criminal law, and Joseph Unger, professor of civil law and a truly creative jurist, all for some time cabinet members, were scholars as well as political advisers. Eduard Suess the famous geologist became also parliamentary leader. Indeed, these intellectuals could give every parliamentary regime distinction, although not all were fully representative of public opinion. Some of them, particularly Eduard Herbst, the chief spokesman of the United Left,[108] were also unduly doctrinaire, adherents of a rigid centralism where it

[108] Professor of law and in the beginning of the liberal era minister of justice.

agreed with their German liberal political philosophy, and opposed to it where national separatism suited the interests that elected them.

In this sense these Liberals advocated for instance the administrative partition of Bohemia, where the Germans represented only a substantial minority, into a Czech and German part while they were opposed to the administrative division of Styria and Tyrol with their Slovene and Italian majorities in the south of both crownlands. In these crownlands taken as a whole the Germans held a majority and therefore looked at the problem from a different angle. These German men of politics differed from the men of St. Paul's Assembly not in their convictions, but in the fact that they were not confined to the empty role of orators but had the opportinuity to act as legislators and some as administrators. Altough their outlook in national and social questions was limited, most German Liberals in public life were men of integrity, who believed to act for the common good, even where they acted just for the middle and upper middle classes. Nevertheless their achievements must not be compared with those of a more egalitarian future whose problems they did not understand, but with the conditions and failures of a past whose policies were rejected except by those representing unwittingly narrow class interests.[109]

The gravest charge that could be made against the Liberals was that they did not adequately represent the urban petty bourgeoisie, the peasants, or labor. Agriculture was to some extent represented by the conservative, clerical groups, although the interests of the big estates owners received first consideration. The urban petty bourgeoisie had some support of national and so-called democratic splinter groups on the left wing of the Liberals. It carried little political weight and secured appropriate political representation only in the two following decades. Labor had no parliamentary representation whatever. Parties, which stood for these interests did not rise until the 1880's. A number of cultural organizations and associations for the support of the sick and unemployed workers in the large cities evolved, which were allowed to represent the completely forgotten man, the blue-collar worker, but only in a strictly nonpolitical manner. Police supervision of what was feared to become a revolutionary movement was tight, and even in terms of the time after 1868 lawful trade-union activities were harassed. Furthermore the incipient labor movement was in general still of a sectarian character and split between

[109] Gustav Kolmer, *Parlament und Verfassung in Österreich,* 8 vols. (Vienna, 1903–1914), see I, 253–403, II, passim; Georg Franz, *Liberalismus* (Munich, 1955), pp. 131–220; Eduard Suess, *Erinnerungen* (Leipzig, 1916), pp. 164–310; Ernst von Plener, *Erinnerungen* (Stuttgart, 1921), II, 1–143; Max Kulisch, *Beiträge zum österreichischen Parlamentsrecht* (Leipzig, 1900), pp. 84–136.

demands for economic cooperatives, unionism, and sometimes rather parochial interests. All stressed primarily the needs for national organization according to Lassalle's ideas, whereas the supporters of international programs were clearly in the minority. They were to win out in the not distant future.[110]

Some labor organizations existed also among the Czechs, who next to the Germans had the most stabilized political life among the Austrian national groups. Here the Old Czechs, led by Palacký's son-in-law Francis Rieger, had stood for the Bohemian *Staatsrecht,* that is, the indivisibility of the Bohemian lands as separate historical body under the Austrian crown. These endeavors received a setback through the Compromise of 1867 and a new attempt for recognition in 1871 favored by the conservative Hohenwart cabinet—to be discussed below—failed likewise. Thus the Czechs were increasingly driven into opposition, and a new party movement, the Young Czechs, in a loose way in existence since the 1860's gained grounds gradually. These Young Czechs were not opposed to the Bohemian *Staatsrecht.* Like the Old Czechs they rejected an administrative partition of Bohemia, demanded by an arrogant German minority. Yet according to the Young Czechs the Old Czechs represented a party that leaned too heavily on the support of the big landowners, mainly the Bohemian aristocracy and the princes of the Church. The Young Czechs wanted a Czech national movement controlled by the interests of commerce and industry, that is, mainly the urban middle class; support of the peasantry should follow. By a policy of intermittent boycott of parliament or diet and a national propaganda in towns but also rural communities they contested the Old Czech leadership. The fact that Palacký himself, the venerable leader of the Old Czechs, attended the Panslav Congress in Moscow in 1867 and endorsed its program already indicated a gradual shift to the idea of ethnic nationalism.[111]

The Poles gained more by cooperation with the imperial government than the Czechs by opposition because imperial control in the distant Carpathian provinces was more difficult to establish than in Bohemia and Moravia; besides the interests of an economically feeble Ruthenian minority could be surrendered to those of the Polish upper classes, whereas the Liberals would never have agreed to a similar treatment of the German minorities in Bohemia and Moravia. Futhermore, it was felt that a dis-

[110] Herbert Steiner, *Die Arbeiterbewegung Österreichs 1867–1889* (Vienna, 1964), pp. 19–144.

[111] Kann, *Nationalitätenproblem,* I, 174–187, 412–417; Joseph F. Zacek, "Palacký and the Austro-Hungarian Compromise of 1867," in L. Holotík and A. Vantuch, eds., *Der österreichisch-ungarische Ausgleich 1867* (Bratislava, 1967), pp. 555–573.

satisfied Polish population at the borders of Russia would endanger the security of the empire. Hence the administration of Galicia was handed over, by administrative decrees between 1867 and 1869 and also parliamentary legislation of 1868, to the three-fifths Polish majority. The Ruthenians fared somewhat better only in the Bukovina with her relative Ruthenian majority. Yet in Galicia the Polish language ruled supreme in courts and schools, from grade level to universities. Government officials from the lowest to the highest rank were mostly Poles, and only in communications with the ministries was German used. The Poles later supported the conservative government in Vienna and were rewarded with high positions in the central administration, even though the government would have been justified to ask for the unconditional support of the Polish big landowners and a gentry whose interests they represented concerning major issues. Yet the Poles, from the aristocratic governor Count Goluchowski[112] to the more moderate and in the days of Kremsier liberal parliamentarians Francis Smolka (later speaker of parliament) and Florian Ziemialkowski (Polish minister without portfolio in various cabinets) enjoyed strategic, geographic, and ethnic advantages, from which the Czechs could not benefit.[113] Even so, it was implicitly understood that the Polish reconciliation with the empire would last only as long as no real chance for the rebirth of a united Poland existed. Obviously the Polish policy of the government did not please the Ruthenians. Their political groups were represented by the formerly liberal national Young Ruthenians and the conservative Old Ruthenians. At the time of the revolution both groups endorsed the Austrian empire idea and were frequently referred to as the Tyrolians of the east, meaning the most faithful of the faithful. Now the Young Ruthenians only thinly camouflaged the association of their interests with those of the Russian Ukrainians, while the Old Ruthenians sympathized more openly with conservative Russians.[114]

The status of the Slovenes remained unsatisfactory. As long as their nationalism was primarily of a cultural nature they had enjoyed the patronage of German liberalism. Now, when they demanded adequate political

[112] For seventeen years governor of Galicia (1849–1859, 1866–1868, 1871–1875). See also Stanislaw Estreicher in *Cambridge History of Poland* (Cambridge, 1951), II, 435–447.

[113] Czechs, and particularly Poles, were frequently represented by the so-called *Landsmannschaftsminister* (cabinet ministers without portfolio), whose sole assignment was to represent the specific interests of their respective national groups.

[114] Kann, *Nationalitätenproblem,* I, 228–231, 329–330, 433–434, 470–471. See also Krupnickyj, *Geschichte der Ukraine,* pp. 254–261.

representation in Styria, and particularly in Carniola where they comprised more than 90 percent of the population but held only one-third of the seats in the diet, they found deaf ears. They continued to follow some of their conservative clerical leaders but at the same time they began to become increasingly interested in the idea of a Southern Slav political union with Croats and Serbs in Austria and especially Hungary.[115]

The Croats, Serbs, and Roumanians in Austria were even more concerned with the fate of their conationals in Hungary than were the Slovenes with the problem of Southern Slav unionism across the whole Habsburg empire. The status of Austrian Southern Slavs and Roumanians left something to be desired, but it was superior to that of their conationals in Hungary who were grossly discriminated against.

But since the majority of these nationalities within the Habsburg monarchy lived in Hungary, satisfactory solutions could not be achieved within the straitjacket of the Compromise. They had to be initiated in Hungary and would subsequently have to affect conditions in Austria.[116]

The situation of the Italians resembled in some ways that of the Poles. In the Trentino in south Tyrol, as well as in the Littoral it was fairly favorable. Even though the administrative separation of Italian and German Tyrol was not achieved, language rights in the diet, courts, and schools were liberal. In Trieste where the Italians had an absolute majority they enjoyed far-reaching autonomy. In Istria, where they were outnumbered by Croats as in Gorizia by Slovenes, they received preferential treatment. The fear of Italian irredentism played a decisive part in the policies of the Austrian government. Whereas the emperor could rely on the loyalty of the Poles as long as the empire lasted, he could not rely on the Italians despite Italy's joining the Austro-German alliance in 1882. The Poles had conationals in Russia and Prussia, but no Polish allied power existed. The Austrian Italians, on the other hand, could be sure of the support of Italy. This meant that Italian irredentism in its activities did not feel necessarily bound to wait for the day of the Habsburg empire's disintegration.[117]

In Hungary, Magyar Hungary that is, liberal predominance was even more marked than in Austria, but even more than in Austria was it

[115] Fran Zwitter, "The Slovenes and the Habsburg Monarchy," in *Austrian History Yearbook*, III:2 (1967), 170–175; see also Toussaint Hočevar, *The Structure of the Slovenian Economic Development 1848–1963* (New York, 1963), pp. 15–117 and Bogumil Vošnjak, *A Bulwark against Germany* (London, 1917), pp. 83–112.

[116] Kann, *Nationalitätenproblem*, I, 254–257, 290–295, 303–305, 441, 455, 458.

[117] Ibid., I, 268–270, 445–446.

focused on political objectives rather than on social issues. Actually the relationship to Austria was perceived as the foremost political problem. The Andrássy cabinet in office from 1867 to 1871, when Prime Minister Count Gyula Andrássy became joint Austro-Hungarian minister of foreign affairs, was backed by the immense authority of Francis Deák, even though he was not a member of the cabinet. Deák and Joseph von Eötvös, the minister of public instruction, could rightly be called genuine liberals in more than in name. The Hungarian Nationality Law and the Hungarian-Croatian Law of Compromise both of 1868, as intended, though not as subsequently administered, show the influence of these men. One might have wished that they had exercised it also in favor or urgently needed agricultural reforms, but most liberals ignored agricultural problems. Reluctant to deal with social problems, their attention was focused on the legal interpretation of the relationship to Austria. Kossuth, then in exile in Torino, denounced the Compromise as betrayal of the nation and stood by the demands for the reestablishment of the Hungarian republic of 1849. The emotional impact of his views was still powerful. The left-wing liberals, later organized in the Independence Party (also called Party of 1848) [118] could not openly endorse the claims for reestablishment of the revolutionary republic. They had to satisfy themselves with demands for the termination of the Compromise; while they publicly accepted the mere Personal Union, that is, recognition of the same ruler as emperor in Austria and king in Hungary, they rejected any other constitutional bonds between the two states. The Independence Party stood at least for one essential progressive measure; introduction of the secret vote in an electoral system which by strict property qualifications and police supervision in favor of the ruling Magyar classes was inferior even to the Austrian franchise laws. But when in 1878 an aristocratic fronde under the leadership of Count Albert Ápponyi accepted the separation program and merged later with the Independence Party, the movement for franchise reform lost its potentially socially progressive character. Heirs to political leadership in Hungary became the so-called Resolution Party of 1861, influenced by the ideas of enlightened conservatives of the reform era, like Baron Siegmund Kemény and Count Paul Somssich. A Calvinist nobleman, Kálmán Tisza, assumed the leadership of this group, and in 1868 presented a program that did not ask for outright abolition but for revision of the Compromise, namely the establishment of a separate Hungarian army,

[118] More correct would have been the name Party of 1849, but reference to 1849, when the Hungarian republic was proclaimed, would have implied a renewed endorsement of treason against the monarchy.

an entirely separate budget, and separate currency and tariff systems. In the elections of 1872 this party secured 116 parliamentary seats against 245 for the government party and 38 for the Party of 1848 on the Left. At this time also the so-called Catholic People's Party, a primarily antiliberal and only nominally populist group, organized itself to the Right of the Deák liberals. The position of the government became increasingly difficult between a right wing that endorsed the Compromise fully and various stronger liberal trends, which disapproved of it in one way or another.

The withdrawal of the aged Deák from politics made it clear that the future belonged to the followers of Kálmán Tisza, who were not saddled with the Magyar concessions made in 1867, although they claimed full credit for those granted by the crown at that time. In consequence of this policy the merger of the government party with the Resolution Party took place in 1875. This was actually the birth year of the Magyar-Hungarian "liberal" machine system as it ruled supreme with short intervals until 1918. Its leader and prime minister from 1875 to 1890 was Kálmán Tisza, frequently referred to as the older Tisza to distinguish him from his more eminent son István. The Tisza regime stood for the prerogatives of Magyar nationalism and national intolerance, conservatism in agricultural questions, industrial expansion, and liberalism in cultural affairs—as far as it pertained to the Magyars. This socially and nationally equally inequitable but in its peculiar way successful regime was maintained by a restricted franchise system, backed by government-directed police power.[119]

The Hungarian-Croatian Compromise of 1868, which granted to the Hungarian Croats a limited autonomy will be discussed under "government in Hungary." At this point we will have to go back to the older concept of a Southern Slav union under Catholic leadership, as it was promoted by Kopitar in the pre-March era. This idea had little appeal to the Serbs, and it could be revived only in a changed form under the auspices of the commanding personality of Josip J. Strossmayer (1815–1905) bishop of Djakovo, a maverick in politics as well as in ecclesiastic questions as his protests against the papal infallibility dogma accepted at the Vatican Council of 1870 proved. Strossmayer believed that at least a cultural union of the Southern Slav peoples was feasible. In pursuit of this objective he promoted, as noted, the establishment of a Southern Slav academy (1868) and a university (1874), both in Zagreb (Agram). Strossmayer supported also the idea that concessions in liturgical questions (primarily the wide recognition of the Old Slavonic Church language in Catho-

[119] Kosáry, *History of Hungary,* pp. 282–298; Carlile A. Macartney, *A Short History of Hungary* (Edinburg, 1961), pp. 171–184.

lic liturgy), could bring the Serbs at least closer to the Southern Slav union. A third device was to work for linguistic assimilation, particularly between Croats and Slovenes. Strossmayer's endeavors corresponded to some degree to those of the Croatian Liberal National Party, whereas the Croatian Rights Party under Ante Starčević's leadership stood for Croatian separatism rather than Southern Slav unionism.

Politically Strossmayer was not successful. The time for linguistic union had passed, neither could accommodation to the rites of the Greek Orthodox Church in the question of Church liturgy exercise great influence on the course of nationalism in the second half of the nineteenth century. Furthermore, the bishop stood for Croatian leadership in Southern Slav affairs, though less directly than Starčević. But since the Serbs, heretofore still loosely affiliated with the Ottoman empire, did not gain their full independence from the Turks until 1878, Croat-Serb rivalry was not yet a major issue. In an ideological-cultural sense, however, Strossmayer furthered the union idea of the Southern Slav peoples substantly, though it finally came about in a way different from that imagined by the colorful bishop. Within the Habsburg empire this union idea was promoted first in the form of trialism, a union of the Austrian and Hungarian Southern Slavs as third major political entity within the Habsburg monarchy. This union would have required an abrogation of the Compromise, but this impractical scheme at least did not collide with the Habsburg empire idea. Since it was not feasible Southern Slav nationalism deviated gradually from the patterns of a Croatian-led trialistic idea within the empire to a unionism under the leadership of those Southern Slav people whose majority lived outside the empire, the Serbs. Trends in that direction became stronger after the Congress of Berlin of 1878.[120]

Before the Serb war of independence against the Turks, the Serbs played only a minor role in the Habsburg empire. Their modest political weight was one reason why Leopold I in the seventeenth century granted them limited autonomous rights in Hungary. Still their political status remained inferior to that of the Croats. That held true for Austrian-administered Dalmatia as well as for Hungary. Even more important, the reincorporation of the Vojvodina into Hungary in 1860 was followed in 1872 by the incorporation of the Military Frontier in Syrmia (Serbian Banat). In 1881 the last part of the Croatian Military Frontier was merged with Croatia. Substantial Serb communities existed in all these terriories. Thus to some

[120] Wendel, *Der Kampf der Südslawen,* pp. 340–396; Guldescu in Eterovich and Spalatin, eds., *Croatia,* II, 40–60. Kissling, *Die Kroaten,* pp. 62–71; Kann, *Nationalitätenproblem,* I, 254–260, 441–443.

extent the Serbs had to foot the bill of the Austro-Hungarian and of the Hungarian-Croatian compromises. The new kingdom of Serbia would probably eventually have become the leader of the Southern Slav national movement in any case, but the governmental surrender of Serb national rights to Magyars and Croats made this development practically a certainty.[121]

In regard to the Hungarian Carpatho-Ruthenians, they lost the limited national autonomy that they had enjoyed under the neoabsolutist regime more as punishment of the Magyars than a rightful concession due to them. Adolf Dobrjanskyi, a Carpatho-Ukrainian himself, was then appointed governor of the four predominantly Ruthenian Hungarian comitats and advanced the cultural and to some extent political autonomy of his people. The pending reconciliation of the crown with Hungary deprived Dobrjanskyi in the early 1860's of his position, and his people of the further protection of their national rights. Almost equally unfortunate were the Slovaks. But here, despite Magyar oppression and efforts to bring about complete Magyarization, an outright program for national autonomy within Hungary, more detailed than the demands of 1848, could be raised openly at a national congress in Turč. Sv. Martin in 1861. This helped to strengthen Slovak national consciousness in the face of continuous pressure for Magyarization.[122]

Most striking was the sellout of Roumanian national rights. As corollary to the October Diploma, the Vienna government promised restoration of the old Transylvanian constitution. In 1863, a new diet declared the union with Hungary as void, and the Roumanians were at the same time finally admitted as fourth Transylvanian nation of equal rights with Magyars, Szekels, and Saxons. A separate Roumanian Orthodox Church was recognized also. In 1867, however, the diet was dissolved and a new one elected with a flagrantly manufactured Magyar majority. It voted, as required, for union with Hungary and thus voted itself out of existence. By 1868 the reincorporation was in substance an accomplished fact. In 1876 the last remainders of autonomy for the four nations were rescinded. No Roumanian deputy was represented in the Hungarian parliament before the

[121] Wayne S. Vucinich, "The Serbs in Austria-Hungary," in *Austrian History Yearbook*, III:2 (1967), 17–20, 24–25; Picot, *Les Serbes de la Hongrie*, pp. 218–342; Ernest Denis, *La Grande Serbie* (Paris, 1915), pp. 138–160.

[122] Ivan Žeguc, *Die nationalpolitischen Bestrebungen der Karpatho-Ruthenen 1848–1914* (Wiesbaden, 1965), pp. 74–81; Václav L. Beneš, "The Slovaks in the Habsburg Empire," in *Austrian History Yearbook*, III:2 (1967), 357–364; René Martel, *La Ruthénie Subcarpathique* (Paris, 1935); Kann, *Nationalitätenproblem*, I, 281–283, 449–450.

1880's and even afterward one Magyar vote in Transylvania weighed as much as about twelve Roumanian votes. A society for Roumanian language and literature led a harrassed existence. While the neighboring kingdom of Roumania could do little to check the excesses of Magyar nationalism in Transylvania, its existence helped to keep the Roumanian national spirit alive.[123]

c) GOVERNMENT IN AUSTRIA

A survey of the legislative work during the first, on the whole liberal, phase of Austrian constitutional government is impressive. After the resignation of Beust as Austrian prime minister in June, 1867, two brothers, the princes Karl and Adolf Auersperg, the first prime minister from 1867 to 1868, the second from 1871 to 1879 guided Austrian parliament toward considerable accomplishments. The fact, that two enlightened high aristocrats stood at the helm of the Austrian government during the main part of that dramatic period, made it easier for crown and conservatives to cooperate with the Auerspergs. This cooperation was not always forthcoming, however, and the liberal era of the so-called citizens' ministries was interrupted by two attempts to install federalist conservative regimes, the first under the Polish Count Alfred Potocki from April, 1870, to February, 1871, the second under his successor, the Austro-German aristocrat Count Siegmund Hohenwart until October, 1871. Mention should also be made that during this whole period the man of the emperor's pronounced personal confidence, Count Edward Taaffe, a conservative, was twice (1867 and 1869–1870) provisional prime minister, as were two able liberal parliamentarians, Professor Leopold von Hasner in 1870 and Dr. Karl von Stremayr in 1879. Fluctuating majorities, Slav federalist opposition, sometimes even boycott of parliamentary proceedings, and finally dissension among the German liberals themselves, were responsible for the political wearing out of administrative-parliamentary leaders. The chief merit for the liberal legislation belonged not so much to the prime ministers, as the ministers in charge of individual departments, such as Josef von Lasser for the interior, Professor Julius von Glaser (minister of justice), Ignaz von Plener (commerce),[124] Brestel (finances), and Hasner and Stremayr, who were more efficient as ministers of public instruction and religious affairs than as prime ministers.

[123] Miron Constantinescu, *Études d'Histoire Transylvaine* (Bucarest, 1970), pp. 9–37; Carlile H. Macartney, *Hungary and her Successors* (London, 1937), pp. 251–275.

[124] From 1860 to 1865 minister of finance.

Matters of education and the separation of education from Church control stood in the foreground of interest for a liberal cabinet. The so-called three May laws in 1868, passed against strong clerical-conservative opposition, established secular jurisdiction in marriage questions and the principle of secular control of education. This doctrine was specified in the general law on elementary and general public education of May, 1869 (*Reichsvolksschulgesetz*). It spelled out the secular structure of the educational system on the grade and public high-school level (*Bürgerschule*). The law guaranteed in most crownlands state-controlled compulsory education; the influence of the clergy was restricted to religious instruction. Hardly any law passed by an Austrian parliament has been so heavily contested through the years, hardly another one was as beneficial for all strata of the population, not excluding the clergy, whose previously controversial position in public life appeared now somewhat eased.

The third of the three May laws dealt in principle with the legal equality of all denominations and the permissible—but still restricted—possibilities of interdenominational marriage. The Concordat of 1855 was severely undermined by this legislation and in August, 1870, it was terminated. The proclamation of papal infallibility at the Vatican Council, only weeks before the Austrian legislative action, had strengthened the forces opposed to the Concordat.

Finally a set of new May laws, passed in 1874, recognized limited government control of the legal status of the Church, and some supervision of Church income and monastic administration. Absolute legal, let alone social, equality of all denominations still did not exist: the Catholic Church had access to income from governmental funds, not open to other denominations. Nevertheless the position of the Church in her external relations was weakened in comparison with her status before 1868, and there were probably more citizens, who believed that liberalism had gone too far than those who held that it had not gone far enough.[125]

Less controversial was the law on general conscription of December 1868, revised in 1889, which required three years of active military service and nine further years in the reserve (*Landwehr*). The liberals passed this unpopular bill with some hesitation.

The electoral reform of 1873, which established direct parliamentary elections in lieu of what had amounted to dietal delegations, has been mentioned. It clearly did not go far enough. Deputies were still elected according to the curia system—big estates owners, chambers of trade and

[125] Weinzierl-Fischer, *Die österreichischen Konkordate*, pp. 99–111; Winter, *Revolution, Neoabsolutismus und Liberalismus*, pp. 158–169.

commerce, towns and rural communities. In some respect the reform simply meant actually the transfer of the curias from the diets into central parliament. It was symptomatic for the inherent lack of social understanding on the part of the liberals, that only few of them offered opposition to these continued restrictions.[126]

In 1862 the parliament, elected on the basis of the February Patent, had approved the promulgation of an Austrian commercial code, the only notable joint Austrian-German judicial legislation, sponsored by the Confederal Assembly in Frankfurt. In 1873 a new code of criminal procedure, drafted by Glaser, the minister of justice, was introduced, which, like the commercial code, is in essence still in force today. Only in comparison with previous conditions could the new code be considered liberal. Innovations like jury trials, equality of status of defense and prosecuting attorney in investigations, and so on were introduced but restricted by qualifying clauses. The introduction in 1875 of a court of administration (*Verwaltungsgerichtshof*), however, was without qualifications beneficial.

Although the accomplishments of the liberal administration were limited by the narrow social outlook of the regime, they were superior to the course of the conservative federalists, who were in power in 1870–1871. Whereas the liberals tried to take care at least of the interests of the urban middle class as they saw them, the federalists considered mainly agricultural demands from the point of view of the big estates owners. The cabinet Potocki had tried vainly to make its peace with the Old Czechs, who resented the Compromise which had left them in the cold. They either vehemently opposed the liberal legislation or boycotted parliament altogether. On many issues they were supported by the Polish parliamentary club and the German clerical conservatives in the provinces.

Count Hohenwart, appointed prime minister in February, 1871, made an effort to come to terms with the Czechs and thereby with Slav and also German conservatism altogether. After cumbersome and protracted negotiations with the Old Czech leaders the cabinet introduced several bills, drafted in cooperation with the Bohemian diet. The so-called Fundamental Articles were to establish a general diet of the three lands of the Bohemian crown (Bohemia, Moravia, and Silesia). Bohemian deputies would no longer be regular members of an Austrian parliament, but merely participate in a Congress of dietal delegates. This arrangement would have approximated the institution of the Austro-Hungarian Delegations. In economic questions far-reaching autonomy was to be granted to

[126] Kolmer, *Parlament und Verfassung*, II, 244–284; Kulisch, *Beiträge zum österreichischen Parlamentsrecht*, pp. 70–136.

the Bohemian administration, to be put now under the jurisdiction of the Bohemian Court Chancery of old rather than under the Ministry of the Interior, as the other crownlands. The validity of the Compromise was nominally recognized, although the special status of the Bohemian lands contradicted the spirit of the Compromise legislation as well as that of the professed equality of status of the Austrian Cisleithanian peoples as stated in the December legislation in 1867.

The Fundamental Articles were accompanied by the draft of a notable nationality law for Bohemia and Moravia. Without agreeing to the German demand for the administrative partition of Bohemia, it provided for the establishment of nationally homogeneous administrative districts. It put the Czech language almost fully on a par with German, each language to be recognized as official in any district where it was the native language of at least a fifth of the population. The draft met also a Czech demand for the command of both languages, Czech and German, as requirement for the appointment of government officials. Separate cultural budgets for both national groups were provided and the diet was to consist of two national curias. The nationality law was controversial in some respects, but provided a reasonable compromise between the Czech and German viewpoint, at least concerning the partition issue. The proposed language reforms were constructive. The fact that this bill was heavily criticized by leaders of both national groups does not speak against its reasonableness. Neither was bilateral opposition the main cause why Hohenwart's program went down to defeat, Fundamental Articles and all.

Chief cause for this failure was the opposition by the Hungarian prime minister, Count Andrássy, who saw acceptance of the Fundamental Articles as a first step toward the federalization of the empire. This might have eventually led to the scrapping of the dualistic system under Magyar and German leadership. Equally important were perhaps reasons of foreign policy—a gentle warning by the German emperor that he would not like to be put in a position where he had to listen to the complaints of a German irredenta in Austria, whose predominance seemed to be threatened by acceptance of the Fundamental Articles. This hint was clear enough, and after the experience of 1866 also painful. The Czechs saw no reason to accept the Nationality Law without the Fundamental Articles and thus the crown was forced to withdraw the whole legislation.

The emperor, after this brief play with the concepts of historic traditional federalism, slightly anachronistic as it was already, returned to the spirit of the Compromise, with its built-in German-Magyar condominium. Beust, the adamant opponent of the Fundamental Articles, was thrown to the wolves, but the Czechs had little opportunity to rejoice. His successor became Andrássy himself who unlike Beust was not encumbered with reminiscences of an anti-Prussian policy as Saxon prime minister in 1866. Yet understanding with Germany after the victories in the war of 1870–1871 was doubly necessary. A distinguished Magyar like Count Andrássy, who subscribed to a pro-German policy, was the man to bring full reconciliation about. The sacrificial lambs were the Czechs; they had been promised favorable consideration of their demands, which were now repudiated. This experience was one of the main reasons why the leadership of Czech policy shifted gradually from the conservative Old Czechs to the radical Young Czechs. The national conflict, not only in the Bohemian lands, had moved again to a higher level.[127]

The fall of the unlucky Hohenwart after a brief intermediate regime of a few weeks was followed by appointment of the cabinet of Prince Adolf Auersperg, which put much constructive legislation on the statute books. At least in one respect the demise of the Hohenwart cabinet was to be regretted. With the prime minister went also his minister of commerce, the Suabian professor of economics, Albert Schäffle, who was also the prime minister's adviser on problems of nationalism. Schäffle had the reputation of being antiliberal, and this supposed quality undoubtedly endeared him to the archconservative Count Hohenwart. Yet he was antiliberal only in the sense of an outdated Manchester liberalism. He proposed the transformation of the socially unrepresentative estates diets into corporate bodies which should give adequate representation to peasants, small business, crafts, and labor at the expense of the aristocratic landowners and big business. Schäffle may be criticized for perceiving these changes only in the frame of corporate ideas. Nevertheless he had more social understanding than his liberal adversaries. He had a better grasp of the problems of nationalism too and hoped for a genuine compromise between all national groups in the Western part of the empire. If that could be accomplished he had little doubt, Hungary would eventually be forced to follow suit. For that reason he had to quit with Hohenwart; he returned to Germany where he rounded out a distinguished scholarly career.[128]

[127] Münch, *Böhmische Tragödie,* pp. 345–363; Kann, *Nationalitätenproblem,* I, 177–185, 414–416.

[128] Albert E. Schäffle, *Aus meinem Leben,* 2 vols. (Berlin, 1905), see I, 172–256, II, 1–111. On the outcome of the crisis see also Friedrich Ferdinand Count Beust, *Aus drei viertel Jahrhunderten,* 2 vols. (Stuttgart, 1887), I, 465–540. Friedrich Prinz, "Die böhmischen Länder von 1848 bis 1914," in Karl Bosl, ed., *Handbuch der Geschichte der böhmischen Länder* (Stuttgart, 1967), III, 135–154.

Schäffle thus became a victim of the multi-national conflict, and the same was true for the Auersperg cabinet. Despite the merits of Prince Adolf Auersperg and some members of his cabinet the ministry was largely responsible for its eventual downfall of long-lasting consequences. The Auersperg cabinet had natural enemies in conservative clericals and conservative aristocratic landowners, largely of Slavic nationality. It lost also the decisive support of the crown in 1878, when it opposed the occupation of Bosnia-Hercegovina. Such attitude would have been farsighted if it had been based on the idea, that an expansion into the Balkans would lead in the long run to a confrontation with Russia. The main argument of the liberals, however, was different, namely that the occupation with the acquisition of territories with Slavic population would endanger the precarious leadership of the Germans in Austria. The over-all motivation was only to a small part one of caution in foreign policy but above all one of national arrogance. One would see too much wisdom in Emperor Francis Joseph as ruler, in assuming that this was the reason why he accepted Auersperg's resignation. The emperor perceived in the German liberal policy, which he did not favor anyway on conservative ideological grounds, a stab-in-the-back attitude, in the face of what he believed to be a chance of enhancing the empire's shaken power position. He never forgave the liberals for this. When the elections, held under the provisional cabinet Stremayr in summer of 1879, turned against the liberals—some 140 liberals and progressives against about 160 German-Czech-Polish conservatives—the emperor gladly turned over the government to the conservative friend of his youth, Count Taaffe. His regime of fourteen years' duration, the longest in Austrian history from the fall of Metternich to 1918, was mainly based on German clerical conservative and Czech and Polish conservative support. None of these groups opposed the occupation. The Czechs and Poles endorsed it, because it would strengthen the position of the Slavs in the empire. Furthermore, they as well as the German conservative-clerical opposition now saw a chance to terminate the rule of the hated liberal regime. There were still occasionally liberal members in Austrian cabinets, not even excluding that of Taaffe himself; yet not only German liberalism but liberalism altogether, seen as powerful ideology, had permanently disappeared from the Austrian political scene. This was the fault of the German liberals themselves, but also it was a symptom of the times, whose new political trends moved in the direction of political intolerance and prejudice. The liberal regime, which had governed in Austria with short intermissions or almost twelve years with fair success, became thus more the victim of the intolerance of others than of its own limitations in regard to nationalist and social issues. This was the tragedy of Austrian liberalism well beyond the German orbit.[129]

d) GOVERNMENT IN HUNGARY

The liberal regime in Hungary, though even more unrepresentative than its counterpart in Austria, introduced some valuable legislation under the leadership of the prime minister, Count Andrássy, and the patronage of Francis Deák. In regard to the Hungarian nationality law of 1868, credit belongs chiefly to the minister of public instruction, Joseph von Eötvös, one of the foremost students of the nationality problems of the Habsburg monarchy, Eötvös believed that its solution rested in a federation of the traditional historic entities on the top and an ethnic administrative organization on the county and community levels. These ideas developed in the writings of this enlightened man in the 1850's could not be materialized in the new Nationality law of 1868 in the face of rising Magyar nationalism (Statute XLIV). The law recognized the right of individuals to their own national language in Church, elementary and intermediate schools, and intercourse with government agencies. It was tied to the status of the individual and did not acknowledge the existence of national groups as political bodies anchored in public law. Nevertheless this statute should not be dismissed in comparison with Article 19 of the Austrian constitutional law 142 of 1867. There the reference to *Stämme*—absent in the Hungarian legislation—implied recognition of national groups only in a very superficial manner. The main difference between the Austrian and Hungarian nationality legislation was rooted in administrative and judicial practice, not in the letter of the law. The Austrian practice, particularly the interpretation by the Reichsgericht and administrative court was admittedly far more liberal than the methods used by the Hungarian administration, enforced lamely by Hungarian courts. Had Eötvös' and Deák's spirit prevailed, the Hungarian treatment of national groups might not have been inferior to that administered by the Austrian authorities. As it were, the lesser successors of these two men interpreted the concept of equality of all members of the Hungarian nation as meaning that the non-Magyar national groups in Hungary

[129] On the liberal legislative record see Kolmer, *Parlament und Verfassung*, I, 253–403, II passim; Richard Charmatz, *Österreichs innere Geschichte von 1848–1907*, 2 vols. (Leipzig, 1909–1911), see I, 84–140, II, 1–10; on the liberal policy concerning the occupation of Bosnia-Hercegovina see Plener, *Erinnerungen*, I, pp. 90–143.

would be treated as equal only if they assimilated, indeed merged, with Magyarism. Magyar national policy was free from racism in so far as it did not base the unequal treatment of minorities on ethnic ancestry but on the demand to give up national identification and accept unconditional conversion to Magyarism. Within these terms the system was willing to recognize equality of all Hungarian citizens, without further consideration of ethnic-racial origin. That this principle, too, violated the right of individuals to preserve their national character, particularly if enforced by discrimination and police chicanery, was neither understood by the great Kossuth nor by his small pseudo-liberal successors.[130]

The second major national law passed in this era was the Hungarian-Croatian Compromise (Statute XXX) of the same year. Like the Austro-Hungarian Compromise, it represented the union between two states, who had the ruler and some institutions in common. Unlike the Compromise of 1867 it was not a real union between equals but officially between unequal states. As for affairs common to Austria and Hungary, Croatia was represented in the Hungarian delegation. As for common Hungarian-Croatian agenda originally,[131] after the incorporation of the Military Frontier, forty Croatian deputies represented the historic land in the deliberations and the voting of the Hungarian parliament whenever joint agenda were at issue. In either case they could be outvoted by the Magyar majority. Common Hungarian-Croatian affairs—in effect, affairs, where the influence of the Magyar majority proved decisive—included taxation, general conscription, defense, commercial treaties, and communications. The autonomy of Croatia was restricted to general internal administration, education, and judicial affairs. Even here the status of the Croatian chief executive, the banus in Zagreb, amounted to a major restriction of Croatia's autonomy. Although he was responsible to the Croatian Sabor, his appointment by the king required approval of the Hungarian parliament. Usually, therefore, the banus was a Magyar, sometimes of nationalistic tendencies. Frequently he played the divide-and-conquer game between Croats and Serbs in Croatia-Slavonia. Thus the Croatian autonomy was limited.[132] Still, the extension of such

[130] Guldescu in Eterovich and Spalatin, eds., *Croatia,* II, 47–60; Macartney, *A Short History of Hungary,* pp. 171–187; Kann, *Nationalitätenproblem,* I, 128–135, 396–400. On Eötvös see ibid, II, 101–107, 327–329; Johann Weber, *Eötvös und die ungarische Nationalitätenfrage* (Munich, 1966), pp. 135–149. On Deák see Steinbach, *Franz Deák,* pp. 29–34.

[131] Croatia was also represented by several members in the Upper House.

[132] Bogdan Krizman, "The Croatians in the Habsburg Monarchy in the 19th Century," in *Austrian History Yearbook,* III:2 (1967), 128–133; Kosáry, *History of*

autonomy to the other non-Magyar groups would have gone a long way to calm the national conflict in Hungary.

Other legislation passed during the Andrássy-Deák era was less controversial. A Hungarian educational law of 1868 was in many ways similar to the Austrian Reichsvolksschulgesetz of 1869. The same similarities are reflected in the Austrian *Wehrgesetz* (defense law) of 1868 (revised 1889) and the Hungarian defense legislation of the same year including the establishment of a Hungarian national militia (the *Honveds*). In 1869 administration and justice were finally separated in Hungary.

With the replacement of Andrássy as prime minister by Count Melchior Lónyaí in 1871, the liberal regime in Hungary became more shady in character. Neither Lónyaí nor his successors up to the appointment of Kálmán Tisza had the authority of Andrássy, the revered revolutionary of 1848. Nor did they have the backing of the great old man of Hungarian politics, Francis Deák. He gradually withdrew from the political scene and died in 1876. The boom-and-bust spirit with its inevitable by-product of corruption, which ended in Austria with the great crash of 1873, existed also in Hungary. The liberals lost in prestige. Except for the enactment of the new code of criminal law in 1878 not much constructive legislation was passed between the resignation of Andrássy as Hungarian prime minister and the year 1879. Tisza, however, managed to steer a middle course between Independents to the left who repudiated the Compromise, revisionists in the center, who wanted to change it, and clerical conservatives to the right, who fully endorsed it.

After the death of Deák and Eötvös in the 1870's all these groups were implicitly agreed on a policy of intransigent Magyar nationalism in a semiliberal dressing. Unlike conditions in Austria there existed, however, no political groups on the Right strong enough to replace the liberal regime. Tisza's economic and social policy had taken the wind out of the sails of Hungarian conservatism. As for the Left, the Independence party of 1848–1849 represented only a relatively small minority. Yet Tisza by making skillful use of the loud but insignificant opposition to the right and left, could pretend that his policy represented a concession to the king-emperor and the Austrian government. In reality, however, the Compromise in military, financial, and above all foreign affairs fully pro-

---

Hungary, pp. 288–290; Kann, *Nationalitätenproblem*, I, 131–132, 398; Pešelj, "Der ungarisch-kroatische Ausgleich vom Jahre 1868," in P. Berger, ed., pp. 169–185. On the Hungarian-Croatian Compromise see also note 107 of this chapter.

tected the political and economic interests of the peculiar brand of Magyar national liberalism.[133]

G. The End of an Era

In Austria, the year 1879 marked the fall of the liberals from power. No similar change occurred in Hungary, although by this time the false front of Magyar liberalism was fully exposed. Notwithstanding its grave shortcomings it had to be taken seriously under Andrássy, Deák, and Eötvös. The same was no longer true under Kálmán Tisza. Mass movements comparable with those of Christian Socials, the Socialists, to a point even the Pan-Germans, almong the Austro-Germans, and the Young Czechs in Bohemia and Moravia did not yet exist in Hungary. On a more limited scale, however, Croatian national parties had begun to develop. Furthermore, an active nationalism in the lands of the Bohemian crown, in Serbia, and Roumania made it clear that Slovak nationalism in upper Hungary, Roumanian nationalism in Transylvania, and Serb nationalism in the Banat, the Vojvodina, and Croatia could not be ignored.

Concerning foreign affairs the conclusion of the Dual Alliance of 1879 between Austria and Germany made it clear that the built-in German-Magyar privileged status established by the Compromise of 1867 was now protected in international relations as well. The Austro-German alliance was dependent on German-Magyar leadership in the Habsburg monarchy. At the same time the alliance meant that Austria-Hungary was shielded from the threat of Panslavism under tsarist police auspices. If not checked by the Dual Alliance it might have led, as noted before, to the early dissolution of the empire, from which tsarist Russia presumably would have profited most. Germany in a Pan-German and Prussian militaristic spirit could have taken the rest.

This danger appeared to be removed now. Germany could rely on Austro-German-Magyar leadership in the Habsburg empire. It did not have to rule in Austria, it could guide the empire by way of the more or less camouflaged predominance of these two national groups. This meant further that constitutional government in the dual monarchy would be secured after a fashion, though, from the point of national and social justice, a highly imperfect fashion. As it were, Austria-Hungary had the chance of peaceful constitutional and social development provided that fairly adequate national and above all social reforms would be introduced. These chances were largely missed.

[133] Kosáry, *History of Hungary,* pp. 182–304; Hanák in E. Pamlényi, ed., VII, 379–390.

Finally, as will be discussed in Chapter VII, the end of the eighteen seventies also brought the decline of pseudoclassic epigone styles in literature, architecture, painting, sculpture, and music. The first traces of naturalism, realism, and functionalism had begun to evolve. An era came to its end, a new one had not yet taken its place, but it began to take shape.

CHAPTER VII

Cultural Trends from Late Enlightenment to Liberalism (From mid-eighteenth century to the 1860's)

Basic cultural trends are all-pervasive in time and place and therefore more or less simultaneous. They penetrate any country, any nation from various directions. The degree of intensity with which new ideas strike various national groups depends on the political and social status of such groups within a country. Exposure to new ideas may leave clearer traces within better-educated strata than within underprivileged ones. This does not mean that greater opportunities offered to one group will necessarily lead to greater or more lasting results. Many factors such as the spread of new ideas into a broader or narrower hinterland, the association with other cultural orbits, degrees of affinity to new mores and old traditions, problems of communications, above all the degree of linguistic development, determine the results. One factor cannot be overstated, namely the difference, and that means the different value judgments, in regard to various cultures. We cannot measure the quality of cultural achievements. We can only judge the intensity of their impact within an environment.

The first main trend in Austrian intellectual history during the period under discussion was pragmatic enlightened reformism under Maria Theresa. After her death under Joseph II it changed into more rigid concepts. The turn of Josephinism to the right under Emperor Francis makes a distinction from genuine conservatism in theory rather difficult. In practice the gradual reversal of the reform policy is easier to see. Centralistic endeavors in the Josephin sense continued but they were increasingly to serve reactionary designs. In other words conservatism in Austria was largely pragmatic in nature. It changed its character in Austrian intellectual history under the influence of romanticism into a movement of far greater philosophical depth. Romanticism in Austria became a highly original movement in its own right. Intellectual endeavors in the Habsburg realms after the shortlived Renaissance era had, apart from the philosophy of the Church, existed mainly on the aesthetic side of general cultural developments in music and the fine arts. The purely intellectual contribution of the Austrian Enlightenment was limited. German classicism in literature and philosophy was a powerful stimulating force but its impact headed almost exclusively from outside. Romanticism, on the other hand, in particular in its historical proclivities, in a country deeply conscious of its traditions, developed there into a more original movement with wider social and political implications.

One factor strengthened its influence further: the renaissance of the Slavic languages and literatures. The word "renaissance" is correct here because a rebirth or reconstruction of past values had occurred. It was, of course, not a revival of attainment in ancient history but of medieval history. Hence we face the cultivation of folklore, sagas, fairy tales, history of the Middle Ages, in other words everything that is dear to the romantic spirit. This was a genuine movement not only among the Slavs but also the Germans, Magyars, and the Latin peoples, who all returned to the dreams of the past, disillusioned by a partly true and partly seeming failure of enlightened rationalism and frustrated reforms.

Still the core of the new tendencies was centered in the Slavic peoples and here these trends changed first their character. Romanticism represented an important aspect of the movement and as such supplied the frame of the Slavic renaissance. But another tendency was the core of this renaissance: the national revolution of the Slavic peoples to come into their own rights. This was in essence a liberal revolution which strove for nationhood, inspired by the achievements of the French Revolution. Again it blended with a stream of similar endeavors among Germans, Magyars, and Latins. Neither the disappointments nor the stimuli of the Enlightenment were forgotten. The political-social demands were on the rise, the traditional historic, largely conservative ones merged with them, but their impact in the new combinations was on the decline. Liberalism was the product of the unequal mixture. It was clear-cut as far as the rights and duties of individual man were concerned. It was contradictory, as was romanticism, in its social aspects. With the advance of urbanization and technology these contradictions were more markedly felt. In literature and philosophy a new realism came in its own, but one which saw the objectives of and limits to the desired expansion of the rights of political man in the maintenance of a social order by means of minor, corrective but not basic changes.

We have thus far referred to changes in intellectual history, which means in our context primarily literature and philosophy. To some extent these observations hold true also for music, theatre, the fine arts, and other cultural activities. However, their development is to a much higher degree dependent on external conditions than purely literary efforts. Consequently they are more strongly bound by tradition than intellectual changes. Major exceptions in regard to the greatest achievements notwithstanding, these disciplines were still strongly penetrated by the spirit of the Baroque and Rococo, at a time when in general in literature and philosophy the Enlightenment had become dominant. Subsequently when Biedermeier, the Austrian bourgeois form of classicism, prevailed in the formative arts, Romanticism became prevalent in the humanities. In fact, the fine arts never developed an original romantic style, but turned to eclectic patterns of historic styles. Only by the end of the nineteenth century, after the liberal era had passed, did the fine arts create again original patterns of their own. In music, such original patterns had existed during the romantic era and continued to exist thereafter.

These observations are not based on value judgments. Cultural activities are responsive to intellectual changes but they do not develop at the speed of abstract mental processes. Out of this incongruity evolves the pluralistic character of a colorful civilization with many facets. Yet with whatever branch of cultural activities we deal in this survey, we are concerned with trends illustrated by the endeavors of men and not with a roll call of the great men and their achievements in Austrian cultural history. Within the very limited range of personalities which can be referred to here a more illustrious name may have to yield to a lesser one if the latter characterizes better prevailing trends.

We will consider the relationship of individuals to the Habsburg empire and within the empire to individual national groups. Personalities born within the empire will be discussed, as well as immigrants from other countries if their residence in Habsburg lands made a cultural contribution. In both cases, self-identification of an individual with a national orbit rather than the language used by him will be the chief determining factor for inclusion.

A. The Austro-German orbit

a) humanities, social sciences, natural sciences

It is not so much the privileged position which the Germans enjoyed exclusively until 1867 and in a more limited sense until 1918 but the extent of the German-language territory which secured them a leading position in so many cultural fields. Furthermore the principles of imperial, aristocratic, and ecclesiastic patronage favored the Germans in the fine arts and music. To the extent to which scholarship was concentrated in the universities, learned societies, and ecclesiastic institutions of higher learning, those close to the capital, Vienna, were favored by greater governmental support than educational establishments in other areas. This was also true for support of scholarly activities in the less formal setting of grants given to individuals by the sovereign or by wealthy aristocrats. The universities did not assume undisputed leadership in higher education until the second half of the nineteenth century. Before that they had been frequently, though meagerly, supported by various kinds of patronage outside the academic domain.

With the rise of the non-German national groups to a more widely recognized cultural life in all spheres of the public domain in the nineteenth century, the German advantage diminished. The field, where German predominance was least obvious, is that of belles lettres, in which the greatness of national achievements was largely independent of a patronage system. The same could not be said for the humanities in a more restrictive sense.

To take a few examples. The humanities in the late eighteenth century made little progress because of censorship in the Maria Theresan era and the utilitarian philosophy of the Josephin regime.[1] In the postwar period of the Franciscan reign three unorthodox theologians, Bernhard Bolzano, Anton Günther, and M. J. Fesl had only a limited influence on the education of academic youth. Bolzano, an enlightened rationalist, was dismissed from his chair at the University of Prague. Of his students, M. J. Fesl, who taught at the seminary in Leitmeritz in northern Bohemia, was likewise a professed rationalist, however, with an affinity to Leibniz's not entirely rationalistic theory of the monads. The Church placed his writings on the index and he himself was confined to a monastery. Günther, the most original of this trio of priestly philosophers,

[1] Robert A. Kann, *A Study in Austrian Intellectual History* (2nd ed. New York, 1973), pp. 146–258.

never obtained a teaching position. His philosophy, a strange combination of scholasticism with Cartesianism, was likewise ostracized by the Church, although Günther escaped Fesl's fate through revocation of his doctrines.[2] He had been influenced by the Romantic Catholic intellectuals from Germany, such as Zacharias Werner, the former playwright, and Johann Emanuel Veith. Both had become ecclesiastic converts, the one from Protestantism, the other from Judaism. Both were much esteemed as preachers by a somewhat decadent society, attracted by their unusual background. The literary historian, aesthetic philosopher, and literary critic, Friedrich v. Schlegel, married to the daughter of Moses Mendelssohn, was for a time employed in the state chancery like Metternich's aides Friedrich von Gentz and Adam Müller. The Protestant Gentz and the circle of Catholic intellectuals, mostly converts, roughly between 1810 and 1830 added lustre to the sober atmosphere of Franciscan government. Yet several of these eminent men, who came from Germany and were attracted by the charming way of life of the Austrian capital, returned, disillusioned by its dreary intellectual climate.[3]

The situation looked better in the nonpolitical sphere. Ernst von Feuchtersleben, professor of medicine, but actually a student of the philosophical aspects of psychosomatic problems, taught unimpeded at the University of Vienna. The Slavists, Batholomäus Kopitar, director of the Court (National) Library in Vienna and Franz von Miklošič, both of Slovene origin, made eminent contributions to comparative philology. The latter remained active well into the second half of Francis Joseph's reign. Two great institutions of learning were established in the pre-March era and under Neoabsolutism. In 1847 the Academy of Sciences was organized, with a philosophic-historical section and a second one dedicated to research in the natural sciences—belatedly in comparison with similar institutions in other countries. In 1854 the Institute of Austrian Historical Research was founded; next to the École des Chartes in Paris it became the foremost school for training in the auxiliary historical sciences. Its first director, Albert Jäger, and Franz von Krones, an outstanding historiographer of Austrian history at the University of Graz, should be mentioned here. In the 1820's, Graz, like Innsbruck, was re-

[2] See particularly Winter, *Romantismus, Restauration und Frühliberalismus im österreichischen Vormärz*, pp. 108–118, 139–144. See also Eduard and Maria Winter, *Domprediger Johann Emanuel Veith und Kardinal Friedrich Schwarzenberg: Der Günther Prozess in unveröffentlichten Briefen und Akten* (Vienna-Cologne, 1972), passim and Eduard Winter ed., *Der Bolzano Prozess* (Berlin, 1944).

[3] Winter, *Romantismus, Restauration und Frühliberalismus im österreichischen Vormärz*, pp. 132–138.

stored to full university rank, which both institutions had lost under Joseph's II policy of radical bugetary trimming.

Jäger, Krones, and the conservative historian of the Austrian revolution of 1848, Joseph A. von Helfert, properly belong in the Francisco-Josephin era. Helfert was not a scholar but a high official in the Ministry of Education. One of Jäger's eminent successors as director of the Austrian Historical Institute at the University of Vienna, Theodor von Sickel, spent many years as director of the Austrian Historical Institute in Rome.[4]

In the social sciences the previously mentioned jurists and political scientists, Joseph von Sonnenfels, Karl von Martini (eminent also as philosopher of natural law), and Franz von Zeiller, the most creative of the Austrian codifiers of civil law, divided their lifework between academic duties and governmental consulting services. They were also entrusted with the specific training of an elite civil service class in the Theresianum. Zeiller's as well as Gentz's and Adam Müller's main contributions were made in the Franciscan era. Gentz, apart from his role as diplomat, was a pioneer theorist in international relations; he was a sophisticated, though somewhat devious enlightened conservative. Adam Müller was an original social philosopher, whose conservatism influenced totalitarian theories of the future. The economist and social historian of revolutionary and postrevolutionary French history, Lorenz von Stein, professor at the University of Vienna in the early Francisco-Josephin era, on the other hand, held a more moderate position with much understanding for radical movements.[5]

In the sciences and applied sciences the late Enlightenment brought only moderate progress. Worth mentioning are the contributions by the botanist Nicolaus J. Jaquin, succeeded by his son Joseph F. at the University of Vienna; another pair of father and son were Joseph J. von Littrow and Karl L. von Littrow, both distinguished astronomers from the Franciscan to the early Francisco-Josephin era. Important were also the contributions of the military mathematician Georg von Vega, still in the late Enlightenment. The importance of technology was recognized by the establishment of the *Polytechnikum* in Graz in 1806 and the

[4] Josef Nadler, *Österreichische Literaturgeschichte* (Linz, 1948), pp. 262 f.; Alfred von Fischel, *Der Panslawismus bis zum Weltkrieg* (Stuttgart, 1919), pp. 125–130; Alphons Lhotsky, *Österreichische Historiographie* (Vienna, 1962), pp. 133–173.

[5] See particularly Golo Mann, *Secretary of Europe: The Life of Friedrich Gentz, Enemy of Napoleon* (New Haven, 1946), pp. 96–313 passim. Karl Mendelssohn-Bartholdy, *Friedrich von Gentz* (Leipzig, 1867), pp. 29–126. On Adam Müller see Jakob Baxa, *Adam Müller* (Jena, 1930), pp. 299–379 and Hans Lang, *Politische Geschichtsbilder zu Anfang des 19. Jahrhunderts* (Aarau, 1944), pp. 40–92. See also Ernst Grünfeld, *Lorenz von Stein und die Gesellschaftslehre* (Jena, 1910).

Technical University (*Technische Hochschule*) in Vienna in 1815. Technological contributions were the invention of the screw propeller for steamships by Joseph Ressel in the late 1820's and, as noted previously, the construction of the Semmering railway, the first alpine mountain railroad by Karl v. Ghega in the 1850's. In railway construction Austria could claim a "first" on the continent, namely, as mentioned in a different context, the opening of the horse-drawn railway between Linz in Upper Austria and Budweis (Budějovice) in Bohemia, in 1832; the first steam locomotive on an Austrian track was operated on a short stretch of the Northern railway in 1837.

A combination of practical and theoretical achievements can be seen in the lifework of the geologist Eduard Suess, to whom Vienna owed its water supply system, which carried water from the Alps to the city. This spectacular achievement of applied science was completed by 1873. One of the greatest theoretical scientists of the earlier Francisco-Josephin era was Gregor Mendel (1822–1884), abbot of the Augustinian monastery in Brno (Brünn), Moravia, whose genetic research, the famous Mendelian laws, were not recognized in their full significance until two decades after his death.

The greatest combined accomplishment of theoretical and applied research was the work of the Viennese School of Medicine. Its fame, from the 1880's to the First World War generally overshadows earlier progress, although Leopold von Auenbrugger in the second half of the eighteenth century pioneered in the field of auscultation. Ignaz Semmelweiss from Buda in Hungary spotted the causes and indicated the prevention of puerperal fever. The anatomist Joseph Hyrtl, the pathologist Karl von Rokitansky, the professor of internal medicine Joseph Skoda, the dermatologist Ferdinand von Hebra, all active before 1848 and in the first half of Francis Joseph's reign, were joined shortly after the revolution by the physiologist Ernst von Brücke. One of the most versatile scientists, he too contributed to what may be called the first flowering period of the Viennese medical school. It extended into the Francisco-Josephin era and led up in the 1870's to the beginning of a new period of momentuous achievements.[6]

b) LITERATURE, THEATER, PRESS

There is a seemingly strange contradiction in the development of German-Austrian literature from the Enlightenment to the rise of a new

[6] Erna Lesky, *Die Wiener medizinische Schule im 19. Jahrhundert* (Graz-Cologne, 1965), pp. 15–160.

liberalism in the 1860's. In the dynamic reform era under Maria Theresa and her sons literary achievements were hardly remarkable. Under the political quietism of the Franciscan and pre-March era and the coming neoabsolutist regime on the other hand, the arts made great progress. It was perhaps the result of a delayed action impact of the great creative efforts across the German borders. Only a generation after the main works of Lessing, Herder, and the early works of Goethe, Schiller, and Kleist were published, we see their distinct effect on Austrian literature. With the spread of Romanticism in Germany the interval between German cause and effect in Austria becomes much briefer and with the new rise of Austrian literature it eventually disappears entirely. Yet there remains something unexplainable about the great Austrian literary achievements. They point to various features of the national character. Could they be fully determined, intellectual history would be dreary and not the fascinating disicpline it is.

Between the death of Abraham a Sancta Clara in 1709 and the rise of the most widely recognized Austrian classic, Franz Grillparzer (1791–1872) the major achievement of Austrian literature rested in the popular comedy, the Punch and Judy shows. Initially tolerated by Maria Theresa, their performances were gradually curtailed and eventually suppressed, largely through the influence of Sonnenfels, who lacked a sense of humor. The popular comedy had its shortcomings[7], but the dreary highbrow tragedies of Heinrich von Collin and Cornelius von Ayrenhoff in the later part of the eighteenth century and the early nineteenth century grew on more sterile ground.[8] Grillparzer's greatness as one of the foremost writers of the German drama rests, indeed, not only on the peculiar combination of romantic, classic, and realistic features in his lifework, but on the fact that it could rise on Austrian grounds where he had no predecessor and very few successors of equal stature. His deep dissatisfaction with what he considered a political climate averse to any intellectual pursuits was linked to an equally profound attachment to his home grounds. In this respect the shy and introvert man represented the am-

[7] Except for reasons of clarification in some specific cases these notes are not meant to refer to individual artists, however great, but rather to general trends. In this respect *Deutsch-österreichische Literaturgeschichte,* 2 vols., ed. Johann W. Nagl, Jakob Zeidler and Eduard Castle (Vienna, various editions), offers the most reliable and comprehensive, though not the most sophisticated presentation.

[8] See Otto Rommel, *Die Alt-Wiener Volkskomödie* (Vienna, 1957); Joseph Gregor, *Geschichte des österreichischen Theaters* (Vienna, 1948), pp. 112–148; Reinhard Urbach, *Die Wiener Komödie und ihr Publikum: Stranitzky und die Folgen* (Vienna, 1973); Kann, *A Study in Intellectual History,* pp. 202–224.

bivalent Austrian national character. He may be considered as the outstanding genuinely Austrian writer also in an imperial sense. Several of his best plays deal with themes not only of Austro-German but Czech and Magyar history. In regard to this topical range of his historical plays he has no equal in the history of Austro-German literature.

Typically Austrian, in different ways, were also two contemporary playwrights of high rank, both actors by profession. Ferdinand Raimund (1790–1836), a comedian with romantic-sentimental tendencies, a keen sense of humor, and poetic gifts, wanted to become a classical tragedian. He did not fully succeed because of his limited education. His outstanding achievements as popular, poetical playwright meant little to him. Johann Nestroy (1801–1862), the other comedy writer and actor, was less sentimental and poetic in his inclinations but he was a superlative student of the human character, a social critic, and an outstanding satirist. The antiintellectualism of the pre-March era lent itself particularly well to satire. The deficiencies of government and the rigid class society offered a challenge to such attacks, yet oppressive measures were not sufficiently brutal to quell subtle opposition. Most writers during the pre-March era and the early reign of Francis Joseph might be called moderate or cautious liberals, such as the playwright Eduard von Bauernfeld and the aristocrat Count Anton Alexander Auersperg who wrote under the pseudonym Anastasius Grün. A warm friend of Slovene cultural endeavors, he turned against the Slovenes as soon as their nationalism began to oppose the rule of the German minority in Carniola. Friedrich Halm (Baron Münch-Bellinghausen), a somewhat shallow playwright but one time a competitor of Grillparzer, is forgotten today, but Friedrich Hebbel (1813–1863) who came to Vienna from the German north has maintained his stature as powerful though somewhat coldly intellectual dramatist. His most interesting diaries show him from a more humane angle. Ludwig Anzengruber (1839–1889), a liberal of anticlerical tendencies, possessed only modest poetic gifts but he introduced the social drama into Austrian literature.

Outstanding was the melancholic lyric and writer of grand epics, Nikolaus Lenau (1802–1850), who came from Hungary but developed into a master of the German language. Of all great Austrian poets he was the only true, radical revolutionary. The most outstanding prose writer of the time was Adalbert Stifter (1805–1868). None before him and none after him brought nature to life the way he did. Like Grillparzer's plays, Stifter's prose transcends the Austro-German orbit. One of his two novels, *Witiko,* deals with Czech history in the high Middle Ages. Uniquely harmonious in his work, Stifter, like Grillparzer, Lenau, and Raimund, was a deeply unhappy man. He ended his life in suicide.

As seen in these brief observations, dramatic literary production and with it the theater rank high in Austrian culture. Joseph II had founded the Burgtheater as court theater and, more important, as Deutsches Nationaltheater, in 1776. It maintained its reputation as the leading German repertoire theater for more than a century and continues to hold a distinguished rank to this day. It served as a unique bond between aristocracy, cultivated bourgeoisie, and intellectuals.[9]

Considering the censorship, at least the first-mentioned two groups were served relatively well by the Austrian press. A *Staatszeitung* of 1724 evolved into the *Wiener Zeitung* of 1780, a local gazette but with literary tendencies still cultivated today. The *Presse* founded in 1848 became the mouthpiece of the liberal bourgeoisie. Gradually it was superseded by the *Neue Freie Presse* founded in 1864, a journal internationally known and respected on account of its excellent correspondents and literary contributors, but edited by journalists of rather limited social understanding and political outlook. The *Vaterland,* founded in 1860, represented Catholic conservative tendencies but after 1874 revealed more insight into social problems than the liberal press.[10] under the influence of a new editor, Karl von Vogelsang.

c) MUSIC

Classical music in Austria reached high levels sooner but more gradually than literature. It would be presumptuous to review it here in a few pages, except for some brief remarks about the external conditions under which it evolved. The fact that the Italian opera beginning with Leopold I and orchestral music even under Maximilian I were largely sponsored by court and aristocracy, played a restrictive role for a long time. The Italian Pietro Metastasio in the eighteenth century held a middle position between court poet and court composer of Emperor Charles VI. His canzonets had much musical charm and his melodrama showed originality. But his contemporary, Ch. W. von Gluck, the composer of operas and orchestral music, was a greater artist. His "Orpheus and Eurydice" is one of the early but greatest operatic works of all times. Gluck could not have achieved what he did, had he not had some security as court conductor

[9] See Rudolf Lothar, *Das Wiener Burgtheater* (Leipzig, 1899); Gregor, *Geschichte des österreichischen Theaters,* pp. 149–195.

[10] Kurt Paupié, *Handbuch der österreichischen Pressegeschichte 1848–1859* (Vienna, 1966), I, 1–12.

for a time. Mozart, on the other hand, received practically no support from the puritan Joseph II who considered his own love for music a luxury if not a vice. Austria's greatest composer died at the age of thirty-five in 1791 after a hectic life which not for a single day of his adulthood had been free of worries about the livelihood of his family.

Joseph Haydn is an example of a great artist who, until his fame as composer was generally recognized, owed a modest degree of security to music-loving artistocrats, above all the Esterházys whose orchestra he conducted. In Beethoven's life the support by aristocrats and in particular by Emperor Francis' brother, Cardinal Archduke Rudolf, was undoubtedly important. Schubert, perhaps the most genuinely Austrian among the greatest composers, lacked support entirely and died in misery. Of these five greatest—Gluck, Haydn, Mozart, Beethoven, and Schubert—all of whom spent the best part of their creative life in Austria, Gluck and Beethoven were not born Austrians, and in a strictly legal sense Mozart, born as subject of the then sovereign Prince Archbishop of Salzburg was not either. The fact that Austria and particularly Vienna became the rallying point for the greatest composers, irrespective of their native country, added to the glory of the city.[11]

Why Vienna became the center cannot be logically deduced. Equal and perhaps superior sponsorship of music existed also at German and Italian courts. Attractions of scenery and a receptive spirit of the people existed in other places as well, and as to interest in musical innovations Vienna was and is more conservative than other centers of music. Tradition and musical receptiveness rather than full understanding on the part of the population were important factors which merely help to explain the setting for a unique phenomenon, whose core remains unexplainable.

d) FINE ARTS

In the fine arts, especially architecture, the impact of external conditions was more obvious. The Baroque, and its derivative the Rococo, were primarily styles expressing the monumental passionate, and later elegant in the service of court, aristocracy, and the Church. The Baroque's last great representative in Austria is the Schönbrunn Palace in Vienna,

[11] The evaluation of Mozart as Austria's greatest composer is based on the assumption that Beethoven might be considered a German. Essentially the question of Mozart's and Beethoven's national affiliation and their comparative greatness is a moot one. The following references are, of course, not meant to refer to musical analyses but exclusively to the relationship of the composers to their Austrian environment. See Heinrich Kralik, *Das Buch der Musikfreunde* (Vienna, 1951) and Karl Kobald, *Wo unsterbliche Musik entstand* (Vienna, 1950).

planned by the elder Fischer von Erlach and completed by Nicola Pacassi. In the late Maria Theresan era a French-influenced Rococo style came to the fore, which however, frequently revealed original classic features. The Gloriette pavilion by Ferdinand von Hohenberg, on a hill overlooking the formal Schönbrunn gardens, and the building of the old university (now the Academy of Sciences) by N. Jadot de Ville Issey are examples of the decorative and graceful but no longer monumental style.

Two of the last of the great fresco painters following the Baroque tradition were Anton F. Maulbertsch and the Italian G. Guglielmi. J. M. Schmidt (the so-called Kremser Schmidt) adopted also the Baroque tradition of dramatic presentation of religious subjects. Martin van Meytens, a portrait painter, deviated from the grand style; in sculpture, Franz Messerschmidt and Wilhelm Byers under Maria Theresa and in particular Franz Anton von Zauner under the young Emperor Francis moved toward a less pretentious style which, on occasion, as the monument of Joseph II by Zauner shows, has noble austerity.

From Joseph II to the revolution of 1848, when frequently shallow replicas of historical designs came into vogue, this pattern of noble and harmonious simplicity and gracefulness led to felicitous artistic creations. Nevertheless this thoroughly original style of neoclassical dignity has not received its full recognition to this day. The Military Medical Academy (I. Cannavale) and the general hospital built under Joseph II in Vienna are masterpieces of the new style. They are also monuments of the social philosophy of the emperor. The gate of the outer Burg square in Vienna by Peter von Nobile and the Schotten monastery by Josef Kornhäusl, both built during the reign of Francis, are like the Fries (Pallavicini) palace, also designed by Hohenberg, further landmarks of this harmonious and dignified architecture.

New vistas were opened in painting. The Nazarene school of religious subjects, represented in particular by Julius Schnorr von Carolsfeld and Joseph von Führich in the pre-March era are less monumental but reveal more feeling than many Baroque paintings, and the eminent Moritz von Schwind (1804–1871), a more imaginative and subtle fresco painter than his Baroque predecessors, excelled in that particular technique. Schwind was also a genre and landscape painter of warmth and charm. In this latter respect he was matched by Ferdinand Waldmüller and later by the highly original Anton Romako, who moved almost imperceptibly toward expressionist tendencies. Friedrich Amerling, Joseph Kriehuber, and in a sense also August von Pettenkofen represented the art of portrait painting in the pre-March and earlier Francisco-Josephin eras. Here, too, a new bourgeois style of more modest designs but wider appeal gradually replaced the courtly tradition.[12]

B. The Magyars

a) Literature

Hungarian intellectual history throughout the Enlightenment lacks somewhat the strong national spirit which had sustained it in general throughout the preceding stormy centuries. The challenge to survival of a proud small nation surrounded by different ethnic groups, ceased to be effective for most of the eighteenth century. This was less a consequence of the peace of Szatmár of 1711, which the Habsburgs imposed on the Hungarian insurrectionists than of the denationalizing western influence of the times. It strengthened the impact of the western-oriented part of the aristocracy and learned professions, secular and clerical. It diminished that of the national nobility and the burghers in the towns. Altogether the small base of the political nation became apparent, from which not only the non-Magyar half of Hungary was excluded but also the major part of the Magyar population itself, the unfree peasants.

Peace with the crown had its social and political advantages, but at the end of Maria Theresa's reign many nobles, and not only the Magyar aristocrats at the court in Vienna, were hardly in full command of the national language. Ecclesiastic and Church-influenced writers on the Catholic and the Protestant sides countered foreign influence, among them the Jesuit priest Ferenc Faludi, a lyric poet of distinction, Janos Illei, a representative of the Jesuit school drama, and Peter Apor (1676–1752), a Transylvanian noble, author of the *Metamorphosis Transylvaniae*. This historiographer of Transylvanian social history deplored the decline of national mores under Habsburg rule. The writer of Calvinist church songs, Paul Ráday, worked for the peace of Szatmár of 1711, and hoped for further reconciliation with the Habsburgs through the Pragmatic Sanction. György Bessenyei (1742–1810) represented the French influence of the tragédie classique and the doctrinaire utilitarian character of enlightened reformism. Laurence von Orczy (1718–1789), an imperial general, likewise exemplified the French school in the form of his poetry, but this literary style was merely the setting of his plea for the revival of the Magyar mores and values of old.

The spirit of national revivalism, brought about largely as protest

[12] Hans Tietze, *Wien* (Leipzig, 1918); Konrad Kaiser, ed., *Romantik und Realismus in Österreich* (Schweinfurt, 1968); Rupert Feuchtmüller and Wilhelm Masch, *Biedermeier in Österreich* (Vienna, 1963).

against the denationalizing policies of Joseph II, made itself clearly felt now. It expressed itself at the end of the eighteenth century and in the first decades of the nineteenth according to the patterns of a new classicism which became oriented toward the Latin rather than the earlier eighteenth-century French tradition. The Pauline priest Benédikt Virág, a lyric of rank who with some exaggeration was referred to as the Hungarian Horace should be mentioned here. Jan Bacsányi (1763–1845), head of the literary circle at Kassa (Košice, Kaschau) in Slovak territory, stood for the breakthrough from the French to the national revolutionary spirit, albeit still in Latinized form. Though only at the fringe involved in the Martinovics Jacobin conspiracy, he remained a political suspect all his life to the authorities, was sent to jail, reprieved, rearrested, and exiled to Austria, where he spent the rest of his life under police supervision. In his esthetic and critical writings even more than in his poetry he should be seen as a vanguard of the coming new national revolution.

Alexander von Kisfaludy (1772–1844), a highly educated officer in the noble guard, represented the national spirit in a more conformist manner. A poet of love poetry, he became also a national tragedian, who selected the topics of his plays from Hungarian history. They were performed in Magyar in Buda in 1790, long before the Hungarian national theater opened in Pest in 1837. The national historical drama was in the pre-March era the great vogue. It was inspired by a patriotic and poetic spirit rather than by concern with historic accuracy. No wonder—the scholarly standards of the national historians of the early nineteenth century, such as István Kulcsár, Isaias Buday, and István Horváth were not very high.

The Hungarian reform period, for ever associated with the inspiring name of Count István Széchenyi, the founder of the Hungarian Academy of Science (1825) furthered socio-economic, cultural and in our particular context literary activities widely and steered skillfully a course which prevented serious molestations by the police regime of the restoration and pre-March eras. Not all new literature was politically oriented. Foreign classicism and Romanticism had primarily an artistic influence on Magyar literary endeavors. This latter aspect is illustrated by the outstanding translations of works of Shakespeare, Molière, and Goethe by the linguistic reformer Ferenc von Kazinczy (1759–1831). Just the same, the thrust of his predominantly literary interests could not protect him under the Franciscan regime. Because of his involvement in the Martinovics conspiracy Kazinczy was condemned to capital punishment. His sentence was commuted, and he spent years in various prisons including the notorious Spielberg in Brünn.

Increasing familiarity with the foreign classics, the rise of national consciousness during the reform period, the influence of contemporary romanticism, and the desire that the cultural nation should transcend the narrow frame of the political one, led to the rise of a new realism with wider popular appeal. Károly Kisfaludi (younger brother of Alexander), the founder of a new literary almanac, *Aurora,* in 1822, represented these new trends as national playwright, and writer of epics and songs. József Katona exemplified them as tragedian, whose interests were focused on Hungarian medieval history.

The national epic and the national historical drama were the concerns of the poet Mihály Vörösmarty (1800–1855), who was actively, deeply, and tragically involved in the Magyar war of independence of 1848–1849. His epic *Zalán's flight*, which glorifies the conquest of Hungary by the Magyars in the ninth and tenth centuries, became a symbolic centerpiece of the new revolutionary, national spirit. Its equivalent in lyrics was Vörösmarty's famous *Szózat* (manifesto) of 1837, which became the lyrics of the national anthem; it symbolizes in sublime language the destiny of "the Hungarian rock surrounded by the Teutonic-Slavic sea."

The Transylvanian aristocrat Baron Miklós Jósika, referred to as the Hungarian Walter Scott, was a novelist of distinction even though his works are out of date today. He, too, was actively involved in the tragedy of 1848–1849. The same held true for Baron József Eötvös (1813–1871), mentioned earlier as one of the great Magyar political thinkers of all time. Political reformer, minister of education briefly in 1848 and then again from 1867 to 1871, and largely responsible for the well-intended but poorly administered Hungarian nationality legislation of 1868, Eötvös was also a poet and writer of social novels. A true humanitarian and advocate of emancipation of the peasants, Eötvös was sceptical about the blessings of Enlightenment and democracy, though he remained opposed to aristocratic prejudices. Baron Zsigmond Kemény, novelist, journalist, and editor, likewise involved in the revolution, did much to extricate Magyar Hungary from an enforced cultural isolation in the postrevolutionary period.

Jointly with Vörösmarty, Alexander Petöfi (1823–1849) represented the revolutionary spirit and the heroic revolutionary sacrifice. His colorful life as traveling actor, his romantic-patriotic lyrics, and his heroic death in the battle of Segesvár in the Hungarian war of independence, all combined to create the portrait of the national martyr-poet true to an ideal type. Yet Petöfi like Kossuth was of non-Magyar descent. His father was of Serb and his mother of Slovak origin. As with Kossuth and other eminent Magyars, this non-Magyar descent strengthened his desire to become a full-fledged Magyar and intensified his patriotism. He succeeded and whatever may be said against the intolerance of Magyar nationalism, the fact that it could triumph within one generation is impressive. John Arany (1817–1882), like Petöfi of peasant stock, like him originally an actor, and like him also an ardent patriot, had the opportunity, not given to Petöfi, to develop his life to the fullest as writer of poetry, epics, and ballads.

The Transylvanian Pál Gyulay (1826–1909) represents the transition to the postrevolutionary generation. As poet, critic, and literary historian he offered a sober analytical self-appraisal of Magyar literature. Mór Jókai (1825–1904) was also actively engaged in the politics of the revolutionary era but as deputy decidedly a moderate. This swimming against the current during the last weeks of the republic in 1849 required as much courage as revolutionary activities. Jókai remained a moderate liberal inside and outside of parliament in the constitutional period after 1860. He became the novelist of the war of independence and, his realistic novels opened a new era of social understanding in literature, although many of them are inferior. Imre Madách (1823–1864), the author of the monumental Magyar Faust drama "The Tragedy of Man" combined realistic and romantic features in his lifework. Michael Horváth became a widely known historian of the reform period and the war of independence. His literary qualifications were largely vitiated by the curse of Magyar historiography: a far too uncritical spirit of nationalism.[13]

b) MUSIC

In the eighteenth century, Hungarian folk music, particularly dance music, was more independent of western influences of the Enlightenment than literature. Orchestral music, performed in the palaces of the great feudal nobles, was primarily that of the Italian and German masters. Ferenc Erkel (1810–1893) was the first distinguished composer of Hungarian national operas. His contemporary Franz Liszt (1811–1886) born close to the German-Magyar language border, as composer of orchestral, choral, and piano literature belongs more in the German than in the Magyar cultural orbit. But like Brahms he was indebted also to Hungarian folk music particularly the Czardas dance music and gipsy songs. But

[13] See Johann H. Schwicker, *Geschichte der ungarischen Literatur* (Leipzig, 1888), pp. 202–833; Julius von Farkas, *Die ungarische Romantik* (Berlin, 1931); Andritsch, ed., *Ungarische Geistesgeschichte*, pp. 115–245.

the great era of Magyar music was still to come, closer to the end of the nineteenth century.[14]

c) FINE ARTS

Throughout the seventeenth century, the Hungarian Baroque produced some outstanding specimens of ecclesiastic architecture in Nagy-Szombat, Györ, and Kassa. But its spread was impeded by the Turkish occupation and the dubious blessings of the wars of liberation (until the peace of Passarowitz in 1718), which also resulted in an extension in time of the Baroque period. In the early eighteenth century Domenico Martinelli reconstructed the royal castle in Buda in Baroque style, Lucas von Hildebrandt designed the palace of Prince Eugene of Savoy in Ráckeve, and Carlo Martino Carlone built that of the Esterházys in Eisenstadt (Kis Marton) somewhat earlier and in a less attractive design. A. Mayerhoffer built the Grassalkovich castle in Gödöllö; later a royal palace, it represented the beginning transition from late Baroque to a French-inspired classicism. In the second half of the eighteenth century J. Fellner was the leading Magyar architect of the new style. He designed the seminary building in Eger (Erlau) and the episcopalian palace in Veszprém (Stuhlweißenburg). The new classicist style after the transition period is exemplified by the Protestant cathedral in Debrecen by Mihály Péchy. More characteristic is the building of the Hungarian national museum in Pest by Mihály Pollak, erected shortly before the revolution. This era was followed by that of the typical revived, but often inimitable neo-historical styles.

The influence of foreign, particularly Italian and German masters was prevalent during the Baroque. The Magyar portrait painter Adám Mányoki in the first half of the eighteenth century was an exception. In the first half of the nineteenth century the foreign pseudo classicism of Thorwaldsen and Canova strongly influenced the Hungarian sculptor István Ferenczy. On the other hand, the Magyar historical school of painting, which developed somewhat later, revealed a more original national style.

Altogether, Hungarian Baroque culture, because of the feudal structure of estates, represented to a greater extent and for a longer time a courtly ecclesiastic and particularly aristocratic culture than Austrian Baroque. Furthermore, the long-lasting foreign domination served as a further impediment to the development of national patterns in the fine arts.

[14] Zoltan Halász, *Ungarn* (Budapest, 1966), pp. 381–392.

These depend to a greater extent on external conditions than the humanities and social sciences. By the turn from the nineteenth to the twentieth century, these formidable obstacles had been successfully overcome.[15]

C. The Czechs

a) language and literature

During the Enlightenment and the subsequent conservative era, well beyond the revolutionary intermission of 1848, the evolution of the Magyar language but for the brief Josephin era was not impeded by outside forces; the predominance of Latin in literary intercourse derived from the feudal structure and changed within the strictly Magyar orbit gradually without much friction. The development and use of the Czech language among educated people, on the other hand, was severely restricted after the battle of the White Mountain. These conditions were only gradually lifted during the later enlightened era. Thus at a time when Magyar literature evolved in a wide range of poetry, plays, and epics, the Czechs had first to revise and to rebuild their national language. They did so successfully within about two generations. The differences in the pace of development referred to above disappeared within the second half of the nineteenth century. In the first half they still prevailed.

In 1769 a learned society for the study of then so-called Bohemian, that is Czech, culture, was founded by the enlightened aristocrats Prince Karl Egon Fürstenberg, Count Ernst Waldstein, Count F. J. Kinsky, and mainly Count Kaspar Sternberg. The mineralogist Ignaz von Born provided the scientific background, the historian Franz Martin Pelzel enriched cultural endeavors in the humanities and social sciences. The first really creative figure in the Czech Slavic renaissance was Josef Dobrovský (1753–1829). Dobrovský, a Jesuit priest before the dissolution of the order in 1773, later an abbé was for a time director of the seminary in Hradiště (near Olomouc) but lived for much of his life in the house of an aristocratic sponsor, Count Francis Nostitz. He considered Czech to be his mother tongue but was aware that because of external suppression and clerical upbringing his command of the native language was limited. All the more impressive were his endeavors to correct that situation—endeavors still for the most part formulated in German or Latin. Dobrovský wrote an Old Slavic grammar in Latin, a pioneer history of the Bohemian

[15] Ibid., pp. 362–372; Julius Pasteiner, "Die Baukunst in Budapest," [Crownprince Rudolf], *Die österreichisch-ungarische Monarchie in Wort und Bild* (Vienna, 1886–1903), *Ungarn*, III, 96–112, 417–421.

language and literature in German, another grammar focused on syntax in German as well as a dictionary of the German and Bohemian (Czech) language. Dobrovský's commanding position as Slavist is uncontested, in particular in the historic significance of his work in the field of general Slavic studies. The work of Josef Jungmann (1773–1847) had more specific philological value in regard to the Czech language. As prefect of the Academic Gymnasium in Prague he wrote a textbook on style in Czech and translated several works by Milton, Pope, Goethe, and Chateaubriand into Czech. Much of his lifework was focused on the compilation of a Czech-German dictionary in five volumes. He also wrote a history of Bohemian literature in Czech. Largely as a result of Jungmann's efforts the authorities finally permitted the teaching of Czech in secondary schools, though not yet as language of instruction. In 1830 Jungmann founded the association for the scholarly cultivation of the Bohemian language and literature. He was the first great Czech Slavist by scholarly, not by ideological and historical standards. Excessive nationalist zeal misled Václav Hanka (1791–1861), the librarian of the Bohemian Museum. He fabricated two allegedly early medieval manuscripts, the Královédvorský and Zelenohorský (Königinhof and Grünberg) manuscripts. According to these documents a fully developed Czech civilization (Kralové Dvur and Zelená Hora) had existed in early medieval Bohemia. Despite this aberration Hanka was a Slavist of considerable knowledge as was František Ladislav Čelakovský, a collector of ancient folksongs and a poet.

Pavel Josef Šafařík (1795–1861), by birth a Slovak, ranks with Dobrovský and Jungmann as the third great Slavist of the Czech renaissance movement. He studied Slavic medieval history and ethnography and wrote also a history of Slavic literature, which started from the assumption of the existence of a comprehensive Slavic mother language, subdivided into the idioms of various Slavic tribes. Šafařík, also distinguished as translator of German classical literature and as poet, may be called an enlightened Panslav, who did not represent integral but humanitarian nationalism. Born in Slovak territory, he spent much of his life in teaching positions in Hungary but became eventually professor of Slavic Philology in Prague and afterward director of the university library there. He represents a scholarly and ideological bridge between the Czech and Slovak language orbits.

František Palacký (1798–1876) was mentioned earlier as distinguished leader in questions of national reform. As national historian of the history of the Bohemian people to 1526, first in a German and then more extensively in a Czech edition, and as collector of the documents of the Hussite wars, he surpasses in scholarly quality contemporary Magyar and Austro-German historiography. One of his students, Václav V. Tomek, wrote a history of Prague, actually a history of the Czechs to the beginning of the seventeenth century, as well as a biography of the Hussite leader Jan Žižka. Tomek was also the historiographer of Prague University, the oldest in the Central European orbit, founded by Emperor Charles IV in 1348. The Germans claimed it to be a German establishment and it was run as German institution until in 1882 a Czech university with Czech language of instruction was finally added. Either university, the German or the Czech, could with equal justification be called the successor to Charles IV's foundation.

The development of theatrical life in Prague was rich and for much of the eighteenth century superior to conditions in any other part of the Habsburg monarchy. It flourished for a long time under German and Italian auspices. In the late seventeenth century the Jesuit drama bloomed in the Czech orbit as in the German Austrian. In the first half of the eighteenth century a theater devoted mainly to the performance of Italian operas and another one for German plays were established under the sponsorship of Count Franz A. Sporck. In 1783 the German National Theater was opened under the sponsorship of Count Francis Nostitz. Here in 1787 Don Giovanni was performed for the first time with Mozart himself conducting. A few years later this theater was dubbed the Theater of the Bohemian Estates or the Estates National Theater. As in Vienna, Punch and Judy shows were performed until the 1770's. An official, though still only interim Czech National Theater, was opened in 1862. The great Bohemian National Theater for plays and operas was built between 1868 and 1891, the new German Theater, whose construction as counterweight to the Czech institution was furthered by the government in Vienna, was opened in 1888. In 1882 another German theater was opened in Brno. In proportion to the much larger Czech population Czech theatrical life was at a disadvantage compared with the German institutions, but this hardly impeded its rich and diverse development in the future.[16]

[16] Hermann Münch, *Böhmische Tragödie* (Braunschweig, 1949), pp. 88–166; Hans Raupach, *Der tschechische Frühnationalismus: Ein Beitrag zur Gesellschafts- und Ideengeschichte des Vormärz in Böhmen* (Darmstadt, 1969), pp. 26–130; A. V. Pypin and V. D. Spasović, *Geschichte der slawischen Literaturen* (Leipzig, 1884), II, part 2, pp. 177–286; František Chudoba, *A Short Survey of Czech Literature*

b) MUSIC

Progress in music became apparent even earlier than in literature, though here, too, German and Italian music came to the fore first. In the early eighteenth century the operas and orchestral pieces of the Austrian (Styrian) composer, J. J. Fux, were performed in Prague, among them an opera in celebration of the coronation of Charles VI as king of Bohemia in 1723. A regular Italian opera stagione existed in Prague as early as 1734, but German operas were offered as well. Mozart's *Marriage of Figaro, The Elopement from the Serail*, and as noted *Don Giovanni* were all performed in the 1780's.

But native Bohemian composers also played a distinguished part. In the eighteenth century it is difficult to classify them as either Czech or German, because in Bohemian lands German or Czech names are no reliable clues in this respect. The Minorit father Bohuslav Černohorský (1684–1742) however, was one of the earliest native orchestral composers who definitely may be considered a Czech. The brothers Franz and Georg Benda (1709–1786 and 1722–1795) followed. The former, concert master of Frederick II of Prussia and an outstanding violin player composed chamber music, the latter mainly operas with Italian librettos. Both left their native country, but Franz Xaver Brixi (1732–1771), composer of ecclesiastic music, remained as chorus conductor at St. Vitus Cathedral. Josephin puritanism and austerity curbed the aristocratic sponsorship of private orchestras as in other parts of the Habsburg realms. Yet in 1803 a symphony orchestra was founded in Prague, and the establishment of a conservatory followed in 1811. Its director, J. F. Kittl (1809–1868), a native of Bohemia, composed symphonies and operas.

In the early nineteenth century opera performances in Italian gradually yielded to German, and in 1820 the first Czech libretto was offered. Venceslav J. Tomásěk (1774–1850) a composer of operas and orchestral music may well be called a Czech, and the two classics Bedrich Smetana (1824–1884) and Antonin Dvořák (1841–1904) were Czechs. Smetana, the

---

(London, 1969), pp. 57–143; Hanuš Jelinek, *Histoire de la Littérature Tchèque* (Paris, 1930–1935), I, 219–393, II, 7–111; Richard G. Plaschka, *Von Palacký bis Pekař* (Graz-Cologne, 1955), pp. 6–35; Oskar Teuber, "Die Theater Prags," in [Crownprince Rudolf] *Die österreichisch-ungarische Monarchie*, vols. *Böhmen*, II, 163–192; Richard Rosenheim, *Die Geschichte der deutschen Bühnen in Prag* (Prague, 1938), pp. 11–27; see also Robert Auty, "Changing Views on the Role of Dobrovský in the Czech National Revival," in Peter Brock and H. Gordon Skilling, eds., *The Czech Renaissance of the Nineteenth Century* (Toronto, 1970), pp. 14–25.

composer of the *Bartered Bride, Dalibor,* and *Libuše* (*Libussa*), ranks among the greatest opera composers of the nineteenth century. His orchestra and chamber music, though somewhat overshadowed by the fame of the *Bartered Bride* and *Dalibor,* were likewise creations of the first order. As composer of numerous operas Antonin Dvořák was not quite of the same rank as Smetana. His chief contribution was in orchestral, choral, and dance music. The national, indeed perhaps nationalistic, element in his music is more pronounced than in that of Smetana. Zdeněk Fibich (1850–1900) may also be considered a genuine national composer of high achievements in regard to operatic and symphonic music. Altogether there is no question, that jointly with the Austro-Germans and later the Magyars, the Czechs hold the first rank in musical creation and production among the national groups under Habsburg rule. In regard to the originality of their national music they had few equals.[17]

c) FINE ARTS

Ecclesiastic and secular Baroque architecture in the Bohemian lands surpasses that in any other part of Central Europe. However, the work of foreign masters such as father and son Fischer von Erlach from Austria, Johann and Kilian Ignaz Dientzenhofer from Germany, and the Italian A. Loragho was of decisive importance. But the embedding of the Baroque palaces and churches in the silhouette and the over-all panoroma of the cities of Bohemia reveals great Czech artistic sensitivity. In the nineteenth century Czech masters recreated the monumental buildings in neohistoric styles of much vigor and, as anywhere else, doubtful originality.[18] Painters representing the nineteenth-century historical school were Gabriel Max (1840–1915) and Václav Brožik (1851–1901) a truly national painter whose work in several ways is related to Makart's art, but was superior in his coloration. Skillful, not ostentatious blending of historical and neohistorical styles remains characteristic for Czech art.[19]

[17] Ottokar Hostinský, "Musik in Böhmen," in [Crownprince Rudolf] *Die österreichisch-ungarische Monarchie,* vols. *Böhmen,* II, 17–60 and Christian von D'Elvert, "Musik in Mähren," vol. *Mähren und Schlesien,* pp. 263–282.

[18] Here the most representative buildings, the Czech National Theater and the Czech National Museum were designed by German architects in the second half of the nineteenth century in a neo Renaissance style (Joseph Zitek and Joseph Schulz).

[19] On fine arts see Jaromir Neumann, *Das böhmische Barock* (Vienna, 1971); Karl Chytic "Malerei und Plastik der . . . Rococozeit" in [Crownprince Rudolf] *Die österreichisch-ungarische Monarchie,* vols. *Böhmen,* II, 378–385, and ibid. Victor Barvitius, "Malerei und Plastik der Neuzeit", pp. 385–432.; Münch, *Böhmische Tragödie,* pp. 470–472.

D. The Slovaks

During the late Enlightenment and the first half of the nineteenth century the struggle between a Catholic Slovak linguistic movement and a Czecho-Slovak movement associated with the Czech Hussite tradition continued. The Catholic endeavors led by Father Antony Bernolák (1762–1813) produced a Slovak grammar and dictionary. A Catholic Slovak literary society, formed as early as 1792 supported these efforts, which were successful, however, only in western Slovakia. While the Czecho-Slovak union movement stressed the historical ties between the two nations, the intent to build up a specific literary national language was not forgotten. The two most eminent leaders were Ján Kollár (1793–1852) and Ludevít Štúr (1815–1856). Kollár must be considered as the great romantic representative of a mystic humanitarian Panslavism. A linguist of rank and collector of Slavic folksongs his fame among northern and southern Slavs was primarily based on his sonnets, published under the title *Slávy dcěra* (*Slava's* Daughter). The glorification of the Slavic mission in Europe was written in a somewhat artificial Czech language of its own with strong Slovak literary associations. Štúr, founder of a Slovak literary journal in the 1840's and professor of literature in Bratislava, edited Slovak folksongs and fairy tales. His pronounced Slovak nationalism collided at points with the literary programs of the Czech intelligentsia. Štúr was an eminent writer and linguist of political tendencies, the priest Jan Hollý (1785–1849) represented a less directly political Catholic romantic Slavism, comparable to Kollár's Protestant Slavism. Hollý translated Greek and Latin classics into Slovak and wrote two national epics, which, like the works of Kollár, extolled national history from a Panslav viewpoint. Another priest, the dome capitular Jura Palkovič (1763–1835), translated the scriptures into Slovak and improved and enlarged Bernolák's dictionary of the Slovak language. His Protestant namesake Jiři Palkovič (1769–1850), professor of Czecho-Slovak language and literature in Bratislava, a collector of Slovak folklore and translator of a Czech bible, promoted Czecho-Slovak linguistic union. Joseph M. Hurban (1817–1888) and Michael M. Hodža (1811–1870) were both Protestant pastors of Czecho-Slovak leanings. The former was also a literary historian and epic writer. The latter, more concerned with politics, was also interested in the language reform in a strictly Slovak national sense. Both became national leaders in the revolutionary era of 1848–1849. The language issue was technically solved by a compromise brought about by Martin Hattala (1821–1903), professor at the Catholic Seminary in Trnava (Tyrnau, Nagyszombat). In his grammar of 1850 he merged the major Slovak idioms, represented in extreme form by Bernolák and Štúr, into a distinct literary language, which despite its Czech roots maintained their Slovak characteristics.

Slovak novels, stories, epics, and lyrics had existed previously. They continued to thrive further after their national identity had been fully recognized, not against but basically with the cooperation of the neighboring Czech people. Problems of the future, when both nations would have to live side by side in the same state, could not yet be clearly envisioned.[20]

E. The Poles

The center of Polish national life in the two decades between the first and third partition was still the area around Warsaw. Afterward for a full generation, the generation of Polish literary Messianism, and romanticism, Paris became the rallying point of political Polish emigration and to a degree of Polish cultural activities. Later, intellectual Poland, though repressed in many ways, had its center of intellectual gravity gradually returned to Russia largely because of the rise of Panslavism among Russians as well as Poles. But another center was in the Republic of Cracow, established at the Congress of Vienna and returned in 1846 to Austrian rule.[21] Cracow, during its republican era had its old medieval university reorganized by the dome capitular Hugo Kołłątaj between 1777 and 1782. A Society of Fine Arts was established there in 1853 and later raised to an academy. The opening of the National Polish Museum followed in 1879. The University of Lwów founded in 1784 as well as the Polytechnicum of 1844 still offered instruction in German. As the result of the administrative semi-autonomy granted to Galicia in 1868, this changed in 1871.

After 1830 the Poles in the Habsburg monarchy were treated better than those in Russia and at least after the suppression of the second Polish revolt of 1863 better than those in Prussia. Yet the evolution of Polish cultural life did not benefit much from these conditions on Austrian territory because Warsaw remained after all the center of the kingdom and the Poles believed that their resurrection could only come from there. Warsaw, not Cracow was also believed to be the future core of Polish culture. The Habsburg empire seemed too feeble ever to be able to guarantee a comprehensive Polish future within its confines. There was, further-

[20] Pypin and Spasović, *Geschichte der slawischen Literaturen,* II:2, 310–352; Ludwig von Gogolák, *Beiträge zur Geschichte des slowakischen Volkes* (Munich, 1963–1972), I, 221–253, II, 1–171 passim, III, 19–31.

[21] Cracow had been also under Austrian rule from 1795–1809.

more, the Ruthenian movement for equality, in particular in eastern Galicia, and the Poles felt, more wrongly than rightly, that the government in Vienna used a *divide et impera* policy by backing up the Ruthenians against them. Whether right or wrong, ill feelings were stronger in cultural life than on the administrative level.

None of the Polish classics such as Mickiewicz, Slovacki, and Krasiński, is directly related to Galician history, but a near-great writer, Count Alexander Fredro (1793–1876) wrote excellent comedies in the style of Molière and had them performed in the national theaters in Cracow and Lwów. Distinguished scholars and academic teachers were the historian of law Anton S. Helcel, and the political philosopher Pawel von Popiel. Both resided in Cracow after its reincorporation into Austria. The medieval-history scholar Karol Szajnocha in Lwów was barred from an academic position because of revolutionary activities in his youth. Notable was the stimulating literary critic Julian Klaczko who wrote mainly in French, until the mid-nineteenth century the language of Polish high society in Galicia.[22]

The glory of Gothic and Renaissance paintings represented by Hans von Kulmbach in the sixteenth century, and wood sculpture in the late fifteenth by the great Veit Stoss were claimed equally for Polish and German culture. The place of birth and training of these men was German, the influence of the environment largely though not fully Polish. Their superb achievements could not be revived by the historical school in the nineteenth century, but some of its outstanding representatives like Jan Matejko (1838–1893), a painter of major historical compositions, and his contemporary Julian Kossak, a portraitist, were fine artists.[23]

F. The Ruthenians

A major factor in the literary history of the Ruthenians in Galicia[24], which came under Austrian rule in 1772 and 1774, was the alienation of aristocracy and intelligentsia from their historic culture. Polish influence

[22] Manfred Kridl, in Bernadotte Schmitt, ed., *Poland* (Berkeley, 1945), pp. 284–310; Manfred Kridl, *A Survey of Polish Literature and Culture* (The Hague, 1967), pp. 317 f.; Count Stanislaus Tarnowski, "Polnische Literatur" in [Crownprince Rudolf] *Die österreichisch-ungarische Monarchie,* vol. *Galizien,* 591–648; Erasmus Piltz, ed., *Poland* (London, 1919), pp. 291–301; Czeslav Milosz, *The History of Polish Literature* (London, 1969), pp. 158–259.

[23] Ladislaus Luszízkiewicz, "Architecture" in [Crownprince Rudolf] *Die österreichisch-ungarische Monarchie,* vol. *Galizien,* pp. 694–720 and Marian von Sokolski, "Malerei und Plastik", ibid. pp. 745–771.

[24] Jointly with the Hungarian Carpatho-Ruthenians the most western branch of the Ukrainian people.

became prevalent and the Ruthenians lost the social and intellectual upper structure of their national group, including a large part of the clergy, to the Poles. The Uniate Church, established by the Union of Brest in 1596, opened Ruthenians a spiritual center, seemingly close enough to their own national tradition, but failed to open to her members the door to equal status in Polish society. In this respect they were not better off than the Ruthenians in the former Turkish Bukovina,[25] where the old orthodoxy continued to prevail. In the Hungarian Carpatho-Ukraine (the Ruthenian territory longest under Habsburg rule, and settled by Ruthenians in the late Middle Ages), opportunities for the development of national life were even more limited than in eastern Galicia.

Much of this changed during the reigns of Maria Theresa and Joseph II. Furthering of Ruthenian seminaries by both rulers in Vienna (1774) and Lwów (1783) and the establishment of the new Polish university in Lwów in 1784 with at least some offerings in the Ruthenian language enhanced the Ruthenian status. These concessions were withdrawn, however, in the early nineteenth century, and teachings in Ruthenian on the academic level resumed only after 1848, on a limited scale. The same applied to conditions at the University of Czernowitz (Cernivtsi, Cernăuţi), founded in 1875. The Maria Theresan-Josephin Ruthenian policy and its continuation after the revolution of 1848, in which the Ruthenian claim for equality with the Poles played its part, helped to reverse the trends of denationalization among the Ruthenian people. In particular the struggle for the use of Ruthenian as language of instruction in public schools was of great significance. Simultaneous tensions in the Russian Ukraine, the nationalist intolerance of the Polish aristocracy and gentry, and the over-all influence of the Slavic renaissance were powerful contributing factors.

These tentative successes of Ruthenian recognition could not immediately lead to major literary achievements. A new conflict, this time not between Ruthenian nationalism and the Polonization process, but between the western Uniate and the eastern Orthodox trends within the clergy, developed in the pre-March period. Supporters of the former, under the leadership of the vicar general of the archdiocese of Lwów, Gregor von Yakhimovych, defended the preservation of the Cyrillic alphabet against the pro-Polish wing, anxious to switch to Latin. At the same time, a conservative trend within the clergy stood for the old Slavic Church language, which meant indirectly communion with the eastern Orthodox Church and Russia. The course of the future however, was neither in a

[25] Under Austrian administration after 1774.

Ruthenian liberal nationalism focused on east Galicia nor in a conservative old Ruthenian linked to tsarism, and least of all in accommodation to Polish culture. The objectives of future generations pointed to a broad Ukrainian cultural nationalism, clearly delineated from Habsburg or Romanov interests and ambitions.

Whether they intended it or not, the first and second generation of Ruthenian literary men under Habsburg rule served this ultimate goal of Ruthenian-Ukrainian nationalism. Three friends, Markiian Šaškevyč (1811–1843), Ivan Vahylevyč (1811–1866), and Iakiv Holováckyj (1814–1888) deserve attention. Shashkevych, a Uniate priest, did for the Ruthenian people on a more elmentary level what the Slavists, Dobrovský, Jungmann, and Šafařik had done for the Czech people. Undoubtedly they and other Slavists had influenced Šaškevyč's lifework. In his collection of folksongs he used the Ruthenian idiom in Galicia. In 1843, Šaškevyč and his friends, despite police chicaneries, published a literary almanac, *Rusalka Dnistrovaia,* and also wrote poetry. Vahylevyč studied Ruthenian history (especially literary history) and ethnography. He translated medieval Ruthenian literature into Polish. Holovaćkyj was for a time professor of Ruthenian language and literature at the University of Lwów, where he was also concerned with the collection of folksongs. His leanings toward the Russians were the strongest among the three; accordingly he had to relinquish his chair eventually. Vahylevič represented a moderately pro-Polish position and Šaškevyč the most definite Ruthenian one.

All three, however—and in this sense they are not so much representatives of Ruthenian as of Ukrainian nationalism—established close contacts with the rising Ukrainian national literature across the Russian border as represented above all by Ivan P. Kotlarewskyj (1769–1838) and the great Ukrainian classic Taras Shevchenko (1814–1861). Within a few decades they were followed by a group of writers, ethnographers, and historians. Whatever the political conflicts between imperial Austrian and Russian interests were, whatever the issues between Ukrainian, Ruthenian, and Russian nationalisms had become, however divisive denominational conflicts between Orthodoxy, Uniate, and Roman Catholic Church might have been, the literary Ukrainian union movement had become irresistible in the half century from the outgoing Enlightenment to the national revolution of 1848. It took only two more decades for this union movement to spread to the isolated Carpatho-Ukraine and to the Bukovina, where the new University of Czernowitz and the literary society Ruska Besida (1868) opened additional gates to cultural Ukrainian unionism. The Ruthenian-Ukrainian literary rise, more an awakening than a renaissance movement, was one of the most successful crusades of Slavic cultural nationalism in the nineteenth century. Its success in east Galicia and the Bukovina were related to changes in the huge Ukrainian hinterland across the Russian frontiers. Such relationship to a majority of ethnic brethren across state boundaries was in itself by no means unique among the national groups in the Habsburg empire. Unique was, however, the joining in common cultural endeavors of two branches of a great nation which had been controlled for generations by alien authorities. The experience of similar outside pressures led to similar cultural objectives.[26]

G. The Southern Slavs

The cultural rise of the Southern Slav peoples in the Habsburg empire from the Enlightenment onward is as much associated with the Slavic renaissance as the rise of other Slavic peoples. What differentiated the Southern Slav renaissance movement from that of other Slavs was the direct, and not merely implied, relationship between endeavors for linguistic and literary union, and those for political union. Similar ideas, as noted before, existed also among Czechs and Slovaks, but not quite simultaneously and in a less specific and politically less realistic sense than among the western Southern Slav nations, Croats, Serbs, and Slovenes.

Yet even there, endeavors to achieve linguistic-literary union, did not mean cultural union and even less political union. The latter was brought about only in a most imperfect manner by the establishment of Yugoslavia in 1918.[27] It took another generation and two world wars to establish a genuine though still imperfect federation on the basis of national equality. Linguistic- literary union has not been accomplished to this day although an accommodation between Croatian and Slovene literature has progressed gradually throughout the romantic stage of the Slavic renaissance and in a less spectacular way ever since. The rise of a true joint Serbo-Croatian literature coincided with the establishment of the first political union in 1918. It has not yet reached its goal. Nevertheless, this cultural union has come closer to materialization after 1918 and increasingly so after 1945. Southern Slav intellectual developments to this day may still be compre-

[26] Emil Ohonowskij, "Ruthenische Literatur" (in Galicia) in [Crownprince Rudolf] *Die österreichisch-ungarische Monarchie,* Vol. *Galizien*, pp. 652–664, Emil Kakužniácki, "Die ruthenische Sprache und Literatur" (in Bukovina), Vol. *Bukowina,* pp. 400–405; Michael Hrushevsky, *A History of Ukraine* (New Haven, 1941), pp. 471–474, 487–493, 495–498.

[27] In this respect, the declaration of Corfu on July 20, 1917 had only declaratory character.

hended largely as a separate process within each of the three nations. Up to 1918 separate analysis is necessary.

a) THE SLOVENES

The Slovenes (smallest of the Southern Slav national groups), pioneers in the translations of the gospels into a Slavic language at the time of the Reformation were pioneers also in grammatical development. The linguistic studies by Adam Bohorič, published in the late eighteenth century, anchored the previously noted sixteenth-century Bible translations of Trubar and Dalmatin into a firm grammatical frame. The Counter Reformation had represented a standstill in linguistic development, although Jesuit influence in the cultivation of the drama and the spread of Italian Baroque opera music had modified the dangers of Slovene cultural isolation.

An era of rapid advance began with the Enlightenment under Maria Theresa as result of the attempts to introduce general education on the elementary level. The consequences exceeded the modest original objectives. One cause was the French occupation of the so-called Austrian Illyrian territories (most of Carinthia, Carniola, Gorizia, Istria, Dalmatia, and southwestern Croatia-Slavonia) from 1809–1814. The French administration cemented the foundations of the relatively brief Austrian reform era and advanced it in higher education. The short duration of this regime blunted tendencies to associate reforms with the impact of suppression by foreign governments.

The Slavic linguistic renaissance was another most important factor in the cultural rise of the Slovenes. A literary almanac had been published in Ljubljana as early as 1779, a newspaper followed in 1797. Both existed only for a few years. Aristocratic sponsorship by Baron S. Zois and a generation later by Anastasius Grün still had to provide a protective shield for the activities of enlightened intellectuals, modest as they were under the Franciscan police regime. At least the bucolic lyrics of Valentin Vodnik (1758–1819) were permissible and a Bible translation could now be undertaken on the Catholic side.

The great and lasting advancement of Slovene literary development came under the auspices of romanticism, but a romanticism with solid scholarly foundations. The previously mentioned linguist and philologist Bartholomaeus Kopitar, director of the Austrian court library in Vienna, was a pioneer in the field of comparative Slavic linguistics and a reformer if not so some extent creator of modern Slovene. He intended to "convert"

Slovene, the most western of the Southern Slav languages, to a bridgehead of western Slavism under Catholic, and by implication Habsburg, sponsorship. He did more. His was the task, largely successfully performed, to give a nation with a solid literary tradition but no political past, a future solely anchored in cultural achievements and political potentialities. Similar developments can be observed among other Slavic peoples but in no instance was the political survival and future so clearly and predominantly based on cultural attainments as in that of the Slovenes.

Kopitar's influence reached beyond the Slovene orbit into that of Croats and Serbs. In regard to general linguistic education and popular cultural activities in the Slovene language his work was supported by the veterinarian Janez Bleiweis, the founder of a journal, *Novice,* in 1843. Through his professional, literary, and political activities he exercised an almost equal influence on peasants, clergymen, and the new writers. He was referred to as father of the nation. Bleiweis inspired also the lyric Francé Prešeren (1800–1849). Kopitar's scholarly student was Fran von Miklosich, who in the following generation became the leading Slavist at the University of Vienna. The primarily apolitical aspect of Slovene literature is shown also by the post-1848 generation of Slovene writers, the lyrics F. Lestvik and Simon Jenko, and the novelist Joseph Jurčić. New and more radical literary developments were to evolve in the last decades of the nineteenth century. The sensitivity for harmony in verse and prose, introduced by the phonetics of Kopitar's scholarship and the art of Prešeren, remained a characteristic feature of Slovene literature.[28]

b) THE CROATS

The rich development of Croatian literature in the school of Dubrovnik from Ivan Gundulić in the early seventeenth century to Nicola Dordić in the late seventeenth and early eighteenth has been mentioned. So have been the literary activities of the national heroes in the late seventeenth century rising in the Croatian north, Counts Francis Frankopan and Peter Zrinski (Zrinyi). Otherwise in the seventeenth century the influence of the Counter Reformation in plays with ecclesiastic subjects was dominant. In general, religious literary trends followed the Jesuit patterns. Secular literature in the late seventeenth century—pseudohistoric epics, glorifying the Habsburg campaigns against the Turks—had little artistic value. Counterreformatory activities, in particular the various seminaries in Italy

[28] Anton Slodnjak, *Geschichte der slowenischen Literatur* (Berlin, 1958), pp. 86–161; Pypin and Spasovič, *Geschichte der slawischen Literaturen,* I, 376–395; Fischel, *Der Panslawismus bis zum Weltkrieg,* pp. 125–130.

for Croatian candidates for the priesthood were focused on missionary activities in the territories occupied for generations by the Turks. This helped to increase Italian cultural influence. It was less prevalent in the literary field than in the fine arts. The monuments of the Venetian renaissance in Dalmatia were followed by a less spectacular but longer lasting influence of the Italian Baroque on Croatian architecture, painting, and sculpture well beyond the coastal lands. In addition to the direct Italian impact in these fields, there was also an influence of German Baroque modified by Italian designs. Croatian folk art preserved its independent, original character during that era, although its influence abroad remained limited.

The direct impact on Croatia of the Enlightenment in the Maria Theresan and Josephin reform era is not as apparent as in regard to the Slovene territories. The constitutional relationship to Hungary and the military character of the Frontier regime help to understand this. Matija Rjelković, a frontier officer from Slavonia (1732–1798), who spent several years during the third Silesian war as prisoner of war in Prussian captivity exhorted his countrymen in a strange epic, *Satir,* to adopt the institutions of the west and to renounce the old customs and folk poetry. With this philosophy he ran counter, not only to a century-old tradition of the past, but also to the romantic tendencies of the literary renaissance movement of the following generation. Its character however, was changed by the previously noted activities of Ljudevit Gaj (1809–1872) whose personality combined features of Romanticism, political nationalism, and political expediency. The last was more apparent than with most other leaders of Slavic renaissance movements.

The idea of cultural union between Croats and Slovenes was not new. The two peoples shared the Catholic-Latin heritage. Furthermore, Kopitar had done much to emphasize the linguistic affinity in his grammatical studies. Yet his concepts of a Catholic-Slav union could be considered political only in a broad ideological sense. Gaj, who had studied at the University of Vienna and was at the same time exposed to Kollár's mystic Panslavism, went further in his political objectives. He pursued them with scholarly achievements inferior to those of Kopitar, but with a superior sense for political timing. He strove for the further-reaching aim of linguistic union of the Serb and Croatian main branches of the Southern Slav orbit to the west of the Bulgarians. He hoped to achieve this union by turning to a southern Dalmatian dialect as basis of a linguistic compromise between Croats and Serbs rather than to insist on subordination to the existing Croatian literary language with its strong western ties. To the extent that the bulk of the Serbs, then still under Turkish rule, was farther removed from the impact of western culture than Croats and Slovenes, this plan appeared to be a Croatian concession to Southern Slav union. Yet as far as the concept of Illyrism was decidedly western, Latin in character and associated with an alleged Roman (Illyrian) tradition along the eastern shores of the Adriatic, it had also an anti-orthodox, anti-Magyar, and pro-Catholic tinge. All three features were agreeable to the pre-March policy of the Austrian government. Various concessions that Gaj obtained, such as the permission to establish an Illyrian Book Foundation and a newspaper with a literary supplement, seemed to indicate smooth relations to the authorities in Vienna. Actually allegations spread by Gaj's orthodox Serb opponents that he was a Metternich agent were probably unfounded. The truth is simply that his activities concurred with the policies of the minister of the Interior, Count Kolowrat, the relatively most enlightened member of the government in Slavic questions. With great skill Gaj had stressed the potential dangers of a Panslav (that meant, pro-Russian) orthodox orientation of the Austrian Southern Slavs. Illyrism, on the other hand, promised a western version of the union movement under Croatian leadership, even though a linguistic understanding with far-reaching concessions to the Serbs had been initiated in cultural matters. The question remained, whether the ties of Illyrism with the Habsburgs could be maintained, if and when a Croatian compromise with the Magyars could be achieved. For the time being Illyrism had mended its political fences with the government in Vienna and had encouraged further cultural advance, unimpeded by governmental actions.

One of its first outstanding literary representatives was Stanko Vraz (1810–1851), a poet who had moved from Slovene territory to Zagreb and had accepted the Croatian (or, in Gaj's terms, the new Serbo-Croatian) language which should follow the southern Dalmatian pattern. Vraz, founder of the literary review *Kolo,* was a collector of folksongs, a lyric poet, writer of ballads, and—characteristic for Croatian literature—satires. Ivan Mažuranić (1814–1890) revived the national epic of the Southern Slav task of defending Christianity. Petar von Preradović (1814–1872), an imperial officer, the most romantic of the new Southern Slav lyrical poets, glorified also the Southern Slav Illyrian mission in the present and future world. The national legal and social historian Ivan Kukuljević, supported the bishop of Djakovo, Josip Strossmayer, in creating the Yugoslav Academy (1851) and the university (1874), both in Zagreb. Luka Botić, who belonged to the school of Mažuranić, perceived in his epic poetry, against mounting parochial Croatian opposition to the

Illyrian unification idea, an even wider union concept, namely the reconciliation of Southern Slav Christianity and Mohammedanism. Here the future problems of Bosnia within a prospective Southern Slav political union were envisaged.[29]

c) THE SERBS

As noted in Chapter IV the Serbs in southern Hungary enjoyed a limited religious and cultural autonomy granted by Emperor Leopold I in 1690–1691. At times restricted, this autonomy never developed beyond the levels of elementary education and church administration. Moreover, during most of the eighteenth century pressures were exerted for cultural union with the Croatians and for Germanization. The first partition of Poland in 1772, which led to the establishment of a Cyrillic printing press in Vienna primarily on behalf of the Ruthenians, offered the Serbs limited facilities for literary publications also but the basic ideas of the Enlightenment reached the Serbs in Hungary, the Banat, and Dalmatia not from Vienna but from Belgrad. Dosjtije Obradović (around 1740 to 1811), a Serb from the Banat who had studied in Vienna and Halle and was impressed by Joseph II's reforms, established an autonomous educational system under over-all Turkish sovereignty after his return to Old Serbia. The autobiography, letters, and essays on practical enlightened philosophy of this remarkable man could be read only with difficulty in Hungary, because the Old Slavonic Church language was used almost exclusively by the clergy and the idiom of the south Hungarian Serbs did not lend itself as yet to the transmission of complex ideas. Obradović and his followers E. Janković, Bishop Lucian Mušicki of Karlowitz (Carlovci), J. Vujić, and others tried with moderate success to raise the standards of the vernacular by translations from the German and Italian.

Largely due to the influence of Kopitar on his foremost student Vuk Stefanović Karadžić (1787–1864) a better solution was initiated. In 1813, Karadžić, born in Serbia and engaged in various revolutionary activities against the Turks, was forced to flee to Vienna where Kopitar prevailed on him to develop and raise a Southern Serb idiom to the literary language of the great Southern Slav hinterland beyond the Sava. Karadžić wrote a Serb grammar in 1814 and edited his famous collection of folksongs admired by Goethe in the revised language. It represented

[29] Paul Diels, *Die slawischen Vöker mit einer Literaturübersicht von Alexander Adamczyk* (Wiesbaden, 1963), pp. 248–253; Franjo Trograncić, "Literature (18th Century)," in Francis H. Eterovich and Christopher Spalatin, eds., *Croatia,* II, 215–239, and K. B. K., "Literature (1835–1895)," ibid. I, 242–256; Zvanc Črnja, *Cultural History of Croatia* (Zagreb, 1962), pp. 281–321.

essentially a combination of Hercegovinian and southern Dalmatian idioms, written in a simplified Cyrillic alphabet.

Karadžić may indeed be called the initiator of the joint Serbo-Croatian literature of the still distant future. In his time, cultural and political traditions and rivalries, beyond the issue of the Latin versus the Cyrillic alphabet, prevented the early amalgamation of the two languages which might have led to the early evolution of a genuine joint Serbo-Croatian literature. Nevertheless, the principles of a common Serbo-Croatian literary language were recognized by the foremost Southern Slav philologists against much opposition of the orthodox, largely pro-Russian, conservative clergy.

Consequently, the first followers of Karadžić came from Habsburg territories in southern Hungary: Branko Radičević, the lyric poet, and Jovan S. Popović, the playwright, in the first half of the nineteenth century, as well as R. Jovan Jovanović, a lyric poet and journalist in the second half. There existed little doubt that the spectacular success of the Slavic renaissance among the Czechs, Polish Messianism, and New Hellenism, all had the effect of strengthening the forces of romantic and gradually liberal nationalism against cultural isolation and an intellectual caste system. Above all, the revised and elevated idioms of the people had prevailed against a decaying and sterile Church language. In fact the new spirit with its double appeal to romantics and liberals initiated by Karadžić was strong enough to give to the Hungarian Vojvodina well into the 1870's the character of an enclave of Serb literary nationalism. The activities of the secret nationalist youth organization *Omladina* until its dissolution in 1872 [30] were particularly significant. Only the establishment of a fully sovereign Serbia in 1878 moved the center of gravity of Serb cultural activities toward the newly strengthened political center.

Major intellectual steps toward this situation had gone on for a century. Their limited success revealed the difficulties resulting from an oppressive and divisive political past. Yet something else became clear: the substantial political achievements brought about by the challenge of a great cultural problem fought against enormous odds.[31]

[30] A dissolution brought about by the anti-Slavic oriented Hungarian government with obliging assistance from the conservative Turkish vassal government in Belgrad.

[31] Ernest Denis, *La Grande Serbie* (Paris, 1915), pp. 86–93; Paul Diels and Alexander Adamczyk, *Die lawischen Völker* (Wiesbaden, 1963), pp. 251–253; Pypin and Spasovič, *Geschichte der slawischen Literaturen,* I, 263–312; Duncan Wilson, *The Life and Time of Vuk S. Karadžić* (Oxford, 1970), pp. 190–313.

H. The Latins

The Italians and Roumanians, separated from each other by the whole length of the Habsburg empire from west to east, had few cultural relations and those that existed were hardly based on ethnic affinity.[32] Affinity was limited in any case by the Slavic streak within the Rumanian nation. They shared the fact, that their cultural history within the Habsburg empire was to a greater degree determined by their conationals across the Habsburg borders than was true of other groups in a seemingly similar position such as the Poles, Ruthenians, and Serbs. The Serbs could develop some limited autonomous cultural life in Hungary before that chance was given to them in Serbia proper. The Poles represented (at least after 1867–1868) a powerful political force within the empire. Even though the cultural center gradually had become Congress Poland again, the weight of the Austrian Poles was bound to be felt within the intellectual life of the whole nation. The Ruthenians went through a different political, religious, and linguistic history than most of the Ukrainian nation. This factor, too, gave their cultural life within the empire considerable significance. Regarding the Italians, the cultural impact of the nation state south of the Trentino and west of the Adriatic was so overwhelmingly powerful, that even the most active cultural life of the Austro-Italians counted relatively little within the Italian cultural body. The Roumanians were a politically suppressed national group in Transylvania, legally until 1863 and practically again after 1867. This was not true to the same degree in the Bukovina, yet here they were slightly outnumbered by the Ruthenians. Furthermore, the history of a permanent separate administration of the crownland goes back only to 1849. Considering these factors it is amazing how diverse Roumanian cultural life in the empire was, even though it too could reflect only its secondary aspects.

a) THE ITALIANS

An active center of Italian enlightened reform ideas existed in Rovereto, where a learned academy was established in 1750. An eminent professor of natural law and member of the legal codification commission under Maria Theresa, Carl Anton von Martini (1726–1800), came from this region. Complete assimilation became so easy for him as for

[32] It might be noted in passing that Morlaks, a group of Roumanian ethnic stock had settled in the Middle Ages in northern Dalmatia. By the eighteenth century they had become completely slavicized, however.

many other distinguished Italians at the center of the imperial administration, that his Italian background was forgotten. Girolamo Tartarotti, his contemporary, remained in the Trentino and became an advocate of legal reforms in the spirit of Beccaria. One of the most interesting personalities in the Rovereto circle was Count Antonio Rosmini-Serbati (1797–1855). A priest, equally versed in philosophy and theology, he was for a time minister of education in the papal state under Pius IX. Rosmini developed an original philosophical system, which tried to combine features of an idealistic and a Cartesian philosophy. In 1849 this doctrine was put on the Index, though by the end of the century it was finally cleared. As for literature, Giovanni Prati (1815–1884), a notable lyric poet and writer of novellas, changed his loyalties from Habsburg to Savoy. Andreas Maffei (1797–1855) became an outstanding translator of Schiller, Goethe, and Milton.

Concerning Dalmatia, the impact of the Italian minority on various aspects of Southern Slav culture, in particular Croatian, had been great throughout the late Middle Ages and early Modern Times. Beginning with the Enlightenment Italian influence declined, although traces were still marked in the nineteenth century, such as those shown by the linguist Tommaseo of Sebenico (1802–1874). When he became involved in anti-Austrian revolutionary activities he had to leave the country. In the Littoral, Capo d'Istria was an Italian cultural center like Rovereto in the Trentino, and in 1793 an academy was established there too. Interests were focused on social reforms. The southward orientation of Italian cultural life in Austria was not only a consequence of the general unification drive but also of the lack of Italian institutions of higher education in the Habsburg empire after 1866. The universities of Padua and Milan, particularly the latter, had been centers of anti-Habsburg activities as long as they were under Austrian administration. The establishment of an Italian university on Austrian soil after 1866, if operated in a free atmosphere of learning, might well have eased the development of irredentism. Alienated Austro-Italian students might have modified their feelings if given the chance to study at an Italian university in their home country. The shortsightedness of the government, but above all German nationalist tendencies prevented this. There was, indeed, little middle ground between integral nationalism and more or less deliberate denationalization, that is, Italian cultural activities of outright irredentist character and those contributions of Italians which merged completely with the central governmental political and educational structure.[33]

[33] Fortunat Demattio, "Italienische Literatur," in [Crownprince Rudolf] *Die*

b) THE ROUMANIANS

The rise of the status of the Roumanians in Transylvania was chiefly related to two events: the introduction of a Uniate Church at the end of the seventeenth century and the conferral of citizenship status on them almost a century later under Joseph II. Both actions helped the suppressed serfs to strengthen their national consciousness. Even though this slow evolution fell short of the attainment of equality with the Magyars, Szekels, and Germans, the member groups of the estates in the three-nation state, these modest concessions sufficed to lay the groundwork for a vigorous evolution of national culture. The Vienna-educated Uniate priest, and subsequently bishop, George Șincai, and his nephew Samuel Klein were coauthors of a new Roumanian grammar *The Element of the Dacian-Roman or Wallach language*. Klein who also had received his theological training in the Uniate seminary in Vienna, edited also a prayer book in the language revised according to the principles of the new grammar. Petru Maior (1754–1821), likewise a Uniate priest, went an important step further in his effort to establish the national identity of the underprivileged Transylvanian Vlachs. After the publication of his sermons his *History of the Origin of the Roumanians in Dacia* came out in 1812. Based in part on previous studies by Șincai this book was indeed a pioneer work of Roumanian national history.[34] George Baritiu (1812–1893), also a historian, became the editor of the first Roumanian-language journal in Transylvania (1838). August Trebonia Laurian (1810–1881) and Nicolas Bălşescu (1819–1852), as early as the 1840's, were editors of a historical journal. Alexander Odobescu (1834–1895) was a distinguished archeologist. Most of these men had a distinctly anti-Magyar orientation, but shared a limited trust in the Austrian government until 1848–1849. Their gradual disappointment in the 1850's and 1860's was one reason why the eminent Roumanian cultural leader, the archbishop Andrei Șaguna (1809–1873), head of the Orthodox Church in Transylvania, stood for a cautious policy of reconciliation with the Magyars. It met considerable opposition among the Roumanians. Yet in several ways the government in Budapest had more reasons to accommodate the Orthodox with

österreichisch-ungarische Monarchie, Vol. *Tirol und Vorarlberg,* pp. 402–416; Anton Zernitz, "Italienische Literatur," in Vol. *Küstenland,* pp. 249–256; Alfred Mussafia, "Italienische Literatur," in Vol. *Dalmatien,* pp. 213–231.

[34] Dacia is generally to be understood as the area of the former Roman province between Tisza river in the west, Carpathians in the north, the Dnjester in the east and the Danube to the south. This territory thus covers only very roughly the Roumanian ethnic area.

their wide backing in the Slavic world to the east than the Uniates. Considerable concessions in regard to Church autonomy and lesser concessions in the Nationality Law of 1868 were made. The prestige of the archbishop, in some ways a parallel figure to that of Strossmayer among the Croats, helped to keep Roumanian policies in Translyvania on an even keel. Şaguna's cultural contributions, in particular the establishment of the journal *Transylvania* for the cultivation of the Roumanian language and literature were instrumental in strengthening national consciousness in an era of steady political oppression.

There was less oppression in the Bukovina. Here Jon Budai-Deleanu (1760–1820) published a Roumanian-German dictionary and a grammar as early as 1805. In 1848, a newspaper was founded in the capital Czernowitz (Cernăuti), a literary journal in 1865. Eudoxious Hurmuzaki (1812–1874) was a historian, well able to handle the medieval sources of Roumanian national history. Roumanian and Ruthenian national cultural progress in the Bukovina suffered indirectly, however, from the German domination of intellectual life, particularly in the capital and the new university founded in Czernowitz in 1875. Apart from the training facilities in theology for the orthodox priesthood it could be called a German institution. Without overt pressure it became clear to young intellectuals in the Bukovina, that a career in the free professions and in government service was easier in the German language orbit than in the Roumanian, whose national base in the Bukovina was much smaller than in Transylvania. Limitations in numbers worked directly as much against the Roumanians here as outright political oppression there. In the light of these difficulties Roumanian cultural progress was indeed impressive.[85]

I. Summary

All things considered cultural life among the national groups of the Habsburg empire had made astounding progress in the era that leads from the Enlightenment to liberalism. For the Austro-Germans it was, of course, easier than for any other national group, except possibly the Italians, to establish a working two-way cultural communications system with the wide German hinterland. Even here the consequences of cultural isolation before the Enlightenment were fully overcome only at the be-

[85] Nicolai Jorga, *Histoire des Roumains de Transylvanie et de Hongrie,* 2 vols. (Bucharest, 1915–1916), see II, 173–305; Johann Sbiera, "Die rumänische Literatur und Sprache," in [Crownprince Rudolf] *Die österreichisch-ungarische Monarchie,* Vol. *Bukowina,* pp. 376–393; Constantin Daicoviciu and Miron Constantinescu, *Brève Histoire de la Transylvanie* (Bucharest, 1965), pp. 326–343; Cornelia Bodea, *The Roumanians' Struggle for Unification, 1834–1839* (Bucharest, 1970), pp. 31–63; Ladislas Makkai, *Histoire de Transylvanie* (Paris, 1946), pp. 284–299.

ginning of the nineteenth century. This did not pertain to the same extent to the Italians, where the cultural community preceded the political union all throughout modern and in part even medieval history. As for the Magyars, the limited range of their language orbit represented a serious impediment. Nevertheless they had become as fully associated with western European literature in the Romantic era as the Poles. In the nineteenth century the Roumanians too had reached a similar stage of literary development in their relations to the west. The linguistic premises for such breakthrough had become fully effective by 1848.

The same had indeed become gradually true for all Slavic national groups in the Habsburg empire. Because of the differences in specific social and political conditions of national groups, their cultural achievements can neither be standardized nor truly compared. It can be said, however, that by mid-nineteenth century, under the powerful impact of the Slavic renaissance, they all had achieved a level of linguistic development which placed intellectual accomplishment within reach, although on political grounds not necessarily within early realization.

The discussion ot one general problem should conclude this chapter: the question of the influence of the cultural achievements of one group within the empire on all others. Only for the Germans was such influence uncontested on an empire-wide scale. A direct impact of Czech on Slovak civilization and of Polish on the superstructure of the Ruthenians is as discernible (though not always as clearly) as for instance that of the Italians on the Croats. But above all the three Southern Slav groups, Croats, Serbs, and Slovenes, each in its own way, shaped general Southern Slav developments. Other influences existed, such as those radiating from and into the Magyar orbit. Yet they were primarily indirect and, in part, imposed on politically weaker national groups. This, of course, is true for the Germans as well. But unlike the German impact, such influences were not outright accepted or rejected but rather digested without specific intent in the course of times. Much of this kind of development can be seen between Magyars on one side and Slovaks and Transylvanian Roumanians on the other. Beyond this, the fascinating problem of cultural interaction between national groups pertains only to the more recent stages of their development. By mid-nineteenth century a process of mutual give and take had become fully conscious in regard to all groups, although it did not take place necessarily on an equal footing. The question will be taken up in the final chapter of this study in regard to the cultural-intellectual development during the last half-century of the empire's existence.

CHAPTER VIII

Decline and Discord (1879-1914)

A. Politics in Austria-Hungary

a) foreign policy

The day after the conclusion of the Austro-German alliance of 1879 Count Andrássy resigned as foreign minister, largely because he had antagonized the German, and particularly the Magyar, liberals and nationalists with the Bosnian occupation. Moreover, although the crown had approved the Austro-German alliance, the emperor still considered it humiliating to have to coordinate his policy from now on with that of Bismarck's Germany, the power in the center of the continental political stage. Andrássy's successor, Baron Heinrich Haymerle, his former aide, was committed to continue this foreign policy. After his sudden death in 1881 he was succeeded by Count Gustav Kálnoky, former ambassador in St. Petersburg, who until his resignation in May, 1895, over an issue of Church prerogatives versus Magyar liberalism pursued a more independent policy. Faithful to the German alliance, but anxious to preserve Austria-Hungary's freedom of action in the Balkans and in particular in relations with Russia, he did not succeed fully in either respect.

The situation faced by Andrássy's successors was focused primarily on the Habsburg empire's relations to Russia, which had been strained from the beginning of the Oriental crisis in 1876 and had certainly not improved after the Congress of Berlin of 1878. In the 1880's, a conservative-inspired Panslav nationalism developed at an accelerated pace in Russia. It was favored by the new tsar Alexander III, who unlike his father assassinated in March, 1881, was neither anxious to preserve cordial relations with Germany nor to keep those with Austria at least on an even keel. The chief battleground between Austria and Russia was the Balkans, as hotly contested spheres of interest of both countries. Here Austria could expect little direct benefit from the German alliance. In his famous Reichstag speech of December, 1888, Bismarck had made it clear that the whole Balkan problem was not worth the sacrifice of the straight limbs of a single Prussian grenadier. The best means to protect and to restrain Austria seemed to him to bring her and Russia to an understanding based on the foundation of monarchic solidarity. This was the premise of the so-called Alliance of the Three Emperors of June, 1881, concluded for three years and renewed for another three years in 1884.

The term "alliance" for the interrelationship between the three empires —in contrast to the genuine Austro-German alliance of 1879—was a euphemistic misnomer because Russia would never have been willing to enter into far-reaching commitments with Austria. Neither would the Austro-German alliance in case of strong Austro-Russian ties have preserved its raison d'être. The covenant was no more than a neutrality agreement between the three powers, which agreed furthermore to consult if the territorial status of Turkey should be threatened. The principle of the closure of the Dardanelles was recognized as well as the Austrian claim to convert the occupation of Bosnia-Hercegovina into permanent annexation.[1] The union between Bulgaria, still a Turkish satellite state, and the autonomous Turkish province East Roumelia was recognized in principle. Since Austria thus seemed safe for the time being from a confrontation with Russia she could afford to reach a profitable agreement of ten years duration with Serbia, whose conclusion was facilitated by liberal subsidies for the absentee sovereign, King Milan. Austria promised to support eventual Serbian expansion in the south, while Serbia pledged even to conclude no agreements with other powers without Austria's approval. Thus the Habsburg empire's predominance in the western Balkans seemed to be well secured.

The conversion of the Austro-German Dual Alliance of 1879 into the Austro-German-Italian Triple Alliance of May, 1882, was meant by Bismarck primarily to strengthen the protection of Germany's western and southern flanks in case of a two-front war with Russia and France. An important secondary objective of this genuine but shaky alliance was to check Italy's designs to liberate at the appropriate time the eastern coast of the Adriatic and the Trentino. This Bismarck strategem, applied

[1] This agreement, which lapsed in 1887, did not preclude the necessity for the approval of the other signatory powers of the Congress Act of 1878.

repeatedly—namely to turn mutual enemies into friends by joining them as junior partners in an alliance—worked no better than the Austro-German-Russian associations, namely the Three Emperors' League of 1873 and the so called Three Emperors' Alliance of 1881 in regard to Austro-Russian relations.

The Triple Alliance of 1882 between Austria, Germany, and Italy, it is true, offered much protection to Italy against a French attack but little additional security to her allies. Germany was hardly in need of Italian support against France. Only in case of the involvement of Austria and Germany in a two-front war against Russia and France could the Italian alliance be of possible use. Yet even this depended on the doubtful assumption of Italian military proficiency and on the reliability of Italy's loyalty to the treaty. Neither Bismarck nor Kálnoky was blind to these facts but they hoped that even a dubious ally was better than a country without commitments that could be won over easily to an opposing camp. Furthermore the very fact of the alliance might put an end to the covert support of Italian irredentist activities in Austria.

A secret alliance with Roumania, concluded in October, 1883, against Russia,[2] soon joined by Germany and Italy, was no more successful. This agreement was based more or less on the two eyes of the Hohenzollern king of Roumania, Carol I, whose loyalty to the Central European powers could be relied on. Although the Roumanians resented the forced cession of southern Bessarabia to Russia in 1878, they were even more interested in the liberation of the Roumanians in Transylvania and Bukovina. This national priority was in part due to the fact, that Austria-Hungary was not as strong a power as Russia. Considering further the French orientation of the ruling classes in Roumania, lack of popular support for this secret alliance was so clearly predictable, that its public disclosure was impossible, despite continuous Austrian and German pressure. Thus the assumption that Roumania would honor a treaty concluded with the lesser evil (Austria) rather than with the bigger one (Russia) because a feeble covenant was better than none, proved to be illusionary.

During the following four years, critical ones in the relationship between the Central European powers and Russia, the effectiveness of the new lineup of alliances was tested. In September, 1885 a revolt in East Roumelia began with the aim to unite the province with Bulgaria. Within

[2] The terms of the treaty did not mention Russia, but the meaning of the alliance was unmistakable.

a year this move succeeded. Its immediate consequences were a Bulgarian conflict with Serbia, in which the advance of Bulgarian troops under the command of the new Bulgarian sovereign Alexander, Prince of Battenberg, was stopped only by an Austrian ultimatum. This was the first in a series of similar Austrian interventions in Balkan affairs but this first time—ironically enough—initiated on Serbia's behalf.

Tsar Alexander III opposed the rule of Alexander of Battenberg, a prince with English dynastic connections, who appeared to him too independent, too liberal, and too western. In the fall of 1886 a Russian-sponsored officers' revolt removed Alexander and restored Russian more or less indirect overlordship in Bulgaria, stepping up the Austro-Russian crisis. The *casus foederis* could now arise for Germany to support Austria over a Balkan issue—the kind of conflict Bismarck wanted to avoid at all costs.

He believed he could do so by assuaging Austria's and—secretly—Russia's concerns as well, but above all to keep his hands at the steering wheel of the Triple Alliance. In early February, 1886, he encouraged Austria's adherence to a British-sponsored agreement of the Mediterranean powers with the exception of France. The declared objective was to maintain the status quo in the Mediterranean and indirectly to block French intentions in regard to Egypt and Russian designs to force the openings of the Dardanelles. Likewise in February, the Triple Alliance was renewed and in view of the critical situation in the Balkans Italy was able to raise her price for further adherence to the treaty: a qualified pledge on the part of the Central European powers to support Italian interests in North Africa against France and—more important for Austria—an agreement that any expansion in the Balkans would entitle the partner to territorial compensations.[3] This concession to future Italian aspirations in the Balkans limited Austria's freedom of action.

Bismark was not naïve enough to put all his policy eggs in the basket of an increasingly illusionary monarchical solidarity of the three eastern empires. He was concerned with a rapid deterioration of German-French relations, due primarily to the unexpectedly fast recovery of France after 1870–1871. More specific issues for the approaching crisis were the dictatorial aspirations of the chauvinist French minister of war, General Boulanger. A frontier incident provoked by Germany in

[3] Exempted from this concession was the conversion of the status of Bosnia-Hercegovina from an occupied to an annexed province. Such change would not entitle Italy to compensatory claims.

Alsace-Lorraine added fuel to the fire. In consideration of such factors Bismarck now moved to direct negotiations with Russia, embodied in the famous secret Reinsurance Treaty of June, 1887.

The first part of the treaty pledged mutual neutrality between Germany and Russia in case of conflict with other powers. Excepted from this obligation were aggressive wars on the part of Germany against France or of Russia against Austria. To put it in other words, Germany was not obliged to support her ally, Austria, in an offensive war against Russia. The determination of what constituted aggression was to be left to the contracting parties. Much has been written on the question, whether this agreement was compatible with the Austro-German alliance of 1879. As far as the letter of the treaty goes, the answer should clearly be in the affirmative. Since the alliance of 1879 was defensive in character, the new German pledge did not conflict with it directly. In regard to the spirit of the agreement we face another problem. The question concerning the differences between offensive and defensive wars appeared even more controversial than it is today. Furthermore, the secrecy of the agreement suggested that Bismarck wanted it to be interpreted entirely according to German interests. This meant in regard to the Balkan questions, to curb Austrian aspirations. As it turned out, if that policy would have been consistently adhered to up to and including the July crisis of 1914, the treaty could have been as much in Austria's as in Germany's interest.

Far less commented on in historical literature was the second part of the agreement, in which Bismarck without knowledge of his Austrian ally promised to recognize a predominant Russian sphere of interests in Bulgaria as well as diplomatic support for Russia's intent to open the Straits. Inasmuch as he prevailed on Austria in December, 1887, to sign a second Mediterranean agreement with Italy and Great Britain, whose objective was to preserve Turkey's control of the Dardanelles and noninterference in Bulgarian affairs, this part of the Reinsurance Treaty represented a clear case of duplicity. At the same time, to pacify Austria's feelings, aroused by Bismarck's refusal to support her openly in Balkan affairs, he agreed to a publication of the Austro-German alliance treaty of 1879. By this time, however, its existence was hardly a secret to the European cabinets. In fact there is good reason to believe that the Austrians suspected the existence of the Reinsurance Treaty as well. Yet for the time being further escalation of the crisis was averted, and with the fall of Bismarck from power in March, 1890, the new German emperor Wilhelm II allowed the Reinsurance Treaty to lapse.

Eastern affairs quieted down briefly and the new prince of Bulgaria,

Ferdinand of Koburg, a former Austrian officer, was recognized by Russia in 1896. In 1897 and 1903 Austria and Russia arrived at agreements to preserve the status quo in the Balkans. At the same time the Ottoman empire was urged to introduce reforms in Macedonia, which should forestall actions by the Balkan states. This was an implied warning to them not to interfere as long as Russia was engaged in other affairs—meaning in particular the impending Russo-Japanese war of 1904–1905.[4]

Seen in a larger frame, political developments appeared ominous enough. The conclusion of the Franco-Russian alliance in 1894, the Franco-British entente in 1904, and the first Morocco crisis of 1905–1906, in which Germany and Austria stood isolated, were major warnings. Added to them must be developments in the western Balkans. In 1889, the corrupt Serbian king Milan, subsidized by Austria, had died, an event which moved Austro-Serbian affairs into less tranquil waters. A pro-Russian nationalist faction in Serbia gained steadily against one in favor of cooperation with Austria. This change of balance paralleled shifts among the Southern Slavs in the Habsburg empire, where political leadership moved gradually from still pro-Habsburg Croatian political direction to the Serbs, who favored secession and the establishment of a Yugoslav state under Serb leadership. These were hopes for the future and not yet definitive political action plans but in June, 1903, the young king Alexander and his consort were brutally murdered by an officers' conspiracy. The replacement of the basically pro-Austrian Obrenovich dynasty by the head of the nationalist and pro-Panslav (pro-Russian) house of Karadjordjevic under Peter I, changed the balance of power in the Balkans, and soon in Europe. From here on not only Serbian national sentiments but Serbian foreign policy became openly hostile to the Habsburg monarchy.

Austria's foreign policy did little to counteract these feelings. On the contrary, a short-sighted economic embargo for the import of Serbian pigs and grain, primarily in the interest of Magyar aristocratic estates owners, aggravated the conflict. It was sharpened further by extreme Austro-German and Magyar nationalism. In October, 1906, the Austrian foreign minister, Count Goluchowski (1895–1906) resigned. He had tried to maintain friendly relations with Russia and thereby indirectly

[4] See William L. Langer, *European Alliances and Alignments* (New York, 1931), pp. 204–250, 323–363. Allan J. P. Taylor, *The Struggle for Mastery in Europe* (Oxford, 1957), pp. 304–325, 370–372; Sidney B. Fay, *The Origins of the World War* (New York, 1938), I, 71–96, 141–151, 354–361. F. R. Bridge, *From Sadowa to Sarajevo: The Foreign Policy of Austria-Hungary, 1866–1914* (London, 1972), pp. 211–277.

with Serbia and was therefore accused by one group of slighting Magyar interests, by another of being too obliging to them. The first group, represented primarily by Magyar aristocrats, argued that Goluchowski had not done enough to represent their economic interests in the economic warfare with Serbia. The second faction was led by the ultraconservative heir apparent Archduke Francis Ferdinand who, opposed to the Magyar establishment, could never quite swallow the terms of the Compromise of 1867. He favored the reestablishment of a centralized empire to be made more acceptable to the Slavs by some limited federalist dressings.

Goluchowski was replaced by an activist foreign minister, the ambassador in St. Petersburg, Count (then Baron) Aerenthal. Worse, a new chief of general staff, General Conrad von Hötzendorf, was appointed a month later at the behest of Archduke Francis Ferdinand. As soon became apparent, he interfered with the direction of foreign policy. His talents as military organizer and strategist could not make up for the fact that here an outright champion of preventive war came into high office. His views ran counter to those of the heir apparent, who had recommended Conrad's appointment on the strength of his military qualifications but not on account of his previously little known political opinions on foreign policy. Conrad believed the difficulties of the monarchy could be solved in good time, namely by a "blood and iron" policy. While his agitation for a preventive war against Serbia and Italy was not immediately successful, the steady demand for action had an emasculating effect on the supporters of a more cautious wait-and-see attitude, until this general, one of the foremost gravediggers of the Habsburg monarchy, finally had his ill-fated way.

Aerenthal, a more sophisticated man than Conrad, was not prepared to advocate preventive war. Unlike the chief of staff he understood that such action might easily lead to a general European conflagration. Yet he, too, believed that some, though more limited, risks had to be taken in an increasingly critical situation. In 1907–1908 he first attempted to strengthen the Austrian position in the western Balkans by promoting a railway project through the Sanjak to Salonika, the chief port in the northern Aegean Sea. Although this scheme presented no threat of war, it indicated a change of the status quo in the Balkans and was objected to by Russia and seen with concern by Britain. Threatening friction with Russia seemed not worth the price, and the Aerenthal plan was dropped but suspicion remained. Soon a new and greater crisis appeared. In July, 1908, the Young Turkish nationalist revolution succeeded in transforming the Ottoman empire, at least on paper, into a constitutional monarchy, proclaimed earlier in 1876 but never carried out. This could have been interpreted to mean that the premises of the Austrian occupation, agreed upon at the Congress of Berlin in 1878, were obsolete. The sultan, still in theory the suzerain of Bosnia-Hercegovina, as from now on allegedly constitutional ruler, could demand restoration of his full sovereign rights in the provinces.

It is doubtful that the Turks would have succeeded by an appeal to the signatory powers of the Congress act to have the occupation terminated. Aerenthal's design to change the occupation into annexation used the revolutionary change in Turkey rather as a convenient pretext. He was more afraid of Southern Slav, particularly Serb, irredentist propaganda in the kingdom, as well as in the occupied provinces and in Croatia. He believed that only annexation could lay the ghost of a Yugoslav state including the Austrian-Hungarian Southern Slav territories. Beyond this he felt that only energetic action on the part of the Habsburg monarchy could dispel the notion of the empire as the second sick man in Europe, whose dismemberment would follow soon after that of Turkey. In this sense his course of action, motivated by understandable concern, represented also a prestige policy. Starting from the assumption that Russia so soon after her defeat in the Far East would not be able to counter an Austrian move backed by German force, he considered the risk of a major conflagration as remote.

Aerenthal played his hands too adroitly. In an entrevue with the Russian foreign secretary Izvolski in mid-September, 1908, in the castle of Buchlau in Moravia, owned by the then Austrian ambassador to St. Petersburg, Count Berchtold, he informed Izvolski of the Austrian intention to change the status of Bosnia-Hercegovina. In return for assurances of Russian acquiescence he promised that Austria would not oppose the opening of the Dardanelles to Russian warships. The Austrian and Russian versions of the conversation are in conflict. According to Izvolski Aerenthal had obscured the fact that the proclamation of the annexation should take place in a matter of weeks. The Austrian foreign minister was unable to repudiate this charge convincingly. On October 6 the annexation of Bosnia-Hercegovina was proclaimed and a feeble constitution, not to say mock constitution, was granted to the provinces. Since no agreement could be reached between Austria and Hungary, in whose territory Bosnia-Hercegovina should have been incorporated, the provinces were to be a condominium of the dual states under the continued administration of the joint minister of finance. As sop to the Turks the evacuation of Austrian troops from the Sanjak was announced at the same time. One day earlier Prince Ferdinand of Bulgaria had proclaimed the severence of the last ties of his country, including Eastern Roumelia, with the Ottoman empire and the acceptance of the proud title of tsar. The timing was shrewdly chosen by Ferdinand, because attention of the great powers would now be fully occupied by the Austrian move and, besides, the Habsburg monarchy would presumably be charged falsely to have initiated the Bulgarian move.

Ferdinand proved to be right. The Austrian annexation, which in no way changed the balance of power in Europe, escalated into a major international crisis. Serbia saw her hopes to establish a Yugoslav empire in the future delayed or shattered. Her government now initiated a passionate campaign of irredentist propaganda linked with warlike threats against Austria. In doing so Serbia had the full propagandist and diplomatic support of Russia and also in a more moderate way that of Britain. Here the fact that in August, 1907 Russia, France's ally, had become also the third partner in the Anglo-French entente—now the Triple Entente—bore fruit for the first time. The Turks were likewise upset, and with legal justification, because the Austrian decision should have been taken only with the consent of all signatories of the Congress Act of Berlin, that is the great powers and Turkey, but not Serbia. Beyond the merits of the case, a major test of strength between the Triple Alliance (actually only the Central Powers) and the Triple Entente was now brewing. Austria yielded in part, at least in regard to her least dangerous opponent, Turkey. In December, 1908, Austria agreed to pay compensation to the Ottoman empire. This did not stop Serbian propaganda and even military preparations backed by Russia. The tsarist government felt doubly betrayed because the Austrian promise to support the opening of the Dardanelles to the Russian navy proved to be worthless in the face of Franco-British opposition to such change. Thus the crisis deepened. Finally in March, 1909, Austria presented an ultimatum to Serbia demanding demobilization and recognition of the annexation under threat of military action. At the same time the German government requested Russia to abandon her support of Serbia, unless she wanted to risk war with Germany. Russia, still weakened by the consequences of the war against Japan, had to back down; this meant that Serbia had to accept the humiliating Austrian ultimatum. Austria-Hungary got away with her violation of the Congress Act of Berlin. Backed by Germany she had secured a major diplomatic victory.

Yet if there ever was a clear case of a Pyrrhic victory, this was an example. Austria had not increased her military power potential. According to some she had actually weakened it by abandoning the Sanjak, although military opinion is divided on this point. The hatred of the Serbs increased and the humiliation of Russia meant that the ruling tsarist regime could not survive another major diplomatic defeat. Unfortunately, the most influential diplomatic and military dignitaries of the Central Powers drew the opposite conclusion. They believed, if Russia had backed down once she would do so again—namely in the July crisis of 1914. Added to this wrong calculation must be the fact, that the annexation accentuated the Southern Slav problem in the Habsburg monarchy further. Thus, Aerenthal's prestige success, anchored primarily in German support, meant that the international crisis as well as the national crisis in the Habsburg monarchy had increased.[5]

With the second Moroccan crisis and the Tripolitanian war by Italy against Turkey in 1911 the international situation deteriorated further. Worse was to come. The outbreak of the first Balkan war in October, 1912, seemed to indicate that the soon to be expected demise of the first sick man in Europe, Turkey, would lead to that of the second, Austria. The liberation of the remaining Slavs in the Ottoman empire would be followed soon by that of the Southern Slavs in the Habsburg monarchy. By this time an unhappy change in the diplomatic command post had taken place. Aerenthal had died in February, 1912, and was replaced by Count Leopold Berchtold, ambassador to the tsar. Although Aerenthal had taken too many risks, he was a circumspect diplomat. He was a man of strong character, who had stood up in 1911 to Conrad's preventive war policy and had forced his resignation. Berchtold was an amiable aristocrat, a man of diplomatic routine, anxious to please and always ready to march with the stronger battalions. Although Conrad was returned to office in 1912, these stronger battalions were still led by the heir apparent, Archduke Francis Ferdinand. He was strongly opposed to any war that could lead to a confrontation with Russia and the revolutionary overthrow of

[5] Bernadotte Schmitt, *The Annexation of Bosnia, 1908–1909* (Cambridge, 1909), passim; Hugo Hantsch, *Leopold Graf Berchtold,* 2 vols. (Vienna, 1963), see I, 115–179; Heinrich Kanner, *Kaiserliche Katastrophenpolitik* (Vienna, 1922), pp. 36–58; Alfred F. Pribram, *Austrian Foreign Policy, 1908–1918* (London, 1923), pp. 24–33; Alexander Musulin, *Das Haus am Ballplatz* (Munich, 1924), pp. 153–171. See also István Diószegi in Fritz Klein, ed., *Österreich-Ungarn in der Weltpolitik* (Berlin, 1965), pp. 230–249; Bridge, *From Sadowa to Sarajevo,* pp. 288–336; Fritz Fellner, *Der Dreibund* (Vienna, 1960), pp. 50–82.

the Habsburg and Romanov dynasties. Just because the opposition to war by this autocrat was not based on humanitarian reasons but on dynastic interests, he had great influence even on the aloof emperor, who was, to say the least, not well disposed to him.

The first Balkan war of 1912–1913—that of a coalition of Bulgaria, Serbia, Greece, and Montenegro against Turkey—ended with the defeat of the Ottoman empire. It was now practically pushed out of Europe. In the second war, the victors, joined by Roumania, coalesced against their former ally, unhappy Bulgaria, whose spoils were considered inordinate. Serbia had been blocked by Austria and Italy from access to the Adriatic, and Greece from the acquisition of southern Albania, but Bulgaria at least was expected to surrender most of her gains to the coalition. The coalition won an easy victory on a three-pronged attack. The major part of Macedonia was now shared by Serbia and Greece, which also gained most of the Aegean coast held by Bulgaria, while Roumania, in possession of the major part of the Dobrudja since 1878, acquired its southern territory now as well. Turkey, which had attacked Bulgaria in a separate campaign in a fourth theater of war, regained Adrianople. From the viewpoint of the Danube monarchy this outcome of the Balkan wars was devastating, except that Austria, this time supported by Italy, had managed to bar Serbia from access to the Adriatic by carrying out Berchtold's pet project, the creation of a supposedly independent but actually at that time not viable Albania. The creation of this satellite state alienated Greece and infuriated Serbia, which had increased in size but had been barred from its justified objective, access to the sea. Even this result was only achieved by two ultimata threatening Serbia and Montenegro with war, if they would not evacuate the Albanian coast. This dangerous device placed the Habsburg monarchy in the eyes of Europe in the role of the big bully. As usual when a big power faces a small one, provocations by the latter were conveniently ignored.

The question may well be asked what risk Austria would have taken if she had allowed Serbia to gain access to the Adriatic. It would have been naïve to assume that such concession would have ended the activities of a government-sponsored Serbian irredentism against the monarchy. On the other hand the moderates in the Serbian government and parliament were not anxious for a confrontation with the big neighbor whose defeat in a major European war could be brought about only at enormous losses to their country. Austrian acquiescence in the acquisition of an Adriatic port by Serbia, linked to an end of the embargo against Serbian agricultural products, might have helped to preserve peace for a period and to gain time.[6] And gaining time, when the explosion of a powder keg threatens, may mean gaining everything.[7]

To Conrad and Berchtold, the former anxious to unloosen the hounds of preventive war, the latter equally concerned not to get into open conflict with either the peace or war party, such considerations were out of the question. The alternatives presented to both men, as they saw it with their limited outlook, were the following: war followed by the dismemberment of Serbia among her neighbors, an economic satellite relationship of the kingdom to Austria-Hungary, or—the course preferred for the time being by Berchtold—to wait and see which way things were going and therupon to set sails to the stronger winds at court. Berchtold did not have to wait long. On June 28, the heir apparent Archduke Francis Ferdinand and his consort were shot in Sarajevo. The perpetrator, like his fellow conspirators, was a Bosnian youth of Serb origin, armed in Belgrad. When he pulled the trigger, history took a decisive turn.

It cannot be the purpose of this study, limited to Austrian history, to offer a detailed analysis of the responsibility for the outbreak of the First World War. This would be impossible without discussing the positions and actions of all major and minor powers involved. But as far as the specific case of the Habsburg empire is concerned a few comments should be made. The archduke was inadequately protected on the day he made his official entry as heir apparent into Sarajevo, the capital of Bosnia. Moreover he made his entry on Vidovdan (St. Vitus day), a day of national mourning, namely the anniversary of the battle of Kossovo of 1389, in which Serbia had lost her independence to the Turks. Obviously neither of these facts suffices to explain either the external conditions or the psychological climate of the assassination. They merely helped to set the stage for the preparation of the act. Not even that much of an argument can be made for the frequently advanced thesis that the archduke was chosen as victim because after his accession to the throne he

[6] The embargo of Serbian cattle and pig imports was only slightly modified by a commercial treaty of 1911. Aerenthal failed in essence to overcome the resistance of the Magyar latifundia owners.

[7] Pribram, *Austrian Foreign Policy*, pp. 33–54; Kanner, *Kaiserliche Katastrophenpolitik*, pp. 59–191; Ernst Christian Helmreich, *The Diplomacy of the Balkan Wars 1912–1913* (Cambridge, Mass., 1938), passim; Fay, *The Origins of the World War*, I, 353–546; Leo Valiani, *La Dissoluzione dell' Austria Ungheria* (Milan, 1966), pp. 9–97; see also Robert A. Kann, "Erzherzog Franz Ferdinand und Graf Berchtold als Aussenminister, 1912–1914," in *Mitteilungen des österreichischen Staatsarchivs*, Vol. 22 (1969), 246–279; and by the same author, *Kaiser Franz Joseph und der Ausbruch des Weltkrieges* (Vienna-Cologne, 1969), passim.

would have met the national demands of the empire's Southern Slav peoples within the frame of the monarchy. According to this view this would have taken the wind out of the sails of Serbian nationalism beyond the frontiers. Suppositions of such kind confound anti-Magyarism with pro-Slavism and autocratic rejection of dualism with concern for multinational democracy. The archduke, his prejudices and feudal bearing notwithstanding, was a man of stature. As for his faculties and serious concern for the future of the empire he stood head and shoulders above the slate of imperial princes, and as for intellectual ability this superiority is true in comparison with the old emperor as well. Little was known in his lifetime about his reform plans, and even that little as far as it met demands of national groups was suspected by them on account of the archduke's feudal, autocratic proclivities.

There is, indeed, every reason to believe that Serb nationalism wanted to destroy the archduke, not because he was considered to be a friend of the Southern Slav peoples, but on the contrary because he was feared to become an oppressor of the Serbs. No doubt about it, the Black Hand terrorist organization in Belgrad selected young Bosnians of Serb nationality for the deed. No doubt either that the perpetrators were trained in Serbia with the active participation of Serbian staff officers. Yet whether these officers acted on orders or even with the full knowledge of the Serbian government under Prime Minister Nicholas Pašić, has not been established with certainty to this day and it may be assumed that it never will be. Further actions of the government in Vienna were thus based largely on surmises. In this respect it speaks for the high standards of the civil service tradition in the empire that the Austrian Foreign Ministry official Friedrich von Wiesner, entrusted with the task of investigating these missing links had the courage to say that he had failed to prove their existence.

Not much equally commendable can be said about his superiors. We have within the plethora of true and unrefuted charges in the war-guilt question a firm tool of evidence in the minutes of the joint Council of Ministers including the chief of general staff. After the authorities in Vienna had assured themselves of the unconditional German support in the coming crisis, a support solicited and (contrary to recent largely unproved suggestions) not freely offered, they began to execute their plans. In this respect, it is true, they were, to say the least, in no way discouraged by German diplomatic and military activities.

In the joint Austro-Hungarian Council of Ministers, the chairman, Count Berchtold, deprived now of the support of the most powerful conservative voice in the antiwar faction, the deceased archduke, declared that diplomatic success against Serbia would lead nowhere as shown in the past. It might be necessary now to destroy Serbia as military threat, even though he knew that this course of action could lead to war with Russia. If action would be put off the international situation might deteriorate further. This opinion including demands for the distribution of major portions of Serbian territory in favor of other Balkan nations and frontier rectifications of unspecified extent for the empire was supported by the other ministers and Conrad, and opposed only to some extent by the Hungarian prime minister, Count Tisza. He demanded the transmission of an ultimatum containing harsh but not unacceptable demands rather than outright war against Serbia. He agreed in case of war to the cession of Serbian territory to other Balkan states, but strongly opposed annexation of further Southern Slav land by the monarchy. The views expressed in this council were kept so highly secret that throughout the war Tisza was generally believed to have been the chief warmonger. He fell as the victim to that erroneous charge, when left-wing Magyar revolutionaries killed him in late October, 1918.[8] In a second ministerial council, held on July 19, Tisza yielded. The only—meaningless—concession which he obtained, was the presentation of an ultimatum to Serbia in lieu of immediate military action. Yet it had been determined already that the terms should be drawn up in a way which would make acceptance by the Serbian government virtually impossible. In regard to the partial dismemberment of Serbia and the frontier rectifications in favor of Austria-Hungary in case of a victorious war—and who would think of a different outcome?—most other ministers, supported of course by Conrad, had their way.

The ultimatum with a time limit of merely forty-eight hours submitted on July 23, contained demands in regard to the suppression of Serb propaganda hostile to Austria and the arrest or punishment of those involved in the assassination plot, which were in part clearly incompatible with the Serbian constitution and the very character of a sovereign state. They required suppression of the basic rights of free expression guaranteed by the constitution in Serbia and, as flagrant violation of sovereignty, the participation of Austrian officials in Serbian investigative-judicial proceedings. The Serbian government, after consultation with the Russian, accepted the major part of the Austrian demands, but rejected those

[8] As to the records of the council of joint ministers see Miklos Komjáthy, *Protokolle des gemeinsamen Ministerrates der österreichisch-ungarischen Monarchie (1914–1918)* (Budapest, 1966).

deemed incompatible with her position as a sovereign and constitutional state. The Serbian government proposed, however, to submit the contested Austrian demands to a decision by the International Court in the Hague. As expected Austria ignored this offer and severed diplomatic relations at once. War was declared three days later on July 28.

The holocaust that followed was only partly of Austria's making, since Austria did not want war with Russia and her allies, yet—and that fact hangs heavily in the balance—Austria was ready to risk it. The assurance given to Russia, that the Habsburg empire did not intend to annex Serbian territory, although obviously untrue, changed little. Russia would not have considered this assurance as a sufficient reason to refrain from further action, and the international chain reaction of events made the whole question illusory.

One further question, apart from the responsibility for the assassination, will always remain unanswered. Conrad was deservedly reputed to be an able strategist and tactician; yet at the same time he was an advocate of war and, as far as the preparations for war were concerned, a bungler. Had it been otherwise, the Austrian armed forces might have been ready for action against Serbia at once, not a full month after the tragedy of Sarajevo. Would not in that case the initial shock and the feeling of monarchic solidarity have been strong enough to prevent a military Russian response? We don't know. But we do know that if Conrad had been as competent a chief of staff as he had been reckless for years in counseling the action against Serbia, the chance to avoid the worldwide conflagration might still have existed. As it was, one half of the Austro-Hungarian troops initially mobilized against Serbia had to be redirected against Russia while en route to the Serbian theater of war. Spread of the conflict a month after the assassination was inevitable.

While Conrad's eagerness had a major share in the responsibility for the events that followed, Berchtold's cynical weakness is hardly less to blame; he went to Conrad's side when the curb of the archduke's powerful restraining hand had disappeared. It is difficult also to absolve the old emperor entirely beyond making allowances for his advanced age. The final decision was taken by him and by him alone. Neither enthusiasm for war nor for revenging the death of an unpopular imperial prince played the major part in the minds of Austria's decision-making "elite." It was rather a cynical gamble that to get the crisis over with was preferable to continued crises. A slight chance of survival might be worth taking the supreme risk. No questions were asked, however, what one really could get over with except the old empire itself and how small the impact of the crises endured was in comparison with those to be expected.

In a larger sense, and this may be an unpopular viewpoint, the empire's peoples were not entirely blameless either. In all warring countries people after half a century of peace had forgotten what war meant and how much more atrocious it would be in the future. Germans and Magyars went to war with cheers and considered those opposed to it as traitors. Yet these opponents, Slavs, Italians, Roumanians, socialists across the empire and some liberals, had done too little to make their voices heard during the time of continued crises from 1908 to 1914. All too easily was the excuse accepted by one camp that it had no power, and by the other that one could not foresee what the consequences of the conflagration might be. It was a sad state of affairs when the hopes of peace hinged on a reactionary like the archduke. All this on either side means not bad intent but tragic callousness.

If one blames Austria it must not be forgotten that Russia backed Serbia without obligation by a formal alliance treaty. Russia did so conscious of the likely outcome. With the fullest understanding of Southern Slav nationalisms it must be admitted also that an Austria, which like any other state believed in a right of self-preservation could not meekly accept disintegration. It is true further that previous diplomatic successes forced at the point of a gun had achieved nothing. This failure might serve as extenuating factor for Austria's rejection of the British proposal to take Belgrad as security and then submit the contested issues to arbitration by the other powers. Yet here insufficient military preparation made it doubtful whether Austro-Hungarian forces would have been able to hold Belgrad. Furthermore, the isolation of the two Central Powers in a coming international conference against the Triple Entente and Italy was certain. The latter, the third partner in the Triple Alliance, declared her neutrality on August 3 and soon began to ask for compensation, not primarily in the Balkans but in the Trentino and the Littoral, that is, in Austrian territory.

Yet all the true or alleged wrongs which, the empire's top officials genuinely believed, had been committed against Austria's existence by the Serb and Italian irredenta as well as by the activities of Russian Panslavism directed from St. Petersburg, should have generated the resolve to avoid war at all costs. Defeat by an overpowering alliance against an empire torn by national strife and an ally eventually to be exhausted by the confrontation with superior man- and seapower, and overwhelming economic strength in regard to raw materials was practically inevitable. What other course could have been taken? Hope, however dim, exists as long as life exists, and the hope for accommodation with Austria's enemies in the future could not be dismissed as long as time could be gained. This argument is not based on hindsight but on common sense. It should have been clear even to those in warring camps on both sides who ignored humanitarian considerations.[9]

b) AUSTRO-HUNGARIAN COOPERATION

The operation of the Compromise between the dual states after 1867 led to a strengthening of the Hungarian position and a corresponding weakening of the Austrian. Nevertheless the differences in Austro-Hungarian relations, as they came to the fore, particularly in the prescribed economic negotiations every ten years, did not seriously undermine the structure of the empire in peace time. The transition to a new currency, based entirely on the gold standard, was effected smoothly in 1892. Henceforward the crown replaced the guilder in a relationship of 1: 2. The joint tariff system had to yield gradually to two separate but almost identical systems.[10] Altogether the replacement of the common tariff and the commercial alliance of 1867 by a mere commercial treaty system in 1907, had fewer direct than indirect economic-political consequences. Henceforward the Hungarian government claimed the right to be a party and signatory to international commercial treaties. This might eventually have served as precedent in the conduct of foreign relations in general. The outbreak of the war in 1914 made this danger meaningless in the face of far greater threats. It should be noted also, that despite protracted wrangling between the representatives of the Austrian and Hungarian governments, there was a peaceful adjustment of the quota for joint expenditures by the two states, in 1867 originally 70 per cent to be paid by Austria and 30 per cent by Hungary, and in 1907 63.4 per cent and 36.6 per cent respectively. Finally, the administration of Bosnia-Hercegovina under the supervision of the joint Austro-Hungarian minis-

[9] Pribram, *Austrian Foreign Policy,* pp. 55–67; Kanner, *Kaiserliche Katastrophenpolitik,* pp. 192–346; Fay, *The Origins of the World War,* II, 547–558; Pierre Renouvin, *The Immediate Origins of the War* (New Haven, 1928), pp. 331–355; Hermann Kantorowicz, *Gutachten zur Kriegsschuldfrage 1914* (Frankfurt am Main, 1967), pp. 413–444; Kann, *Kaiser Franz Joseph und der Ausbruch des Weltkrieges;* contrary to the varying opinions cited above, Hugo Hantsch, *Leopold Graf Berchtold,* 2 vols. (Graz, 1963), II, pp. 541–647 and Musulin, *Das Haus am Ballplatz,* pp. 195–248. See also Vladimir Dedijer, *The Road to Sarajevo* (New York, 1966); Fritz Klein in F. Klein, ed., *Österreich-Ungarn in der Welpolitik, 1900–1918,* pp. 155–162; Fritz Fischer, *Der Krieg der Illusionen: Die deutsche Politik von 1911–1914* (Düsseldorf, 1969), pp. 542–585.

[10] The most important of these exceptions became the introduction of a surtax on sugar imports between the two dual states in 1907.

try of common finances did not lead to major friction between the dual states.[11]

More serious were conflicts in the military sphere. Here differences in the Austrian and Hungarian versions of the Compromise provided the Hungarian government with a convenient handle to avoid the passing of the annual quota of draftees in time, as prescribed in the common Defense Law of 1868 (revised 1889). This quota, in line with the population increases, went steadily up, so the Hungarian government was in the position to exercise pressure to exact concessions from the crown. They led to a gradual weakening of the common defense structure and an undermining of the principle of the common language of command: German.

From 1902 to 1912, when defense legislation could finally be passed, a continuous crisis existed in these respects. A hortatory imperial manifesto, issued after the annual maneuvres of 1903 at Chlopy—"Joint and unified as they have been, shall my armed forces remain . . ."—was of little avail. The institution of national Hungarian regiments using Magyar as language of command gained steadily in practice, if not in principle. The national Hungarian militia (the Honveds), which by law were under the exclusive jurisdiction of the Hungarian government, increased in political importance in comparison with its counterpart, the Landwehr and Landsturm in Austria, who played a more modest and entirely nonpolitical role. In fact it was largely the demand for a Hungarian national army, which in Hungary in 1905–1906 led to the only really critical situation in Austro-Hungarian relations between 1867 and October, 1918. It will be discussed below in connection with Hungarian domestic developments. Yet even this crisis was weathered for the time being as long as the Compromise, at least in foreign affairs, stood the test of time—although such time clearly was running short. That the service obligation—three years in the line for the common soldier and one year only for reserve officers candidates who had passed the equivalent of a higher secondary education—was essentially undemocratic in a social sense in both dual states is another matter.[12] All kinds of major and minor differences between Austria and Hungary notwithstanding,

[11] Adolf Beer, *Der Staatshaushalt Österreich-Ungarns* (Prague, 1881), pp. 444–509; Heinrich Benedikt, *Die wirtschaftliche Entwicklung der Franz Joseph Zeit,* Vienna, 1958), pp. 104–118. Kristina M. Fink, *Die österreichisch-ungarische Monarchie als Wirtschaftsgemeinschaft* (Munich, 1968), pp. 51–81; Peter Hanák, in Ervin Pamlényi, ed., *Die Geschichte Ungarns* (Budapest, 1971), pp. 399–479.

[12] See Edmund Bernatzik, *Die österreichischen Verfassungsgesetze mit Erläuterungen* (Vienna, 1911), pp. 688–713; Gmeiner, *Grundzüge der Verfassung Ungarns,* pp. 119–125.

this simple fact symbolized the basic solidarity of interests in the alliance between the German and Magyar social superstructure.

B. Cisleithanian Austria

a) domestic administration

The centralistic governmental structure in a country increasingly weakened by national strife faced great difficulties. They affected the stability of the administration. Thus in Germany, where the powers of the legislative branch of government were encumbered with limitations similar to those in Austria, only five chancellors headed the cabinet between 1871 and 1917. In the dual states of the Habsburg empire the situation was different. Hungary had seventeen prime ministers and Cisleithanian Austria twenty [13] during that period. Several of them in Austria headed mere caretaker governments during protracted crises, some governed by emergency decrees while parliament was recessed on the strength of Article 14 of the basic statute 141 of 1867.

Important during that period were the cabinets headed by Count Taaffe for a tenure incredibly long under Austrian conditions (1879–1893), Windischgrätz (1893–1895), and Badeni (1895–1897) with brief caretaker or transitional cabinets in between and afterward until 1900, when Körber (1900–1904) took office. The Koerber cabinet was followed by the ministries Gautsch (1904–1906) and Beck (1906–1908), again with a provisional cabinet sandwiched in between. Of the following three cabinets, only that headed by Count Stürgkh (1911–1916) was very significant. With his assassination in the midst of the First World War the next to last chapter in Austrian history was closed.

Although the Austrian cabinets were not technically dependent on a confidence vote of parliament, successful conduct of business was possible only if the legislature did not obstruct the activities of the executive branch of government, as frequently happened during the second part of the era under discussion from the fall of Badeni in 1897 to 1914. In this sense the composition of parliament and the political party structure was of vital importance. It will be discussed in the next section.

After direct but not equal franchise was introduced in 1873, the deputies were no longer delegates of the diets but elected by the voters as members of parliament. Still, they presented four very unequal social curias—large estates owners, chambers of commerce and trade, towns,

[13] Actually even more cabinets held office during that period, but some prime ministers in Austria (Gautsch, Körber) and in Hungary (Wekerle and the younger Tisza) headed several ministries.

and rural communities. Membership in these curias depended on landed property or tax contributions (with a minimum of ten guilders annually). This eliminated practically all urban and rural daily wage earners and a sizable part of the small peasants and craftsmen. Due to obvious social pressures, resulting mainly from industrialization in the towns and dissatisfaction of indebted peasants in rural communities, the property qualifications were lowered from ten to five guilders in 1882. This, of course, changed little, but from here on the question of electoral reforms tending in the direction of general, equal, male franchise came more to the attention of the public. Demands of bourgeois parties catering to the vote of the so-called little man still carried more weight than socialist calls to action. Taaffee himself proposed a compromise solution in 1893 according to which the four curias of voters should remain intact but general franchise should be introduced in the two lower curias of towns and rural communities, qualified mainly by the requirements of literacy and at least token tax contributions. This proposal was turned down by conservatives and German liberals. Taaffe's main motivation for the reform was the belief that the extension of the franchise to the agricultural and industrial workers would diminish the acuteness of the national conflict, led primarily by the educated and half-educated middle class. Their influence on the conduct of public affairs should be reduced now. Whether this assumption was right or wrong, Taaffe had failed and he resigned. In 1896 under Badeni the basic features of the Taaffe reform became law in somewhat changed form. A new, fifth, curia of voters was added to the existing four. It would elect 72 deputies in addition to the existing body of 353. This fifth curia was based on the principle of general franchise, curbed, however, by the fact, that a number of voters in other curias obtained an additional vote in the fifth curia. Even now five and a half million voters in this new curia elected only 72 deputies, as compared to the 85 elected by some 5,000 large estates owners in the first curia and 21 deputies by the limited number of members of the chambers of trade and commerce. Nearly 400,000 propertied voters in the towns elected 118 deputies and almost 1,500,000 in the rural communities 129.[14]

The electoral reform of 1896 was more a product of social pressure than the reform attempts of 1893 and in line with the figures given above it

[14] Gustav Kolmer, *Parlament und Verfassung in Österreich* (Vienna, 1910), VI, 152–172; William A. Jenks, *Austria under the Iron Ring, 1879–1913* (Charlottesville, Va., 1965), pp. 293–302; Kulisch, *Beiträge zum österreichischen Parlamentsrecht*, pp. 97–143.

was still unsatisfactory. Victory for the rising demands for general, male franchise seemed possible only, if the forces working for social progress would coalesce with those fighting for a better national equilibrium. This finally occurred in 1907 and brought the electoral reform campaign in the western half of the monarchy to a successful conclusion.

Actually the representation of the relatively privileged national groups in parliament was never as disproportionately high as the parliamentary composition in regard to national wealth. The leading German position in Austria rested less on inordinate parliamentary strength than on an economically privileged status anchored in various educational and social advantages.

The Germans like the Poles lost some seats in parliament, the Czechs gained correspondingly slightly in parliamentary strength. The relatively most favorable national quota of the Italians remained almost untouched like those of the Roumanians and of the Austrian Croats and Serbs. Main winners of the reform in regard to national objectives were Slovenes and Ruthenians. The former increased the percentage of their representation by more than 25 per cent. The previously grossly underprivileged Ruthenians had their national quota more than doubled. Still, it remained well below par. Yet these changes as to national distribution were not decisive. They could not have a major impact in the eleven years left to the empire. Even if it had not disintegrated so soon after the passage of the reform, it is highly unlikely that the new franchise order could have substantially affected the course of events. Whatever major changes came about and were to be expected resulted more from the shifts in the social than in the national composition of parliament, brought about by the elections of 1907 and 1911 under the new legislation. The representation of the still predominantly conservative small peasants was strengthened, that of more radical labor in relative terms somewhat weakened. This state of affairs did not make major changes in peace time likely.[15]

The formation of the Taaffe cabinet in 1879 represented a switch from the German liberal regime to a coalition of Poles, moderate and conservative Czechs, and German Catholic Conservatives as the so-called Iron Ring around German liberalism. The fourteen-year life span of this cabinet, in which neither the prime minister nor any of his colleagues were outstanding personalities, can be explained by several factors. Brilliancy was the least quality the emperor looked for. In fact original ideas were sus-

[15] See William A. Jenks, *The Austrian Electoral Reform of 1907* (New York, 1950), pp. 126–198; Britta Skottsberg, *Der österreichische Parlamentarismus* (Göteborg, 1940), pp. 104–110.

picious to him. He did not have to fear their injection in the course of government by the old friend of his youth Taaffe, whom he could fully trust. Besides, Taaffe had come to power at the top of a rising current of conservatism, not only in Austria, but also in Germany and France. This trend continued well into the 1890's and Taaffe fell from power when he cautiously tried to change it with his electoral reform proposals of 1893. Yet although not endowed with brilliance Taaffe was skilled in administrative and legislative matters. In social questions he was not an outright reactionary. A cynic, like several Austrian statesmen from Kaunitz and Metternich on, he is credited with saying that the secret of government in Austria consists in keeping all national groups in a state of well-tempered dissatisfaction. There was some truth in these words. Neither able nor capable to introduce comprehensive national reforms, Taaffe avoided at least the pitfalls of an outright German course and met Slavic demands to the limited extent that led neither to their nor to the German liberals' open parliamentary revolt. The liberals, organized in 1881 under the misleading label United Parliamentary Left (Vereinigte deutsche Linke), pitied themselves on account of alleged governmental discrimination, while they continued to enjoy all privileges of the dominant ethnic and social group as before. Yet this mild deviation from the German course sufficed to secure for Taaffe the support of the Czechs, among whom the Young Czechs gained steadily ground against the Old Czechs. The prime minister also managed to keep the backing of the Poles. With this support Taaffe had the Austrian railway net expanded, the port facilities of Trieste improved, and above all and for the first time a policy of social reforms initiated—still modest, but notable in comparison to other countries. In seven years, from 1883 to 1889, workers' health and accident insurance, limitations of the working day to eleven hours (!), trade and craft inspectorates to enforce these and other measures, were introduced. In part, the fear of a growing Socialist movement, which had constituted itself for the first time as a united political party at Hainfeld in Lower Austria in 1888, accelerated then long overdue and largely insufficient reforms. Yet the workers and their leaders could be credited only with a rather indirect influence at that time. Apart from the policy of governmental expediency to weaken the liberal middle and upper middle class, a genuine interest existed in social questions as expression of Christian concern, as represented for instance in the writings of Karl von Vogelsang. Its impact on public opinion may have been greater than that of a socially still isolated labor class.[16]

[16] Jenks, *Austria under the Iron Ring,* pp. 158–220.

Contemporaries of the Taaffe era would have considered one event during that period as of paramount importance in the shaping of Austrian history: the suicide of Crownprince Rudolf, probably as the consequence of a illicit love affair. Allegations that fear of discovery of a conspiracy between Rudolf and Hungarian aristocrats against the emperor were the real reason for his death could never be proved. The crown prince's suicide and the initial attempts by the government to hush it up damaged the prestige of the devout Catholic dynasty. More important, Rudolf's death was felt to be a shattering blow to the German liberals, who esteemed the archduke as their ideological ally. Such philosophy can indeed be deduced from the archduke's partly secret intercourse with liberal writers and journalists and some of his public speeches. On the other hand, we know now from his papers, published after 1918, that in foreign affairs he followed an imperialist policy in the east, which might have led to a major war with Russia. Considering the shifty, tense, and in the last years of his life neurotic features of the crown prince's character, there is little reason to believe that his reign would have offered an auspicious future for Austria. By a macabre twist of fate his death is related to the disintegration of Austria, because Archduke Francis Ferdinand succeeded Rudolf as heir apparent. The new heir's death at Sarajevo opened the gate for the apocalyptic riders in 1914.[17]

After Taaffe's resignation a ministry headed by the conservative aristocrat Prince Alfred Windischgrätz (1893–1895) returned the United German Left—actually a center party—for a span of two years into the ranks of the government coalition. Meanwhile the growing radicalization of the Czechs led to their withdrawal from support of the cabinet. This ministry fell as the result of a conflict concerning the national language problem in southern Styria, this time a minor issue between Germans and Slovenes. The national conflict increasingly became the most conspicuous though not necessarily the most basic issue during the last two decades of Austrian government.

In June, 1895, Count Casimir Badeni, governor of Galicia, was appointed prime minister, with a program to solve the issue in one of the most sensitive areas of binational strife: Bohemia. As we have seen, Badeni's cabinet tackled first the problem of electoral reform. This piecemeal legislation was rated at that time a considerable political success. Under Badeni the last outstanding legislative judicial compila-

[17] Oskar von Mitis, *Das Leben des Kronprinzen Rudolf,* revised edition by A. Wandruszka (Vienna, Herold, 1971). Kann, *Nationalitätenproblem,* II, 186–191, 351–354.

tion in Austria, the Code of Civil Procedure was enacted in 1895. Credit belonged, of course, primarily to the efforts of previous cabinets. Furthermore a revised and from the point of social justice improved system of graded personal income tax was passed by parliament in 1896. Yet Badeni's name is primarily associated with what should have been his supreme achievement and turned out to be his catastrophic failure, the attempt to settle the national language conflict between Czechs and Germans. The language problem at issue will be discussed in section B-c. Badeni's reform proposals, though not the methods which he employed, were basically constructive. But the violent obstruction and counterobstruction which they encountered dealt Austrian parliamentarism a blow from which it never recovered.[18]

Badeni's successors as prime ministers tried to patch up the conflict by minor concessions to the Czechs but in substance they wanted to restore the status before his reform attempts in favor of the Germans. In doing so they encountered stiff Czech opposition without, however, securing the support of the Germans. Accordingly only an unsatisfactory procrastination could put off the collision of opposing Czech and German forces, concomitant with any comprehensive attempts to solve national problems.

The ministry headed by Ernst von Körber (1900–1904), an ingenious and capable bureaucrat, came close to the settlement of the language issue in Bohemia, and yet Körber failed, too, possibly in part because the heir apparent Archduke Francis Ferdinand feared a decline of the influence of the crown as arbiter between the feuding parties.[19] Körber also hoped to divert national demands from their sterile track by advancing Austrian industrial programs, particularly the communication system. He succeeded to a point, but he could not make the parties agree to a concept of economic priorities before national priorities. Thus his cabinet too fell largely over the language issue, this time because of Czech opposition. The ministries Paul von Gautsch (1904–1906) and Max von Beck (1906–1908), tackled again the question of electoral reform. Beck, one of the ablest statesmen throughout the last decades of the empire's existence actually succeeded in this respect, as he did in bringing about a new ten-year lease of life for the Austro-Hungarian economic settlement.

[18] Kolmer, *Parlament und Verfassung,* VI, 1–351 passim; Berthold Sutter, *Die Badenischen Sprachenverordnungen von 1897* (Graz-Cologne, 1960–1965), II, 402–418, 442–445.

[19] See Rudolf Sieghart, *Die letzten Jahrzehnte einer Grossmacht* (Berlin, 1932), pp. 462 f.; see also Alfred Ableitinger, *Ernest von Körber und das Verfassungsproblem im Jahre 1900* (Vienna-Cologne, 1973), pp. 82–121.

Yet as the socialist leader Victor Adler put it, political democracy was like air, you could not live without it, but you could not live from it alone. Thus general equal franchise could not save the empire, apart from the fact that Beck himself had to resign because the archduke Francis Ferdinand could not tolerate it that one of his intimate advisers would lend the emperor his services as prime minister before his own accession. The last prime minister appointed in peacetime, Count Karl Stürgkh (1911–1916), became the initiator of wartime absolutism in Austria and one of its major victims. His adjournment of parliament in March, 1914, with resort to Article 14 (basic statute 141 of 1867) in the face of national obstruction was no longer considered as extraordinary measure, yet it paved the way for the elimination of parliament until May, 1917. Even more important, it deprived the Austrian peoples in the July crisis of 1914 of the opportunity to raise their voices through elected representatives and to force the Conrads and Berchtolds to listen to them. This was the supreme tragic effect of temporary absolutist government in Austria[20]

b) POLITICAL PARTIES

The emphasis given to national problems throughout the period 1879–1914 does not mean that social problems were of secondary importance in Cisleithanian Austria. Conflicts between labor, petty bourgeoisie, and capital, and between industry and agriculture, and various cultural problems played as important a role as in any other country. Yet the accentuation of the national problem means, that the broad issues of social conflict were by and large channeled into the bed of diverse narrow national interests.

Thus during the era under discussion some forty political parties, organized in about twenty parliamentary clubs, operated or more often obstructed the course of government. The party names and club affiliations were continuously changing which would make it confusing to discuss here in detail the intricacies of the parliamentary lineup. National groups were represented by one or more deputies, who stood for different social and cultural interests, conservative, agrarian, clerical, liberal, later

[20] Technically foreign policy was beyond the purview of the Cisleïthanian Austrian parliament, practically the members had the opportunity to alert public opinion to its problems.

On the legislative and administrative record of the whole period from 1879–1904 see Kolmer, *Parlament und Verfassung,* Vols. III to VIII. On the same subject, with chief emphasis on the administration, the less sophisticated and interpretative work by Alois von Czedik, *Zur Geschichte der k.k. österreichischen Ministerien 1861–1916,* 4 vols. (Teschen-Vienna, 1917–1920).

also socialist. These deputies of the nine recognized Cisleithanian national groups were organized in loose roof organizations, such as the Czech or Polish club, the German United Left, or since 1910 the so-called German Nationalverband, which comprised about ten political parties. Of major parties only the German Christian Socials almost to the end of the First World War and the Socialists all throughout stayed clear of these clubs, which put strange political bed fellows together. They were frequently linked by nothing but national interests, or more often national prejudices.

The decline of the German liberals discussed in Chapter VI had led to a political regrouping in the elections of 1879. This proved that the industrial management sector—in international affairs German-oriented and in church-state and cultural relations, anticlerical—had become too small a base to govern Austria. Too small, that is, as long as it was no longer propped up by an unjust franchise system. This was still the case. Thus the decline of the German liberals was as yet only moderate in the elections of 1886 (loss of fifteen seats). Even after those of 1891 some 170 Germans faced about 160 Slav deputies. A Latin Italian-Rumanian group did not dip the scales. It was rather the support of the German conservatives and various pacts with the German liberals, which enabled Count Taaffe to continue in office after the Young Czechs, the actual victors, had left the government coalition. A new German party, the Christian Socials, as yet with only fourteen members, appeared in the newly elected parliament. Also nearly a score of German nationalist deputies had split by that time from the rank of the liberals. The elections of 1897, which followed Badeni's very limited franchise reform, almost doubled the number of Christian Social deputies. The Young Czechs now fully dominated Czech politics, and the conservative Old Czechs, who a generation before had monopolized Czech party politics, disappeared from the scene. In this parliament Socialists (fifteen in number) showed up for the first time.

In 1901 the German moderate Left lost some seats to the German national Right, the Young Czechs to the German Agrarians and both Christian Socials and Socialists lost slightly, a circumstance partly to be explained by a conservative trend, which followed the Badeni crisis and partly by the intricacies of the franchise law. In the elections of 1907, the first elections held under general equal and secret male franchise, all this changed more radically in a social than in a national sense. The Christian Socials increased their number now from twenty-two to sixty-eight, and in the election of 1911, the last to be held in imperial Austria, to seventy-six. Even more spectacular was the rise of the Socialists from ten to eighty-seven in 1907, followed by a slight decline to eighty-two in 1911. The German national radicals, divided in various splinter groups, continued to decline. Yet their influence on public opinion continued to be greater than could be deduced from their parliamentary representation, which had never exceeded about 5 per cent of all parliamentary seats. The electoral reform gave Slovenes and particularly Ruthenians some more adequate parliamentary representation. Thus the Slavs now held a relative majority against the Germans. This, however, was obscured by the fact that the numerically strongest party, the Socialists, who were officially not committed in the national conflict, had their largest representation in German territory and leaned somewhat to the German side. Moreover, the last cabinets barely managed to survive by fluctuating support from the moderate, conservative, and clerical parties; at that, with little regard to national affiliation. The Polish club of about seventy-five deputies remained as the most solid progovernmental block.

Of the new parties, or perhaps more correctly party movements, the decisive changes occurred in the German orbit. The greater leverage of German parties is explained by the incongruous franchise system, until 1918 by the tradition of the centralistic system, and by a control of key economic positions including German dominance of the primary newspapers: the liberal *Neue Freie Presse,* after 1888 the socialist *Arbeiter Zeitung,* and after 1894 the clerical *Reichspost.* Radical German nationalism, on the other hand, cannot be associated with any specific major paper, but rather with a series of rapidly appearing and disappearing dailies and periodicals.

By 1879 German liberalism in a parliamentary sense comprised many conflicting trends and group interests, among them few genuine progressives, and more adherents of a capitalist industrialist system, whose liberalism was expressed chiefly in their aversion to social legislation, anticlericalism and anti-Semitism. There were further tendencies to give the petty bourgeoisie, small crafts and trades, a better representation. Labor had practically no representation and agriculture only a negligible one within the liberal tent.[21] Pervasive throughout the left as well as right wing of liberalism was a noticeable, but officially not yet acknowledged anti-Semitic trend, deeply anchored in the Austrian tradition and attributed to an alleged inordinate influence of the Jews in the political,

[21] A small Viennese-centered left wing of the Liberals under the leadership of deputy Ferdinand Kronawetter represented to a limited degree interests of labor in the 1880's and 1890's. It was soon superseded by the Socialists. German spokesmen for agrarian interests were as yet chiefly clerical conservatives.

cultural, and economic life of the liberal era. No single party could in the long run serve all these interests. New alignments were clearly shaping up.[22]

In September, 1882, some left-wing German liberals in Linz drew up the so-called Linz program with emphasis on national and social questions. Participants were the nationalist radical deputy Georg von Schönerer (1842–1921), the young lawyer Robert Pattai, the writer Engelbert Pernerstorfer, the young physician Victor Adler (1852–1918), and the historian Heinrich Friedjung. Of these four, Schönerer soon became the leader of the nationalist Pan-German racist movement in Austria, and Pattai became a prominent right-wing Christian Social parlamentarian. Pernerstorfer was to become a prominent representative of moderate German national trends in the future Social Democratic party, and Adler its founder and undisputed leader. Friedjung, like Adler of Jewish background, soon dropped out of politics, but as the only one of the four remained faithful to the old liberal program.

The Linz program asked for the union of all German-speaking Austrian lands, including Bohemia and Moravia. Administrative separation of Dalmatia and Galicia from the bulk of the Austrian lands was demanded to secure a solid German majority in parliament. German should become the state language. The Austro-German alliance supplemented by a customs union was to be anchored in the constitution.[23] Relations to Hungary were to be reduced to purely dynastic ties.[24]

The racial factor—the exclusion of Jews from the new movement and as far as possible from public life—was still lacking in these postulates. But within two years Schönerer added demands to that effect as basic principles to the program of the German National Association. Joined to it was a passionate anti-clericalism, the "Los von Rom" movement. Anticlericalism was fed by opposition to the infallibility dogma of the Vatican Council of 1870. In that respect the program was part of the liberal heritage. But in another it was anchored in racialism and attacked a double-faced enemy, Christian universalism and liberal pseudo-egalitarianism. Hence the slogan: "Ohne Juda, ohne Rom, bauen wir den deutschen Dom."

Hitler glorified Schönerer in *Mein Kampf,* but deplored Schönerer's

[22] Jenks, *The Austrian Electoral Reforms of 1907,* pp. 176–214; Julius Sylvester, *Vom toten Parlament* (Vienna, 1928), pp. 16–44; Kann, *Nationalitätenproblem,* II, 225–232, 365–368.

[23] Public opinion had long surmised the existence of an Austro-German alliance of 1879 made public only in February, 1888.

[24] Kann, *Nationalitätenproblem,* I, 98–99, 294.

lack of organizational talent. Because of this deficiency Pan-Germanism never reached great parliamentary strength and split up in mutually feuding sectarian movements. Criticism of Schönerer's and his ideological friends' deficiencies, as seen from Hitler's viewpoint, may have been valid. Yet lack of organization was hardly the main reason why the parliamentary strength of the movement never was at par with its ideological impact. Schönerer, Karl H. Wolf, and other bitterly feuding Pan-German leaders, never themselves believed that they had a chance of bringing about the success of their program in its most radical form. It would have meant the splitup of the Habsburg monarchy, whose German crownlands would have been joined to the Reich, further, the creation of Slavic satellite states, the reduction of the Jews to helots, and the replacement of the Catholic Church by a strange kind of Protestantism, similar to the German Christianity of the totalitarian future.

These were dream goals, which could not be achieved while the Habsburg empire was still at least nominally a great power. Propagation of this program in parliament meant a wasting of votes. Yet just because these were dream goals—to the majority of the Austro-Germans still those of bad dreams—they were discussed and promoted in all kinds of private associations, such as athletic clubs (*Turnvereine*) or the powerful German School Association (*Deutscher Schulverein*). In particular, government officials in the lower and middle ranks, who by law were restricted in their political activities, found here an outlet to work for their "cultural" interests. In this sense the seeds of the movement had a powerful impact—which could be harvested half a century later.[25]

In the meantime many of its sympathizers voted secretly for a rival party, whose leader, whatever his weakness, could not be charged with lack of organizational ability. Dr. Karl Lueger, a lawyer (1844–1910), came originally from the liberal fold, like Schönerer. Lueger, not less a demagogue than Schönerer, but more skillful a tactician, saw a chief weakness of liberalism in the pauperization of crafts and small shopkeepers in the face of rising industrialization. He was also concerned with the lot of the small peasants, whose forest and pasture lands were gradually taken over by saw mills and the big estates owners. To fight these conditions was certainly justifiable but Lueger realized that a fight on purely economic issues directed against the rich would deprive him of

[25] Paul Molisch, *Geschichte der deutschnationalen Bewegung in Österreich* (Jena, 1926), pp. 106–266 passim; Andrew G. Whiteside, *Austrian National Socialism before 1918* (The Hague, 1962), pp. 14–15, 60–66, 81–86; Kann, *Nationalitätenproblem,* I, 98–102, 376–382.

support of the establishment. Like Schönerer, he saw the best means of promoting his program in deflecting it from the abstract issues to a personified enemy, allegedly responsible for these conditions, the Jew, and in particular the liberal Jew. As seen from an intellectual and not a social viewpoint, Lueger appealed to basically more conservative strata. To them liberalism in literature, press, theater, and universities appeared as what later became known as cultural bolshevism. Statements like the one by the Christian Social local politician H. Bielohlavek, in the Viennese city council, "I am fed up with books, you find in books only what one Jew copies from another" or Lueger's own publicly expressed opinion that the liberal scholars should shut up, until one of them could invent artificial grass which a real cow could eat, were specimen of the new movement's propaganda techniques.[26]

The fact that Lueger's followers, radical in verbiage but basically conservative in sentiments, did reject Pan-Germanism and remained faithful to the Church, did not diminish their vitriolic anti-Semitism, although it was anchored in social causes and at least officially not in racial ones. In practice the distinction was frequently negligible. The Christian Socials, developed from a merger of various antiliberal associations (1885–1888) to a political party organization. This changed the image of clericalism in Austria radically. The new party rejected moderation, the stand against demagogy and religious and political prejudices taken by the Austrian episcopate. The lower clergy, on the other hand, widely realized the propaganda value of the Lueger program, and its adherents had reason to rejoice that the image of a union of Catholicism with conservatism, as represented by the German Catholic People's party in the Alpine lands, were rapidly superseded by the new movement.

It was to become more radical in words than in deeds. Only gradually did it become clear that craftsmen and small shopkeepers could no longer be saved in the face of widespread industrialization. Lueger, though more mindful of the social problems of the impoverished urban lower middle class than the Pan-Germans, made his peace with industry as long as it was not "officially" Jewish controlled. As for the peasantry, a scion of one of the richest landowning aristocratic families, Prince Alois Liechtenstein became one of the leaders of the party. The Christian Socials, better adapted to the image techniques of modern times than the liberals, became the chief carriers of the policies of the establishment with the elections of 1907. This remained true till 1918 and well beyond.

[26] See Kann, *A Study in Austrian Intellectual History,* pp. 108–110 and the sources quoted there.

If this process of evolution had been realized sooner by men more sophisticated than Francis Joseph's advisers, the confirmation of Lueger's election as mayor of Vienna in the face of a routed liberal party would not have met the stubborn refusal from the crown, which in the end only helped Lueger to establish himself more firmly in the saddle of the mayoralty.[27] The emperor finally yielded in April, 1897, and found that the Christian Socials in government—though as yet only local government—were more moderate than as members of an entirely irresponsible opposition.

No general conclusion can be drawn from this experience—least of all in regard to national socialism in whose accession to power the reverse proved to be true. The Christian Socials were in essence never a revolutionary party. They supported the existing structure of the dual monarchy. They stood firmly against Magyar tendencies to weaken the Compromise of 1867, and their leader, apart from his doubtful demagogic talents, had uncontested ability as administrator. Neither did Lueger lack a measure of social consciousness in regard to urban ecology, transfer of public utilities to the public domain, conservation of natural resources, and other reform measures.[28]

While Lueger's record in this respect was quite good, it was good only on the local level and it certainly was not good enough even in its farther reaching social demands to meet the needs of the underprivileged labor class. Here help could only be self-help by labor. It resulted in the decisions of the Hainfeld Congress December 30, 1888, to January 1, 1889, which established a common platform of the various trends and factions within the labor movement, syndicalism, economic cooperative tendencies and trade unionism. Above all, the desire for a joint political program was met.

The anarchistic adherents of individual action had previously done the image of labor great harm in the eyes of public opinion. Terror had little direct influence on the modest social reform program of the Taaffe regime, but it had led to repressive measures such as the infamous an-

[27] Fearful of the allegedly revolutionary character of the Christian Social party, the emperor denied Lueger between 1895 and 1897 four times confirmation of his election as mayor of Vienna, although the majority behind him increased after every one of the undemocratic dissolutions of the town council, ordered by the authorities.

[28] Kurt Skalnik, *Dr. Karl Lueger* (Vienna, 1954), pp. 53–165; on the history of the Christian Socials see Reinhold Knoll, *Zur Tradition der christlichsozialen Partei* (Graz-Cologne, 1973); Hugo Hantsch, *Geschichte Österreichs* (Graz, 1947), II, 442–446, 458–459; Kann, *Nationalitätenproblem,* I, 102–104, 380–383.

archist law of 1886 which exempted major political crimes from the jurisdiction of jury trials. The new Social Democratic party under the leadership of Victor Adler stated its clear intention to fight for improvement of social conditions and against exorbitant demands of the military, the big landowners, and industry according to democratic principles, in parliament. The only extraparliamentary means used—seldom enough—was to be strikes and demonstrations. The latter were used effectively in the struggle for equal general franchise. Altogether the program was to be understood as extension of social reform measures rather than as demands for socialization. They were not seriously raised in imperial Austria.

As mentioned, the Pan-German movement benefited from support from the lower and middle Austrian bureaucracy, the lower judiciary, and altogether from the provincial middle-class intelligentsia. This greatly helped the radical German Nationals to establish an influence far beyond the parliamentary strength expressed in numbers of votes. The Christian Socials in their later history could count on the help of the establishment, the Social Democrats (as supporters of democratic means to socialist ends) had economic change going for them. With the rapid progress of industrialization in the cities and the slower advance in agriculture, the ranks of the labor force—from here on organized labor—would inevitably swell. It may be added that a sizable section of the leadership, including that in the lower echelons came from the liberals. They were equally alienated by the lack of social understanding in the liberal party machine, operative in the United Left and later the *Nationalverband* (a roof organization of bourgeois German parties), as by Christian Social and Pan-German slogans. Much progress was thus achieved in adult education and various cultural activities, above all in the establishment of a well-written and reasoned labor press.

In 1899 the Social Democrats in the nationality program of Brünn (Brno) affirmed, at least indirectly, adherence and loyalty to a reformed Austrian empire. This program called for the solution of the nationality problem by a broad system of territorial autonomy for the various national groups. Yet labor had national problems of its own. In 1911 the Czech party separated from the over-all Austrian Cisleithanian organization, because of alleged inordinate German influence in the leadership. Not entirely without reason. A residue of Marx's and Engels' ideological inheritance, national prejudices were still noticeable in the ranks of German-Austrian labor. Yet the differences could have been bridged just as much as the deficiencies of the program of territorial autonomy which did not do justice to the problem of minorities in nationally mixed areas. More important was the fact that labor and its leadership believed in the future of a restructured Austrian empire. The government ignored this cooperative outlook.[29]

The Pan-Germans by their partial control of the lower and middle bureaucracy influenced the course of government. In the last decade of the monarchy, the Christian Socials were frequently represented in the cabinets and had considerable indirect influence even before. The Socialists, from the standpoint of the government, were considered to be beyond the social pale of official collaboration, despite inofficial and occasional contacts with some right-wing socialist advocates of national and cultural reforms, like Karl Renner and Engelbert Pernerstorfer. This is not to say that the Austrian government perceived the Socialists as the *vaterlandslose Gesellen* as the German emperor Wilhelm II did. At this time the loss of a great opportunity was caused more by adherence to a stuffy tradition, than by fear of social revolution.

c) ISSUES OF THE CONFLICT BETWEEN THE NATIONAL GROUPS

The struggle for national equality on the part of the underprivileged national groups against the privileged elite was complex enough in theory, but even more difficult to solve in practice. In many cases privileged national groups were unwilling to yield advantages, nor were they compelled to do so. In other instances underprivileged national groups asked in theory for nothing but equality, but as soon as it seemed to be achieved or within reach, this attitude changed to implied demands for national predominance in some areas. All this may have been due to a general human weakness, particularly characteristic in the national struggle, namely the inability to project oneself into the position of the other fellow, in this case the other national group, whether privileged or deprived.

Strangely, while the basic issues of the national conflict were certainly broad, the fight usually raged over very specific points, often seemingly insignificant except to legalistic minds and often incomprehensible to the broad masses. This latter aspect of the problem may have had its roots in part in the bureaucratic structure and tradition of the Austrian

[29] Ludwig Brügel, *Geschichte der österreichischen Sozialdemokratie,* 5 vols. (Vienna, 1922–1925), see IV, and V, 10–143; Hans Mommsen, *Die Sozialdemokratie und die Nationalitätenfrage im habsburgischen Vielvölkerstaat, 1867–1907* (Vienna, 1963), I, 88–450 passim. Kann, *Nationalitätenproblem,* I, 104–108, 383–384 and, concerning the national question, II, 160–182, 342–351.

state. Discussion of a few particularly significant problems may illustrate the point.

The core issue of the national problem was the language question in nationally mixed areas. The problem was important in schools and in the communications between individual citizen and government in matters of administration and court proceedings as well as in communications between government agencies. The court-backed practice in grade and secondary schools was that minorities of at least 20 percent in any given area were entitled to schools or at least classes with instruction in the vernacular of the students. In higher education, chiefly gymnasiums and universities, the question was more complex. The Windischgrätz cabinet fell because of German National opposition to Slovene parallel classes in a gymnasium in Cilli (Celje) in southern Styria. German violent opposition also prevented the establishment of an Italian law faculty in Innsbruck in 1904. On the other hand, the partition of the German university in Prague in a German and a Czech institution was accomplished peacefully in 1882, and the separation of the boards of education followed there in 1890. The Polish university in Lwów gradually set up a number of chairs with instruction in Ruthenian and the Croatian university of Zagreb, established in 1874, was significant also for Austrian Southern Slav students.

Storm centers of strife in the nationally mixed areas were the crownlands with the culturally most advanced population, particularly Bohemia with its roughly three-fifths to two-fifths relationship between Czechs and Germans. Here the distinction between language of the land (*Landessprache*) and language customary in the lands (*landesübliche Sprache*) has to be introduced. The former notion meant that a language of the land was any language spoken as vernacular by at least 20 percent of the people. That applied to Bohemia and Moravia in regard to the Czech and German languages, in Silesia to the Polish as well.[30] According to a language ordinance of 1880, administrative actions should be taken in the language in which they were initiated by an individual party with interpreter service provided for the other party, if necessary. The other concept, the language "customary in the land" was for the Germans in Bohemia and Moravia the language prevalent in any given district. The Czechs did not recognize any distinction between the two concepts in

[30] According to the official Austrian census of 1910, 63.2 percent Czechs and 36.8 percent Germans lived in Bohemia, 71.8 percent Czechs and 27.6 percent Germans in Moravia, and 43.9 percent Germans, 31.7 percent Poles, and 24.3 percent Czechs in Silesia.

these two crownlands. The Germans stressed the importance of the distinction. It looked like a hair-splitting theoretical issue, yet in practice the consequences were far-reaching.

The Czechs demanded that the Czech language should, on historical grounds be the only official language throughout the two crownlands, even in German districts. The Germans on the other hand held that the official language should be only the one customary in any given district—in the German districts, German. The Germans thereby promoted the administrative separation of Bohemia and Moravia as historic entities, in a Czech and German part. This view was opposed by the Czechs who considered the lands of the Bohemian crown as historically Czech lands once united under the crown of St. Wenceslav. The Czech position would have been stronger if they had taken the same position in regard to Silesia where they were outnumbered by Germans and Poles. There they wanted to perceive the national problems of Silesia as part of a Czech entity of all lands of the Bohemian crown rather than as crownland with German recognized as official language throughout. Even more subjective was the German position. Except for the unjustified demand for full administrative partition of Bohemia, the German position would have been arguable there as well as in Moravia, if the Germans had been ready to agree to recognition of the same principles in predominantly Slovene southern Styria or in the Italian part of South Tyrol (the Trentino). Here the Germans insisted that the historic lands must be administered as entities with German majorities, even though Slovenes and Italians had a clear majority in the South of both crownlands.

As for the language of administration, a further bone of contention was the administrative practice in regard to a tripartite concept of language use: first, an "external" language used in communicating with the interested parties, second an "internal" language used within the government agencies for the agenda not to be communicated to the parties, and third the so-called "innermost" language used between lower and higher government agencies, in particular in communicating between the crownland administrations and the ministries in Vienna. The struggle for the use of the internal language in the administration of Galicia was won by the Poles in 1868, by the Czechs not until the 1890's and only in part.[31]

Prime Minister Count Badeni, appointed in 1895, believed he could settle the enervating Czech-German language conflict in Bohemia and

[31] Kann, *Nationalitätenproblem,* I, 186–199, 416–420; Rudolf Sieghart, *Die letzten Jahrzehnte einer Grossmacht,* (Berlin, 1932), pp. 397–402.

Moravia by two language ordinances of 1897 which provided simply for the conduct of business in both languages, Czech and German throughout the crownlands. Badeni consequently ordered that all public officials in Bohemia and Moravia would have to acquire a sufficient command of both national languages within three years. Otherwise they would lose their office. Badeni hoped that if this plan succeeded it could correspondingly be introduced in other crownlands.

Few Czech officials lacked a sufficient knowledge of German, the second language of most educated people in the empire. Few Germans, on the other hand, had a commensurate knowledge of Czech which many arrogantly considered to be the inferior language of a small people. Other Germans simply believed it was too difficult to learn and of only limited practical use. Many took Badeni's decrees as insult and challenge to their feeling of national superiority. German nationalists and liberals started filibustering in parliament. Badeni might have attempted to compromise on the time limit of three years and thus might have split the opposition to his basically valid principles. He put himself in the wrong, however, by trying to break the filibuster by the questionable tactics of introducing a new order of parliamentary procedure. The filibuster now turned to open violence in parliament, and spilled from there into the streets of Vienna and Graz as well as the German towns of Bohemia. The earlier German nationalist and German liberal oppositions were now supported by Christian Socials and Social Democrats and the battle was joined on the opposing sides by almost all Czechs, but also Southern Slavs, and some Ruthenian and Polish deputies. The police dragged a score of deputies from the halls of parliament. Riots in the streets ensued and the emperor had to yield to force and dismiss Badeni. The following cabinets modified and in 1899 rescinded the decrees. Czech filibuster replaced the German filibuster practically to the end of the empire. Open violence had ceased but so had a working system of Austrian parliamentarism. It was generally recognized now that Austria was torn far too much by internal conflict to allow for evolutionary reforms of the centralistic system.[32]

Actually it was not only blind obstinacy and nationalist prejudices, which were responsible for this state of affairs. Both existed on either side of the conflict, though they were more conspicuous in the German camp. Yet a fundamental lack of understanding of the political process

[32] Kolmer, *Parlament und Verfassung,* VI; Münch, *Böhmische Tragödie,* pp. 405–458; Berthold Sutter, *Die Badenischen Sprachenverordnungen von 1897* (Graz-Cologne, 1960–1965), I, passim, II, 50–175.

in regard to the handling of minorities prevailed in all Europe, not only in Austria. It was widely held that the key to the solution of the national problem in mixed areas was territorial autonomy for the settlements of various ethnic groups. To make them nationally homogeneous would have required, however, the establishment of such small districts, that their administration would have become unmanageable. But in larger administrative areas territorial autonomy could in effect mean the subordination of substantial scattered minorities to a narrow majority. Reform proposals of this kind, though frequently advanced, thus missed their objective of national justice. The ingenious Socialist deputy, Dr. Karl Renner (1870–1950) later chancellor of the first and second Austrian republics and eventually head of state, proposed another scheme, so-called personal autonomy. This meant that national status corrected was not to be conferred on the population in a nationally mixed territory but linked to the individuals themselves, regardless of their domicile. People could register in a public record book as nationals of their own choosing. They were then eligible to vote in a national curia, German, Czech, or whatever, for a predetermined number of deputies. Some public agenda, particularly the most controversial cultural-educational matters, were to be administered by nationally homogeneous agencies. In 1905 a compromise of this kind was reached between Czechs and Germans in Moravia, another in 1910, between Ruthenians, Roumanians, Germans, and Jews in the Bukovina,[33] and the enactment of a third in Galicia between Poles and Ruthenians was only blocked by the outbreak of the First World War.

The principle of personal autonomy, even though it was a more sophisticated instrument of national justice than that of territorial autonomy, would not in the long run have resolved the problems of national conflict. In the last analysis most national groups in the Habsburg empire, like any other who were or felt to be oppressed, wanted statehood and not just national equality based on a perfect legal structure. Personal autonomy though more equitable than territorial autonomy, actually seemed

[33] Kann, *Nationalitätenproblem,* I, 199–201, 331–335, 420–421, 471–472, and by the same author "Karl Renner," *Journal of Modern History,* XXIII (1951), 243–249. Austrian legal practice did not recognize the Jews as a separate national group in terms of Article XIX of the basic law 142 of 1867. Neither did the majority of Jews desire such recognition. After 1900, however, the rise of Jewish national sentiments, furthered by the new Zionist movement, led increasingly to demands for separate Jewish national status, particularly in the crownlands with the relatively largest Jewish population, Galicia and Bukovina. The national compromise of 1910 in the Bukovina met these demands halfway by incorporating a number of dietal seats reserved for Jews into the German curia.

farther removed from the semblance of the desired identity of nation and state. The nation appeared to be anchored in the public records rather than in conspicuous territorial jurisdiction, however limited. Nevertheless, as long as the empire lasted within the setting of the centralistic systems in the dual states, personal autonomy could have provided national justice to a degree which no other institutional system could grant under existing conditions. Moreover, reforms on this basis precluded the sweeping innovations of a federal structure, which probably could not have been brought about without conflicts with Hungary and ensuing intervention from neighboring countries. Thus, although the personality principle would not have solved the Austrian national problems, it might have helped to arrest the creeping disease of national disintegration for some time. This, however, was the most a desperately sick patient could have hoped for.

d) INDIVIDUAL NATIONAL GROUPS AND NATIONAL CONFLICT

German political developments have been sketched in the preceding survey of political party movements. Major problems of the Czechs have likewise been touched upon. Here, the national leadership of the former Old Czech leader, František Rieger, was superseded in the early 1890's by the brilliant Young Czech parliamentarian Dr. Karel Kramář who tended in the direction of a moderately conservative Panslavism. His predecessors in the leadership of the new movement, Dr. Karel Sladkovský, a revolutionary of 1848, and the brothers Dr. Edvard Grégr and particularly Julius Grégr, had given it a decidedly pro-Russian orthodox orientation. Only shortly before and during the First World War were western associations equally cultivated. The Young Czechs, who displayed various features of an intransigent nationalism, at the same time had no more understanding for social questions than the German liberals. The party had reached its peak around 1897 and from then on had to share representation of Czech interests with an agrarian and a so-called National Socialist party, actually a moderately left oriented liberal group, to the right of the Socialists. After 1900 the great personality of Thomas G. Masaryk (1850–1937), former Young Czech deputy and after 1900 leader of the small moderately left liberal Realist party, became the ideological leader of the Czech people. The future founder of the first Czech republic secured this position not by parliamentary maneuvering but by the strength of his personality, his humanitarianism, his courage in the fight against prejudices, and his scholarly wisdom. Not yet ready to abandon Austria, his program between 1900 and 1914 consisted in demands for social and political justice, to be brought about by evolutionary reform. It honors the Czech people that they acknowledged the moral leadership of a man, who in imperial Austria did not share, desire, or lay claim to any of the paraphernalia of power on which political careers are generally based in parliamentary systems.[34]

As for the Poles, steady cooperation with the government continued on the basis of the Galician administrative autonomy. It secured the Poles, at the expenses of the Ruthenians, farther-reaching language rights than the Czechs had ever possessed in imperial Austria. Gradually, however, clouds came up on the political horizon. The anti-Polish policy of the Bülow cabinet in Germany and in particular Prussia (1900–1909) also led to a radicalization of Polish nationalism in Austria. Resentment was stirred up earlier, with the Austrian electoral reforms of 1907, which increased the number of Ruthenian parliamentary seats, chiefly at the expense of the Polish representation. A Polish-Ruthenian compromise, although never enacted because of the outbreak of the World War, forced the Poles to new concessions. It resulted largely from fear of the activities of a Ruthenian irredenta in case of a conflict with Russia. Several political leaders, only losely affiliated with the establishment of the Polish Szlachta, played a role here, especially Roman Dmowski of the new National Democratic party, which was pro-Russian, anti-German, anti-Ruthenian, and anti-Semitic. Unorthdox in the sense of the Polish club in the Austrian parliament were also the policies of the leader of the Polish socialists, Ignacy Daszýnski, a brilliant parliamentary orator. Neither Daszýnski nor Dmowski had as yet a large following in Galicia, but the personalities of these men were powerful enough to destroy the image of a monolithic conservative Polish policy. A contribution to this effect was also made by the agrarian leader of the Small Peasant party, Wincenty Witos, like Daszýnski a prime minister of the future Polish republic, of which Dmowski was to become a foreign minister.[35]

The Ruthenians in the era under discussion were a national group on

[34] Münch, *Böhmische Tragödie,* pp. 553–627; Jan Havránek, "The Development of Czech Nationalism," *Austrian History Yearbook,* III:2 (1967), 248–260; Kann, *Nationalitätenproblem,* I, 197–209, 419–424; Horst Glassl, *Der mährische Ausgleich* (Munich, 1967), passim.

[35] Wilhelm Feldman, *Geschichte der politischen Ideen in Polen seit dessen Teilungen 1795–1914* (Osnabrück, 1964), pp. 298–304, 401–431; Estreicher in *Cambridge History of Poland,* II, 449–460; Piotr S. Wandycz, "The Poles in the Habsburg Monarchy," *Austrian History Yearbook,* III:2 (1967), 279–286; Józef Buszko, "Revolutionäre Bewegungen in Österreich-Ungarn zu Anfang des 20. Jahrhunderts und die Teilnahme von Polen daran," *La Pologne au XIIe Congrès International des Sciences Historiques à Vienne* (Warsaw, 1965), pp. 101–114; Kann, *Nationalitätenproblem,* I, 228–233, 433–434.

the upswing in Austria. It was an ominous sign of the creeping disintegration of the empire that such changes of national status for the better did rather weaken than strengthen loyalty to the empire. Among the Ruthenians, the pro-Ukrainian Young Ruthenians outnumbered the orthodox pro-imperial Old Ruthenians in parliamentary representation by four to one in 1907 and more than ten to one in 1911. The relationship was to some extent similar to that between Old and Young Czechs, although corresponding to their firmer grip on the national representation, the loyalty of the Young Ruthenians was considerably more doubtful than that of the Young Czechs before 1914. At that time the Young Ruthenians had succeeded to have a language law passed by the Galician diet which secured near equality with the Poles, except for communications with the central authorities and continued inferiority as to university education. In the Bukovina they achieved full equality with the other major national groups by the previously discussed crownland compromise of 1910. Able leaders were Julijan Romančzuk, founder of an Ukrainian National Council in East Galicia in the 1880's, and the younger E. Lewyckyj, an expert in the intricate language problems of multinational areas. Both, Romančzuk and Lewyckyj, in principle favored an understanding with the Poles.[36]

Of the empire's Southern Slavs nearly 3,000,000 lived in Hungary including Croatia-Slavonia, more than 2,000,000 in Austria, and less than 2,000,000 in Bosnia-Hercegovina (population census of 1910). Bosnia-Hercegovina represented a wholly Southern Slav territory, in which the proportional relation between Serbs and Croats was about two to one. In Hungary including Croatia-Slavonia, the Southern Slavs at that time had a share of 14 percent within the total population of whom nearly two-thirds were Croats, the remainder Serbs. In Austria only 7.3 percent of the population were Southern Slavs, of whom more than three-fifths were Slovenes, the remainder Serbo-Croats.[37]

On the basis of these population figures it would have been reasonable to assume that the Southern Slav union movement, the genuine leitmotif of Southern Slav politics in the era from 1879 to 1914, should have started

[36] Borys Krupnicky, *Geschichte der Ukraine* (Wiesbaden, 1963), pp. 242–263; Ivan L. Rudnitzky, "The Ruthenians under Austrian Rule," *Austrian History Yearbook*, III:2 (1967), 407–429.

[37] The Austrian official statistics, unlike the Hungarian, did not distinguish between Croats and Serbs and comprised both groups under the heading of Serbo-Croats. On linguistic and religious grounds it is impossible to assign the 34 percent Mohammedans of the total Bosnian population to either Croats or Serbs. There is no doubt, however, that according to ethnic principles they must be recognized as Southern Slavs.

in Bosnia, and if not there in Hungarian-controlled Croatia. Actually until about 1903 the center of the movement was in Austria and later in Serbia, for the following reasons. Until 1908 Bosnia-Hercegovina was an occupied territory under the administration of an enlightened absolutism in regard to agriculture, industrial development, and communications. This regime had little regard for claims of national autonomy and less for social justice on behalf of the exploited peasants. The grant of a crownland constitution at the time of the annexation in 1908 changed little. This anachronistic estates' constitution exposed bills passed by the Bosnian diet to the threefold veto of the joint Ministry of Finance and of the Austrian and Hungarian parliaments. Yet even if the new crownland constitution had been more democratic, it presumably would not have made much difference. By 1903, with the replacement of the pro-Austrian Obrenović dynasty in Serbia by the pro-Russian house of Karadjordjević the kingdom had moved definitely into the sphere of Panslav agitation and alliances hostile to Austria. Presumably this change in Serbian attitudes would have happened anyway because of the inevitable trend toward integral nationalism even without the violent events of 1903 in Belgrad. In any case, Southern Slav nationalism had now become largely irredentist, and a strong irredentist movement could be directed effectively only from abroad. In domestic policies the harassment tactics of the Hungarian government continued, not only in Hungary proper but also in Croatia. Here the banus, Count K. Khuen-Hédervάry (1883–1903) and most of his successors would play Serbs and Croats against each other. Accordingly concerted Southern Slav action generating from Zagreb became increasingly difficult.

Before the twentieth century, Croatian-Serb rivalries and not Serb irredentism had primarily impeded the union movement. The Croats in the Habsburg empire, a historic national group of long standing endowed with autonomous rights in Hungary, had consistently claimed leadership of Southern Slav national interest. They had considered the orthodox Serbs as a junior, culturally less advanced partner of their nation. Undoubtedly remnants of the traditions of Illyrism played also a part, not intended by its ancestor Ljudevit Gaj. Yet the influence of the conservative late nineteenth century and prewar twentieth century Croatian leaders Ante Starčević (founder of the Party of Right) and later Josip Frank (founder of the Party of Pure Right) [38] was declining. Both

[38] "Right" to be understood as Croatian rights, interpreted and represented by a conservative party. In this sense the policies of the later Frank party were even more out of line with the course of Southern Slav unionism than those of Starčević.

parties were strongly national Croatian, which meant in the case of Frank's followers pro-trialist under Croatian leadership but above all strongly anti-Serb. Neither of them could deliver the goods of a trialistic program which would have given the Southern Slavs under Croatian leadership equal constitutional status with Austria and Hungary. Neither did these politicians understand the social problems of the poor peasants, particularly in Serbia and the Serb regions of Bosnia, but to a lesser extent in all other Southern Slav territories as well. Gradually it became clear that, irrespective of national claims, Serbs and Croats had many social issues in common. The new peasant party under Ante and Stjepan Radić and the new Croatian Progressive party represented such issues in the past prewar decade.

A remarkable change of policies took place in 1905, when the Croatian opposition was disappointed by emperor-king Francis Joseph's legally correct refusal to negotiate with Austrian Croatian deputies from Istria and Dalmatia on behalf of their oppressed brethren in Hungarian-controlled Croatia-Slavonia. The Croatian opposition leaders now decided to cooperate with the Magyar anti-dualistic Independence party. In return for Croatian support the nationalist Magyar opposition pledged a liberal interpretation of the Hungaro-Croatian compromise of 1868 (the *Nagodba*), as well as initiation of democratic reforms in Croatia. The Magyar and the Croatian opposition also agreed on the demand that Dalmatia should be joined to the triune kingdom. On October 4, 1905, this understanding was endorsed by a convention of Austrian and Hungarian-Croatian deputies in opposition to their governments, in Rijeka (Fiume). Two Austrian Croats from Dalmatia who were not exposed to the vengeance of the government in Budapest, Frano Supilo and Dr. Ante Trumbić, subsequently Yugoslav minister of foreign affairs, took a leading role in these proceedings.

Less than two weeks later twenty-six Austro-Serb deputies agreed in the resolution of Zadar (Zara) in Dalmatia to the program of Rijeka. A second, this time joint, Croatian-Serb meeting at Zadar coordinated common objectives still further. Croats and Serbs declared now to be one nation, bound to fight for the same program. This political philosophy, however, was endorsed neither by the People's party, the adherents of the old Starcević party of Right, nor by Frank's Party of Pure Right. Undisputed Croatian leadership in a Southern Slav union program was then still the foremost issue. Even a party anchored in a socially broader base, the new Peasant party under the charismatic leadership of Stjepan Radić, did not suport the Croat-Serb coalition of Zadar but came out for somewhat vague ideas of broad, empirewide federal objectives.

Yet the policy of the strong Croat-Serb coalition operative in the diet in Zagreb was not destroyed from inside but from outside, because of the nationalist intransigence of the Magyar Independence party which, in 1905, formed the nucleus of the so-called Hungarian coalition government. It stood in strong opposition to the previous and future semiliberal establishment. In 1907, the intolerant nationality policy of this regime imposed, contrary to previous promises, a new Magyarizing language legislation on Croatia. It was answered by Croatian obstruction in the Hungarian parliament and an electoral victory of the Croat-Serb coalition which by now had reversed its collaboration with the Hungarian government.

The coalition opposed the annexation of Bosnia-Hercegovina in 1908, a major factor in the high-treason trial of Zagreb in 1909 against the Serb leaders of the coalition.[39] A subsequent libel suit in Vienna showed that the convictions in this trial were largely based on forged evidence, probably with the foreknowledge of Austro-Hungarian authorities. The defendants of Zagreb were fully exonerated in a legal sense, and the unscrupulous methods of Hungarian political justice were proved. The nonjudicial question of loyalty of those convicted in Zagreb to the Habsburg monarchy was, of course, a different matter.

After suspension of the Croatian constitution of 1912 as sanction for obstructionism, the new Tisza government in Hungary succeeded to paper over the conflict with Croatia by withdrawing the objectionable language legislation. Strict adherence to the Nagodba of 1868 was pledged again. Yet in essence none of the major problems between Hungary and Croatia were solved because they were all caused by the broad ethnic issue, not by the constitutional problem in a narrow sense. In this respect a genuine long-range understanding on joint Serbo-Croatian policies beyond declaratory statements and issues of immediate concern may have been still remote as far as the majority of both peoples in the empire was concerned. But a common opposition, supported by a strong majority, against Austria-Hungary's foreign policy, against the nationalistic spirit of the Hungarian government, and less directly against discrimination in Austria came ever more clearly to realization. Such was the situation when war broke out in July, 1914.[40] To be sure, the union program

[39] The issue will be touched upon again in the context of Hungarian domestic policy in Section C: a of this chapter.

[40] Wendel, *Der Kampf der Südslawen*, pp. 385–620; Rudolf Kissling, *Die Kroaten* (Graz-Cologne, 1956), pp. 62–90; Dimitrje Djordjević, "The Serbs as an Integrating and Disintegrating Factor," *Austrian History Yearbook*, III:2 (1967), 70–82; Carlile A. Macartney, *The Habsburg Empire 1790–1918* (New York, 1969), pp.

of Zara (Zadar) in its full extent has not been fulfilled to this day because of the undeniable difference in cultural and social structure and tradition between the Serbs and Croats.

The sizable Slovene minorities in the crownlands of Styria and Carnithia were strongly discriminated against by Germans. Their status was better, though still in some respects not fully equal with that of the Germans, in Carniola, where they represented a majority of more than 90 percent. In Goricia too, where they also formed an absolute majority, the government favored the Italian minority. In all these crownlands Catholic conservative leadership was dominant among the Slovenes. It represented Slovene interests with some success. In 1885, in return for support of the Taaffe government the Slovenes secured a more adequate representation in the diet of Carniola where previously 6 percent Germans had held two-thirds of all seats. They also gained considerably by the electoral reform of 1907; limited language rights were secured in Carinthia and Styria. Consequently, in 1912 the conservative Slovenes and Croats, united by the common Roman-Catholic tradition, in the declaration of Ljubljana (Laibach) came out for a Croat-Slovene union, in effect an anti-Serb alliance. This Slovene policy, however, led by the clerical conservative Dr. Antonin Korošec, was opposed by the small group of Socialists who stood for a comprehensive concept of Southern Slav union, including not only Serbs but Bulgarians as well. Eventually the liberal national movement gained the upper hand also among the Slovenes; this development was indeed inevitable even though the majority of Slovene deputies in the Austrian parliament and in the diet in Carniola were still conservative. One of their leaders close to the Christian Socials was Father (Prelate) Janez Krek. But the Slovenes, the smallest of the Southern Slav national groups, had nowhere to go except in conjunction with the Croats. In Austria they were an isolated group. Thus when the Croats saw the need for a common program with the Serbs, it was clear that the Slovenes would have to join under the flag of Southern Slav unionism. This unionism, however, could not be materialized as long as the Compromise of 1867 was in force, and that meant practically as long as the empire lasted. Neither trialism stood a chance, nor even less subtrialism,

---

767–770; Mirjana Gross, *Vladavina Hrvatsko-Srpske Koalicije 1906–1907* (Beograd, 1960), pp. 228–232, and by the same author *Povijest Pravaške Ideologije,* (Zagreb, 1973), pp. 223–429, 431–440; Stanko Guldescu in Francis H. Eterovich and Christopher Spalatin, eds., *Croatia,* II, 50–70; see further, Denis, *La Grande Serbie,* pp. 130–165; See also note 51 in this chapter. Kann, *Nationalitätenproblem,* I, 254–264, 290–298, 441–443, 455–456.

the concept of subordination of a union of the empire's Southern Slavs as a junior partner of minor rights to the dual states. Trialism was opposed by the Austro-Hungarian establishment, subtrialism was rejected by the Magyars and the Southern Slavs themselves. The fact that the largest body of Serbs in the Habsburg monarchy lived in Bosnia as the oppressed brethren at the gates of the Serbian kingdom voided the possibility of a solution within the empire. This was one reason why unionism was promoted from Serbia. Even if the governments of the dual states had agreed to a trialistic solution within the empire, the time for its realization had run out with the nineteenth century.[41]

As for the Latin national groups, united in the Austrian parliament under a loose roof organization, the *Unio Latina,* the Roumanians in Cisleithanian Austria represented less than 1 percent of the total population. Most of them lived in the Bukovina, where their national rights were adequately secured by the compromise, incorporated in the crownland constitution of 1910.[42] This does not mean that the Austro-Roumanians considered this as a definitive solution. Such a solution was perceived only in a union with their brethren in Hungarian Transylvania and those in the independent Roumanian kingdom. The fact that Roumania was Austria-Hungary's ally, although only in secret, put at least some limited restraint on irredentist propaganda from outside. The Austro-Roumanians could thus settle for a temporary, fairly comfortable arrangement with the government. The struggle for Roumanian rights under conditions not comfortable but outrageous took place in Hungary. In the context of the discussion of Hungarian political conditions we will return to the Roumanian problem.

If it has been said that the secret Roumanian alliance impeded irredenta activities against the monarchy, it seems to be suggestive that this consideration should doubly apply to the status of the Italians in the empire. In this case Italy was not only a secret but a publicly professed partner of the Triple Alliance. Things worked out quite differently, however. Roumania was a relatively small Balkan state, possibly in need of Austrian and German support against Russia. Italy was at least nominally a great power, and courted by Germany and the Russo-France counter alliance. There was no reason for the Italian government to refrain from the support of irredentist activities and to pay more than lip-service respect to

[41] Fran Zwitter, "The Slovenes and the Habsburg Monarchy," *Austrian History Yearbook,* III:2 (1967), 173–182; Kann, *Nationalitätenproblem,* I, 305–307, 459.

[42] Richard Wenedikter, "Bukowina," in Karl Gottfried Hugelmann, *Das Nationalitätenrecht des alten Österreich* (Vienna, 1934), pp. 724–734; Kann, *Nationalitätenproblem,* I, 332–335, 471–472.

the Austrian protestations. Up to the end of the 1880's these anti-Austrian activities were partly curbed by the fact that the Italian population in the Trentino, to the south of German South Tyrol, was largely oriented toward Catholic conservatism and opposed to radical liberal forces in Italy. The same could not be said for the Austrian Littoral and particularly not for Trieste. Here the liberals and Socialists were definitely on the march. In fact, in 1911 the future martyr of the Italian irredenta in Austria, the Socialist Cesare Battisti, was elected to parliament even in the Trentino. Italians had reason to complain about the brutal and stupid German opposition which denied them a university on Austrian soil. Still they enjoyed a limited administrative autonomy in the Trentino. Furthermore, the disinclination of Austrian bureaucracy to officiate in a Slavic language applied less to Italian. As for the Littoral, the Italians enjoyed a privileged status concerning linguistic rights in comparison with the absolute Slovene majority in Goricia and Gradisca and the relative Serbo-Croatian majority in Istria. Privileges for the Italians were even stronger in Dalmatia, where the Italians represented less than 3 percent of the population, compared with more than 96 percent Serbo-Croats. Concerning representation in parliament, the Italians were the one group that elected a deputy with fewer votes than even the Germans. Inasmuch as the Italians were the smallest national group in Austria (about three-quarters of a million) this generosity—partly meant to be a concession to the unpleasant ally in the South—had little long-range significance. No constellation was conceivable in which the Italians, if given the opportunity, would not turn against the empire and join their conationals in the kingdom. Counterarguments, which refer to the relatively superior standard of living of the Austro-Italians as compared with the Italians in the mother country frequently do not acknowledge that the superiority applies only to Italian averages and only in part to Lombardy and Venetia, the neighboring provinces. Yet even if the standards of living of the Austro-Italians would have been much higher and those in the kingdom even lower, the course of events is inevitable for a small minority bound to a vast ethnic majority across the border, when the hour strikes.[43]

[43] Robert K. Greenfield, "The Italian Problem of the Austrian Empire," *Austrian History Yearbook,* III:2 (1967), 501–526; Georg Pockels, "Tirol," and Alfred Manussi-Montesole, "Die Adrialänder," in Hugelmann, *Das Nationalitätenrecht,* pp. 545–568 and 569–684; Theodor Veiter, *Die Italiener in der österreichisch-ungarischen Monarchie* (Vienna, 1965), pp. 7–92. On the attitude of the Italian government to the issue of irredentism in Austria, see the memoirs of the Austrian ambassador to Italy, 1904–1910, Heinrich von Lützow, *Im diplomatischen Dienst der k. & k. Monarchie* (Munich, 1971), pp. 110–171.

C. Hungary

a) domestic administration and party structure

The Kálmán Tisza cabinet of 1875—liberal in terms of a hardly restrained Manchester liberalism—continued in office until 1890. It required a skillful tactician to remain in the saddle so long, when the Magyar position was attacked by the nationalities on the one side and within Magyarism itself from the other for alleged subservience to Austria. By maintaining a grossly unrepresentative franchise system, based on gerrymandering, Tisza was capable of containing the opposition of the suppressed national groups. It was different with the opposition from the Left, radical in national terms and rather moderately left in social ones, as represented by the Party of 1848. Its parliamentary members were not to be appeased by concessions concerning the interpretation of the Compromise, according to them dictated by Vienna. Actually the Hungarian establishment was threatened more by dissension within its own ranks. The so-called united opposition of 1878 organized in 1892 as National Party, and led by the brilliant Count Albert Apponyi and Dezsö Szilágyi illustrated this well. These more conservative nationalists, like the members of the Independence party, were serious when they asked for revision of the Compromise, yet they were quite content with business as usual in regard to social questions. Their representatives came after all from the same class as the supporters of the government. A candidate for parliament stood little chance for election if he did not represent the social interests of the Magyar upper and middle class, preferably rural but possibly urban as well. As for the national question, the opposition had objected to a defense bill, which offered the Hungarian Honveds a field of activity too limited in their view. In 1888–1889 serious trouble arose about the passage of the general defense bill, which the opposition and many government supporters rejected as an undue bow to the hated German language of command in the armed forces. Faced by these difficulties Tisza took the opportunity to resign in 1890 over a minor issue, the question of the recognition of Hungarian citizenship of the exile Louis Kossuth.

Under the elder Tisza, particularly because of the efforts of Gabriel von Baross, minister of commerce, public works and communications, much had been done to centralize and improve the railway and canal system including the major problem of preventing Danube floods. Commerce and industry prospered to a degree under the system. Yet little had been done to tackle the closely related nationality and social problems. The unsatisfactory state of both was illustrated by the at times violent flareup of anti-Semitism particularly in the countryside. As in Austria it was partly based on racial ethnic features and partly on social issues. Yet there were also different aspects. The heavy immigration of Jews from the east—even larger than the substantial immigration to Austria—played a major part. The number of Jews in Hungary between 1870 and 1914 nearly doubled to almost one million as compared with an over-all population increase of only about one-third during that period. That meant an increase from 3.7 percent to almost 5 percent of the total population.[44] This anti-Semitism could not take umbrage at the unquestionable Jewish loyalty to the country. Charges that Jews were the spearheads of the leftist revolutionary movement were taken seriously only after the turn of the century. The splendid Jewish contribution to Hungarian social and cultural life could not be questioned, except in the problematical sense that the Jews had progressed more than any other national group. It was charged also that some Magyarized Jews wanted to be more Magyar than the Magyars themselves in their stand against the demands of the nationalities for equal rights. Furthermore it was held that sizable strata of the economically and culturally most advanced Jews, who originally had come from eastern Europe, considered Hungary as a transit station on their path to further migration to the west. After they had moved to the west their place was taken by poor Jews from Russia and Poland. Thus Hungary had to pay the bill for westernization to the advantage of other countries. These were real problems, although hardly problems for which the Jews could be blamed in terms of individual responsibility. Inasmuch as anti-Semitism is an indication of unjust social conditions, these were certainly not improved by the Tisza government.[45]

[44] Comparable figures for Austria would be an increase from 820,000 to 1,300,000 during the same period. The Jews in Austria represented little more than 4 percent of the population in 1870 and still less than 5 percent in 1910. Both the Austrian and Hungarian figures are based, of course, on religious and not ethnic racial statistics, which can only be surmised. Yet as far as they can be surmised, conversions on the whole pertained mainly to the upper strata of the Jewish population. See also Robert A. Kann, "Hungarian Jewry during Austria-Hungary's Constitutional Period (1867–1918)," *Jewish Social Studies,* VII:4 (1945), 357–386. See also the excellent study by William O. McCagg, *Jewish Nobles and Geniuses in Modern Hungary* (New York, 1972), pp. 48–109.

[45] Gusztav Gratz, *A Dualizmus Kora: Magyaroszag Törtėnete 1867–1918* (Budapest, 1934), I, 204–269; Kosáry, *History of Hungary,* pp. 282–304; Berthold Sutter, "Die innere Lage Ungarns vor dem ersten Weltkrieg in der Beurteilung deutscher

The next cabinet, headed by Count Gyula Szapáry (1890–92), followed in principle the Tisza policy with a slight deviation toward the Independence party. Just the same the national opposition forced Szapáry's resignation over the question of increased administrative centralization versus the historic comitat (county) system. The comitats could indeed have become the basis of a grassroot democracy on the local level, working its way gradually toward genuine nationwide democratic institutions. Actually this institution served the Independents mainly to protect historic privileges in a parochial sense.[46]

Szapáry's successor as prime minister was Alexander Wekerle (1892–1895), a statesman experienced in economic questions. Endowed with considerable political skill and an equal degree of opportunism, he tried to reconcile the Independence party. Liberals and Independents saw eye to eye on major issues, such as curbing of the power of the Church, which seemed to the nationalists to impair Hungarian independence and to the liberals to suppress freedom of conscience. In 1895, against considerable conservative opposition, obligatory civil marriage was introduced and mixed marriages between Catholics, Protestants, and Jews were legalized. This was an extraordinary feat of legislation in a predominantly Catholic country under the rule of a devout dynasty, which, however, to the national opposition appeared to be a foreign one. This legislation undoubtedly contributed to Wekerle's fall, although as skillful compromiser he was called to the office of prime minister twice again.[47]

The new prime minister, Baron Deszö Bánffy (1895–1899) tried to win favor with the liberals by continuation of the anticlerical policies and with the Magyar nationalists by a particularly ruthless Magyarization policy in Transylvania. Yet the old stratagems did no longer work. Bánffy lost the confidence of the ruling Liberal party, when he agreed to have the ten-year economic compromise ratified by parliament, even though it had to be octroyed in Austria by emergency degree. He preferred to resign over this issue rather than by reason of a more immediate conflict with the papal nuncio.[48]

Under Bánffy the gradual splitup of the huge government party began. The left wing of the Liberals joined the opposition under the leadership

Diplomaten," *Südostdeutsches Archiv* (Munich, 1970–1971), XIII, 119–194, XIV, 188–224; McCagg, *Jewish Nobles and Geniuses,* pp. 111–166.

[46] Gratz, *A Dualizmus Kora,* I, 270–335.

[47] Ibid., pp. 306–334; Moritz Czáky, *Der Kulturkampf in Ungarn* (Graz-Cologne, 1969), pp. 29–110; see also Bucsay, *Geschichte des Protestantismus in Ungarn,* pp. 176–178.

[48] Gratz, *A Dualizmus Kora,* I, 336–393; Czáky, *Der Kulturkampf in Ungarn.*

of the younger Andrássy, who was later to become the empire's last minister of foreign affairs in 1918. Furthermore, a new Catholic People's party began to make some headway, which promoted a program similar to that of the Austrian Christian Socials. Also, Magyar industrial labor began to stir and accepted the Austrian Hainfeld program of 1889 as political objective. This meant in essence the gradual shift from mere trade unionism[49] supplemented by some modest welfare legislation concerning rural cooperatives and industrial workers' sick and unemployment benefits, to a genuine political program.

Prime Minister Kálmán von Szell (1899–1903) succeeded once more to reconcile the rifts between government and Independents. But his cabinet, like that of Tisza before him, stumbled over the defense bill including intense parliamentary opposition to the hated German language of command. Here even more so than in Austria the deep causes of social unrest and dissension were covered up by passionate conflicts over secondary issues of national prestige. Still they could generate trouble. A cabinet under the banus of Croatia Khuen Héderváry (1903), a man much hated by all Southern Slavs, failed to solve the conflict. The king-emperor's manifesto to the armed forces of September 1903 made it clear that he was not prepared to yield on the issue of unified command.[50] He now entrusted Kálmán Tisza's son, (Count) István Tisza (1861–1918) with the formation of the government, with the understanding that the new prime minister's cabinet (1903–1905) would be able to ram the essential defense legislation through parliament. From his standpoint Francis Joseph could not have selected a better man, even though the task before him exceeded his powers. The younger Tisza, a courageous and stubborn character, made of much sterner stuff than his father, deeply believed in the mission of a Magyar Hungary as first among equals in the Compromise. At the same time he considered the Compromise as the supreme guarantee of safety for this Magyar-controlled Hungary, surrounded by Germans, Slavs, and Roumanians, to whom he was unwilling to make concessions. Since the Compromise could not survive without the passage of the defense bill, Tisza forced it through parliament by approximately the same kind of dubious tactics which Badeni had used in Austrian parliament—and with little better results. The new elections

[49] Recognized in Hungary, though with various restrictions, by legislation of 1872 and 1884. See Tibor Süle, *Sozialdemokratie in Ungarn* (Cologne-Graz, 1967), pp. 1–74.

[50] Gratz, *A Dualiszmus Kora,* I, 394–413, II, 1–26. Kosáry, *History of Hungary,* 304–310.

held in January, 1905, on a doubtful constitutional basis led to a crushing defeat of the government majority. The parliamentary opposition gained 229 parliamentary seats, 159 of them held by the Independence party alone. It was the good fortune of the government in Vienna that this now powerful party was led by a paper tiger, Ferenc Kossuth, whose main attraction rested in the charismatic name of his father.

Francis Joseph was ready to appoint a new coalition government consisting of the Independence party, the Catholic People's party, and the Andrássy Liberals, provided they would drop the demand for the revision of the Compromise, in particular in regard to the creation of a Hungarian national army. When the coalition refused, a nonparliamentary interim government under Geza von Fejerváry, a general faithful to the old Habsburg army tradition, remained nevertheless in office (1905–1906). Parliament was recessed several times and freedom of assembly and press curtailed. In 1906 parliament was altogether dissolved by a royal military commissioner. A tax strike of incensed voters threatened and it seemed out of the question to have the annual recruit quota passed by legal means. Just at this critical juncture when the possibilities of either revolution or permanent royal absolutism had to be faced, the coalition surrendered. It actually took office under Alexander Wekerle (1906–1910), but—and this was the decisive qualification—under the terms of the Compromise of 1867, unchanged in basic matters. The success of the coalition, led by the feeble younger Kossuth, had thus become meaningless and a new sweeping electoral victory, in which some Socialists entered parliament for the first time, changed matters little.

Actually the crown was the victor by a simple but effective device. It had introduced a general, equal franchise reform bill in parliament. The adoption of this reform would have toppled the Hungarian political and social structure. No doubt it would have given the nationalities at least a near-majority and together with the Magyar Left (People's party and Socialists) probably a majority. This would have meant the victory of small peasants and agricultural and industrial workers, welcome neither to the Magyar establishment nor to the crown. In the face of a threatening social revolution the coalition dropped the political revolution. This concurred fully with Francis Joseph's intention. He supported the Austrian electoral reform to a measure, but there he was under greater pressure from industrial labor and better organized political organizations of national groups than those existing in Hungary. The only power close to the crown which took the Hungarian franchise reform seriously was the heir apparent, Archduke Francis Ferdinand—not because he wanted to democratize the empire, but because he hoped to take Magyar aspirations one peg down. This opened vistas of possibly revising if not revoking the Compromise after his accession to the throne.

The outcome of the crisis had proved convincingly that the national prestige issues raised by the coalition and supported in an underhand way by the Liberals were not taken seriously enough to move the Magyar masses to a revolution against the crown. This held doubly true for the other national groups. At the same time the crisis had shown that the Magyar establishment, divided in political matters but united in defense of social privilege, was strong enough to block radical political and social changes. The status quo continued with minor changes until a truly revolutionary situation arose in the fall of 1918.[51]

Under the coalition an industrial insurance act was passed and a new code of civil procedure was prepared, and adopted by the following government in 1910. Yet in regard to the nationality issue, the minister of education, Court Apponyi, managed to push the process of Magyarization and concomitant suppression of the nationalities further by the Education Act of 1907. It made government subsidies of the sectarian schools among non-Magyar national groups dependent on expanded use of the Magyar language among teachers and students. Apponyi was seconded by Minister of Commerce Ferenc Kossuth, who infringed on Croatian language rights, contrary to the Hungaro-Croatian Compromise of 1868.

The coalition government had disappointed its supporters, particularly the truly liberal left wing under Gyula Justh. It had embittered the opposition. It felt that the strength of the Habsburg empire had suffered from the protracted conflict about the interpretation of the Compromise, while the coalition had not secured one single tangible concession. The restricted political nation eligible to vote, was tired of this performance and gave the former Liberals, headed now by Tisza a large majority. He organized the 237 parliamentary members of his party as National Labor party, which indicated the obvious truth that liberalism was neither in vogue any longer nor had it ever been the genuine leitmotif of the party. But parliament was not yet ready to accept the leadership of the strong man Tisza. Two transitional cabinets, Khuen Hédervåry (1910–1912) and Lukács (1912–1913), followed. They had to face strong opposition in Croatia by Croatians and Serbs alike. In particular the latter had scored a major propaganda victory in 1908–1909, when the previously noted mis-

[51] Gratz, *A Dualizmus Kora,* II, 127–170; Kosáry, *History of Hungary,* pp. 304–311; Julius Miskolczy, *Ungarn in der Habsburger Monarchie* (Vienna, 1959), pp. 170–181; Kann, *Nationalitätenproblem,* I, 135–138, 399–401.

carriage of justice in a treason trial in Zagreb against Serb politicians was exposed in the eyes of Europe by a subsequent jury trial in Vienna. The evidence admitted by the court in Zagreb was fabricated, but the anti-Habsburg and anti-Magyar sentiments of the defendants were genuine. This added indeed an element of satire to a tragedy.[52]

In 1912 labor troubles of major proportions followed, including aborted attempts at a general strike in support of the franchise reform in Hungary. In 1913 parliament was ready for a new Tisza regime (1913–1917). A defense bill could finally be passed in parliament. A course was initiated according to which the government was ready to live up to the provisions of the Compromise in terms of the narrowest interpretation of joint Austro-Hungarian affairs. But this sufficed to strengthen somewhat the military forces of the empire and thus it was hoped its position in international relations. As Tisza saw it, this policy stood for rejection of any concessions to the nationalities, particularly in the question of franchise reform; and as for Magyars and non-Magyars alike, repression of a progressive social reform movement. Surely this course of action was outdated, but if one man could give it at least a new brief lease of life it was the puritan Tisza, an incorruptible man of determination, ability, and political blindness.[53]

b) PROBLEMS OF THE CONFLICT BETWEEN THE NATIONAL GROUPS

The Southern Slav problem in the empire including Hungary has been discussed briefly in section B-c of this chapter on the nationality problems in Austria, since the union movement because of political restrictions could not start from Hungarian soil. Further references to the over-all nationality problems in Hungary have been made also throughout the preceding subsection C-a. It is necessary, however, to consider some remaining national issues germane exclusively to Hungary, especially that of the Slovaks. Suppression, tightened after conclusion of the Compromise, increased further under the regime of Kálmán Tisza (1875–1890). The activities of the Slovak literary society Matica were suspended, several high schools closed, and Magyarization by governmental pressure at its ugliest promoted by the Hungarian writer Bela Grünwald, an adherent of

[52] Here the Austrian historian Heinrich Friedjung, who had testified to the genuineness of incriminating documents, probably forged with full knowledge of the Austrian legation in Belgrade, had to make a humiliating confession of having been deceived. Friedjung's personal good faith was not in doubt, but his judgment was exposed as deplorable. See Kann, *Nationalitätenproblem,* I, 293–296, 455–456.

[53] Gratz, *A Dualizmus Kora,* II, 170–281; Miskolczy, *Ungarn in der Habsburger Monarchie,* pp. 181–194.

Apponyi. What made the Slovak situation especially difficult was the fact, that the Church autonomy granted to the Greek Orthodox, Greek Catholic, and Uniate churches, from which Carpatho-Ruthenian and Serb national aspirations benefited at least to some extent, was of no help to the partly Lutheran and partly Catholic Slovaks. The Roman Catholic Church cautiously refrained as far as possible from taking sides in the national struggle and the Lutherans were not granted full Church autonomy by the government. Individual Protestant pastors and Catholic priests, the former represented by Martin Rázus (1888–1937), the latter by Father Andrej Hlinka (1864–1938) were leaders of the movement for Slovak autonomy within Hungary and godfathers of the Slovak People's party, which gained seven seats in the Hungarian parliamentary elections of 1906. Under the existing oppressive conditions this was to be rated as a great success. The so-called Cernová massacre of the same year in which about a dozen people were killed in a brutal attack by Hungarian gendarmery when a new church was dedicated in Hlinka's birthplace, was a blow directed against his charismatic leadership of the peasants. Eventually, by spring 1918, Hlinka, steadily harassed and several times imprisoned by the Hungarian authorities, turned to the concept of Czecho-Slovak union. None of the Slovak leaders could more strongly rely on the loyalty of his followers.

Some Slovak intellectuals, among them Milan Hodža, now a member of the Hungarian parliament, had hoped for help from Archduke Francis Ferdinand. But communications between this future prime minister of Czechoslovakia and the heir apparent, whether they related to federalization of the empire or a Slovak territorial autonomy within Hungary, never went beyond a vague blueprint stage. That much seems suggestive: in peacetime the majority of Slovak nationalists favored autonomy within Hungary rather than union with the Czechs. This program was promoted increasingly after 1895, in particular by Thomas G. Masaryk, in the so-called Hlasist movement (deriving its name from the journal *Hlas,* The Voice).[54]

[54] Ludovit Holotík, "The Slovaks: An Integrating or a Disintegrating Force?" *Austrian History Yearbook,* III:2 (1967), 389–393; Robert W. Seton-Watson (Scotus Viator), *Racial Problems in Hungary* (London, 1908), pp. 161–204, 339–351; Gilbert L. Oddo, *Slovakia and its People* (New York, 1960), pp. 148–154; László Katus, "Über die wirtschaftlichen und gesellschaftlichen Grundlagen der Nationalitätenfrage in Ungarn vor dem ersten Weltkrieg," *Die nationale Frage in der österreichisch-ungarischen Monarchie 1900–1918* (Budapest, 1966), pp. 149–216; Joseph M. Kirschbaum, *Slovakia* (New York, 1960), pp. 54–57; Kann, *Nationalitätenproblem,* I, 281–285, 449–451; Hanák, in Ervin Pamlényi, ed., *Die Geschichte Ungarns,* pp. 471–480.

Deplorable was the situation of the Carpatho-Ruthenians who had seen their best days of limited national recognition under the neo-absolutist Bach regime. National repression initiated after 1867, increased here too, but the Uniate Church could give the conservative Ruthenians at least some protection, whereas the liberals were helped to a limited degree by the cultural-linguistic activities sponsored by the Basilius Association founded in Ungvár in 1865. More pronounced liberal in character was the Unio publishing house, established, likewise in Ungvár, in 1902.[55]

The 2 million Germans in Hungary are frequently not counted among the suppressed nationalities. They took in some measure advantage of the privileged position of their kin in Austria and even more of the German alliance which was so dear to Magyar national interests. The Germans in the Zips, in the Slovakian mining towns, and the Saxons in Transylvania, whose history in Hungary could be traced to the High Middle Ages, were in a better position than the so-called Danube Swabians, most of whom had immigrated in the later part of the eighteenth century. The Magyarization process affected these old German communities with their well-established social structure less than the newer wave of immigration in the south. For these Germans conversion to Magyarism was made easier than for any other nationality in Hungary and members of these groups like Alexander Wekerle and Gustav Gratz became ranking statesmen in Hungarian political life. This meant in effect that the Nationality Law of 1868 was adhered to by authorities in relation to the Hungarian Germans. It did not mean, however, any recognition of their national group as political entity. The founding of the Hungarian German People's party in 1905 was to promote the preservation of the national identity of the Germans as national group and not merely as individuals.[56]

More serious, even from the Magyar point of view, was the problem of Roumanian nationalism, thinly camouflaged though it was by the secret alliance and the cordial relationships between the Austrian and German dynasties and the Roumanian Hohenzollern king. The program of the Transylvanian Roumanians, drawn up by a Roumanian national party in Transylvania had consistently been the restoration of the historic Transylvanian autonomy, comparable with the status of Croatia-Slavonia. This

[55] Ivan Žeguc, *Die nationalpolitischen Bestrebungen der Karpatho-Ruthenen 1848–1914* (Wiesbaden, 1965), pp. 72–119; René Martel, *La Ruthénie Subcarpathique* (Paris, 1935), passim.

[56] Harold Steinacker, *Austro-Hungarica* (Munich, 1963), pp. 249–266; 298–311; Raimund F. Kaindl, *Geschichte der Deutschen in Ungarn* (Gotha, 1912), pp. 54–104; Geza C. Paikert, *The Danube Swabians* (The Hague, 1967), pp. 8–47.

movement was supported by the Roumanian Cultural League, founded in Bucharest in 1891. Its goals were after all objectives compatible with loyalty to the empire and the Hungarian crown, but incompatible with persistent Magyar national intransigence. The outcome of the Hungarian state crisis of 1905–1906 was disappointing. It did not, as hoped for, lead to equal franchise, of which the nationalities would have been chief beneficiaries. The Apponyi educational laws of 1907 changed conditions for the worse. Attempts by Archduke Francis Ferdinand to reconcile the Roumanians by vague promises of territorial autonomy or federal status, as exemplified by the rather primitive federation plans of the Transylvanian Roumanian Aurel Popovici offered too little and came too late. Now it became increasingly clear, though it was never stated in so many words, that nothing but union with the kingdom across the Carpathians could solve the Roumanian question. Further repressive Magyar measures could only add fuel to a fire that could no longer be extinguished.[57]

All things considered, the Magyar nationality policy after 1867 and particularly under Kálmán Tisza and afterward was not always as atrocious as pictured by the various national irredenta movements. The fairly liberal Hungarian nationality law of 1868 was respected at certain times in dealings with individual national groups, though never with all of them at the same time. Absent, however, was the understanding for the desire not only of individuals but of national groups for identification in the form of autonomy, whether territorial or personal. Lacking also was the understanding that national discrimination, added to social discrimination, aggravated the lot of the socially underprivileged non-Magyar peasant and worker still further. Social and political dissatisfaction, illustrated by increased emigration were symptoms of a situation waiting for an explosion that was bound to happen.

D. Economic developments in Austria-Hungary

By the beginnings of the 1880's Austria had recovered from the aftereffects of the great stock exchange crash of 1873. Austrian and Hungarian agriculture and industry progressed, though due to the differences in national wealth, social stratification, and per capita income at a rather

[57] Miron Constantinescu, *Études d'Histoire Transylvaine* (Bucharest, 1970), pp. 27–43; Stephen Fischer-Galati, "The Roumanians and the Habsburg Monarchy," *Austrian History Yearbook*, III:2 (1967), 442–449 and ibid., Andrei Oteta, "The Roumanians and the Disintegration of the Habsburg Monarchy," 463–476; Horváth, *Die Geschichte Siebenbürgens*, pp. 150–155; Ladislas Makkai, *Histoire de Transylvanie* (Paris, 1946), pp. 325–334.

different pace. Beginning with the 1890's an over-all crisis began in European countries with a surplus of agricultural products resulting from the import of cheap wheat and cattle from the Americas and Australia. Furthermore, the tense political situation in the Balkans, the friction between Germany and the western powers, which closed the western financial markets to the Habsburg empire, had their effect on the balance of trade. It had been consistently active from 1876—three years after the crash—to 1898, though intermittently by rather low margins. It became passive in 1898 for the first time, when the breakup of the Austro-Hungarian Compromise appeared to be a distinct threat. Exports then rallied again, but the balance of trade became definitely passive after the annexation crisis of 1908–1909.

In economic relations between Austria and Hungary the basic, though at times modified, position was the Hungarian promotion of a free-trade policy. It would assure the export of Hungarian agricultural goods to Austria, and it was hoped, to the European market in general, while export possibilities of Hungarian industry, though increasing, were still of secondary concern. Austria, on the other hand, whose agricultural interests were declining in over-all economic terms, favored a protective-tariff policy, which would support her growing industrialization. Hungary's export to Austria throughout the era under discussion amounted to more than 70 percent of the country's over-all export. The bulk of these exports consisted in agricultural products. Hungarian imports from Austria—chiefly industrial products— in the last prewar decade slightly exceeded in value the exports to Austria. Altogether, the economic relationship between the dual states was certainly close, although it operated with increasing friction. Such friction had become inevitable because it was no longer a relationship between a mixed industrial-agricultural and an agricultural economy but now between two thoroughly mixed economies. Of these the Austrian economy paid increasing attention to its industrial needs while, partly for political reasons, it could not neglect agricultural interests, including those of the small peasants. Hungary now showed a relatively greater rise in the industrial sector. While the agricultural sector was still dominant, the pattern of exchange of Hungarian agricultural versus Austrian industrial goods became more problematical, because Germany became a strong competitor for industrial exports to a Hungarian economy, whose demands for industrial quality goods were steadily on the rise.

A few figures will help to illustrate the point. In 1900 about 58 percent of the Austrian population were engaged in agriculture compared with 68 percent in Hungary including Croatia. Industry employed 22 percent of the working population in Austria, 14 percent in Hungary. The corresponding figures for commerce and transportation were 7 percent as against 5 percent. Altogether the gap between the social structure of the two states was steadily narrowing. It remained wide, however, within the social structure of individual occupations. Austria's agriculture consisted primarily of small and middle-sized homestead farms with a sprinkling of large estates in the possession of the aristocracy and of some monasteries. Some of these properties were inordinate in size but the situation in Hungary was more striking. Small homesteads, which could not provide for the livelihood of a family even with the most modest standard of living, were owned by more than half of the agricultural population, versus 3,000 people or institutions (aristocrats and religious establishments) who owned almost half of the arable land of the country. This situation influenced not only socioeconomic but also political conditions including foreign affairs. Thus it would have been to the best interest of the empire to fight Southern Slav irredentism heading from Serbia by a liberal customs policy. Yet this ran counter to the interest of the Magyar latifunda owners, and after 1906 an embargo on the import of Serbian pigs had to be imposed. Street demonstrations of Austrian industrial workers against the rising meat prices followed. Two years later, in the year of the annexation crisis, Serbian agricultural imports were drastically reduced. In 1911 the mentioned slight liberalization of this policy occurred. The *tertius gaudens* in this economic warfare was the German empire which in some respects replaced the Habsburg monarchy as trade partner of Serbia. The brunt of the damage was to be borne by the Austrian workers but in the last analysis by all peoples of Austria-Hungary. It would be naïve to suggest that the Austro-Serbian conflict could have been reconciled by a liberal trade policy. Yet, like with the previously discussed alternative of letting Serbia gain access to the Adriatic, a Serbian economy tied by agreement and not pressure to the empire, presumably would not have presented the united anti-Austrian front, to which Serbs of all parties subscribed between 1908 and 1914.[58]

[58] Herbert Matis, *Österreichs Wirtschaft 1848–1913* (Berlin, 1972), pp. 342–447; Fink, *Die österreichisch-ungarische Monarchie als Wirtschaftsgemeinschaft*, pp. 51–76; Kann, *Werden und Zerfall des Habsburgerreiches*, pp. 80–88, 121–134; Stefan Pascu, Tibor Kolossa, Jan Havránek, *et al.*, Die Agrarfrage in der *österreichisch-ungarischen Monarchie 1900–1918* (Bucarest, 1965), passim; Miskolczy, *Ungarn in der Habsburger Monarchie*, pp. 138–194; see further, Iván Berend and György Ranki, "Nationaleinkommen und Kapitalakkumulation in Ungarn 1867–1914," and Laszlo Katus, "Economic Growth in Hungary during the Age of Dualism (1867–

Magyar intransigence, in addition to increasing food prices directly, also indirectly increased production costs of Austrian industry. One reason why this industry could not stand up to the economic policy of the Magyar magnates was the preponderance of middle-sized and small industrial establishments. More than three-fifths of them employed less than fifty workers each. Consequently they had little political leverage.

The center of Austrian industry remained the three crownlands of the Bohemian crown. It comprised three-fifths of all Austrian industrial establishments and production and nearly two-thirds of all persons employed in industry, primarily in textile, glass, and paper production and increasingly also in iron-ore processing and machine-manufacturing. In agricultural products, sugar-beet planting, particularly in Moravia, became the single most important combined agricultural-industrial export article. Furthermore the Skoda works in Plzeň (Pilsen) became the chief armament center of the empire. Bohemia with her rich mineral resources of coal, tungsten, tin, uranium, and radium was not only the center of the metallurgical industry, but also of the mining of these resources in the empire. These mines were even richer than those in northern Hungary.

Lower Austria continued to be a second important center of textile and paper industry and of manufactured luxury goods of various kinds, particularly leather, china, and furniture. In this latter respect the large lumber resources in the Alpine lands were important. Significant was also the machine industry in Lower and Upper Austria, armament works in Steyr and chemical industry in Carinthia and Carniola. The utilization of the Galician oil wells increased. One of the most important Austrian industrial corporations was the Alpine Montan Gesellschaft, founded in 1881, which mined the rich iron resources of northwestern Styria. Yet the major foundries and furnaces of the company were in Moravia and Bohemia. Only a few larger steel-producing plants operated in Styria.

Economically favorable was the expansion of the Austrian railroad net, in particular the construction of the scenic Arlberg route between the Swiss frontier and Tyrol, and the Tauern railroad which added to the Brenner route a second important connecting link between Vienna and the south across the Alps. Considering the fact that Austria's only access

1913)," both in Ervin Pamlényi, *Social Economic Researches in the History of East-Central Europe* (Budapest, 1970), pp. 11–34, 35–127; Alexander von Matlekovits, *Das Königreich Ungarn* (Leipzig, 1900), II, 491–567; Guillaume Vautier, *La Hongrie Économique* (Paris, 1893), pp. 201–483; Hanák in Pamlényi, ed., *Die Geschichte Ungarns,* pp. 408–437; Ákos Paulinyi, "Die sogenannte gemeinsame Wirtschaftspolitik Österreich-Ungarns" in Adam Wandruszka and Peter Urbanitsch eds., *Die Habsburgermonarchie 1848–1918* (Vienna, 1973–), I., pp. 567–604.

to shipping was by an inland sea, the Adriatic, the expansion of the Austrian Lloyd Triestino to the largest commercial shipping company in the Mediterranean was highly satisfactory, as was the development of the Austrian Danube Steamship Company, which carried freight from the German frontier to the Black Sea.

In Austrian agriculture, sugarbeet plantations in Moravia and potato plantations in Galicia could be efficiently run, but farming in the Alpine and Karst lands to the south was in a state of continuous crisis. The homesteads were too small, farm labor in the mountains strenuous, and the climate too harsh to raise crops at prices which could compete with the Hungarian large-scale production, particularly in wheat. Beef cattle in the Alpine territories could not compete with the Hungarian imports because of the high fodder costs, and cheaper meat could not compete with the lower-quality beef cattle raised in Galicia. The Austrian mountain peasant in general was in debt, which commenced usually as soon as he came into possession of the farm. First he had to carry the debts incurred by his father, secondly he had to pay off his brothers' and sisters' share in the inheritance, and he could do neither without mortgaging his homestead. Most Alpine peasants concentrated on dairy products, fruit, and sometimes vegetables, but these rarely sufficed to earn the livelihood for a whole family. The answer was in many cases a forced selling out to the lumber companies or to the big estates owners who changed pastures and fields to forests, a transaction which combined the pleasure of enlarged hunting facilities with the opportunity of profitable sales to the lumber mills. If the Austrian mountain peasant could have been assisted it would have been by cheaper credits and a channeling of production into more specialized products. But the major problem of merging the smallest farms to units of at least twenty acres, which could support a family, was not solvable without far-reaching government intervention. This, like farm subsidies, was out of the question in prewar Austria. But although it was uncertain how the mountain peasants could be helped, the tariff war with Serbia was counterproductive.[59]

As for Hungary including Croatia-Slavonia, the competitive superiority of Hungarian agriculture was not only based on the economic power of the big estates owners. Climate, soil conditions, and centuries of experience of the labor force favored large-scale agricultural operations,

[59] H. Matis and K. Bachinger, "Österreichs industrielle Entwicklung," ibid., pp. 105–229; Benedikt, *Die wirtschaftliche Entwicklung in der Franz Joseph Zeit,* pp. 104–181; März, *Österreichische Industrie und Bankpolitik in der Zeit Franz Josephs I.,* pp. 213–362; Tremel, *Wirtschafts- und Sozialgeschichte Österreichs,* pp. 324–372; Matis, *Österreichs Wirtschaft 1848–1913,* pp. 371–383.

which could not be pursued to the same extent in Austria. Still, without the introduction of protective tariffs Hungarian agriculture could hardly have weathered the wheat crisis, which threatened in the 1890's, an era of European tariff warfare, largely because of flooding of the market with cheap American crops. Some enlightened reformers like Count Alexander Károlyi and Ignaz von Darányi helped by establishing farmers' cooperatives and credit societies, but these measures barely touched the social problems of the small farms. The Hungarian agrarian Socialist movement was a response to the hardship endured. Surely the Hungarian small peasant was no better off and the agricultural worker even worse off than his Austrian counterpart. Heavy emigration to overseas countries was the consequence. It occurred in spite of the fact that the gross product from the over-all point of the national economy was relatively larger, cheaper, and for crops and cattle of better quality, than in the western part of the empire.

Much of the Hungarian industry benefited from its close link with agriculture, especially flour mills, sugarbeet refineries, distilling of spirits, and agricultural machinery. Hungarian textile and leather industry was likewise tied to agriculture. The rich mineral resources in the north fed the new armament industry in the vicinity of Budapest. The railroad net expanded almost tenfold between 1867 and 1907. Altogether the Hungarian economy, despite its grave deficiencies in the distribution of the national product, was basically sounder than the Austrian.[60]

In Bosnia-Hercegovina, finally, the Bosnian serf-peasant, the Kmet, a hereditary lease holder, who owed one-third of his earnings to the landlord, was the most exploited agricultural worker in the empire. After 1908, reforms were introduced attempting to convert the land of the Kmets to free property by government loans. Because of the outbreak of the war in 1914 the reforms had little effect and nobody knows whether much more would have been done if there had been no war. After 1878 the Bosnian administration under the Joint Ministry of Finance had introduced tobacco and potato plantations and sugarbeet production. Cattle-raising was considerably improved. Yet much good that could have come

[60] Matlekovits, *Das Königreich Ungarn,* I, 189–616; II, passim; Iván Berend and György Ranki, "Das Niveau der Industrie Ungarns zu Beginn des 20. Jahrhunderts im Vergleich zu dem Europas," in Vílmos Sándor and Peter Hanák, eds., *Studien zur Geschichte der österreichisch-ungarischen Monarchie* (Budapest, 1961), pp. 267–289; Solle, *Sozialdemokratie in Ungarn,* pp. 112–163; Hanák in Pamlényi, ed., *Die Geschichte Ungarns,* pp. 438–441, 466–471; I. T. Berend and G. Ranki, "Ungarns wirtschaftliche Entwicklung 1849–1918" in A. Wandruszka and P. Urbanitsch eds., *Die Habsburgermonarchie 1849–1918,* I, pp. 462–520.

of these reforms was voided by the poor communication system. The Hungarian government vetoed the construction of a railroad between Bosnia and Dalmatia, since this Austrian crownland was claimed as a fief of the crown of St. Stephen. Thus Bosnian agricultural products were barred from cheaper transport by sea. Furthemore, the main wealth of Bosnia, the huge forests, was largely in the hands of Austrian and Hungarian lumber mills. The logs were processed in Bosnia, but the chief profits were made by Austrian and Hungarian businessmen.

Bosnia might have been even worse off under Turkish administration, but it was certainly not well enough off under the Austrians to blunt the drive of nationalist unionism in the occupied and subsequently annexed land.[61]

[61] Kurt Wessely, "Die wirtschaftliche Entwicklung von Bosnien-Herzegowina," ibid., pp. 528–566. Ferdinand Schmid, *Bosnien und die Hercegovina unter der Verwaltung Österreich-Ungarns* (Leipzig, 1914), pp. 297–566; Peter R. Sugar, *Industrialization of Bosnia-Hercegovina 1878–1918* (Seattle, 1963), pp. 33–220 passim; Ernest Bauer, *Zwischen Halbmond und Doppeladler: 40 Jahre österreichische Verwaltung in Bosnien-Hercegovina* (Vienna, 1971), pp. 115–178.

CHAPTER IX

World War and Dissolution (1914-1918)

Austria-Hungary's last war and the subsequent dissolution has inspired more literature than any other period in the empire's history. Chief reason for this abundance is not only the interest in the disappearance of a great and old political body from the stage of history, a major event in itself, but in particular the interest in the fate of the national groups involved in the dissolution process. To some of them the last phase of the empire's history appears to be the first glorious chapter of their newly gained or regained national sovereignty.

The historian who deals with the evolution and the disintegration of an empire in four centuries cannot take this forward-looking position. To him the dissolution must be primarily linked to the past and not to the future, legitimate as the other viewpoint may be, as seen from the angle of national philosophy. If we look backward, we will recognize the significance of the great historical process of the dissolution. Yet we will have to look at it in the proper perspective against the background of a full and diverse history of four centuries. In this sense the disintegration process is an important chapter in the history of the Habsburg empire, but after all just one chapter in a long chain of events. Therefore this study cannot allot to these four years space out of proportion to the total time covered by this book. History deals with the evolution, the maturity, and the decay of thought and action in time. What happened within a few war years is in essence only an abstract of a long-drawn-out process of decline.

A. Conduct of the War

a) Foreign Affairs

A new and unique factor in the analysis of the empire's foreign relations during the war period is the impossibility, apparent particularly during the last years of the war, to separate foreign from domestic policies. The gradual secession of the national groups as part of their state-forming process belongs in both spheres. The decisive steps were no longer taken in coordination with Vienna. In fact national leaders were frequently either unwilling or unable to keep in touch with the government. Beginning with the summer of 1918 the foreign policy conducted by the Joint Ministry of Foreign Affairs became an empty shell, though its significance had by then been in marked decline for at least a year. In the following survey it is necessary to recognize distinctions as far as possible, between actions taken from the weakening seat of imperial power and the national centers. This means that in this first section we will discuss foreign relations as they were still conducted from Vienna. The actions of the various national movements, as far as they pertain to foreign relations, will be surveyed in sections dealing with the national crisis in Austria and Hungary.

During the first half of the war the two chief problems of foreign policy were the coordination with allied Germany and the efforts to prevent Italy from joining the Entente powers. The hope that Italy might honor her commitments to the Triple Alliance was shaky due to the problematical nature of Austro-Italian relations in any case. Yet Austria had failed to consult with her southern neighbor before presenting an ultimatum to Serbia, hence Italy could claim that she was not bound to support the Habsburg empire. During the second half of the war, which begins for Austria with the accession of Charles I after the death of Emperor Francis Joseph on November 21, 1916, several decisive shifts occurred in problems of chief concern to the government. The first was the unsuccessful but protracted attempts to terminate the war by secret peace negotiations. The second, rather transitory one, was the conclusion of peace with revolutionary Soviet Russia and with Roumania, which like Italy had changed from an ally to an opponent. The third supreme, desperate, belated, and wholly unsuccessful endeavor was to establish peace by open negotiations on the basis of sweeping concessions to prevent the dissolution of the empire.

Of the issues listed here the relationship to Germany will be discussed in one of its most important aspects, the military one. The Italian problem was a diplomatic one during the first year of the war. As early as August 4, even before Austria was formally at war with the Entente powers,[1] did Italy declare her neutrality, preceded in that respect by one day by Roumania, the secret ally. The Italian declaration, which for tactical reasons did not yet terminate her technical adherence to the Triple Alliance treaty was based on the assumption that Austria's war against Serbia represented not a defensive but an aggressive war. Moreover, Italy claimed that she had not been notified in time about the Austrian ultimatum to Serbia; hence the *casus foederis* had not occurred. Both these assertions were arguable but both were predictable. Undoubtedly the war against Serbia was defensive to a degree in its motivations, but not in a legal technical sense. As for informing Italy in accordance with the terms of the Triple Alliance in good time before the ultimatum, it would probably have led to a leak to Russia and Serbia. This fact alone is a drastic demonstration of the adventurous character of the Berchtold-Conrad policy.[2]

Within a few weeks after the declaration of neutrality on the strength of Article VII of the Triple Alliance treaty, Italy raised demands for compensation for Austrian conquests in the Balkans. The Italian government made it clear that she was not primarily interested in parcels of newly conquered territory, but in Austrian lands, that is, the Trentino, part of the Littoral, and various Dalmatian islands although specific demands were not immediately made. It was of little concern to Italy that these claims were clearly in conflict with the terms of the alliance, which referred to compensations in regard to newly annexed territories and not merely temporarily occupied ones. Since November 1914 the crown was under pressure by Germany, represented at the Quirinal by the pro-Italian former chancellor Prince Bülow as ambassador, to accede

[1] The Austrian declaration of war on Serbia occurred on July 28, on Russia on August 6; the British and French declaration of war on Austria on August 12; the Belgian declaration of war not until August 28. Berchtold had obviously hoped to avoid a formal break with the Western Powers similar to the German attitude towards Italy, after the latter had declared war on Austria in May, 1915.

[2] According to the terms of the fourth renewal of the Triple Alliance Treaty, Article VII, a full exchange of opinion between Austria and Italy before the presentation of the ultimatum to Serbia would have been required. The Austro-Hungarian Foreign Ministry merely informed the Italian government two days in advance of the presentation of the ultimatum and even then only in general terms. The text of the ultimatum was transmitted only after the notification of the Serbian government. See Ludwig Bittner, *et al.*, eds., *Österreich-Ungarns Aussenpolitik*, 8 vols. and index vol. (Vienna, 1930), see VIII, 538–642 passim.

as far as possible to Italian demands. If treaty rights did not support them, a deteriorating military situation certainly did. In the beginning of January, 1915, Count Berchtold was ready to yield in regard to the cession of the Trentino and of parts of the Albanian coastline. The latter concession would have been less controversial, from the Austrian viewpoint, because it did not apply to territory of the empire. In regard to international law it was a highly dubious proposition.

Berchtold was firmly opposed by Tisza, who saw in the cession of the Trentino an ominous precedent for potential Roumanian demands for the cession of Transylvania. This argument, the voluntary abandonment of territories of the multinational empire as precedent for demands by other states and national groups, was certainly powerful. But so was the need to prevent the opening of a new theater of war, particularly at a time when the German offensive in the west had come to a permanent halt and the Russians had pierced the Carpathian defense line at some points. The ill-fated Berchtold could not cope with this difficult situation and surrendered his office, which for the sake of the monarchy's welfare he should never have accepted. His successor was Baron (later Count) Stefan Burian, a former Hungarian diplomat and later joint minister of finance. He was a serious, less cynical official than Berchtold, but his long-winded, legalistic, and unimaginative policy made him as incapable a minister of foreign affairs as his predecessor had been. In March, 1915, when Burian was finally ready to offer cession of the Trentino, Italy also demanded large parts of territories in the Littoral and Dalmatian islands. Worse, it had become clear that she could get them from an alliance with the Entente powers as well—in fact more easily—than from Austria. In the beginning of April Italy had finally formulated a compensation program to an extent, which clearly would have made Austria's maritime position untenable, although for the time being a mere sweeping autonomy of Trieste was asked for in lieu of outright annexation. Yet by this time Italian public opinion and leading government circles had moved away from the idea of gaining their objectives by pressure, not to say blackmail, rather than by alignment with the Entente powers. On April 26, 1915, a secret pact of London between Italy and the Entente powers was signed. According to its terms, if Italy joined the war on the side of the Entente within four weeks she should obtain the Trentino, Goricia, Gradisca, Istria, Trieste, the most important Dalmatian islands, and the southern part of Dalmatia. This unfortunate treaty which considerably exceeded the ethnic boundaries of territory settled by Italians, became a major stumbling block for any subsequently conceivable peace negotiations between Austria and the Entente powers. Besides, the treaty represented a source of future friction between Italy and Yugoslavia. When Burian, in early May, 1915, limped behind events and offered the Trentino plus a strip of Isonzo territory, the game was clearly up. Italy continued negotiations in a halfway manner for appearance's sake until she was ready to strike. Her declaration of war occurred on May 23, 1915. The conflict with Italy became the only part of the war which even in the long run remained popular with a majority of the Austrian and Hungarian peoples. They felt deeply embittered by the Italian action and took it as a real breach of faith.

Could Austria have prevented this turn of events? It is unlikely for two reasons, both of major consequence for further developments. First, in view of the history of the wars of 1859 and 1866, Italian public opinion felt strongly that the country must not owe the liberation of Italian territory to smart diplomatic dealings and pressure on Austria but to a genuine national military effort. Secondly, the question of the timing of the transfer of the ceded territories in case of an Austro-Italian deal represented insoluble difficulties. Immediate cession, as demanded by Italy, would have laid Austria open to attacks from the south at any time of Italy's choosing. Postponement until the end of the war made it highly probable that Austria, except in case of outright defeat, would refuse to honor a deal concluded under severe pressure. Italy's security to keep the conquered territory depended indeed on Austria's defeat, which meant the dismemberment of the empire. Among the powers allied against the Danube monarchy Italy was the only one thus at least indirectly committed before 1918 to the empire's dissolution. Naturally she hoped and endeavored to win her allies over to that objective. In this sense the entry of the Italian forces into the war with Austria, even though Italy's military strength was not equal to her ambitions, was perhaps the most fateful strike against the empire throughout the war.[3]

In October, 1914, Turkey had joined the war on the side of the Central Powers under considerable German pressure. The Ottoman empire had more to fear from a Russian-British than from a German-Austrian victory. The Turkish entry into the war put Bulgaria in a squeeze. The

[3] Allan J. P. Taylor, *The Struggle for Mastery in Europe 1848–1918* (Oxford, 1957), pp. 544–548; Karl von Macchio, *Wahrheit: Fürst Bülow und ich in Rom 1914/15* (Vienna, 1931), pp. 25–135; Count Stefan Burian, *Drei Jahre: Aus der Zeit meiner Amtsführung im Kriege* (Berlin, 1923), pp. 11–51; Leo Valiani, *La Dissoluzione dell'Austria Ungheria* (Milan, 1966), pp. 97–138; Angelo Tamborra, *L'Idea de Nazionalità e la Guerra 1914–1918* (Trento, 1963), pp. 16–19; Arthur J. May, *The Passing of the Habsburg Monarchy 1914–1918* (Philadelphia, 1966), I, 170–202.

danger of attack from west and east on the one side and the chance to take revenge on Serbia on the other, forced the cunning king of Bulgaria to take the big jump rather than to wait out the war crisis. In September, 1915, Bulgaria became a partner of what from now on was called the Quadruple Alliance. Now a contiguous territory from the Vosges in the west to Anatolia in Asia Minor was under control of the Central Powers. But Britain dominated the seas and Russia, though several times indecisively defeated, seemed to have a nearly inexhaustible pool of manpower at her disposal; hence Bulgaria's entry into the war could merely delay the inevitable. It was certainly offset in August, 1916, by Roumania's declaration of war against the Central Powers. This action resulted from the conviction that the Central Powers were doomed, rather than from the consideration that Hungarian Translyvania was a more valuable objective than Russian Bessarabia.[4]

In early November, 1916, the Central Powers proclaimed the establishment of conquered Congress Poland as independent kingdom of Poland. This restoration was one of the clumsiest diplomatic moves of the German chancellor Bethmann Hollweg and the more obtuse Burian. The paper independence under Allied occupation was expected to pay dividends by the recruiting of Polish soldiers for the cause of the Central Powers. Apart from this, the deceitful proclamation already had become obsolete by the tsarist government's pledges for the reestablishment of a united Greater Poland under Russian auspices. Thus the promise of the Central Powers did not open the way for the restoration of Poland—on the contrary, it meant the perpetuation of the contradictory relationship between a satellite condominium of the Central Powers and the continuation of the Austrian regime in Galicia and the German one in West Prussia and Poznan.[5]

On November 21, 1916, Emperor Francis Joseph died close to the end of the sixty-eighth year of his tragic reign.[6] Fate spared him the tribulation of

[4] Frank G. Weber, *Eagles on the Crescent: Germany, Austria and the Diplomacy of the Turkish Alliance 1914–1918* (Ithaca, 1971), passim. Gerald Silberstein, *The Troubled Alliance: German Austrian Relations 1914–1917* (Lexington, Ky., 1970), pp. 129–247; Burian, *Drei Jahre*, pp. 52–61, 103–108.

[5] Bernadotte E. Schmitt, "The Polish Problem in International Politics," in W. F. Reddaway, J. H. Penson, *et al.*, eds., *Cambridge History of Poland* (Cambridge, 1950–1951), II, 481–489; Werner S. Conze, *Polnische Nation und deutsche Politik im ersten Weltkrieg* (Cologne-Graz, 1958), pp. 46–257; Burian, *Drei Jahre*, pp. 62–87, 254–264; see also Heinz Lemke, "Die Regierung Stürgkh und die Pläne zur Teilung Galiziens," in Fritz Klein, ed., *Österreich-Ungarn in der Weltpolitik, 1900–1918* (Berlin, 1965), pp. 267–283.

[6] Personal tragedies of his reign—apart from the political decline of the empire —were the execution of his brother Maximilian in Mexico in 1867, the suicide of

witnessing the breakup of the Habsburg monarchy. He was succeeded by his grand nephew Archduke Charles, a young man in no way superior to his predecessor in intellectual ability and second to him in consistency and, naturally, experience. In domestic and above all in foreign policy there were important differences between the two rulers. Francis Joseph, in part due to his age and tradition, was averse to change, in particular in relations to the German ally. He would in all probability have continued the war to the bitter end as the faithful, though hardly cheerful, junior partner of the German alliance. Charles, married to the Italian-born Princess Zita of Bourbon-Parma, whose brothers served in the Belgian army,[7] had an entirely different outlook. Neither Charles nor his more energetic consort were disloyal to the German alliance, but the new emperor was not raised in the tradition of Austria as the presiding power in the German Confederation and of the Habsburgs as Holy Roman emperors. To him, the alliance meant less than the genuine independence of the Habsburg empire. The aim of achieving peace, if possible by coordinated action with Germany, if necessary by going it alone, dominated his thinking from the beginning of his brief reign to its tragic end.

Now the second phase of the diplomatic history of the war, the Austrian attempt to obtain peace began. On December 12, 1916, the Quadruple Alliance in a clumsy and arrogant manner declared to the world its readiness to enter into peace negotiations, without however even hinting at the restoration of Belgium and Serbia within their prewar boundaries. Germany did not indicate either that a compromise on the French claim to the return of Alsace-Lorraine was feasible. Obviously this first official attempt to initiate peace negotiations in the works already before Charles' accession, was bound to fail. In December, 1916, the new emperor, who wanted a more flexible and ingenious foreign minister than the dreary Burian, appointed Count Ottokar Czernin, former confidant of Archduke Francis Ferdinand, and until recently minister to Bucharest, as Burian's successor.[8] Czernin was a highly controversial personality. More flexible, more original in his thinking and more energetic than either Burian or Berchtold, this intelligent German-Bohemian aristocrat

Crownprince Rudolf in 1889, the assassination of the Empress-Consort Elisabeth by an Italian anarchist in 1898, and finally the assassination of the heir presumptive in Sarajevo in 1914.

[7] As claimants to the French crown, scions of the House of Bourbon could not serve in the French armed forces.

[8] See Robert A. Kann, "Count Ottokar Czernin and Archduke Francis Ferdinand," *Journal Central European Affairs,* XVII:11 (1956), 117–145.

was also more neurasthenic, more mercurial in temper and unpredictable in his course of action than his predecessors. The unfortunate war situation and the contradictions in Czernin's personality were in part the cause for the gifted man doing as much damage to the empire as his predecessors.[9]

General semiofficial attempts by President Wilson to initiate peace negotiations introduced only days after the sterile declaration of the Quadruple Alliance, were met by a negative response from the Entente powers. The beginning of the unrestricted U-boat warfare by Germany on February 1, 1917, opposed only feebly and vainly by the Austrian authorities, sounded the death knell for efforts to rally public opinion in all warring countries behind efforts to end the war without annexations to be made or reparations to be paid on either side, as proposed by Pope Benedict XV in the summer of 1917.[10] In this situation the Austrian and German governments were agreed that each was entitled to make secret contacts of its own with Entente representatives. The respective ally had only to be informed about the general fact of such contacts, which might eventually lead to peace negotiations, to be conducted and concluded jointly by all partners of the alliance. A whole host of such secret attempts on the German as well as on the Austrian side were made subsequently, none of them to any avail. Chief stumbling blocks were generally the German unwillingness to compromise on the question of Alsace-Lorraine and to agree to the unconditional restoration of a fully sovereign Belgium. The Austrians, on the other hand, declined to agree to the terms of the secret treaty of London of April, 1917, whose provisions had in a general way come to the knowledge of the Central Powers. Here the British and French governments, much to their own disliking, were bound to support the inordinate Italian demands in full.

Austria as the weaker partner in the alliance of the Central Powers was less feared by the Entente Powers than Germany. It seemed to some Entente diplomats Austria might be agreeable to a separate peace. In any case she had the better chance in secret peace negotiations to arrive at mutual understandings of the problems, if not at agreements. In 1917 such secret discussions, among others, were held between the Austrian diplomat Count Nikolaus Revertera and the French diplomat Count Abel St. Armand, as well as between the former Austrian ambassador to

[9] Burian was actually his immediate predecessor (after Berchtold) and his immediate successor as well.

[10] Wolfgang Steglich, ed., *Der Friedensappell Benedikts XV. vom 1. August 1917 und die Mittelmächte: Diplomatische Aktenstücke* (Wiesbaden, 1970), pp. 1–22.

the Court of St. James, Count Albert Mensdorff-Pouilly and the South African Prime Minister, General Jan Christian Smuts. In these latter negotiations Smuts drew the picture of a huge Central and Central Eastern European federation or confederation headed by Emperor Charles, provided the Habsburg empire would leave the German alliance and make the necessary concessions to Italy. This vague scheme could probably never have materialized, and if so such a structure would hardly have outlasted the drying of the signatures on the treaty. Even if Italy would ever have agreed to such a plan, a highly unlikely contingency, most member states of the new federal or confederal structure would undoubtedly have seceded soon to attain fully sovereign statehood. Apart from this, Czernin refused to entertain notions of Austria's betrayal of the alliance with Germany, and with good reasons. As he saw it, irrespective of the moral question involved, such efforts would have permanently alienated the dominant national groups, Austro-Germans and Magyars, the pillars of the Compromise of 1867, while at this late stage of the war support of the empire's Slavic and Latin populations could have been gained, if at all, only temporarily.

Thus, not much significance should be attached to those attempts, except for one, the so-called secret Sixtus negotiations, held from March to May, 1917, between the emperor and his consort and Prince Sixtus of Parma, one of her brothers, who served as semiofficial representative of the French and British governments. Czernin, according to most sources, was only partly informed about these negotiations held secretly in the imperial castle of Laxenburg, ten miles to the south of Vienna. According to the disputed accounts of the empress and her brother Sixtus, however, Czernin had full knowledge of the proceedings. The negotiations in themselves were no more remarkable than any other secret pourparlers held between other negotiators, except that the emperor and his authority were directly involved. On the other hand, a Bourbon prince was a poor choice in the eyes of French as well as German (and German-Austrian) public opinion in case the negotiations would have been successful and would eventually have been made public. Yet there was little reason to worry about this point, since they floundered like previous contacts on the cliffs of the terms of the treaty of London, which would have made the Habsburg empire for all practical purposes a land-locked country.

The important fact about the so-called Sixtus negotiations was neither their outcome, nor even the personalities of their august participants but the circumstances, under which they were disclosed to the public opinion of the world, more than a year after their termination. The emperor had committed the uncautious act of handing over to Prince Sixtus a letter for transmittal to the French president Poincaré, which included the clause that Charles "would by all means at his disposal support the justified demands for the return of Alsace-Lorraine to France." It is highly unlikely that Czernin as a statesman with at least some professional diplomatic experience would ever have agreed to such assurances in writing, which, however justified in themselves, contradicted the terms as well as the spirit of the Austro-German alliance.

For reasons not fully clarified to this day, the foreign minister in a public speech of early April, 1918, alluded to French attempts to enter into secret peace negotiations with Austria. Probably he had meant to refer to St. Armand's conversations with Revertera, whereas the new French prime minister, the tough Clemenceau, understood Czernin's remarks as reference to the Sixtus negotiations, which were initiated on the imperial and not on the French side. In the course of an exchange of widely publicized assertions and denials between Czernin and Clemenceau, about the still obscure negotiations, the latter hinted at the emperor's personal involvement; Czernin denied this. Thereupon Clemenceau had the whole so-called Sixtus letter published in fascimile. The fallout of this revelation was widespread and serious beyond expectations, since feeble and hopeless dementis showed the matter only in a worse light, as seen from the point of view of Austrian credibility. In this respect the challenge to the emperor's truthfulness did greater damage than that to the correctness of Czernin's statements.[11]

The emperor, though clearly motivated by a desire for peace, exercised however in all ill-advised and less than frank manner, had exposed himself as a man who, in three respects, could not be trusted: by his own peoples, particularly the Austro-Germans and Magyars, by the German ally, and in practice most serious, by Clemenceau and Lloyd George, the British and French prime ministers. To the Magyars and Germans within and across the border he had become the man who had gone back on the alliance and what it stood for. To the allied representatives he appeared now as a negotiator whose discretion was not to be trusted, and who, in a pinch, would rather deny the obvious than face the consequences. Undoubtedly as far as the matter of discretion was concerned, Czernin was largely to blame. Unquestionably also, extenuating moral circumstances spoke for the more flagrant lapse of the hapless emperor. Unfortunately

[11] See Robert A. Kann, *Die Sixtusaffäre und die geheimen Friedensverhandlungen Österreich-Ungarns im ersten Weltkrieg* (Munich, 1966), pp. 9–90 passim. Ingeborg Meckling, *Die Aussenpolitik des Grafen Czernin* (Vienna, 1969), pp. 314–358.

his good intentions were not matched by prudence and consistency to stand by his words. In this regard Charles' cable to Emperor Wilhelm, in which he denied everything and pledged that his answer to Clemenceau's "lies" were to be given by the Austrian artillery in the west, did little good before friend and foe alike. As for the latter it made matters worse.

Yet all this was almost incidental. Imperial Austria in the eyes of the leading allied statesmen from now on lacked sufficient credibility to continue or to take up further meaningful negotiations. Two months after the public scandal of the exposure of the Sixtus affair the French government recognized the Czechoslovak National Council as representative official agency of the Czech people, followed within days by similar American and within weeks British action. Austria, now sitting between two chairs, had to commit herself even more fully to the iron grip of the German alliance as made clear to the world by the visit of Charles to the German emperor at the German headquarters at Spa August 14, 1918. The Austrian emperor had to disown his independent peace policy and with it perhaps the last hopes for the future of his empire. The brilliant but intemperate Czernin had to yield his office to the deplorable Burian, now minister of foreign affairs for the second time, which added only satire to the tragedy.[12]

The miserable outcome of the Sixtus affair was only one important factor in the impending collapse. An even more serious one, were the national revolutions, evolving with increasing speed at home but directed largely from abroad. These developments will be reviewed in a separate section. The third major factor was the response of the Austro-Hungarian authorities to the extraordinary events of the Russian March revolution and also the Roumanian defeat. Russia, after the February revolution of 1917 under Kerensky's leadership, had resolved to continue the war, a decision hailed by the western powers not merely for military but also for ideological reasons. Now the great alliance against the Central Powers appeared no longer encumbered and compromised by the impact of tsarist absolutism. Yet in November of the same year the Bolsheviks overthrew the moderate pro-Western Kerensky government, never to relinquish power again. Within weeks, they decided to withdraw from the war, and, if world revolution could not be accomplished now, at least a separate peace with the Quadruple Alliance would open the chance for unrestricted revolutionary development within the country and revolutionary propaganda abroad. The armistice and peace negotiations between

[12] Edmund von Glaise-Horstenau, *Die Katastrophe* (Vienna, 1929), pp. 205–234; Kann, *Nationalitätenproblem,* II, 260–291, 376–385.

the Quadruple Alliance, the Soviet Union, and a separate Ukrainian delegation started in mid-December, 1917, at Brest-Litovsk. With the Ukraine these negotiations were concluded on February 9, 1918, by a peace treaty. A new, nominally independent state was recognized.

Negotiations with the Soviet delegation under Trotsky's skillful leadership proved to be difficult. Hostilities were in fact resumed in early February, 1918, when the Soviets refused to accept the extremely harsh demands of the Central Powers. Actually they were no longer willing or able to offer military resistance. On March 3, the Soviet delegates were forced to return to the conference table and to sign a peace treaty on the dotted line.

Sound reasoning on the part of the Central Powers would have demanded that the peace terms agreed upon should have been moderate, in part to blunt the effective revolutionary Soviet propaganda, chiefly, however, to show to a world deeply impressed by President Wilson's Fourteen Point peace program of January 6, 1918, that the Central Powers now so close to defeat in the west, were, as victors in the east, more moderate than Allied propaganda would have it. The German and Austrian peace delegations, the former headed by the German secretary of foreign affairs Richard von Kühlmann, the latter by Count Czernin, and both under pressure of the German high command, actually did the opposite. They showed the world the brutality of an imposed German peace. The treaty of February 9, which recognized the Ukraine as a sovereign state, actually a merely camouflaged German-Austrian condominium to be ruled by right-wing groups, opened the prospects of further revolutionary change. Moreover, the cession of the Cholm district in Congress Poland to the new state and the announcement of the partition of Galicia in a western Polish and an eastern Ukrainian crownland embittered Austro-Polish relations from here on to the end of the empire.

Yet the Ukrainian "bread treaty," as it was called, promised substantial grain imports from the east and thus relief from the desperate food situation in Austria. Even these expectations were only partly fulfilled. But if there was some justification for the Ukrainian treaty in regard to the determination of boundaries with Poland, there was none for that with the Soviet Union, enforced by the German High Command and meekly acquiesced to by the Austrian authorities. Kurland, Lithuania, Livonia, and Estonia were meant to become German vassal states under German princelings, although the Hohenzollern empire had collapsed before the spoils could be divided between the various German dynasties. Congress Poland and Finland, now to be nominally independent, might at least indirectly have become German satellite states within the *Lebensraum* scheme directed toward the east. As for imperialistic designs they were second only to those of Hitler three decades later. A German peace was thus exposed to the world as true *Siegfrieden* and the last illusion that Austria could be more than a satellite with this system was shattered.[13]

Roumania had capitulated like Russia in December, 1917. Peace was concluded at Bucharest on May 7, 1918. This treaty was less important though just as harsh. It divided the Dobrudja between Austria, Germany, and Bulgaria, gave the Carpathian passes to Hungary, and handed over the rich Roumanian oil wells to the Central Powers for a number of years. From here on the Habsburg monarchy did no longer have to worry about the results of secret peace feelers or about a negotiated peace. In the face of what had happened in the east, both concepts had lost their meaning.[14]

In view of the desperate military situation Austria-Hungary on September 4, 1918, submitted a request to all warring nations to start peace negotiations at once. This move made without any diplomatic preparations was rejected off hand by the Entente. That it violated also the agreement with Germany concerning joint peace negotiations had become an academic question.

On October 4, the last joint Austro-German diplomatic action followed the breakdown of the Bulgarian front in the southern Balkans which opened the way for the Entente armies into Hungary. Austria and Germany now offered acceptance of Wilson's Fourteen Points as basis of peace negotiations, but clearly this concession came too late. As far as Austria was concerned it would have involved the evacuation of Russian territory and the restoration of Serbia, Montenegro, and Roumania as well as the acceptance of frontiers with Italy based on the ethnic principle. Even the establishment of a free Poland comprising the Austrian and Prussian Polish territories could be swallowed in the hope that at least the trunk of the Habsburg empire could be preserved. This hinged on Point Ten, which demanded opportunity for autonomous development for the people of Austria-Hungary. When Wilson, on October 18, 1918, rejected this offer with reference to the fact that autonomy in lieu of national self-

[13] Wolfgang Steglich, *Die Friedenspolitik der Mittelmächte 1917/18* (Wiesbaden, 1964), I, 313–415; Henryk Batowski, *Rozpad Austro-Wegier, 1914–1918* (Warsaw, 1965), pp. 147–152; Ottokar Czernin, *Im Weltkrieg* (Vienna, 1919), pp. 289–347; Richard von Kühlmann, *Erinnerungen* (Heidelberg, 1948), pp. 518–568; Wolfdieter Bihl, *Österreich-Ungarn und die Friedensschlüsse von Brest-Litovsk* (Vienna, 1970), pp. 35–130.

[14] Czernin, *Im Weltkrieg*, pp. 351–366; Kühlmann, *Erinnerungen*, pp. 550–562.

determination had become anachronistic by this time, the long-pending death sentence for the empire was, so to speak, officially pronounced.

What happened from now on, when all serious negotiations took place with the representatives of the Austro-Hungarian nationalities rather than the Joint Ministry of Foreign Affairs, is comparable to the frantic and senseless knocking about of a drowning man. On October 24 the luckless Burian resigned and was replaced by the liberal Hungarian Count Andrássy, whose bitter task was to terminate the German alliance, concluded by his father nearly four decades earlier.

Emperor Charles with his limited comprehension of affairs, overstrained by the blows of fate of the last two years, believed that this desperate act taken at this late hour would enable Austria to gain a separate peace. Naturally the offer was made in vain and Austria could at least have been spared an unnecessary further humiliation. On November 2 Andrássy resigned and a powerless ruler lacking a viable government behind him failed to appoint a successor. On the following day, after the collapse of the Italian front, the armistice between Austria-Hungary and the Entente powers was signed. Here Italy acted on behalf of the Great Alliance. The agreement permitted free movement of Entente troops on Austrian soil, unilateral disarmament, evacuation of Tyrol south of the Brenner pass, surrender of the Litoral and Dalmatia. Moreover, because of a dubious Italian interpretation of the time of the termination of hostilities, which earned cheap laurels for a foe of greater ambitions than military prowess, nearly 400,000 Austrian troops became prisoners of war. On November 11, the emperor formally relinquished his claims to participation in the government of Cisleithanian Austria and approved in advance of the form of government of the new Austrian republic. This somewhat ambiguous action was meant to get around the formal necessity of abdication. Yet neither abdication nor mere withdrawal from participation in governmental affairs was of practical significance any longer.

Notable is the fact that the German High Command after the signing of the Austrian armistice, in the wake of the German collapse ordered the march of German troops into Austria. Only the outbreak of the German revolution on November 9 prevented the spread of hostilities to Austrian soil north of the Alps. This military decision so desperate in nature and taken at so desperate a time made it doubly clear that the notion of an Austrian withdrawal from the Dual Alliance at an earlier stage, when Germany was in full command of her military forces, had been illusionary.

A final over-all observation on Austrian foreign policy may be in order at this point. Taking a view across the centuries, such policy was no more aggressive than that of other major powers, and if we distinguish between basic motivations and their execution probably even less so. Against the Turks, the French, the Prussians, the Italians, and finally the Russians, the Habsburg empire's five most powerful opponents through four centuries, Austria was by and large in essence in a defensive position. This does neither preclude nor excuse individual aggressive actions. On the whole, however, they were rare.

Neither can it be said that the foreign policy of the empire was in general conducted by men inferior in skill or vision to the statesmen of other countries. In a decisive period between mid-eighteenth and mid-nineteenth century the opposite was true. It was regrettable that in the supreme crisis leading to the World War and all through it men of inferior qualifications were at the helm. Yet it would be a simplification of history to say that even this fact was decisive.

What distinguished the foreign policy of the Habsburg empire from that of other great powers, and what definitely contributed to its decline and ultimate downfall, first, was the incongruity of its national composition which has been discussed throughout this study. It was impossible to subordinate the foreign policy of the multinational empire to the concept of the nation state. Yet, a less obvious fact, it could not be subordinated to distinct and clear-cut historic and geographic notions either. The historic traditions within the Habsburg empire, ancient and venerable as they were, ran across those of other states, and the geographic boundaries were drawn in the course of history partly by defense needs, but more often by almost accidental opportunities, hardly ever by clearcut objectives forged and maintained through the centuries. Hence the loss of non-contiguous territories in Italy, southwestern Germany, the Netherlands, and hence the acquisition of others, Galicia, Bukovina, and Bosnia. In neither case did long-established historic or geographic-economic ties ease the integration of such territories in the empire or make their loss particularly difficult. Similar examples can be found also in the history of other powers, but there they represented in the main rather the exception, in the Habsburg empire they represented the rule.

These facts do not obviate the existence of strong, ancient, and in many ways culturally beneficial traditions for the people under Habsburg rule and well beyond to the east, west, north, and south. They were not homogeneous, however, not well directed, not strong enough to guarantee the survival and least of all the revival of the Habsburg empire. It was the very tragedy of this situation that the essentially defensive position of the Habsburg empire in history was primarily not a consequence of moral strength but of inherent, deeply rooted political weakness. No foreign policy could in the long run succeed against such odds.

b) MILITARY AFFAIRS

In the war, the Habsburg empire with a population of 52,000,000 people lost 1,200,000 killed; 3,500,000 were wounded and 2,200,000 became prisoners of war, of whom an unspecified but large number never returned. Even in the briefest survey of the military events that led to this tragedy, one must also consider the operations in theaters of war, particularly on the western front, where Austrian forces, except for some units of heavy artillery, did not participate. Nominal head of the armed forces, until the death of the old emperor, was Archduke Frederick, reputed to be a better businessman than soldier. Actually leader of military operations was the chief of staff Conrad. Disregarding his damaging prewar political interventions, he was in some ways an ingenious strategist, but also a man of erratic temper, tense and difficult in his dealings with the German ally. Until December, 1914, the Balkan army was under the command of General Potiorek who had sloppily handled security measures at the time of the assassination of Sarajevo. Potiorek on December 2, 1914, the anniversary of the emperor's coronation, laid Belgrade at "his majesty's feet," but had to evacuate the city the next day with the sacrifice of lives of thousands of soldiers. Upon this act of Byzantinism he was belatedly cashiered. His replacement was Archduke Eugene, an able soldier, who distinguished himself later also in the Italian theater. After the death of Francis Joseph, the new emperor whose military experience was negligible, nominally assumed the supreme command, with no better results than his colleagues in such function, the German emperor and the Russian tsar. Conrad, equally difficult as subordinate and commander was now replaced by the more amenable General Arz von Straussenburg as chief of staff. Conrad in turn was given the command of the armed forces in South Tyrol, in which region he could claim expert knowledge. Yet an overambitious offensive of his in the spring of 1918 backfired and he was forced to resign. A man with far better than average gifts had on balance done great harm to the empire. As for other generals, some were poor like the archdukes Joseph Ferdinand and Peter Ferdinand, whose command was almost exclusively anchored in their exalted rank, some like the Croatians Svetozar Boroević von Bojna on the Isonzo front and Stephan Sarkotić von Lovćen on the Balkan front, were outstanding representatives of the Military Frontier tradition in the Habsburg armies.

The small Austrian navy, which owed its development largely to the interest of the archduke Francis Ferdinand and the excellent command of Grand Admiral Anton Haus, could defend the Austrian shores successfully against the superior Italian navy. All things considered the armed forces of the empire fought well until October, 1918. Except for some Czech regiments, which went over to the Russian enemy, and a number of individual deserters, usually from Slavic units, they served with dedication and almost complete disregard of the nationality conflict raging on the home front.

The over-all strategy of the war on the part of the Central Powers was geared to that of the stronger ally, Germany. During the second part of the war, Hindenburg and Ludendorff were in charge of the German General Staff. They directed also in a general way the common efforts of the Allies under the nominal command of the German emperor, although the Austrian emperor had reserved his veto power.

The German Schlieffen plan of 1905 provided that the main German forces should immediately after outbreak of the war be sent to the west with the objective of knocking out France before a British army could arrive on French soil. Meanwhile only small German detachments would face the Russians in East Prussia, while the bulk of the Russian armies, by far the largest of all warring countries, should be contained by Austrian forces, until such time—middle of September—when the French were expected to be defeated and the German armies could be transferred to the Russian front.

The plan failed. In early September, 1914, the German armies were checked in their advance toward Paris and the Channel by the French and British armies at the Marne. The initiative lost there was never regained. As for the east, the Germans with the support of some troops transferred from the western front (possibly just the ones lacking in the decisive battle at the Marne) routed the Russians in East Prussia under Hindenburg. Still, this spectacular success did not change the situation decisively. The Austrian armies, in early August in accordance with prearranged plans, had taken the offensive in Galicia, but by the end of the month they had to yield to numerically superior Russian forces. Accordingly the offensive was reversed. On September 1, the official Austrian war communique announced to an unprepared and stunned population the often-quoted sentence "Lemberg (Lwów) still in our possession." The following day the Russians took the city. The Austrians incurred enormous losses, particularly among the active officers, and withdrew to the Carpathians. Yet even this defense line was pierced at points in November.

Russian troops entered Hungarian mountain territories, though not yet the Hungarian plains. With determined effort and considerable German support the front could be held, and in early May, 1915, combined Austrian-German forces took the offensive, broke through the Russian front at Gorlice, and by late summer had conquered most of Poland and Lithuania. Conrad and Hindenburg's predecessor as Germany's chief of staff, the brilliant General von Falkenhayn, was credited with the planning of this operation. Still, in one respect it failed in its objective. It had been hoped that the great offensive would deter Italy from joining the Entente. But the treaty of London was signed two weeks before the offensive started.

Meanwhile events in the Balkan theater of war required Austrian attention. As mentioned before, the Austrian army against Serbia under an inferior general had done poorly against the fine Serbian troops, particularly well trained in new techniques of guerrilla warfare. By December, 1914, Serbian soil was cleared of Austrian forces. But when Bulgaria joined the Central Powers it was possible to start a new and now successful offensive against Serbia. In October, Austrian and German forces attacked from the west and Bulgarians from the east. In December, 1915, Serbia and Montenegro were conquered.

While the Austrians had not distinguished themselves particularly on the Balkan front, they stood up well to the task of fighting the Italian foe in a third major theater of war. Since the bulk of the Austrian armies was engaged against Russia and Serbia, their troops were vastly outnumbered by the Italians. Still, in eleven bloody battles along the river Isonzo from May, 1915, to September, 1917, the Italian forces, superior in numbers but not comparable to the qualities of the Serbian army, had gained hardly more than ten miles. Between October and December, 1917, they were in fact routed at Caporetto at the gate to the Italian plains. Three hundred thousand Italians became prisoners of war and an even greater number went over as deserters, by far the greatest number in any combatant force. Had it not been for French and British help, Italy would have been knocked out of the war. The strain on all fronts made it impossible for the Central Powers to send reinforcements to the southwestern front although they might have been of decisive importance.[15] The wear and tear of the war had become too great for the armies of the Central Powers, particularly after the first American forces appeared on the western front and opened up vast untapped resources of manpower. Even more

[15] The theory that the German high command did not want to defeat Italy completely, since in that case Austria would have lost interest in the war, cannot be proved.

important, the effect of the allied naval blockade on the food supply of the armies and the demoralizing effect of the worse food conditions on the home front made themselves increasingly felt.

In June, 1918, the Italians stopped a new Austrian offensive, started from South Tyrol, at the river Piave; a final ill-conceived offensive in late October, when the empire was in a process of dissolution already, was checked at the same fatal river. Hungarian troops left the front at that time and returned to their country, which was on the brink of revolution. In this critical situation in fall 1918 British troops broke through the Austrian front line and Italians followed. With British help the decisive Italian victory of Vittorio Veneto was thus secured.

As for the eastern front, from the end of June to September, 1917, the Russian forces under General Aleksej Brusilov started a major thrust, in which they reconquered East Galicia and the Bukovina. More than half a million soldiers, mostly Austrians, were captured by the Russians. With German help the defeat and retreat, primarily attributable to poor Austrian generalship, could be halted and the situation brought under control again. By July, 1917, East Galicia was reconquered, and the Bolshevik October offensive put an end to further Russian resistance. Still, the defeat of 1917 had increased Austrian dependency on Germany.

In the meantime, Roumania had decided to take the plunge and join the great coalition. In late August, 1916, the kingdom declared war on the Central Powers and its army invaded Transylvania. In one of the most brilliantly executed operations of the war joint Austrian and German forces under Falkenhayn took the counteroffensive in late September and, supported by Bulgarians from the south, took Bucharest in early December. The Roumanian danger had passed.

Still, Roumania was a relatively minor foe. The decisive—be it well understood, purely military—cause of the breakdown of the Central Powers, apart from the consequences of national conflict and economic attrition, was the German defeat in the west and the failure of the unrestricted U-boat warfare. By spring, 1918, in particular with the arrival of large American forces in France, the conclusive turn of the military operations had become fully evident. By August, 1918, the German forces were in full retreat. Shortly afterward, in September, the collapse of the Bulgarian forces was of great impact. By the end of the month, an Entente army, assembled in Salonica on Greek soil,[16] broke through the Bulgarian

[16] Greece had entered the war on the side of the Western Allies in June, 1917, but a provisional government established under Venizelos in Crete had sided with the Allies as early as September, 1916.

frontline at Monastir. Bulgaria capitulated, and thereupon the path to the Danube and Hungary was open to the Entente armies. The Central Powers could not hold the line in a new major theater of war. In this sense, the Italian victory at Vittorio Veneto was the mere aftermath to a decisive turn of events, reached previously in a political as well as in a military sense. Notwithstanding great efforts and enormous sacrifices of men on all sides, the powers bound to win because of military and economic strength, but also because of the superiority of a democratic ideology, had prevailed.[17]

B. Domestic developments in Austria-Hungary

a) wartime absolutism and wartime constitutionalism in austria

The national problems had driven the Habsburg empire into the war, the same problems led to a political situation, in which it could not survive defeat. It was doomed to dissolution. The development of these national problems during the war in Austria and Hungary will have to be discussed in separate sections. At this point it is necessary to survey the setting, in which these explosive changes occurred.

The primary factor in domestic policies during the first part of the war was the decision of the Austrian prime minister, Count Stürgkh, approved of by Emperor Francis Joseph, to keep parliament adjourned. This move allowed for unrestricted censorship of the press, resort to extraconstitutional military courts in political matters, prohibition of assemblies, and in general of the curtailment of civil rights (*Grundrechte*), guaranteed to the Austrian peoples in the basic state law 142 of 1867.

These curtailments could not have occurred as easily, if parliament, sent home by the government in March, 1914, had remained in session. As noted before, a session of parliament during the crisis following the assassination in Sarajevo might conceivably have saved the peace. Yet without condoning Count Stürgkh's unconstitutional action, from his pragmatic point of view he had good reason to stick to it. The loyalty of the great majority of Germans and Magyars—not excluding the So-

[17] On the over-all course of military operations see Rudolf Kissling, *Österreich-Ungarns Anteil am ersten Weltkrieg* (Graz, 1958). See further, Franz Conrad von Hötzendorf, *Aus meiner Dienstzeit, 1906–1918* (Vienna, 1921–1925); see Vols. IV and V and Oskar Regele, *Gericht über Habsburgs Wehrmacht* (Vienna, 1968). See also Imre Gonda in Fritz Klein, ed., *Österreich-Ungarn in der Weltpolitik* (Berlin, 1965), pp. 162–182; Gerhart Ritter, "Die Generalstäbe und der Kriegsausbruch," in Wolfgang Schieder, ed., *Erster Weltkrieg: Ursachen, Entstehung und Kriegsziele* (Köln, 1969), pp. 283–308.

cialists until 1917—was uncontested almost to the end of the war. Most Slavs in the first war years probably wanted to sit things out and see which way things were turning, irrespective of the prompting of the political exiles from abroad. The best the government could hope for was thus a loyalty on short notice of complete reorientation, depending on a radical change of the military situation. As for some groups—the Ruthenians after the Russian occupation of Galicia, the Serbs, and the Italians—it would have been illusory to count even on conditional loyalty. On the other hand, swelled by the military power of the great German ally, the demands of the Austro-German nationalists became more sweeping. The expression of their feelings of arrogant nationalist superiority was hardly hampered by the absolutist war government. All things considered, Stürgkh had indeed good reason to expect that a convocation of the Austrian parliament in wartime would not lead to responsible discussions between different political and national groups, which would give the world the impression of a free people divided as to means but united as to overall purpose. In lieu of this, one could expect passionate opposition against the outrages of military justice, of death sentences, imprisonment, and trial of political leaders in star-chamber proceedings without due process of law.[18] The increasingly critical food situation aggravated by the fact that Hungary refused to send food supplies to Austria, would have evoked storms of indignation.[19] All this could conceivably have been accepted and free discussion on these points might have done some good. Yet an open debate, which would have challenged obligations of loyalty to the empire, was another matter. When parliament could finally reassemble at the end of May, 1917, representatives of some Slavic national groups gave more or less veiled notice of possibly severing their allegiance to Austria. Fear of such a situation had made convocation of parliament unacceptable for the Stürgkh cabinet. A state which is faced by dilemmas of this kind has lost its raison d'être.

Stürgkh, no vicious tyrant but a bureaucrat of German centralistic tendencies, who like most Austrian high dignitaries despised noisy obstructionism and filibustering in parliamentary proceedings thus held to his course. In October, 1916, he was shot dead by an Austrian left-wing

[18] Stürgkh, though a prime mover of wartime absolutism, opposed the illegal and ruthless interference of the Supreme High Command with civil government and due process of law. See Christoph Führ, *Das k. u. k. Armeeoberkommando und die Innenpolitik in Österreich* (Vienna-Cologne, 1968), pp. 15–159 passim. On the Stürgkh administration during the war see Alois von Czedik, *Zur Geschichte der k. k. österreichischen Ministerien,* IV, 432–524.

[19] Hungary, however, supplied the armies in the field with food.

Socialist, Friedrich Adler, son of the party leader, Victor Adler. Stürgkh's assassination was the first open act of defiance against the war regime in any country and a storm signal that the Socialist International, shattered by the nationalist furor of the July crisis of 1914, would become alive again. The events which led to Stürgkh's assassination had not done credit to Austria. In the public trial, reported extensively in the press, Adler in an open break with wartime absolutism was enabled to turn his defense into an indictment of the regime.

Sentenced to death and later reprieved by Emperor Charles, Adler, who had attacked an unjust cause by unjustifiable means became the most celebrated international revolutionary leader in prison. He used his popular appeal resulting from a revolutionary deed in 1919 to rally the Austrian workers against a Communist putsch—a curious twist of history. In 1916, the impact of Adler's action and of his subsequent trial on public opinion was great enough to pierce the power of absolutism.[20]

In another political trial, which preceded that of Adler, court proceedings in the country were subject to severe criticism. From May, 1915, to November, 1916, Dr. Karel Kramář, the brilliant Young Czech leader, was tried for high treason by a military court in secret and sentenced to death by hanging. Whether Kramář was a determined enemy of the Habsburg empire before he underwent this gruesome experience, is debatable. That he became one after he had been amnestied in July, 1917, is certain. From here on he ranks among the staunchest champions of the complete independence of his people.[21]

Stürgkh's successor was expected to modify the system of wartime absolutism. Ernest von Koerber, who had been prime minister from 1900 to 1904, was one of the more enlightened and experienced administrators. His tenure of office bridged only the last months of Francis Joseph's and the first one of Charles I's reign. His resignation had three reasons. First, he believed the planned convocation of the Austrian parliament to be premature, but the young emperor wanted to present himself to his peoples as soon as possible as constitutional monarch. Secondly, Koerber objected to far-reaching concessions to Hungary about to be offered in the negotiations on a new ten-year compromise. The new emperor, on the other hand, did not want to disturb his relations to Hungary with too

[20] See [Friedrich Adler], *Friedrich Adler vor dem Ausnahmegericht* (Berlin, 1919) and Ronald Florence, *Fritz* (New York, 1971), passim; Robert A. Kann, "Am Beispiel Friedrich Adlers" in *Neues Forum,* XIII:154 (1966), 601–603 and XIII:155–156, 727–730.

[21] [Karel Kramář], *Der Hochverratsprozess Kramář* (Vienna, 1919).

adamant a position. The compromise, finally passed under Ernst von Seidler, Koerber's second successor, represented a middleground position. On this point reasonable men might differ, yet on the third and most important one Koerber was certainly right. He was firmly opposed to Charles' almost immediate coronation in Hungary, or more precisely to his taking the coronation oath before Austro-Hungarian relations and the conflicts in the Austrian and Hungarian versions of the Compromise of 1867 would have been straightened out. After Charles had taken the coronation oath, the question of federal reform in the whole empire could be ruled out, and according to the Hungarian position even in Cisleithanian Austria alone. In this oath the king-emperor had to pledge that he would preserve the territorial and constitutional integrity of Hungary. This made any prospective changes in the Compromise legislation legally impossible.

Furthermore, as will be remembered, the Compromise was based on the promise of constitutional government in Austria, and this meant according to Hungarian theory the Austrian constitutional laws of 1867. Actually, Charles' commitments went further. If he had any leverage to persuade the Hungarian prime minister, Count Tisza, and the Hungarian parliament, that franchise should be extended and at least some kind of national autonomy granted to the non-Magyar national groups, such opportunity existed only before the coronation. Now the well-meaning young Charles wanted all these reforms, yet inexperienced, shifty, and anxious to please everybody all the time, he succumbed to Tisza's entreaties to take the coronation oath and hope for the best afterward. Koerber, who foresaw this development, resigned.[22]

New appointments in the first month of Charles' reign included that of the somewhat mystically inclined Autro-German centralist, Count Arthur Polzer-Hoditz, one of his former tutors as chief of the emperor's personal cabinet. The key positions were given to two men who had belonged to his uncle the late Archduke Francis Ferdinand's brain trust, the Bohemian feudal lords Count Ottokar Czernin as foreign minister and Count Heinrich Clam-Martinic as Austrian prime minister. Clam-Martinic was offered the position as a second choice, because Czernin had declined.[23] Clam-Martinic could be described as a moderate conservative,

[22] Czedik, *Zur Geschichte der k. k. österreichischen Ministerien,* IV, 525–565; Gratz, *A Dualizmus Kora,* II, 338–363; May, *The Passing of the Habsburg Monarchy,* I, 422–447; Kann, *Nationalitätenproblem,* II, 236–248, 369–372.

[23] A previous offer made to Dr. Alexander Spitzmüller, former Minister of Commerce, had been withdrawn on Czernin's insistence.

basically German, but moderately so in outlook, with many noble Czech connections. As a former adviser of Francis Ferdinand, he was considered to be a friend of some form of limited national autonomy in the language questions and administrative matters in general. In no way did he support federal programs. Under Clam-Martinic, parliament after three years of absolutism was reconvened on May 30, 1917. This was about all he accomplished. His outworn program of limited national autonomy was rejected by the German nationalists as ignoring the historical leading position of the Germans in Austria. To most Slavs represented in the Reichsrat on the other hand, Clam's plans appeared too vague and noncommittal, and the radicals felt that the time for reform had passed altogether. To paraphrase a German saying, it was a program that would not tempt a dog to leave the warm corner behind the stove. Clam-Martinic gladly relinquished his office in mid-June, 1917.[24] His qualifications as prime minister had been poor, but those of his successor, Ernst von Seidler, were poorer. An official in the Ministry of Agriculture and, like Polzer, a former tutor of Charles, he assumed office, first of a provisional nature and then as regular prime minister until mid-August, 1918. A narrow-minded German centralist, unimaginative and stubborn, he did what could be expected from a man of his caliber, essentially nothing. Nevertheless, under Seidler, but at the personal initiative of the emperor, an amnesty was issued for political prisoners. It was strongly criticized by the military, especially Conrad, the determined foe of subversive activities. It was also condemned by the German nationalists. On the other hand, the amnesty did not have the hoped for impact on the Slavic nationality representatives in parliament. Yet with the benefit of hindsight we know that it was a step in the right direction. In fact it succeeded for a time to blunt the appeal of the propaganda of the political emigrants abroad.

During the second half of Seidler's tenure the political crisis was aggravated. In January, 1918, a wave of strikes occurred in the munitions and other armament factories, particularly in and around Vienna. Here workers at starvation rations and wages had to toil frequently under the sanction of martial law. They were frozen in their civil jobs, but stood now under military discipline and had to work for token military pay. These strikes were influenced by the Socialist Left under the leadership of Otto Bauer, who had returned from captivity in a prisoner of war camp in Russia. Ominous was also, in February, the sailors' mutiny in the

[24] Felix Höglinger, *Ministerpräsident Heinrich Graf Clam-Martinic* (Graz-Cologne, 1964).

Austrian naval base at Kotor (Cattaro) in southern Dalmatia. It was suppressed but, in spite of some executions, because of Socialist intervention not with quite the same harshness as otherwise might have been the case. Still, the Socialist Right under the influence of Karl Renner remained completely loyal to the German alliance, and this position, on the whole supported by the German-oriented party leader Victor Adler, carried the day for the time being.

The Seidler regime had failed, largely because of the insoluble character of most of the empire's political problems at that time. But Seidler, revealing an extraordinary degree of political insensitivity, wanted to solve the national issue in Bohemia at this late hour by administrative partition in national districts, so hateful to the Czechs. In August, 1918, he resigned, but such were the contradictions in the nature of the weak emperor, that he appointed this nonentity chief of cabinet, although Seidler, in his German-centralistic proclivities was opposed to the emperor's principles.[25] Seidler's successor was Baron Max von Hussarek, a conservative, devout, and erudite former minister of education, who tried to reconcile the Southern Slavs by conversion of the dualistic into a trialistic system. After the declaration of Corfu of July 20, 1917, in which Southern Slav leaders from Serbia and émigré leaders from the empire announced the formation of a future united Southern Slav state comprising Croats, Serbs, and Slovenes, Hussarek's plan appeared completely anachronistic. Even if the problem had not been settled in the meantime from outside, he had as little reason to hope that the Hungarian government would be willing to change the Compromise of 1867 as that a new Poland would be willing to be tied to the dying Habsburg monarchy. Concerning both issues he hoped against hope. If reforms could not be reached in negotiations with Hungary a shortcut was necessary. A crown council of October 15 approved of an imperial manifesto which proclaimed the conversion of Cisleithanian Austria into a federation of national member states. Hungary was to be reconciled by a clause which promised that the lands of the Hungarian crown should not be affected by this constitutional change.

By this move, the emperor hoped that President Wilson might be persuaded to accept the Habsburg empire's adherence to the Fourteen Point program as a basis for peace negotiations. Within two days Charles had

[25] Glaise-Horstenau, *Die Katastrophe,* pp. 235–264; Arthur Count Polzer-Hoditz, *Kaiser Karl* (Vienna, 1929), pp. 386–552; Helmut Rumpler, *Max Hussarek* (Graz-Cologne, 1965), pp. 22–103; Richard G. Plaschka, *Cattaro-Prag: Revolte und Revolution* (Graz-Cologne, 1963), pp. 15–192; Ludwig Brügel, *Geschichte der österreichischen Sozialdemokratie* (Vienna, 1922–1925), V, 329–340.

learned that his naïve action—belated as to content, precipitate as to manner of execution—had doubly misfired. The manifesto issued on October 16 fell far short of the assurances given by the Entente powers to Czechs, Southern Slavs, and Poles. This was known to almost everybody, and on October 18 even to the emperor. At that time Wilson rejected the peace notes of the Central Powers which had accepted the Fourteen Points in principle, as no longer in line with actual developments.

Emperor Charles and Baron Hussarek might have been forgiven, for attempting the impossible, if they had announced the proclamation of an empire-wide federation plan with the slim hope that this would meet at least a partly positive response in Austria and even in Hungary. The manifesto, as issued on October 16, however, was a farce. The pledge to preserve the integrity of Hungary meant that Croatian, German, Roumanian, Serb, and Ruthenian territories would remain divided. Thus the manifesto was to have created not a federation of national groups but of truncated splinter groups. All the emperor got in response was the declaration of the Hungarian government that Charles' action, according to the previously discussed Hungarian constitutional theory, was in violation of the Compromise of 1867. With this rejection the Realunion with Austria had ended. What remained for a few weeks was the personal union of merely the same ruler in both states. The emperor had been forewarned of these developments by the Hungarian Prime Minister Wekerle's strong dissent in the crown council of October 15. By this time the process of disintegration had proceeded so far that little attention was given any longer to the momentous act of severing the Realunion with Hungary.[26]

Hussarek resigned, and on October 27 the last imperial cabinet under Professor Heinrich Lammasch took office, a former professor of criminal and international law in Vienna and a champion of peace through the war years. Members of the new government were the distinguished constitutional historian Josef Redlich and a future chancellor of the Austrian republic, professor of moral theology, Ignaz Seipel.

It could not even be said, paraphrasing Sir Winston Churchill, that this cabinet presided over the disintegration of the empire—the cabinet could merely watch it. When Lammasch came into office the national governments seceding from Austria were either in the saddle already or in the process of establishment. Lammasch could do nothing but resign within a fortnight. His resignation did not even mark the end of imperial Austria, but just the disappearance of a symbolic government without power.

[26] Helmut Rumpler, *Das Völkermanifest Kaiser Karls vom 16.X.1918* (Vienna, 1966), passim; Kann, *Nationalitätenproblem,* II, 284–288, 382.

Lammasch's resignation coincided with a final imperial manifesto of November 11, which announced Emperor Charles' withdrawal from participation in the government of German-Austria (Deutschösterreich) and approval of her form of government. This act of state was not the end of the disintegration process but merely the end of the illusion that imperial Austria had still been in existence until November 11, 1918.[27]

b) WARTIME GOVERNMENT IN HUNGARY

Prewar Hungary is generally pictured as a country more opposed to national and social reforms than Cisleithanian Austria. This study does not take exception to such interpretation, but the war aims of the Magyar nationalists, unlike those of the Austro-German nationalists, were not focused on the support of Germany's annexation program but on the preservation of the Magyar dominant position in Hungary. This implied in principle opposition to territorial gain of non-Magyar territories which would further imperil the precarious Magyar position in Hungary. Besides, charges against the Hungarian franchise system were certainly justified, but it has to be admitted that Magyar national pride kept parliament in session from the first to the last day of the war and opened thus a forum for the free discussion of public affairs. In contrast to this, Austrian parliament, elected by general franchise, meekly submitted for almost three years to continued prorogation of its meetings. True, the government in Hungary could rely on the support of a pseudo-liberal, by no means truly democratic majority, whereas in Austria genuine liberalism never succeeded in coming to power. Still, respect for a constitutional history dating back to the *Bulla aurea* could not be matched by a similar vigorous tradition in Austria.

Tisza had firm control of the government throughout the first half of the war. The food situation in Hungary was far better than in Austria, but not entirely because of larger production and better soil conditions. In Hungary, as well as in Austria, the food crisis was largely due to manpower shortage and poor transportation facilities, resulting from the severe demands of the armed forces on labor and railways. At least the first and major one of these problems could be handled better on the large Hungarian estates with their agricultural machinery than on the small mountain farms in Austria.

[27] Zbyněk A. B. Zeman, *The Break-Up of the Habsburg Empire 1914–1918* (London, 1961), pp. 119–176; Josef Redlich, *Schicksalsjahre Österreichs 1908–1919: Das politische Tagebuch Josef Redlichs,* 2 vols. (Graz-Cologne, 1953–1954), I, 307–318, II, 214–218, 287–291, 361–363, 383–385; see also Kann, *Sixtusaffäre,* pp. 81–84.

Tisza failed, however, in the understanding of the nationality and franchise problems. As late as September, 1918, he shouted to a Southern Slav delegation in Bosnia: "May be we will have to perish but before that we will still have the strength to crush you."[28] He opposed stubbornly the modest efforts to give the vote to soldiers who had served at the front. Such refusal was, by then, an untenable position even in Magyar Hungary. Possibly Tisza's aversion to any concessions was based on the fact, that Count Michael Károlyi had become the chief proponent of reforms. In the summer of 1916 this aristocratic frondeur broke away from Andrássy's and Apponyi's Independence party and established his own left-wing party club. Károlyi's demands for national autonomy, general franchise, and breaking up of the big estates were unacceptable to Tisza in principle, but even more hateful was to him the fact that these demands were proposed by a man whom he considered to be a traitor to his class. To be sure he liked the left-wing intellectuals not much better, the sociologist Oscar Jászi foremost among them. Their allegiance to western democratic principles was to him evidence of decadence bordering on treason. Even more firmly did he reject socialist programs.

In May, 1917, Tisza, whose pride, stubbornness, and probably also Calvinist creed were objectionable to King Charles, was forced to resign, though he remained the leader of the parliamentary majority.[29] His successor for a few months was the more amenable Count Moritz Esterházy. Because of Tisza's and his supporters' opposition he failed to have a limited franchise reform bill passed. In August, 1917, he was replaced by that shrewd compromiser, Alexander Wekerle, who managed at least to conclude the negotiations on the economic compromise. But in regard to the nationality question he did not come closer to a solution than Tisza and a bill introduced in December, 1917, to liberalize somewhat the franchise system was stalled in parliament. The government did little to prevent this. Actually the so-called Democratic Bloc for Electoral Rights consisting of members of the Károlyi party and several liberal groups, among them Vilmos Vázsonyi and his followers as genuine moderates and Oscar Jászi's adherents to the left, were probably no longer interested in solving controversial problems within the dualistic system. The main objective of such groups—with the exception of the Vázsonyi faction—

[28] Glaise-Horstenau, *Die Katastrophe,* p. 287.

[29] Gratz, *A Dualizmus Kora,* II, 318–352; Ludwig Windischgrätz, *Vom roten zum schwarzen Prinzen* (Berlin, 1920), pp. 197–210; Glaise-Horstenau, *Die Katastrophe,* pp. 67–112, 267–308; Hanák, in Ervin Pamlényi, ed., *Die Geschichte Ungarns,* pp. 480–495.

was to propagandize the franchise question as one of the issues to be solved in the coming revolution. Not even the prime minister could be considered any longer as reliable supporter of the establishment, as his attitude proved in response to the imperial manifesto of October 16, announcing the conversion of Cisleithanian Austria into a federation. Yet when Wekerle declared the Realunion as void and the personal union as last remaining tie between Austria and Hungary, he had little choice. He was forced now to satisfy not the king but Károlyi and the rising radical Left, but particularly the National Council established on October 23. Charles, ill-advised as so often before, yielded to pressure and Károlyi was appointed prime minister on October 31 [30] with the hope, that the revolution could now be prevented. In fact, it was accelerated. The same day Tisza, fearless to the last, was killed by red guardists, and the following day Károlyi asked to be absolved from his oath of allegiance to the king. Charles complied and Károlyi was henceforward only responsible to the nation. Archduke Joseph, the head of the Hungarian Habsburg line, played a dubious role in this affair. Yet King Charles could hardly be criticized for bestowing the seal of office on a man if he could have been expected to bring about the essential social and national reforms. Károlyi succeeded in this at best only to a limited extent, his good intentions notwithstanding. King Charles, as ruler a failure himself, had handed over the government of Hungary to an aristocratic enfant terrible, certainly his intellectual superior, but a dilettante without any gifts of statesmanship in domestic or foreign policy. The man who as prime minister had proclaimed the Hungarian republic on November 11, 1918, had to relinquish power as head of state in March, 1919, to spend most of the remaining thirty-six years of his life in exile as backseat critic of political events.[31] Károlyi had failed to secure more favorable armistice terms for the country, to put into practice his reasonable agricultural reforms, and to bring the country closer to the bitter necessity of reconciliation with its neighbors. These were all formidable tasks, but the man, so keen as social critic, so effective as speaker for the radical opposition, had accomplished nothing but to hand over the country—involuntarily to be sure—to a Communist dictatorship which in turn paved the

[30] After Wekerle's resignation and before Károlyi's appointment, a moderate cabinet under Count Janos Hadik had been in office for two days. Gratz, *A Dualizmus Kora,* II, 352–388.

[31] Except for a brief return to Hungary in 1946 and a subsequent tenure of two years as ambassador to France, 1947–1949. When Károlyi resigned then in justified protest to Stalinist outrages in Hungary, he had proved again his lack of political foresight after his return to Hungary.

way for the more sterile and at least in its beginnings equally harsh dictatorship of the Right.

Yet this was not the bankruptcy of an individual's policy, it was the failure of the century-old system, which had divided the role of leadership and opposition both within the establishment. Even men who did not merely feign such opposition like the Apponyis and Andrássys but were serious about it, had to come from the ranks of the ruling oligarchy. No wonder that Károlyi failed to comprehend the spirit of the new revolutionary times, just as his intellectual supporters, who had received their political training in the coffee houses of Budapest. To the peasants and workers they remained just as much alien as the unhappy count, who cuts such an unhappy figure in Hungarian history, all his noble dreams and personal sacrifices notwithstanding.[32]

C. The conflict between the national groups comes to a head

The supreme crisis in this struggle, the deadly disease of the multinational empire during the war, can be understood only in conjunction with a purview of military and political events. The steady deterioration of the position of the Central Powers in these respects affected the strategy and the success of the political emigrants abroad. It made, of course, its influence on domestic developments felt as well, where wartime censorship in the long run was of little avail. Furthermore, the increasingly desperate food situation had its primary impact on the home front.[33]

Probably no other single factor contributed as much to the radicalization of the masses. History has shown repeatedly that people can put up for a long time with the suppression of civil liberties by wartime absolutism, and that they may accept heavy war casualties as inevitable; but mothers just won't tolerate the slow starvation of their children while the fathers are absent in the service of an unpopular war machine. The vari-

[32] Kosáry, *A History of Hungary,* pp. 377–384; Oscar Jászi, *Magyariens Schuld, Ungarns Sühne* (Munich, 1923), pp. 1–66; Michael Károlyi, *Fighting the World* (New York, 1925), passim; Kann, *Nationalitätenproblem,* I, 142–146, 402–404; Hanák, in Ervin Pamlényi, ed., *Die Geschichte Ungarns,* pp. 499–513.

[33] See General Ottokar Landwehr von Pragenau, *Hunger: Die Erschöpfungsjahre der Mittelmächte 1917/18* (Vienna, 1931), passim. In 1917–1918 Landwehr was chief of the joint Austro-Hungarian food committee (Gemeinsamer Ernährungsausschuss). See also Wilhelm Winkler, *Die Totenverluste der österreichisch-ungarischen Monarchie* (Vienna, 1919); Iván T. Berend and György Ranki, "Ungarns wirtschaftliche Entwicklung 1849–1918" in A. Wandruszka and P. Urbanitsch eds., *Die Habsburgermonarchie 1848–1918* (Vienna, 1973–), I, 520–527. Prinz Ludwig Windischgrätz, *Vom roten zum schwarzen Prinzen* (Berlin, 1920) pp. 156–314.

ous hunger revolts, the naval mutiny, and the munition workers' strikes of January, 1918, contributed strongly to the formulation of the social demands, which became an intrinsic factor in the November revolutions of 1918. Although there is not necessarily a direct connection between national programs, hunger revolts, and demands for social reform, there is a strong indirect connection. People, who have chronic grievances (as was the case with the nationality issues), are apt to perceive all social ills as related to them and to blame the government accordingly. The war had largely started as a struggle over nationality issues and in this sense all the evils resulting from it could be linked to Austria-Hungary's stubborn refusal to comprehend and to attempt to solve the Southern Slav problem before the assassination of Sarajevo. Moreover, the inter-nationality conflict could no longer be focused primarily on points of national honor and prestige, belabored by the tiresome oratories of semi-intellectuals. Socialist propaganda had effectively fought such outworn slogans. Genuine socialist theorists like Otto Bauer, Karl Renner, and others had made it abundantly clear that nationality discrimination involved social discrimination as well and that its first and chief victims were the underprivileged class of industrial and agricultural workers.

a) CISLEITHANIAN AUSTRIA

Of the concomitant causes discussed above, the desperate food situation and increased social radicalism were more strongly felt in the more industrialized western part of the empire than in Hungary. They have to be understood as the orchestral accompaniment to the problems discussed below. The political leverage of the Austro-Germans had steadily increased during the war. Before the reconvening of parliament in May, 1917, this strength was largely the result of the influence of the German alliance. With the radicalization of Slav national movements, which included even the estrangement of the largely conservative Polish parliamentary club, the government now depended almost entirely on German support. The radical German national wing of the essentially nationalist German Nationalverband tried to take advantage of this situation by promoting a national program, irrational even in peace and absurd in war. The demands presented, for instance, in the so-called Osterbegehrschrift of 1915 included the separation of Galicia and possibly also of Dalmatia and Bukovina from the bulk of the Austrian lands to assure an artificial German majority. German was then to become the official state language and Bohemia was, on the basis of these achievements, to be divided in German and nationally mixed, but not Czech administrative districts. The Austro-German alliance was to be incorporated in the constitutional laws of the dual states. But these and other reform plans of the same kind were not just day dreams of beer-consuming German secondary-school teachers. In late summer, 1918, while the western powers had already recognized the various national councils on a provisional basis and the German western front was pierced, the German parties in Austria voted for an old pet project, the establishment of a German district court in Trautenau in Bohemia, a foolish move ignored by the Czechs.[34]

Such aberrations from sanity were common but there were exceptions. The moderate German national parliamentary leader in Bohemia, Rudolf Lodgman von Auen, strove honestly and vainly for a German-Czech compromise making no claims for German cultural superiority.[35] The Social Democrats opposed the German nationalist program with greater energy during the second half of the war than they had ever done in peacetime, while the Christian Socials, though not fully committed to the policy of the Nationalverband, supported to a degree its political program for the recognition of a privileged German position anchored in constitutional law, in other words a German state nation in Austria. Such policies were to a considerable extent influenced and furthered by the *Mitteleuropapogramm* of the German progressive pastor Friedrich Naumann, published first in 1915. Naumann, who in social questions showed considerable understanding, cannot be classified as a crude German imperialist, even though he promoted a program which would have gone beyond the dreams of the earlier nineteenth-century German economic semiimperialists Friedrich List, Karl Friedrich von Bruck, and the federalist Constantin Frantz. Naumann wanted to "contitutionalize" the Austro-German alliance and supplement it by a customs union and a strictly coordinated military defense system. The commanding position in this setup would have been held by Germany. Austria would have enjoyed little more than autonomy, although this was not spelled out in so many words.

Naumann looked with satisfaction on a Germanization policy in Austria, but even more strongly did he recommend continuation of Magyarization in Hungary, because he rightly assumed that the Magyars, embattled by Slavs and Roumanians, would be the strongest champions of

[34] Molisch, *Geschichte der deutschnationalen Bewegung,* pp. 238–265; Kann, *Nationalitätenproblem,* I, 96–102, 375–382; II, 244–252, 370–374; Zeman, *The Break-Up of the Habsburg Empire,* 84–94, 116–118, 147–176.

[35] Kann, *Nationalitätenproblem,* II, 247–248, 372.

Mitteleuropa. Naumann's program received strong support from the German Right, but also from German and Magyar moderate rightist and center parties, in addition to that of the right-wing Socialist Karl Renner, and of the Magyar leftist Oscar Jászi.

To do justice to Naumann, he was in many ways more moderate than the German military and industrialist annexionist establishment. Precisely for these reasons he was an all the more valuable ally for these interests. Personally a man of integrity, he made the program of industry and military forces appear respectable and idealistic in the eyes of the middle class. It found considerable support within the German Nationalverband in Austria. Although the emperor was opposed to it, Czernin, though not fully committed to Naumann's ideas, hoped that accommodation in the direction of a customs union could persuade the German military around Hindenburg and Ludendorff to make concessions to the Entente in regard to Alsace-Lorraine and Belgium. In this respect like in so many others, Czernin was to be disappointed.[36]

Thus the German policy of the government, the Nationalverband, the Christian Socials, and until the outbreak of the war largely that of the Socialist, had failed. Still, most Austro-Germans, the only ones of the empire's peoples, remained loyal to the crown and the imperial government to the end. The convocation of a provisional national assembly for German-Austria on October 21, 1918, consisting of the German deputies in the Austrian parliament was merely a response to the break-away movement in full swing among all other national groups in the empire. No political initiative can be seen in this inevitable action, and this is also true for the proclamation of a provisional German-Austrian constitution on October 30. It declared German-Austria (Deutschösterreich) to be a part of the coming German republic. German-Austrian parliamentarians believed—as it turned out with good reasons—that an independent and hence isolated German-Austrian republic would alone be held responsible for the actions and commitments of the dissolving empire. The "Anschluss" under existing conditions was a natural reaction to this concern. Even German-Austrian persistence in regard to the Anschluss, after it had become clear that the union with Germany would be of no help

[36] Friedrich Naumann, *Mitteleuropa* (Berlin, 1915); Gustav Gratz and Richard Schüller, *Die äussere Wirtschaftspolitik Österreich-Ungarns: Mitteleuropäische Pläne* (Vienna, 1925); Droz, *L'Europe Centrale,* pp. 217–222; Kann, *Nationalitätenproblem,* II, 252–260, 373–377. See also Leon Grosfeld, "Mitteleuropa und die polnische Frage," in *La Pologne au XIIe Congrès International des Sciences Historiques à Vienne* (Warsaw, 1965), pp. 115–132.

in freeing the country from the stated liabilities, can be understood. At least German-Austria would not be entirely set apart.

For obvious psychological and less obvious political reasons it was impossible now to retreat voluntarily from the position taken on October 30. The proclamation of the German-Austrian republic on November 12 took cognizance of this situation. It followed the emperor's relinquishment of his constitutional rights and his approval of the constitutional pattern of the new Austria. The people's failure to identify fully with the new state, from which the coming republic was to suffer so much, was probably more the result of lack of popular initiative in its creation than—as widely assumed—the identification of the new state with defeat and the empire's dissolution. The Anschluss movement after 1918–1919 which must be distinguished from that during the revolutionary crisis, still represented this fear of initiative. It was primarily a response to untoward events and less the fullfillment of a program, though idealistic motives should not be denied.[37]

The Czechs were the national group whose policies were most clearly directed by political émigrés and whose political strategy proved most successful. These émigrés were guided since 1914 by the towering personality of Thomas G. Masaryk, who combined in an ideal manner a western outlook and western political connections with a deep understanding of Russian Slavism. He also had the good fortune to be relieved of much routine work and squabbles, so irksome among political exiles, by the consummate, but controversial skill of Edvard Beneš. Masaryk's and Beneš's leadership benefited from the fact that Kramář was removed from the political arena for almost three years, up to the July amnesty of 1917, because of the ordeal of his trial and later confinement. As little as the leaders abroad wished for this situation, Kramář with his conservative orientation toward Russian tsarism, was the only representative Czech until the Russian March revolution of 1917 who could have deflected the western course charted by the political émigrés under Masaryk's guidance.

Leadership by the prominent parliamentarians at home was indeed uninspiring and was harshly criticized by Beneš. Allowances had to be made for the fact that the exiles abroad were free to express their opinion and to conduct their policies accordingly. Similar action undertaken in

[37] Charles A. Gulick, *Austria from Habsburg to Hitler,* 2 vols. (Berkeley-Los Angeles, 1948), I, 43–65; Walter Goldinger, *Geschichte der Republik Österreich* (Vienna, 1922), pp. 9–22; Karl R. Stadler, *The Birth of the Austrian Republic 1918–1921* (Leiden, 1966), pp. 17–32.

Austria would have led to high-treason proceedings by Austrian military courts, as was the case in regard to Kramář and other Czech leaders. Émigrés abroad criticized the Czech parliamentarians in Vienna and Prague not quite fairly for undue caution. Actually and understandably, up to the beginning of 1918 they were not clear themselves about their political aims. The Czech declaration at the reopening of the Austrian parliament in May, 1917, asked for the conversion of Austria into a multinational federation and the establishment of the lands of the Bohemian crown and of the Hungarian Slovak territories as one of its member states. In no way could such plans be considered as treasonable. Even the Epiphany Declaration of 1918 of the Czech parliamentary and dietal deputies of the lands of the Bohemian crown, which asked for the right of national self-determination, did not break off all bridges to a future within the Habsburg empire. Yet only a few months later after the revelations of the Sixtus affair had destroyed all hopes for a separate peace of the western powers with Austria-Hungary, did the French in late June, 1918, recognize the Czech National Council in Paris as the political body which represented the Czech nation. Almost simultaneously the U.S. government issued a declaration which interpreted Point Ten of the Fourteen Points program not in the sense of comprehensive autonomy but of self-determination directed toward independent statehood. This statement was supplemented by the Pittsburgh Declaration of the representatives of Czech and Slovak organizations in America, which was issued with the cooperation of Masaryk. According to this document, the Slovaks would form an autonomous nation within the new Czechoslovak state. These developments were made inevitable by the participation of Czech legions consisting of prisoners of war and deserters from the Austro-Hungarian armed forces in the battles in all theaters of war, but particularly their operations on the Russian front and their subsequent tribulations in Siberia.

Masaryk, realist that he was, did not consider the proclamation of the Czech National Council in Prague as the government of the new Czechoslovak republic on October 28, 1918, to be the formative act in creating statehood. This constitutional transaction was to him merely recognition of the inevitable, after the Austrian authorities had yielded quietly and thus had avoided a hopeless struggle. According to Masaryk, the decisive actions were the official recognition of the new state in mid-October, first by France and a few days later by the United States. The deep attachment of the Czechoslovak republic to France and the trauma following its betrayal by the Third French Republic in 1938 have their roots in this mid-October action of 1918. All things considered, none of the national groups seceding from the empire had a representation abroad which worked as determinedly and skillfully for statehood. Recognition of this truth must not overshadow another one: there were no people either who through the centuries had quietly prepared themselves better for the revival of the past in the setting of a deeply tragic future.[38]

The fact that the Czechs were settled entirely in Cisleithanian Austria and even jointly with the Slovaks still entirely in Austria-Hungary, whereas the Polish nation was partitioned between three empires, played an important part during the war. Neither problem could be solved then, but the Polish issue, which had to be faced on the national and international levels, generated greater difficulties. The existing rift between various Polish political factions was only one cause but not the main one that Polish national organizations were less effective than the Czech representation abroad. The primary cause was the character of the Polish problem as bargaining issue within the two great alliances, on one side between the western Entente powers and the more directly involved tsarist empire, and on the other between the Central Powers themselves. In both cases the Poles from the start of the war were directly engaged in negotiations with one or the other partitioning power to whom Poles individually were bound to owe allegiance. In the beginning of the war this meant further that these Poles were more objects of discussion than participants in them. The conspiratorial character of the Czech liberation movement was largely absent in the Polish situation. This does not mean that at least tacit support of the Polish freedom movement by the Poles themselves in Austria as well as in Prussia and Russia was absent. It does mean that it becomes practically impossible to perceive the Polish struggle for independence in any of these countries in isolation.

Polish nationalism before the war was suppressed more severely in Prussia than in Austria. The Prusso-German wartime administration, in which the commanding generals in every province practically took over important functions of civil government, restricted the possibilities of Polish political activities. Russian Congress Poland had been, since summer 1915, in the hands of the Central Powers and remained so except for the strip of territories reconquered during the Brusilov offensive the following summer and then lost by the Russians again. Thus public Polish political activities during the war were primarily concentrated in Galicia

[38] Thomas G. Masaryk, *Die Weltrevolution* (Berlin, 1925), pp. 386–435; Edvard Beneš, *Der Aufstand der Nationen* (Berlin, 1928), pp. 555–696; Zeman, *The Break-Up of the Habsburg Empire* (London, 1961), pp. 217–245.

and in Congress Poland under the administration of the Central Powers. Russia was soon eliminated as a directly codetermining factor, but not so as an indirect one. The tsarist government at the beginning of the war had promised to restore a united Poland including the Austro-Polish and Prusso-Polish territories under the tsar. In domestic policies this would have meant roughly a restoration of the Polish status on a larger scale than that existing between 1815 and 1830. This promise was vaguely implemented by the appointment of a joint Russo-Polish committee, which was supposed to work out the specifics of a new Polish autonomy. The formation of this commission coincided with the conquest of Congress Poland by the armies of the Central Powers after the breakthrough of Gorlice in spring, 1915, and its task therefore became meaningless. More seriously was taken the announcement by the new government under Prince Georgij Lvóv as temporary prime minister and Alexander Kerensky, then minister of justice, after the outbreak of the Russian March revolution of 1917 that a truly independent Poland should be restored. The outcome of the Russian November Revolution confirmed the notion that from the Russian side any claims for the reconquest of Poland had been dropped, although the frontier issues remained open. These were the intangibles which the Austrian and German policy in regard to the Poles had to face.

It was largely the Austrian tolerance toward Polish nationalism based on half a century of cordial relationship with the Polish club in parliament, which facilitated the establishment of a Polish national committee under the leadership of Joseph Pilsudski on the socialist Left, supported by Roman Dmowski on the moderate Right. A Polish Legion was established now, a move for which preparations had been made before the outbreak of the war with the tacit approval of the Austrian government. It failed to understand, however, that Pilsudski and his followers presented a philosophy different from that of the Szlachta members in the Polish parliamentary club in Vienna. We noted earlier the disappointing effect of the stillborn declaration of November 5, 1916, by the Central Powers, which promised the establishment of an independent Congress Poland—actually rather a joint Austro-Hungarian-German satellite state or condominium which should serve as recruiting station for the Allied armies. The promise of an expansion of the Galician autonomy followed; it was supposed to console the Austrian Poles for their disappointment in the November declaration. It had no practical impact.

From here on the situation moved from bad to worse from the Austrian point of view. The Poles in conquered Congress Poland and those in

Galicia, Poznań, West Prussia, and Prussian Silesia resented the division of Russian Poland under two separate Austrian and German military administrations. The establishment of a Polish state council in Warsaw as merely advisory body, primarily to the German military administration, offered small comfort. Pilsudski, the man of the hour and the future, rejected the demand that Polish troops should take an oath of allegiance to the military command of the Central Powers and was thereupon detained in Germany. This arrest of the highly popular leader squashed the hopes of creating a Polish legion loyal to the Allied cause. In fact the Russo-Polish members, whose loyalty to the Central Powers was suspected, had to be ousted from the legion. The Austrian and Prussian Poles on the other hand were bound to serve in the regular military units of the countries whose citizenship they held.

Meanwhile the process had begun of disposing of or bartering the Polish conquest to the mutual benefit of the Central Powers, or, as seen from the angle of Berlin and Vienna, to the advantage of one or the other of them. Originally the German government would have been ready to have a Congress-Polish state in a satellite relationship linked to Austria. This might possibly have served as compensation for expected more sweeping German conquests. Bethmann-Hollweg, however, objected to the union of Russian Poland with Galicia because such union would have raised hope for the liberation of the Polish minority in Prussia, which, as will be remembered, was more seriously suppressed than the Austrian Poles in Galicia. Obviously this "solution" could not be made palatable to any Polish nationalists, however moderate. Czernin as foreign minister was willing to reverse this course and to agree to the affiliation of a Congress Poland augmented by Galicia with Germany, if the German emperor's government would be willing to remove the gravest obstacle to peace and agree to the return of Alsace-Lorraine to France and to the unconditional restoration of Belgian sovereignty. Czernin's policy would have looked better if he had not tacked another condition to his proposal, namely a free hand for Austria in Roumania. This could have meant an affiliation of Roumania and Transylvania as a satellite state within Austria-Hungary. The German government saw in this proposal a shift in the balance of the Central Powers to the advantage of Austria. Yet even if Germany had been amenable to Czernin's proposal Tisza was not. He objected to any open or camouflaged trialistic solution which would have established Poland plus Galicia or Roumania plus Transylvania as third partner in a revised Compromise of 1867. He was, however, subsequently generous enough to accept the annexation of substantial parts of Roumanian territory and their incorporation into Hungary.

Neither of these solutions, even if agreed to between diplomats, would have been acceptable to the people directly affected. There were also other obstacles. The planned settlements of the Polish question would have established a dangerous precedent in regard to the Southern Slav problem, as the Austro-Hungarian authorities saw it. Furthermore, the Austro-German nationalists, although they had constantly asked for the administrative separation of Galicia from the bulk of the Austrian territories, were opposed to the establishment of a Slavic state as equal partner of Austria and Hungary.

To add to these rising troubles, Czernin had to agree in Brest-Litovsk to the transfer of the Congress-Polish Cholm district to the Ukraine. Even though this concession was largely justified on ethnic grounds, it violated the concept of the historic frontiers of Poland and led to the permanent alienation of the Polish club in the Austrian parliament. From now on it ceased to support the government. Yet this club could hardly speak for the interests of the nation on the rapid march toward unification and restoration, although its members had come out for the establishment of an all-Polish state comprising the Austrian, Prussian, and Russian Poles. Affirmation of a constitutional tie of such a state with Austria-Hungary by the loyal conservative Austro-Poles was no longer to be taken seriously. The club dissolved in mid-October, 1918, and now the leadership of Polish affairs was clearly in the hands of a Polish committee in Cracow, in conjunction with a regency council in Warsaw that had switched from mere advisory to executive functions. On November 3, 1918, the Polish republic was proclaimed in Warsaw. This outcome was clearly predictable but the further difficulties to establish the frontiers of the new state in the east and the ordeal it had to undergo two decades later were still unpredictable. Clearly, diplomatic bargaining by the Central Powers on the strength of temporary military success was built on sand. It could neither overcome the concerted will of the affected peoples, nor the powerful historic tradition of the dream of a resurrected Poland, whose long awaited hour had finally struck.[39]

The Polish problem was complicated further by the Ruthenian question. The Polish-Ruthenian compromise which had been negotiated for

[39] Batowski, *Rozpad Austro Wegier,* pp. 162–211; Bernadotte E. Schmitt, ed., *Poland* (Berkeley-Los Angeles, 1945), pp. 70–85; Werner Conze, *Polnische Nation und deutsche Politik* (Cologne-Graz, 1958), pp. 307–403; Czernin, *Im Weltkrieg,* pp. 271–287; Kann, *Nationalitätenproblem,* I, 231–238, 434–435.

years between the two national groups in Galicia and which should have come into force in July, 1914, fell through with the outbreak of the war. A wave of hysteria now swept through the unhappy crownland. To the Polish feeling of national superiority was added that of patriotic ardor; the Ruthenians were accused of being disloyal and traitors to the cause of the Central Powers. Logic is not a strong element in nationalism and the fact that the Poles themselves became increasingly inclined to break away from Austria did not diminish the zeal with which these charges were voiced.

The Russian invasion of Galicia put the Ruthenians in a quandary. It affected the conservative pro-Russians and the liberal pro-Ukrainians alike. Cases of collaboration with the enemy undoubtedly occurred. They did not justify mass arrests and executions, often with the flimsiest evidence. The persecution of the Ruthenians in Galicia, and to a lesser extent in the Bukovina and in Hungary, was a sorry chapter in the history of the nationality struggle during the war. Whether the Polish-Ruthenian compromise could ever have been enforced, if the war had ended in a stalemate is an open question. Yet it is clear that an Austrian solution was out of the question after the Ukraine had been recognized as sovereign state in early Febuary, 1918. The establishment of a western Ukrainian republic on October 19, comprising also the Hungarian Ruthenian territory, was largely obviated by the seizure of East Galicia by Polish troops. Further developments, the proclamation, in January, 1919, of a united Ukrainian republic now independent from great power control in the west, but soon subject to a far stricter one from Bolshevik Russia, converted the country after a bloody civil war into a member republic in the Soviet system. These events culminated in the preliminary (October, 1920) and permanent (March, 1921) peace treaties of Riga between the Soviet Union and a Soviet Ukraine which, however, acted hardly as free agent. For all practical purposes this meant that the western powers had relinquished their interests in the major part of the area. But they had retained some control through the western Ruthenian branch by way of France's allies, of whom Poland was to control East Galicia, Roumania, the Bukovina; Czechoslovakia was to control the Carpatho-Ukraine—ethnically the most absurd solution.

Some of these problems transcend the scope of this study. Yet the unpredictable irony of history led to a strange result, related to our topic. The Ruthenian people in Galicia and in the Bukovina, who had violently demanded the breakup of the empire, remained for another two decades under foreign rule, those in Hungary for almost thirty years. In the first two instances the Polish administration, despite the treaties for the protection of minorities under the sponsorship of the League of Nations, was harsher than the Austrian. To the Austrian government, Ruthenians represented after all an important counterweight to Polish nationalism. The Carpatho-Ukrainians in Czechoslovakia were better off than when under Hungarian rule, yet they remained as isolated from their conationals as before. All these three groups of the western branch of the Ukrainian people achieved only belatedly national recognition and unification in the Soviet Union, but at the price of submission to a totalitarian regime.

The thrust of these observations is not that the Ruthenians were necessarily better off under Austrian rule than under a Soviet regime. Such comparisons are irrelevant, because the choice between a dissolving empire and a new Ukrainian state did not exist. The former, irrespective of the preferences or aversions of the Ruthenians was on the way out, the future of the latter was as yet unpredictable. This unpredictability of history even at short range is, indeed, the lesson to be derived from the destiny of this ethnic group. The path of the Ruthenians conjointly with the Ukrainian mother nation to independent statehood seemed clearer than that of other Slavic peoples. The line-up of a western-supported Poland in the conflict with the Soviet Union had permanently destroyed that possibility by 1921 as it appears now, but could not be foreseen then.[40]

As pointed out before, the Italian question in the Habsburg empire during the war represented a severe roadblock to the establishment of either a separate peace of Austria-Hungary or a joint one of both Central Powers with the Entente. The situation created also a serious military problem. By 1915 it had become clear that the Austrian maritime crownlands and South Tyrol would be lost in case of an Italian victory. Certainty of this loss stiffened the Austrian war efforts in the southwest, but it made also Italy the most determined champion of the dissolution of the empire since a landlocked Habsburg empire could never have accepted such mutilation in the long run.

The Austro-Italians in the Trentino and the Litoral were accordingly hardly camouflaged supporters of complete separation. Even the supporters of boundary lines along ethnic frontiers in Tyrol, the so-called Salurnisti, yielded at the beginning of the war to the views of the champions of a strategic frontier reaching as far north as the Brenner pass.[41]

[40] Michael Hrushevsky, *A History of the Ukraine* (New Haven, 1941), pp. 500–555; Czernin, *Im Weltkrieg*, pp. 313–351.

[41] The language frontier at Salurn is about sixty miles to the south of the Brenner pass.

Even the martyr of Italian irredentism, the Socialist Cesare Battisti, at the beginning of the war converted to the more radical view. Many Austro-Italian clericals, who up to the end of the nineteenth century had supported concepts of autonomy within Tyrol, had shifted to the radical line even earlier than Battisti. The prince bishop of Trento, Dr. Cölestin Endrici, during the last years of the war a staunch irredentist, had to be confined to German-Austrian territory, outside of his diocese.

The radicalization of the Italian claims was in some respects no longer primarily directed against Austria but against Yugoslavia in the making. Italy expected Yugoslavia to become after the war a highly unpleasant neighbor at the shores of the Adria. Thus the abandonment of the ethnic principle for strategic frontiers gave Italy an inordinately large part of Istria and, hardly justified, a string of Dalmatian islands, as well as by illegal seizure Fiume (Rijeka) in 1919. All these land grabs were largely meant to be precautionary measures against future Yugoslav expansion. Nevertheless, the true or frequently alleged suppression of Italians by Austria served as motivation for these actions. Allied propaganda had understandably publicized widely the shameful circumstances of Battisti's execution.[42] It is true nevertheless that the Austro-Italians, even in wartime, were on the whole better treated than irredentists among other national groups. Respect for Italian culture and the notion of inevitable separation may have played a part here, in spite of the fact that the war against Italy was the most popular facet of World War I in Austria. Yet the issue of moderate or harsh treatment of Italian nationals in Austria had little effect in the face of inexorable historical contingencies.[43]

b) HUNGARY

There is an important difference between the action and philosophy of the Austro-German and the Magyar nationalists. The Austro-German nationalists were dominated by the Pan-Germans in the Reich and approved of a German annexation program. It would serve them in the Habsburg empire but also and even better in case the empire would

[42] At the beginning of the war Battisti had fled to Italy to participate as officer in the Italian campaign against Austria. Captured by the Austrians in summer of 1916 he was, as Austrian subject, legally correctly condemned to death. Yet this fact does not excuse the hideous circumstances of the execution of this brave man.

[43] Bernhard Schloh, in Franz Huter, ed., *Südtirol* (Vienna, 1965), pp. 293–297; Anton M. Zahorski-Suchodolski, *Triest* (Vicuna, 1962), pp. 46–62; Valiani, *La Dissoluzione dell'Austria Ungheria,* pp. 344–413; Tamborra, *L'Idea de Nazionalitá e la Guerra 1914–1918,* pp. 89–115; Theodor Veiter, *Die Italiener in der österreichisch-ungarischen Monarchie* (Vienna, 1965), pp. 93–108; Claus Gatterer, *Cesare Battisti* (Vienna, 1967), pp. 49–114.

dissolve and they would be given the opportunity to join Germany. As for oppressive tactics against the non-Magyar groups in Hungary, the Magyars outdid the Austro-Germans because they had much wider opportunities in a country more clearly under Magyar domination than Cisleithanian Austria under German. But, as noted, the Magyars had the primary interest of preserving the status quo, that is, to prevent the incorporation of further Slavs and Roumanians into Hungary, because it would make the Magyar position more precarious. Although during the *quid pro quo* negotiations between the Central Powers Tisza had agreed to the incorporation of substantial Roumanian territories into Hungary, this agreement was a transitory phase of the negotiations with Roumania in winter and spring of 1918. The cession of Roumanian Carpathian passes, as determined eventually in the otherwise very harsh treaty of Bucharest in May, 1918, while not justified on ethnic grounds, was limited in nature. Tisza's original attitude reflected the Hungarian response to what was considered to be treason by a former ally. Inasmuch as the Roumanian alliance was secret, this attitude was more unreasonable than the Austrian in regard to Italy's switch from the Triple Alliance to the Entente. The most that can be said in defense of the handling of the nationality question by the Hungarian establishment during the war is that it subsequently somewhat modified its position. Tisza had at least the virtue of consistency. He stubbornly opposed the extension of franchise except for soldiers who had been decorated for outstanding bravery at the front. So-called Magyar moderates, such as Baron Gyula Szilassy, promoted a vague and contradictory concept of general franchise linked to further Magyarization efforts, apparently in accordance with Naumann's prescriptions. The aristocratic frondeur Prince Louis Windischgrätz, on the other hand, proposed extended but not general franchise. More sophisticated were the proposals of the left-wing liberal intellectual Oscar Jászi, minister for national minorities under the Károlyi regime. Jászi, a scholar, was stronger endowed with critical faculties than with an understanding of practical politics. He criticized the weakness of the imperial Austrian and Hungarian system, but his reform proposals were interesting but unrealistic—they included a modified acceptance of Naumann's Middle Europe, an imperial federation anchored in the "Big Five" (Germans, Magyars, Czechs, Poles, and Croats), and a cantonal reorganization of Hungary according to the Swiss pattern.[44] Just as unclear were the notions of his chief, Károlyi, who at various times had supported

[44] Czernin, *Im Weltkrieg*, pp. 349–366; Károlyi, *Fighting the World*, pp. 398–400; Jászi, *Magyariens Schuld, Ungarns Sühne*, pp. 233–239; Kann, *Nationalitätenproblem*, I, 83, 141–145, 372, 402–404; II, 8–9.

proposals for national autonomy, federalization of Hungary, a Danube confederation, and only as last resort national self-determination. If possible, he as well as Jászi wanted to pursue their reforms within the frame of the historic frontiers of Hungary, obviously impossible even in peacetime. To do Jászi and Károlyi justice, it should be noted that they had proposed their programs in times when their promotion required considerable political courage. In the question of the change of the Hungarian franchise system to a democratic one, the record of both men was clear and straightforward.

Concerning the Hungarian national groups, the alternatives in regard to the Roumanian problem were either continued suppression or secession and union with the kingdom. Hopes entertained by Czernin during his tenure as Austrian minister to the Roumanian court (1913–1916), that a Roumanian kingdom enlarged by Transylvania could be brought into a satellite relationship to Austria-Hungary, were illusory during the critical war years. Even earlier, in spring, 1914, only the imaginative Czernin himself took them seriously. As for Roumania, it may be doubted that a more generous peace than that concluded in May, 1918, in Bucharest, could have changed matters substantially. That treaty divided the Dobrudja between the Central Powers and Bulgaria, turned over a number of Carpathian villages and some mountain passes to Hungary, but kept the oil wells under the joint administration of the Central Powers. A more moderate attitude might—perhaps—have impressed the western powers, but hardly Roumania herself. When the process of the Habsburg empire's disintegration had begun, the outcome was inevitable. Roumania resumed the war against an enemy that in a military sense no longer existed and hardly in a political sense either. Thus between the end of November and the first of December, 1918, the kingdom brought about the union with Transylvania, the Banat, and the Bukovina with little military efforts. In fact, Roumania which so long had been sitting on the fence, waiting for the highest bid from the Central Powers and Russia cashed in eventually from both. The state gained southern Bessarabia from the Soviet Union as well. These acquisitions made Roumania for two decades the most conspicuous winner of all the countries involved in the war. Yet history rarely repeats itself. The extent of the territorial gains, which in east and west transcended the ethnic boundaries, led to tragic involvement of the country in the struggle between Hitler Germany, her satellites, and the Soviet Union. The Second World War brought more severe tribulations for Roumania than those endured during the First World War.[45]

[45] Daicoviciu and Constantinescu, *Brève Histoire de la Transylvanie,* pp. 372–389; Nicolas Jorga, *History of Roumania* (London, 1925), pp. 258–265; Erich Prokopo-

In theory it would have been easy for the Slovaks to plan for an intra-Hungarian solution, because the Slovaks were, in substance, confined to northern Hungarian territories.[46] Magyar oppressive nationality policies thwarted such possibilities before, and even more so during the war. At the same time political persecutions had driven a relatively large number of Slovak leaders into exile, such as Milan Štefánik and Stefan Osuský. Popular leaders in the country who may have been amenable to the autonomy concept within Hungary, like Father Andre Hlinka and Milan Hodža (the future Czechoslovak prime minister) could do little under Hungarian wartime absolutism, even though Hodža was a member of parliament. It was small wonder therefore, that the Slovak political émigrés came under the leadership of the Czechs. In April, 1918, at the congress of the suppressed nationalities in Rome, Czechs and Slovaks were represented by a joint delegation and the final resolution passed there proclaimed a joint political future.

The difficulties in the Czech-Slovak relationship which were to become an intrinsic part of the history of the first and second Czechoslovak republics received little attention before the hour of victory. Besides, the substantial number of Slovak immigrants to the United States cared little about ethnic and political differences between the two nations. As noted above, the Pittsburgh declaration of June 30, 1918, agreed upon between Thomas G. Masaryk, himself of Slovak descent, and the American Slovak leaders confirmed the union of Czechs and Slovaks in the new state. The promise of autonomy for the Slovaks in the future republic presented no difficulty then, though it turned out later that it meant too sweeping a concession to the Czechs and too little to the Slovaks. These problems, however, were not anticipated in the days of joy about the bloodless separation from the Habsburg empire. The proclamation of the new Czechoslovak republic by the National Council in Prague on October 28, 1918, was followed the next day by a solemn concurring resolution of the Slovak National Council on October 29 at Turčiansky Sväty Martin on Slovak soil. No serious offer of an alternative solution within Hungary had been made to the Council by the Hungarian government to that day. The Károlyi cabinet of October 31, had it come to power a few weeks

witsch, *Die rumänische Nationalbewegung in der Bukowina und der Dako-Romanismus* (Graz-Cologne, 1965), pp. 130–159; Miron Constantinescu, *Études d'Histoire Transylvaine* (Bucarest, 1970), pp. 43–113.

[46] An unspecified but substantial number of people of Slovak descent lived in Austria in particular in Bohemia, Moravia, and also in Lower Austria. The official Austrian national statistics, however, failed to recognize the Slovaks as ethnic group separate from the Czechs.

earlier, could hardly have changed matters. Yet, not too little was offered to the Slovak people but nothing. They took the only possible course of union with the Czechs, because reform within Hungary had become anachronistic and independent statehood would have exposed the Slovaks to expansionist pressures from the east without any protection from outside.[47]

The national evolution of the Southern Slavs was discussed in the preceding chapter in the context of Austrian developments, because the union movement, fully suppressed in Hungary before the war, could be initiated cautiously from Austrian soil. The history of the three Southern Slav peoples in Austria-Hungary is so closely interwoven that only joint discussion can clarify the issue. Therefore it would seem logical to survey the situation during the war from the angle of the Serbian kingdom, whose position in the union movement had become commanding. Yet analysis of events in Serbia beyond the realm of international relations would transcend the scope of a study of the history of the Habsburg empire. Accordingly the next best alternative seems to be to place this final discussion of the question in the context of the national crisis in Hungary where a substantial relative majority of the empire's Southern Slavs lived.[48] This discussion pertains to an era when police suppression of the union movement was no longer effective.

A new impetus for the Southern Slav union movement did not have to wait for the July crisis of 1914. It began with the outbreak of the first Balkan war in October, 1912, when the fight for the liberation of Serbian territory from the grip of the first sick man in Europe, the Ottoman empire, began. The sympathies of all Southern Slav peoples in this struggle were definitely on the side of Serbia. To some extent this situation reversed itself briefly after the assassination of the archduke in Sarajevo. Now sizable rightist elements in Croatia and many of Croatian stock in Bosnia, as well as many Slovenes, turned against the Serbs. The attacks on individual Serbs and the wrecking of Serb stores should be considered as mob action rather than as expression of the popular will, but the majority of the empire's Croats and even more so Slovenes sided then with the imperial cause. Field Marshal Boroević, in command at the Isonzo

[47] Jozef Lettrich, *History of Modern Slovakia* (New York, 1955), pp. 43–58; S. Harrison Thomson, *Czechoslovakia in European History* (Princeton, 1953), pp. 276–325; Victor S. Mamatey, *The United States and East Central Europe 1914–1918* (Princeton, 1957), pp. 29–34, 282–284, 336–339; Kann, *Nationalitätenproblem,* II, 283–286, 450–451.

[48] The Southern Slavs in Austria and Bosnia-Hercegovina combined outnumbered those in Hungary only by a ratio of approximately four to three.

front and Colonel General Sarkotić, who held a command in the Balkans [49] were popular military leaders, who represented the Croatian Military Frontier tradition at its best. A Southern Slav legion, consisting of prisoners of war and deserters, organized by the Entente, on the other hand, had fewer than 20,000 members. In effectiveness it could not be compared with the famous Czech legion. Rumors about the extent of concessions to Italy made by the Entente at the expenses of the Southern Slavs in the secret London treaty of April, 1915, restrained the desire to establish contacts with the western powers. Accordingly, Croatian and Slovene sympathies could largely be kept in line with the interests of the Habsburg monarchy.

This state of affairs did not change much during the first three years of the war. The Slovene parliamentary leader, Anton Korošec, in a letter of January, 1917, to the Austrian prime minister, Count Heinrich Clam-Martinic, expressed the loyalty of the Slovene people, and other Slovene leaders, the priests Ivan Sustersič and Janez Krek, cooperated with the Austro-German Christian Socials, in particular with the conservative wing of the party.

At the reopening of the Austrian parliament at the end of May, 1917, the Croatian-Slovene position shifted to some extent. Now the union of all Southern Slavs within the empire was asked for, that is, in effect, a trialistic solution. Such demands, which had been raised before, did not challenge the role of the dynasty directly. This program was now fully (that is, in a less anti-Serb vein) supported by the Frank party in Croatia and to a substantial part by the high Roman Catholic clergy under the leadership of the archibishop of Sarajevo, Josef Stadler. It was still understood also that the dominant role in this union project should accrue to the largest Southern Slav national group on Austro-Hungarian soil, the Croats.

Yet all this represented only one side, and as it turned out the less significant one, of the whole story. In the later years of the war, particularly in 1918, Magyar pressure decreased under the new banus of Croatia, Anton von Mihalovich, a moderate Croatian nationalist. Now the movement for union with the Serbs in the kingdom came into the open, aided by the Croatian Socialists but also by the peasant party under Stjepan Radić and at least indirectly by members of the high clergy. With such support it had become respectable. At the same time, the Yugoslav political émigrés in London made their weight felt under

[49] Sarkotić was also the last imperial and royal governor of Bosnia-Hercegovina; see also Bauer, *Zwischen Halbmond und Doppeladler,* pp. 140 f.

the leadership of the Croatian democrat Ante Trumbič, who had split with the conservatives. The Declaration of Corfu of July 20, 1917, proclaimed the coming union of Serbs, Croats, and Slovenes in a future Yugoslavia. To the two latter national groups as well as to the Serbs in the empire this meant, of course, a shift of allegiance from the house of Habsburg to the Karadjordjević dynasty. The shift for all three was no longer a major problem.

The Rome congress of the oppressed nationalities in the spring of 1918 recognized the union of the Southern Slav peoples, but to avoid trouble with Italy at a critical juncture of the war the delegates abstained from asking for the determination of boundaries at this time. This postponement of the decision in regard to foreign relations can be understood better than the failure to agree upon federal principles in the organization of the new state. Yet both omissions had regrettable consequences. The first led to inequitable ethnic boundaries to the disadvantage of the Southern Slavs and, thereforee, to protracted differences with Italy. The second, a built-in autonomous system in a still largely centralized state —to Croats and Slovenes merely a greater Serbia—made the establishment of a royal dictatorship in 1929 possible.

The Declaration of Corfu, proclaimed after deliberation of the Croatian and Slovene political exiles with the Serbian government, was an important political step. This does not mean that events in the monarchy were of lesser significance. Serbia led the union movement, but the decisive question was, whether the Southern Slavs in the Habsburg empire were willing and able to keep up with the program activated abroad.

The Serbs in the camp of the western Allies had not only the advantage of unimpeded propaganda facilities, supported by the government in exile. Their resistance in the struggle against the Austrian, German, and Bulgarian armies, the sacrifice of nearly one-third of the population of Serbia in that fight, appeared to many Southern Slavs within the empire as the most convincing factor in favor of Serbian leadership.

Against these feelings stood the different western historic, religious, and cultural tradition of Croats and Slovenes. While the question of union with the Serbs was still not clarified within the Habsburg empire, the establishment of national councils in Carniola, Dalmatia, Bosnia, and on October 6 one in Zagreb for all Southern Slav peoples under Habsburg rule, proceeded smoothly and practically unimpeded by the Austrian and even Hungarian governments. These councils were agreed that the union of the Southern Slav peoples in the Habsburg empire was imperative and that the trialistic or subtrialistic solutions[50] ventilated by the crown but rejected by Hungary had as little chance of success as the unhappy Hussarek manifesto of October 16, 1918. This conviction in itself led to the compelling conclusion that the Habsburg dynasty, split between an Austrian Dr. Jekyll and a Hungarian Mr. Hyde, could not bring about this union and would have to quit. This quandary moved the union movement close, but not close enough, to the final agreements with Serbia. The Slovenes remained largely opposed to a regime under the orthodox Karadjordjević dynasty and would have preferred a republican government. Radić, the Croatian peasant leader, wanted to emphasize the federal or preferably the mere confederal character of the union. He proposed three heads of state, only one of them to be the king of Serbia. Yet these differences notwithstanding, union with Serbia was to be the over-all objective. By the end of October, 1918, the national councils had agreed in principle to the transformation of Serbia into the SHS (Serbian, Croatian, Slovene) state. Even the emperor had in a way sanctioned this solution by implication by handing over the Austro-Hungarian navy to the evolving new Yugoslavia on October 31.[51]

Within the empire, the Slovene leader Korošec informed the western powers of the formation of a Croatian National Council as the legal representation of the Southern Slav peoples within the dissolving Habsburg monarchy. This declaration did not conflict with the union agreement. It was meant primarily to secure Croatian and Slovene participation in the coming peace conference. But the expectations of the Austro-Hungarian Southern Slavs were disappointed because Serbia alone was represented at the peace conference. This rejection added fuel to a protest movement against unification under Serbian leadership in a greater Serbia rather than in a genuine tripartite federation. By the end of November, however, the National Council in Zagreb yielded and the new centralized Yugoslavia, with weak safeguards for national autonomy within the three-nation state, was proclaimed on December 1, 1918. An uninterrupted series of crises and renewed frightful bloodletting in the Second World War followed before a genuine federal structure was agreed upon with great difficulties in 1945 and enacted finally in 1946.

Thus the Southern Slav peoples had succeeded in the midst of a bloody war to bring about peaceful secession from the Habsburg empire. By

[50] As noted, a subtrialistic solution meant the division of the empire in three component parts, of whom the third, the Southern Slav unit, should be subordinated to Austria and Hungary.

[51] Within days, however, the navies of the Western powers divided the bulk of the Austro-Hungarian navy among themselves.

putting off the determination of the frontier question according to ethnic principles and the transformation of the union into a genuine federation, they had not eliminated any of their basic difficulties. Besides, they had to yield to Italian annexionist actions, soon to be aggravated by Fascist imperialism. For their failure to settle the constitutional issue they had to pay by more than two decades of latent civil war. The unsolved crises in domestic and foreign affairs were directly related to the Yugoslav tragedy during the Second World War. The union movement in 1918–1919 had fully succeeded in severing by then anachronistic bonds. It had failed to break the ground and to establish ground rules for a viable political organization in internal and international relations.[52]

D. A final reflection on the dissolution process

The abundance of studies dealing with the disintegration of the Habsburg empire may roughly be divided into two overlapping groups. One holds that the impetus to the dissolution of Austria came from forces outside the empire, the other sees domestic problems as the main cause. In the first case a merely contributory role is assigned to the national groups at home. In the second the exile organizations represent the supporting cast. The former view perceives the causes mainly in the activities of the political exile organizations abroad and their influence on the policies of the Wilson administration in the United States and the British and French governments.[53] For Italy such extraneous influence of exile organizations was hardly necessary. In the group of studies which assigns chief responsibilities to political exile organizations, we find those who defend the role of the Habsburg empire in Europe as balancing factor and sometimes even glorify it as a model how different nationalities can live together in peace and prosperity as long as they are not misled by agitators. It is also pointed out that numerous original and well-perceived reform plans in the last years of the empire's peacetime existence were

[52] Fran Zwitter, "Les Problèmes Nationaux dans la Monarchie de Habsbourg," 122–128, and by the same author "The Slovenes and the Habsburg Monarchy," *Austrian History Yearbook,* III:2 (1967), 182–188; Bogumil Vošnjak *A Bulwark Against Germany* (London, 1917), pp. 213–263; Bogdan Krizman, "The Croatians in the Habsburg Monarchy, *Austrian History Yearbook,* III:2 (1967), 113–115, 144–158; Kissling, *Die Kroaten,* pp. 97–127; Dušan A. Lončarević, *Jugoslawiens Entstehung* (Vienna, 1929), pp. 633–660; Hermann Wendel, *Der Kampf der Südslawen* (Frankfurt, 1925), pp. 621–755; Josef Matl, *Südslawische Studien* (Munich, 1965), pp. 58–102; Guldescu in Francis H. Eterovich and Christopher Spalatin, eds., *Croatia,* II, 82–96; Denis, *La Grande Serbie,* pp. 298–322; Kann, *Nationalitätenproblem,* I, 306–308, 459, II, 285–287, 383.

[53] Mamatey, *The United States and East Central Europe, 1914–1918,* pp. 380–384.

promoted by such men as the right wing socialist Karl Renner in regard to personal autonomy, the liberal Transylvanian Roumanian Aurel Popovici concerning territorial autonomy, or the ultraliberal Magyar Oscar Jászi, who recommended a combination of both. It is held further that as far as change was necessary, political ideas developed within the empire provided also the means to effect this change.

Such views, which gradually have been muted within the past decade by more critical ones, may appear simplistic, but they are so only insofar as they picture the Habsburg empire as paradise on earth. The reform plans on the whole were drawn up by men of political sophistication, though perfect solutions were out of the question. Their projects were bound to fail above all because the first premise, the genuine intent of preserving the empire, was lacking. However, the view that the empire could have been saved by ingenious reform plans but was destroyed at the initiative of outside forces (a view supported by sizable groups within the empire), can advance stronger evidence. Only the two privileged national groups, Austro-Germans and Magyars, took no initiative to secede until the last weeks of the war. Even then they acted more or less on the spur of necessity but not of preference. For all other national groups, the decisive actions for secession were engineered by outside forces, not necessarily though primarily by exile organizations, but also, as in regard to the Italians and Roumanians, by governments in sympathy with the objectives of irredenta movements. If we accept this with due consideration of the social revolutionary factors involved in the disintegration process, we can make a convincing case for the following propositions. The belief that the empire was destroyed primarily by outside forces is held by those who confirm the existence of a cultural and political mission of the Habsburg empire, but not by those alone. One may be critical of the empire's policies, may consider its continued existence in the twentieth century as anachronistic, and still believe that the empire was destroyed from outside.

The other view is that the empire failed to solve the nationalities problem, failed to adjust itself to overdue social changes, and rushed into a war whose outcome, practically any outcome—win, draw, or lose—would have worse consequences for the Habsburg monarchy than those of gradual yielding in the Balkan questions and other contested issues of nationalist conflict. The defenders of the Habsburg empire's position in history can easily prove that a string of political defeats in international relations as well as on the home front would have set dangerous precedents which might have led to disintegration. Yet it would be difficult to assert that all concessions would have involved risks as great as war.

The adherents of the view that the Habsburg empire was responsible for its doom and died, to paraphrase Marx, as a consequence of its inherent contradictions, usually cite and analyze a long list of sins of commissions and omissions stretching through the centuries. This study does not follow this technique, partly because the deficiencies of the Habsburg empire have been spelled out in these pages and repetition would add little. Partly, however, because I believe that all the wrongs put together would not have made the doom of the empire inevitable. I reject theories of historical inevitability. I believe at the same time, that the intrinsic causes for the dissolution did not come from outside but from within the empire. One can affirm at a certain point in time the necessity of the empire's fall on the strength of domestic inadequacies without condemning the empire's position and achievements in history. I reject blanket condemnation as much as uncritical glorification and shallow hopes for restoration. The empire can never be restored because all its social premises have been destroyed.

In rejecting theories of historical inevitability I do not deny that individuals and nations in certain phases of their history may set actions which can never be reversed. Such irreversibility is not the result of a historical law but simply of lack of time. When Austria-Hungary in condoning the war with Serbia committed suicide from fear of death, the dual monarchy lost the only chance it had to survive: namely by the help of time itself. The decline could probably have been slowed down or even stopped by various constellations in international politics. When the brittle political body of the empire joined the war, a time limit was set for its continued existence—namely that necessary to arrive at a military decision. This decision, from the beginning of the war probably an unfavorable one for the Central Powers, sealed its doom. It seems equally clear that victory, an almost paradox possibility, would have merely aggravated the nationalities problem. An annexionist policy would probably have been pursued in that case; it would presumably have led within a short time to either further wars or revolutions, probably both. The improbability of a negotiated peace—in itself the least dangerous alternative—is shown by the failure of the secret peace negotiations. Even if they had succeeded it seems illusionary that a weakened Habsburg empire, now deprived of the support of a strong Germany, would have had as good a chance to survive as if it had never taken up arms.

As for domestic causes, the engineers of the empire's dissolution abroad were products of the intelligentsia of the various national groups at home. To a point they were also agents of coming social revolutions. Masaryk, Beneš, Trumbič, Dmowski, Stefánik, and many other lesser leaders became alienated at home and carried the conflict germinated there abroad. Although they succeeded partly because of their political skill and above all due to the help they received from the western powers, they could never have attempted what they did if the conditions they worked for to change, had not existed at home. Thus the search for the prime cause is in this case not a question who comes first the hen or the egg, a fallacious logical problem based on the inevitable lack of evidence by observation. Such evidence is not lacking in the case of the Habsburg empire. There we know what caused the conditions, which enabled the political émigrés to become successful. This study supports the second view that the causes of disintegration were to be found on the home front and merely supported by forces abroad.

In one respect, however, I dissent from both views, the one which holds that the causes for destruction are to be found primarily abroad and the other which perceives them primarily at home. My dissent pertains to the single point on which both views agree, namely that the dissolution process of the Habsburg empire marks the end of an era. Neither do I believe that the Habsburg demise heralds the beginning of a new one. As will be discussed in the final chapter, a new period had been evolving for several decades already.

CHAPTER X

New Beginnings: Cultural Trends from the 1860's to 1918

The dissolution of the empire represented merely a stage in the evolution of a new, highly promising era of cultural developments. Gradually it had come into existence, even before the advent of the new century and it continued after 1918. The maturation of these developments has not come to an end in our days and is subject to further expansion.

To sketch this intellectual process requires some change from the lineup of the national groups presented in Chapter VIII. There we have started with the politically leading national groups, the Germans and Magyars, followed by the Czechs, to whom the Slovaks were attached for ethnic reasons. Discussion of the two northeastern national groups, the Poles and Ruthenians followed. Then the Southern Slavs from West to East (Slovenes, Croats, and Serbs) were discussed. The two Latin groups, Italians and Roumanians, came at the end. This organization was appropriate on political and geographical grounds. Since it is not our aim to rank national groups according to a rating of cultural merits, the factor of priorities in this respect could be disregarded.

The situation, as it presents itself in this final chapter is different. We still do not intend to classify national groups according to a system of cultural achievements. But we may well ask ourselves, how much the members of these national groups, who were settled in Habsburg territories contributed to cultural progress that outlasted the empire. Some ethnic groups which taken as a whole made great cultural contributions to European civilization, could not make a comparable impact with the splinter groups of conationals in the Habsburg monarchy. Would it then be appropriate to proceed according to a scheme, in which the nations, whose confines were fully within the borders of the empire, would receive priority? This means Croats, Czechs, Magyars, Slovaks, Slovenes. Yet such a lineup would reflect the true situation only to a limited extent. Both, Slovenes and Slovaks, though settled fully within the territory of the empire, had fewer specific though not fewer general cultural achievements to show during the last half century of the Habsburg monarchy's existence than for example the Austrian Poles, who represented only a minority of their nation as a whole. The stress here is put on the attribute: specific. We are not concerned with the issue of major or minor cultural achievements but with the question to what extent such achievements were integrated into the cultural history of the Habsburg empire. The Slovene cultural activities merged increasingly with the Southern Slav union movement, in particular with the aspects of it inspired by the Croats. Essentially the same holds true for the relationship of the Slovak cultural activities with those of the Czechs during the period under discussion. The Austro-Germans, on the other hand, though only a branch of the German-speaking people became outstanding in the evolution of ideas of lasting cultural significance for the empire as a whole and beyond. Similar achievements could be observed in the Magyar and Czech orbits and to a lesser extent in those of Croats and Poles. We will attempt to clarify in the following, that these developments were not the result of an innate superiority of any national group, but of a continuation of historical, socioecological, and psychological factors. Other national groups could fully compete with these attainments, if we look at them either as part of nations as a whole or in conjunction with related ethnic groups, and not merely as fragmentary groups within the empire. Accordingly, if we want to build a case for our thesis it is suggestive to work "from the outside." This means to begin with those national achievements which had a less direct impact on the new cultural germination within the empire referred to above. From the outer fringe we will proceed to the contributions considered most outstanding in our mentioned terms of reference. Accordingly we will begin with a brief survey of the situation among the Latin groups, Italians and Roumanians. In doing so we will not be concerned primarily with the uncontested achievements of these nations as a whole, but with those of their conationals within the empire. They had to be interested in the first place with creating the political premises for participation in the cultural life of the entire nation, that is, the life of their conationals across the borders. Specific cultural activities within the empire beyond those of a political national character frequently had to come afterward.

Poles and Ruthenians in the empire formed a geographic though not a cultural and ethnic entity. The cultural contributions of both groups were outward-directed, especially in the last decades of the empire's existence. Many cultural advantages favored the Poles in this respect in comparison with the Ruthenians. Of the Southern Slavs, the Serb position was almost completely focused on cultural trends outside the monarchy beyond the right banks of the Sava and the Drina rivers. As for the two Catholic Southern Slav national groups, Croats and Slovenes, the achievements of the latter appear no longer as distinct as they did at the time of the Slavic renaissance. They were increasingly influenced by the Croats. Even though the Croats moved toward the Southern Slav union movement, Croatian culture during the period under discussion was still largely shaped by the affiliation with the Habsburg empire. To some extent trends which outlasted the empire began to develop within the sphere of this influence. Similar developments are more fully true for Magyars, Czechs, and Austro-Germans. In particular the last-mentioned formed a center of cultural intercommunications. The language conflict between Czechs and Germans in the lands of the Bohemian crown, though exacerbated by a domineering German attitude, does not contradict this. In fact it focused attention on Czech-German cultural interrelationship. For this reason the Czech position in this survey is placed close to that of the Germans.

The Slovaks are discussed here jointly and briefly with the Czechs. But, much as their political national struggle progressed successfully, the Slovak specific cultural contributions, like those of the Slovenes, became less easily identifiable than in previous periods. A partial explanation may be that the national struggle of the small national groups of peoples without independent political history within the Habsburg empire consumed an increasing part of their national energies in the last decades of Austria-Hungary's existence.

Magyars and Austro-Germans represent the two cases where, jointly with that of the Czechs, our thesis can be demonstrated most convincingly. In regard to Magyars as well as Czechs German influence was of great significance, but significance with a difference. We are faced by a mutual Czech-German cultural penetration, a kind of osmosis. On the conscious level the Czechs rejected German influence; indirectly they were exposed to it as were the Germans to that of the Czechs. Many advantages rested here with the larger nation.

In regard to the Magyars, opposition to German influence did not exist nearly to the same degree. Conflict occurred there on the political level between the Cis- and Transleithanian administrations, but not on the cultural-national between Germans and Magyars. It might have existed if this influence would have come primarily from German-Austria. Actually it came chiefly from Germany, where the young Magyar intelligentsia had become indoctrinated with German culture. The Austro-Germans might have been considered to represent a threat to the Magyar position, not so the Germans in the Reich, who were welcomed as allies against a Panslav danger. To the Czechs such distinction was meaningless, since as neighbors of the Reich they were as much exposed to cultural and possibly political penetration from Germany as from the Austro-German lands.

In accordance with these considerations we will discuss the Magyars after the Czechs, and finally the Austro-Germans. Either directly or via Germany the major new cultural trends became most spectacular here. In line with the foregoing we will have to discuss the cultural achievements of Czechs, Magyars, and particularly Germans at relative greater length than the other national groups. Again, no value scheme is involved here, but merely the question of pertinence to our problem.

A. The Latins (Italians and Roumanians)

A shift of cultural activities from the Trentino to Trieste became increasingly marked after the middle of the nineteenth century among the Austro-Italians. The steady economic rise of Austria's only major commercial port city, made Trieste at the same time also the center of public political activities as distinguished from the symbiosis of quietism and irredentism prevalent in Trento and surroundings. This rural area, in which clericalism was still relatively strong, did not have the economic strength to establish cultural facilities on a large scale. For this reason the Austrian government considered it safer, at the beginning of the twentieth century, to establish an Italian law school in Trento rather than in Trieste, and an artificial *furor teutonicus* prevented operation of the project even in Innsbruck, the German-speaking capital of Tyrol. Antonin Gasoletti, a neoromantic lyric, was perhaps the last major poet, who in the second half of the nineteenth century headed from the environment of Trento. In the social sciences, the patriotic martyr Cesare Battisti from Trento made an important contribution to the geography of the region.

Trieste, which in the later part of the nineteenth century succeeded to the cultural position which the Trentino had held during the Enlightenment, could afford to develop an Italian theater, a city orchestra, and an art gallery. Literary life surpassed soon that of any other region of the Litoral or of the Trentino. Here was also the seat of "Legio Nazionale" (the Italian national association). Domenico Rossetti, a contemporary of Gasoletti, still followed the romantic tradition. Yet Riccardo Pittieri represented already the neoromantic ultranationalist spirit of Gabriele D'Annunzio. Scipio Slataper, a remarkably original prose writer and a lyric introduced new realistic trends. His autobiography *Il mio Carso* of 1912, which pictured the multinational character of the Littoral as seen from the point of view of Italian nationalism, received more attention in Italy than in Austria. Italo Svevo, influenced by the art of Proust, in the early twentieth century made an important contribution to the psychological novel and Umberto L. Saba, who died almost forty years after the First World War, was another distinguished prose writer and lyric. Altogether the cultural efforts of the Austro-Italians proved convincingly that they could not be held down by an alien and unsympathetic, though not oppressive government. At the same time it must be conceded that no major new cultural trends originated from these regions during the last decades of the empire's existence.[1]

Although a larger number of all Roumanians lived in Habsburg territory, especially Hungary, than, proportionally, Italians, the center of cultural activities remained Bucharest and not Hungarian Koloszvár (Cluj, Klausenburg) or Austrian Czernowitz (Cernăuti). One factor in this respect was the severe suppression of Roumanian cultural activities by the Hungarian government. It was difficult to publish Roumanian literature on Hungarian territory and even more difficult to promote it. Lyrics and fictional prose were suspected of irredentist propaganda. All the more impressive were literary activities in the late nineteenth and early twentieth centuries, when oppressive measures were at their height. George Coşbuc from Transylvania was a remarkable lyric; Jan Slavici, was a versatile native of Hungary proper, who distinguished himself as a prose narrator of Roumanian peasant life and of fairy tales, as well as a playwright. He became a successful editor of the *Journal Tribuna* in Sibiu (Nagyszeben, Hermannstadt). The lyrics and rural novels of the Transylvanian Octavian Goga parallel in some ways Slavici's works.

Least impeded by the authorities was the writing of regional national

[1] Fortunat Demattio, "Literatur in Tirol und Vorarlberg: Die italienische Literatur," in [Crownprince Rudolf], *Die österreichisch-ungarische Monarchie,* Vol. *Tirol,* pp. 410–416; Anton M. Zuhorsky-Suchodolski, *Triest* (Vienna 1962), pp. 150–164.

history, and here we meet contributions like those of A. Papiu Ilarion, who, particularly in the third quarter of the nineteenth century, distinguished himself as writer of Roumanian national history in Transylvania. His equal and contemporary was Eudoxius Hurmuzaki, the son of a Roumanian political leader, who resided in Cernăuți (Czernowitz, Chernivtsi) and wrote a voluminous but still incomplete history of the Roumanians. Those in the Habsburg empire received special consideration. This work, whitten partly in German and partly in Roumanian, and largely based on original sources, is still rated as an important contribution to the subject matter.[2]

B. The Ruthenians and Poles

Ruthenian culture in Austria became increasingly oriented toward outward centers. The old tripartite division between Austrian-, Russian-, and Ukrainian-oriented cultural trends shifted gradually toward the Ukrainian conationals across the border. Ukrainian culture by the end of the nineteenth century had become the mainroad of Ruthenian civilization. Beginning with the 1860's and 1870's, the influence of the journal *Prawda,* published in L'viv (Lwów, Lemberg) was important. The ideas of the previously mentioned Ukrainian poet Taras Shevchenko (1814–1861), radiated from the Russian East Ukraine into Galicia. Ivan Franko (1856–1916), the greatest modern Ruthenian writer in the Habsburg monarchy, equally distinguished in his lyrics, stories, and novels, which deal largely with social problems, represented a moderate pro-Ukrainian orientation. The ethnographer Volodymyr Hnatiuk and the Ruthenian historian at the University of Lwów, Mykmailo Hrushevs'kyi stood even more distinctly for the Ukrainian national movement. The same holds true for Osyp Fed'kovych, a poet, who lived in the Bukovina, where the literary society Russka Besida represented both the pro-Russian and the gradually victorious Ukrainian cultural movement. It might be added here that the University of Chernivtsi founded in 1875, furthered Ruthenian cultural activities only to a limited extent beyond the orbit of the theological faculty. The same held even more true for the Roumanian position in the academic life of the Bukovina. This university furthered the Germanization of the educated upper strata of the crownland and was only of indirect benefit for the training of the young Ruthenian and

[2] Daicoviciu and Constantinescu, *Brève Histoire de la Transylvanie,* pp. 326–358; Jakal Negruzzi and George Bogdan-Duică, *Geschichte des rumänischen Schrifttums* (Wernigerode, 1892), pp. 136–232; Nicolae Jorga, *Histoire des Roumains de Transylvanie et de Hongrie,* 2 vols. (Bucharest, 1915–1916), II, 306–401.

Roumanian intelligentsia. The Ruthenian national struggle took place in several theatres, above all in confrontations with Russian orthodoxy and Polish nationalism. Therefore, the advancement of the Ukrainian cultural movement, which spread to the remote corners of the Hungarian Carpatho-Ukraine (Carpatho-Ruthenia) was all the more remarkable. There, cultural associations like the Basilius Society and subsequently the more liberal Unio Society exercised a notable influence. Evmenij Sabov, a literary historian, furthered the national objectives. Altogether the policies of tsarism in Russia, which suppressed the Russian Ukrainians even more severely than the Hungarian government did in regard to the Carpatho-Ruthenians, actually strengthened the Carpatho-Ruthenian national resistance movement.[3]

For the Poles, Cracow (Kraków) with its ancient Jagiellonian university of 1364, its Academies of Science and Fine Arts, was as much the cultural center of Polish activities in Austria as Lemberg (Lwów) was that of political activities.[4] Michael Bobrzyński, one time governor of Galicia and Polish minister in the Koerber and Clam-Martinic cabinets during the war, must be considered a great national Polish historian, whose presentation was based not on a glorified nostalgic longing for the Poland of old but on a critical approach to the bygone kingdom's unsolved social problems. Joseph Szujski (1835–1883), professor of history in Cracow, wrote a history of Poland in a more traditional, conservative vein. At the same time he was also an effective representative of the national historical drama and, like Bobrzynski, engaged in Polish politics in the Austrian Reichsrat. Count Stanislaus Tarnowski, a colleague of both men and president of the Polish Academy of Science, made a similar contribution to the history of Polish literature. K. Estreicher distinguished himself in the auxiliary historical sciences. S. Pawlicky was a historian of classical philosophy. In the sciences, Ladislaus Natanson and Marian Smolchowski were widely known physicists; the latter was one of the early explorers of atomic theory.[5]

Juljan Falat (1852–1929), the director of the Academy of Fine Arts, was

[3] Michael Hrushevsky, *A History of Ukraine* (New Haven, 1941), pp. 483–513; Žeguc, *Die nationalpolitischen Bestrebungen der Karpato-Ruthenen 1848–1914,* pp. 92–100; Emil Ohonowskij, "Ruthenische Literatur," in [Crownprince Rudolf], *Die österreichisch-ungarische Monarchie,* Vol. *Galizien,* pp. 660–665 and Emil Kakužniácki, "Die ruthenische Sprache und Literatur," in Vol. *Bukowina* of the same work, pp. 401–405.

[4] The university (of 1784) and technical university there, though in size surpassing the institutions of higher learning in Cracow, had not the same standing in Polish tradition.

[5] Erasmus Piltz, ed., *Poland* (London, 1919), pp. 296–313.

active during the same period as one of the early representatives of Polish impressionism. One of his successors as director of the Academy was the sculptor Ksawery Dunikowski, who had moved from impressionism to a monumental and austere symbolism. The influence of both men on modern Polish art extended beyond the dissolution of the empire.[6] In literature, too, Cracow became a dynamic center of new ideas, fully effective after 1918. Lucjan Rydel (1870–1918) was a widely known dramatist, but the most interesting and diverse literary personality was Stanislav Wyspiański, a poet and playwright, but at the same time a painter of mystic tendencies. Wyspiański also had interesting ideas about architecture. Yet his genius had no opportunity to put in practice his plans of blending modern architecture schemes with medieval Polish village architecture. S. Przybyszewski, likewise from Cracow, was as talented as Wyspiański, but the topics of his writings were more specialized. They were influenced by the sex problem according to Freudian theories and the literary works of Strindberg. S. Brzozowski, a young Socialist in the prewar period, rejected extreme individualism and promoted ideas of mass culture. Stanislaus Kozmian and his successor Tadeusz Pawlikovski were foremost representatives of the pattern-forming theater in Cracow. One young Galician Pole, Józef Wittlin, who reached manhood only during the First World War was the author of one of the best novels on the Ruthenian peasant milieu ever written. It reveals no trace of Polish national prejudice.[7]

Yet all these men were nationalists to a greater or lesser degree, but generally in a creative sense. This nationalism, whether in history, the sciences, or literature and the fine arts exercised in its achievements a greater influence beyond the Polish orbit and thereby within the over-all Austrian sphere than the works produced by the members of the other national groups considered thus far. In part this may be due to the fact, that the Austrian Poles played a more important role within their nation than the Austro-Italians or Ruthenians. In some respect the Polish cultural achievements emanating from Galicia and in particular from the

[6] Ibid., pp. 352–378; Ladislaus Luszczkiewicz, "Die Architektur," pp. 706–708 and Marian von Sokolowski, "Malerei und Plastik," pp. 756–771 both in [Crownprince Rudolf], *Die österreichisch-ungarische Monarchie,* Vol. *Galizien;* Irone Piotrowska, "Fine Arts," in Bernadotte E. Schmitt, ed., *Poland,* pp. 311–322.

[7] Stanislaus Count Tarnowski, "Polnische Literatur," in [Crownprince Rudolf], *Die österreichisch-ungarische Monarchie,* Vol. *Galizien,* pp. 635–648; Piltz, ed., *Poland,* pp. 330–343; Manfred Kridl, "Polish Literature" in Bernadotte E. Schmitt, ed., *Poland,* pp. 284–310; Roman Dyboski, "Literature and Learning in Poland since 1863," in *Cambridge History of Poland* (Cambridge, 1951), II, 535–566; Manfred Kridl, *A Survey of Polish Literature and Culture* (The Hague, 1967), pp. 350–471; Czeslaw Milosz, *The History of Polish Literature* (London, 1969), pp. 281–379.

Cracow area belong to those which not only the Poles but imperial Austria have transmitted to the postwar world.

C. The Serbs, Croats, and Slovenes

For the Serbs, the days of Slavic romanticism and the Slavic renaissance had gone, when Karadžić could consider Vienna a focal point of communications with Slavists from other nations. Now Belgrad had become the main center of Serb cultural activities. Of the last generation before the First World War, the lyric Veljko Petrović, came originally from and returned in later life to the southern Hungarian plains, but spent his most creative years in Serbia. Otherwise, Bosnia-Hercegovina, the most recently acquired Habsburg domain with the proportionally largest Serb population became the most important area of Serb cultural activities outside of the kingdom. It seems that the province nearest to central Serbia, the Hercegovina, had the closest cultural ties to the kingdom also. Vojislav Ilić, a lyric writer who died as a young man, headed from there. So did Aleksa Santić, a nationalist playwright and lyric, whose poetry, at the turn of the nineteenth century reflects the scenery and sentiments of his Hercegovinian home territory and the strong desire for Southern Slav union. Ivo Andrić from central Bosnia, the novelist and Nobel prize winner of the future, born in 1894, represents a bridge between imperial and royal Habsburg and future Yugoslav Bosnia. Although he portrayed the imperial administration of Bosnia with great sensitivity and knowledge, he and the other writers mentioned above were outward directed toward Serbia. Their works can hardly be considered as part of a composite civilization within the Habsburg empire.[8]

The situation was different with the Catholic Slovenes, an ethnic group fully within the borders of the Cisleithanian part of the empire. Yet it was not as different as it might have been expected from the nation, from which had come Kopitar, Miklošič, and Prešeren, all champions and examples of a kind of Austro-Slavism. Josip Stritar (1836–1923), poet-novelist, essayist, and editor of the Slovene literary journal *Zvon,* published in Vienna since 1870, was one of the last Austro-Slavists, yet one more nationalist than his predecessors. Ivan Tavčar, from Ljubljana (Laibach), a many-sided talent equally distinguished as lyric, novelist, and playwright, may be

[8] Matthias Murko in Paul Hinneberg, ed., *Die osteuropäischen Literaturen und die slawischen Sprachen* (Leipzig, 1908), pp. 233–238; Anton Hadžić, "Die serbische Literatur," in [Crownprince Rudolf], *Die österreichisch-ungarische Monarchie,* Vol. *Kroatien-Slavonien,* pp. 149–152; Josef Matl, *Südslawische Studien* (Munich, 1965), pp. 494–526.

considered as the pioneer of Slovene literary realism and symbolism with Socialist leanings, who had overcome the naturalistic tendencies, which had not been particularly fruitful in Slovene literature. Other realists were Janko Kersnik and Fran Lestvik, the former primarily a lyric, the latter a novelist and playwright. Oton Župančič, also from Ljubljana, who died in 1949, a lyric and creator of modernized folk poetry represented expressionist tendencies in Slovene literature. Dragotin Kette stood for similar sentiments in a perhaps less sophisticated manner. All these men were not as concerned with the union movement as the Austrian and Hungarian Serbs. At the same time they cannot be considered as representatives of Austro-Slavism either. It had entered its period of decline with the passing of the Slavonic renaissance even among the one fully Austro-Slav nation, the Slovenes.[9]

More complex were developments among the Croats, in particular those in the triune kingdom and in Dalmatia. The Southern Slav union movement had made enormous political progress during the last prewar decades and the Serb political ascendancy became stronger. Yet in the cultural realm Serb and Croatian cultural endeavors and achievements could still be separated clearly in a linguistic as well as in a cultural sense. Center of Croatian literary activities was Zagreb, where the main literary journal of the 1880's and 1890's the *Vijenac* (wreath) became the arena for the struggle between the conservatives and the young radicals, a conflict that continued in the main cultural association, the *Matica Hrvatska* (Croatian cultural national association). Literary radicalism, however, was not identical with political and national radicalism.

By the end of the nineteenth century we have to distinguish between three main literary trends among the Croats, all of which represented the *Moderna,* a movement characterized by a deepening interest in psychological interpretation, skepticism, and interest in the new literary trends represented by the Russians, Scandinavians, and French. This development was clearly shown in the school of Zagreb with particular emphasis on Dostoevsky, Ibsen, and later Strindberg. Here nationalism was a by-product of the literary revolution. The so-called school of Prague where many young Croats studied at the Czech university, represented, to a much higher degree, national-social objectives. A kind of Austrian north-south Panslavism became rather effective. In Vienna, on the other hand,

[9] Slodnjak, *Geschichte der slowenischen Literatur,* pp. 158–324; Gregor Krek, "Die slovenische Literatur," in [Crownprince Rudolf] *Die österreichisch-ungarische Monarchie,* Vol. *Kärnten, Krain,* pp. 442–448; Murko in Paul Hinneberg, ed., *Die osteuropäischen Literaturen und die slawischen Sprachen,* pp. 230–231, 237; Matl, *Südslawische Studien,* pp. 529–540.

the Croats who studied at the university were also influenced by the *l'art pour l'art* trends of the period, as exemplified by Baudelaire and Verlaine, and consequently less radical in political questions. All these currents eventually merged with the mainstream of Croatian nationalism and Southern Slav unionism. Yet the very existence of these diverse trends in Croatian cultural history confirmed ties between the new brands of cultural nationalism and the institutional traits and traditions of the Habsburg monarchy.

Evgenij Kumičić (1850–1904), a writer in the second half of the nineteenth century, still represented the influence of Zola's and perhaps Turgenev's naturalism. The outstanding representative of the era between national romanticism and naturalism was August Šenoa (1838–81). This encyclopedic talent, as literary critic, stage manager, lyric, and epic poet, as well as author of realistic village stories and the historical novel *Baron Ivica,* influenced Croatian intellectual life lastingly in the coming age of the *Moderna.* Silvije Kranjčević (1865–1908), already an adherent of the *Moderna,* became a lyric poet of social tendencies. Mihovil Nikolić, another lyric poet, can be considered as a neoromantic of sentimental idyllic tendencies, in contrast to Vladimir Vidrić who in his poetry stood for a sensual, hedonistic spirit unusual in the rich poetry of Croatian literature.

Ivo Vojnović, who came from Dubrovnik in Dalmatia, rates as the greatest modern Croatian dramatist, whose symbolism superseded the naturalist tendencies which were still dominant in Petar Petrović-Pecija's plays. Miroslav Krleža (1893–), a more original artist, revealed in his plays but particularly in his novels a strange combination of a revolutionary and a pantheistic spirit. At the time when this survey ends, in 1918, he, like the Serb Andrić, had given a mere foretaste of his great talents. All three writers were still active in the new Yugoslavia.

August Matoš, critic and essayist in the last prewar decades was an impressionist influenced by French literature. Branko Vodnik, who died in 1926, was a scholarly literary historian whose interests were focused largely on nineteenth-century Illyrism.[10]

As for music, German and Italian influences were strong throughout the nineteenth century and afterward. Vatroslav Lisinski (Ignatz Fuchs),

[10] K.B.K. on literature in F. H. Eterovich and C. Spalatin, eds., *Croatia,* I, 253–272; Nicola Andrić, "Ergänzung zur croatischen Literaturgeschichte in [Crown-prince Rudolf] *Die österreichisch-ungarische Monarchie,* Vol. *Kroatien, Slawonien,* pp. 137–149; Murko in Paul Hinneberg, ed., *Die osteuropäischen Literaturen und die slawischen Sprachen,* pp. 231–233, 237–238; Matl, *Südslawische Studien,* pp. 455–492.

1819–1854, was a composer of operas, and after him Ivan Zajc, a prolific creator of vocal music and author of the historical opera *Nicola Šubić-Zrinski* dominated the musical scene in Zagreb. Yet the truly original contributions to modern music were made in the main only after 1918. In the fine arts, on the other hand, an original Croatian school of architecture, painting, and sculpture was in full bloom already in the nineteenth century. Bartol Felbinger (1785–1871), a successful student of a neoclassical style, became the chief architect of a modernized Zagreb. Viktor Kovačić (1874–1924) introduced modern functionalism into Croatian architecture. In painting, Vlaho Bukovac, (1855–1922) who had studied in Paris, stood for academic realism in the setting of large compositions; Josip Račić and Miroslav Kraljević were late impressionists and portrait and landscape painters. The pioneer of modern Croatian sculpture was the Dalmatian Ivan Rendić (1849–1932), teacher of the Dalmatian Ivan Meštrović (1883–1962), whose art superseded impressionism. Meštrović's genius cannot be classified, but undoubtedly his art was related to expressionism. Meštrović who had studied at the Academy in Vienna and who later lived in Italy, Switzerland, Great Britain, and the United States was recognized everywhere as a towering Southern Slav artist. His originality blended well with the tradition of national culture. At the same time his great lifework is a symbol for the many trends which tied Croatian art to the empire and have radiated from there into the world.[11]

D. The Slovaks

The Slovak contribution to the establishment of independent statehood in 1918 was equal to that of the Czechs and in regard to support by conationals abroad, particularly in the United States, perhaps superior. The same cannot be said in regard to nineteenth and twentieth century Slovak cultural developments, but there were substantial contributions. In the late nineteenth century Svetozár Hurban Vajanský was a representative of Slovak poetry, attuned to the atmosphere of the Tatra mountains. He promoted the national cause and fought Magyarism in his epical work. Pavol Orszagh-Hviezdoslàv (1849–1921), the most important Slovak

[11] Fedor Kabalin on music in Eterovich and Spalatin, eds., *Croatia,* I, 283–287; Ruža Bajurin on architecture, sculpture, painting, *ibid.*, pp. 323–345. See further on music Diels, *Die slawischen Völker,* pp. 296 and ibid., on fine arts, pp. 287; Ferdo Miler on music and Isidor Kršnjavi on fine arts in [Crownprince Rudolf], *Die österreichisch-ungarische Monarchie,* Vol. *Kroatien, Slawonien,* pp. 168–176; see further Matl, *Südslawische Studien,* pp. 447–448; Zvanc Črnja, *Cultural History of Croatia* (Zagreb, 1962), pp. 319–336.

novelist of the period, was interested in the life and customs of the Slovak rural gentry. Martin Razus was another novelist of the time.

Václav Chaloupecký (1882–1951), a Czech scholar at the University of Bratislava, was the historian of Slovak relationship to the Hussite movement. He represented a link between Czech and Slovak historiography. Vítĕslav Novák became the great authority on Slovak folk music and a distinguished composer of orchestral music. Altogether Czech and Slovak bonds in the second half of the nineteenth century and in the early twentieth were better reflected in political cooperation than in cultural associations. Yet one was in many ways the premise for the other.[12]

E. The Czechs

Czech culture, regardless of national objectives, was related to the over-all Austrian culture because Germans and Czechs had lived so closely together for many centuries that a kind of osmosis between literary, musical, artistic, and scholarly activities resulted. The strong migration of Czechs and Germans to Vienna played an additional important part. The intensified national conflict between the two peoples after the revolution of 1848 did not impede this cultural interchange, and in some respects furthered it. The renewed rapid Czech cultural rise beginning with the Slavic renaissance inspired national objectives. They helped to further Czech cultural and cultural-political activities which made them competitive with developments in the German-Austrian orbit. Every gifted young German from Bohemia or Moravia who moved to German Austria to make his professional artistic, literary, or scholarly career, benefited from this twofold, intertwined background. Every Czech, who was given the opportunity of a professional career in Bohemia or Moravia profited in the same way from the German cultural heritage which coexisted in these lands. As soon as the political and social privileges, on which it was based, could be successfully challenged, benefits for the Czechs outweighed previous disadvantages. It might be suggestive to review Czech and German cultural trends in the Bohemian lands jointly. It is not done here because most culturally outstanding Sudeten Germans

[12] Alexander Adamczyk, in Paul Diels, *Die Slawischen Völker* (Wiesbaden, 1963), pp. 222–224; Friedrich Prinz, "Die volkskulturellen Grundlagen: b) Die Slowakei," in Karl Bosl, ed., *Handbuch der Geschichte der böhmischen Länder* (Stuttgart, 1969), IV, 287–299; Otto Rade, in Leonid I. Strakhovsky, *Handbook of Slavic Studies* (Cambridge, 1949), pp. 494–495; Samuel Czambel, "Die slovakische Sprache und Literatur," in [Crownprince Rudolf], *Die österreichisch-ungarische Monarchie,* Vol. *Ungarn,* V, 443–446.

(the Germans in the lands of the Bohemian crown) moved eventually into the German-Austrian geographical orbit. For reasons of greater clarity it is preferable to discuss the Sudeten Germans with the Austro-Germans. Besides, joint treatment might obscure the individualistic character of Czech culture. Yet, whether treated jointly or separately, whether acknowledged or not by the parties concerned, interchange between two great cultures at the time under discussion was in many ways beneficial.

a) LITERATURE AND PRESS

We will remember that early nineteenth-century Czech literature was dominated by the work of great linguistic scholars. Because most educated Czechs were fully conversant with German development, the belles lettres in their own language were less articulate. Karel Hynek Mácha (1810–1836), a lyrical poet influenced by Byron's romanticism, was one of the earliest widely known Czech writers whose lifework can be separated from scholarly activities. Yet there were few like him at that time. The situation changed rapidly in the course of the second half of the century. Jan Neruda (1834–1891) was a lyric and story writer superior to Mácha and so was the writer of social novels Jakub Arbes. Svatopluk Čech, who died in 1908, took the subjects of his novels largely from the dynamic late medieval and reformation history of his people. He did so in a more critical and in part satirical vein than most contemporary writers of historical novels, such as Alois Jirásek, whose topics likewise covered the Hussite period but also that of national oppression in the seventeenth and eighteenth centuries. More realistic was the work of Božena Němcová (1829–1862) whose peasant novels represented a first in Czech literature. Němcová, one of the many significant women writers in Czech literature, distinguished herself also as collector and editor of sagas and fairy tales. Of great influence throughout the late nineteenth and early twentieth century was Jaroslav Vrchlický (pseudonym for Emil Frída), 1853–1912, professor of comparative literature at the Czech University in Prague and life member of the Austrian House of Lords. Vrchlický was a lyric and epic poet and writer of tragedies and comedies. His chief contribution was perhaps the elegance of his language and his splendid translations into Czech of German, French, and Italian classics. Otakar Brežina (pseudonym for Václav Jebavy, 1868–1929), a lyric of mystical tendencies, was probably influenced by Nietzsche. He was a political prose writer and oriented toward realism.

A powerful lyrical poet was Petr Bezruč (1867–1959). His Silesian songs whose topics were the intertwined social and national problems of a highly industrialized area, were translated into German by Franz Werfel. A writer of more pronounced political tendencies was Viktor Dyk who wrote radical nationalist and social novels. Josef Svatopluk Máchar (1864–1942), a brilliant writer of literary feuilletons and political prose who resided in Vienna for many years, supplemented Dyk's work. He later became inspector general of the armed forces of Czechoslovakia. Karel Čapek (1890–1938), friend and biographer of T. G. Masaryk, was an expressionist novelist and an author of highly original social utopian plays. He shared international fame with Jaroslav Hašek (1883–1923), creator of the immortal figure of the sly, seemingly naïve but actually complex Czech saboteur soldier Schwejk in the First World War. With all credit due to Hašek's outstanding talent, it is questionable whether the fame of Schwejk has not spread too far for the good of the Czech national image. Schwejk represents one trait in the Czech character, that of cunning and calm composure, which served underground resistance so well during a long period of oppression. Yet Schwejk does not personify the straightforward and heroic Czech national character.

The previously mentioned greatest journalist of the nation, Karel Havlíček (1821–1856) is the splendid example of a writer who managed to either outwit or defy censorship. In the oppressive pre-March period he made his liberal national views known to his people. Julius Grégr, the editor of *Národni Listy* (Nationalblatt) in the liberal era of the 1860's and 1870's upheld Havliček's tradition successfully. *Čas* (The Times), founded in 1886 as a weekly and continued as a daily since 1900, represented, under T. G. Masaryk's editorial guidance, the blending of the old liberalism with the new socially progressive forces.[13]

b) FINE ARTS

Karel Purkyně (1834–1868), son of a famous physiologist, Jan E. Purkyně, was a student of Courbet and introduced the strong relationship to French schools into Czech painting. But in a sense he and his other teacher, Josef Mánes (1820–1871), who had received his training in Munich, were the last eminent and still traditional nineteenth-century painters among the Czechs. Antonín Chitussi (1847–1891) and Antonín Slavíček (1870–1910) were landscape painters; the former was influenced

[13] Prinz, "Das kulturelle Leben (1867–1939)," in Karl Bosl, ed., *Handbuch der Geschichte der böhmischen Länder,* IV, 213–216; Münch, *Böhmische Tragödie,* pp. 291–296, 475–486; Eduard Goldstücker, ed., *Weltfreunde: Konferenz über die Prager deutsche Literatur* (Berlin, 1967), report by Paul Reimann, pp. 7–31; Hanuš Jelinek, *Histoire de la Littérature Tchèque,* 3 vols. (Paris, 1933–1935), see II, 113–347, III, 11–146, 195–242.

by the plain-air Barbizon school, the latter could be considered an impressionist. Max Švabinský (1873–1962), likewise originally an impressionist, became a portraitist and graphic artist. Emil Filla and Rudolf Kremlička were influenced by Picasso. The most outstanding artist among these painters was possibly Jan Zrzavy (1890–1971).

As for sculpture, the last distinguished traditionalist was Václav Levy (1820–1870). The first representative of the modern school was a student of Mánes, Josef Václav Myslbek (1848–1922), creator of the St. Wenceslas equestrian monument in Prague, in more than one way the symbol of Czech independence. Ladislas Šaloun, about two decades younger than Myslbek, designed the Hus monument in Prague, a work of equal symbolic significance as Myslbek's statue but of somewhat controversial artistic merit. Jan Štursa, somewhat younger than Šaloun, and likewise an impressionist, revealed in his art the influence of Rodin. In general, French influence on the Czech fine arts is perhaps stronger than that of any other nation.

The transition from the eclectic pseudo-historical styles to modern art was particularly rapid. The architects Josef Gočár (1880–1945) and his contemporary Jan Kotěra could already be considered representatives of functionalism.[14]

c) MUSIC

It is convincing evidence for the greatness of Czech music that the trio of Smetana, Dvořák, and Fibich soon found congenial successors. Josef Suk (1874–1935), Dvořák's son-in-law, was an inventive and colorful composer of orchestral and chamber music. Leoš Janáček (1854–1928), a Moravian, composer of the operas *Jenufa* and *The Sly Little Fox,* revealed spiritual relationship to Mussorgskij. At the same time, Janáček represented the Czech national spirit in his operatic work as well and clearly as Smetana. Jaromir Weinberger, the composer of *Švanda the Bagpiper,* continued the tradition of the national popular opera in a milieu of national folklore.[15]

d) SCHOLARSHIP

Czech scholarship which could point to a proud and rich tradition, benefited from the division of the ancient University of Prague, in 1882,

[14] Münch, *Böhmische Tragödie,* pp. 470–475; Prinz, "Das Kulturelle Leben (1867–1939)," in Karl Bosl, ed., *Handbuch der Geschichte der böhmischen Länder,* IV, 207–209.

[15] Prinz, "Das kulturelle Leben (1867–1939)," in Karl Bosl, ed., *Handbuch der Geschichte der böhmischen Länder,* IV, 209–211; Münch, *Böhmische Tragödie,* pp. 495–500.

into Czech and German institutions. The establishment of the Czech Academy of Arts and Sciences in 1894 had the same effect. Now the organizational frame which had heretofore been missing, helped in educating a new academic generation. Only a few highlights can be touched upon here. In historical disciplines the tradition of Palacký's scholarship was further expanded. Václav Tomek, a student of his and his liberal colleague at the Reichstag of Vienna, and Kroměříž (Kremsier) in 1848–1849 eventually became a conservative national historian, as shown in his biography of Žižka and his history of Prague—at the same time a monumental history of the Bohemian kingdom. His legal political concept was practically that of the Bohemian Staatsrecht, namely the lands of the Bohemian crown as separate unit of the Habsburg empire. Anton Gindely, his colleague, the historian of the Counter-Reformation in Bohemia and of the Thirty Years' War, may be considered as the most Austrian, the most supranational of the Czech historians. His sovereign command of sources was not entirely matched by originality of thought and stimulating presentation. Josef Kalousek, twenty years younger than Tomek and about ten years younger than Gindely, was the distinguished biographer of the great Luxembourg ruler Charles IV, but also a too uncritical defender of tradition in the dispute about the authenticity of the Královedvorský (Königinhof) and Zelenohorský (Grüneberg) manuscripts. A historian of greater scholarship was Jaroslav Goll (1846–1929) who studied the organization of the Bohemian Brethren church structure and the diplomatic aspects of the Thirty Years' War in relation to Bohemia. Goll who had close ties to German and Austro-German historians was the first fully modern Czech historian. The second of equal distinction was Josef Pekař (1870–1937), whose work on Žižka superseded that of Tomek as much as his study on Wallenstein that of the Austro-German historian Srbik.

Among many distinguished scholars in the humanities and social sciences too numerous to mention here, the orientalist and linguist Bedřich Hrozný (1879–1952) proved the Indo-German origin of cuniform writings. H. Jireček (1829–1909) was an authority on Slavic legal history, and the Moravian professor of criminal law, František Weyr, was one of the first who fully comprehended and promoted the significance of Hans Kelsen's pure theory of law. T. G. Masaryk should also be mentioned here as social philosopher, although his great scholarly contribution to the understanding of Russian intellectual history is overshadowed by his political fame. In the sciences, Czech progress, introduced by the physiologist Jan E. Purkyně in the first half of the 19th century, was as great as in the other fields of knowledge. But the breakthrough to world attention came only after the First World War when the financial resources of the Czech University in Prague were no longer those of an Austrian provincial institution.[16]

The great Czech influence on Austrian culture is one of the strongest factors which injects into achievements of the Austro-German orbit some fertile traits different from those of purely German culture. Yet, in regard to Czech culture, much as it was to prosper later, the year 1918 represented the end of an age. The unique interrelationship between Czech, German, and German-Jewish culture declined in the different setting of the new state in which the primacy of Czech culture was firmly established. With the end of the interwar period, this interrelationship ceased. After 1918 a new broadening and deepening of an ancient civilization was on the rise in the Bohemian lands. Yet a unique brand of multinational culture of high and strong achievements was on the way out.

F. The Magyars

Much that has been said about the Czechs is also true for the Magyars. There was a strong cultural relationship between the Hungarian and the Austrian orbit in general. This meant in particular a sizable movement of the intelligentsia and of artists from Budapest to Vienna. Yet the Magyars who moved to the West in the second half of the nineteenth century were not to the same degree indoctrinated with German culture as the Czechs. On the other hand, there was less friction between individual Germans and Magyars than between Czechs and Germans. The conflicting issues between Czechs and Germans were national problems, which touched closely upon the feelings of the individuals, those between Magyars and Germans in essence problems of state-craft, which did not affect individuals as closely as national problems.

a) Literature and Press

Jókai was followed by a brief period of relative stagnation in Magyar literature. Geza Gárdonyi (1863–1922), an author of historical and peasant novels and stories filled this void with some other authors of lesser rank. Ferenc Herczeg (1863–1954), editor of the literary periodical *Új Idök* (New Times) a neoromantic writer of original historical novels and

[16] Jelinek, *Histoire de la Littérature Tchèque,* III, 245–330; Münch, *Böhmische Tragödie,* pp. 488–492; Prinz, in Karl Bosl, ed., *Handbuch,* IV, 188–195; Richard G. Plaschka, *Von Palacký bis Pekař* (Graz-Cologne, 1955), pp. 27–90; Erna Lesky, *Purkynĕs Weg, Wissenschaft, Bildung und Nation* (Vienna, 1970), passim.

stories, represents the transition to the modern spirit in a conservative Catholic way. In his time he was respected as a favorite author of high society. Ferenc Molnár (1878–1952) who went into exile during the Second World War is more difficult to place. Many playwrights and critics who see evidence of genius in the fact that they themselves are unable to draw characters true to life, to hold the attention of the audience with their dialogue, or to write clear prose, look down on Molnár's unheard-of success, who excelled in all these respects. Accordingly, his amusing and witty plays were considered second-rate entertainment literature. Yet after his death even critics had to recognize what the general public had felt all along, that the creator of the character of the gangster Liliom, of the play *The Swan,* of the children's novel *The boys of St. Paul's Street* was a truly modern poet of the first rank.

Still it could be held that Molnár spent as great a part of his life in Viennese coffeehouses as in those of Budapest and that he was just as much at home in Paris and later seemingly (but not actually) in New York. In that sense he may be called a great writer, but a typical Magyar writer only with qualifications. In this respect, Endres Ady (1877–1919), rates first in modern Magyar literature. This scion of the gentry, who was a chief contributor to the new literary journal *Nyugat* (West) was a radical, influenced by contemporary thought on Marxism and psychoanalysis, and in a literary sense by French impressionism. Ady, who spent some years of his youth in Paris, was impressed by the lyrics of Rimbaud, Baudelaire, and Verlaine. But in his collections of poetry *New Poems* 1906 and *Blood and Gold* 1908 he remained independent. The same is true for his impressive later epics. Ady can be classified neither as impressionist nor as expressionist. If he had lived to an old age he would probably have been called an existentialist, because his fear of life and infatuation with death became increasingly demanding. In another way it is difficult to conceive that a genius like Ady would not have changed his philosophy if he had survived the two world wars. Mihály Babits as the editor of *Nyugat,* a friend and colleague of Ady, was more versatile, though less grandiose. Equally distinguished as lyrical poet, playwright, and author of novels and stories, he died like Ady as a young man. Yet while Ady was perhaps wrongly associated by the public with the Left, Babits, whose symbolism was difficult to understand, was attacked by Right and Left alike.

Easier to comprehend were the numerous novels and stories by Zsigmond Móricz (1879–1942) which represented the various conflicts in Hungarian society. Móricz was one of the few, who frankly discussed the problem of anti-Semitism. Dezsö Kostolányi (1885–1936) was the most conservative representative of the new generation; he could be considered a distinct impressionist at a time when impressionism had passed its zenith. As individualist and l'art pour l'art aesthete this eminent poet and writer of psychological novels had little use for the revolutionary lyrics of Ady.

A few remarks may be added here about the press in Hungary, a country, whose urban society and particularly urban intellectuals consisted largely of avid newspaper readers. An evil institution taken over from the West was the boulevard journalism represented by *Az Est,* (The Evening), whereas *Pesti Hirlap* (Budapest Journal), possibly the most influential paper in Budapest, stood for middle-class liberalism, anticlericalism, and largely chauvinism as well. After 1900 the official socialist paper *Nepszáva* (voice of the people) became a daily, that did much to promote a Marxian program. The novel approach of this journal also interested non-Marxian intellectuals. Altogether Magyar Hungary had many brilliant journalists with linguistic gifts in several western languages. Some journalists who went into exile after the accession to power by the Horthy regime distinguished themselves subsequently as journalists in Austria, Germany, France, and the United States. Standards of journalistic integrity in Hungary were not always commensurate to the journalistic talents of Magyar writers.[17]

b) FINE ARTS

In painting, Miklos Barabás (1810–1896) represented the neoclassicism of the old school, Mihály Zichy (1827–1896) neoromanticism. Victor Madarăsz's art revealed French romantic influence and Gyula Benczúr stood still for the large-scale traditional paintings of historical topics from national history. The same was true of Mihály von Munkácsy (1844–1890) some of whose paintings revealed the spirit of early impressionism. Fülop Laszló (1869–1937) was a portraitist of high society in western Europe before the First World War.

[17] Tibor Klaniczay, József Szander, Miklos Szabolcsi, *Geschichte der ungarischen Literatur* (Budapest, 1963), pp. 152–215; Johann H. Schwicker, *Geschichte der ungarischen Literatur* (Leipzig, 1888), pp. 833–927; Josef Remenyi, *Hungarian Writers and Literature* (New Brunswick, N.J., 1964), pp. 146–370; Antal Siviasky, *Die ungarische Literatur der Gegenwart* (Bern, 1962), pp. 13–47; Zoltan Horváth, *Die Jahrhundertwende in Ungarn: Geschichte der zweiten Reformgeneration (1896–1914)* (Neuwied, 1966), pp. 176–203, 267–283, 373–412; on the press, ibid., pp. 302–715. Andritsch, *Ungarische Geisteswelt,* pp. 245–273; William O. McCagg, *Jewish Nobles and Geniuses in Modern Hungary* (New York, 1972), pp. 71–74; see also for background reading William M. Johnston, *The Austrian Mind: An Intellectual and Social History 1848–1938* (Berkeley, 1972), pp. 335–350.

The first painter of the modern impressionist school was Pál Szinyei Merse (1845–1920). Károly Ferenczy, who was influenced by the French Barbizon school and particularly Jozsef Rippl-Ronai in his early work, were other characteristic representatives of the modern school, Rippl-Ronai of the then ultra modern Secession. Most of these modern painters were still influenced by the Magyar equivalent of the French Barbizon school, that of Nagybánya.

In sculpture the traditionalists were longer in control. István Ferenczy (1792–1856) was a student of the neoclassicism of Canova and Thorwaldsen. Miklós Izsó (1831–1875) created true-to-life portrait plastics in the traditional style. Only János Fadrusz' (1858–1903) art introduced a transitional stage to the modern spirit. Fülop Ö. Berk (1873–1945) represented it in full.

Hungary's architecture had a full share of the eclectic pseudo-historical styles of the nineteenth century. Frigyes Fresl (1821–1884) stood for neoromantic motives, Miklos Ybl for the neo-Renaissance, while Imre von Steindle, the architect of the monumental, somewhat pompous, Hungarian parliament, combined Gothic and Renaissance features in his work. Ödon Lechner (1845–1914), however, became an interesting representative of a modern style. He worked for a compromise between the secessionist trend in the fine arts with the designs of historic Hungarian folk art.[18]

c) MUSIC

Czech, German, and Magyar music in their great achievements reveal mutual influence. Combined they represent the essence of musical heritage developed in the Habsburg empire and transmitted from there to the world. The specific Magyar contribution rests primarily in the blending of modern with folk- including gipsy music. Ernst v. Dohnányi (1877–1960) and Jenö Hubay (1858–1937) were composers of traditional opera and symphonic music. Both, and this is characteristic for Magyar music, were practizing artists also, Dohnányi as pianist and Hubay as violinist. Bela Bartók (1881–1945) creatively injected the themes of old folk tunes into modern music. He was also a musicologist of rank. Zoltan Kodály (1882–1967), for nearly a generation the great old man of Magyar music, was the composer of choral work, a sophisticated brief opera and symphonic music. His *Psalmus Hungaricus* like Bartók's *Kossuth* symphony was a landmark of a new style. Bartók and Kodály were the outstanding composers in contemporary music who raised cliché concepts of

[18] Lajos Németh in *Ungarn* (Budapest, 1966), pp. 371–380; Horváth, *Die Jahrhundertwende*, pp. 217–223, 425–433.

pseudo-romantic folk music and standard patterns of national music to new emotional and intellectual levels.

One should also mention the Magyar contribution to the operetta. The two best known names of the light muse were Imre Kálmán, composer of the *Czardas Princess* and Franz Lehár of the *Merry Widow*. The center of gravity, however, of the musical activities of these two more gifted than distinguished musicians was Vienna rather than Budapest. Finally it should be noted that one of the most outstanding German conductors, Arthur Nikisch, and the Bohemian-born Austrian composer Gustav Mahler, were both consecutively directors of the excellent Hungarian national opera house in Budapest. All things considered, Magyar music beginning with the second half of the nineteenth century, gave as much to Czech and German musical developments as it received from their music.[19]

d) SCHOLARSHIP

Humanities and Social Sciences

In the humanities one might mention first two great literary critics. Georg Lukács (1885–1971) was an independent neo-Marxist philosopher, equally conversant in the field of philosophy and literature. Most of his internationally known, though often controversial work was done after the First World War and therefore has to remain outside of this discussion. Yet his penetrating study on the evolution of the modern drama was published in 1911, and his equally interesting work on the theory of the novel, though published only after the war, was largely completed by 1918. Baron Lajos Hatvany (1860–1961), the scion and black sheep of a wealthy Magyar industrialist family of Jewish background, who was forced to spend much of his life in exile, was a literary critic, essayist, and writer of sophisticated and entertaining novels dealing with the problems of Jewish assimilation in prewar Hungary.

Armin Vámbéry (1832–1913) became a famous Turkologist of international reputation. Gustav Beksics (1847–1906), a distinguished liberal historian, was primarily interested in Hungarian constitutional and national problems. Henrik Marczali (1856–1910) was likewise an authority on Hungarian constitutional history and on the enlightened era. Two representative late-nineteenth and twentieth-century Magyar historians

[19] András Pernye in *Ungarn,* pp. 390–399; Horváth, *Die Jahrhundertwende,* pp. 204–216, 413–424; Stefan Borsody, "Modern Hungarian Historiography," *Journal of Modern History,* XXIV:15 (1952), 398–405; Andritsch, *Ungarische Geisteswelt,* pp. 273–281.

were Gyula Szekfü (1883–1955) and Bálint Hóman (1885–1951). Szekfü was a versatile, though not very consistent Magyar historian, who vacillated according to the spirit of the times between Right and Left. Still, his work on state and nation, his biographies of the younger Rákóczi in exile and of Gabriel Bethlen, and his *The State of Hungary,* were specimens of outstanding scholarship as was his share in the five-volume work History of Hungary written by him and Hóman. Hóman, the great Hungarian medievalist, wrote the two first volumes of this monumental work. Convicted for his pro-German policy as minister of education during the early part of the Second World War, he died in prison. Characteristic for Hungarian historiography, as indeed for Hungarian history in general, is the emphasis put on institutional and particularly constitutional problems.

The Hungarian contribution to sociology was focused largely on the nationality problem. Oscar Jászi (1875–1957), minister of nationalities in the Károlyi administration 1918–1919 is usually considered as a social historian if judged by his contributions to the analysis of the Habsburg empire and the Hungarian revolutions of 1918–1919. Yet his studies on nationalism, published before the First World War in Hungary and not yet translated into a western language, characterize him primarily as sociologist. An original sociological thinker along biological lines was Bódog Somló (1873–1920). A philosophy of law, strongly influenced by Spencer's positivist sociology, owes much to Gyula Pikler (1864–1934). The greatest sociologist and social philosopher of Magyar origin was Karl Mannheim (1893–1947), student of Max Weber. Mannheim's *Ideology and Utopia* owed much to his early education in Hungary, although he never held a chair at a Hungarian university because scholars found a better sounding board in the west than in the narrow Magyar-language orbit of Hungary. The migration of Hungarian scholars to the west, however, was also in part the result of Hungarian national chauvinism, anti-Semitism, and beginning with the March revolution of 1919 to this day the totalitarian influences from the Right and Left.[20]

Sciences

Ignác Semmelweiss (1818–1865), who spent the best part of his professional career in Vienna, is credited with the momentous introduction of antiseptics into obstetrics, an invention which he could put through only against enormous odds of the prejudices and hurt vanities of his

[20] Horváth, *Die Jahrhundertwende,* pp. 86–104; Johnston, *The Austrian Mind,* pp. 365–379; McCagg, *Jewish Nobles and Geniuses,* pp. 102–112, 142–148.

colleagues. Ányos Jedlick (1800–1885) made an original contribution to electrophysics and József Petzval (1807–91), in his later life professor in Vienna, was a pioneer in photographic optics. Lorand Eötvös, president of the highly reputed Hungarian Academy and minister of education from 1894 to 1895, was an eminent scientist in the field of geophysics. The commanding position in physics which issued from Hungary into the world was yet to come. Endree Högyes (1847–1906) became a famous neurologist. Hungarian contributions to science are richer during the period under discussion than those of the Czechs who were their equals in other fields. Hungary's position within the dualistic system provided particularly the university in Budapest with means comparable only to those offered to the University of Vienna. Just the same, decentralization of institutions of high learning in the Habsburg empire, as far as it went, enriched cultural progress.[21]

Altogether Magyar cultural achievements, because of the ethnic isolation of the nation, had greater difficulties in breaching the language barrier than even the small Slavic national groups with their interrelated languages. Yet greater challenges led also to greater stimuli. None of the peoples under Habsburg rule has succeeded to a wider degree in injecting its major cultural attainments in the western languages to the world across its borders. In doing so—and this is the second most remarkable fact—the nation has fully preserved its national identity. The reasons are as apparent in the cultural field as in any other: Magyars have always considered this national identity as the most precious treasure of their stormy history.

G. The Austro-German orbit

This subheading differs in character from the preceding ones, which refer to national groups but coincides with the one selected in Chapter VII. It has been chosen after some deliberation. In the center of the empire we have to deal with actions on two levels. First Austro-German cultural contributions and, of equal importance, but not identical though largely overlapping, cultural contributions within the Austro-German geographical and social orbit. It should be reemphasized that the following survey can offer only a highly selective picture, in which individuals will be sometimes referred to for the sake of illustrating a trend rather than because they were necessarily the greatest in their field of activity.

[21] Helen Antal, *Ungarn* (Budapest, 1966), pp. 261–263.

a) LITERATURE, PRESS, THEATER

Marie von Ebner-Eschenbach (1830–1916), the daughter of a Moravian aristocratic family, is generally reputed to be Austria's greatest woman poet. The setting of her novels is largely that of her Moravian homeland. Frequently the aristocracy residing on their country estates and so well known to her by origin and environment, plays an important part in her writings. Yet usually the peasants, not the nobles are the heroes. A strong feeling for social justice permeates Ebner-Eschenbach's work. She frequently portrays the Moravian peasant as Peter Rosegger (1843–1918) does the Styrian peasant. The social outlook of both writers is thus similar, although their social origin was vastly different. Rosegger was the son of the poorest type of mountain peasants and wrote on the basis of experience gained by an outlook from below, where Ebner-Eschenbach was primarily motivated by social injustices observed from above. Both share a similar social philosophy, with the difference, however, that a sprinkling of German nationalism in Rosegger's writings is alien to Ebner-Eschenbach.

The Tyrolian physician Dr. Karl Schönherr (1869–1943) was one of the most gifted dramatists of the period. His peasant characters as well as the intellectuals, frequently taken from his own medical profession, are sketched in a simplified but in his best works monumental realism tending toward expressionism. The modern impressionist and later expressionist age in Austrian literature is represented by the Viennese Arthur Schnitzler (1862–1931), Hugo von Hofmannsthal (1874–1929), Richard Beer-Hofmann (1866–1945), and Peter Altenberg (1859–1919, original name Richard Engländer). Schnitzler, the oldest of them, was only fifteen years older than Hofmannsthal, the youngest. The best known today is still undoubtedly Schnitzler, a physician, son of a Jewish academic upper middle class family in Vienna. Schnitzler is known today primarily on account of his plays and here in part because of the erotic but never coarse tinge in some of them. His outstanding prose, particularly his novellas, are not as well remembered as they should be. Schnitzler is the prototype of the apolitical, but by no means l'art pour l'art writer. His topics are the basic conflicts of men through the ages, love, death, reality, dream. Social questions are not ignored, but are presented as personal, not as general problems. His philosophy of life in several ways influenced by his great contemporary, Sigmund Freud. Though the setting of Schnitzler's plays is frequently the educated Austrian upper burgher class, this does not mean that Schnitzler wanted to be identified with it. His themes of lasting human significance—and that keeps his oeuvre alive—were illustrated by the conflicts within the class of people Schnitzler knew best. Essentially they are human throughout. Richard Beer-Hofmann was closer to problems alien to Schnitzler, the relation between individual and nation, man and God. His work, small in volume with emphatic attention to immaculate form, was largely focused on the problems of the Jew from biblical history to his own age. Hugo von Hofmannsthal shares with his friends the great concern for a noble and purified prose. A cultured man with sensitivity pertaining to all major themes of world literature, he was not particularly original but an outstanding connoisseur and editor of classical works. He was also the author of noble, though somewhat academic essays and of a sensitive lyric. Hofmannsthal's ability to understand the work of others made him the congenial writer of the texts of Richard Strauss's most famous operas. It would be inappropriate to call these texts mere librettos. Peter Altenberg was the typical member of the Bohème in his daily life; his field was the small but carefully written sketch of daily impressions. He was the most impressionist of these four great writers and the only one who stayed with this trend to the end of his life.

Anton Wildgans (1881–1931), author of dramas, epics, and lyrics, though almost within the age group of the others, outgrew impressionist tendencies. An artist of great emotional power he came close to expressionism. Wildgans' work is marred to some extent by jingo patriotism at the beginning of the First World War and a tendency to work himself into extreme passion. Still, with some of his lyrics and some of his prose more than with his dramatic work, he belonged to the notable writers of his day. The same cannot be said for the versatile talents of a Hermann Bahr who has to be mentioned here chiefly because of his vacillating position between various trends in literary history. From naturalism to impressionism, expressionism, and symbolism, he represented all styles in his plays and prose work. In politics he navigated with skill between socialism, liberalism, radical nationalism, and finally devout Catholicism.

Richard von Schaukal (1874–1942), who moved from Brünn (Brno) to Vienna, was an essayist, but primarily a lyric who upheld traditional conservative and religious values. Georg Trakl (1887–1914), wrote pessimistic poetry, which reveals extraordinary powers of vision and formal beauty. He ended his life through suicide. The highly gifted Franz Werfel (1880–1945) from Prague belongs in this context only with the expressionist works of his radical youth. The novels which made him famous were written after 1918. The critic and prose writer Karl Kraus (1874–1936), according to his self-description, was the servant of the word, the foe of shoddy journalism. It was his interesting theory that extreme care in cultivation of a clear and fully correct language determines in a decisive way the course of human relations. Whether Kraus' own style complied fully with his stiff demands remains, however, debatable. Kraus, for more than thirty years editor and eventually the only contributor to the journal *Die Fackel* (The Torch) was a highly aggressive personality, in permanent conflict with Austrian journalism and most of his fellow writers. Inasmuch as he too moved through various political strata, by and large from the Left to the Right, it was not hard for him to find opponents and it was even easier to pick quarrels with smooth and insincere writers. Though Kraus's cantankerous and morbidly vain character left much to be desired, he had outstanding merits in much of his prose and to some extent as eminent lyric. Whatever may rightly be said against his character and excessive introvert disposition, his passionate protest against the First World War, expressed in his monumental drama *The Last Days of Mankind,* is a work of genius and intellectual courage.

Here may be the appropriate place to refer to two writers, originally from Prague, whose place is easier to establish in world literature than in relation to German-Austrian letters. Rainer (René) Maria Rilke (1875–1926) led a restless life, impeded further by his poor health and his fragile nervous system. He could work only intermittently, but his lyrics are considered by many in the western world as the greatest to have originated on Austrian soil. His sonets and elegies reveal strong romantic and pantheistic tendencies. The fear of life and death, seemingly overcome in his last works, leads frequently to his evaluation as early existentialist. His impact on world literature is greater than that of any other Austrian lyric before and after him.

Franz Kafka (1883–1924) shares with Rilke a fame abroad unsurpassed by any other writer in modern Austrian literature. Yet although his stories and later novels represent, according to many, expressionist abstractions as their main characteristic, a certain realism, as shown in Kafka's impressions of the Prague of his youth in its mystical-gloomy attraction, is more obvious in his writings than in Rilke's. They both share the great fear of death, and the urge for salvation. Symbolism plays a predominant role in Kafka's almost magically powerful prose in its mixture of reason and phantasmagories.[22]

[22] Johann W. Nagl, Jakob Zeidler and Eduard Castle, *Deutsch-österreichische Literaturgeschichte* (Vienna, 1899–1937), IV, 833–866, 1355–1358, 2119–2120; Josef Nadler, *Literaturgeschichte Österreichs* (Linz, 1948), pp. 356–480; Claudio Magris, *Der habsburgische Mythos in der österreichischen Literatur* (Salzburg, 1966); Allan Janik and Stephen Toulmin, *Wittgenstein's Vienna* (New York, 1973), pp. 33–91; Johnston, *The Austrian Mind,* pp. 357–361.

As for the press so bitterly attacked by Kraus, the three leading German-Austrian dailies by the end of the nineteenth century were the *Neue Freie Presse*, the Socialist *Arbeiter-Zeitung*, and the Catholic *Reichspost*. The *Neue Freie Presse* had the smallest popular support and the widest recognition among the intelligentsia and the well-to-do classes in the country and abroad. It was German-liberal in an economic, anticlerical sense, capitalistic, and strongly dynastic. What gave the paper added appeal was the roster of excellent literary writers and occasional contributors from the highest ranks of government. A staff member was the founder of Zionism, Theodor Herzl (1860–1904) who, however, was forbidden to promote his cause in the paper because it offended the feelings of the assimilatory Jewish bourgeoisie, represented by the editor in chief, Moritz Benedikt. The *Arbeiter-Zeitung,* edited by Victor Adler, the leader of the party, and Friedrich Austerlitz, a brilliant young journalist, conducted a brave fight against social injustice. Considering the fact that the means at the disposal of the paper were limited, the intellectual level of its simple, lucid, but never banal discussions of complex social problem was as noteworthy as the devotion to the cause of workers' education in general. The *Reichspost,* under the management of Friedrich Funder was strictly pro-Austrian in a so-called black-yellow, anti-Magyar, anti-German-nationalist sense. To leave no doubt that this latter position did not imply any conciliation with liberalism, the devout clerical paper was, in Lueger's spirit, strongly anti-Semitic. The German nationalist press, because of poor political organization, was represented only by numerous dailies and weeklies of relatively small circulation. Their cumulative influence was nevertheless considerable.[23]

Of the Viennese theaters, the Opera reached the summit of its achievements in the late nineteenth and early new century under the musical leadership of Gustav Mahler. The other state theater, the Burgtheater, founded by Joseph II as National Theater in 1776 but actually operated as imperial court theater, had its most glorious era behind it by this time. When the performances were still given in the modest old house, the so-called Old Burgtheater under the management of Heinrich Laube (from 1849–1867), a former Young German radical, they were unexcelled in the whole German language orbit. After Laube, under Franz von Dingel-

[23] Kurt Paupié, *Handbuch der österreichischen Pressegeschichte 1848–1959,* 2 vols. (Vienna, 1961–1966); Adam Wandruszka, *Geschichte einer Zeitung: Das Schicksal der 'Presse' und 'Neuen Freien Presse'* (Vienna, 1958); Janik and Toulmin, *Wittgenstein's Vienna,* pp. 77–81.

stedt, director from 1872 to 1881, the theater still maintained its high reputation and improved it, in fact, in regard to scenery and costumes. To Laube, who had focused his attention exclusively on the spoken word, the external aspects of the stage had meant little. When the Burgtheater moved into a huge, richly decorated new palace in 1888, the cultivation of the spoken word on the stage, whether prose or verse, declined. Moreover, the theater remained out of tune with literary developments, a factor more widely resented in the age of new mass education than previously. Dr. Max Burkhardt, a new manager, tried to improve matters in this respect in the 1890's and introduced the plays of Ibsen and Gerhart Hauptmann to the stage of the court theater. In essence he fought a losing battle. The master of the imperial household, the supreme chief of the theater, insisted that the theater and its repertoire must always be kept within the bounds of the imperial-royal tradition. Revolutionary changes and experiments, therefore, ought be banned from this hallowed ground. The Burgtheater as court theater always retained a respectable level of quality but while it could never claim literary leadership it lost its primacy in theatrical techniques as well. The Deutsches Volkstheater, opened in 1889 under private management, was expected to be unimpeded by courtly etiquette which plagued the Burgtheater. The new theater was to cultivate modern plays and popular Austrian dramatic literature. It succeeded to some extent but never gained the prestige that the Burgtheater had in the era of Laube as the model for excellent standards of performance and as the school of graceful living for aristocracy and upper burgher class. New theaters, some more radical than the Volkstheater and some more ready to cater in their offerings to a popular preference for the operetta, were established. But the leadership in offerings of plays of literary interest and new experimental stage techniques by the turn of the century had passed on to Berlin.

Austrian impressionism in literature had established patterns to be followed widely in western literature, as had the Austrian stage before the last quarter of the nineteenth century in the German orbit.[24]

b) FINE ARTS

The most celebrated painter of the 1870's and 1880's was Hans Makart (1840–1884). He was much admired for his presentation of female beauty in the manner of Rubens, partly in the setting of semi-historical, huge

[24] Joseph Gregor, *Geschichte des österreichischen Theaters* (Vienna, 1948), pp. 196–253; Rudolf Lothar, *Das Wiener Burgtheater* (Vienna, 1899), pp. 124–203.

compositions, partly in sensual female portraits in a pseudo-Greek frame. Colorful, highly decorative, but somewhat sloppy in his drawings and his technique of painting which made his shining colors fade after a few years, Makart was a symbol for the eclectic and essentially superficial make-believe taste of the period. Hans Canon (1829–1885) followed the same pseudo-historical and pseudo-allegorical but not equally sensual pattern. A greater though less ostentatious artist was Anton Romako (1834–1889) whose landscapes herald future expressionism. The work of the woman landscape painter Tina Blau (1845–1916) was more clearly impressionistic. Her and Romako's equal was Rudolf von Alt (1812–1905) likewise a painter of landscapes and also of picturesque city views, who started out in the manner of the eighteen-century Venetian artists, the Canalettos, and ended his long life as adherent of the plain-air school. Alt in his old age represented a transitional stage to the modern school. Its foremost representative and one of the most gifted artists on Austrian soil, whose fame has been revived in recent years, was Gustav Klimt (1867–1918). A founder of the new modern school, represented by the Sezession, Klimt's highly original combination of a simplified realism with an ornamental style and a brilliant sense of color gave to his composition of portraits but also allegorical subjects a more genuine sensuality than the showy art of Makart. Egon Schiele (1890–1918) followed the pattern of Klimt. His style is less ornamental and more expressionist than that of his master. The third outstanding representative of the modern school, definitely expressionist in his portraits and grand compositions, was Oskar Kokoschka (1886–   ) an artist equally impressive as painter and writer. His art too, like that of Klimt, had considerable influence beyond the Austrian borders.

Sculpture in Austria was more strongly associated with the traditional than painting. Anton Fernkorn (1813–1888) was the creator of two great equestrian statues (Archduke Charles and the more monumental Prince Eugen of Savoy) in the big outer courtyard of the Hofburg in Vienna. Kaspar von Zumbusch (1830–1915) created the biggest, but certainly not most beautiful monument on Austrian soil, that of Maria Therera in Vienna. The statue of the empress is surrounded by a host of oversize statues of her advisors and generals, some of them on horseback. Decorative and monumental in character it is what time and place primarily asked for. The later nineteenth and early twentieth century artists Viktor Tilgner (sculptor of the elegant Mozart monument) and Hans Bitterlich (monument of Empress Elisabeth) deviated from the monumental pseudo-naturalistic style to a more pleasing simpler one. Edmund Hellmer followed this trend with the Goethe monument and the memorial to the liberation from the Turks in St. Stephan's cathedral.[25]

Most characteristic of all branches of fine art of a period is usually architecture. This can be understood by the fact, that the architect, due to the costs of his works in skilled labor and money, is more dependent on public or private support than the painter and—to some degree—the sculptor. He is therefore bound to make more concessions to the wishes of his sponsors than other artists. It means further that his work is more closely linked to the social conditions of time and place than theirs.

The great architects of the second half of the nineteenth century were the designers of what is frequently referred to as *Ringstrassenarchitektur*. That means the eclectic, pseudo-historical styles of the new monumental boulevard encircling the inner city of a Vienna, that was on its way to becoming now a great city, not only as previously by tradition but also by population figures. The Ringstrasse represents the power of the imperial House, that of the rising new industrial and financial bourgeoisie, but above all the will to represent or make believe greatness. At the same time this architecture of the Gründer period that exploded in part in the big crash of 1873 did not lack taste and the artistic sensibility inherent in the talents of the German-Austrian people. The new architecture offered an interesting compromise.

The best work of the period was also one of its earliest, the Opera house in Italian Renaissance style, erected in the 1860's by Eduard Van der Nüll and August von Siccardsburg. Public criticism of this noble building in a rich but not yet lavish setting drove Van der Nüll to suicide and Siccardsburg to an untimely death due to nervous exhaustion a few weeks later. Gradually the Viennese became used to the new blending of historical styles by the so-called three great building barons, the Dane Theophil von Hansen, the German Friedrich von Schmidt, and the Austrian Heinrich von Ferstel. Hansen, perhaps the most gifted of the three, was attracted by classical Greek designs, which he blended with Renaissance motives in the palaces of the Viennese Academy of Fine Arts, the Musical Association (*Musikvereinsgebäude*), the stock exchange, and several apartment houses. All these buildings, though not quite in line with modern taste, were commodious, monumental, and dignified. A misconception, however, was his main work the House of Parliament, the most "Greek" of his works, not because it was unattractive in itself, but because it did not fit in the surroundings—a Greek temple in a Baroque city. Schmidt, though a lesser

[25] Destroyed during World War II. His subsequent Johann Strauss monument was a relapse to previous pseudo-naturalistic tastelessness.

artist than Hansen, did better with the city hall, which combined Renaissance and Gothic features and did not look nearly as strange in its more spacious surroundings than the Parthenon-like parliament. Ferstel was the designer of the pseudo-Gothic Votiv Church, also an early work of the period. As all-too-faithful, all-too-regular replica of late medieval French cathedrals, this in many ways commendable work reveals artificial sweetness which its great models lack. Ferstel was also the designer of the main building of the University in Italian Renaissance style and here some of the failings of the Ringstrassen architecture came glaringly into the open. An inordinate part of the space available was used for two monumental staircases, while many lecture halls and offices are inadequate. According to a sarcastic joke which contained a good deal of truth, the university was built for the opening ceremonies by the emperor and not for faculty and students. What was true for the university was doubly true for the new Burgtheater and the two imperial museum buildings. In both instances a fourth building baron, Karl von Hasenauer (1833–1894), an epigone to the other three, had botched the noble original plans of the brilliant Saxon architect Gottfried Semper. The Burgtheater is not only richly but overlavishly decorated, but when it was opened one could not see the stage well from most seats. An expensive partial rebuilding was necessary which, however, could not remedy fully the basic deficiencies to this day. Even more inappropriate was the distortion of Semper's plans by Hasenauer for the buildings of the imperial museums. The domes are discordant with the basic designs, the vestibules and staircases overdecorated. In the Museum of Fine Arts, lavishly ornamented and guilded high exhibition halls smother the objects shown there. These last epigone Ringstrassen buildings reveal an architecture in decay, which in its beginnings and at its height had great merits. Yet these merits pertained chiefly to the palaces of the inner city. The main shortcomings of the Ringstrassen style rested in the fact, that it was indiscriminately copied in the apartment buildings for the poor, the so-called "rent barracks", (*Zinskasernen*) where plaster took the place of stone and marble, and the money spent on superfluous and ugly decorations in cheap material was taken from the funds which should have been spent on lacking essentials.

Otto Wagner (1841–1918), one of the early members of the *Sezession* (the symbol of a new style evolving around the turn of the century) broke finally with the eclectiv pseudo-classical pattern. His architecture, as shown in several churches, private and public buildings, presents a curious and sometimes startling blending of an incipient functionalism with simplified historical motives. The results are in his best works outstanding, in others still notable. But this is typical for the pioneer artist. Two of his students, Joseph Olbrich, designer of the Sezession's exhibition building, and Josef Hoffmann, were on the way to a more complete functionalism. Its full-fledged representative was Adolf Loos from Moravia (1870–1933) who abandoned the ornament and make-believe decorations in architecture completely and designed the so-called House without Eyebrows, that is, without window ornaments. According to contemporary critics, its vicinity to the imperial castle (the Hofburg) made it a petrified *crimen laesae majestatis*. Adolf Loos, like Kokoschka also a brilliant writer, promoted his ideas in essays on various aspects of esthetics. They still make interesting reading today, after his views which appeared paradox in his time have met general acceptance.

Indeed, while the Austrian pseudo-historic architecture was in line with similar developments elsewhere in Europe, the architecture of Wagner, Olbrich, Hoffmann, and Loos has had a genuine avant garde impact on architectural developments in the new and old worlds to this day.[26]

c) MUSIC

The greatest period in Austrian music, and perhaps in the music of western civilization altogether, were the two generations between the rise to manhood of Josef Haydn and the death of Beethoven and Schubert in the pre-March era. As with Beethoven, new lustre came to Austrian music when another outstanding German composer who followed the classic pattern, Johannes Brahms, took up permanent residence in Vienna. He resided there from 1869 to his death in 1897. Thus the supreme achievements of Brahms in symphonic and chamber music, his requiem and many of his Lieder are associated with the musical atmosphere of Vienna. Anton Bruckner (1824–1896), episcopal organist in Linz, Upper Austria, took up his headquarters in Vienna a few years later. His grandiose symphonic work is as reminiscent of the Austrian Baroque as that of Brahms is of German neoclassicism. The third great, somewhat younger symphonic composer, Gustav Mahler (1860–1922), for ten years director of

[26] Karl Oettinger, Renate Wagner, Franz Fuhrmann and Alfred Schmeller, *Reclams Kunstführer Österreichs*, 2 vols. (Stuttgart, 1961); Hans Tietze, *Wien* (Berühmte Kunststätten, Vol. 67) (Leipzig, 1918), pp. 279–312; Fritz Novotny, *Anton Romako* (Vienna, 1954); Emil Pirchan, *Gustav Klimt* (Vienna, 1956); Oskar Kokoschka, *Schriften: 1907–1955* (Munich, 1956); Renate Wagner, ed., *Die Wiener Ringstrasse: Bild einer Epoche* (Vienna-Cologne, 1969), Vols. I and II; Elisabeth Lichtenberger, *Wirtschaftsstruktur und Sozialstruktur der Wiener Ringstrasse* (Vienna-Cologne, 1970), passim; Robert Waissenberger, *Die Wiener Sezession* (Vienna, 1970), passim.

the Vienna Opera, represented a highly emotional neoromantic style. Hugo Wolf (1860–1903), an outstanding Lieder composer, in particular in the spirit rather than in the style of Italian and Spanish music, created also an opera *Corregidor,* which is undeservedly forgotten today. For a time it was perhaps the enormous influence of Richard Wagner and later in a different way that of Richard Strauss which discouraged Austrian musicians to emulate masters of the old opera and the new musical drama. Only Johann Strauss, the younger (1825–1899), composer of unparalleled and widely celebrated Viennese waltz music, filled a lacuna, perhaps precisely because he did not want to compete with the very great. Two of his operettas, *Der Zigeunerbaron* (the *Gipsy Baron*) and *Die Fledermaus* (The Bat) are frequently considered light comic opera; yet it does not impair the musical brilliance of *Die Fledermaus* if one refers to it as operetta.

The great pioneer of modern music in Austria, radiating from Austria to the world was Arnold Schönberg (1874–1951). From free harmonic composing—atonality—he moved to the stricter frame of the twelve-tone scale. Yet, revolutionary as these changes in harmonics were, Schönberg still preserved the classical structure of symphonic and choral works. Of his students, the most outstanding one was Alban Berg (1885–1935), the creator of the opera *Wozzek*. A revolutionary work of creative genius, it was worthy of the teachings of Berg's master. In connection with the new atonal music the teacher of the theory of music, Heinrich Schenker (1868–1935) should be mentioned.

In this silver age of music in Austria musical life was rich. The philharmonic concerts of a world-renowned orchestra under various conductors of high rank remained unparalleled in continental Europe. Yet after the resignation of Mahler in 1906 the Opera never fully regained its former brilliance, although performing artists and the superb orchestra continued to be of the highest quality. In other respects musical development left something to be desired. The operetta, an art form for masters like Johann Strauss and even Franz Lehár, Imre Kalman, or Oskar Straus (the composer of *Waltz Dream*) became increasingly trivial under lesser successors, accommodating the musical taste of the masses. This cheap musical export article found its unlamented end roughly with the outbreak of the Second World War. As for serious though no longer classical music, the new era from Mahler to Schönberg and Berg gave powerful incentives to musical developments across the world.[27]

[27] Heinrich Kralik, *Das Buch der Musikfreunde* (Vienna, 1951), pp. 94–199; Franz Farga, *Die Wiener Oper* (Vienna, 1947), pp. 196–313; Lothar Fahlbusch

d) SCHOLARSHIP

Austrian scholarship during the half century under discussion here struck a middle line between the traditional and the revolutionary. The former pertains by and large to the historical disciplines, the latter to the natural sciences. In the social sciences we meet both, but with strong tendencies toward new vistas.

Humanities

In the humanities Theodor von Sickel (1828–1908) from Germany, at some time director of the Austrian Institute for Historical Research at the University of Vienna and director of the Austrian Historical Institute in Rome, was an outstanding medievalist and teacher of the auxiliary historical sciences. Oswald Redlich, the biographer of Rudolf von Habsburg, likewise a distinguished medievalist, was at the same time a keen student of the seventeenth and eighteenth century. Josef Redlich from Moravia (1869–1936), a liberal parlamentarian has remained to this day the unexcelled biographer of Francis Joseph and a constitutional historian of first rank. Alfons Dopsch, an original social historian of early medieval history, explored the continuity of development from ancient to medieval times. August Fournier, biographer of Napoleon, and Heinrich von Srbik (1878–1951) biographer of Metternich, were first-rank historians from an intellectual and literary point of view, though Srbik's studies on the German unification idea were marred by national prejudices.

Of outstanding musicologists Eduard Hanslick from Prague (1825–1904), is frequently remembered chiefly for his criticism of Wagner. Actually he was a pioneer scholar in musical esthetics. Guido Adler, from Moravia (1855–1941) became the meritorious editor of the *Denkmale der Tonkunst in Österreich.*

Exciting were developments in philosophy. Theodor Gomperz from Brünn (Brno) (1832–1912) held the middle-ground between intellectual history and philosophy. His great work *Griechische Denker* (Greek Thinkers) is still worth reading from a literary point of view. Entirely new ideas were introduced by Franz Brentano from Germany (1838–1917). He was the scion of a family which had given much to German scholarship and arts. Brentano, a former Catholic priest, was secularized

---

ed., *Eduard Hanslick, Musikkritiken* (Leipzig, 1972); Richard Specht, *Das Wiener Operntheater* (Vienna, 1919); Marcel Prawy, *Die Wiener Oper* (Vienna, 1969).

and then married the daughter of a Viennese patrician family. This marriage because of the denominational impediments of Austrian marriage legislation, cost him his chair at the University of Vienna and he had to continue his teaching as unpaid lecturer. Brentano, an adherent of philosophical realism, rejected the idealistic philosophy of Kant as dominated by intent and replaced it by a doctrine of psychic phenomena, consisting of concepts, judgments, and feelings not of the senses but of the heart. His metaphysics are characterized by a Christian liberal theism. The liberal aspects in philosophical teaching were taken up by Friedrich Jodl from Germany (1844–1914) who adhered to a materialistic monism.

But Brentano's teaching had a greater significance because of its influence on the theory of phenomenology, developed later by Edmund Husserl from Moravia (1859–1938). Husserl rejected psychologism in logic by proving the existence of *a priori* logical laws. His phenomenology is a combination of an analytical and intuitive discipline. Judgments derive from immanent intuition, as so-called intuitive evidence. This philosophy in turn had great influence on the existentialism promoted by Martin Heidegger. Thus the chain of thought unloosened by Husserl ranks among the most important trends in modern philosophy. Original were also the ideas of Christian von Ehrenfels (1859–1932), a philosopher of diverse interests, at the German university in Prague. He may be considered as a pacemaker for the development of Gestalt psychology. In regard to important and lasting influence the teachings of the great Jewish philosopher of religion, Martin Buber (1878–1965), who attempted to direct Jewish orthodox theology with its emphasis on the law to the personal I-Thou relation to God, made a profound impact on Protestant theology and religious philosophy.

The "Viennese circle" of neopositivism, in which Moritz Schlick from Germany (1882–1936) exercised leadership, played an important and different role. It stood for pure empiricism and aprioristic logics in the sense of Husserl. Unlike Husserl this school saw a solution to the psychophysical problem in physical terms. Yet the most brilliant representative of the philosophy of the Viennese circle, which penetrated the western world, deviated eventually from its doctrines. Ludwig Wittgenstein (1889–1951) Professor at Cambridge University recognized a kind of metaphysics. He perceived the world as the totality of connections between objects, that is, the facts. But statements are facts, too. Logics are not concerned with reality. The connection between thinking and being cannot be expressed in words, it can merely be recognized and indicated by symbols. This is the basis of a new semantics, according to which philosophy is criticism of language, a doctrine which in different ways confirms and develops conclusions of the linguistic German-Bohemian philosopher, Fritz Mauthner (1849–1923), a generation before Wittgenstein. The three main works of Wittgenstein the *Tractatus logico-philosophicus* of 1921, the *Philosophical investigations,* and *Remarks on the foundation of mathematics*—the latter two published after his death—rank with the most important contributions of philosophical thought of our century. In few other fields of human knowledge have ideas developed or initiated on Austrian soil become as all-pervasive as those in modern philosophy.[28]

Social Sciences

In the social sciences Austria produced outstanding legal scholars whose fame transcended the confines of the country's legal system. Joseph Unger (1828–1913), in the liberal Auersperg era member of the cabinet, was an outstanding theorist in general civil law. Anton Menger (1841–1906), professor of civil procedure and as Socialist a truly *rara avis* in the Austrian academic world, wrote about the unfair treatment of the poor in civil law, an unfairness largely brought about not by discrimination but by the application of a mechanic system of equality. Franz Klein (1854–1926), from 1906 to 1908 attorney general and chief archiect of the Austrian Code of Civil Procedure with its principle of free judicial evaluation of evidence saw the basic ideas of his code accepted by other countries. Edmund Bernatzik, professor of constitutional law, was an authority on the complex problems of nationality legislation. One of the greatest Austrian legal scholars after Zeiller, the chief compilator of the Austrian Code of Civil Law of 1811, was Hans Kelsen from Prague (1881–1973). His theory of pure law which perceives the state not as a social or political order but as a system of law, has been studied, emulated, developed around the globe as has no other work by a contemporary legal scholar. It was on many occasions not only criticized on a scholarly basis but sneered at by some of his colleagues and their followers in Austria, in part due to misunderstanding of new ideas and in part due to racial prejudices. Kelsen's theory has met most challenges; and the constitution of the Austrian republic, of which he was the author after the collapse

[28] Alphons Lhotsky, *Österreichische Historiographie* (Vienna, 1961–1962), pp. 174–223; Richard von Mises, *Positivismus* (Cambridge, Mass., 1951); Norman Malcolm, *Ludwig Wittgenstein* (London, 1958); Allan Janik and Stephen Toulmin, *Wittgenstein's Vienna* (New York, 1973) pp. 120–201; Johnston, *The Austrian Mind,* pp. 181–220, 290–307. On philosophy in Austria see also Albert Fuchs, *Geistige Strömungen in Österreich: 1867–1918* (Vienna, 1949), pp. 199–226.

of the empire, is again the law of the land after it had been abolished during the National Socialist occupation.

Here may be the place to inject some remarks about the Austrian peace movement, although it is connected with the academic world only in the person of Heinrich Lammasch (1853–1920), professor of criminal and international law at the University of Vienna. During the war he spoke out for peace in the Upper House, was Austria's last prime minister for two weeks, and made several notable scholarly contributions to the concept of international arbitration in theory and practice. Most impressive, however, was the example of his sincere and courageous personality. Bertha von Suttner, born in Prague in 1843 as Countess Kinsky, died in Vienna just a month before the outbreak of the First World War. No scholar, and a promoter of the peace idea primarily by strength of emotional appeal, this author of the novel *Die Waffen nieder* was awarded the Nobel peace prize in 1905. The same honor was awarded to Alfred H. Fried (1864–1921) in 1911. As founder of the German and Austrian peace societies he took an unpopular stand for his cause during the war.

World famous became the so-called Austrian School of Economics including its later sociological ramifications. In originality it ranks close to the Austrian contributions to philosophy. Karl Menger (1840–1921), Eugen von Böhm-Bawerk from Moravia (1851–1914), and Friedrich von Wieser (1857–1926), all three professors of economics at the University of Vienna were pioneers of new doctrines, the latter two also cabinet members (Böhm-Bawerk as minister of finance 1900–1904 and Wieser minister of commerce 1917–1918). They developed a theory of marginal profit, and beyond it one of economic value altogether. Wieser, the youngest of the original founders of the school proved himself also as original social thinker in his study *Recht und Macht,* 1910. The younger members of the Austrian school carried its findings into the Anglo-Saxon world and developed them further. With the exception of Ludwig von Mises (1881–1973) equally distinguished as economic historian and theorist, they belong already to the generation active after the First World War. The connecting link between old and new generation was Joseph Schumpeter from Moravia (1883–1950), an economist and sociologist and a powerful and original thinker. He became one of the leading critical historians of economic theory in his time and in his *Capitalism, Socialism, and Democracy* (first ed. 1942) a highly perceptive critic of Marxism, who at the same time recognized the power and originality of Marx's thought.[29]

[29] Fuchs, *Geistige Strömungen in Österreich,* pp. 5–275 passim; Ludwig von Mises, *The Historical Setting of the Austrian School of Economics* (New Rochelle,

Natural Sciences

From the 1870's to the beginning of the new century the Austrian medical school held almost uncontested leadership in the western world. It was lost after the dissolution of the empire, partly for economic reasons. Karl von Rokitansky from Bohemia (1804–1878) became the best-known anatomic pathologist of his time. He established his discipline in a sense as the foundation of medical education altogether. Theodor Billroth from Germany (1829–1894), a musical close friend of Brahms, became the leading surgeon of the Viennese school and with it of an era. His achievements include new findings in histology, pathological anatomy, and anesthesiology. Hermann Nothnagel from Germany (1841–1905) was a versatile teacher of internal medicine who was equally competent in physiology and pathology of the heart, the nervous and the intestinal system. Contrary to Billroth he was also dedicated to liberal principles. Of international fame and a Nobel prize winner was the bacteriologist Karl Landsteiner (1868–1943), discoverer of the blood groups. Clemens von Pirquet (1874–1929), professor of pediatrics, was a pioneer in the study of allergies and serum disease, and the first to use the tuberculin test. No medical discipline has contributed more to the reputation of the Viennese school than medical psychology and psychiatry. Theodor Meynert from Germany (1833–1892) perceived psychiatry primarily as exploratory science and contributed in this sense greatly to the study of the human brain. Richard von Kraft-Ebbing, on the other hand, his successor, also from Germany (1840–1902), understood psychiatry rather as descriptive science. In this sense he wrote a comprehensive textbook of psychiatry and another one of forensic psychopathology. He was succeeded by Julius von Wagner-Jauregg (1857–1941), who was awarded the Nobel prize for his discovery of the treatment of progressive paralysis by malaria therapy.

The most widely known Austrian scientist and perhaps most widely known Austrian of this century is, of course, Sigmund Freud (Freiberg, Moravia 1856—London, 1939). It is impossible in these pages to do justice to his theory and therapy of psychoanalysis which penetrated the western world, particularly in its wide anthropological and cultural ramifications. In strange and sad contrast to Freud's genius and fame are the impedi-

---

1969); Rudolf A. Metall, *Hans Kelsen: Leben und Werk* (Vienna, 1969); Wilhelm Weber, "Hundert Jahre österreichische Nationalökonomie an der Universität Wien," *Studien zur Geschichte der Universität Wien,* (Graz-Cologne, 1962), pp. 104–125; Johnston, *The Austrian Mind,* pp. 318–320.

ments which blocked his academic career on Austrian soil. This is more often than not explained with the anti-Semitism which in its most hideous National Socialist form drove Freud into exile at the age of 82. And yet the basic reason for the harassments he was subjected to before his expulsion derive presumably more from an even more powerful motivation than racial prejudice: fear. Freud's contemporaries everywhere—not only in Austria—shrank from the consequences which his exploration of the subconscious and unconscious in the human psyche might have on their lives. It remains a problem of the future to determine whether those who loudly proclaim and frequently misapply and vulgarize Freud's momentous findings in sundry disciplines do not merely overcompensate those fears which the preceding generation not more sincerely but more patently professed. Josef Breuer (1842–1925) Freud's early collaborator and originator of the first observations leading to the development of the new discipline was also a highly original physiologist. Alfred Adler (1870–1937), originally a student of Freud, deviated from the less than tolerant master's doctrines and introduced the concept of *Individualpsychologie,* which replaced the sex factor as source of neurosis by the conflict between the urge for social position and the often dismal social reality. His school, too, greatly influenced psychiatric therapy in England and the United States and like psychoanalysis it developed in substance outside of the academic frame. Even Freud had only the honorary title of professor and never held a chair at the University of Vienna.

In the natural sciences outside of medicine, developments in physics were most conspicuous. Christian Doppler (1803–1853) made an important contribution to the theory of sound and light waves. The work of Josef Loschmidt from Bohemia (1821–1895) on the theory of molecules was of high practical and theoretical significance. Ludwig Boltzmann's (1844–1906) findings supplemented Loschmidt's research on molecular theory. He also succeeded in proving the correctness of J. C. Maxwell's electromagnetic theory of light. But of the greatest importance were the achievements of the genius of Ernst Mach from Moravia (1838–1916). They are of equal importance for physics, physiology, and philosophy. He made contributions to mechanics, physiology of the senses, and to a functional philosophy which considers causal connections as purely speculative. The progress of neopositivism and the theory of relativity in physics are closely connected with Mach's creative thoughts. Great technological contributions to applied physics were made by Carl Auer von Welsbach (1858–1928) who introduced gas lighting and a type of electric bulb, and by Robert von Lieben, an amateur physicist who made the basic invention of the amplifier tube in the development of early radio technique.

Reference should be made also to the great geologist Eduard Suess (1831–1914). From the 1870's to the 1890's this scholar was also a leading Austro-German liberal deputy who fought for educational reforms.[30]

H. Conclusions

Of the more than eighty outstanding men discussed in this last section, twenty were born in the lands of the Bohemian crown—generally Bohemia or Moravia—and most of them moved sooner or later to German-Austria, usually to Vienna. Two came from Hungary and sixteen from Germany. Almost a dozen left the country again, either for Germany or the United States. Among the men who were in their thirties and forties by 1918 the impact of the subsequent National Socialist persecutions of Jews played an important part. Yet this does not explain the whole problem of emigration which went on steadily after 1918.

Some facts stand out. Not all personalities discussed here were Austrians by citizenship, but they all spent at least a good part of the most creative period of their lives in Austria. Irrespective of their citizenship, ethnic origin, or religious affiliation, they used German as their native language and were immersed in the culture of the Austro-German orbit. Yet this was no unmixed Austro-German culture. Those who came from the Bohemian lands were also influenced by the blending of the Austro-German and Czech cultural setting. Furthermore—and because of the scope of this work it cannot be shown in these pages—many of those born within the Austro-German orbit were only second-generation Austro-Germans. Their parents and grandparents had come from the Bohemian lands, Hungary, Galicia, the Bukovina, and other parts of the empire. It should be added also that the sizable number of Germans from the Reich who settled in Austria added an important and stimulating element to cultural conditions in German-Austria. This is true also for the many and varied challenging ideas which radiated to the world at large from the Habsburg empire in its political decline. We are faced here no longer with the Austro-Germans in isolation or the Austro-German orbit by itself, but with that orbit as center and intersection of crossroads of the empire's

[30] Erna Lesky, *Die Wiener medizinische Schule im 19. Jahrhundert* (Vienna-Cologne, 1965), pp. 119–632; Fuchs, *Geistige Strömungen in Österreich: 1867–1918*, pp. 202–212, 227–247; John T. Blackmore, *Ernst Mach* (Berkeley, 1972), passim.

peoples from east and west, north and south. The cosmopolitan character of the empire and the fertile seeds which began to grow there frequently blossomed and bore fruits in another country.

Was it then the cosmopolitan character of intellectual and artistic Vienna as symbol of both a multinational and a supranational culture, which led to outstanding achievements? The question seems all the more puzzling, since this atmosphere was in so many ways in conflict with the narrow-minded, bigoted, and prejudiced aspects of political party life, which long before Hitler drove many of Austria's best sons into isolation at home or exile abroad.

Before we attempt to deal with this problem, two others have to be clarified. In the first place, there does not exist any fully satisfactory or comprehensive explanation why great intellectual and artistic achievements occur in one country at a certain time and not in another at a different one. It is largely the combination of inexplicable psychological and biological factors with more obvious socialeconomic ones which defy a full elucidation of the phenomenon. For that reason intellectual history becomes so fascinating and in some respects so enigmatic a subject.

The other point to be clarified is this. If we say that the last half century of the empire's existence produced works and ideas which had a greater influence on the world than anything that had been created in Austria before, this does not necessarily mean that the Austrian cultural achievements during the last decades of its history were superior to any previous ones. Magnificent as they were, the older Fischer von Erlach in the late seventeenth and early eighteenth century was probably a greater architect than any of his nineteenth and twentieth-century successors. Grillparzer's standards as a dramatist and Stifter's as a prose writer were not fully equaled by the following generations, and the great musical classics of the late eighteenth and early nineteenth centuries remained unmatched by posterity.

This is not true in all fields, but in some it is obvious. Why then the more pervasive influence of ideas developed in Austria in the later period in philosophy, economics, medicine, musical theory, fine arts, and in several other areas? Improvements in communications may have played its part, but it is uncertain to what degree. Unheard-of progress in this respect in the contemporary world has not been matched by equally unique cultural achievements. Even genuine greatness, we well realize, offers not more than a partial explanation. Its full recognition in presence and future is to a large measure dependent on unpredictable social and political conditions. The multinational character of the empire and in particular the multinational background in the ancestry of great Austrians may presumably have been an important, though not fully provable factor. Yet at least limited negative proof is possible here. Austrian cultural fertility has been steadily declining after the dissolution of the empire, a process that has been slowed down but not come to its end by now. In the postwar decades economic misery and later National Socialist oppression played an important part; yet today, in a more prosperous era, the cultural prospects look possibly somewhat, but not conspicuously, more promising. In the East Central European succession states, political suppression has greatly impeded cultural development. The one state which until 1938 resembled most closely the multinational character of the Habsburg empire, the Czechoslovak republic, could also point to significant cultural achievements, and in any case to the relatively most liberal political atmosphere. This factor has been consistently overlooked by German, Magyar, and Polish nationalism.

This does not mean to say that a multinational setting is an essential precondition of cultural development, but presumably it is a favorable one. People in the democratic Austrian republic share with those in Yugoslavia and the East Central European states in the Russian orbit, a keen sense of intellectual curiosity and full appreciation of esthetic harmony and beauty. These gifts, provided they can be exercised under socially acceptable conditions of political freedom, herald the possibility of future cultural attainments which may well reverse present-day trends. In the Habsburg monarchy such accomplishments, however, were achieved under ethnic and political conditions different from any existing in the East Central European states now. Social inequality was unquestionably greater. But so was in several areas political and cultural freedom throughout the last decades of the empire's existence.

Yet, if reference has been made to the momentous cultural achievements of the pre-March period in the Habsburg empire, which was surely a period of political suppression under a police regime, does that not contradict the assumption that such freedom is a favorable precondition for great attainments? I do not acknowledge the existence of such a contradiction. In the first place this suppression was not always as severe as that which we have been watching in our time in many a country under totalitarian rule. Secondly, Austrian police absolutism did not require active participation of the intellectual and the artist in support of government policy. On the contrary, this regime wanted him to stay away from interference in public affairs. The totalitarian state of today recommends the active involvement of the intellectual and the artist to a higher degree than that of anybody else. This particular factor is an almost insurmountable barrier for the promotion and spread of creative thought. We do not suggest that Austrian conditions between 1814 and 1848 were ideal, but they allowed creative men to resort to the flight into a fancy world outside the reach of police power. By no means, however, am I ready to accept the view, held by some, that commanded restraint from participation in public affairs and the permissible flight into irreality created particularly favorable conditions for cultural development. These conditions were merely a lesser evil than totalitarian control, and the existence of such lesser evils gives convincing testimony for the greatness of the Austrian genius since it proved to be fully capable of overcoming serious impediments.

More suggestive as contributing factor to outstanding cultural attainments in another consideration which pertains again directly to the last decades of the empire's existence. There seems to be much truth in the ancient saying *victi victoribus leges dederunt.* It applies impressively to the cultural conquest of the Greeks in east and west after Alexander the Great had destroyed the last shreds of Hellenic political independence. Cultural stimuli are with much better grace accepted from a state which does not present any longer the danger of cultural penetration in the service of a dreaded political supremacy. Psychological resistance is weakened in such cases as we can see in more recent times in the strong influence of French civilization on the victorious German empire after 1871 and conversely of the culture of the Weimar republic on France after 1918. Admittedly this is only one factor which helps to understand the easing of difficulty in the transmission of cultural ideas. It does not explain the basically unexplainable causes for the great achievements of the human spirit. Yet, whether explainable or not, facts they are, namely the greatness, the originality, and the wide appeal abroad of the Habsburg empire's cultural accomplishments and of the wealth of ideas generated there in the last century of its existence. The chain reaction of cultural stimuli makes it conceivable that this cultural impact may last even longer than the four centuries of political development reviewed in this study. In this sense, what has been suggested at the outset of this chapter seems to be true. At the time when the political history of the Habsburg empire ended, the history of its cultural message to the world in an ever-more widening sense had just begun.

CHAPTER XI

Bibliographical Essay

A complete bibliography about the main topics discussed in the preceding chapters may fill a volume of the size of this study. Consequently only a relatively narrow selection can be offered in this bibliographical essay.

The principles on which the selection is based are the following. Priority is given to literature in West-European languages. This means primarily works in German, because more items have been published in this language than in all other Western languages combined. Next, significant works in English will be cited, and some in French and Italian. Studies in the various languages of the national groups represented in the Habsburg empire will be listed in the first place in English translation and only if none exists in German.[1]

But where standard works dealing with the broad aspects of the problems discussed in this volume are covered neither fully in Western languages nor by translations into Western languages, some representative works in the vernacular of the national groups will be cited. The same is true in general for a selected number of works in non-Western languages. References to national bibliographies, in particular if bibliographies published in Western countries are not sufficiently comprehensive, are likewise listed in non Western languages. The literature in the national languages published in this century has come up amazingly fast in quantity and quality, and therefore such extension of the bibliography is often imperative.

[1] If translations in both languages are available, the one based on the most recently revised edition in the original language will be chosen. German translations of English works will in general be referred to in the first place, if they represent revised editions of the original work.

As for the principles of selection, the yardstick applied in general is scholarly and literary standing of a work, secondly that it illustrates a specific viewpoint with particular clarity, thirdly that it is the only one which covers a specific important fact. Preference is given to modern works. Older ones, which have for years been out of print and are not available in most substantial libraries in this country, are listed only if their paramount historic importance in the field demands inclusion.

It may have been suggestive to organize the bibliography like the text itself in ten main sections. This has not been done because the same topics occur several times in the book in different chronological and national settings. In many cases such division of the bibliography would have required repeated listing of the same item in a number of places. As the bibliography stands now, attention is focused on topical divisions and only in the second place on chronological order. This organization should help to reduce the necessity of multiple listings. Furthermore, to keep this bibliographical essay within reasonable bounds, a fairly large number of works will be found only in the footnotes. This is true of monographs on specific topics or of works which have been referred to only in a few instances. On the other hand, in view of the desired representative character of this bibliography, a number of works, in particular in Slavic languages which have not been used, are included in this essay. It is meant to be in the first place a selective bibliography on the topic in general, irrespective of its relationship to the text of this book.

ORGANIZATION OF BIBLIOGRAPHICAL ESSAY:

I. The Habsburg Empire: General Works
- A) Geography
- B) Histories of the Habsburg Empire including Comprehensive Bibliographies
- C) Dissolution of the Empire
- D) Foreign Relations to 1914
- E) Economic and Social History
- F) Cultural History
- G) Party Ideologies
- H) Nationality Problems in the Habsburg Empire: General Survey
- I) Churches
- J) Armed Forces
- K) Constitutional Problems and Administration
- L) Primary Sources (Records) in Domestic Affairs and Foreign Relations
  - (a) In Domestic Affairs
  - (b) In Foreign Relations.
- M) Historiography
- N) Biography, Reference Works
- O) Serials and Newspapers
- P) Statistics
- Q) Bibliography

II. Literature on the History of the National Groups
- A) The Austro-Germans
- B) The Magyars
- C) The Italians
- D) The Roumanians
- E) General Slavic Intellectual and Linguistic History
- F) The Czechs
- G) The Slovaks
- H) The Poles
- I) The Ruthenians
- J) The Southern Slavs
  - (a) The Croats
  - (b) The Slovenes
  - (c) The Serbs

I. The Habsburg Empire: General Works

a) geography

Carl von Czoernig, *Ethnographie der österreichischen Monarchie,* 4 vols. (Vienna, Hof- und Staatsdruckerei, 1849–1857), is a standard work as yet only in parts outdated. Leon Dominian, *Frontiers of Language and Nationality in Europe* (New York, Holt & Co., 1917), is a useful reference work on ethnic questions. Konard Kretschmer, *Historische Geographie von Mitteleuropa* (Munich, R. Oldenbourg, 1904), and more recently Richard H. Osborne, *East Central Europe* (New York, F. A. Praeger, 1967), are notable surveys. See also George W. Hoffmann, "The Political-Geographical Bases of the Austrian Nationality Problem," in *Austrian History Yearbook,* III:1 (Houston, Rice University Press, 1967).

The most comprehensive work is [Rudolf, Crownprince of Austria-Hungary, sponsor], *Die österreichisch-ungarische Monarchie in Wort und Bild,* 24 vols.(Vienna, Österreichische Hof- und Staatsdruckerei, 1886–1902). It appears outdated more in style and appearance than in substance. This work, written in general by outstanding authorities in the field, offers frequently excellent surveys on descriptive geography, economic policies, social institutions, and cultural developments in the empire.

b) histories of the habsburg empire including comprehensive bibliographies

No fully satisfactory history of the Habsburg empire exists in any language, but some in German are relatively most adequate. This factor is not due to any alleged German cultural supremacy but a consequence of the centuries-old political dominance of the German-speaking people in the empire. A substantial number of these works are by intent fully objective, but they were still written from the vantage point of German centralism.

Hugo Hantsch, *Die Geschichte Österreichs,* 2 vols. (Graz-Cologne, Styria, 4th and 5th edition, 1968–1969), is one of the good modern works written from such traditional German centralist viewpoint. Franz von Krones, *Handbuch der Geschichte Österreichs,* 4 vols. and index vol. (Berlin, Th. Hofmann, 1876–1879), is a valuable, concise, somewhat dry, but reliable presentation of facts, supported by comprehensive bibliographical references. The history of the nineteenth century, however, is merely sketched. Alfons Huber, *Geschichte Österreichs,* 5 vols. (Gotha, F. A. Perthes, 1885–1896), Vol. II, 13th and 14th centuries, revised by A. Lhotsky

(Vienna, Böhlau, 1967) is still valuable. Franz M. Mayer, *Geschichte Österreichs mit besonderer Berücksichtigung des Kulturlebens,* 2 vols. (Vienna, W. Braumüller, 1909), is a readable presentation (German centralist viewpoint). Raimund F. Kaindl, Hans Pirchegger and Anton A. Klein, *Geschichte und Kulturleben Deutschösterreichs,* 3 vols. (Vienna, Braumüller, 1958–1965), is a revised edition of the original work, confined primarily to the German-Austrian orbit. It does not come up to the literary standards of the original work. Victor L. Tapié, *Monarchie et Peuples du Danube* (Paris, Fayard, 1969), is one of the best modern studies of the empire as a whole. This work has been published in English under the title *The Rise and Fall of the Habsburg Monarchy* (New York, Praeger, 1971). Adam Wandruszka, *Das Haus Habsburg* (Vienna, Verlag für Geschichte und Politik, 1956) (available also in English translation) covers the dynastic bond which held the empire together through the centuries. See in this respect also Robert A. Kann, "The Dynasty and the Imperial Idea," *Austrian History Yearbook,* Vol. III:1. Erich Zöllner, *Geschichte Österreichs* (Vienna, Verlag für Geschichte und Politik, 3d edition 1966) is a very sound, factual history written from the German centralist viewpoint (good bibliography).

Sixteenth Century

Heinrich Ullmann, *Kaiser Maximilian I,* 2 vols. (Stuttgart, Cotta, 1884–1891, reprint 1968), offers important background material. Hermann Wiesflecker, *Kaiser Maximilian I,* 1 vol. (Vienna, Verlag für Geschichte und Politik, 1971; Vols. II–IV in preparation) is expected to become a new standard biography and at the same time a history of the late Renaissance in the hereditary lands. In the evolution of the Habsburg empire Ferdinand I is perhaps the most important figure. A major modern biography is needed, but Wilhelm Bauer, *Die Anfänge Ferdinands I.* (Vienna, Braumüller, 1907) and Franz B. von Bucholtz, *Geschichte der Regierung Ferdinands I.,* 8 vols. and appendix volume with documents (Vienna, Schaumburg & Co., 1831–1838; reprinted with excellent introduction by Berthold Sutter available), an old, partly outdated but still valuable standard work, takes its place. László Makkai, *Die Entstehung der gesellschaftlichen Basis des Absolutismus in den Ländern der österreichischen Habsburger* (Budapest, Akadémiai Kiado, 1960), offers an interesting social analysis of the reign of Ferdinand I written from a Marxian viewpoint. Moritz Ritter, *Deutsche Geschichte im Zeitalter der Gegenreformation und des 30-jährigen Krieges 1555–1648,* 3 vols. (Stuttgart, Cotta, 1889–1908), is still useful. Karl Brandi, *Reformation und Gegen-*

formation (Munich, Bruckmann, 1960), is a modern standard work and Johann Loserth, *Reformation und Gegenreformation in den innerösterreichischen Ländern im 16. Jahrhundert* (Stuttgart, Cotta, 1898), gives a thoroughly documented presentation of the Protestant position.

Seventeenth Century

Bernhard Erdmannsdörffer, *Deutsche Geschichte vom Westfälischen Frieden bis zum Regierungsantritt Friedrichs des Großen,* 2 vols. (Berlin, Grote, 1892–1893), is a somewhat pedestrian but objective work which may be considered to be a continuation of Ritter's work (see above). Hans Sturmberger, *Ferdinand II. und das Problem des Absolutismus* (Munich, R. Oldenbourg, 1957), is a perceptive study of the leading counterreformatory ruler of the first half of the century. See also Josef V. Polišenský, *The Thirty Years War* (Berkeley and Los Angeles, University of California Press, 1971) and C. V. Wedgwood, *The Thirty Years War,* listed more fully under I:D. Oswald Redlich, *Weltmacht des Barock: Österreich in der Zeit Leopolds I.* (Vienna, R. Rohrer, 1961), offers a fairly comprehensive picture of the second half of the century. Max Braubach's monumental biography of *Prinz Eugen von Savoyen,* 5 vols. (Vienna, Verlag für Geschichte und Politik, 1963–1965), is significant for the understanding of the political history of the late seventeenth and early eighteenth centuries.

Eighteenth Century

The historiography of this period is largely personalized and focused on some outstanding personalities. Hanns Mikoletzky, *Österreich: Das grosse 18. Jahrhundert* (Vienna, Bundesverlag für Wissenschaft und Kunst, 1967), offers an over-all presentation and Oswald Redlich, *Das Werden einer Grossmacht: Österreich 1700–1740* (Brünn-Vienna, R. Rohrer, 1942), serves as excellent introduction into the political history of Austria's evolution to great-power status. The standard work of the middle period of the era is still Alfred von Arneth, *Geschichte Maria Theresias,* 10 vols. (Vienna, Braumüller, 1863–1879). Although technically a biography of the empress, this work is in the first place a history of her reign. Eugen Guglia, *Maria Theresia: Ihr Leben und ihre Regierung,* 2 vols. (Munich, R. Oldenbourg, 1917), is valuable in the same sense. George P. Gooch, *Maria Theresa and other Studies* (London, Longmans, Green & Co., 1951), includes some perceptive essays. Alexander Novotny, *Staatskanzler Kaunitz* (Vienna, Hollinek, 1947), is a readable brief biography of one of Austria's greatest diplomats. Here, a more comprehensive work is needed. See further, Friedrich Walter, *Die Theresianische Staatsreform von 1749* (Vienna, Verlag für Geschichte und Politik, 1958). Paul von Mitrofanov, *Joseph II.*, 2 vols. (Vienna, C. W. Stern, 1910), is still the best, though in some respects outdated biography of the emperor. Useful are also the brief studies, François Fejtö, *Un Habsbourg Revolutionaire: Joseph II,* (Paris, Plon, 1953); Paul P. Bernard, *Joseph II,* (New York, Twayne, 1968) and by the same author *Jesuits and Jacobins: Enlightenment and Enlightened Despotism in Austria* (Urbana, University of Illinois Press, 1971); T. C. W. Blanning, *Joseph II and Enlightened Despotism* (London, Longman, 1970). A new comprehensive biography of Joseph II, comparable in scholarly standards to the excellent one of his brother by Adam Wandruszka, *Leopold II.*, 2 vols. (Vienna-Munich, Herold, 1965), is needed.

Nineteenth and Twentieth Century

Viktor Bibl, *Der Zerfall Österreichs,* 2 vols. (Vienna, Rikola, 1922–1924), perceives the beginning of the disintegration process of the empire in the early nineteenth century and continues this story to 1918 (German national viewpoint). Allan J. P. Taylor, *The Habsburg Monarchy: 1809–1916* (London, Hamilton, 1951), is a readable and sophisticated brief presentation, marred, however, by a predilection for unprovable paradox conclusions. Richard Charmatz, *Österreichs innere Geschichte 1848–1907* (Leipzig, Teubner, 1909–1911), is a useful, concise survey (liberal viewpoint). See further Arthur J. May, *The Hapsburg Monarchy: 1867–1914* (New York, Norton, 1951), a readable presentation and Carlile A. Macartney, *The Hapsburg Empire, 1790–1918* (New York, Macmillan, 1969), a somewhat controversial, but interesting and perceptive presentation. Adam Wandruszka and Peter Urbanitsch eds., *Die Habsburgermonarchie 1848–1918* (Vienna, Österreichische Akademie der Wissenschaften, 1973–) is designed as collective work of 8 volumes, covering all aspects of the history of the Habsburg empire throughout the indicated period. So far vol I, *Die wirtschaftliche Entwicklung,* has been published.

Gustav Kolmer, *Parlament und Verfassung in Österreich,* 8 vols. (Vienna, Fromme, 1902–1914), (German liberal viewpoint), covers the parliamentary history from 1848 to 1904 in a chroniclelike but nevertheless interesting manner (indispensable). Alois von Czedik, *Zur Geschichte der k.k. österreichischen Ministerien (1861–1916)*, 4 vols. (Teschen, Prochaska, 1917–1920), is likewise an essential but far less interesting reference tool. The works of Kolmer and Czedik are confined to the institutional history of Cisleithanian Austria.

Of more specialized studies see Hanns Schlitter, *Aus Österreichs Vormärz* (Vienna, Amalthea Verlag, 1920), Part 1 Galizien und Krakau; Pt. 2 Böhmen; Pt. 3 Ungarn; Pt. 4 Niederösterreich (useful, and based on thorough archival research). Joseph A. von Helfert, *Geschichte der österreichischen Revolution,* 2 vols. (Freiburg i. B., Herder, 1907), presents the conservative viewpoint; Ernst Violand, *Die soziale Geschichte der Revolution in Österreich* (Leipzig, O. Wigand, 1850), a liberal viewpoint. Heinrich Friedjung, *Österreich von 1848–1860,* vols. I and II/1 (Stuttgart, Cotta, 1908–1912), is a masterly but incomplete history of the neoabsolutist era. See further Eduard Winter, *Frühliberalismus in der Donaumonarchie* (Berlin, Akademieverlag, 1968). William A. Jenks, *Austria and the Iron Ring 1873–93* (Charlottesville, University of Virginia Press, 1965), is the first solid study focused on the Taaffe administration.

The two outstanding biographies for the period are Heinrich von Srbik, *Metternich: Der Staatsmann und der Mensch,* 3 vols. (Munich, Bruckmann, 1925–1954) and Josef Redlich, *Kaiser Franz Joseph von Österreich* (Berlin, Verlag für Kulturpolitik, 1928); in English *Emperor Francis Joseph of Austria* (New York, Macmillan, 1929).

c) DISSOLUTION OF THE EMPIRE

Henryk Batowski, *Rozpad Austro Wegier 1914–1918* (Wroclaw, Zaklad Narodowy im. Ossolińskich-Wydawnictwo, 1965) and Leo Valiani, *La Dissoluzione dell'Austria Unghera* (Milano, Casa Editrice Il Saggiatore, 1966), now available in English as *The End of Austria-Hungary* (New York, Knopf, 1973), use some new material. Z. A. B. Zeman, *The Break-up of the Habsburg Empire 1914–1918* (London, Oxford University Press, 1961) and by the same author *A Diplomatic History of the First World War* (London, Weidenfeld & Nicolson, 1971). See also Arthur J. May, *The Passing of the Habsburg Monarchy 1914–1918,* 2 vols. (Philadelphia, University of Pennsylvania Press, 1966). All three works are significant recent contributions in English.

Robert A. Kann, *The Habsburg Empire: A Study in Integration and Disintegration* (2nd ed. New York, Octagon, 1973), published in German under the title *Werden und Zerfall der Habsburgermonarchie* (Graz-Vienna, Styria, 1962) discusses briefly the integration as well as the disintegration process of the empire. Robert A. Kann, *Die Sixtus-affäre und die geheimen Friedensverhandlungen Österreich-Ungarns im ersten Weltkrieg* (Vienna, Verlag für Geschichte und Politik, 1966), offers new material on the secret peace negotiations. On the peace negotiations with the Soviet Union and the Ukraine see Wolfdieter

Bihl, *Österreich-Ungarn und die Friedensverhandlungen von Brest-Litovsk* (Vienna-Cologne, Böhlaus Nachf., 1970). Edmund von Glaise-Horstenau, *Die Katastrophe* (Vienna, Amalthea Verlag, 1929), is a readable study written from the viewpoint of German centralism. Oscar Jászi, *The Dissolution of the Habsburg Monarchy* (Chicago, University of Chicago Press, 1929), is the best study on the social aspects of the problem. Josef Redlich, *Austrian War Government* (New Haven, Yale University Press, 1929), discusses the wartime administration in Cisleithanian Austria. Gutav Gratz and Richard Schüller, *The Economic Policy of Austria-Hungary in its External Relations* (New Haven, Yale University Press, 1928), emphasizes the Middle Europe concept of economic union between the two Central Powers. Victor S. Mamatey, *The United States and Eastern Central Europe* (Princeton, Princeton University Press, 1957), is a comprehensive study in diplomatic history on the interrelationship between U.S. foreign policy and the dissolution process. Its counterpart in regard to Great Britain is Harry Hanak, *Great Britain and Austria-Hungary during the First World War* (London, Oxford University Press, 1961). Gordon Brook Sheperd, *The Last Habsburg* (New York, Weybright and Talley, 1968), a biography of the last emperor Charles offers some interesting new material. A recent study are the minutes of the international congress "Herbst 1918," edited by Richard G. Plaschka and Karlheinz Mack under the title *Die Auflösung des Habsburgerreiches* (Vienna, Verlag für Geschichte und Politik, 1970). See finally Richard G. Plaschka, Horst Haselsteiner, Arnold Suppan, *Innere Front. Militärassistenz, Widerstand und Umsturz an der inneren Front der Donaumonarchie, 1918,* 2 vols. (Wien, Verlag für Geschichte und Politik, to be published 1974).

D) FOREIGN RELATIONS TO 1914

The standard histories of the Habsburg empire are also the most informative works on its foreign relations in the sixteenth and seventeenth centuries. Beginning with the eighteenth century, monographs are of increasing importance. Franz von Krones, *Handbuch der Geschichte Österreichs,* Vols. II, III (listed under I:B) is not an inspiring but a thoroughly reliable guide for the empire's diplomatic history in the sixteenth and seventeenth centuries. For the Reformation and early Counter Reformation era see Karl Brandi, *Kaiser Karl V.,* 2 vols. (Munich, Bruckmann, 1937–1941). For the interrelationship of the policies of the German and Spanish Habsburg lines see Helmut G. Königsberger, *The Habs-*

burgs and Europe, 1516–1660 (Ithaca, Cornell University Press, 1971). There is no finer book on the diplomatic issues of the Thirty Years War than Cecily V. Wedgwood, *The Thirty Years War* (London, Cape, 1944). For the diplomatic history of the reign of Leopold I and those of his sons and successors Joseph I and Charles VI, see Oswald Redlich, *Weltmacht des Barock: Österreich in der Zeit Leopolds I.* (see under I:B) and by the same author *Das Werden einer Grossmacht: Österreich 1700–1740* (Brünn, R. Rohrer, 1942).

Important are also Heinrich von Srbik, *Wien und Versailles 1692–97* (Munich, Bruckmann, 1944) and Max Braubach, *Versailles und Wien von Ludwig XIV. bis Kaunitz* (Bonn, Rohrscheid, 1952).

Alfred von Arneth, *Geschichte Maria Theresias* (see I:B) is still the best over-all presentation of the diplomatic history during the forty years of the empress' reign from 1740 to 1780. For the discussion of the Polish question during that period see Herbert H. Kaplan, *The First Partition of Poland* (New York, Columbia University Press, 1962).

Of older works, Albert Sorel, *The Eastern Policy in the Eighteenth Century* (London, Methuen and Co., 1898) and John A. R. Marriott, *The Eastern Question: A Historical Study in European Diplomacy* (Oxford, Clarendon Press, 1951), slightly revised and supplemented from the original edition of 1917, are still reliable and informative but in some respects outdated in regard to the sources used.

A comprehensive diplomatic history of the Habsburg empire from the outbreak of the French Revolution in 1789 to the Congress of Vienna in 1814–1815 has not yet been written. A number of monographs of high scholarly standards, some of which have been referred to in the notes to Chapter V, Sections A and J, must take their place. Only a few can be mentioned here. Golo Mann, *Secretary of Europe: The Life of Friedrich Gentz, Enemy of Napoleon* (New Haven, Yale University Press, 1946), is a sophisticated study on a key figure in diplomatic history, but the lack of a scholarly and bibliographical apparatus diminishes the value of this work. Enno E. Kraehe, *Metternich's German Policy* (Princeton, Princeton University Press, 1963), Vol. I "The Contest with Napoleon: 1799–1814;" and Rudolfine von Oer, *Der Frieden von Pressburg* (Munich, Aschendorff, 1965), are important.

For the so-called conference period after the Congress of Vienna, C. Irby Nichols, *The European Pentarchy and the Congress of Vienna* (The Hague, M. Nijhoff, 1971), is very useful. Henry A. Kissinger, *A World Restored: Metternich, Castlereagh and the Problems of Peace 1812–22* (Boston, Houghton Mifflin, 1957), offers a sophisticated analysis.

A brief and challenging, though in regard to documentation somewhat outdated survey is Richard Charmatz, *Geschichte der auswärtigen Politik Österreichs im 19. Jahrhundert,* 2 small volumes (Leipzig, K. G. Teubner, 1912–1914). An up to date diplomatic history is R. F. Bridge, *From Sadowa to Sarajevo: The Foreign Policy of Austria-Hungary, 1866–1914* (London, Routledge & Kegan Paul, 1972).

For the intervening period from the end of the conference period 1822, to the Austro-Prussian war of 1866, see four well-documented perceptive studies: Elisabeth Andics, *Das Bündnis Habsburg-Romanow* (Budapest, Akadémiai Kiadó, 1963) and for the Crimean war crisis Bernard Unckel, *Österreich und der Krimkrieg* (Lübeck-Hamburg, Mathiesen, 1972); Paul W. Schroeder, *Austria, Great Britain and the Crimean War* (Ithaca, Cornell University Press, 1972) and Wilfried Baumgart, *Der Friede von Paris 1856* (Munich, R. Oldenbourg, 1972).

The core of Austrian foreign policy, the German question, is covered in Heinrich von Srbik, *Deutsche Einheit: Idee und Wirklichkeit vom Heiligen Reich bis Königgrätz,* 4 vols. (Munich, Bruckmann, 1935–1942), *grossdeutsch* romantic outlook and Heinrich Friedjung, *Der Kampf um die Vorherrschaft in Deutschland 1859–1866,* 2 vols. (Stuttgart, Cotta, 1897–1898), German liberal viewpoint. In essence this brilliantly written classic is still valuable. The 8th edition is abridged.

Austro-Italian relations until 1866 have been somewhat neglected in Austrian historiography. All the more welcome are the monographs by Richard Blaas, "Die italienische Frage und das österreichische Parlament 1859–1866," *Mitteilungen des österreichischen Staatsarchivs,* Vol. 22 (1969), 151–244 and by the same author "Il Problemo Veneto nella Politica Estera Austriaca del Periodo 1859–1866," *Archivo Veneto,* Serie V, XXX (1967), 39–157, and *Tentativi di Approcio per la Cessione del Veneto* (Venice, Tipografia Commerciale, 1966). For an interpretation close to the Italian viewpoint see William R. Thayer, *The Life and Times of Cavour,* 2 vols. (New York, Houghton Mifflin, 1914), see Vol. II.

For the 1870's see the somewhat longwinded but in terms of diplomatic history informative biography by Eduard von Wertheimer, *Graf Julius Andrássy und seine Zeit,* 3 vols. (Stuttgart, Deutsche Verlagsanstalt, 1910–1913), and the fine study by William N. Medlicott, *The Congress of Berlin and After: A Diplomatic History of the Near Eastern Settlement 1878–1880* (London, Methuen, 1938).

For the 1870's with particular regard to the eastern question, see John A. R. Marriott, *The Eastern Question,* as noted above, Chapters XIII–XV, 346–432. For the two last decades of the empire's history see Fritz Klein, ed., *Österreich Ungarn in der Weltpolitik 1900–1918* (Berlin, Akademie Verlag, 1965), Marxian interpretation. See further, the interesting analysis by Stephan Verosta, *Theorie und Realität von Bündnissen: Heinrich Lammasch, Karl Renner und der Zweibund (1897–1914)*, (Vienna, Europa Verlag, 1971) and Alfred F. Pribram, *Austrian Foreign Policy, 1908–1914* (London, Allen and Unwin, 1923), a brief masterpiece. Three significant studies are also Bernadotte E. Schmitt, *The Annexation of Bosnia, 1908–1909* (Cambridge, University Press, 1937); Fritz Fellner, *Der Dreibund: Europäische Diplomatie vor dem Ersten Weltkrieg* (Vienna, Verlag für Geschichte und Politik, 1960) and Ernst Christian Helmreich, *The Diplomacy of the Balkan Wars 1912–1913* (Cambridge, Mass., Harvard University Press, 1937); see further Friedrich Engel-Janosi, *Geschichte auf dem Ballhausplatz* (Graz, Styria, 1963).

For world war diplomacy see I:C (Dissolution of the Empire); for collections of documents see I:L (b), (Primary Sources, Records on Foreign Relations). Biographies which have an important bearing on foreign policy but are not exclusively focused on foreign policy are found in I:B.

E) ECONOMIC AND SOCIAL HISTORY

A comprehensive economic and social history of the Habsburg empire does not exist. Although some of the following publications are of high scholarly quality, they do not fill this gap completely. Ferdinand Tremel, *Der Frühkapitalismus in Inner Österreich* (Graz, Leykam, 1954), is confined to the eastern Alpine territories. By the same author, *Wirtschafts- und Sozialgeschichte Österreichs: Von den Anfängen bis 1955* (Vienna, Deuticke, 1969) carries the author's research within the confines of the German-Austrian lands to the present. A counterpart of this work for Hungary is Zsigmond P. Pach, *Die ungarische Agrarentwicklung im 16.–17. Jahrhundert* (Budapest, Akadémiai Kiadó, 1964). In a wider geographical context, see for early modern history also Ingomar Borg, ed., *Der Aussenhandel Ostmitteleuropas 1450–1650: Die ostmitteleuropäischen Volkswirtschaften in ihren Beziehungen zu Mitteleuropa* (Vienna-Cologne, Böhlaus Nachfolger, 1973). See further, Gustav Otruba, *Die Wirtschaftspolitik Maria Theresias* (Vienna, Bergland Verlag, 1963). Louise Sommer, *Die österreichischen Kameralisten in dogmengeschichtlicher Darstellung* (Vienna, C. Konegen, 1920), is an excellent study of the evolution of economic theory in seventeenth- and eighteenth-century Austria. Valuable is also Jerome Blum, *Noble Landowners and Agriculture in Austria, 1815–1848* (Baltimore, Johns Hopkins Press, 1946). Eduard März, *Österreichische Industrie und Bankpolitik in der Zeit*

Franz Josephs I. (Vienna, Europa Verlag, 1968), liberal; and Heinrich Benedikt, *Die wirtschaftliche Entwicklung in der Franz Josephs Zeit* (Vienna, Herold, 1958), conservative, offer insight into an era of rapid economic change. More comprehensive is Herbert Matis, *Österreichs Wirtschaft 1848 bis 1913* (Berlin, Duncker & Humblot, 1972). See further, Kristina Maria Fink, *Die österreichisch-ungarische Monarchie als Wirtschaftsgemeinschaft* (Munich, R. Trofenik, 1968), which strongly affirms the economic unity of the empire. These studies are supplemented by Hans Mayer, ed., *100 Jahre österreichische Wirtschaftsentwicklung 1848–1918* (Vienna, Springer, 1949) and Stefan Pacsu, Tibor Kolassa, Jan Havránek et al., *Die Agrarfrage in der österreichisch-ungarischen Monarchie* (Bucarest, Academy, 1965). Friedrich Naumann, *Mitteleuropa* (Berlin, Reimer, 1915), is the main work that promoted the concept of German economic expansionism in the Habsburg monarchy after the end of the First World War. Vilmos Sandor and Peter Hanák, eds., *Studien zur Geschichte der österreichisch-ungarischen Monarchie* (Budapest, Akadémiai Kiadó, 1961), comprises interesting essays on various aspects of nineteenth century economic developments in the empire, as seen from a Marxian viewpoint. See in this respect also Ervin Pamlényi, *Social-Economic Researches on the History of East-Central Europe* (Budapest, Akadémiai Kiadó, 1970). Nikolaus von Preradovich, *Die Führungsschichten in Österreich und Preussen 1804–1918* (Wiesbaden, Steiner, 1955), gives an interesting pioneer study on the selection of leadership. See also the previously noted works by G. A. Gratz and R. Schüller, O. Jászi, and R. A. Kann noted under I:C, and *Die österreichisch-ungarische Monarchie in Wort und Bild,* under I:A.

See further Wandruszka and Urbanitsch eds., *Die Habsburgermonarchie 1848–1918* (see I:B) and Ivan T. Berend and György Ranki, *Economic Development in East Central Europe in the 19th and 20th Centuries* (New York, Columbia University Press, 1974), the latter work published after completion of this study.

F) CULTURAL HISTORY

Johann W. Nagl, Jakob Zeidler and Eduard Castle, *Deutschösterreichische Literaturgeschichte,* 4 vols. (Vienna, Fromme, 1899–1937), is the most comprehensive German-Austrian literary history. Josef Nadler, *Literaturgeschichte Österreichs* (Salzburg, O. Müller Verlag, 1951), is a briefer and readable, but less objective one (German nationalist tendency). Claudio Magris, *Der Habsburgische Mythos in der österreichischen Literatur* (Salzburg, O. Müller Verlag, 1966), relates literature to the imperial idea. See also Robert Blauhut, *Österreichische Novellistik des 20. Jahrhunderts* (Vienna, Braumüller, 1966). As for fine arts, Reinhardt Hootz, ed., *Kunstdenkmäler in Österreich,* 2 vols. (Munich, Deutscher Kunstverlag, 1966), stresses architecture. Hans Tietze, ed., *Wien: Kultur, Kunst, Geschichte* (Vienna, Epstein, 1931), is an excellent cultural history of the capital. On history of the stage see Josef Gregor, *Geschichte des österreichischen Theaters* (Vienna, Donau Verlag, 1948).

Concerning the Austrian Renaissance at the court of Maximilian I, see Kurt Adel, ed., *Conrad Celtes* (Graz, Stiasny Verlag, 1960) and the important monograph by Alphons Lhotsky, *Thomas Ebendorfer* (Stuttgart, Hiersemann, 1957). For the transition period from late Renaissance to early Baroque see R. J. W. Evans, *Rudolf II and his world. A Study in Intellectual History, 1576–1612* (Oxford, Clarendon Press, 1973). In regard to Baroque art, see Therese Schüssel, *Kultur des Barock in Österreich* (Graz, Stiasny Varlag, 1960) and Werner Hager, *Die Bauten des deutschen Barock 1690–1770* (Jena, Diederichs, 1942) and Jaromir Neumann, *Das böhmische Barock* (Vienna, Forumverlag, 1971). As for intellectual history from the late seventeenth to the early nineteenth century, see Robert A. Kann, *A Study in Austrian Intellectual History: From late Baroque to Romanticism* (2nd ed. New York, Octagon, 1973), published in German under the title *Kanzel und Katheder* (Vienna, Herder, 1964). Intellectual history in the seventeenth and early eighteenth centuries is covered more broadly in Eduard Winter, *Barock: Absolutismus und Aufklärung in der Donaumonarchie* (Vienna, Europa Verlag, 1971) and by the same author *Frühaufklärung* (Berlin, Akademie Verlag, 1966). For the problem of Josephinism, see also by Eduard Winter, *Der Josefinismus und seine Geschichte* (Brünn, R. Rohrer, 1943), left-wing interpretation. Fritz Valjavec, *Der Josephinismus,* second revised edition (Vienna, Verlag für Geschichte, 1945), national liberal and Herbert Rieser, *Der Geist des Josephinismus und sein Fortleben* (Vienna, Herder, 1963), Roman Catholic interpretation.

Regarding intellectual history in the early nineteenth century, see Eduard Winter, *Romantizismus: Restauration und Frühliberalismus im österreichischen Vormärz* (Vienna, Europa Verlag, 1968). For the following period and by the same author, *Revolution, Neoabsolutismus und Liberalismus in der Donau Monarchie* (Vienna, Europa Verlag, 1969); Albert Fuchs, *Geistige Strömungen in Österreich, 1867–1918* (Vienna, Globus Verlag, 1949), left-wing interpretation. While the works by E. Winter and A. Fuchs meet high scholarly standards, a comprehensive, fully impartial presentation of the subject is still needed. William

M. Johnston, *The Austrian Mind: An Intellectual and Social History 1848–1938* (Berkeley and Los Angeles, University of California Press, 1972), is a first, largely successful attempt to offer a full-fledged Austrian intellectual history. Allan Janik and Stephen Toulmin's interesting *Wittgenstein's Vienna* (New York, Simon and Schuster, 1973), covers in part the same ground but is focused on Vienna. See further, Robert Waissenberger, *Die Wiener Sezession* (Vienna, Jugend und Volk Gesellschaft, 1971). Concerning the rise of Austrian medical science to world fame, see the excellent work by Erna Lesky, *Die Wiener Medizinische Schule im Neunzehnten Jahrhundert* (Cologne-Vienna, Böhlaus Nachfolger, 1965).

On cultural history of the Habsburg empire, see also under I:A, [Rudolf, Crownprince] *Die österreichisch-ungarische Monarchie in Wort und Bild.*

G) PARTY IDEOLOGIES

See Adam Wandruszka's perceptive "Österreichs politische Struktur," in Heinrich Benedikt, ed., *Geschichte der Republik Österreich* (Vienna, Verlag für Geschichte und Politik, 1954), Pt. II on the origins of the political party system among the Austro-Germans. See further Johann Christoph Allmayer-Beck, *Der Konservatismus in Österreich* (Munich, Isar Verlag, 1959) and Georg Franz, *Die deutschliberale Bewegung in der Habsburgischen Monarchie* (Munich, Callway, 1955) and by the same author, *Kulturkampf: Staat und katholische Kirche in Mitteleuropa* (Munich, Callway, 1954), both books are written from a German national viewpoint. See further Paul Molisch, *Geschichte der deutschnationalen Bewegung in Österreich* (Jena, Fischer, 1926), German national interpretation.

Concerning the Socialist movement in Austria see Ludwig Brügel, *Geschichte der österreichischen Sozialdemokratie,* 5 vols. (Vienna, Verlag der Volksbuchhandlung, 1922–1925) and in a popular presentation Jacques Hannak, *Im Sturme eines Jahrhunderts: Volkstümliche Geschichte der sozialistischen Partei Österreichs* (Vienna, Verlag der Wiener Volksbuchhandlung, 1952), both works present the Socialist viewpoint. For the early history of the labor movement see Herbert Steiner, *Die Arbeiterbewegung Österreichs 1867–1889* (Vienna, Europa Verlag, 1964).

H) NATIONAL ISSUE IN THE HABSBURG EMPIRE: GENERAL SURVEYS

Hugo Hantsch, *Die Nationalitätenfrage im alten Österreich* (Vienna, Herold, 1952), is a brief and useful general survey. Robert A. Kann,

The Multinational Empire: Nationalism and National Reform in the Habsburg Monarchy 1848–1918, 2 vols. (New York, Columbia University Press, 1950 and New York, Octagon Press, 1964 and 1970), is a more extensive study which includes a comprehensive bibliography. The revised and enlarged German edition of this work *Das Nationalitätenproblem der Habsburgermonarchie,* 2 vols. (Vienna-Cologne, Böhlaus Nachfolger, 1964), includes considerable additional material, particularly in the chapters on the Slavic national groups. The bibliography is brought up to 1964. Franz Zwitter in collaboration with Jaroslav Šidak and Vaso Bogdonow, *Les Problems Nationaux dans la Monarchie des Habsbourg* (Beograd, 1960), offers an interesting unorthodox Marxian interpretation and useful bibliographical information, particularly on modern Slavic literature. Peter Hanák, ed., *Die nationale Frage in der österreichisch-ungarischen Monarchie* (Budapest, Akadémiai Kiadó, 1966), presents in most contributions various views prevailing in countries, which belong to the Eastern European Communist bloc. As for legal problems, Ludwig Gumplowicz, *Das Recht der Nationalitäten und Sprachen in Österreich-Ungarn* (Innsbruck, Wagner, 1879), is the pioneer work in the legal aspects of the national problem. Karl Gottfried Hugelmann, ed., *Das Nationalitätenrecht des alten Österreich* (Vienna, Braumüller, 1934), is a more recent, important collection of contributions to the same issue. Theodor Veiter, a student of Hugelmann, offers in his *Das Recht der Volksgruppen und Sprachminderheiten in Österreich* (Vienna, Braumüller, 1970), a kind of continuation of Hugelmann's work for the Austrian republic. Yet in many ways this volume comments also on the national problems of the Habsburg monarchy. The viewpoint of both works is predominantly *grossdeutsch.* Hans Mommsen, *Die Nationalitätenfrage und die Sozialdemokratie im Habsburgischen Vielvölkerstaat* (Vienna, Europa Verlag, 1963), offers a good analysis of the Socialist viewpoint represented in the theories of such Socialist classics as Karl Renner, *Das Selbstbestimmungsrecht der Nationen* (Vienna, Deuticke, 1918) and Otto Bauer, *Die Nationalitätenfrage und die Sozialdemokratie,* 2d edition (Vienna, Verlag der Volksbuchhandlung, 1924). The conservative equivalent to these works is Ignaz Seipel, *Nation und Staat* (Vienna, Braumüller, 1917). See further, in Peter F. Sugar and Ivo J. Lederer, eds., *Nationalism in Eastern Europe* (Seattle, University of Washington Press, 1969), the chapters on the Czechs by Joseph F. Zacek, on the Magyars by George Barany, on the Poles by Peter Brock, on the Roumanians by Stephen Fischer-Galati, and on the Southern Slavs by Ivo J. Lederer.

I) CHURCHES

Ernst Tomek, *Kirchengeschichte Österreichs,* 3 vols. (Innsbruck, Tyrolia, 1935–1959), is the uncompleted standard work on the history of the Catholic Church in Austria. Vols. II and III cover the period from the Reformation through the Enlightenment. Josef Wodka, *Kirche in Österreich* (Vienna, Herold, 1959), is a briefer useful survey. See further, Erika Weinzierl, *Die österreichischen Konkordate von 1855 und 1933* (Vienna, Verlag für Geschichte und Politik, 1960). On the relationship of Church policies to the national problem see Friedrich Engel-Janosi, "The Church and the Nationalities," *Austrian History Yearbook,* III:3, (1967) and ibid. Emanuel Turczinsky, "The National Movement in the Greek Orthodox Church in the Habsburg Monarchy."

On the problem of Josephinism in relation to the Church see Eduard Winter, *Der Josefinismus: Die Geschichte des österreichischen Reformkatholizismus 1740–1848* (Berlin, Ritter and Loening, 1962); Herbert Rieser, *Der Geist des Josefinismus und sein Fortleben* (Vienna, Herder, 1963) and Charles H. O'Brien, *Ideas of Religious Toleration at the Time of Joseph II* (Philadelphia, American Philosophical Society, 1969). See further, Ferdinand Maass, *Der Frühjosephinismus* (Vienna, Herold, 1969), ecclesiastic viewpoint. The indispensible documentary collection is Ferdinand Maass, *Der Josephinismus,* 5 vols. (Vienna, Herold, 1951–1961), which covers the period from 1760 to 1850 (conservative-ecclesiastic interpretation). On the relationship between governmental and ecclesiastic authorities with particular regard to the problem of censorship in the eighteenth century see Grete Klingenstein, *Staatsverwaltung und kirchliche Autorität im 18. Jahrhundert* (Vienna, Verlag für Geschichte und Politik, 1970). See also Eduard Hosp, *Kirche Österreichs im Vormärz, 1815–1850* (Vienna, Herold, 1971).

On the history of Protestantism, see Grete Mecenseffy, *Geschichte des Protestantismus in Österreich* (Graz-Cologne, Böhlaus Nachfolger, 1956) and the work by J. Loserth listed under I:B.

J) ARMED FORCES

See Eugen Heischmann, *Die Anfänge des stehenden Heeres in Österreich* (Vienna, Österreichischer Bundesverlag, 1925). Oskar Regele, *Der österreichische Hofkriegsrat 1556–1898* (Vienna, Österreichische Staatsdruckerei, 1949). Hugo Schmid, *Heereswesen,* 2 vols., 3d edition (Vienna, Selbstverlag H. Schmid, 1915). See further, Günther E. Rothenberg, "The Habsburg Army and the Nationality Problem in the Nineteenth Century, 1815–1914," *Austrian History Yearbook,* III:1 (1967); Walter Wagner, *Geschichte des k.k. Kriegsministeriums, 1848–1888,* 2 vols. (Graz-Cologne, Böhlaus Nachfolger, 1966–1971); Nikolaus von Préradovich, *Die Führungsschichten in Österreich,* as listed under I:E. See further Thomas M. Barker, *Raimondo Montecuccoli and the Thirty Years War: a military intellectual and his battles* (Albany, State University of New York Press, to be published 1974).

K) CONSTITUTIONAL PROBLEMS AND ADMINISTRATION

Hermann I. Bidermann, *Geschichte der österreichischen Gesamtstaatsidee, 1526–1804* (Innsbruck, Wagner, 1867), is an incomplete, original attempt to perceive the evolution of the Habsburg empire as a combination of legal and political factors. Otto Brunner, *Land und Herrschaft: Grundfragen der territorialen Verfassungsgeschichte Österreichs im Mittelalter,* 4th revised edition (Vienna-Wiesbaden, R. Rohrer, 1959) presents a more modern approach for the medieval period. See also Helmut G. Koenigsberger, *Estates and Revolution* (Ithaca, Cornell University Press, 1971). Alfons Huber, *Österreichische Reichsgeschichte,* 2d revised edition by Alfons Dopsch (Vienna, A. Tempsky, 1901), is a masterpiece in the field of constitutional and administrative history. However, the work carries the story only to the 1870's. Ernst C. Hellbling, *Österreichische Verfassungs- und Verwaltungsgeschichte* (Vienna, Springer, 1956), a presentation not on a par with that of Huber-Dopsch but with some additional bibliographical information, covers the topic to the end of the Second World War. See also Otto Stolz, *Grundriss der österreichischen Verfassungs- und Verwaltungsgeschichte* (Innsbruck-Vienna, Tyrolia, 1957), a brief survey; and most recently Friedrich Walter, *Österreichische Verfassungs- und Verwaltungsgeschichte von 1500–1955* (Vienna-Cologne-Graz, Böhlaus Nachfolger, 1972). See also Hermann Baltl, *Österreichische Rechtsgeschichte,* 2nd enlarged ed. (Graz, Leykam, 1972), a brief survey with emphasis on medieval and early modern history.

Josef Ulbrich, *Das österreichische Staatsrecht,* 3d revised edition (Tübingen, J. C. B. Mohr [P. Siebeck], 1909), is a reliable constitutional history. Its counterpart for the eastern part of the empire is Heinrich Marczali, *Ungarisches Verfassungsrecht* (same publisher, 1911). Josef Redlich, *Das Österreichische Staats- und Reichsproblem,* vol. I/1, vol. I/2 (notes and documents), vol. II (Leipzig, P. Reinhold, 1921), is a monumental torso which covers Austrian constitutional history from 1848 to 1867. Beyond this, the work offers deep insight into the political problems and ideas which arose in the Habsburg empire in the eighteenth and later nineteenth centuries. See further, Louis Eisenmann, *Le Compromis Austro-Hongrois de 1867* (Paris, G. Bellais, 1904), the thus-far best analysis of the Compromise. Strictly factual but more limited in scope than Eisenmann's work is Ivan Žolger, *Der staatsrechtliche Ausgleich zwischen Österreich und Ungarn* (Leipzig, Duncker and Humblot, 1911). See further, Max Kulisch, *Beiträge zum österreichischen Parlamentsrecht* (Leipzig, Duncker and Humblot, 1900). Britta Skottsberg, *Der österreichische Parlamentarismus* (Göteborg, Elanders, 1940), offers a perceptive and reliable analysis.

Three works on administrative history are significant: Ignaz Beidtel, *Geschichte der österreichischen Staatsverwaltung (1740–1848)*, ed. by Alfons Huber, 2 vols. (Innsbruck, Wagner, 1896–1898); Thomas Fellner, *Die österreichische Zentralverwaltung,* completed by Heinrich Kretschmayr, 3 vols. (Vienna, Holzhausen, 1907); and Friederich Walter, *Die österreichische Zentralverwaltung* (1792–1848), 2 vols. (Vienna, Holzhausen, 1956), (a continuation of T. Fellner's work).

L) PRIMARY SOURCES (RECORDS) IN DOMESTIC AFFAIRS AND FOREIGN RELATIONS

(*a*) *Domestic Affairs*

Ferdinand Maass, ed., *Der Josephinismus,* as quoted under I:J, offers for the first time a nearly complete record of the pertinent documents of the history of Josephinism in Austria from 1760 to 1850. Anton Springer, ed., *Protokolle des Verfassungsausschusses im österreichischen Reichstage 1848–1849* (Leipzig, S. Hirzel, 1885) and Alfred von Fischel, *Die Protokolle des Verfassungsausschusses und die Grundrechte* (Vienna, Gerlach and Wiedling, 1912), are in several ways as important as the records of the proceedings of the general assembly at Vienna and Kremsier themselves, *Verhandlungen des ersten österreichischen Reichstages,* 5 vols. (Vienna, Kremsier, 1848–1849). See further, Heinrich von Srbik, *Quellen zur deutschen Politik in Österreich 1859–1866,* 5 vols. (Munich, R. Oldenbourg, 1934–1938). The volume on the Austrian nationality legislation, edited and interpreted by Edmund Bernatzik, *Das österreichische Nationalitätenrecht* (Vienna, Manz, 1917), is an indispensable source.

(*b*) *Foreign Relations*

Concerning the transactions of the Congress of Vienna, see Johann L. Klüter, ed., *Der Wiener Congress in den Jahren 1814 und 1815,* 9 vols. (Erlangen, Palm und Ende, 1815–1819). Regarding the documentation of the Congress of Berlin, see Alexander Novotny, *Studien zur Geschichte des Berliner Kongresses 1878* (Graz-Cologne, Böhlaus Nachfolger, 1971)

Vol. I. As first two volumes of a new comprehensive series, *Die Protokolle des österreichischen Ministerrates (1848–1867)*, introduced by Friederich Engel-Janosi, the following have been published: "Einleitungsband" by Helmut Rumpler and Section VI, Vol. I, "Ministerium Belcredi," edited by Horst Brettner-Metzler (both Vienna, Österreichischer Bundesverlag, 1970–1971), cover foreign and domestic agenda. A Hungarian series covering the period 1867–1918 will follow. Miklos Komjáthy, ed., *Protokolle des gemeinsamen Ministerrats der österreichisch-ungarischen Monarchie (1914–1918)* (Budapest, Akadémiai Kiadó, 1966) is important for the understanding of wartime government.

Alfred F. Pribram, ed., *The Secret Treaties of Austria-Hungary 1879–1914,* 2 vols. (New York, Fertig, 1969, reprint of the English edition), translated from the German *Die politischen Geheimverträge Österreich-Ungarns 1879–1914* (Vienna, Braumüller, 1920), is an imperative tool for the study of diplomatic history. The same is true for Ludwig Bittner, Alfred F. Pribram, Heinrich von Srbik and Hans Übersberger, eds., *Österreich-Ungarns Aussenpolitik von der bosnischen Krise 1908 bis zum Kriegsausbruch 1914,* 8 vols. and index vol. (Vienna, Österreichischer Bundesverlag, 1930). This is the major Austrian publication of documents pertaining to the prehistory of the First World War.

As for the immediate prehistory of the war, the official collection *Österreichisch-Ungarisches Rotbuch: Diplomatische Aktenstücke zur Vorgeschichte des Krieges 1914* (Vienna, Staatsdruckerei, 1914), are incomplete and unreliable but their deficiencies were largely corrected by the publication of supplements in two parts in 1919. Interesting is also the selection by Roderich Goos, *Das Wiener Kabinett und die Entstehung des Weltkrieges,* 2d edition (Vienna, Seidel, 1919). See further, *Österreichisch-Ungarisches Rotbuch: Diplomatische Aktenstücke betreffend die Beziehungen Österreich-Ungarns zu Italien, 20. Juli 1914 bis 23. Mai 1915* (Vienna, Manz, 1915) and *Österreichisch-Ungarisches Rotbuch: Diplomatische Aktenstücke betreffend die Beziehungen Österreich-Ungarns zu Rumäniem vom 22. Juli 1914 bis 27. August 1916* (Vienna, Manz, 1916).

M) HISTORIOGRAPHY

Heinrich von Srbik, *Geist und Geschichte vom deutschen Humanismus bis zur Gegenwart,* 2 vols. (Salzburg, O. Müller Verlag, 1950–1951) and Alfons Lhotsky, *Österreichische Historiographie* (Vienna, Verlag für Geschichte und Politik, 1962), are the major contributions to the historiography of Austrian history written in German. See also more recently Paul Schroeder, "The Status of Habsburg Studies in the United States," and Fritz Fellner and Friedrich Gottas, "Habsburg Studies in Europe," both in *Austrian History Yearbook,* III:3 (1967) and R. John Rath, "Das amerikanische Schrifttum über den Untergang der Monarchie," in Richard G. Plaschka and Karlheinz Mack, eds., *Die Auflösung des Habsburgerreiches,* listed under I:C. For historiographical information on the individual national groups see part II of this chapter.

N) BIOGRAPHY, REFERENCE WORKS

Constantin von Wurzbach, *Biographisches Lexikon des Kaisertums Österreich 1750–1850 (1859),* 60 vols. (Vienna, Hof- und Staatsdruckerei, 1856–1891), is an important biographical source. For the later part of the period and the first half of the nineteenth century it is being supplemented by *Österreichisches Biographisches Lexikon, 1815–1950,* ed. by Leo Santifaller and Eva Obermayer-Marnach (Graz-Cologne, Böhlaus Nachfolger, 1957-). *Neue österreichische Biographie 1815–1918,* ed. originally by Anton Bettelheim (Vienna, Amalthea Verlag, 1923-), is a selective biographical work of respectable literary quality (so far eighteen volumes). Austrian biography in German has to be supplemented by *Allgemeine deutsche Biographie,* 60 vols. including appendixes and necrologies (Leipzig, Duncker and Humblot, 1875–1912) and after 1945 by *Neue deutsche Biographie,* 6 vols. so far (Berlin, Duncker and Humblot, 1953).

O) SERIALS AND NEWSPAPERS

Mitteilungen des Institutes für österreichische Geschichtsforschung (MIÖG), 1880– , various publishers and slightly varying titles currently published by Böhlaus Nachfolger, Graz-Cologne, is the standard scholarly journal on Austrian history in German language. *Mitteilungen des österreichischen Staatsarchivs* (MIÖSTA), (Horn, Berger, 1948–), publishes articles and monographs, based primarily on research in Austrian archives. The national academies of the succession states to the Habsburg empire publish likewise serials based on historical research in their countries.

In English, see the *Austrian History Yearbook* (Houston, Rice University, 1965– annual) and *Central European History* (Atlanta, Emory University, 1968– quarterly). Various serials on Slavic history published in Great Britain and the United States contain significant articles.

Of newspapers see particularly the following journals which outlasted the empire: *Neue Freie Presse* founded in 1864 (German liberal), *Reichspost* founded in 1894 (Catholic conservative), *Arbeiter-Zeitung* founded 1889 (Socialist); all three published in Vienna. On the bibliography of the press in German see the work by K. Paupié, listed under

I:Q; on the press in other national languages see the references listed under bibliographies in II:B to M.

P) STATISTICS

The official Austrian and Hungarian statistical publications are *K. K. Österreichische Staatische Zentralkommission, Österreichisches statistisches Handbuch* (Vienna, A. Hölder, 1880– annual, with slightly varying title) and *L'Office Central Royal Hongrois de Statistique Annuaire Statistique Hongrois,* (Budapest, Athenaeum, 1893–1918); both series are of high quality.

The Magyarizing tendencies in the Hungarian statistics are not reflected in any outright distortion of figures but rather in the manner of presentation. The survey volumes at the end of every decade, 1880, 1890, etc. are of particular importance. Of older works on statistics see the one by Czoernig listed under I:A and Wilhelm Winkler, *Statistisches Handbuch der europäischen Nationalitäten* (Vienna, Braumüller, 1931). See also the bibliography on statistical sources in R. A. Kann, *Nationalitätenproblem,* Vol. II, Appendix I, listed under I:H and the monographs listed in Appendix I of this study.

Q) BIBLIOGRAPHY

Karl and Mathilde Uhlirz, *Handbuch der Geschichte Österreichs und seiner Nachbarländer Böhmen und Ungarn,* 4 vols. (Vienna, Böhlaus Nachfolger, 1927–1944). The first volume covering Austrian history until 1526 has been published in a revised second edition by Böhlaus Nachfolger, Graz-Cologne, 1964. This work in conjunction with the History by Franz von Krones (see under I:B) contains presently the most comprehensive bibliography on the political and administrative history of the Habsburg empire. Richard Charmatz, *Wegweiser durch die Literatur der österreichischen Geschichte* (Stuttgart, Cotta, 1912) is a useful brief bibliographical survey. The most up-to-date bibliographical work on current literature with emphasis on works in German and English is Eric H. Boehm and Fritz Fellner, *Österreichische historische Bibliographie—Austrian Historical Bibliography* (Santa Barbara, Calif., Clio Press, 1965- annual volumes) compiled by Herbert Paulhart and Günther Höde with the cooperation of Wolfdieter Bihl. Fully up to date are also the important bibliographies by Paul L. Horecky, *East Central Europe* (Chicago, University of Chicago Press, 1969) and by the same author and publisher *South Eastern Europe* (1969). Chief emphasis is put on the history of the national groups to the present rather than of the empire itself. See also

F. R. Bridge, *The Habsburg Monarchy 1804–1918: Books and Pamphlets Published in the United Kingdom between 1804 and 1918, a Critical Bibliography* (London, School of Slavonic and East European Studies, University of London, 1967).

Apart from the standard bibliography on German historiography by Dahlmann-Waitz, see E. Zöllner (under I:B) and for recent literature also *Austrian History Yearbook* (under I:O) and *Österreichische historische Bibliographie* as noted above. On nationalism, see R. A. Kann, *Das Nationalitätenproblem* and Fran Zwitter, *Les Problèmes Nationaux dans la Monarchie des Habsbourg* (particularly good on modern Slavic literature), (both listed under I:H).

On the bibliography of the press see Kurt Paupié, *Handbuch der österreichischen Pressegeschichte,* 2 vols. (Vienna, Braumüller, 1960–1966); on that of the labor movement see Herbert Steiner, ed., *Bibliographie zur Geschichte der österreichischen Arbeiterbewegung* (Vienna, Verlag des österreichischen Gewerkschaftsbundes, 1962).

II. Literature on the History of the National Groups

Many of the following items, like some of the previously listed ones, are to a greater or lesser extent tinged with the spirit of nationalism. This does not mean, however, that the topic is focused necessarily on the national issue. It does mean that most of these works were written from a national viewpoint.

A) THE AUSTRO-GERMANS

Most of the works on the Austro-Germans are covered in the sections of the preceding Part I. To them, the following works which, at least in part, emphasize aspects of nationalism, may be added.

Paul Molisch, *Briefe zur deutschen Politik in Österreich* (Vienna, Braumüller, 1934), Wilhelm Schüssler, *Österreich und das deutsche Schicksal* (Stuttgart, Deutsche Verlagsansstalt, 1918), and Heinrich von Srbik, *Österreich in der deutschen Geschichte* (Munich, Bruckmann, 1936) represent the *grossdeutsch* position. Heinrich von Srbik, *Deutsche Einheit: Idee und Wirklichkeit vom heiligen Reich bis Königgrätz,* 2 parts in 4 vols. (Munich, Bruckmann, 1936), is an important contribution to the analysis of Austria's role in the history of the German unification movement. See also Andrew G. Whiteside, *Austrian National Socialism before 1918* (The Hague, Nijhoff, 1962). For bibliographical information see the bibliographical section I:Q.

Important autobiographies and diaries written from different viewpoints are Ernst von Plener, *Erinnerungen,* 3 vols. (Stuttgart, Deutsche Verlagsanstalt, 1926), German liberal; Eduard Suess, *Erinnerungen* (Leipzig, Hirzel, 1916), German liberal; Friedrich Funder, *Mein Weg vom Gestern ins Heute* (Vienna, Herold, 1952), Christian Social; Rudolf Sieghart, *Die letzten Jahrzehnte einer Grossmacht* (Berlin, Ullstein, 1932), conservative; Joseph M. Baernreither, *Fragmente eines politischen Tagebuches* (Berlin, Verlag für Kulturpolitik, 1928), enlightened conservative; Fritz Fellner, ed., *Schicksalsjahre Österreichs: Das Politische Tagebuch Joseph Redlichs 1908–1919,* 2 vols. (Graz-Cologne, Böhlaus Nachfolger, 1953), German progressive. No fully adequate scholarly biographies of major political figures such as Victor Adler, Karl Lueger, Georg von Schönerer have as yet been published.

B) THE MAGYARS

The standard Hungarian history is Bálint Hóman and Gyula Szekfü, *Magyar Történet,* 5 vols. (Budapest, Egyetemi Nyomda, 1935–1936). There is no single adequate history of Austria from the Middle Ages to modern times in English, but there are several on Hungary. Dominic G. Kosáry, *A History of Hungary* (Cleveland, Benjamin Franklin Society, 1941), is a stimulating survey. See further, Denis Sinor, *History of Hungary* (London, Allen and Unwin, 1959); C. A. Macartney, *Hungary: A History* (Edinburgh, University Press, 1962) and Sandor de Bertha, *La Hongrie Moderne de 1849 á 1901* (Paris, Plon Norritt, 1901). An interesting modern work is Erik Molnár, Iván T. Berend, et al., eds., *Magyaroszag Törtènete* (Budapest, Gondolat Konyvkiado, 1967), 2 vols. The most recent history of Hungary written strictly from the viewpoint of the prevailing party ideology in the country is Ervin Pamlényi, ed., *Die Geschichte Ungarns* (Budapest, Corvina, 1971). The work offers much new material on socioeconomic and some on political history but it is onesided in its interpretation and in its bibliographical references. It has been published in Hungarian and German. Julius Miskolczy, *Ungarn in der Habsburger-Monarchie* (Vienna, Herold, 1959), discusses the relationship of the lands of the Hungarian crown to the empire in a conservative, by and large pro-imperial manner. A standard work on the era from 1867–1918, as seen from the dualistic constitutional angle is Gustav Gratz, *A Dualizmus Kora: Magyaroszag Törtènete 1867–1918,* 2 vols. (Budapest, Magyar Szemle Társasag, 1934). P. Hanák interprets the same problem from the Communist viewpoint with greater emphasis on socioeconomic factors in *Austrian History Yearbook,* Vol. III:1. Heinrich Marczali, *Ungarische Verfassungsgeschichte* (Tübingen, J. C. B. Mohr

(P. Siebeck), 1910) and by the same author *Hungary in the Eighteenth Century* (Cambridge, Mass., Harvard University Press, 1910), are both translations of distinguished works by a notable Magyar historian. See also Bela Király, *Hungary in the late Eighteenth Century* (New York, Columbia University Press, 1969), a significant study with new material. On the following period of reform, see George Barany, *Stephan Széchenyi and the Awakening of Hungarian Nationalism 1791–1841* (Princeton, Princeton University Press, 1968). For a Marxian interpretation of this period see Erzsébet Andics, *Metternich und die Frage Ungarns* (Budapest, Akadémiai Kiadó, 1973).

Hungarian social and economic history: Count Paul Teleky, *The Evolution of Hungary and its Place in European History* (New York, Macmillan, 1923), is the work of an ardent Magyar revisionist after the First World War. Written with intellectual honesty, the study contains much useful factual information although the interpretation may frequently be challenged. Alexander (Sandor) von Matlekovits, *Das Königreich Ungarn,* 2 vols. (Leipzig, Duncker and Humblot, 1900), (translated from the Hungarian), is a useful survey. Zsigmond P. Pach, *Die ungarische Agrarpolitik im 16. und 17. Jahrhundert* (Budapest, Akadémiai Kiadó, 1964), (referred to in I:E), informative. See further, Sonja Jordan, *Die kaiserliche Wirtschaftspolitik im Banat im 18. Jahrhundert* (Munich, R. Oldenbourg, 1967) and Konrad Müller, *Siebenbürgische Wirtschaftspolitik unter Maria Theresia* (Munich, R. Oldenbourg, 1961). See also the previously listed work by V. Sandor and P. Hanák, *Studien zur Geschichte der österreichisch-ungarischen Monarchie,* under I:D.

Nationalism: Josef Weber, *Eötvös und die ungarische Nationalitätenfrage* (Munich, R. Oldenbourg, 1966) discusses the national philosophy of the outstanding political thinker and would-be empire reformer. Paul Bödy, *Joseph Eötvös and the Modernization of Hungary, 1840–1870* (Philadelphia, American Philosophical Society, 1972), extends this analysis to the topic of administration. Julius Szekfü, *État et Nation* (Paris, Les Presses Universitaires de France, 1945), translated from the Hungarian, is a study of great importance.

Cultural history: J. H. Schwicker, *Geschichte der ungarischen Literatur* (Leipzig, W. Friedrich, 1888), is an older conservative, but still useful work. More modern in outlook is Josef Reményi, *Hungarian Writers and Literature* (New Brunswick, Rutgers University Press, 1964). See Julius von Farkas, *Die ungarische Romantik* (Berlin, W. de Gruyter, 1931). See further Johann Andritsch, ed., *Ungarische Geisteswelt* (Baden-Baden,

Holle, 1968) and Antal Sivirsky, *Die ungarische Literatur der Gegenwart* (Bern, Francke, 1962). One of the rare books which offers more than the title promises, namely an analysis of major factors in Hungarian intellectual and social history, is William O. McCagg, *Jewish Nobles and Geniuses in Modern Hungary* (New York, Columbia University Press, 1971).

Two important studies which discuss the gradual ascendancy of the Left in Magyar intellectual life are Zoltan Horváth, *Die Jahrhundertwende in Ungarn* (Neuwied am Rhein, Luchterhand, 1966), translated from the Hungarian, and Tibor Süle, *Sozialdemokratie in Ungarn* (Cologne-Graz, Böhlaus Nachfolger, 1967).

Historiography: See Stephan Borsody, "Modern Hungarian Historiography," *Journal of Modern History* (1952) and for the Communist period Francis S. Wagner, *A Magyar Történetirás új útjai 1945–57* (Washington, D. C., 1956).

General reference: *Ungarn* (Budapest, Corvina, 1966).

Bibliography: Dominic Kosáry, *Bevezetés a Magyar Történelem Forrásaiba és Iodalmába,* 2 vols. (Budapest, Magyar Tudományos Akadémia, 1951–), (for the period to 1825); see further, *Magyar Történeti Bibliográfia 1825–1867* (Budapest, Academy, 1950–), and *Magyar Nemzeti Bibliográfia* (Budapest, National Széchényi Library, 1946–), classified according to subject matter.

c) THE ITALIANS

Most studies in Italian on the Austro-Italian problem written before 1918 represent the irredentist viewpoint; most studies in German, written after 1918, the revisionist one. See L'Adriatico, *Studio geographico storico e politico* (Milano, Fratelli Treves, 1915) and Virginio Gayda, *L'Italia d'oltre confine* (Torino, Fratelli Bocca, 1915). See further Angelo Tamborra, *L'Idea di nazionalitá e la guerra 1914–1918* (Trento, Congresso di Storia di Risorgimento Italiano, 1963). As for regional studies, see Giuseppe Borghetti, *Trento Italiana* (Firenze, Barbéra, 1903); Cesare Battisti, *Il Trentino, ilustrazione statistico-economico* (Milan, Ravà et Co., 1915) and Giorgio Roletto, *Trieste ed i suoi problemi* (Trieste, Borsatti, 1952).

In English see Kent R. Greenfield, "The Italian Nationality Problem of the Austrian Empire," *Austrian History Yearbook,* III:2 (1967). As for literature in German see Hans Kramer, *Die Italiener unter der österreichisch-ungarischen Monarchie* (Vienna, Herold, 1954); Theodor Veiter, *Die Italiener in der österreichisch-ungarischen Monarchie* (Vienna, Verlag für Geschichte und Politik, 1965); Michael Mayr, *Der italienische*

Irredentismus im Entstehen und seine Entwicklung, vornehmlich in Tirol, 2d edition (Innsbruck, Tyrolia, 1937); Adam Wandruszka, *Österreich und Italien im achtzehnten Jahrhundert* (Vienna, Verlag für Geschichte und Politik, 1963).

Bibliography: See Attilio Pagliani, *Catalog generale della libreria italiana,* 8 vols (Milan, Associazione tipografico libraria italiana, 1901–1905) continued by *Quaderni e riviste d'Italia: repetorio biliografico* (Rome, 1958–). For literature in German see the above-listed work by H. Kramer.

D) THE ROUMANIANS

The standard work on Roumanian history is Nicolae Jorga, *Istoria Românilor,* 10 vols (Bucarest, Roumanian Academy, 1935–1939). A complete translation in French is out of print. Abridged editions of this work have been published in English, French, and German. Relatively most comprehensive of these shorter versions is the German edition: *Greschichte des rumänischen Volkes im Rahmen seiner Staatsbildungen,* 2 vols. (Gotha, F. A. Perthes, 1905–1911). In English see particularly Robert W. Seton-Watson, *A History of the Rumanians* (Cambridge, Cambridge University Press, 1934).

On the Roumanians in the Habsburg monarchy, see Mathias Bernath, *Habsburg und die Anfänge der rumänischen Nationsbildung* (Leiden, Brill, 1972) and Stephan Fischer-Galati, "The Roumanians and the Habsburg Monarchy," *Austrian History Yearbook,* III:2 (1967). On the dissolution of the Habsburg empire with particular regard to the Roumanian problem see Constantin Daicoviciu and Miron Constantinescu, *Destramarea Monarhiei Austro-Ungare 1900–1918* (Bucarest, Editura Academei, 1964). On the Roumanians in Hungary including Transylvania see Theodor V. Păcătianu, *Cartea de aur: sau luptele politice-nationale al e Românilor de sub coroana ungară,* 8 vols. (Sibu, Tipografia arhidiecezană, 1904–1915). For briefer presentations see Miron Constantinescu, *Études d'Histoire Transylvaine* (Bucarest, Academy, 1970) and Constantin Daicoviciu and Miron Constantinescu, *Brève Histoire de la Transylvanie* (Bucarest, Academy, 1965), the classic Nicolae Jorga, *Histoire des Roumains de Transylvanie et de Hongrie,* 2 vols. (Bucarest, Gutenberg, 1915–1916), somewhat outdated, and the scholarly study by Keith Hitchins, *The Rumanian National Movement in Transylvania 1780–1849* (Cambridge, Mass., Harvard University Press, 1964). On the Magyar viewpoint, see Eugen Horváth, *Transylvania and the History of the Rumanians* (Budapest, Sârkány, 1935) and Ladislas Makkai, *Histoire de Transylvanie* (Paris, Press Universitaires de France, 1946). See also Konrad Müller, *Siebenbürgische Wirtschaftspolitik unter Maria Theresia* (Munich, R. Oldenbourg, 1961). On the Roumanians in the Bukovina, see Erich Prokopowitsch, *Die rumänische Nationalbewegung in der Bukowina und der Daco-Romanismus* (Vienna-Cologne, Böhlaus Nachfolger, 1965).

Bibliography: See Andrei Veress, *Bibliografia română-ungară,* 3 vols. (Bucarest, Certea Românească, 1931–1935) and the above-listed works on Transylvania by C. Daicoviciu and M. Constantinescu, and on the Bukovina by E. Prokopowitsch. See also *Studiĕ revistă de istoria,* (Bucarest, Academy, 1948).

E) GENERAL SLAVIC INTELLECTUAL AND LINGUISTIC HISTORY

See Hans Kohn, *Die Welt der Slawen,* 2 vols. (Frankfurt am Main, S. Fischer, 1960) and by the same author, *Panslavism: Its History and Ideology* (New York, Vintage Books, 1960). On Panslavism see also the excellent older study by Alfred von Fischel, *Der Panslawismus bis zum Weltkrieg* (Stuttgart, Cotta, 1919). As general reference see further Francis Dvornik, *The Slavs in European History and Civilization* (New Brunswick, Rutgers University Press, 1962) and Leonid Strakhovsky, ed., *A Handbook of Slavic Studies* (Cambridge, Mass., Harvard University Press, 1949). Paul Diels, *Die slawischen Völker* (Wiesbaden, O. Harrassowitz, 1963), excellent. Paul Hineberg, *Die osteuropäischen Literaturen und die slawischen Sprachen* (Berlin-Leipzig, Teubner, 1908). An older work, translated from the Russian, is rich in facts and still useful: A. N. Pypin and V. D. Spasovič, *Geschichte der slawischen Literaturen,* 2 parts in 3 vols. (Leipzig, Brockhaus, 1880–1884). Of some use is still Gregor Krek, *Einleitung in die slawische Literaturgeschichte* (Graz, Lenschner, 1887). Of greater importance are the works by Dmitry Cizevsky, *Comparative History of Slavic Literature* (Nashville, Vanderbilt University Press, 1971) and by the same author *Outline of Comparative Slavic Literature* (Boston, American Academy of Arts and Sciences, 1952).

Bibliographies: See Robert J. Kerner, *Slavic Europe: A Selected Bibliography* (Cambridge, Mass., Harvard University Press, 1918) and more recently Jirina Sztachova, *Mid Europe* (New York, Mid European Studies Center, 1953). For more extensive bibliographical information see the references in the subsections on the individual Slavic national groups.

F) THE CZECHS

See Robert J. Kerner, ed., *Czechoslovakia* (Berkeley and Los Angeles, University of California Press, 1945), is a useful general survey on political, cultural, and socioeconomic history. Václav Novotný, Kamil Krofta and Josef Macek, eds., *České Dějiny,* 3 vols. in 16 parts (Prague, J. Laichter, 1912–1966), is a comprehensive history still in progress. So far it is the standard work on Czech medieval history. Still valuable are Ernest Denis, *Fin de l'Independence Bohême,* 2 vols. (Paris, A. Colin, 1890) and by the same author *La Bohême depuis la Montagne Blanche,* 2 vols. (Paris, Leroux, 1903). Both works together cover Bohemian history from the middle of the fifteenth to the end of the nineteenth century. Karl Bosl, ed., *Handbuch der Geschichte der böhmischen Länder,* 3 vols. (Stuttgart, A. Hiersemann, 1967–1970), Vols. I, III, IV: Vol. I on medieval history; Vol. III on nineteenth and twentieth centuries; Vol. IV on the history of the republic (Vol. II on early modern history not yet published.) Hermann Münch, *Böhmische Tragödie* (Braunschweig, G. Westermann, 1949), is excellent on German-Czech relations. To be recommended is also Elizabeth Wiskemann, *Czechs and Germans* (London, Oxford University Press, 1938). In English, S. Harrison Thomson, *Czechoslovakia in European History* (Princeton, Princeton University Press, 1953) and Robert W. Seton-Watson, *History of the Czechs and Slovaks* (London, Hutchinson and Co., 1943) are useful one-volume surveys. Outstanding relatively brief but comprehensive histories in Czech language are Kamil Krofta, *Dějiny Československé* (Prague, Janda, 1946); see also Josef Macek, et al., eds., *Přehled československých dějin,* 3 vols. in 4, (Prague, Akademie věd, 1958–1960), of which vols. 1–3 pertain to Czech history until 1918 (Marxian interpretation); and a standard work by Václav Novotný, ed., *Dějiny in Československá vlastivěda* (Czechoslovak Encyclopedia), 2 vols. (Prague, Sfinx, 1932–1933).

Of monographs, see Robert J. Kerner, *Bohemia in the Eighteenth Century,* revised edition edited by Joseph F. Zacek (Orono, Academie Internationale, 1969). Of other significant monographs see Hans Raupach, *Der tschechische Frühnationalismus* (Darmstadt, Wissenschaftliche Buchgesellschaft, 1969) and Stanley Z. Pech, *The Czech Revolution of 1848* (Chapel Hill, University of North Carolina Press, 1970); Christian Stölzl, *Die Ära Bach in Böhmen: Sozialgeschichtliche Studien zum Neoabsolutismus 1849–1859* (Munich, R. Oldenbourg, 1971), offers important new insight in socioeconomic problems of the neoabsolutist era in Bohemia.

See further, the two valuable studies by Friedrich Prinz, "Die böhmischen Länder von 1848–1914" and "Das kulturelle Leben (1867–1939) vom österreichisch-ungarischen Ausgleich bis zum Ende der ersten tschechoslowakischen Republik," both published in Karl Bosl, ed., *Hand-*

buch der Geschichte der böhmischen Länder, Vol. III, the second ibid. Vol. IV. On the dissolution of the empire from the Czech viewpoint see Jan Opočenský, *The Collapse of the Austro-Hungarian Monarchy and the Czechoslovak State* (Prague, Orbis, 1928). Two important autobiographies, focused on the disintegration period, are Edward Beneš, *My War Memoirs* (London, Allen & Unwin, 1928) and *Thomas G. Masaryk* (New York, F. Stokes, 1927), both translated from the Czech.

On Czech constitutional history, see Ernst Birke and Kurt Oberdorffer, eds., *Das böhmische Staatsrecht in den deutsch-tschechischen Auseinandersetzungen des 19. und 20. Jahrhunderts* (Marburg/Lahn, Elvert, 1960). On Czech nationalism, largely discussed also in most of the works mentioned above, see further Jan Havránek, "The Development of Czech Nationalism," *Austrian History Yearbook,* III:2 (1967).

On Czech literary history, see Count Francis Lützow, *A History of Bohemian Literature* (London, Heinemann, 1907); and more important Hanuš Jelinek, *Histoire de la Littérature Tchèque,* 3 vols. (Paris, Editions du Sagittaire, 1930–1935), and more briefly Frantisek Chudoba, *A Short Survey of Czech Literature* (New York, Kraus, 1969).

On Czech historiography see Richard G. Plaschka, *Von Palacký bis Pekař* (Vienna-Cologne, Böhlaus Nachfolger, 1955).

Strongly contested are statistics of the Bohemian lands, particularly of Bohemia herself. Three good works written from different viewpoints are Alfred Bohmann, *Bevölkerungsbewegungen in Böhmen 1847–1947, mit besonderer Berücksichtigung der nationalen Verhältnisse* (Munich, Collegium Carolinum, 1958); Heinrich Rauchberg, *Die Zahlenverhältnisse der Deutschen und Tschechen in Böhmen* (Munich, Callway, 1900); and V. Srb and M. Kučera, "Vývoj obyvatelstva českých zemí v XIX, století," in *Statistika a demografie,* I (1959).

Bibliography: *Český časopis Historický, Bibliografie vědecké práce o české, minulosti za posledních čtyřicet let 1895–1934* (Prague, Česká Akademie, 1935). Josef Macek, Václav Husa and Branislav Varsík, eds., 25 *Ans d'Historiographie Tschechoslovaque 1935–1960* (Prague, Czechslovak Akademy, 1960). See also Otakar Odložilík, "Modern Czech Historiography," in *Slavonic and East European Review* (1930).

G) THE SLOVAKS

For brief surveys see Jozef Lettrich, *History of Modern Slovakia* (New York, Praeger, 1955) and Jozef Mikus, *La Slovakie dans le Drama de l'Europe 1918–1950* (Paris, Les Ills d'Or, 1955). Robert W. Seton-Watson, *Racial Problems in Hungary* (London, Constable and Co., 1908), is a first in Western languages which called attention to the discrimination against Slovaks under Magyar administration. See further, Ludwig von Gogolák, *Beiträge zur Geschichte des slowakischen Volkes,* 3 vols. (Munich, R. Oldenbourg, 1963–1972), Vol. I, *Die Nationswerdung der Slowaken und die Anfänge der tschechoslowakischen Frage (1526–1790)*; Vol. II, *Die slowakische nationale Frage in der Reformperiode Ungarns (1790–1848)*; Vol. III, *Zwischen zwei Revolutionen (1848–1919).* In Slovak language see František Bokeš, *Dejiny Slovenska a Slovákov od najstarších čias po oslobodenie* (Bratislava, Slovak Academy, 1946); Ludovit Holotík, ed., *Dejiny Slovenska,* 2 vols. (Bratislava, Slovak Academy, 1961–1968); Ján Tibenský, *Slovensko: dejiny* (Bratislava, Obzor, 1971), all three Marxian interpretation.

On early modern Slovak history see Ludovit Holotík and Anton Vantuch, eds., *Humanizmus a renesancia na Slovensku v 15.–16. storočí* (Bratislava, Slovak Academy, 1967). On the evolution of the Slavic renaissance among the Slovaks in the eighteenth and early nineteenth centuries, see Ján Tibenský, ed., *K'počiatkom slovenského narodného obrodenia* (Bratislava, Slovak Academy, 1964) and Endre Arató, "A szlovák nemzeti mozgalom a forradom elott (1845–1848)," in *Szazadok* (Budapest, 1948), Magyar Marxian interpretation.

On the position of the Slovaks in the Habsburg empire see Ernest Denis, *La Question d'Autriche: Les Slovaques* (Paris, Delagrave, 1917); Václav L. Beneš, "The Slovaks in the Habsburg Empire: A Struggle for Existence," and Ludovit Holotík, "The Slovaks: An Integrating or a Disintegrating Factor?" Both essays were published in *Austrian History Yearbook,* III:2 (1967). See also *Studia Historica Slovaca* (Bratislava, Slovak Academy, 1963–).

Bibliography: Ludovit V. Rizner, *Bibliografia pisomníctva slovenského,* 6 vols. (V. T. Sv. Martine, Náklodom Matice Slovenskej, 1929–1934). See further, as listed under II:F, J. Macek, et al., eds., 25 *Ans d'Historiographie Tschechoslovaque.*

H) THE POLES

Bernadotte Schmitt, ed., *Poland* (Berkeley and Los Angeles, University of California Press, 1945), is a good survey on political, cultural, and socioeconomic history. Of other surveys see, above all, William F. Reddaway, J. H. Penson, Oscar Halecki, Roman Dyboski, eds., *The Cambridge History of Poland,* 2 vols. (Cambridge, Cambridge University Press, 1950–1951), a work equally strong on political and intellectual history. It does not deal primarily but still adequately with the Poles in Galicia.

A valuable modern survey is Alexander Gieysztor, Stefan Kieniewicz, Emanuel Rostworowski, et al., *History of Poland* (Warsaw, Polish Scientific Publishers, 1968); on developments in Galicia, see particularly pp. 486–490, 496–499, 540–546, 577–579, 602–605, 616–628 by Stefan Kieniewicz and Henryk Werezycki. Wilhelm Feldman, *Geschichte der politischen Ideen in Polen seit dessen Teilungen* (Osnabrück, Zeller, 1934), is a standard work on the political ideologies dominant in divided Poland. An outstanding work on Polish cultural history is Manfred Kridl, *A Survey of Polish Literature and Culture* (New York, Columbia University Press, 1956) translated from the Polish. Exclusively focused on literature is Czeslaw Milosz, *The History of Polish Literature* (London, Macmillan, 1969). See also Oscar Halecki, *A History of Poland,* 2d edition (New York, Roy, 1956). In Polish language, Alexander Brückner, Wlodzimierz Antoniewicz, et al., *Polska jej dzieje i kultura,* 3 vols. (Warsaw, Nakl, Trzaski, Everta i Michaleskiego, 1927–1932), is still a standard history.

On the Poles in Galicia see also Konstanty Grzybowski, *Galicja 1848–1914: historii ustroju Austrii* (Cracow, Academy, 1959); Hanns Schlitter, *Aus Österreichs Vormärz,* Part 1, "Galizien und Krakau," as listed in Part I:B; furthermore Piotr S. Wandycz, "The Poles in the Habsburg Monarchy," and Henryk Wereszycki, "The Poles as Integrating and Disintegrating Factor," both essays in *Austrian History Yearbook,* III:2 (1967) and Kazimierz Chledowski, *Pamietniki,* 2 vols. (Wroclaw, Biblioteka narádowa, 1951), Stefan Kieniewicz, *Rewolucja Polska 1846 roku: wybór zródel* (Wroclaw, Biblioteka narádowa, 1950), a counterpart to Schlitter's work.

Bibliography: See Karol J. Estreicher, *Bibliografia Polska,* thus far 34 vols. and 4 supplementary vols. (Warsaw, Cracow, Academy, 1872–). This comprehensive Polish bibliography is in a continuous state of revision. The standard modern historical bibliography is Jan Baumgart et al., eds., *Bibliografia historii polskiej* (Cracow, Historical Institute of the Polish Academy of Sciences, 1952–), annual publication. See further, Ludwik Finkel, *Bibliografia historii polskiej,* 3 vols. (Cracow, Academy, 1906; reprint Warsaw, 1955), covers Polish history to 1815; Tom Wsterny, ed., *Bibliografia Historii Polski 1815–1914* (Warsaw, Państwowe Wydawnictwo Naukowe, 1954) supplements Finkel's bibliography. In English see Sigmund S. Birkenmayer, ed., *Bibliography of Polish Literature in English* (University Park, Pennsylvania State University Press, 1971). For brief bibliographical information see also the above listed work by Bernadotte Schmitt, ed., *Poland.*

I) THE RUTHENIANS (WEST UKRAINIANS)

For general surveys, see Michael Hrushevsky, *A History of Ukraine* (New Haven, Yale University Press, 1941) and by the same author, *The Historical Evolution of the Ukrainian Problem* (London, Garden City Press, 1915). Both were translated from the Ukrainian, like Dmytro Doroshenko, *History of the Ukraine* (Edmonton, Institute Press, 1929). See also Borys Krupnyckyj, *Geschichte der Ukraine von den Anfängen bis zum Jahre 1917* (Wiesbaden, O. Harrassowitz, 1963).

On the Galician Ruthenians, see Ivan L. Rudnytsky, "The Ukrainians in Galicia under Austrian Rule," in *Austrian History Yearbook*, III:2 (1967); on the Ruthenians in the Bukovina, see Adrian Văleanu, "The Question of Bukovina—then and now," *Journal of Central European Affairs*, V (Boulder, Col. 1945–1963 annual); on the Carpatho-Ruthenians, see Ivan Žeguc, *Die nationalpolitischen Bestrebungen der Karpatho-Ruthenen 1848–1918* (Wiesbaden, O. Harrassowitz, 1965). See also René Martel, *La Ruthénie Subcarpathique* (Paris, P. Hartmann, 1935).

In Ruthenian language see K. Levyts'kyi, *Istoriia politychnoi dumky Halyst'kykh Ukraintsiv, 1848–1914*, 2 vols. (Lwiw, 1929). See further on the Young Ukrainian movement, Ivan Franko, *Moloda Ukraina: providni idei i epizody* (Lwiw, Ukrains'ko rus'ka vydavnica spilka, 1910).

The best comprehensive reference work in English is *Ukraine: A Concise Encyclopedia*, ed. by Volodymyr Kubijoviyč, 2 vols. (Toronto, University of Toronto Press, 1963–1967). This work discusses all aspects of Ruthenian political, cultural, and socioeconomic life.

Bibliography: Ivan Mirtschuk, *Geschichte der ukrainischen Kultur* (Munich, Isar Verlag, 1957) and by the same author, *Handbuch der Ukraine* (Leipzig, Harrassowitz, 1941) and *Ukrainian Review* (London, Association of Ukrainians in Great Britain, 1954–   ).

J) THE SOUTHERN SLAVS

General: See Georg Stadtmüller, *Geschichte Südosteuropas* (Munich, R. Oldenbourg, 1950). L. von Südland (Pilar), *Die südslawische Frage und der Weltkrieg* (Vienna, Manz, 1918), conservative. Hermann Wendel, *Der Kampf der Südslawen um Freiheit und Einheit* (Frankfurt a. M., Societas Druckerei, 1925), Socialist-liberal. Dušan A. Lončarević, *Jugoslawiens Entstehung* (Vienna, Amalthea Verlag, 1929), Serb viewpoint. On the Southern Slav action movement as seen from the Croatian angle see Ivan Mučič, *Hrvatska politika i Jugoslavenska ideja* (Croatian Politics and the Yugoslav Idea), (Split, Vlastita naklada, 1969). On Illyrism see Fran Zwitter, "Illyrism et Sentiment Yougoslave," *Le Monde Slave,* (Paris, April–June, 1933) and Alfred Fischel, *Der Panslawismus,* listed under I:E. On intellectual history, see Josef Matl, *Südslawische Studien* (Munich, R. Oldenbourg, 1965).

For reference, see Werner Markert, *Jugoslawien* (Cologne-Graz, Böhlaus Nachfolger, 1954).

a) THE CROATS

Rudolf Kissling, *Die Kroaten* (Vienna-Cologne, Böhlaus Nachfolger, 1956), is written from a strictly conservative viewpoint. See further Stanko Guldescu, *The Croatian-Slavonian Kingdom 1526–1792* (The Hague, Mouton, 1970). On cultural and social history, see Francis H. Eterovich and Christopher Spalatin, *Croatia: Land, People, Culture,* 2 vols. (Toronto, University of Toronto Press, 1964–1970); Zvane Crnja, *Cultural History of Croatia* (Zagreb, Office of Information, 1962) and Ante Kadić, *From Croatian Renaissance to Yugoslav Socialism: Essays* (The Hague, Mouton, 1969). For the same period, with emphasis on ideological history see Mirjana Gross, *Povijest Pravaške Ideologije* (Zagreb, Institute of Croatian History, 1973).

A standard history of the Croats is Ferdo Šišic, *Pregled povijesti hrvatskoga naroda* (Zagreb, Matica Hrvatska, 1962), thoroughly revised by Jaroslav Šidak. The work was first published in 1873. Of great importance is Jaroslav Šidak, *Provijest Hrvatskoga Naroda 1860–1914* (Zagreb, Školska Knjiga, 1968). For the same period, with emphasis on ideological history, see Mirjana Gross, *Provijest Pravaške Ideologije* (Zagreb, Institute of Croatian History, 1973).

On the military border, see the two studies by Günther Rothenberg, *The Austrian Military Border in Croatia 1522–1747* (Urbana, University of Illinois Press, 1960) and *The Military Border in Croatia 1740–1881* (Chicago, University of Chicago Press, 1966), also Nikolaus von Preradovich, *Des Kaisers Grenzer: 300 Jahre Türkenabwehr* (Vienna, F. Molden, 1970). See further Heeresgeschichtliches Museum, *Die K. K. Militärgrenze* (Vienna, Österreichischer Bundesverlag, 1973) covers all Military Frontiers of the Habsburg empire (comprehensive bibliography).

On the Croat status within the Habsburg empire, see Charles Jelavich, "The Croatian Problem in the the Habsburg Monarchy in the Nineteenth Century," *Austrian History Yearbook,* III:2 (1967) and ibid. Bogdan Krizman, "The Croatians in the Habsburg Monarchy in the Nineteenth Century."

Bibliography: The two above-listed essays by Jelavich and Krizman, and Fran Zwitter, *Les Problèmes Nationaux dans la Monarchie des Habsbourg* listed in section I:P, provide adequate bibliographical information.

b) THE SLOVENES

In English see Dragotin Lončar, *The Slovenes: A Social History from the earliest Times to 1910* (Cleveland, American Yugoslav Printing and Publishing Co. 1931). See further, Anton Slodnjak, *Geschichte der Slowenischen Literatur* (Berlin, De Gruyter, 1958) and for the Slovene position within the Habsburg monarchy, Fran Zwitter, "The Slovenes in the Habsburg Monarchy," *Austrian History Yearbook,* III:2 (1967) and Bogumil Vošnjak, *A Bulwark against Germany* (London, Allen & Unwin, 1917). On Slovene economy within the Habsburg empire, see Toussaint Hočevar, *The Structure of Slovenian Economy 1848–1963* (New York, Studia Slovenica, 1963).

See Josir Mal, *Zgodovina slovenskega naroda najnovejša doba* (V Celje, Družba sv Mokorga, 1928–1929); Edvard Kardelj (Sperans), *Razvoj slovenskega narodnega Vprašanja,* 2d edition (Ljubljana, Državna Založba Slovenije, 1957) and Bogo Grafenauer, *Zgodovina slovenskega naroda,* 5 vols. (Ljubljana, Kmečka knjiga, 1954–1962), revised editions in progress.

Bibliography: See the above-listed essay by F. Zwitter and his *Les Problèmes Nationaux,* listed under I:H and I:Q.

c) THE SERBS

Josef K. Jireček, *Geschichte der Serben,* 2 vols. (Gotha, Perthes, 1911), revised and enlarged Serbian edition by Jovan Radonić (Beograd, Naučna knjiga, 1952), the emphasis is on medieval history. Stanoje Stanojević, *Istorija srpskoga naroda,* 3d edition (Beograd, Izdavačka knjižarnica Napredak, 1926), is a useful general presentation on political history. On the evolution of political thought see Vaso Cubrilović, *Istorija politicke misli u Srbiji XIX veku* (Beograd, Prosveta, 1958).

As for the Serb position within the Habsburg monarchy, see Wayne S. Vucinich, "The Serbs in Austria Hungary" and Dimitrije Djordjević, "The Serbs as an Integrating and Disintegrating Factor," both essays in *Austrian History Yearbook,* III:2 (1967) and Dušan J. Popović, *Srbi u Vojvodini,* 3 vols. (Novi Sad, Matica srpska, 1957–1963). A basic recent biography is Duncan Wilson, *The Life and Time of Vuk S. Karadžić* (Oxford, Clarendon Press, 1970).

For general reference see the work by W. Markert, *Jugoslawien,* listed under II:J and Alfred Stead, ed., *Serbia by the Serbians* (London, W. Heinemann, 1909).

Bibliography: *Bibliografija Jugoslavije* (Beograd, Bibliographical Institute, 1945–) and, of older works, Emile Picot, *Les Serbes de Hongrie* (Prague, Gregr & Dattel, 1873) and Ernest Denis, *La Grande Serbie* (Paris, Delagrave, 1915). In English see the essays by W. S. Vucinich and D. Djordjević in *Austrian History Yearbook,* III:2 (1967) and Joel M. Halpern, *Bibliography of English Language Sources on Yugoslavia* (Amherst, University of Massachusetts Press, 1969).

On Bosnia-Hercegovina see Ferdinand Schmid, *Bosnien und die Herzegowina unter der Verwaltung Österreich-Ungarns* (Leipzig, Veit & Co., 1914); Peter F. Sugar, *Industrialization of Bosnia-Hercegovina 1878–1918* (Seattle, University of Washington Press, 1964), and Ernest Bauer, *Zwischen Halbmond und Doppeladler* (Vienna, Herold, 1971). See also Nikola Stojanović, *Bosanska Kriza 1908–1914* (Sarajevo, Veselin Masleša, 1958). See further Dorde Pejanović, *Stanovništvo Bosne i Hercegovine* (Belgrad, Srpska Akademija Nauka, 1955) and Dominik Mandié, *Bosnia i Hercegovina* (Chicago, Croatian Historical Institute, 1960), Vol. I (Croatian viewpoint).

APPENDIXES

APPENDIX I

Population and Nationality Statistics

Official statistics as well as other scholarly statistical studies in the Habsburg empire were in many respects excellent. They came into existence during Maria Theresa's reign and became a permanent institution in the Restoration era. Beginning with the Neoabsolutist era these statistics were compiled on an empire-wide scale. After 1867 a regular census every ten years was introduced in both dual states and from thereon separately handled by both administrations.

Statistics up to 1829 were compiled mainly for the purpose of taxation and military conscription. The use of this unquestionably valuable material for population statistics is, however, to some extent impaired by several factors: First, statistical estimates fluctuated in regard to the extent of the territories scrutinized at different times. Second, the correctness of these estimates varied considerably in different parts of the Habsburg domains. They are relatively most reliable in the Alpine Hereditary and Bohemian lands. Finally, statistical policies differed also in regard to the inclusion of military forces, migratory workers, and, beyond this, nontaxable individuals altogether. Beginning with the establishment of a separate government agency for statistical services in 1829 and the work of its directors, Anton v. Baldacci and Karl v. Czoernig, the quality of the work done improved greatly and quickly.

This did not apply in the same degree to early estimates of nationality statistics. In this respect scientific statistics exist in the dual states only after 1867, in Bosnia-Hercegovina only in the twentieth century. Even then, allowance has to be made for the fact that Croatians and Serbs were counted in Austria as Serbo-Croats, while in Hungary they were only beginning to be considered at all with the late eighteen-eighties, but after that were tabulated properly as Croats and Serbs separately. Slovaks are not to be found in Austrian nationality statistics at all and are listed there under Czechs. Jews were not recognized as a separate nationality either in Austria or Hungary, except in the crownland of Bukovina after 1909.

The belated introduction of reliable nationality statistics in the Habsburg empire undoubtedly had many disadvantages, but in a seemingly paradoxical way, it had one major favorable effect, namely that of safeguarding nationality statistics against gross nationalist distortions. By the time these statistics were officially introduced in Cisleithanian Austria, the national groups there protested effectively against such transgressions. Consequently, exaggerated claims raised by various nationalities cancelled each other in the final tabulations. No such influence could be conceded to the non-Magyar groups in Hungary, apart from Croatia-Slavonia. Yet even in Hungary, at least the influence of public opinion abroad and the publication of the works of members of non-Magyar national groups in French and English outside of Hungary had a beneficial effect. In any case, here too one cannot adduce evidence for major distortions of official statistical figures themselves. Statistical bias is by and large apparent in the gerrymandering of administrative districts to the disadvantage of minorities rather than in outright juggling of figures.[1]

A. Population statistics

Population:	*1773*	*1780* *	*1786*	*1789*
The Habsburg domains exclusive of Lombardy and the German Vorlande according to official statistics and estimates by F. Gürtler, which are generalized here	18,875,000	17,435,000	20,600,000	21,000,000
	1840	*1842*		
The Habsburg domains including Lombardy-Venetia according to official statistics and estimates of S. Becher, generalized here	36,600,000	37,500,000		

* The differences between the figures of 1773 and 1780 are probably caused by revised estimates of the population in Galicia.

[1] For the sources used here, see subsection IP in the bibliographical chapter. To these the following works may be added: Konrad Schünemann, *Österreichs Bevölkerungspolitik unter Maria Theresia* (Berlin, Deutsche Rundschau G.m.b.H., 1935);

	1787	*1850*
Hungary, according to official statistics and estimates of G. E. Hollos, in round figures	8,000,000	11,550,000

Population figures on the basis of official statistics after 1867:

	Cisleithanian Austria	Hungary including Croatia-Slavonia	Bosnia-Hercegovina	
1869	20,345,000	15,417,000	1895	1,604,000 (estimate)
1880	22,144,000	15,642,000	1910	1,932,000
1890	23,895,000	17,349,000		
1900	26,151,000	19,255,000		
1910	28,572,000	20,886,000		

Habsburg empire

1857	(including Lombardy Venetia)	32,216,000
1869	(without Lombardy-Venetia)	35,812,000
1880	(without Bosnia-Hercegovina)	37,786,000
1890	(without Bosnia-Hercegovina)	41,224,000
1900	(without Bosnia-Hercegovina)	46,974,000
1910	(including Bosnia-Hercegovina)	51,390,000

Alfred Gürtler, *Die Volkszählung Maria Theresias und Josefs II* (Innsbruck, Wagner, 1909); and Siegmund Becher, *Die Bevölkerungsverhältnisse der österreichischen Monarchie* (Vienna, A. Doll's Enkel, 1846). (All of these works are excellent.) See in this respect also Gustav Otruba, *Die Wirtschaftspolitik Maria Theresias* (Vienna, Bergland Verlag, 1963). There exists no equally reliable work on early nonofficial nationality statistics. Franz Schuselka's *Ist Österreich deutsch?* (Leipzig, Weidmansche Buchhandlung, 1843) offers an interesting estimate which is, however, weighted in favor of the Germans. Statistical estimates pertaining to population figures prior to the reign of Maria Theresa are based almost entirely on conjecture.

As to Hungarian statistics for earlier periods, see Aloys Kovács, *Développement de la population de la Hongrie depuis la cessation de la domination turque* (Budapest, Pesti Könyonyimda riszvény túrsasay, 1914); Étienne Hollos, "Le développement pendent les 200 dernières années de la population Hongroise dans le bassin des Carpathes," in *Journal de la Société Hongroise de Statistique* (Budapest), XII (1934): 154–160. See also "Die Bevölkerung Ungarns zur Zeit Josephs II. Die Hauptergebnisse der Zählungen von 1784–1787," *ibid.* XVI (1938): 168–181; and G. Thirring, "Les recensements de la population en Hongrie sous Joseph II," *ibid.* IX (1931): 201–247. In the same volume see also Bela Földes, "Les minorités et les statistiques des nationalités," pp. 441–474.

For the history of population statistics in the Habsburg empire see Ernst Mischler and Josef Ulbrich, eds., *Österreichisches Staatswörterbuch,* 4 vols. (Vienna, Hölder, 1905–1909); see vol. IV, pp. 848–852.

B. Statistics of religious affiliation in 1910

Cisleithanian Austria	
Catholics incl. Uniates	91.0 percent
Greek Orthodox	2.3
Protestants	1.9
Jews	4.7
Hungary including Croatia-Slavonia	
Roman Catholics	52.1 percent
Greek Catholic rites	9.7
Calvinist Protestants	12.6
Lutheran Protestants	6.4
Unitarians	0.3
Jews	4.5
Bosnia-Hercegovina	
Greek Orthodox	43.2 percent
Mohammedans	32.2
Roman Catholics	23.0
Jews	0.6
Empire totals	
Catholics (incl. Roman Catholics, Greek Catholic and other Uniate rites)	77.2 percent
Protestants	8.9
Greek Orthodox	8.7
Jews	3.9
Mohammedans	1.1

C. Nationality statistics

ESTIMATES BY F. SCHUSELKA IN *Ist Österreich Deutsch* [LEIPZIG, 1843]:

Territory	Number	Nationality
The lands belonging to the German Confederation, that is the lands of the Bohemian crown, the Alpine hereditary lands including Carniola, Trieste, Gorizia, Gradisca, and parts of Istria	5,615,000	Germans
	5,235,000	Slavs
	350,000	Italians
	11,200,000	*Total*
Galicia and Bukovina (no breakdown between Poles and Ruthenians)	4,350,000	Poles and Ruthenians
	150,000	Germans
	4,500,000	*Total*
Dalmatia (no ethnic breakdown)	370,000	*Total*
Lands of the Hungarian crown, including Croatia-Slavonia and Military Frontier	5,500,000	Slavs
	5,300,000	Magyars
	1,200,000	Germans
	1,000,000	Vlachs (Roumanians)
	13,000,000	*Total*

Empire totals of 1843

15,465,000	Slavs
6,965,000	Germans
5,300,000	Magyars
1,000,000	Vlachs (Roumanians)
350,000	Italians
29,080,000	*Total*

OFFICIAL STATISTICS AND ESTIMATES BY E. HOLLOS AND A. KOVÁCS:

Magyars within the total population of Hungary, in	1787	39 percent
"	1850	41.6 "
"	1869	45.5 "

OFFICIAL NATIONALITY STATISTICS IN PERCENTAGES:

Cisleithanian Austria

	1880	*1890*	*1900*	*1910*
Germans	36.8	36.1	35.8	35.6
Czechs (incl. Slovaks)	23.8	23.3	23.2	23.0
Poles	14.9	15.8	16.6	17.8
Ruthenians	12.8	13.2	13.2	12.6
Serbo-Croats	2.6	2.8	2.8	2.7
Roumanians	0.9	0.9	0.9	1.0

Lands of the Hungarian crown including Croatia-Slavonia

	1880	*1890*	*1900*	*1910*
Magyars	41.2	42.8	45.4	48.1
Germans	12.5	12.2	11.1	9.8
Slovaks	11.9	11.1	10.5	9.4
Roumanians	15.4	14.9	14.5	14.1
Ruthenians	2.3	2.2	2.2	2.3
Croats	—	9.0	8.7	8.8
Serbs	—	6.1	5.5	5.3

Bosnia-Hercegovina (estimates of 1910)

Croats	21
Serbs	42
Mohammedans	34

Empire totals of 1910

Germans	23.9
Magyars	20.2
Czechs	12.6
Slovaks	3.8 (estimate)
Croats	5.3
Serbs	3.8

Mohammedan Serbo-Croats in Bosnia-Hercegovina	1.2 (estimate)
Poles	10.0
Ruthenians	7.9
Roumanians	6.4
Slovenes	2.6
Italians	2.0

APPENDIX II

The Rulers

The Austrian Habsburg and Habsburg-Lorraine rulers from the middle of the fifteenth century to 1918.

Differences as to the time of election of individual rulers to the status of king of Bohemia, Hungary, and Holy Roman emperor are noted only where they are of political significance. Elections to the dignity of Roman (German) king during the life time of the ruling emperor are disregarded, because such elections signify only the right to succession.

A. HABSBURG RULERS

Albrecht II	king of Bohemia and Hungary 1437 German king 1438–1439
Friedrich III	German king 1440 emperor 1452–1493
Maximilian I	1493–1519 (emperor 1508)
Charles V	emperor 1519–1556
Ferdinand I	regent in the hereditary lands 1521 king of Bohemia and Hungary 1526 king of Croatia 1527 emperor 1556–1564
Maximilian II	emperor 1564–1576
Rudolf II	king of Hungary to 1608 king of Bohemia to 1611 emperor 1576–1612
Matthias I	king of Hungary 1608–1618 king of Bohemia 1611–1617 emperor 1612–1619
Ferdinand II	king of Hungary 1618–1637 king of Bohemia 1617–1637 emperor 1619–1637

Ferdinand III	emperor 1637–1657
Leopold I	king of Hungary 1655 king of Bohemia 1656 emperor 1658–1705
Joseph I	emperor 1705–1711
Charles VI	emperor 1711–1740

B. HABSBURG-LORRAINE RULERS

Maria Theresa of Habsburg	1740–1780 crowned queen of Hungary 1741 crowned queen of Bohemia 1743 empress consort 1745
Married to Francis Stephan of Lorraine	emperor 1745–1765
Joseph II	emperor 1765–1790 (until 1780 merely co-regent in Habsburg lands)
Leopold II	emperor 1790–1792
Francis (II) I	Holy Roman emperor 1792–1806 emperor of Austria 1804–1835
Ferdinand I	emperor of Austria 1835–1848
Francis Joseph	emperor of Austria 1848–1916 crowned as king of Hungary 1867
Charles I	emperor of Austria 1916–1918

APPENDIX III

Chronology

The following selective dates pertain to political history only. They are merely meant to provide a broad frame in whose setting frequently more important socioeconomic and cultural changes should be placed. Concerning the reigns of the Habsburg rulers see the preceding Appendix II.

1521	Treaty of Worms between Charles V and Ferdinand I concerning the latter's regency in the Lower Austrian duchies.
1522	Treaty of Brussels concerning the separation of the Spanish and Austrian lines of the Habsburg dynasty and Ferdinand's rule in all Austrian lands.
1526/VIII	Death of Louis II of Hungary and Bohemia in the battle of Mohács
1526/X	Ferdinand I elected king of Bohemia
1526/XI	Ferdinand I elected king of Hungary
1527/I	Ferdinand I elected king of Croatia
1529	First siege of Vienna by the Ottoman Turks under Suleiman the Magnificent
1541	Buda incorporated as pashalic in the Turkish empire
1545–1563	Council of Trento
1546–1555	Schmalcaldic war
1554	Issuance of the order of partition of the hereditary lands to take place after the death of Ferdinand I
1568	Major concessions to Protestant noble estate in Upper and Lower Austria by Maximilian II
1578–1580	Beginning of Counter Reformation in the hereditary lands during the reign of Rudolf II
1593–1606	Turkish war
1609	Rudolf II's Letter of Majesty grants major concessions to Protestant nobles and royal towns in Bohemia
1614	General diet in Linz

1615	General diet in Prague
1618	Defenestration of Prague
1620	Battle of the White Mountain
1621	Succession treaty under Ferdinand II
1627	Vernewerte Landesordnung for Bohemia
1629	Edict of Restitution
1630	Election of Prince George Rákóczy as prince of Transylvania
1634	Assassination of Wallenstein
1648	Westphalian peace treaty
1653–1654	Imperial diet of Regensburg declared in permanence
1663–1664	War against the Turks
1666	Conspiracy of Hungarian magnats
1667–1668	First war of Devolution
1672–1678	Second war of Devolution
1683–1699	Second Turkish war of Leopold I
1683	Second siege of Vienna by the Turks
1686	Reconquest of Buda
1688–1697	War of the League of Augsburg
1687–1688	Diet of Pozsony (Pressburg)
1690–1691	Diploma Leopoldinum for the Serbs in Hungary and for Transylvania
1699	Peace of Karlowitz with Ottoman power
1700	Death of Charles II of Spain
1701–1714	War of the Spanish Succession
1703	Mutual succession pact between the sons of Leopold I
1704	Election of Prince Francis II Rákóczy as prince of Transylvania
1711	Peace of Szatmár between Charles VI and the Hungarian rebels
1713	Peace of Utrecht
1712–1723	Pragmatic Sanction about the succession in the Habsburg lands
1714	Peace of Rastatt
1714	Peace of Baden
1716–1718	Turkish war
1717	Conquest of Belgrad
1718	Peace of Passarowitz
1719	Founding of Ostendian Trading Company
1733–1735	War of the Polish succession
1737–1739	Turkish war
1740–1742	First Silesian war
1741–1748	War of the Austrian succession
1744–1745	Second Silesian war
1753	Count (Prince) Kaunitz state chancellor
1756–1763	Seven Years' war (Third Silesian war)
1765–1780	Joseph II coregent

1772	First partition of Poland
1775	Acquisition of the Bukovina
1778–1779	War of the Bavarian succession
1781	Toleration Patent
1788–1791	Turkish war
1790	Treaty of Reichenbach between Austria and Prussia
1792–1797	War of the First Coalition against France
1793	Second partition of Poland between Russia and Prussia
1795	Third partition of Poland
1797	Peace of Campo Formio
1797	Congress of Rastatt
1799–1801	War of the Second Coalition
1801	Peace of Luneville
1803	Reichsdeputationshauptschluß of Regensburg
1804	Proclamation of Austrian empire
1805	War of the Third Coalition
1805	Peace of Pressburg (Pozsony)
1806	Continental blockade established
1806	Abdication of Francis (II) I as Holy Roman emperor
1808	Establishment of Austrian national militia (Landwehr)
1809	Austrian war against France
1809	Uprising in Tyrol
1809	Count (Prince) Clemens Lothar Metternich appointed minister of foreign affairs
1809	Peace of Schönbrunn
1810	Marriage of Napoleon I with Marie Louise, daughter of Francis I
1811	Austrian state bankruptcy
1813–1814	Austria joins coalition against France
1814/III	First occupation of Paris
1814/IV	Abdication of Napoleon
1814/V	First Peace of Paris
1814/IX–1815/VI	Congress of Vienna
1815/III–VI	Napoleon's regime of hundred days
1815/VI	Charter of German Confederation adopted
1815/VII	Second occupation of Paris
1815/IX	Holy Alliance
1815/XI	Second Peace of Paris
1819	Karlsbad Decrees
1820	Definitive Charter of German Confederation
1821–1848	Metternich state chancellor
1833	German customs union
1846	Incorporation of Cracow
1848/III	Outbreak of the revolution. Invasion of Lombardy by Piemontese troops
1848/V	Opening of St. Paul's Assembly in Frankfurt
1848/VI	Slav Congress in Prague

1848/VII	Opening of Reichstag in Vienna
1848/VIII	Evacuation of Lombardy by Piemontese troops
1848/X	Emancipation of peasants passed by Reichstag in Vienna
1848/X	Beginning of Hungarian revolution
1848/X	October revolution in Vienna
1848/XI	Prince Felix Schwarzenberg prime minister
1848/XI	Reopening of Reichstag in Kremsier
1849/III	Dissolution of Reichstag of Kremsier and promulgation of octroyed Stadion constitution
1849/III	Reopening of war with Piemont-Sardinia
1849/IV	Hungarian National Assembly declares Habsburg dynasty deposed
1849/V	Russian military intervention in Hungary agreed upon
1849/VIII	Hungarian capitulation at Világos
1849/VIII	End of insurrection in Lombardy and Venetia
1850	Customs union between Austria and Hungary
1850	Olmütz (Olomuc) agreement between Austria and Prussia
1851/XII	New Year's Eve Patent, which reintroduces absolutism
1852	Death of Prince Schwarzenberg
1853–1856	Crimean war
1855	Concordat between Holy See and Austria
1859	Austro-French Piemontese war
1860	Restoration of Hungarian constitution of 1848
1860/X	October Diploma
1861/II	February Patent
1863	Assembly in Frankfurt under Emperor Francis Joseph's chairmanship
1864	Danish-Austro-Prussian war
1865	Gastein Convention
1865	Suspension of constitution
1866/IV	Prusso-Italian alliance
1866/VI–VII	Austro-Prussian-Italian war
1867	Austro-Hungarian Compromise
1867/XII	Austrian constitutional laws
1870	Termination of Concordat with Holy See
1872	Three Emperors' League
1878	Congress of Berlin
1878	Occupation of Bosnia-Hercegovina
1879	Austro-German Alliance
1881	Three Emperors' Alliance
1882	Triple Alliance
1882	German National Association founded
1887	Christian Social Association in Vienna founded
1889	Social Democratic Party founded
1897	Dr. Karl Lueger confirmed as mayor of Vienna
1897	Badeni crisis

1905	Hungarian state crisis
1907	Introduction of general equal franchise in Austria
1908	Annexation of Bosnia-Hercegovina
1914/III	Adjournment of Austrian parliament
1914/VI	Assassination of the heir apparent Francis Ferdinand
1914/VII	Austrian ultimatum and declaration of war on Serbia
1914/VIII–1918/XI	World War I
1915/V	Italian declaration of war
1917/V	Reopening of Austrian parliament
1917/VII	Southern Slav Declaration of Corfu
1918/III	Peace treaty of Brest-Litowsk with Soviet Union
1918/VIII–IX	De facto recognition of Czechoslovakia's independence by Great Britain and the United States
1918/X	Termination of the Austro-Hungarian *Realunion*
1918/X	Declaration of independence of Czechoslovakia
1918/XI	Proclamation of Polish republic
1918/XI	Renunciation of the emperor's executive powers
1918/XI	Proclamation of Austrian republic
1918/XI	Proclamation of the United Kingdom of Serbs, Croats, and Slovenes

APPENDIX IV

Maps

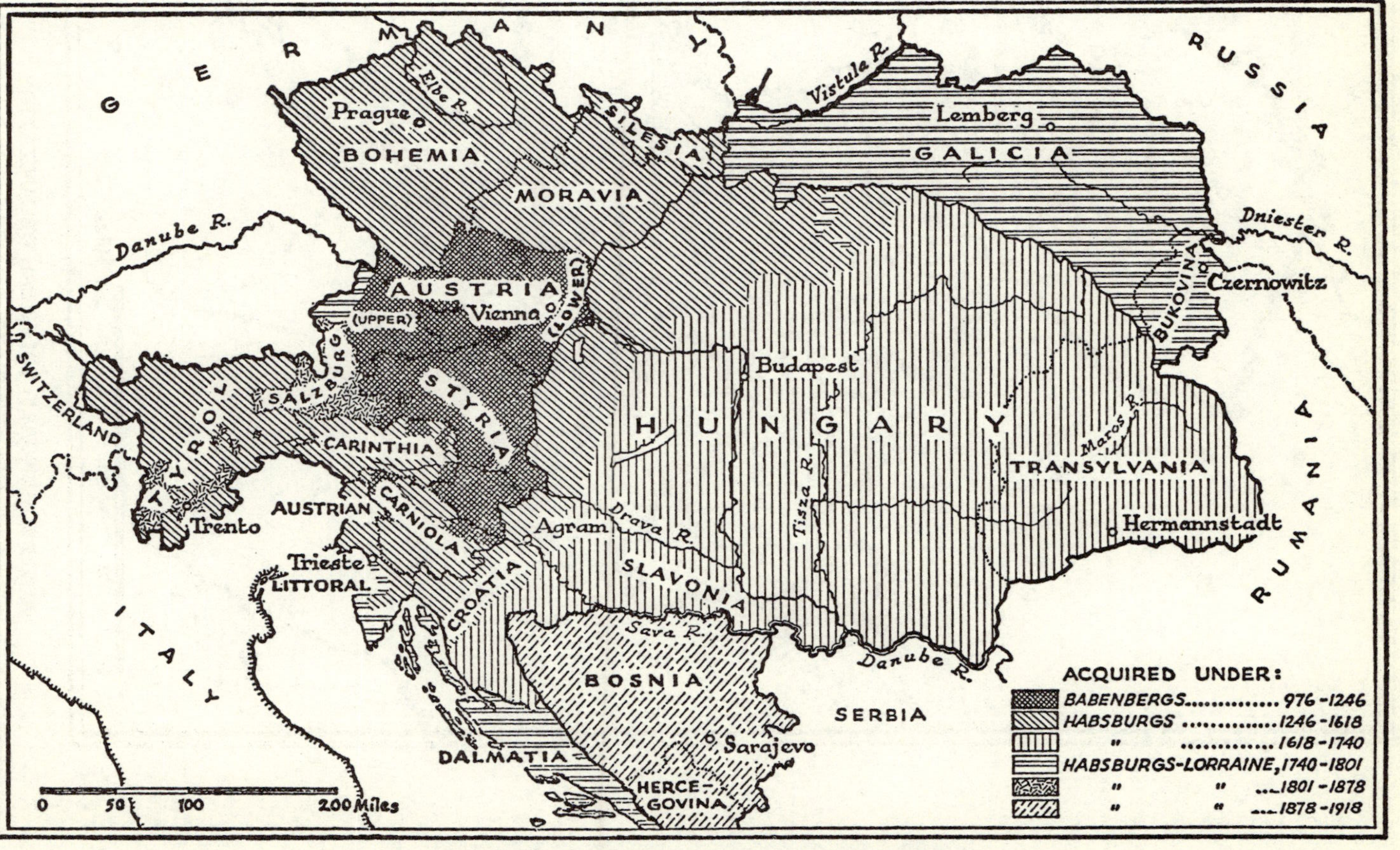

AUSTRIA-HUNGARY, HISTORICAL DEVELOPMENT

Only changes within the boundaries from 1878–1918, including the occupied and in 1908 annexed territory of Bosnia-Hercegovina, are shown on this map.

AUSTRIA-HUNGARY, POLITICAL ORGANIZATION

Names of crownland capitals and one-time capitals of historicopolitical units

vithin Hungary and Bosnia-Hercegovina are underlined.

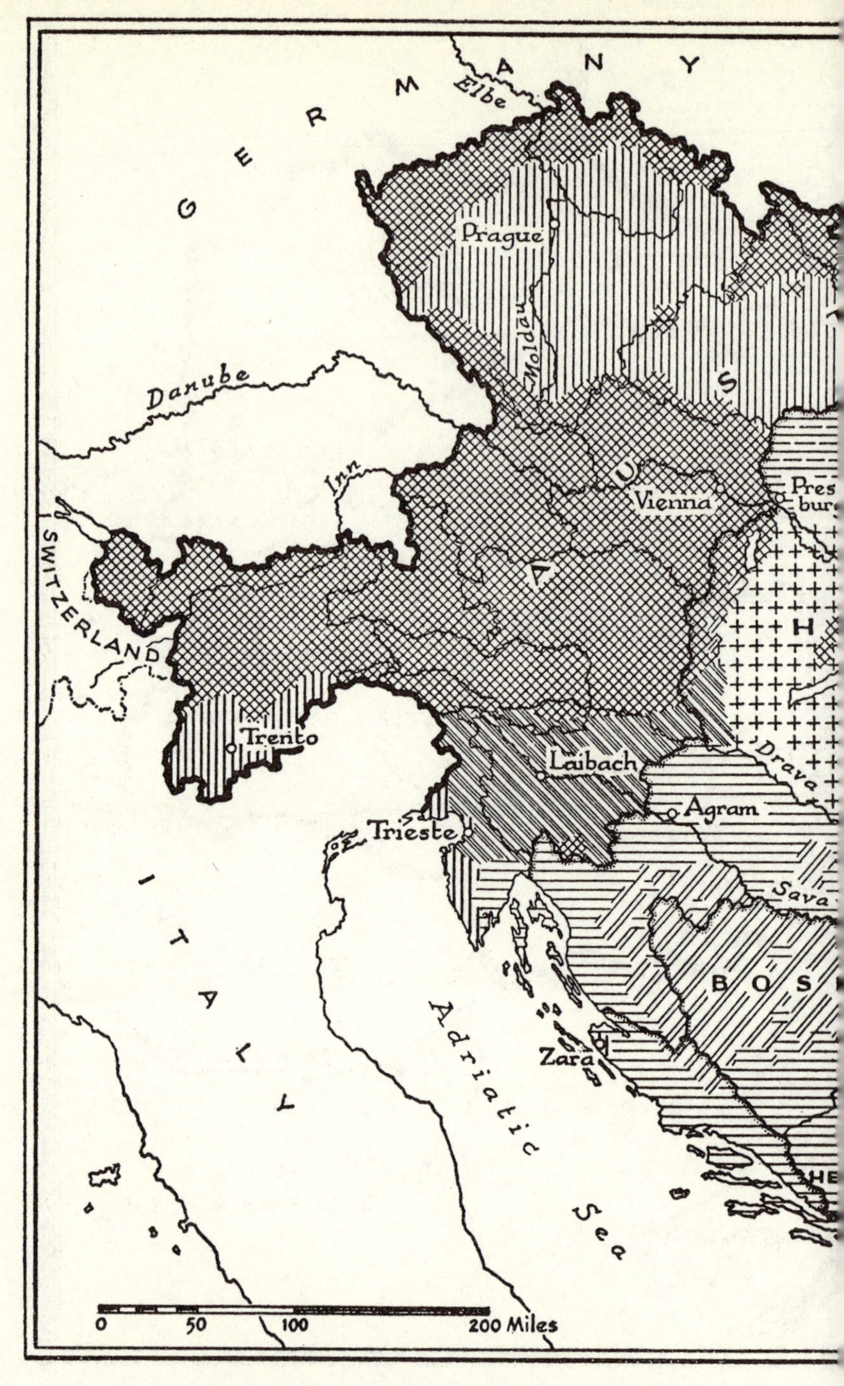

AUSTRIA-HUNGARY, NATIONAL GROUPS

Only national groups representing more than 50 percent of the population in a

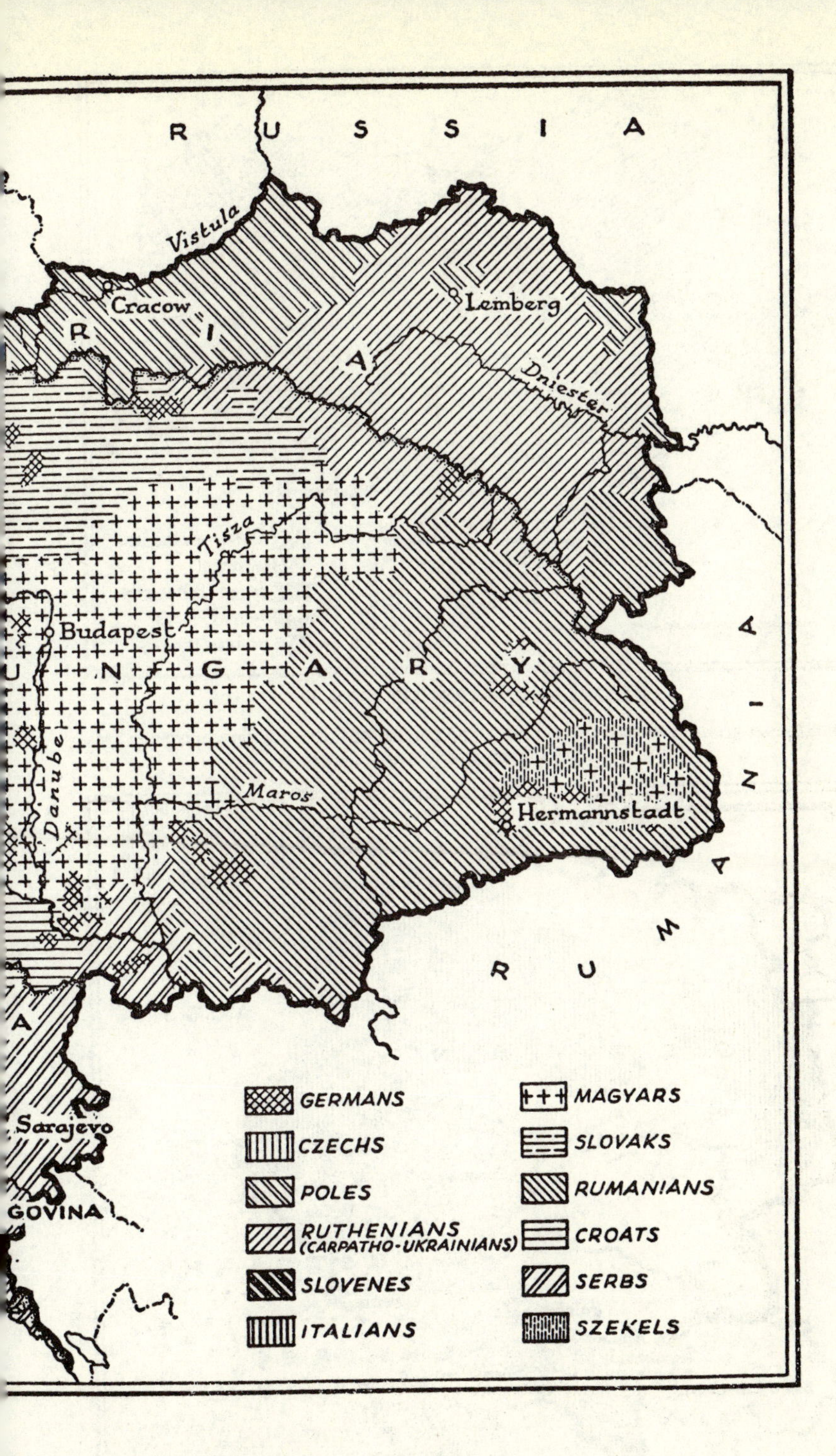

given area are shown on this map.

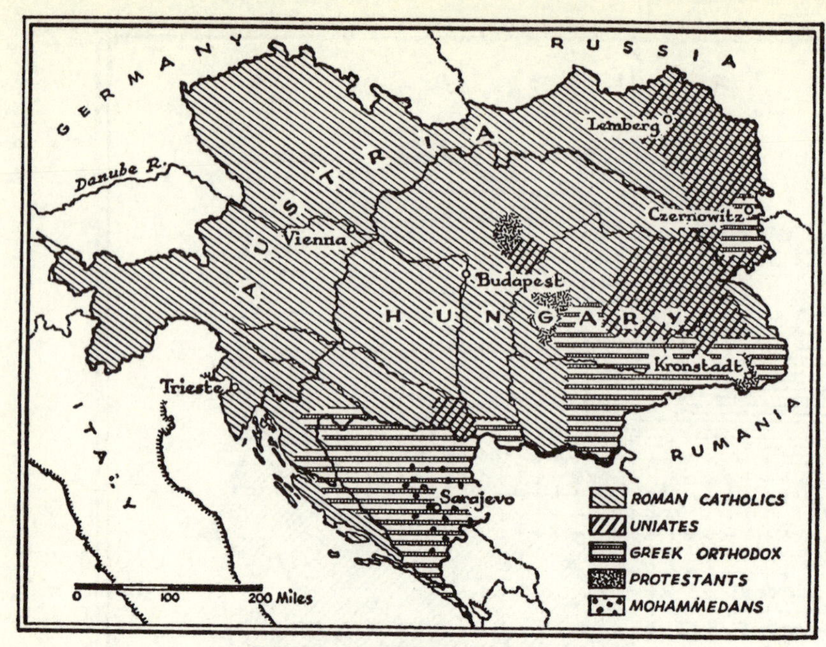

AUSTRIA-HUNGARY, RELIGIONS

Only religious groups representing more than 50 percent of the population in a given area are shown on this map.

THE AUSTRIAN EMPIRE AND THE GERMAN CONFEDERATION
1815–1866

Index

An *n* after a page number refers to discussion of a specific entry in a note. Subdivisions of historical subjects are in general listed in chronological order, others in alphabetical order. The names of royalties, except for some specific instances, are listed in anglicized form. Otherwise, the spelling of names either in anglicized form or in one of the vernacular languages of the Habsburg empire is determined in each individual case by the assumed familiarity of the reader with the listing used.

Errata

page 138, lines 33-35 *should read* The University of Salzburg was founded as a Benedictine institution in the 1620s and that of Innsbruck as a Jesuit institution in the 1670s.

page 166, line 21 *for* between Inn *read* to the east of Inn

page 203, line 21 *for* As for education *read* As for the language problem

page 220, lines 24-26 *should read* secured Tyrol, Vorarlberg, the rich western territories Burgau, Eichstädt, Lindau, the bishopric of Passau, and the southern part of Brixen and

page 221, line 3 *for* and the elimination of Prussia *read* and the attempted elimination of Prussia

page 236, line 14 *should read* neither requested nor even welcomed support of his policies by the masses

page 238, lines 13-15 *should read* Changed by several piecemeal revisions and one major one in 1852, it remained in force until 1974.

page 245, line 14 *should read* intervention in support of the Bourbon regime in Spain, a

page 252, note 7 *delete* the incomplete reference *and add* W. R. Thayer, *The Life and Times of Cavour* (Boston, 1914) I, 77-106.

pages 259, 288, 301, 306, 309, 354, 448, 487, 517, in notes *for* Kissling *read* Kiszling

pages 282, note 32; 341, note 101; 595, lines 9, 13, and 24, *for* Ludovit *read* L'udovit

page 306, line 10 *for* semi-dictorship *read* semi-dictatorship

page 315, note 72 *for* hung *read* hanged

page 326, line 20 *should read* presided over by

page 331, line 27 *should read* after the validity

page 347, line 17 *should read* as their predecessors in the opposition in the parliament of 1873

page 353, lines 3-4 *for* At this time *read* Only in 1895

page 362, line 30 *should read* Hungarian administration enforced by Hungarian courts.

page 363, lines 17-21 *should read* As for common Hungarian-Croatian agenda, forty Croatian deputies represented the historic land in the deliberations and the voting of the Hungarian parliament whenever joint agenda were at issue.[131] They could be outvoted by the Magyar majority.

page 391, line 29 *for* 1774 *read* 1774/5

page 403, lines 10-11 *should read* George Sinçai and Samuel Klein nephew of the great bishop John Micu (Klein) were coauthors of a new Roumanian grammar *The Element of the Dacian-Roman or Wallach language.*

page 442, lines 13-14 *should read* This meant that national status was not to be conferred

page 451, line 21 *should read* Inasmuch as next to the Roumanians the Italians

page 466, note 60, line 5 *for* Solle *read* Süle

page 478 line 22 *for* An even more serious one, were *read* Even more serious were

page 490, line 28 *for* Autro-German *read* Austro-German

page 507, line 28 *should read* peace treaties of Riga between Poland, the

page 509, line 25 *for* contingencies *read* necessities

page 511, line 4 *should read* obviously impossible in peacetime.

page 512, line 10 *for* wartime absolutism *read* wartime administration

page 517, line 27 *should read* model of how different nationalities

page 537, line 28 *should read* his study on Wallenstein outranks that of

page 540, line 21 *for* commensurate to *read* commensurate with

page 543, line 7 *should read History of Hungary*

page 547, line 11 *should read* and was to some extent

page 547, line 25 *for* Austrian lyric *read* Austrian lyricist

page 553, line 11 *for* paradox *read* paradoxical

page 554, line 7 *for* to emulate *read* from emulating

page 557, line 20 *for* archiect *read* architect

page 573, line 18 *should read* Shepherd

page 574, line 10 *for Versailler read Versailles*

page 576, line 13 *add* R. A. Kann, *Erzherzog Franz Ferdinand Studien* (Munich, Oldenbourg, 1976).

page 581, lines 14-15 *for* Herbert Rieser *read* Herbert Rütten

page 584, line 25 *for* two parts *read* three parts

page 588, line 23 *for* Norritt *read* Nourritt

page 594, line 4 *should read the Rise of the Czechoslovak State*

page 594, line 6 *should read* and Thomas G. Masaryk, *The Making of a State,* (New York, F. Stokes, 1927),

page 595, line 12 *for* all three Marxian interpretation *read* the last two works Marxian interpretations.

page 607, *Cisleithanian Austria* table, *should include* between "Ruthenians" and "Serbo-Croats" the following:

Italians	3.1	2.9	2.8	2.7
Slovenes	5.2	5.0	4.6	4.5